# The Winchcombe and Coventry Chronicles:
## Hitherto Unnoticed Witnesses to the Work of John of Worcester

Medieval and Renaissance Texts and Studies

Volume 373

# The Winchcombe and Coventry Chronicles: Hitherto Unnoticed Witnesses to the Work of John of Worcester

## Volume One: Introduction and Commentary

*Edited and translated by*
Paul Antony Hayward

ACMRS
(Arizona Center for Medieval and Renaissance Studies)
Tempe, Arizona
2010

Published by ACMRS (Arizona Center for Medieval and Renaissance Studies)
Tempe, Arizona


**Library of Congress Cataloging-in-Publication Data**

John, of Worcester, 12th cent.
[Winchcombe chronicle]
The Winchcombe and Coventry chronicles : hitherto unnoticed witnesses to the work of John of Worcester / edited and translated by Paul Antony Hayward.
p. cm. -- (Medieval and Renaissance texts and studies v. 373)
Texts in Latin with English translations; commentary in English.
Includes bibliographical references and index.
ISBN 978-0-86698-421-8 (acid-free paper)
1. Great Britain--History--Anglo-Saxon period, 449-1066--Early works to 1800. 2. Great Britain--History--Norman period, 1066-1154--Early works to 1800. 3. Great Britain--History--Angevin period, 1154-1216--Early works to 1800. 4. Monastic and religious life--England--History--To 1500--Early works to 1800. 5. Monastic and religious life--History--Middle Ages, 600-1500--Early works to 1800. 6. Manuscripts, Latin (Medieval and modern)--England--London--Facsimiles. 7. John, of Worcester, 12th cent.--Manuscripts--Facsimiles. 8. John, of Worcester, 12th cent. Winchcombe chronicle. 9. John, of Worcester, 12th cent. Coventry chronicle. 10. British Library. I. Hayward, Paul Antony. II. John, of Worcester, 12th cent. Coventry chronicle. III. Arizona Center for Medieval and Renaissance Studies. IV. Title. V. Title: Coventry chronicle.
DA150.J64 2010
942.01--dc22
2010023455

*Cover Art:*

London, B.L., MS Harley 3775, fol. 34r (Coventry Chronicle: opening leaf)

∞
This book is made to last. It is set in Adobe Caslon Pro,
smyth-sewn and printed on acid-free paper to library specifications.
*Printed in the United States of America*

*For My Teachers*
*Christopher N. L. Brooke*
*(1927–)*
*and*
*Valerie I. J. Flint*
*(1936–2009)*

# Table of Contents

## Volume I:
## Introduction and Commentary

# Volume Two:<br>Texts and Translations

## Texts and Translations



## Appendices



## Indices

# Preface

The present study is part of a larger project, the subject of which is the great outburst of historical activity that took place in England after the Norman Conquest. The intention is not, however, to focus on the most famous works of the period, on works such as William of Malmesbury's *Gesta regum* and *Gesta pontificum Anglorum* or Eadmer's *Historia novorum*, but on the many lesser texts, on the many strange miscellanies, breviate chronicles, and hagiographical tracts which were produced at this time, in the hope that they will shed new light on the major works in much the same way that the Early Music movement has helped modern audiences to understand the music of composers such as Monteverdi, Handel, and Bach. I am referring to the way in which one hears Johann Sebastian Bach's Magnificat in D major afresh having heard and analysed its model, the Magnificat in C major by his predecessor as Cantor of the Thomaskirche in Leipzig, Johann Kuhnau (1660–1722). There is no denying that Kuhnau's work is the lesser of the two, being rather less sophisticated and a shade too sentimental; but it offers insights into the context in which Bach was working—as to the task confronting him when he came to write his setting. For it was devised for the same liturgical purpose, it subdivides the text into different numbers in almost the same way, it employs almost the same musical forces, and it uses similar imagery. Hearing Kuhnau's version allows one to better appreciate the nuances and originality of Bach's setting. It is the present author's hope that the subtleties and originality of the greatest historians of the post-Conquest period—William of Malmesbury, Henry of Huntingdon, and Geoffrey of Monmouth—will be better understood when we know more about the many lesser texts which were composed in this period. To this end, the author has published several articles to date and two more books are now in hand. The present instalment is focused on two breviate world chronicles which are perhaps the most important examples of this historical sub-genre to survive from the century after the Norman Conquest. They are, indeed, examples of what this project is all about, as they shed new light on one of the most active but least appreciated of early twelfth-century historians—namely, John of Worcester.

Thanks must be given to a number of scholars, above all Julian Harrison. The present volume was originally to be a jointly authored edition of the chronicles in the two Cotton manuscripts, Tiberius E.IV and Faustina B.I. However, new discoveries, above all that of the *Coventry Chronicle*, altered the shape of the project, and differences over the interpretation of the data meant that that idea was abandoned. Our discussions and exchanges of information have nevertheless been to the great advantage of the present volume, for which its author is most grateful. These debts—including those to Julian's unpublished work on the Norman Annals, on the reception of Marianus Scotus in England, and on the manuscripts in the Cotton collection—are specified in greater detail in the footnotes below. Thanks are also due to several other scholars: to Patrick McGurk, for lending the draft of his forthcoming edition of the *Chronicula*'s annals as far as 1066; to Bernard Meehan for sharing his thoughts about the series of entries in the *Winchcombe Chronicle* which concern the abbots of Winchcombe; to Andrew Jotischky, to John Thorley, and especially to Martin Brett for giving their attention to sections of the text. The errors and misunderstandings that remain are, of course, the author's responsibility.

It is also a pleasure to thank the staff of the manuscript and rare book departments of the Bodleian Library, Oxford, the British Library, London, the John Rylands Library, Manchester, and Trinity College Library, Dublin. Thanks are due to them all, but none have had to put up with as many demands as the staff of the interloans department of Lancaster University Library. Their help and forbearance are much appreciated. One must also thank the institutions and publishers—including Cetedoc and Brepols, the Bibliothèque nationale de France, and the Deutsches Institut für Erforschung des Mittelalters—that have helped to make texts available on the World Wide Web or in searchable databases (such as the CLCLT CD-Rom, the MGH Online, and Gallica). Enabling one to work from almost anywhere, these sites and databases have been of immense value to the present project—a debt which is, alas, scarcely reflected in the notes below. It is important to indicate, therefore, how much the efforts of the scholars who have created these tools are appreciated. Two institutions provided financial support without which the research for this book could not have been undertaken: the University of Otago funded two research campaigns in the British Library—in early 2002 and early 2003; Lancaster University also provided a grant which funded further work at London, Oxford, and Gloucester in 2004.

The process of preparing a challenging text for publication was much advanced by the skill and learning of the staff at the Arizona Center for Medieval and Renaissance Studies, not least Leslie B. MacCoull and Todd Halvorsen, for which I am most grateful.

This study is dedicated to my postgraduate supervisors, Christopher N. L. Brooke and Valerie I. J. Flint. Both have been keen scholars of twelfth-century historical writing, both have contributed much to our knowledge of the great monasteries of the Severn Valley and of their intellectual life, and I remain indebted to them both for defining many questions which have continued to drive my own development as an historian. I hope that its contents meet with their approval.

P.A.H., July 2009

# List of Figures and Tables

# List of Plates

I. MS. Oxford, Corpus Christi College, 157, p. 56 (lower half).
This plate reproduces the second nineteen-year cycle in the Easter tables among the prelims to the holograph MS of John of Worcester's *Chronica chronicarum*. As the inscription in red at the foot of the page explains, the first series of annals (covering AD 19–37) is placed on the left-hand side, the second (covering AD 551–569) is on the right, whilst the third (covering AD 1083–1101) is distinguished with a gamma, 'Γ'. This approach is the same as that used in the Easter tables of the Hereford MS of Marianus Scotus's *Chronica chronicarum* (that is, London, B.L., Cotton Nero C.V, fols. 19v–26r). They also offer precisely the same explanation at the foot of folio 19v. The same system is used in other versions of Marianus's tables (e.g. MS. Cambridge, U.L., Kk.5.32, fols. 61r–74v).

II. MS. London, B.L., Cotton Tiberius E.IV, fol. 13r.
*Winchcombe Chronicle*: annals for AD 809–811, and the Winchcombe foundation charter, all of which is the work of scribe $T^{1}$.

III. MS. London, B.L., Cotton Tiberius E.IV, fol. 22v.
*Winchcombe Chronicle*: annals for AD 1121–1130, illustrating the changeover between scribes $T^{1}$, $T^{11}$, and $T^{12}$. The first phase ends with the first item under AD 1122; the second begins with the final item under that year. Note also the double column chronological apparatus.

IV. MS. London, B.L., Cotton Tiberius E.IV, fol. 27r.
*Winchcombe Chronicle*: annals for AD 1178–1181, illustrating the work of scribe $T^{14}$.

V. MS. London, B.L., Harley 3775, fol. 34r.
*Coventry Chronicle*: opening leaf with annals for VA 1 to VA24/AD 2, illustrating the work of scribe $H^{1}$. Note also the dominical letters in the right-hand margin.

VI. MS. London, B.L., Harley 3775, fol. 65v.
*Coventry Chronicle*: the annals for 1185 to 1188, illustrating the beginning of the third major continuation (from AD 1187, if not 1185). At least two scribes may be distinguished here: $H^7$, who is responsible for lines 1–6, and $H^8$, who is responsible for the remainder. I say 'at least' because there is some variation in letter forms—in, for example, the *h* of *hoc* which opens the annals for 1187 and 1188—which gives a little cause for doubt as to whether these annals were written by a single scribe.

# Abbreviations

AD — Anno Domini

*ACad.* — *Annales Cadomenses*, ed. André DuChesne, *Historiæ Normannorum scriptores antiqui* (Paris: DuChesne, 1619), repr. by Francis Maseres in *Historiæ Anglicanæ circa tempus conquestus Angliæ a Guilielmo Notho, Normannorum duce, Selecta Monumenta* (London: J. White, 1807), 355–66. Annals of Saint-Étienne, Caen, covering AD 633 to 1293.

*ACestr.* — *Annales Cestrienses; or Chronicle of the Abbey of S. Werburg, at Chester*, ed. Richard C. Christie, The Record Society for the Publication of Original Documents relating to Lancashire and Cheshire 14 (London: Printed for the Record Society, 1886). Covering AD 1 to 1297.

Alexander and Temple, *Illuminated MSS in Oxford* — J. J. G. Alexander and Elzbieta Temple, *The Illuminated Manuscripts in the Oxford College Libraries, the University Archives and the Taylor Institution* (Oxford: Clarendon Press, 1985).

*AG* — *Annales Gemmeticenses*, ed. Jean Laporte in *Les annales de l'Abbaye Saint-Pierre de Jumièges, chronique universelle des origines au XIIIe siècle* (Rouen: Cerf, 1954). Annals of Jumièges, covering AD 12 to 1265.

*ALD* — *Annales Lindisfarnenses et Dunelmenses*, ed. Wilhelm Levison and Hans Eberhard Meyer, *Deutsches Archiv für Erforschung des Mittelalters* 17 (1961): 447–506, at 478–89. Annals produced at Durham, covering AD 532 to 1199.

AM — Anno mundi

*AMSM* — *Annales Montis sancti Michaelis*, ed. Leopold Delisle, *Chronique de Robert de Torigni, abbé du Mont-Saint-Michel, suivie de divers opuscules historiques de cet auteur et de plusieurs religieux de la méme abbaye*, Ouvrages publiés par la société de l'histoire de Normandie, 2 vols. (Rouen: A. Le Brument, 1872–1873), 2:214–30. Annals of Mont-Saint-Michel: edited imperfectly omitting everything for the period between AD 30 and 875, except for an addition s.a. 708.

*APW* — *Annales prioratus de Wigornia*, ed. Luard, *AM*, 4:355–564. Cited by annal number. Parts of this text are also reproduced below in Appendix A.

*ARF* — *Annales regni Francorum inde ab a. 741 usque ad a. 829*, ed. Friedrich Kurze, *MGH SSRG* 6 (Hannover: Hahn, 1895). Cited by annal number.

*ASBD* — *Annales sancti Benigni Divionensis*, ed. Georg Waitz, *MGH SS*, 5:38–50. A set of annals covering AD 753 to 1178.

*ASC* — *Anglo-Saxon Chronicle.* Cited by the usual manuscript sigla and annal numbers where precision is required.

*ASC Coll.* — *The Anglo-Saxon Chronicle: A Collaborative Edition*, ed. David N. Dumville and Simon D. Keynes, 23 vols. (Cambridge: D. S. Brewer, 1983–): vol. 1, *MS F: Facsimile Edition*, ed. David N. Dumville (2003); vol. 3, *MS A*, ed. Janet M. Bately (1986); vol. 4, *MS B*, ed. Simon Taylor (1983); vol. 5, *MS C*, ed. Katherine O'Brien O'Keeffe (2000); vol. 6, *MS D*, ed. G. P. Cubbin (1996); vol. 7, *MS E*, ed. Susan E. Irvine (2004); vol. 8, *MS F*, ed. Peter Baker (2000); vol. 10, *The Abingdon Chronicle, A.D. 956–1066 (MS C with references to BDE)*, ed. Patrick W. Conner (1996); vol. 17, *The Annals of St Neots with* Vita Prima Sancti Neoti, ed. David N. Dumville and Michael Lapidge (1984).

*ASN* — *Annales sancti Neoti*, ed. David N. Dumville in *ASC Coll.*, 17:1–107. Annals drawn from Norman and English sources, covering 43 BC to AD 914.

Asser — Asser, *De rebus gestis Ælfredi*, ed. William H. Stevenson, *Asser's Life of King Alfred together with the Annals of Saint Neots erroneously ascribed to Asser*, rev. Dorothy Whitelock (Oxford: Oxford University Press, 1959), 1–96. Cited by section number.

*AT* — *Annales monasterii de Theokesberia*, ed. Luard, *AM*, 1:43–180. Cited by annal number.

*AU* — *Annales Uticenses*, ed. Augustus Le Prévost, *Orderici Vitalis Angligenæ, coenobii Uticensis monachi, Historiæ Ecclesiasticæ Libri Tredecim*, 5 vols. (Paris: Renouard, 1835–1855), 5:139–73. Annals of Saint-Évroult, covering AD 1–1503.

AV*Chron.* — Ado of Vienne, *Breviarum chronicorum ab origine mundi ad sua usque tempora, id est ad regnum Ludouici Francorum regis cognomento Simplicis, an. Domini dccclxxx* (Paris: Morelius and Warancore, 1561).

Baker and Holt, *Gloucester and Worcester*
Nigel Baker and Richard Holt, *Urban Growth and the Medieval Church: Gloucester and Worcester* (Aldershot: Ashgate, 2004).

B.A.V. Biblioteca Apostolica Vaticana

BC Before Christ

B*CS* *Cartularium Saxonicum: A Collection of Charters Relating to Anglo-Saxon History*, ed. Walter de Gray Birch, 3 vols. and index (London: Whiting, 1885–1899). Cited by charter number.

Bede, *CM* Bede, *Chronica maiora seu de sex aetatibus mundi*, ed. Charles W. Jones, CCSL 123B (Turnhout: Brepols, 1977), 463–535.

Bede, *DTemp.* Bede, *De temporibus*, ed. Charles W. Jones, CCSL 123C (Turnhout: Brepols, 1975–1980), 585–611.

Bede, *DTR* Bede, *De temporum ratione*, ed. Charles W. Jones, CCSL 123B (Turnhout: Brepols, 1977), 263–544.

Bede, *HE* Bede, *Historia ecclesiastica gentis Anglorum*, ed. Bertram Colgrave and R. A. B. Mynors, OMT (Oxford: Clarendon Press, 1969). Cited by book and chapter.

*BHG* *Bibliotheca Hagiographica Graeca*, ed. François Halkin, SH 8, 3rd ed. (Brussels: Société des Bollandistes, 1957); with *Novum Auctarium*, ed. idem, SH 65 (Brussels: Société des Bollandistes, 1965).

*BHL* *Bibliotheca Hagiographica Latina*, *Antiquae et Mediae Aetatis*, SH 6, 2 vols. (Brussels: Société des Bollandistes, 1898–1899); with *Novum Supplementum*, ed. Henryk Fros, SH 70 (Brussels: Société des Bollandistes, 1986).

B.L. British Library

Blair, *Church* John Blair, *The Church in Anglo-Saxon Society* (Oxford: Oxford University Press, 2005).

B.n.F. Bibliothèque nationale de France

Bod.L. Bodleian Library

Brett, "John" Martin Brett, "John of Worcester and his Contemporaries," in *The Writing of History in the Middle Ages: Essays Presented to Richard William Southern*, ed. Ralph H. C. Davis and John M. Wallace-Hadrill (Oxford: Clarendon Press, 1981), 101–26.

Brooke, *CWB* Christopher N. L. Brooke, *The Church and the Welsh Border in the Central Middle Ages*, Studies in Celtic History 8 (Woodbridge: Boydell Press, 1986).

Brooks, *Canterbury*
Nicholas P. Brooks, *The Early History of the Church at Canterbury: Christ Church from 597 to 1066* (Leicester: Leicester University Press, 1984).

Byrhtferth, *Enchiridion*
Byrhtferth of Ramsey, *Enchiridion*, ed. Michael Lapidge and Peter S. Baker, EETS, s.s. 15 (Oxford: Early English Text Society, 1995).

Byrhtferth, *Vita Oswaldi*
Byrhtferth of Ramsey, *Vita S. Oswaldi archiepiscopi Eboracensis* (*BHL* 6374), ed. James Raine, *Historians of the Church at York and its Archbishops*, RS 71, 3 vols. (London: Longmans, 1879–1894), 1:399–475.

*Cart. Gloc.* *Historia et cartularium monasterii sancti Petri Gloucestriae*, ed. W. H. Hart, RS 33, 3 vols. (London: Longmans, 1884–1893).

*Cart. Worcs.* *The Cartulary of Worcester Cathedral Priory (Register I)*, ed. Reginald R. Darlington, PPRS n.s. 38 (London: J. W. Ruddock, 1968).

*CBMLC* *Corpus of British Medieval Library Catalogues*, ed. Richard Sharpe et al., 17 vols. (London: British Library in association with the British Academy, 1990–); vol. 1, *The Friars' Libraries*, ed. K. W. Humphreys (1990); vol. 2, *Registrum Anglie*, ed. R. A. B. Mynors, R. H. and M. A. Rouse (1995); vol. 3, *Libraries of the Cistercians, Gilbertines and Premonstratensians*, ed. David N. Bell (1992); vol. 4, *English Benedictine Libraries: The Shorter Catalogues*, ed. Richard Sharpe, James P. Carley, Rodney M. Thomson, and Andrew G. Watson (1995); vol. 5, *Dover Priory*, ed. William P. Stoneman (1999); vol. 6, *The Libraries of the Augustinian Canons*, ed. Teresa Webber and Andrew G. Watson (1998); vol. 7, *The Libraries of Henry VIII*, ed. James P. Carley (2000); vol. 8, *Peterborough Abbey*, ed. Karsten Friis-Jensen and James M. W. Willoughby (2001); vol. 9, *Syon Abbey with the Libraries of the Carthusians*, ed. Vincent Gillespie and A. I. Doyle (2001); vol. 10, *The University and College Libraries of Cambridge*, ed. Peter D. Clarke (2002).

CCCM Corpus Christianorum Continuatio Medievalis (Turnhout: Brepols, 1966–).

*CCM* *Corpus consuetudinum monasticarum*, ed. Kassius Hallinger et al. (Siegburg: F. Schmitt, 1963–).

CCSL Corpus Christianorum Series Latina (Turnhout: Brepols, 1953–).

*C&S I* — *Councils and Synods with Other Documents Relating to the English Church*, vol. 1, *A.D. 871–1204*, ed. Dorothy Whitelock, Martin Brett, and Christopher N. L. Brooke, 2 pts. (Oxford: Oxford University Press, 1981).

Chaplais, "Original Charters" — Pierre Chaplais, "The Original Charters of Herbert and Gervase, Abbots of Westminster (1121–1157)," in *A Medieval Miscellany for Doris Mary Stenton*, ed. Patricia M. Barnes and C. F. Slade, PPRS 76, n.s. 36 (London: J. W. Ruddock, 1960), 89–110.

Chaplais, "Some Diplomas" — Pierre Chaplais, "Some Early Anglo-Saxon Diplomas on Single Sheets: Originals or Copies?," *Journal of the Society of Archivists* 3 (1965–1969): 315–36.

*Chronicula*[1] — See JW below.

*Chronicula*[2] — Gloucester Continuation to John of Worcester's *Chronicula* (G, fols. 113v24–151v). Cited by reference to the AD year as given in the edition by Reginald R. Darlington, Patrick McGurk, and Jennifer Bray, *The Chronicle of John of Worcester*, OMT, 3 vols. (Oxford: Clarendon Press, 1995–), 3:154–289 (where the text is reported in the form of variants from JW*CC*) and 290–305 (where the final year or so of the text is reported in full).

Coates, *EMB* — Alan Coates, *English Medieval Books: The Reading Abbey Collections from Foundation to Dispersal* (Oxford: Oxford University Press, 1999).

Coggeshall — Ralph of Coggeshall, *Chronicon Anglicanum*, ed. Joseph Stevenson, RS 66 (London: Longmans, 1875). Cited by page number.

Colker, *TCD* — Marvin L. Colker, *Trinity College Library Dublin: Descriptive Catalogue of the Medieval and Renaissance Latin Manuscripts*, 2 vols. (Dublin: Scolar Press, 1991).

*Coventry* — The Coventry Chronicle as edited and translated below. Superscript numbers are used to distinguish the main phases of the chronicle: thus, *Coventry*[1] refers to the first phase, down to 1122.1.

Cowdrey, *Lanfranc* — H. E. J. Cowdrey, *Lanfranc: Scholar, Monk, and Archbishop* (Oxford: Oxford University Press, 2003).

Cubitt, *Church Councils*
Catherine Cubitt, *Anglo-Saxon Church Councils, AD. 650–850* (Leicester: Leicester University Press, 1995).

Darlington — Reginald R. Darlington, "The Winchcombe Annals, 1049–1181," in *A Medieval Miscellany for Doris Mary Stenton*, ed. Barnes and Slade, 111–37.

Delaborde — *Oeuvres de Rigord et de Guillaume de Breton*, ed. H. François Delaborde, Société de l'Histoire de France 210 and 224, 2 vols. (Paris: Renouard, 1882–1885).

Devizes — Richard of Devizes

*AW* — *Annales monasterii de Wintonia*, ed. Luard, *AM*, 2:3–125. Cited by annal number.

*CTR* — *Chronicon de tempore regis Richardi primi*, ed. John T. Appleby, *The Chronicle of Richard of Devizes of the Time of King Richard the First* (London: T. Nelson, 1963). Cited by page number.

Diceto — Ralph de Diceto. Cited by annal number (and page where apposite).

*AChron.* — *Abbreviationes Chronicarum*, ed. William Stubbs, *The Historical Works of Master Ralph de Diceto*, RS 68, 2 vols. (London: Longmans, 1876), 1:3–263.

*YH* — *Ymagines historiarum*, ed. Stubbs, *Historical Works of Ralph de Diceto*, 1:291–440; 2:3–174.

Domesday — *Great Domesday Book*, ed. Ann Williams, R. W. H. Erskine and G. H. Martin, 31 vols. (London: Alecto, 1987).

Dugdale, *Antiquities*
William Dugdale, *The Antiquities of Warwickshire Illustrated from Records, Leiger-Books, Manuscripts, Charters, Evidences, Tombs and Armes; Beautified with Maps, Prospects and Portraitures* (London: T. Warren, 1656).

Dugdale, *Monasticon*
*Monasticon Anglicanum: A History of the Abbies and other Monasteries, Hospitals, Friaries and Cathedral and Collegiate Churches*, ed. William Dugdale et al., 6 vols. in 8 pts. (London: Longmans, 1817–1830).

Eadmer, *HN* — Eadmer, *Historia novorum in Anglia*, ed. Martin Rule, RS 81 (London: Longmans, 1884).

*EEA* — *English Episcopal Acta* (London: Oxford University Press for the British Academy, 1980–): vol 1, *Lincoln 1067–1185*, ed. D. M. Smith (1980); vol. 2, *Canterbury 1162–1191*, ed. C. R. Cheney and B. E. A. Jones (1986); vol. 3, *Canterbury 1193–1205*, ed.

C. R. Cheney and E. John (1986); vol. 4, *Lincoln 1186–1206*, ed. D. M. Smith (1986); vol. 5, *York 1070–1154*, ed. J. E. Burton (1988); vol. 6, *Norwich 1070–1214*, ed. C. Harper-Bill (1990); vol. 7, *Hereford 1079–1234*, ed. J. Barrow (1993); vol. 8, *Winchester 1070–1204*, ed. M. L. Franklin (1993); vol. 9, *Winchester 1205–1238*, ed. N. Vincent (1994); vol. 10, *Bath and Wells 1061–1205*, ed. F. M. R. Ramsey (1995); vol. 11, *Exeter 1046–1184*, ed. F. Barlow (1996); vol. 12, *Exeter 1186–1257*, ed. F. Barlow (1996); vol. 13, *Worcester 1218–1268*, ed. P. M. Hoskin (1997); vol. 14, *Coventry and Lichfield 1072–1159*, ed. M. L. Franklin (1997); vol. 15, *London 1076–1187*, ed. F. Neininger (1999); vol. 16, *Coventry and Lichfield 1169–1182*, ed. M. L. Franklin (1998); vol. 17, *Coventry and Lichfield 1183–1208*, ed. M. L. Franklin (1998); vol. 18, *Salisbury 1078–1217*, ed. B. Kemp (1999); vol. 19, *Salisbury 1218–1228*, ed. B. Kemp (2000); vol. 20, *York 1154–1181*, ed. M. Lovatt (2000); vol. 21, *Norwich 1215–1243*, ed. C. Harper-Bill (2000); vol. 22, *Chichester 1215–1253*, ed. P. M. Hoskin (2001); vol. 23, *Chichester 1254–1305*, ed. P. M. Hoskin (2001); vol. 24, *Durham 1153–1195*, ed. M. G. Snape (2002); vol. 25, *Durham 1196–1237*, ed. M. G. Snape (2002); vol. 26, *London 1189–1228*, ed. D. P. Johnson (2003); vol. 27, *York 1189–1212*, ed. M. Lovatt (2004); vol. 28, *Canterbury 1070–1136*, ed. M. Brett and J. A. Gribbin (2004); vol. 29, *Durham 1241–1283*, ed. P. Hoskin (2005); vol. 31, *Ely 1109–1197*, ed. N. Karn (2005).

EETS — Early English Text Society

  o.s. — original series (1864–).

  s.s. — supplementary series (1970–).

*EGC* — *Earldom of Gloucester Charters: The Charters and Scribes of the Earls and Countesses of Gloucester to A.D. 1227*, ed. Robert B. Patterson (Oxford: Clarendon Press, 1973).

*EHR* — *English Historical Review*

*EKAft.* — *English Benedictine Kalendars After A.D. 1100*, ed. Francis Wormald, HBS 77 and 81, 2 vols. (London: Harrison, 1939–1946).

*EKBef.* — *English Kalendars Before A.D. 1100*, ed. Francis Wormald, vol. 1, *Texts*, HBS 72 (London: Harrison, 1934).

Eyton — Robert W. Eyton, *Court, Household and Itinerary of King Henry II* (London: Taylor, 1878).

*Fasti* Diana E. Greenway et al., eds., *John Le Neve: Fasti Ecclesiae Anglicanae 1066–1300* (London: Institute of Historical Research, University of London, 1968–).

Finberg, *ECWM* H. P. R. Finberg, *The Early Charters of the West Midlands*, Studies in Early English History 2, 2nd ed. (Leicester: Leicester University Press, 1972).

Foot, *Veiled Women*
Sarah Foot, *Veiled Women*, Studies in Early Medieval Britain 1, 2 vols. (Aldershot: Ashgate, 2000).

Freeman, *Narratives of the New Order*
Elizabeth Freeman, *Narratives of the New Order: Cistercian Historical Writing in England, 1150–1220*, Medieval Church Studies 2 (Turnhout: Brepols, 2002).

Gameson, *Manuscripts*
Richard Gameson, *The Manuscripts of Early Norman England (c.1066–1130)* (London: Published for the British Academy by Oxford University Press, 1999).

*GCO* *Giraldi Cambrensis Opera*, ed. John S. Brewer, James F. Dimock, and George F. Warner, RS 21, 8 vols. (London: Longmans, 1861–1891).

GCS Die Griechischen christlichen Schriftsteller der ersten drei Jahrhunderte, 53 vols. (Leipzig: Hinrichs, 1897–1969).

Gervase Gervase of Canterbury, *Chronica*, ed. William Stubbs, in *The Historical Works of Gervase of Canterbury*, RS 73, 2 vols. (London: Longmans, 1879–1880), 2:84–594.

Gillingham, *Richard I*
John Gillingham, *Richard I*, Yale English Monarchs (New Haven: Yale University Press, 1999).

GM Geoffrey of Monmouth, *The* Historia regum Britanniae *of Geoffrey of Monmouth*, vol. 1, *Bern, Burgerbibliothek, MS.568*, ed. Neil Wright (Cambridge: D. S. Brewer, 1985).

Gransden, *HWE* Antonia Gransden, *Historical Writing in England*, 2 vols. (London: Routledge and Kegan Paul, 1974–1982).

Gransden, *LTH* Antonia Gransden, *Legends, Traditions and History in Medieval England* (London: Hambledon Press, 1992).

Greatrex, *BR* Joan Greatrex, *Biographical Register of the English Cathedral Priories of the Province of Canterbury, c.1066–1540* (Oxford: Clarendon Press, 1997).

Gullick, "Manuscripts of the *Collectio Lanfranci*"
Michael Gullick, "The English-Owned Manuscripts of the *Collectio Lanfranci* (s.xi/xii)," in *The Legacy of M. R. James: Papers from the 1995 Cambridge Symposium*, ed. Lynda Denison (Donnington: Shaun Tyas, 2001), 99–117.

Harrison, "New Discoveries"
Julian Harrison, "New Discoveries among the Cotton Manuscripts," *Monastic Research Bulletin* 8 (2002): 23–33.

Hart, *ECEE* Cyril R. Hart, *The Early Charters of Eastern England*, Studies in Early English History 5 (Leicester: Leicester University Press, 1966).

Hart, *ECNE* Cyril R. Hart, *The Early Charters of Northern England and the North Midlands*, Studies in Early English History 5 (Leicester: Leicester University Press, 1975).

Hart, *Learning and Culture*
Cyril R. Hart, *Learning and Culture in Late Anglo-Saxon England and the Influence of Ramsey Abbey on the Major English Monastic Schools*, 2 vols. in 3 pts. (Lampeter: E. Mellen Press, 2002).

*HBC* *Handbook of British Chronology*, ed. E. B. Fryde et al., 3rd ed. (London: Royal Historical Society, 1986).

HBS Henry Bradshaw Society Publications (London: For the Society, 1891–).

*HDSBH* *Handbook of Dates for Students of British History*, ed. Christopher R. Cheney and Michael Jones, Royal Historical Society Publications 4, 2nd ed. (London and Cambridge: Cambridge University Press, 2000).

*Hist. Abbend.* *Historia Ecclesiae Abbendonensis*, ed. John Hudson, *The History of the Church of Abingdon*, OMT, vol. 2 (Oxford: Clarendon Press, 2002–). Cited by part and section number.

*Heads I* David Knowles, Christopher N. L. Brooke, and Vera C. M. London, eds., *The Heads of Religious Houses, England and Wales*, vol. 1, *940–1216*, 2nd ed. (Cambridge: Cambridge University Press, 2001).

Heimann, "Dublin, Trinity College, MS 53"
Adelheid Heimann, "A Twelfth-Century Manuscript from Winchcombe and its Illustrations, Dublin, Trinity College, MS 53," *Journal of the Warburg and Courtauld Institutes* 28 (1965): 86–109.

HF*Chron.* Hugh of Fleury, *Hugonis Floriacensis monachi Benedictini Chronicon*, ed. B. Rottendorf (Münster: Bernard Raesfeld, 1638).

HH Henry, archdeacon of Huntingdon, *Historia Anglorum (History of the English People)*, ed. and trans. Diana E. Greenway, OMT (Oxford: Clarendon Press, 1996). Cited by book and chapter.

Hollister, *Henry I*
C. Warren Hollister, *Henry I*, ed. Amanda Clark Frost, Yale English Monarchs (New Haven: Yale University Press, 2001).

Holtzmann, *PUE* *Papsturkunden in England*, ed. Walther Holtzmann, 3 vols., Abhandlungen der Gesellschaft der Wissenschaften zu Göttingen: Philologisch-historische Klasse, n.F. 25; 3.F. 14–15, 33 (Berlin: Weidmann, 1930–1952).

H&S *Councils and Ecclesiastical Documents relating to Great Britain and Ireland*, ed. Arthur W. Haddan and William Stubbs, 3 vols. (Oxford: Clarendon Press, 1869–1871).

Hughes, "Welsh Latin Chronicles"
Kathleen Hughes, "The Welsh Latin Chronicles: *Annales Cambriae* and Related Texts," *Proceedings of the British Academy* 59 (1973): 233–58; repr. in eadem, *Celtic Britain in the Early Middle Ages*, ed. David N. Dumville, Studies in Celtic History 2 (Woodbridge: Boydell Press, 1980), 67–85.

Jocelin of Brakelond
Jocelin of Brakelond, *Cronica de rebus gestis Samsonis, abbatis monasterii Sancti Edmundi*, ed. and trans. Harold E. Butler (London: T. Nelson, 1949).

JL *Regesta pontificum romanorum ab condita ecclesia ad annum post Christum natum MCXCVIII*, ed. Philipp Jaffé, Wilhelm Wattenbach, Samuel Loewenfeld et al., 2 vols. (Leipzig: Veit, 1885–1888).

John, "Sources" Eric John, "A Critical Study of the Sources of the Winchcombe Annals" (MA thesis, University of Manchester, n.d.).

Jones, *BP* Charles W. Jones, *Bedae pseudepigrapha: Scientific Writings Falsely Attributed to Bede* (Ithaca: Cornell University Press, 1939).

JW John of Worcester. Cited by AD annal number except where page numbers are indicated.

*CC* *Chronica Chronicarum*, ed. and trans. Darlington, McGurk and Bray, *Chronicle of John of Worcester*. For the sections of JW*CC* not covered in the volumes of this edition that were available at the time of writing (i.e. volumes two and three) reference is made to the manuscripts (especially, the autograph C) using the sigla set out below.

*Chronicula*[1] John of Worcester's *Chronicula* from G, fols. 37r–151v. Cited by reference to the Marianan (VA) years, but sometimes, as the text varies, by reference to Dionysian (AD) years.

Kauffmann, *Romanesque Manuscripts*
Claus M. Kauffmann, *Romanesque Manuscripts, 1066–1190*, Survey of Manuscripts Illuminated in the British Isles 3 (London: H. Miller, 1975).

Ker, *Books, Collectors and Libraries*
Neil R. Ker, *Books, Collectors and Libraries: Studies in the Medieval Heritage*, ed. Andrew G. Watson (London: Hambledon Press, 1985).

Ker, *English Manuscripts*
Neil R. Ker, *English Manuscripts in the Century after the Norman Conquest* (Oxford: Clarendon Press, 1960).

Keynes, *Councils of* Clofesho
Simon D. Keynes, *The Councils of* Clofesho, Eleventh Brixworth Lecture 1993 / Vaughan Papers in Adult Education 38 (Leicester: Department of Adult Education, University of Leicester, 1994).

Knowles, *MO* David Knowles, *The Monastic Order in England, 940–1216*, 2nd ed. (Cambridge: Cambridge University Press, 1963).

*Landboc* *Landboc sive registrum monasterii beatae Mariae Virginis et Sancti Cenhelmi de Wincelcumba*, ed. David Roycc, 2 vols. (Exeter: William Pollard, 1892).

Landon Lionel Landon, *The Itinerary of Richard I with Studies on Certain Matters of Interest Connected with his Reign*, PPRS n.s. 13 (London: J. W. Ruddock, 1935).

Lapidge, "Germanus"
Michael Lapidge, "Abbot Germanus, Winchcombe, Ramsey and the Cambridge Psalter," in *Words, Texts and Manuscripts: Studies in Anglo-Saxon Culture Presented to Helmut Gneuss on the Occasion of his Sixty-Fifth Birthday*, ed. Michael Korhammer (Woodbridge: D. S. Brewer, 1992), 99–129.

Lapidge, "A Metrical Calendar"
Michael Lapidge, "A Tenth-Century Metrical Calendar from Ramsey," *Revue Bénédictine* 104 (1984): 326–69; repr. in idem, *Anglo-Latin Literature, 900–1066* (London: Hambledon Press, 1993), 343–86.

*Liber diurnus* — *Liber diurnus Romanorum pontificum*, ed. Hans Foerster (Bern: Francke Verlag, 1958). The formulas are cited by reference to the numbering of the Vatican MS. (Archivio Segreto Vaticano, Misc. Arm. XI.19), here edited on 77–180.

Levison, *EC* — Wilhelm Levison, *England and the Continent in the Eighth Century* (Oxford: Clarendon Press, 1946).

*LHF* — *Liber Historiae Francorum*, ed. Bruno Krusch, *MGH, SS rer. merov.* 2:215–328.

Liebermann, *ANG* — *Ungedruckte anglo-normannische Geschichtsquellen*, ed. Felix Liebermann (Strassburg: K. J. Trübner, 1879).

Love, *Three Lives* — *Three Eleventh-Century Anglo-Latin Saints' Lives*, ed. Rosalind C. Love, OMT (Oxford: Clarendon Press, 1996).

*LPont.* — *Le Liber Pontificalis: Texte, introduction et commentaire*, ed. Louis Duchesne and Cyrille Vogel, 3 vols. (Paris: E. Thorin, 1886–1957).

Luard, *AM* — *Annales monastici*, ed. Henry R. Luard, RS 36, 5 vols. (London: Longmans, Green, 1864–1889).

Marianus — Marianus Scotus, *Chronica chronicarum*, in London, B.L., MS Cotton Nero C.V, fols. 27r–159r. Cited by AD annal number or, where relevant, folio.

Meehan, "MSS of James Ussher" — Bernard Meehan, "The Manuscript Collection of James Ussher," in *Treasures of the Library, Trinity College Dublin*, ed. Peter Fox (Dublin: Royal Irish Academy for the Library of Trinity College Dublin, 1986), 97–110.

*MGH* — *Monumenta Germaniae Historica*

- *AA* — *Auctores antiquissimi*, 15 vols. (Berlin: Weidmann, 1877–1919).
- *CRF* — *Capitularia regum Francorum*, 2 vols. (Hannover: Hahn, 1883–1897).
- *CE* — *Capitularia Episcoporum*, 4 vols. (Hannover: Hahn, 1984–2005).
- *Epp.* — *Epistolae* (Berlin: Weidmann, 1887–).
- *Epp. Sel.* — *Epistolae Selectae in usum scholarum*, 5 vols. (Hannover: Hahn, 1887–1891).
- *SSRG* — *Scriptores rerum Germanicarum in usum scholarum separatim editi*, 63 vols. (Hannover: Hahn, 1871–1987).

*SS rer. Merov.*
*Scriptores rerum Merovingicarum*, 7 vols. (Hannover: Hahn, 1885–1951).

*SS* *Scriptores*, 30 vols. (Hannover: Hahn, 1826–1934).

*MLGB* Neil R. Ker, *Medieval Libraries of Great Britain: A List of Surviving Books*, 2nd ed. (London: Royal Historical Society, 1964).

*MLGBS* Andrew G. Watson, *Medieval Libraries of Great Britain: A List of Surviving Books: Supplement to the Second Edition* (London: Royal Historical Society, 1987).

*MMBL* Neil R. Ker and Andrew J. Piper, *Medieval Manuscripts in British Libraries*, 5 vols. (Oxford: Clarendon Press, 1969–2003).

MS. Manuscript

Mynors and Thomson, *Hereford Cathedral Library*
R. A. B. Mynors and Rodney M. Thomson, *Catalogue of the Manuscripts of Hereford Cathedral Library* (Cambridge: Published on behalf of the Dean and Chapter of Hereford Cathedral by D. S. Brewer, 1993).

Newburgh William of Newburgh, *Historia Rerum Anglicarum*, ed. Richard Howlett, *Chronicles of the Reigns of Stephen, Henry II, and Richard I*, RS 82, 4 vols. (London: Longmans, 1884–1889), 1:1–408, and 2:409–53. Cited by book and chapter.

Newton Robert R. Newton, *Medieval Chronicles and the Rotation of the Earth* (Baltimore: John Hopkins University Press, 1972).

*ODNB* *Oxford Dictionary of National Biography from the Earliest Times to the Year 2000*, ed. H. C. G. Matthew and Brian Harrison, 60 vols. and index (Oxford: Oxford University Press, 2004).

OMT Oxford Medieval Texts (Oxford: Clarendon Press, 1950–).

*Orderic* *The Ecclesiastical History of Orderic Vitalis*, ed. Marjorie Chibnall, OMT, 6 vols. (Oxford: Clarendon Press, 1968–1980).

Orphen, *Ireland* Goddard H. Orphen, *Ireland under the Normans, 1169–1333*, 4 vols. (Oxford: Clarendon Press, 1911–1920).

Paris, *CM* Matthew Paris, *Chronica Majora*, ed. Henry R. Luard, RS 57, 7 vols. (London: Longmans, 1872–1883).

*Peerage* George E. Cokayne, *The Complete Peerage of England, Scotland, Ireland, Great Britain and the United Kingdom*, ed. Vicary Gibbs et al., 13 vols. in 14 pts. (London: St Catherine, 1910–1959); vol. 14, *Addenda and Corrigenda*, ed. Peter W. Hammond (Stroud: St Catherine, 1998).

Pseudo-Isidore — *Decretales Pseudo-Isidorianae*, quoted from the *halb-kritischen* edition which has been put online through K.-G. Schon's *Projekt Pseudoisidor* (http://www.pseudoisidor.de/). Cited by reference to decretal and, where the file can be downloaded in pdf format, the page number (e.g "II Clemens p. 45").

*PL* — *Patrologiae cursus completus: series latina*, ed. J.-P. Migne, 221 vols. (Paris: J.-P. Migne, 1844–1864). Cited by volume and column number.

Planta, *MSS in the Cottonian Library*

Joseph Planta, *Catalogue of the Manuscripts in the Cottonian Library, deposited in the British Museum* (London: British Museum, 1802).

PPRS — Publications of the Pipe Roll Society (London: Wyman and Sons, 1884–).

RH — Roger of Howden

*Chron.* — *Chronica*, ed. William Stubbs, *The Chronicle of the Reigns of Henry II and Richard I*, RS 51, 4 vols. (London: Longmans, 1868–1871). Covers the history of England from the age of Bede to 1201, being a compilation derived from earlier histories as far 1169.

*GHS* — *Gesta regis Henrici secundi Benedicti abbatis*, ed. William Stubbs, *The Chronicle of the Reigns of Henry II and Richard I, AD 1169–1192*, RS 49, 2 vols. (London: Longmans, 1867). Covers the years from 1169 to 1192.

Rollason, *Symeon of Durham*

*Symeon of Durham, Historian of Durham and the North*, ed. David W. Rollason, Studies in North-Eastern History 1 (Stamford: Shaun Tyas, 1998).

*RRAN* — *Regesta regum Anglo-Normannorum, 1066–1154*, ed. H. W. Carless Davis, Charles Johnson, and H. A. Cronne, 4 vols. (Oxford: Clarendon Press, 1913–1969).

*RRAN Will.* — *Regesta regum Anglo-Normannorum: The Acta of William I (1066–1087)*, ed. David Bates (Oxford: Clarendon Press, 1998).

RS — Rolls Series: Rerum Britannicarum Medii Ævi Scriptores, or Chronicles and Memorials of Great Britain and Ireland during the Middle Ages (London: Longmans, 1858–).

RT — Robert of Torigni

*Access.* — *Accessiones ad Sigebertum*, ed. R. Howlett, *Chronicles of the Reigns of Stephen, Henry II, and Richard I*, RS 82, 4 vols. (London:

Longmans, 1889), 4:3–60. A chronicle covering AD 94–1100 which incorporates much material from the Norman Annals in a form closely related to *AMSM*. The Rolls Series edition is preferred here to that of Delisle, because it provides greater guidance as to Robert's sources.

*Chron.* — *Chronica*, ed. Howlett, *Chronicles of Stephen, Henry II, and Richard I*, 4:81–315.

S — Peter H. Sawyer, *Anglo-Saxon Charters: An Annotated List and Bibliography* (London: Royal Historical Society, 1968). Cited by charter number.

s.a. — sub anno

SD — Symeon of Durham

*HR* — *Historia Regum*, ed. Thomas Arnold, *Symeonis monachi opera omnia*, RS 75, 2 vols. (London: Longmans, 1882–1885), 2:3–283. Cited by section number.

*LDE* — *Libellus de Exordio atque Procursu istius, hoc est Dunhelmensis, Ecclesie—Tract on the Origins and Progress of this the Church of Durham*, ed. and trans. David W. Rollason, OMT (Oxford: Clarendon Press, 2000). Cited by book and chapter.

*SEHD* — Florence E. Harmer, *Select English Historical Documents of the Ninth and Tenth Centuries* (Cambridge: Cambridge University Press, 1914).

SH — Subsidia Hagiographica

Sharpe, *HLW* — Richard Sharpe, *A Handlist of the Latin Writers of Great Britain and Ireland before 1540*, Publications of the Journal of Medieval Latin 1 (Turnhout: Brepols, 1997).

Sims-Williams, *RLWE*
Patrick Sims-Williams, *Religion and Literature in Western England, 600–800*, Cambridge Studies in Anglo-Saxon England 3 (Cambridge: Cambridge University Press, 1990).

Smith, *MSS Bibl. Cotton.*
Thomas Smith, *Catalogus Librorum Manuscriptorum Bibliothecæ Cottonianæ* (Oxford: Sheldonian Theatre, 1696).

Stevenson, "Domesday Survey"
William H. Stevenson, "A Contemporary Description of the Domesday Survey," *EHR* 22 (1907): 73–84.

Story, *Carolingian Connections*
Joanna Story, *Carolingian Connections: Anglo-Saxon England and Carolingian Francia, c. 750–870*, Studies in Early Medieval Britain 2 (Aldershot: Ashgate, 2003).

Thomson, *St Mary of the Meadows*
A. Hamilton Thomson, *The Abbey of St Mary of the Meadows Leicester* (Leicester: Leicestershire Archaeological Society, 1949).

TM*Chron.* Thomas of Marlborough, *History of the Abbey of Evesham*, ed. and trans. Jane Sayers and Leslie Watkiss, OMT (Oxford: Clarendon Press, 2003). Cited by section number.

U.L. University Library

VA *Verior Assertio*, i.e. the "corrected chronology" of Marianus Scotus.

Walther, *Initia* Hans Walther, *Initia carminum ac versuum medii aevi posterioris latinorum: Alphabetisches Verzeichnis der Versanfänge mittellateinischer Dichtungen*, 2nd ed. (Göttingen: Vandenhoeck and Ruprecht, 1969).

Wallis Faith Wallis, trans., *Bede: The Reckoning of Time*, Translated Texts for Historians 29 (Liverpool: Liverpool University Press, 1999).

Warner and Gilson, *Royal and King's MSS*
George F. Warner and Julius P. Gilson, *Catalogue of Western Manuscripts in the Old Royal and King's Collections in the British Museum*, 4 vols. (London: British Museum, 1921).

Webber, *Scribes and Scholars*
Teresa Webber, *Scribes and Scholars at Salisbury Cathedral, c. 1075–c. 1125* (Oxford: Clarendon Press, 1992).

Williams, *English and the Conquest*
Ann Williams, *The English and the Norman Conquest* (Woodbridge: Boydell Press, 1995).

*Winchcombe* The Winchcombe Chronicle as edited and translated below.

*Winchcombe*[1] The first phase, from VA 1 to AD 1122.

*Winchcombe*[2] The second phase, from AD 1123 to 1181.

WM William of Malmesbury

*GP* *De gestis pontificum Anglorum libri quinque*, ed. N. E. S. A. Hamilton, RS 52 (London: Longmans, 1870). Cited by book and section number.

*GR* *Gesta Regum Anglorum*, ed. and trans. R. A. B. Mynors, Rodney M. Thomson, and Michael Winterbottom, OMT, 2 vols. (Oxford: Clarendon Press, 1998–1999). Cited by book and section number.

*HN* *Historia Novella: The Contemporary History*, ed. Edmund King, trans. K. R. Potter, OMT (Oxford: Clarendon Press, 1998).

*VW* *The* Vita Wulfstani *of William of Malmesbury*, ed. Reginald R. Darlington, Camden Society 3rd ser. 40 (London: Royal Historical Society, 1928).

# Introduction

# Prologue: The Historical Significance of the Chronicles

The two annalistic chronicles edited and translated in the present volume were both produced during the twelfth century for monastic communities in England. The longer of the two was produced at Winchcombe Abbey, and for this reason it is here designated the *Winchcombe Chronicle*. The evidence for the provenance of the shorter chronicle is less conclusive: its continuations were certainly added at a religious house in the central midlands, and there are good, albeit not particularly straightforward, grounds for thinking that that community was the Priory of Coventry Cathedral—grounds which are sufficiently strong to allow us to name it the *Coventry Chronicle*.[1] Each is preserved in a single manuscript: the former in MS. London, B.L., Cotton Tiberius E.IV, folios 1r–27v (hereafter "T"),[2] the latter in MS. London, B.L., Harley 3775, folios 34r–67v and 73r (hereafter "H"). They are, moreover, closely related to each other. Both begin with the Incarnation of Jesus Christ, and the great majority of their annals down to 1122 appear to derive from the same common root, a lost chronicle for the existence of which there is also evidence in a number of thirteenth- and fourteenth-century compilations. In *Winchcombe* this common root has been expanded with the addition of much new material; in *Coventry* it appears to have been abbreviated a little. With their entries for 1123 they part company: *Winchcombe* was later extended with a single continuation bringing its coverage of events down to 1181, whilst *Coventry* was extended in perhaps as many as twelve different stages bringing its coverage down to 1202. The historical value of these chronicles has two different dimensions, since they speak, on the one hand, to a number of precise questions pertaining to the study of English history between the late eighth and the late

[1] The problem is discussed in detail in chap. 4 below.

[2] *Winchcombe*'s annals were also used in the making of a second chronicle which may also have been produced at the abbey. A fragment of that chronicle covering 1049 to 1232 survives in MS. London, B.L., Cotton Faustina B.I, fols. 12r–29v. Darlington treated this text as another witness to *Winchcombe*, but so much material has been added to it that it is better seen as a new work. It is discussed below along with other lesser witnesses to the common root in chap. 5, § d, below.

twelfth centuries, and on the other, to a number of broader problems in the study of monastic culture, of medieval historiography, and indeed of the long-term history of historical writing itself. It will be best to proceed by outlining their significance with regard to the former issues before turning to the latter, since this will permit more economy in the introduction of explanatory information.

The two chronicles provide, first of all, material which sheds light on several issues in the history of Anglo-Saxon and Angevin England. The foundation documents preserved in the *Winchcombe Chronicle* are of some significance, for example, for the study of the last century of the Mercian kingdom and its church, since the minster at Winchcombe lay at the centre of a vast lordship that made it one of great churches of the ninth century. This lordship was assembled by one of the last great Mercian kings, Cenwulf (796–821), when he founded the minster as a burial church for himself and his family. The chronicle preserves the only medieval copy of his alleged foundation charter, and the only copies of the papal privileges which Cenwulf obtained from Leo III (795–816) and Paschal I (817–824) apart from those in the abbey's thirteenth-century cartulary. There are problems with these documents—all of them show signs of having been forged or retouched—but all can be rescued to some extent, making the status of *Winchcombe*'s versions of them a matter of some consequence for our knowledge of this period in the history of the Mercian hegemony.[3] The continuations to both chronicles also preserve a little information of some importance for the study of late twelfth-century English history. The continuation to *Winchcombe* contains a number of otherwise unknown items, most belonging to the section of the reign of Henry II (1154–1189) which it covers—that is, the twenty-seven years between 1154 and 1181. Some of its most striking information concerns the earls of Gloucester. *Winchcombe* is, for example, unique among the chronicles of this period in crediting Earl William with the capture of Earl Robert of Leicester at the Battle of Fornham (1173.6). Since they were composed at the house where the chronicle was maintained, as opposed to being borrowed from other sources, the later continuations to *Coventry* contain rather more information which is otherwise unreported. Much of it relates to appointments and obits, but the third extended continuation, that which covers 1187 to 1190, has some material of greater value. This continuation is more detailed than the rest, and it offers some unique insights as to how the spin that Richard I's court was putting on events such as his final quarrel with his father, Henry II (1188.5, 1189.1), and his postponement of his departure for the Third Crusade (1190.1) was received by those in the middle tiers of the English ecclesiastical establishment.

But with the exception of these items, there is no disguising the absence of much new or important data of the traditional kind in the two chronicles

[3] The early history of Winchcombe and the extent of the charters' contamination by forgery is discussed in detail in the commentary on *Winchcombe* 787.2, 811.1–3, and 818.3 below.

edited and translated here. The common root is almost entirely comprised of items which are reported with more accuracy and in greater detail elsewhere, chiefly in John of Worcester's *Chronica chronicarum*. Much the same is true of the additional matter which was inserted into the text when it was first copied at Winchcombe and of the continuation which was later appended to the text. Most of this material can also be found elsewhere, in the prelims to John's *Chronica chronicarum*, in his *Chronicula*, in Gervase of Canterbury's *Chronica,* and in the *Annals of Tewkesbury*. The way in which the two chronicles handle their material also fails to impress. The author who created the common root made some glaring errors. He faithfully reproduced garbled material,[4] and he often misplaced material in relation to the root's twofold chronological apparatus. That is, he often inserts material as though his sources were using the Marianan rather than the Dionysian *Anno Domini* system, dislocating these additions by some twenty-two years from their proper place in the sequence of events.[5] The chronological apparatus also caused problems for the scribes who copied the common root for the Coventry version. Using the Dionysian years as their guide, they often allowed dislocations to creep into the Marianan years, distorting the overall shape of the chronicle. In truth, the two chronicles add little to the established repertoire of narrative sources. Rather, their significance lies chiefly in what they have to say about certain historiographical questions.

Indeed, the specific problem in the study of English history to which they speak most loudly is that of explaining the work of John of Worcester. John is presently recognised as the author of the Worcester *Chronica chronicarum* and *Chronicula*, two of the more important sources for the study of Anglo-Saxon and Anglo-Norman history.[6] And, as has already been indicated, the two chronicles edited below are both full of entries which *echo* the contents of John's known works. The vast majority of these items were transmitted through a common root, but some were received by other means: the redactor of the first phase of *Winchcombe*, for example, combined the common root with items from one of the auxiliary texts which John prepared as adjuncts to his *Chronica chronicarum* and *Chronicula* (namely, the revised version of his "Papal Annals"), whilst most of the material in the first of the continuations added to *Coventry*, that covering 1123

[4] E.g. *Winchcombe* 824.3.

[5] The problem occurs most often with items taken from the Norman Annals, which follow the Dionysian system: e.g. *Winchcombe* 890 (rightly 912), 950 (rightly 972), 968.2 (rightly 988?), 974 (rightly 996).

[6] His position among a wider network of historians active in his day is explored in Martin Brett, "John of Worcester and his Contemporaries," in *The Writing of History in the Middle Ages: Essays Presented to Richard William Southern*, ed. Ralph H. C. Davis and John M. Wallace-Hadrill (Oxford: Clarendon Press, 1981), 101–26, hereafter Brett, "John". Readers unfamilar with John of Worcester and the nature of his work are directed to chap. 2, § a, below.

to 1150, is derived from a version of the *Chronica chronicarum* which extended down to 1138. But it is the common root and the strength of its relationship with John's work which is of most interest. Judging by the items shared by the various witnesses,[7] the common root was a substantial annalistic chronicle which covered the period from the Incarnation down to 1122 and one which, like both of the known works of John, employed the revised chronology of Marianus Scotus. This much is almost certain, since *Winchcombe* and *Coventry* use the same two-column chronological apparatus in which the years of the Incarnation are given according to both Dionysius Exiguus and "the Gospel truth" as defined by Marianus Scotus.

The strength of the relationship between the common root and the known works of John raises a number of questions. How, to begin with, should it to be understood? Should the common root and its descendants, *Winchcombe* and *Coventry*, be seen as evidence for the reception of John's works? If so, can they be made to yield insights into the way in which *Chronica chronicarum* was compiled similar to those provided by other near-contemporary chronicles which incorporate material borrowed from it, chronicles such as the *Historia regum* attributed to Symeon of Durham?[8] Or is the relationship to be explained in a different way? Might the common ancestor be, for example, an as-yet-unidentified work by John himself? It certainly has many attributes which point in this direction: it was produced within his lifetime, it used the Marianan chronology he was so keen to promote, it was full of material related to the history of Worcester Cathedral, and the items which *Winchcombe* and *Coventry* derived from it show signs of having been reworked in ways which are typical of his compositional method. If, moreover, the common ancestor is the third of John's works to be identified, what can it contribute to our understanding of his methods, of the contents of his library, and above all, of what he was trying to achieve as an historian? The question of exactly what John was trying to achieve is one which affects the status of all the evidence that has been derived from the *Chronica chronicarum*, yet it remains far from being satisfactorily resolved. Historians of Anglo-Saxon and Anglo-Norman England have tended to assume that John was a relatively straightforward historian whose aim was to accumulate information about England's past by gleaning was to be had from whatever sources he could find and by attaching it to the scaffolding provided by Marianus.[9] But this all too convenient

[7] Other witnesses to the existence of this common root, in particular three chronicles which appear to intrude a number of items directly from this source, are discussed in chap. 5 below.

[8] See Brett, "John," esp. 119–20.

[9] See, for example, Elisabeth M. C. van Houts, "Historical Writing," in *A Companion to the Anglo-Norman World*, ed. Christopher Harper-Bill and eadem (Woodbridge: Boydell Press, 2002), 103–21, at 112–13. Van Houts treats *Chronica chronicarum* as a Latinised version of the Anglo-Saxon Chronicle, contrasting it unfavourably with Eadmer's

view falls foul of John's authorship of *Chronicula*, for the existence of this strange, breviate, version of the former text belies the theory that he was merely interested in accumulating data. It shows that his aims as an historian were more complex than have been supposed. If the common ancestor is also one of John's works, then that would seem to compound the difficulties with the usual view, since it would imply that he produced not just one, but now two breviate alternatives to *Chronica chronicarum*.

The answers to these questions will no doubt remain a matter of some debate; but no matter what the exact solutions, the strong relationship which the shared root exhibits with John of Worcester's works is also important in a broader sense. For it helps to show that the production of annalistic chronicles was not, as is often assumed, a random process, but a matter of compiling a text that was intended to perform a particular task. This much is clear from the way in which the common root covers exactly the same ground as John's *Chronica chronicarum* and *Chronicula*—that is, the whole of the sixth age from the Incarnation down to 1122—and uses much the same material—a mixture of items derived from Marianus Scotus and from various English and, to a lesser extent, Frankish and Norman sources—whilst presenting that material in an entirely different way from the other two works. It matters not whether the common root was produced by John himself or exactly how its author produced it—that is, whether it was produced by abbreviating *Chronica chronicarum* and by adding the few items not found there, or by making a different selection of the items in John's working notes or the books which he had gathered in his *atelier*. For no matter what the precise method involved, the point remains the same: the common root was the product of a conscious decision to create an alternative version of this material in a *particular generic format*. It is true that one of the root's descendants, *Coventry*, was continued with many brief additions which look as though they were added according to a random process, but most of these continuations continue the pattern established by the common root.

*Historia novorum* and citing Brett, "John," 125, for his comments on John's "resolute if blinkered interest in the dates of men's deaths and the succession to ecclesiastical offices." Kauffmann, *Romanesque Manuscripts*, 87, writes that down to 1095 *Chronica chronicarum* consists "mainly of a translation into Latin of the Anglo-Saxon Chronicle grafted onto a world history compiled by Marianus Scotus." Chris Given-Wilson, *Chronicles: The Writing of History in Medieval England* (London: Hambledon Press, 2004), 158–59, gives more emphasis to the Marianan component, but he still sees John as an historian whose aim was to recover "the story of the English people." These views of John reflect the seemingly ineluctable influence of a long-standing tradition in which it has been the norm to print and discuss only those parts of his works which were relevant to the study of the English nation-state—that is, those parts which could be assimilated to the grand narrative of the rise of England. It is the contention of the present study that John's project needs to be understood, above all, in relation to his monastic context.

There are, moreover, strong clues as to the task for which the common root was intended in its contents and in the way in which it was adapted and continued by the makers of *Winchcombe* and *Coventry*. The contents of the common root suggest, to begin with, that the task was related to the discipline of computus: many items refer to events of computistical significance such as the junction-points in the great paschal cycle, whilst the interest taken in phenomena such as evolution of the political topography of both the Frankish and the Anglo-Saxon worlds echoes the geographical and spatial interests found in computistical reference books. There is, secondly, something about the pragmatic way in which *Winchcombe* and *Coventry* adapt and continue the common root which is redolent of the needs of the teaching context. Though they are very different in character, their manuscripts also suggest that the role which these chronicles played was related to the teaching of computus. *Winchcombe*, on the one hand, was part of a large computistical collection which has been aptly described as a school-book, and there is clear evidence in its palaeography (in the fact that the scribe who copied the first phase of the chronicle also executed the calendar, various tables, and the diagrams) that the chronicle was identified as a useful addition to the collection. *Coventry*, on the other hand, is preserved in a rather ugly bundle of five quires: apart from a short poem the chronicle is the only item in these leaves, but the manuscript also shows a connection with computus in so far as a later scribe went through the entire chronicle, from back to front, entering in the margin the dominical letter(s) for each year—an addition which cannot easily be explained except as an attempt to produce a teaching aid, as an attempt to provide a visual illustration of the attributes of this computistical device.

These findings are significant because the reasons why annalistic chronicles were compiled remain a matter of uncertainty. Chronicles of this kind are a ubiquitous feature of the manuscript record, yet their functions are obscure because they rarely offer clear evidence as to why they were compiled. Annalistic chronicles seldom have prefaces,[10] nor do they offer any internal commentary on their own contents. In the absence of obvious evidence, scholars have got away with projecting onto them some rather gratuitous theories as to why they were produced. The desire, for example, to extract the few unique nuggets of fact that these sources typically contain without having to trouble oneself with the possibility that the reporting of these items may have been affected by an agenda of some kind has given rise to the view that annalistic chronicles are the products

---

[10] An exception to the rule is the preface found in various copies of the Hyde-Reading-Worcester group of chronicles and printed from *APW* in Luard, *AM*, 4:355. On this group of chronicles, see chap. 1, § a, below; on the preface and the reasons why it appears with some but not all of the chronicles that comprise this group, see Noel Denholm-Young, "The Winchester-Hyde Chronicle," *EHR* 49 (1934): 85–93, at 88. Gervase's *Cronica* also has a preface, but this chronicle is better understood, not as an annalistic chronicle, but as a hybrid with many of the characteristics of rhetorical history: see chap. 1, § f, below.

of a primitive and jejune interest in collecting historical data. The theory is that annals were produced by "merging" whatever earlier annals were to hand and by continuing the resulting confection with the addition on an almost year-by-year basis of notices recording recently reported events.[11] The problem with this approach is not that there are no nuggets of fact to be had, but that it is wasteful, unduly negative, and erroneous, in so far as close analysis of chronicles such as *Winchcombe* and *Coventry* suggests that agendas were at work in the selection of material, albeit ones of a pedagogical rather than a political character. Indeed, the example provided by the present chronicles points the way towards a much more positive evaluation of the historical value of the annalistic chronicle, one which encourages scholars to see such texts as evidence for the workings of the monastic classroom. The observation that there is a relationship between the production of annalistic chronicles and the teaching of computus is hardly new, but the exact nature of that connection remains obscure, and scholars have often defined it in vague terms. The evidence of *Winchcombe* and *Coventry* helps to show that that relationship was more precise and purposeful than is often assumed—namely, that chronicles of this kind were used to provide the background understanding of time necessary for a genuine grasp of the issues and methods involved in calculating dates, and that they were also used in conjunction with computistical manuals to illustrate various aspects of this science.

The questions to which *Winchcombe* and *Coventry* speak are, in conclusion, mostly of an historiographical character, but they are by no means insignificant. These chronicles ask us to rethink our theories as to the nature of John of Worcester's project, they help to clarify the functions of the annalistic chronicle and to define its relationship to other kinds of historical text, and they provide insights into the historical culture of the twelfth-century monastery. That is, they provide insights as to the intellectual beginnings from which many of the major historical writers active at this time—figures such as William of Malmesbury and Gervase of Canterbury—developed their ideas about the wider world. The organisation and contents of *Winchcombe* and *Coventry* will be discussed in detail in chapters two to four below. It will be helpful to begin, however, by examining the issues raised by annalistic chronicles and the theories as to their function and significance that presently hold sway. This topic will, therefore, be treated presently in chapter one.

---

[11] This assumption underpins, not only much empiricist exploitation of annals, but also much theory-driven "reflection" on the historical qualities of annalistic chronicles: e.g. Jerzy Topolski, "Historical Narrative: Towards a Coherent Structure," *History and Theory* 26 (1987): 75–86, at 78: "The annalist just flatly recorded facts *as they occurred.* When reporting on a given fact he did not activate his knowledge about what happened earlier, and since he was a contemporary of the facts he recorded he was unable (even had he felt the need to do so) to reflect on what happened later, including the consequences of the facts recorded by him" (my italics).

# Chapter One: Towards a Better Understanding of the Annalistic Chronicle

## (a) Some Definitions

To begin with some definitions, the term "annalistic chronicle" may be said to apply to *any* record of the past which is organised according to a year-by-year format, a trait which distinguishes these histories from those which organise their material on a thematic basis or according to irregular units of time, such as the reigns of a kingdom's rulers.[1] The chronicles edited below are examples, however, of a specific type of annalistic chronicle which seems to have flourished in England during the twelfth and thirteenth centuries. These chronicles attempt to cover the sixth age of the world—that is, every year from the Incarnation (or the Nativity of John the Baptist) down to the time when they were compiled.[2] When an example fails to cover all of the sixth age, it is usually because the manuscript in which they are preserved begins or ends imperfectly, or because it is a late example where a chronicle of this kind has been reworked for a new purpose. When, moreover, as often happens in their coverage of the more distant past, they fail to provide any items for a given year, the year-number is almost always

[1] On the many different types of chronicle that can be identified in the manuscript record, see David N. Dumville, "What is a Chronicle?," in *The Medieval Chronicle II: Proceedings of the Second International Conference on the Medieval Chronicle, Drieberger/Utrecht, 16–21 July 1999*, ed. Erik Kooper, Costerus n.s. 144 (Amsterdam: Rodopi, 2002), 1–27. Useful starting points for the discussion of chronicles also include Michael McCormick, *Les annales du haut moyen âge*, Typologie des sources du moyen âge occidental 14 (Turnhout: Brepols, 1975), esp. 11–21.

[2] For the concept of the six ages of the world, see Augustine, *De civitate Dei*, 22.30, ed. Bernhard Dombart and Alfons Kalb, CCSL 47–48 (Turnhout: Brepols, 1955), 2:862–66. On Augustine's role in defining the concept and its development by Isidore and Bede, see Michael I. Allen, "Universal History 300–1000: Origins and Western Developments," in *Historiography in the Middle Ages*, ed. Deborah M. Deliyannis (Leiden: Brill, 2002), 17–42 (esp. 31–35); Hildegard L. C. Tristram, *Sex aetates mundi: Die Weltzeitalter bei den Angelsachsen und den Iren* (Heidelberg: Winter, 1985), esp. 19–30.

retained.[3] The annals in these chronicles tend to be brief. They rarely assemble more than two or three notices for a single year, and their coverage of a given year rarely exceeds more than one hundred words. Indeed, it is not unusual for them to cover two or three decades on a single page, especially in their earlier sections. They tend, finally, to favour the inclusion of certain types of material, namely:

1. The obits and successions of the emperors of Rome, including those of the Frankish and German heirs to the title.
2. The obits and successions of the kings of the Franks.
3. The obits and successions of local rulers, such as the kings of the various English kingdoms and the dukes of the Normans.
4. Major shifts in political topography, such as the threefold division of the kingdom of the Franks in 843.
5. The successions (or perhaps more often the floruits) of the bishops of Rome.
6. The papal acts which have created the church as a sacramental institution, such as rulings as to format and content of the liturgy and as to work and appearance (that is, the hair and vestments) of the clergy.
7. The spread of Christianity, especially its arrival in Gaul and Britain.
8. The persecutions of the Catholic Church.
9. The obits and successions of the local metropolitan.
10. The obits and successions of the diocesan bishop.
11. The obits and successions of the heads of the community at which the chronicle was produced.
12. The floruits or obits of major writers such as Jerome, Augustine, Cassiodorus, and so on. These writers are usually Christian, but these chronicles sometimes include entries for pagan scientists such as Pliny.

12\. Dedications and foundations of major churches.

13\. Hagiological events such as deaths of saints and the translations or enshrinements of their relics.

14\. Prodigies and portents.

15\. Famines and other disasters.

---

[3] In the parlance that has emerged around this subject, such years or annal-numbers are said to be *barren* as opposed to those which are *fruitful*. These are awkward usages since they imply that there was always an intention always to include something, and it is by no means certain that this is so.

The category may be described, in short, as comprising breviate world chronicles that cover the Sixth Age of the World in an annalistic format—there is no convenient label.[4] With the exception of *Winchcombe* and *Coventry*, the most interesting twelfth-century English examples of this sub-type comprises a series of chronicles based on the so-called Norman Annals and mostly associated with houses located in the southeast. These chronicles may be listed as follows:[5]

1. London, B.L., Cotton Claudius C.IX, fols. 12v–17v (s.xii$^{2}$, Worcester)
2. London, B.L., Cotton Nero A.VIII, fols. 2r–41r (s.xii$^{med}$, Rochester?)
3. London, B.L., Cotton Nero C.VII, fols. 216r–223v (s.xii$^{med}$, Canterbury)
4. London, B.L., Cotton Nero D.II, fols. 234r–241r (s.xii$^{1}$–s.xiii$^{in}$, Battle Abbey)
5. London, B.L., Cotton Vespasian D.XIX, fols. 53r–70v (s.xii$^{1}$–s.xiii$^{in}$, Ely or St Swithuns, Winchester?)
6. London, B.L., Cotton Vitellius A.XVII, fols. 1r–16r (s.xii$^{med}$–s.xii$^{2}$, Chichester)
7. London, B.L., Royal 4.B.VII, fols. 211r–218v (s.xii$^{ex}$, Rochester)
8. Vatican City, B.A.V., Reg. lat. 147, fols. 61r–69v (s.xii$^{2}$, Lewes)[6]

To explain, the term "Norman Annals" refers to a group of annalistic texts ultimately derived from a chronicle now lost which was probably compiled and continued at Rouen Cathedral from the middle of the eleventh century if not

[4] These chronicles are to be distinguished, in short, from both the "larger annalistic chronicles" and the many "world-chronicles" that take a non-annalistic format, such as Ralph Niger's *Chronica*, ed. Hanna Krause, *Eine englische Weltchronik des 12. Jahrhunderts* (Frankfurt: P. Lang, 1985), 1–308. On the many different types of larger annals that emerged between the ninth and thirteenth centuries, see Elisabeth M. C. van Houts, *Local and Regional Chronicles*, Typologie des sources du moyen âge occidental 74 (Turnhout: Brepols, 1995), and, for the latter part of the period, Given-Wilson, *Chronicles*, passim. On the category of the "world-chronicle", see Karl H. Krüger, *Die Universalchroniken*, Typologie des sources du moyen âge occidental 16 (Turnhout: Brepols, 1976), esp. 21–23. See also Anna Dorothee von den Brincken, *Studien zur lateinischen Weltchronistik bis in das Zeitalter Ottos von Freising* (Düsseldorf: M. Triltsch, 1957); Brian Croke, "The Origins of the Christian World Chronicle," in *History and Historians in Late Antiquity*, ed. idem and Alanna M. Emmett (Sydney: Pergamon, 1983), 116–31.

[5] Nos. 1–4 and 6–7 were edited or collated, sometimes only in part, in Liebermann, *ANG*, 35–49, 51–55, 61–83, 86–89. No. 5 remains unprinted.

[6] Partly ed. Felix Liebermann, "The Annals of Lewes Priory," *EHR* 17 (1902): 83–89.

earlier.[7] The items in the extant versions which indicate their origins comprise items concerned with the successions of the archbishops of Rouen, with various local Neustrian saints, and with, from the coming of the Normans to Rouen in 876, the deeds of the Counts of Rouen. The surviving versions are all related as far as the beginning of the eleventh century to a set of Easter-table annals from the abbey of Saint-Bénigne, Dijon,[8] which suggests that their common root may derive from a version of this chronicle which travelled to Normandy with the help of the connections established by the reformer William of Volpiano. In the wake of the monastic revival in early eleventh-century Normandy (though probably not until the very end of the eleventh century)[9] the Rouen version of this chronicle was circulated among the monasteries and cathedrals that had been re-established in the duchy. Each made its own transcript, sometimes reworking the Latin but invariably continuing it with other material. Each of the surviving versions offers, therefore, a slightly different selection of entries from the Rouen version together with various other items. The most accessible of these Norman versions may be listed as follows:

9. Avranches, Bibliothèque municipale, 211, fols. 67r–77v (s.xii$^{1}$, Mont-St-Michel)[10]
10. Paris, B.n.F., lat. 10062, fols. 130r–160v (s.xii$^{1}$–xvi$^{in}$, St-Évroult)[11]
11. Paris, B.n.F., lat. 11885, fols. 24–35 (s.xiii$^{in}$, St-Évroult)
12. Rouen, Bibliothèque municipale, 1132, fols. 216v–222r (s.xii$^{ex}$, Jumièges)

[7] The origins and transmission of the Norman Annals are discussed by Jean Laporte, *Les annales de l'Abbaye Saint-Pierre de Jumièges* (Rouen: Cerf, 1954), 8–11; by Leopold Delisle, "Chroniques et annales diverses," in *Histoire Littéraire de la France*, vol. 32 (Paris: Imprimerie Nationale, 1898), 182–264 (esp. 194–212); by Oswald Holder-Egger in *MGH SS*, 26:488–90; and by David N. Dumville in *ASC Coll.*, 17:xliii–xlvi.

[8] *Annales sancti Benigni Divionensis*, ed. Georg Waitz, *MGH SS*, 5:38–50, hereafter *ASBD*.

[9] Laporte, *Les annales de Jumièges*, 10, suggests that the annals were first transcribed at Saint-Évroult around 1098, at Mont-Saint-Michel around 1100, at Saint-Étienne around 1100–1106, and at Jumièges soon after that date.

[10] Partly ed. Leopold Delisle, *Chronique de Robert de Torigni, abbé du Mont-Saint-Michel, suivie de divers opuscules historiques de cet auteur et de plusieurs religieux de la même abbaye*, Ouvrages publiés par la société de l'histoire de Normandie, 2 vols. (Rouen: A. Le Brument, 1872–1873), 2:207–30, hereafter *AMSM*. Delisle's edition omits everything for the period between AD 30 and 875, except for an addition s.a. 708. For the remainder reference has been made to the manuscript.

[11] Ed. Augustus Le Prévost, *Orderici Vitalis Angligenæ, coenobii Uticensis monachi, Historiæ Ecclesiasticæ Libri Tredecim*, 5 vols. (Paris: Renouard, 1835–1855), 5:139–73, hereafter *AU*.

13. Vatican City, B.A.V., Reg. lat. 553, pt. ii, fols. 153r–168r (s.xii$^{ex}$, St-Wandrille; s.xiii$^{in}$, Rouen)[12]

14. Vatican City, B.A.V., Reg. lat. 703A (s.xii$^{med}$, St-Étienne, Caen)[13]

It needs to be stressed that of the surviving Norman versions only the *Annals of Mont-St-Michel* and the *Annals of St-Évroult* are earlier than the mid-twelfth century, and that some are much later in date than the earliest English versions. One or two lightly adapted copies of the common root must have reached England soon after they began to circulate in Normandy. Furthermore, by around 1125 at the latest, entries from these Norman exemplars or English versions of them were being used to amplify other chronicles, the contents of which were dominated by English material, such as the *Annals of St Neots*[14] and the E- and F-texts of the *Anglo-Saxon Chronicle.*[15] Were someone to attempt a reconstruction of the "original" Annals of Rouen in all their details, he or she would need to give as much attention to the various English texts as to their Norman counterparts. For present purposes, however, the crucial point is that although their coverage of events is much thinner, the various versions of the Norman Annals are chronicles of much the same type as *Winchcombe* and *Coventry*. It is striking, indeed, that many of them begin as do *Winchcombe* and *Coventry* by reporting the nativities of both John the Baptist and Jesus Christ,[16] a phenomenon which begins to suggest that the compiler of the common root of the latter texts might well have taken the Norman Annals as one of his models.

Another relevant group of chronicles survives in at least six versions which may be listed as follows:

1. Cambridge, Corpus Christi College, 59, fols. 158v–180r (s.xiii$^{1}$, Merton)

[12] Ed. Laporte, *Les annales de Jumièges*, 21–111, hereafter *AG*. As Laporte explains, these MSS derive from the *Annals of Jumièges*.

[13] Ed. André DuChesne, *Historiæ Normannorum scriptores antiqui* (Paris: DuChesne, 1619), repr. by Francis Maseres in *Historiæ Anglicanæ circa tempus conquestus Angliæ a Guilielmo Notho, Normannorum duce, Selecta Monumenta* (London: J. White, 1807), 355–66, hereafter *ACad.*

[14] Ed. David N. Dumville, *ASC Coll.*, 17:1–107, hereafter *ASN*. *ASN* is utilised below as a further witness to the Norman Annals down to the year AD 914, where it ends.

[15] For discussion, see Susan E. Irvine in *ASC Coll.*, 7:lxxxviii–xc; Peter S. Baker in *ASC Coll.*, 8:xxxii–xxxiv.

[16] Number 1 begins imperfectly with AD 43, number 14 likewise with AD 633; numbers 2–7, 9, 12 and 13 begin with the birth of John the Baptist; numbers 8, 10 and 11 begin with the Incarnation.

2. London, B.L., Cotton Caligula A.X, fols. 65r–193r (s.xiv$^{in}$–xiv$^{2}$, Worcester)[17]
3. London, B.L., Cotton Faustina A.VIII, fols. 120v–146v (s.xiii$^{1}$, Southwark); Oxford, Bod.L., Rawlinson B.177, fols. 192r–286v (s.xiv$^{in}$, Southwark)
4. London, B.L., Cotton Vespasian E.IV, fols. 153r–201v (s.xiii$^{2}$, Reading)[18]
5. London, B.L., Harley 231, fols. 1r–71v (s.xv, Bermondsey)[19]
6. Oxford, Bod.L., Bodley 91, fols. 103r–127v (s.xiii$^{2}$, Hyde Abbey, Winchester)

These chronicles are all preserved in later medieval manuscripts and all distort the underlying model, but their annals down to about 1220 (the points of departure vary) depend to differing degrees on an earlier annalistic chronicle which almost certainly belonged to the sub-category under discussion.[20] The version which seems to preserve this root-text in its purest form may be that associated with Southwark. Southwark was a house of Augustinian canons, but a number of the items variously reported by these texts suggest that the root was itself based on an earlier chronicle produced at a Cluniac house in central France, perhaps La Charité-sur-Loire. It seems to have been at her daughter house of Bermondsey that it was first continued in England, possibly having arrived soon after it was founded in 1089. Having been extended into the early thirteenth century, it then

---

17 Cited as *APW*, this chronicle is discussed further in chap. 5 below. It departs from the usual pattern in as much as it suppresses the year-numbers of blank annals.

18 Luard, *AM*, 4:355–492, prints in small type those annals which were reproduced in *APW*; Liebermann, *ANG*, 182–202, prints the annals for 1202 to 1262, as these were omitted by Luard. The provenance depends mostly on two additions in a hand different from that which copies the text as a whole, which relate to Reading and which appear under 1199 and 1200 (fol. 175r). See Coates, *EMB*, 70, 72, 159–60.

19 Ed. Luard, *AM*, 3:423–87.

20 See Martin Brett, "The Annals of Bermondsey, Southwark and Merton," in *Church and City, 1000–1500: Essays in Honour of Christopher Brooke*, ed. David Abulafia, Michael Franklin, and Miri Rubin (Cambridge: Cambridge University Press, 1992), 279–310 (esp. 281); M. Tyson, "The Annals of Southwark and Merton," *Surrey Archaeological Collections* 13 (1926): 24–57; Denholm-Young, "Winchester-Hyde Chronicle," 85–93; Liebermann, *ANG*, 173–82; Gransden, *HWE*, 1:319, 333. These chronicles are by no means ideal examples of the present type, but they help to illustrate the margins of this sub-genre and the way in which it was distorted in the thirteenth century when the study of annalistic texts began to be disassociated from the study of computus. Several also figure in the discussion below (esp. chap. 5), and are helpfully introduced at this point.

became the basis of these chronicles.[21] But whatever the exact relationship between them, the crucial point for present purposes is that they exhibit much the same generic format as *Winchcombe* and *Coventry*. In the annals extending down to around 1200 they show much the same priorities in the selection of material; indeed, they offer more thorough coverage than the Norman Annals of certain topics, not least the early history of the Franks,[22] and the early history of the church as a sacramental institution.[23] The later manuscripts often omit substantial blocks of year numbers,[24] but the original almost certainly numbered all (or perhaps almost all) the years of the Sixth Age. Two, interestingly, begin with a summary account of the six ages of the world.[25]

Further examples could also be cited, but enough have been identified to show that there flourished in twelfth- and thirteenth-century England a type of historical text which may be described as the "breviate world chronicle in annalistic format". This chapter will attempt to show how historians might best exploit chronicles of this and similar kinds, and it will be useful to begin by examining the ideas about annalistic chronicles that currently hold sway and their intellectual roots.

---

[21] Brett, "Annals of Bermondsey," esp. 285 and 288. The existing annals of Bermondsey are, however, a much distorted version of the text underpinning the entire complex. See also Rose Graham, "The Priory of La Charité-sur-Loire and the Monastery of Bermondsey," in eadem, *English Ecclesiastical Studies: Being Some Essays in Research in Medieval History* (London: Society for Promoting Christian Knowledge, 1929), 91–124.

[22] Note esp. Faustina A.VIII, s.aa. 383, 431, 438, 469, 488, 499, 615, 631, 646, 649, 653, 660, 684, 689, 694, 714, 738, 740, 742, 752. The series has been thinned out in Vespasian E.IV, s.a. 383, 431, 469, 476, 488, 500, 607, 631, 646, 653, 679, 684, 738, 740, 742.

[23] E.g. Faustina A.VIII, s.aa. 72, 85, 94, 103, 122, 132, 142, 153, 157, 179, 188, 213, 230, 260, 263, 270, 274, 282, 313, 320, 324, 349, 371, 407, 422, 426, 443, 493, 497, 498, 592; Vespasian E.IV, s.aa. 72, 85, 86, 103, 122, 132, 142, 153, 157, 179, 189, 230, 260, 263, 270, 274, 282, 313, 319, 324, 349, 371, 407, 422, 426, 443, 493, 497, 498, 562 (*recte* 592).

[24] In its treatment of the sixth to ninth centuries the chronicle in Vespasian E.IV is especially muddled: it omits numbers for 570 to 613 (causing the insertion of extra entries for 595 and 607 at the foot of fol. 163), for 618 to 623, for 685 to 738, for 748 to 780, for 784 to 812, and so on. Some these errors were carried over in turn into Cotton Caligula A.X, the annals in which take Vespasian E.IV as their core text. See chap. 5, § a, below.

[25] E.g. Vespasian E.IV, fol. 153r; *APW*, 356. It should be noted that not all of the existing texts begin with the Incarnation: the Annals of Merton cover 1066 to 1240; those of Bermondsey begin in 1042.

## (b) The Problem of the Annalistic Chronicle

These texts have seldom enjoyed much esteem, especially among the more intellectually inclined, and the attitude is by no means a recent development. Indeed, Cicero gave his great authority to contempt for records of this kind with his discussion of historical writing in his *De oratore*, a dialogue set in 91 BC but written in 55 BC.[26] He there divides such historical works as had been written in Latin into two categories, the first comprising those which were modelled on the public annals maintained by the Pontifex Maximus: "Many have taken up this kind of writing and have left behind them unembellished memoranda of times, persons, places, and deeds . . . and as long as what is said makes sense, they consider brevity of expression alone to be praise."[27] This category clearly refers to the many annalistic works that were produced during the final centuries of the Roman Republic. Judging by what other writers say about them and by the contents of the fragments they quote, most seem to have used a year-by-year format with the years dated *ab urbe condita* or *a Remo et Romulo* or by the magistrates of the year, and to have been manufactured, as were the majority of medieval annals, by the collation and continuation of earlier historical works of much the same kind. Cicero calls them *annalium confectio*.[28] Their contents are said to have comprised notices recording disasters, eclipses, portents, prodigies, and the names of the annual officials. Cicero's other category of historical writing comprised those works which attempted to invest the past with *sonus vocis*, the qualities of the orator's voice—a category which refers to the "rhetorical monograph" as developed by writers such as Coelius and Sallust. Taking Thucydides as their model, historians of this kind usually told the story of a distinct episode from the recent past, often a war or a crisis that had befallen the state. They organised the contents

---

[26] For the entire passage, see Cicero, *De oratore libri tres*, 2.51–64, ed. Augustus S. Wilkins (Oxford: Clarendon Press, 1902). For the generic models available to the earliest Latin historians, see T. P. Wiseman, "Practice and Theory in Roman Historiography," *History* 66 (1981): 375–93; Christina S. Kraus and Anthony J. Woodman, *Latin Historians*, Greece & Rome New Surveys in the Classics 27 (Oxford: Oxford University Press, 1997), esp. 2–3.

[27] *De oratore*, 2.53: "Hanc similitudinem scribendi multi secuti sunt, qui sine ullis ornamentis monumenta solum temporum, hominum, locorum gestarumque rerum reliquerunt. . . . Et, dum intellegatur quid dicant, unam dicendi laudem putant esse brevitatem."

[28] *De oratore*, 2.52. For the methods of the annalists, see Stephen P. Oakley, *A Commentary on Livy, Books VI–X*, 4 vols. (Oxford: Clarendon Press, 1997–2005), 1:72–99; on the pontifical annals, see Bruce W. Frier, *Libri Annales Pontificum Maximorum* (Rome: American Academy in Rome, 1979). See also A. S. Gratwick in *The Cambridge History of Classical Literature*, vol. 2, *Latin Literature*, ed. E. J. Kenney and W.V. Clausen (Cambridge: Cambridge University Press, 1982), 149–52.

of their works in accordance with the narrative requirements of the story itself rather than by fitting into a long-term historical framework.

For Cicero it was this latter type alone which was worthy of attention. He derides the annalists for their failure to ornament their texts: they are "mere narrators."[29] It is to be hoped, he argues, that Latin writers will follow the example of Greek historians such as Thucydides, who introduced so many details (*res*) into his writings that the number of his ideas (*sententia*) is almost the same as the number of his words.[30] The historian ought to invest his narrative with distinction by deploying a variety of colours, and he should so arrange his words that they present a regular and continuous flow of language.[31] Cicero goes on, moreover, to define the issues which the historian ought to address in his narrative. He ought, for example, to pass judgement on the passage of events and to identify the causes of what happened: when writing about the counsel that was given in affairs of state the writer should say what he approves; when writing about the events that followed he should record not only what was done and said but also the manner in which things were done and said; and when writing about the outcome he should set out the reasons why the episode turned out as it did, regardless of whether it was through accident, good judgement, or sheer daring that the conclusion in question was reached.[32] Cicero's problem, in short, was that annals were lacking in both aesthetic appeal and the kind of forensic analysis which would enable the elites who ran the Republic to learn from their mistakes.

Though few modern historians are bothered by their want of literary refinement, many still find annals deficient for their failure to satisfy as narrative and as analysis.[33] It is certainly true that the way in which annalistic chronicles present

---

29 *De oratore*, 2.54: "Non exornatores rerum, sed tantum modo narratores fuerunt."

30 *De oratore*, 2.56.

31 *De oratore*, 2.54: "Caelius neque distinxit historiam varietate colorum neque verborum conlocatione et tractu orationis leni et aequabili perpolivit illud opus."

32 *De oratore*, 2.63. It is at this point that Cicero's ideals come closest to those of the modern academic, but see Anthony J. Woodman, *Rhetoric in Classical Historiography* (London: Croom Helm, 1988), 70–116, who stresses Cicero's advocacy of the application of rhetorical techniques to history.

33 On the perceived "failings" of annals as narrative history, see Hayden V. White, "The Value of Narrativity in the Representation of Reality," *Critical Inquiry* 7 (1980): 5–27; repr. in idem, *The Content of the Form: Narrative Discourse and Historical Representation* (Baltimore: John Hopkins University Press, 1987), 1–25. White's essay has much to be said for it, not least for its insistence that annals and chronicles ought be treated as "*alternatives* to, rather than failed anticipations of, the fully realized historical discourse that the modern history form is supposed to embody" (5). He never entirely succeeds, however, in escaping the Whiggish perspective that afflicts discussions of the form (see below). See also Robert F. Berkhofer, *Beyond the Great Story: History as Text and Discourse* (Cambridge, MA: Harvard University Press, 1995), esp. 37; and Morton White, *Foundations of Historical Knowledge* (New York: Harper and Row, 1965), 4.

their material makes them look most unlike a conventional narrative: they consist of chronologically ordered lists of happenings or events; they make no attempt to connect these items together with statements alluding, say, to causal links; they do not provide the series of events with a conclusion or an outcome. They often begin with a significant juncture like the Incarnation or the foundation of the house at which they were compiled,[34] but their texts end *in medias res*, without having achieved closure or a denouement. It is often hard to identify an underlying subject which they might conceivably be about: it is often possible, as has been shown above, to draw up a list of favoured topics, but it is often hard to identify a central theme, a point of view, or an interpretation that has influenced the choice of material or the way in which it has been treated. As Robert Bartlett says of the continuation to *Winchcombe*, "although there are certain recurrent topics of interest, it would be too much to claim that there is a theme to these annals and items of very miscellaneous nature follow one another in disjointed succession."[35] The entries themselves, furthermore, eschew analysis and comment in favour of the description of what happened: they seldom attempt to explain the event, to identify its causes, to explore its consequences, or to discuss its significance. They have, as one scholar puts it, "no identifiable narrative voice."[36] The entries seem to lack critical depth, being, as another historian puts it, "factual but 'stupid' and 'random'."[37] For these reasons, annalistic chronicles have often been considered unworthy of serious attention except in so far as they can be mined for a few useful facts which can be used to construct a real history.

There have been a number of well-meant attempts to rescue annals from this disdain, perhaps the most influential of which was that developed by Reginald Poole. In a series of elegant lectures delivered in 1924, he attempted to invest even the most rudimentary forms of the genre with new value by arguing that they were important witnesses to the origins of modern analytical history. He distinguished some four stages in the development of the medieval chronicle, each represented by a different type: the first was represented by the brief annals often found in the margins of Dionysian tables used for the calculation of the date of Easter; the second by the annalistic chronicle in which brief descriptions

34 Easter table annals are the only annalistic sub-genre which does not *by type* begin at a significant starting point, a fact which is sometimes disguised by the way in which the other texts have been edited or sometimes by the loss of material from the beginnings of their manuscripts.

35 Robert Bartlett, *England under the Norman and Angevin Kings, 1075–1225*, New Oxford History of England (Oxford: Clarendon Press, 2000), 617.

36 White, "Narrativity in the Representation of Reality," 6.

37 John O. Ward, "Some Principles of Rhetorical Historiography in the Twelfth Century," in *Classical Rhetoric and Medieval Historiography*, ed. Ernst Breisach, Studies in Medieval Culture 19 (Kalamazoo: Medieval Institute Publications, 1985), 103–65, at 106.

of events were listed according to the year of the Lord's Incarnation in which they took place; the third by a more expansive kind of chronicle which attempted to list all the significant events of a given year; and the fourth by "chronicles on the point of becoming histories," texts which do not restrict themselves to recording events but which begin to explore their significance and the causal links between them.[38] Poole's grand narrative reaches its climax with the St Alban's chroniclers whom he credits with developing the chronicle to the point where it had become "history";[39] but there is no doubting that its *telos*—that the *implicit* end point towards which it looks—lies in the emergence of history as an academic discipline in the nineteenth and twentieth centuries. He futher identifies as evidence for the links in the chain various hangovers from the earlier stages in the later genres. Thus he sees the presence of "barren entries" in the earliest annalistic chronicles—that is, the practice of listing years even when there was nothing to be recorded for them—and the absence in many of these texts of entries that extend beyond a single line as a remnant of the generic model from which they were derived: Easter table annals.[40] The suggestion, in other words, is that annals and chronicles deserve the attention of scholars for much the same reasons as evolutionary biologists study the fossilized bones of the first hominids.

There is certainly something about these chronicles which suggests that they represent a "starting-point", but the chronological distribution of the evidence implies a different pattern of development from that suggested by Poole. For when we look at the manuscript record we find that the various sub-types of annalistic chronicle evolved alongside one another rather than in sequence. If we look, for example, at England in the twelfth century, when *Winchcombe* and *Coventry* were produced, we find Easter table annals, breviate world chronicles, and, to a lesser extent, the fuller chronicles produced by writers such as Roger

[38] Poole nowhere specifies "four different stages" but this is pretty much what is implied by *Chronicles and Annals: A Brief Outline of their Origin and Growth* (Oxford: Clarendon Press, 1926). Note especially the words used to signal turning points in the argument (26, 33–34, 41, 52–53, 64, 67, 73). Poole's approach is developed by Charles W. Jones, *Saints' Lives and Chronicles in Early England* (Ithaca: Cornell University Press, 1947), esp. 9–12; McCormick, *Les annales*, esp. 11–21; Denis Hay, *Annalists and Historians: Western Historiography from the Eighth to the Eighteenth Centuries* (London: Methuen, 1977); and Bernard Guenée, *Histoire et culture historique dans l'Occident médiéval* (Paris: Aubier Montaigne, 1980), esp. 203–7.

[39] Poole, *Chronicles and Annals*, 73. William of Malmesbury and William of Newburgh are the two other English writers whom Poole ranks as "historians": *Chronicles and Annals*, 53, 67.

[40] Poole, *Chronicles and Annals*, 28, 41–42. Poole believed that the practice of using the Incarnation to provide the fixed point from which events were dated was invented *by accident* when annals were first entered in the margins of Dionysian Easter tables, for in contrast to those of Victorius and other early computists, these tables took the year in which Jesus was born as their start point: *Chronicles and Annals*, 9, 19–26.

of Howden flourishing *at the same time*. There are at least twelve manuscripts containing Easter tables that have annals in their margins which were begun or continued in England during the twelfth century, as can be seen from the following list:[41]

1. Cambridge, St John's College, A.22, fols. 111r–118v (s. xii$^{2/4}$, Reading)[42]
2. Cambridge, Trinity College, O.7.41, fols. 9r–22v (s.xii, Colchester)[43]
3. Cambridge, U.L., Kk.5.32, fols. 61r–74v (s.xii$^{1/4}$, England, possibly the southwest)[44]

---

41 Note that this list excludes the Hereford MS of Marianus Scotus's *Chronica chronicarum* (that is, MS. London, B.L., Cotton Nero C.V, fols. 3r–161v, hereafter N) and the various MSS of John of Worcester's *Chronica chronicarum*. Including them would add a further six examples to the list, since all except the Evesham fragment include an Easter table with extensive series of annals, each slightly different from the others (see chap. 2, § a, below). It is arguable that the annals in the margins of N, fols. 19v–26r, ought to be included, even though the original layer of text is of Continental origin. For an early twelfth-century hand has added four items, including two that relate to England: that is, the notices *Ordinatio Wlfstani episcopi* on fol. 26r (alongside 1062) and *Obierunt Wlstanus et Robertus episcopi* on fol. 19v (alongside 1095). The other two additions are for the elections of Hildebrand and Wibert to the papacy (alongside 1074 and 1084).

42 Ed. C. W. Previté-Orton, "Annales Radingenses Posteriores, 1135–1264," *EHR* 37 (1922): 400–3. The first run of entries ends in 1162. See also Coates, *EMB*, 42–43, 71, 147.

43 The provenance depends on a run of thirteenth-century additions to the chronicle: see M. R. James, *A Descriptive Catalogue of the Manuscripts in the Library of Trinity College, Cambridge*, 4 vols. (Cambridge: Cambridge University Press, 1900–1904), 1:380–81.

44 This version of the great paschal cycle as-adapted-by-Marianus seems to be one of the earliest of those now extant, since its entries extend only as far as 1100, the latest being the obit for *Willelmus rex iunior* (fol. 61v). The layout of both the tables and the annals is similar to that of number 10. There are hardly any clues as to the manuscript's provenance, its most distinctive obits being those for a monk called Maurus (d. 1098) and, in a different hand from the other additions, for Roger de Montgomery (d. 1094). Monks called Maurus are attested in this period at Canterbury, Rochester, and Worcester (see Greatrex, *BR*, 321, 620, 845). The entries cover several but not all of the bishops who died in the late 1090s, namely Wulfstan II of Worcester (d. 1095), Walkelin of Winchester (d. 1098), and Osmund of Salisbury (d. 1099). They omit Remigius of Dorchester/Lincoln (d. 1092), Herfast of Thetford (d. 1094), Robert of Hereford (d. 1095), and William of Durham (d. 1096). The eleventh-century calendar with which the tables are presently bound (fols. 50r–55v; ed. *EKBef.*, no. 6) is often thought to have been produced in the southwest: see Helmut Gneuss, *Handlist of Anglo-Saxon Manuscripts: A List of Manuscripts and Manuscript Fragments Written or Owned in England up to 1100*, MRTS 241 (Tempe: Arizona Center for Medieval and Renaissance Studies, 2001), no. 26.

4. Durham, Cathedral Library, Hunter 100, fols. 27v–41r (s.xii$^{1}$, Durham)[45]
5. Glasgow, U.L., Hunterian 85 (T.4.2), fols. 11r–27v (s.xii$^{1}$, Durham)[46]
6. London, B.L., Cotton Caligula A.XV, fols. 132v–139r (s.xi$^{2}$–xiii$^{1}$, Canterbury)[47]
7. London, B.L., Cotton Nero C.VII, fols. 80r–84v + Oxford, St John's College, 17, fols. 139r–155v (s.xii$^{in}$–s.xvii$^{1}$, Thorney)[48]
8. London, B.L., Cotton Vespasian D.XIX, fols. 71r–82r (s.xii$^{in}$, England?)[49]
9. London, B.L., Harley 3667, fols. 1r–2r (s.xii$^{2/4}$–s.xii$^{ex}$, Peterborough)[50]
10. London, B.L., Royal 8.E.XVIII, fols. 94r–96v (s.xii$^{2/4}$–s.xii$^{ex}$, Reading)[51]
11. Oxford, Bod.L., Auct. F.3.14, fols. 120br–132v (s.xii$^{1}$, Malmesbury)
12. Paris, B.n.F., lat. 9376, fols. 30r–31r (s.xii$^{2/4}$, Tewkesbury)[52]

The Easter table annals in Cotton Caligula A.XV may represent the earliest English example of a chronicle of this kind: the original hand entered the annals for 988 to 1073, and another eighteen provide the entries down to 1202.[53]

---

[45] Ed. Wilhelm Levison and Hans Eberhard Meyer, "Die 'Annales Lindisfarnenses et Dunelmenses': kritisch untersucht und neu herausgegeben," *Deutsches Archiv für Erforschung des Mittelalters* 17 (1961): 447–506, at 455–56. For the most recent dating and description, see A. Borst, ed., *Schriften zur Komputistik im Frankenreich von 721 bis 818*, MGH: Quellen zur Geistesgeschichte des Mittelalters 21, 3 vols. (Hannover: Hahn, 2006), 1:226.

[46] Ed. Levison and Meyer, "Annales Lindisfarnenses et Dunelmenses", 478–89, hereafter *ALD*.

[47] Ed. Peter S. Baker, *ASC Coll.*, 8:129–34. For a reproduction, see Ker, *English Manuscripts*, plate 8a.

[48] Ed. Cyril R. Hart, "The Anglo-Saxon Chronicle of Ramsey Abbey," in *Alfred the Wise*, ed. Jane Roberts, Janet L. Nelson, and Malcolm Godden (Cambridge: D. S. Brewer, 1997), 78–86, and Cyril R. Hart and T. M. Halliday, "The Thorney Annals," *Peterborough's Past: The Journal of the Peterborough Museum Society* 1 (1982–1983): 15–34.

[49] See Harrison, "New Discoveries," 30–31.

[50] Ed. Liebermann, *ANG*, 13–14.

[51] Ed. Liebermann, *ANG*, 9–12. See also Coates, *EMB*, 42–43, 153–54.

[52] Ed. René Poupardin, "Notes annalistiques de l'Abbaye de Tewkesbury," in *Mélanges d'histoire offerts a M. Charles Bémont* (Paris: F. Alcan, 1913), 99–104.

[53] Whether Cotton Caligula A.XV is the "earliest" example of such a chronicle depends on whether one regards as annals the "necrological" entries found in earlier tables such as those in MS. London, B.L., Cotton Titus D.XXVII, fols. 14v–21r, and those

It would be a mistake, however, to infer from this pattern that Easter table annals were a later development, that they emerged after the fuller kinds of annalistic chronicle. For it is to be expected that many examples of this type will have been destroyed, since the tables in whose margins they were placed were a highly ephemeral type of text. As soon as such tables were out of date (and examples of such tables usually cover some three to five nineteen-year cycles instead of the full twenty-eight required to complete the great paschal cycle),[54] one had either to extend them or, as must often have happened, to replace them. Onto the rubbish heap will have gone many earlier examples of annals of this kind.[55] Rather, what this kind of evidence shows is that the various sub-genres of chronicle *flourished alongside one another.*

Perhaps the most stark example of this phenomenon is that provided by the Abbey of St-Évroult in Normandy, where a version of the Norman Annals laid out in four columns alongside paschal tables covering the full 532-year cycle was produced at the same time as one of its monks began writing a monumental *Historia Ecclesiastica* in eleven books focused on the Norman churches and their

---

in MS. Oxford, Bod.L., Bodley 579, fol. 53r-v. The former set of tables has sixteen obits which are printed in *Ælfwine's Prayerbook (London, British Library, Cotton Titus D.xxvi + xxvii)*, ed. Beate Günzel, HBS 108 (London and Rochester: Boydell Press, 1993), 109–10; the latter has seven obits which are printed in *The Leofric Missal*, ed. Nicholas A. Orchard, 2 vols., HBS 113–114 (London and Rochester: Boydell Press, 2001–2002), 2:86–87. Both MSS are hybrids in as much as they combine liturgical components with a small but substantial computistical collection: in the former, this section occupies the first eight quires (Titus D.XXVI, fols. 2r–56v) and it includes a copy of Ælfric's vernacular computus (fols. 30r–54r); in the latter, the computus occupies quires 7, 8, and 9 (Bodley 579, fols. 38v–58r).

[54] This statement refers to manuscripts of these tables more generally. Most of the tables in the present list cover the great paschal cycle as a whole, and that probably goes a long way towards explaining their survival. The tables in numbers 2, 3, and 10, for example, are versions of the Easter tables-cum-annals of Marianus Scotus and cover the full 532-year paschal cycle. Their annals are related as far as their notice for the succession of the antipope "Wibert" (1085). In nos. 4 and 5, they cover the full paschal cycle. In 7 the first set of tables covered 532 to 1421, and a second covering 1422 to 2612 was added in the fifteenth century. See Hart and Halliday, "Thorney Annals," 15.

[55] Jones, *Saints' Lives and Chronicles*, 10. There is, as Jones points out (9 and n. 22), strong evidence for the antiquity of the practice of inserting annals in computistical tables, since there is a marginal annal alongside the year 501 in the Gotha copy of the fifth-century Easter tables of Victorius. See, likewise, Dumville, "What is a Chronicle?," esp. 3, 7. The significance of this evidence has been questioned, however, by Rosamond McKitterick, *History and Memory in the Carolingian World* (Cambridge: Cambridge University Press, 2004), esp. 97–100, who sees the habit of entering annals in the margins of Easter tables as a phenomenon which really took off only after the Carolingians promoted the use of AD-dating. Cf. Kenneth Harrison, *The Framework of Anglo-Saxon History to A.D. 900* (Cambridge: Cambridge University Press, 1976), esp. 45.

benefactors.[56] Indeed, the person who entered the annals for 1087 to 1140 in these tables was Orderic Vitalis, the author of this *Historia*.[57] Orderic began the latter work around 1114 and completed it in 1141; the *Annals of St-Évroult*, on the other hand, were continued until 1503, whilst the abbey never again produced a history of the stature of the *Historia*. A similarly glaring contrast is evident at Malmesbury, where a series of annals in the margins of another set of tables covering the great paschal cycle (MS. Oxford, Bod.L., Auct. F.3.14, fols. 120br–132v) was being continued at the same time as William of Malmesbury was writing his *Gesta regum* and *Gesta pontificum Anglorum*. The additions are in a variety of small and scarcely distinguishable hands, but Ker thought that at least one of them was in William's own hand.[58] The latest addition is that for the election of Theobald as archbishop of Canterbury in 1139 (fol. 120cv). A third example is provided by the cathedral priory at Durham, where the so-called *Annals of Lindisfarne and Durham*, another set of Easter table annals, were being compiled and copied at the same time as Symeon was writing his *Libellus de Exordio atque Procursu istius, hoc est Dunhelmensis, Ecclesie*.[59] These annals have also been identified as a product of Symeon's own hand.[60] If Poole's theory were valid, with each of his types being a better version of its predecessor, then the production of "proper history" ought to have rendered the more "primitive" types of chronicle obsolete;

---

[56] Ed. Marjorie Chibnall, *The Ecclesiastical History of Orderic Vitalis*, OMT, 6 vols. (Oxford: Clarendon Press, 1968–1980), hereafter *Orderic*.

[57] For the various items in this manuscript which are in Orderic's hand, see *Orderic*, 2:200; *Catalogue des manuscrits en écriture latine portant des indications de date, de lieu ou de copiste*, ed. Charles Samaran and Robert Marichal, 7 vols. (Paris: Centre national de la recherche scientifique, 1959–1984), vol. 3, pt. 1, 151; Leopold Delisle, "Notes sur les manuscrits autographes d'Orderic Vital," in *Matériaux pour l'édition de Guillaume de Jumièges*, ed. Jules Lair (Paris: Nogent-le-Rotrou, 1910), 7–27 (esp. 14–15).

[58] Neil R. Ker, "William of Malmesbury's Handwriting," *EHR* 59 (1944): 371–76, at 364–65. The entry reads *Henricus rex Anglorum regnauit ann' xxxv et super hoc a nonis aug' usque ad kl' decemb'* (fol. 120bv), and echoes a passage in WM*HN*, i.11. The entries for 1066 to 1139 were printed and discussed by Stevenson, "Domesday Survey," 81–82. The MS and the evidence for its Malmesbury provenance is discussed in Stevenson, "Domesday Survey," 78–84.

[59] Ed. David W. Rollason, *Tract on the Origins and Progress of this the Church of Durham*, OMT (Oxford: Clarendon Press, 2000), cited as SD*LDE*.

[60] Symeon was responsible for the tables and the annals as far as 1063 in MS. Glasgow, U.L., Hunterian 85, fols. 11r–27v (at fols. 18r–24v), and it is likely that the annals were compiled at Durham in the early part of the twelfth century: see Levison and Meyer, "Annales," 458–506; Michael Gullick, "The Hand of Symeon of Durham: Further Observations on the Durham Martyrology Scribe," in Rollason, *Symeon of Durham*, 14–31, at 29 (no. 30); Joanna E. Story, "Symeon as Annalist," in Rollason, *Symeon of Durham*, 202–13, at 207–9 and plates 39–41.

but there is in fact little sign that this happened.[61] The medieval evidence suggests, indeed, that the development of historical writing followed a *radial* rather than a *linear* pattern, one in which established genres gave rise to a greater variety of types like the spreading branches of a large and leafy tree. As Dumville puts it, "chronicling . . . diversified."[62]

The truth, moreover, is that the annalistic chronicle has never ceased to prosper, for forms of historical writing flourish in our own time which are not dissimilar to the medieval manifestations of the genre. A good example is the historical atlas as manifested in books such as the *DTV–Atlas zur Weltgeschichte*, better known in the English-speaking world as *The Penguin Atlas of World History*.[63] This book has many of the features of an annalistic chronicle: it is laid out in a diagrammatic fashion, it uses colour and bold type to highlight important events, it is concerned (of course) with the long-term evolution of the political topography of the world, and, on the pages opposite its maps, it sets out in double columns and in tabular fashion a summary history of the region in question. Consider, for instance, its treatment of English history from 1087 to 1154:[64]

> 1087–1100 William II (Rufus). William I's eldest son Robert (Curthose) inherited the Duchy of Normandy. After William's death his younger brother
>
> 1100–35 Henry I had himself crowned king. He defeated Robert at Tinchebray (1106) and reunited Normandy and England.
>
> 1107 The Concordat of Westminster terminated the investiture struggle . . . The king forced the nobility to

[61] It was perhaps only with the gradual disappearance of the need for clerics to calculate the date of Easter that the practice of adding annals to Easter tables finally died out. As far as England is concerned, this development probably began with the intensification of conciliar organisation after the Norman Conquest, but it was probably completed only in the early modern period with the availability of cheap printed almanacs. But note that items were still being added to the Easter table annals in MS. Oxford, St John's College, 17, fols. 139r–155v, in the early seventeenth century, after it had arrived in Oxford: see Hart and Halliday, "Thorney Annals," 15; Dumville, "What is a Chronicle?," 20.

[62] "What is a Chronicle?," 3. But cf. McCormick, *Les annales*, 13, for whom the 12th century was the period when the rhetorical and annalistic forms of history "converged" to produce increasingly exhaustive chronicles of the kind developed by Roger Howden.

[63] For the original version, see Hermann Kinder and Werner Hilgemann, *DTV–Atlas zur Weltgeschichte* (Munich: Deutscher Taschenbuch-Verlag, 1964–1966); for the first English edition, see eidem, *The Penguin Atlas of World History*, trans. Ernest A. Menze with maps designed by Harald and Ruth Bukor, 2 vols. (Harmondsworth: Penguin, 1974–1978).

[64] Kinder and Hilgemann, *Atlas of World History*, 161. The cross-references have been omitted.

1127 recognise his daughter Mathilda (widow of the Emperor Henry V . . . ) as heiress to the throne. She mar. Count Geoffrey of Anjou (1128), who was nicknamed 'Plantagenet' ('sprig of broom' — after his helmet decoration).

Henry I est. an exchequer (scaccarium), to which the sheriffs . . . of the shires had to account for their income (rents and feudal income) on 'pipe rolls' (pipe-shaped rolls of annual accounts, after 1130/31) at Easter and Michelmas (29 Sep.). The tribute paid to the vikings (Danegeld) became a general tax.

1135–54 Stephen of Blois. After Mathilda's landing in England (1139) a period of anarchy ensued (civil wars), which strengthened the position of the nobility and Church.

Though the type of event recorded has been altered under the influence of nineteenth- and twentieth-century administrative history, the format and approach are in essence those of an annalistic chronicle. The text comprises a series of disconnected notes; it makes no attempt to explain the causes of events, and it omits much that would help in the development of a proper explanation. Some reference to the death of Henry I's son in the White Ship disaster would have helped, for example, to explain how and why Matilda became his successor. It is instructive to note also that academic attitudes towards texts of this kind tend to be similar to those towards medieval chronicles. Consider, for example, Richard Vinen's review of Hywel Williams' *Cassell's Chronology of World History*. Vinen begins by disavowing mockery, but as a university-based historian—he teaches modern history at King's College, London—he cannot help being sarcastic about the book: he expresses admiration for the industry involved in producing a volume that covers some 135,000 years in 765 pages, but cannot avoid noting its Anglocentrism and its emphasis on phenomena that are amenable to dating (battles, embassies, coronations, and elections) as opposed to those that matter for academic historians (social, cultural, and intellectual developments); "for all its pretensions", he concludes, it "has a mad kind of brilliance."[65]

If the development of the annalistic chronicle has a modern *telos*, it surely lies not in the "Oxford Historical Monograph", but in books such as these. They are vastly superior in terms of accuracy and coverage to their medieval counterparts, but they exhibit many of the same generic tendencies. It seems to this contributor that the qualities of the annalistic chronicle are so alien to those of analytical history that these texts are best approached by accepting at the outset that the priorities of their authors were entirely different from those of the modern academic—or of a Roman aristocrat like Cicero. To understand these

[65] "Breaking News from Constantinople," *Times Literary Supplement* (16 September 2005), 9: a review of Hywel Williams, *Cassell's Chronology of World History* (London: Cassell, 2005).

artefacts we need to set aside all pretensions to elitism. The simple truth is that the annalistic chronicle cannot be redeemed by pretending that it is an ancestor of academic history.

## (c) The Social Context

Modern analogies do, however, have some insights to offer, for the genre's affinities with the modern historical atlas and world chronology point to a more effective way of looking at these texts. The success of the *DTV–Atlas zur Weltgeschichte*—volume one was reprinted for the thirty-sixth time in 2005, volume two for the thirty-eighth time in 2004[66]—shows that books of this kind serve a genuine need, and there is little doubt that it is, above all, newcomers to history who use them. Books of this kind are often compiled by historians of recognised stature, but they are usually intended for people who have recently discovered an interest in the past—who are setting out on the process of acquiring historical knowledge and of constructing of an internal map of how the histories of various peoples and places relate to one another. This kind of interest in the past arguably represents a crucial stage in the development of a person's historical awareness, one which a teacher or parent might well be keen to nurture before introducing them to the questions of method and perspective that confront all serious attempts to study the past. Thus, the advertising blurbs on the most recent imprints of the *DTV–Atlas zur Weltgeschichte* commend the book to the school pupil, the university student, and the general reader.

Medieval monasteries were also concerned with educating people from a relatively basic starting point. This was especially true of the Benedictine houses, since many of their recruits were presented to them as children by their parents.[67] Orderic Vitalis, for example, was given by his father to the abbey of St-Évroult when he was ten.[68] An idea of just how large a proportion of a community the

[66] The atlas has also been translated into French, Italian, Japanese, Spanish, and Swedish as well as English: see Jeremy Black, "Historical Atlases," *Historical Journal* 38 (1994): 643–67, at 656.

[67] For recent treatments of the origins of oblation, see Mayke de Jong, *In Samuel's Image: Child Oblation in the Early Medieval West*, Brill's Studies in Intellectual History 12 (Leiden: Brill, 1995), 16–55, 126–45; Patricia A. Quinn, *Better than the Sons of Kings: Boys and Monks in the Early Middle Ages*, Studies in History and Culture 2 (New York: P. Lang, 1989), 13–44. John Boswell, *The Kindness of Strangers: The Abandonment of Children in Western Europe from Late Antiquity to the Renaissance* (Harmondsworth: Penguin, 1988), 228–55, and Joseph H. Lynch, *Simoniacal Entry into Religious Life from 1000 to 1260* (Columbus: Ohio State University Press, 1976), 36–60, focus upon economic and social factors which conspired to support the practice.

[68] *Orderic*, 6:552–55.

underage monks might comprise is given by the *Liber vitae* of the New Minster, Winchester. The principal scribe who began the necrology in 1031 entered two lists of monks: the first consisted of some seventy-seven deceased monks, the second some thirty-seven who comprised the community at that time.[69] Noting their ranks in descending order from Abbot Ælfwine (1031–1057), the list includes seventeen priests, eleven deacons, and nine children. Thus oblates would seem to have made up approximately one-quarter of the community in 1031. Subsequent additions to the list appear to record each member's status at the time of their admission to the Minster. They indicate that almost all subsequent monks entered as children.[70] At any given moment, therefore, a significant proportion of the inmates of a Benedictine monastery will have been oblates and novices. Orderic had received an education for some five years at a school in Shrewsbury before he came to St-Évroult,[71] but most oblates will have been illiterate when they arrived at their monasteries. Indeed, Bede states that his kinsmen gave him to Monkwearmouth when he was seven so that he could be "educated by the venerable abbot Benedict."[72] Much of an abbey's resources will have been devoted, therefore, to the training of these oblates for the monastic life, and this is reflected in the attention given to this issue in customaries and commentaries on the Benedictine

[69] MS. London, B.L., Stowe 944, fols. 20v–21v (ed. Jan Gerchow, *Die Gedenküberlieferung der Angelsachsen, mit einem Katalog der* Libri Vitae *und Necrologien*, Arbeiten zur Frühmittelalterforschung 20 [Berlin: de Gruyter, 1988], 324 [no. B]): 'NEWA' and 'NEWB'. I follow Gerchow's reconstruction of how the book was compiled: see Gerchow, *Die Gedenküberlieferung*, 155–85 (esp. 161 and 178). The main scribe added the names of two more boys before later continuators took over. See also *The Liber Vitae of the New Minster and Hyde Abbey, Winchester (British Library Stowe 944)*, ed. Simon D. Keynes, Early English Manuscripts in Facsimile 26 (Copenhagen: Rosenkilde and Bagger, 1996), 90–91. As Keynes notes elsewhere, the list is unique among English necrological records for the eleventh and twelfth centuries: see idem, 'The *Liber Vitae* of the New Minster, Winchester," in *The Durham* Liber Vitae *and its Context*, ed. David W. Rollason et al., Regions and Regionalism in History 1 (Woodbridge: Boydell Press, 2004), 149–63 (esp. 159–60), and compare the lists of Durham monks edited by Andrew J. Piper, "The Early Lists and Obits of the Durham Monks," in Rollason, *Symeon of Durham*, 161–201, at 178–85.

[70] MS. London, B.L., Stowe 944, fols. 21v–22r (ed. Walter de Gray Birch, *Liber Vitae: Register and Martyrology of New Minster and Hyde Abbey*, Hampshire Record Society Publications [London: Simpkin, 1892], 35–36): of the 32 new monks up to about 1077, 27 are listed as children, 2 are unspecified, 2 are listed as deacons, 1 as a priest and 1 as a *conversus* and a priest. These categories are discussed in Christopher N. L. Brooke, *The Monastic World 1000–1300* (London: Elek, 1974), 88.

[71] *Orderic*, 6:552–53.

[72] Bede, *HE*, v.24: "educandus reverentissimo abbati Benedicto."

Rule.[73] It seems likely that some attention was probably also given to the production of reading matter for adolescent oblates and novices.

Annalistic chronicles are aptly seen as suitable texts for beginners: their grammar and vocabulary is not always straightforward, but it is simpler than that of most historical texts; they avoid the difficult problems of interpretation that would emerge as soon as the topic of causation was raised; and, above all, they include a range of sensational and dramatic events which might well arouse the interest of a young monk—natural disasters, prodigies, battles, and so on.[74] Indeed, this kind of target audience might well help to explain why the most well-known of English annalistic chronicles—the various versions of the *Anglo-Saxon Chronicle*—were still being continued in the vernacular in the eleventh and even the twelfth centuries even though successive reform movements had established higher standards of Latinity in most monasteries. It is true that many later annalistic chronicles were produced for monasteries belonging to orders such as the Cistercians who had rules against admitting children;[75] but there is much evidence that they were still offered oblates and that they accepted them,[76] and these houses will still have had, in any case, to confront the problem of educating recruits who arrived with little education.[77]

---

[73] See, for example, Lanfranc, *Decreta Cantuariensibus transmissa*, esp. §§ 109–10, ed. David Knowles and Christopher N. L. Brooke, *The Monastic Constitutions of Lanfranc*, OMT (Oxford: Clarendon Press, 2002), 170–75. On the spiritual and intellectual education of children in monasteries more generally, see de Jong, *In Samuel's Image*, 145–55; eadem, "Growing up in a Carolingian Monastery: Magister Hildemar and his Oblates," *Journal of Medieval History* 9 (1983): 99–128; Quinn, *Boys and Monks*, esp. 46–48, 53, 111–15, 123–24, 156–59, 165–66; Jean Leclercq, "Pédagogie et formation spirituelle du IVe au IXe siècle," in *La scuola nell'Occidente latino dell'alto medioevo*, Settimane di studio 19 (Spoleto: Centro Italiano di Studi sull'Alto Medioevo, 1972), 255–90; Pierre Riché, "L'enfant dans la société monastique au XIIe siècle," in *Pierre Abélard—Pierre le Vénérable: les courants philosophiques, littéraires et artistiques en Occident au milieu du XIIe siècle*, ed. R. Louis et al. (Paris: Éditions du Centre national de la recherche scientifique, 1975), 689–701.

[74] Cf. White, "Narrativity in the Representation of Reality," 10: "Everywhere it is the forces of disorder, natural and human, the forces of violence and destruction that occupy the forefront of attention."

[75] The statutes of 1157 raised the minimum age for admission as a novice from fifteen to eighteen: *Statuta capitulorum generalium ordinis Cisterciensis*, ed. Joseph Canivez, Bibliothèque de la Revue d'histoire ecclesiastique, 8 vols. (Louvain: Bureaux de la Revue, 1933–1941), 1:62 (§ 28).

[76] See Joseph H. Lynch, "The Cistercians and Under-Age Novices," *Cîteaux: Commentarii Cistercienses* 24 (1973): 283–97.

[77] Thus the *Instituta generalis capituli* of ca. 1147, ed. Chrysogonus Waddell, *Narrative and Legislative Texts from Early Cîteaux*, Cîteaux: Studia et Documenta 9 (Pontigny: Citeaux, 1999), 490–91 (§ 80), provide for the teaching within the monastery of *pueri* who had arrived as novices or as monks from other orders.

Monasteries had, moreover, a powerful reason for providing their monks with a basic knowledge of the past, for they needed to identify in each new generation of monks at least one or two with an understanding of time strong enough to allow them to manage their observance of the Christian liturgy. To explain, there was in every monastery an official who was responsible for managing its religious services.[78] He was usually known as the *cantor*, but sometimes as the *armarius*, because he also looked after the abbey's books which were stored in an *armarium* or cupboard. One of the many skills required of the holders of this office was the ability to co-ordinate three different time-cycles — the solar year, the lunar month, and the seven-day week. The problem was that these cycles did not neatly divide into each other,[79] whilst each controlled the timing of different series of religious services: the solar year governed the dates of the feasts of the saints; the weekly cycle controlled the round of Sunday services and the choice

[78] For an English customary that provides a relatively thorough account of the work involved in organising the liturgy (which is here divided between the cantor and his assistant, the succentor), see the *Customary of the Benedictine Monasteries of St Augustine, Canterbury, and St Peter, Westminster*, ed. Edward M. Thomson, HBS 23, 28, 2 vols. (London: Henry Bradshaw Society, 1902–1904), 1:90–101; for Cluniac customaries, see *Liber tramitis aevi Odilonis abbatis*, ed. Peter Dinter, *CCM*, 10:238–39, and esp. Bernard, *Ordo Cluniacensis*, § 14, ed. Marquard Herrgott, *Vetus disciplina monastica* (Paris: Charles Osmont, 1726), 134–364, at 161–64. Lanfranc's *Decreta Cantuariensibus transmissa*, § 86, covers only the finer details of the office, presumably because its essentials were so well known that they did not need to be established. The thirteenth-century *Customary of the Benedictine Abbey at Eynsham in Oxfordshire*, ed. Antonia Gransden, *CCM*, 2:161–68, concentrates on the organisation of the library and scriptorium, but also emphasises the high level of erudition required of candidates for the office. It should also be noted that in the eleventh and twelfth centuries, a distinction was often made between the *armarius* or *cantor* and the weekly cantor, a "choir-master" who was in effect his deputy: see Margot E. Fassler, "The Office of the Cantor in Early Western Monastic Rules and Customaries: A Preliminary Investigation," *Early Music History* 5 (1985): 29–51 (esp. 43–48).

[79] The solar year comprises 52 weeks (or 364 days) and 1¼ days; the lunar year comprises 12 months of 29½ days (or 354 days) and is eleven days shorter than the solar year of 365¼ days. It takes 28 years before the weekly cycle and the year cycle will again coincide, some 19 years before the lunar and solar cycles will again coincide, and 532 years before the series of Easter dates will again repeat themselves. The issues are explained in Roger T. Beckwith, *Calendar and Chronology, Jewish and Christian: Biblical, Intertestamental and Patristic Studies*, Arbeiten zur Geschichte des antiken Judentums und des Urchristentums 33 (Leiden: Brill, 1996); Charles W. Jones, *Bedae opera de temporibus* (Cambridge, MA: Mediaeval Academy of America, 1943), 1–122 (esp. 55–75); Faith Wallis, trans., *Bede: The Reckoning of Time*, Translated Texts for Historians 29 (Liverpool: Liverpool University Press, 1999) (hereafter Wallis), xxxiv–lxiii; Byrhtferth, *Enchiridion*, xxxiv–xxxix. For a gentle introduction to the issues of time reckoning, see now Leofranc Holford-Strevens, *The History of Time: A Very Short Introduction* (Oxford: Oxford University Press, 2005).

of psalms to be sung in the liturgy of the hours; the impact of the lunar cycle was felt through its role in the timing of Easter, which fell on the first Sunday after the first full moon following the vernal equinox. The date of Easter could vary by as much as thirty-five days between 22 March and 25 April, and the timing of the services that comprised the Lenten and Easter seasons depended on it.[80] The upshot is that no two years in succession were ever celebrated in the same way; rather, a different combination of prayers and chants would be needed for the majority of services throughout the entire year. The monastery needed, in short, to find among its novices one or two who were capable of working out in detail how the different cycles of time would affect the celebration of the liturgy in a given year. A science known as *computus*, "reckoning" or "time studies", had evolved in order to provide assistance with this task. Indeed, a number of scholars had developed tools which greatly simplified the processes involved, the most important of which were the Easter tables devised by Dionysius Exiguus and the liturgical calendar as refined by scholars such as Bede (d. 734) and Abbo of Fleury (d. 1004). They had also written manuals on how to use these tools, the most important of which was Bede's *De temporum ratione.*[81]

Accuracy in the use of these tools was crucial because it affected the most essential of the roles that the monastery played in medieval society—its role in offering up prayer to God on behalf of others. Extensive programmes of communal worship and prayer had been central to monasticism as it was actually practiced in western Europe since at least the sixth century, its patrons' need for prayer having meshed with ascetic practices which used the recitation of sacred texts as a tool for disciplining the self. The idea was contrary to Augustine's teachings on divine grace, but it was widely believed that ritual *correctly* performed by those who led the purest lives was more likely to attract divine favour for its sponsors on earth.[82]

---

[80] For an introduction to the Christian year, see P. G. Cobb, "The History of the Christian Year," and K. Donovan, "The Sanctoral," in *The Study of Liturgy*, ed. C. Jones et al., 2nd ed. (London: Society for Promoting Christian Knowledge, 1992), 455–84; or Olaf Pedersen, "The Ecclesiastical Calendar and the Life of the Church," in *The Gregorian Reform of the Calendar*, ed. George V. Coyne, Michael A. Hoskin, and idem (Vatican City: Pontificia Academia Scientiarum, 1983), 17–74.

[81] Ed. Charles W. Jones, CCSL 123B (Turnhout: Brepols, 1977), 263–544, hereafter Bede, *DTR*. For a brief catalogue of early medieval computistical texts, see Alfred Cordeliani (*recte* Cordoliani), "Les traités de comput du haut moyen âge (526–1003)," *Archivum latinitatis medii aevi (Bulletin du Cange)* 17 (1942): 51–72; and for a statement of the fundamental importance of computus to early medieval scholarship, see Isidore of Seville, *Etymologiarum sive Originum Libri XX*, 3.4, ed. Wallace M. Lindsay, 2 vols. (Oxford: Clarendon Press, 1911).

[82] The fundamental pattern was established by the Merovingians and the Carolingians: see Barbara H. Rosenwein, "Perennial Prayer at Agaune," in *Monks and Nuns, Saints and Outcasts: Religion in Medieval Society: Essays in Honor of Lester K. Little*, ed. Sharon Farmer and eadem (Ithaca: Cornell University Press, 2000), 37–56 (esp. 53–56);

This belief was reflected in the Carolingian regime's insistence that monasteries and cathedral schools should adopt an educational programme which would help them to deliver accuracy in the performance of prayer. In the *Admonitio generalis* of 789, Charlemagne insisted that every monastery and cathedral was to teach boys the psalms, notation, song, computus, grammar, and the editing of sacred texts so that the books which were used by those praying to God could be corrected.[83] Their schools were to be open to the laity as well as those intended for a religious career, and "notation" *may* refer to the writing of shorthand rather than, as seems more natural, music;[84] but this was a curriculum geared to the needs of institutions whose role was offer up liturgical prayer on behalf of others. It was, moreover, a curriculum in which computus played a prominent part. This much is borne out by the manuscript record, for many Carolingian copies of computistical tracts and tables are still extant.[85] Communities that failed, moreover, to achieve competence in this curriculum risked being humiliated in public and being reformed by higher authorities. Charlemagne wrote, for example, to his abbots expressing his dismay at finding vulgar expressions (*sermones inculti*) in the letters which he had received from monasteries that were praying to God on his

---

Mayke de Jong, "Charlemagne's Church," in *Charlemagne: Empire and Society*, ed. Joanna E. Story (Manchester: Manchester University Press, 2005), 103–35 (esp. 119–25); eadem, "Carolingian Monasticism: The Power of Prayer," in *The New Cambridge Medieval History*, vol. 2, *c.700–c.900*, ed. Rosamond McKitterick (Cambridge: Cambridge University Press, 1995), 622–53 (esp. 630, 649).

[83] *Admonitio generalis*, § 72, ed. Alfred Boretius, *MGH CRF*, 1:60: "Psalmos, notas, cantus, compotum, grammaticam per singula monasteria vel episcopia et libros catholicos bene emendate, quia saepe, dum bene aliqui Deum rogare cupiunt, sed per inemendatos libros male rogant." Monasteries would later be released from the obligation to educate the children of the laity as well as their own *pueri* (see Council of Aachen in 817, § 5, ed. Joseph Semmler, *CCM*, 1:474), but some continued to educate clerical *scholastici* for roles in the secular church (see de Jong, "Carolingian Monasticism," 643–44).

[84] Cf. Bernhard Bischoff, *Latin Palaeography: Antiquity and the Middle Ages*, trans. Daíbhí Ó Cróinin and David Ganz (Cambridge: Cambridge University Press and the Medieval Academy of Ireland, 1990), 81 and n. 208, 173–74.

[85] Some forty-five of the known MSS of Bede, *DTR*, date from between ca. 775 and ca. 850, and most of these have a continental provenance. For a full list, comprising some 245 MSS, see CCSL 123B, 242–56; for a list of eighth- and ninth-century MSS, see Wesley M. Stevens, *Bede's Scientific Achievement*, Jarrow Lecture 1984 (Newcastle: St Paul's Church, 1985), 39–42. See also idem, "*Compotistica et Astronomica* in the Fulda School," in *Saints, Scholars and Heroes: Studies in Medieval Culture in Honour of Charles W. Jones*, ed. Margot H. King and Wesley M. Stevens, 2 vols. (Collegeville, MN: Hill Monastic Manuscript Library, 1979), 2:27–63.

behalf. "Those who seek to please God by living rightly," he grumbled, "should not neglect to please him by speaking rightly!"[86]

Much the same complex of ideas and practices governed the role of monasticism in English society. Indeed, King Alfred took almost the same view of the work of the church as Charlemagne when he attributed the misfortunes of the English to the clergy's neglect of learning: God was punishing the nation because the clergy could not recite the divine services with understanding.[87] King Edgar was made to take almost the same view of the need for liturgical conformity as Louis the Pious when he insisted that the monasteries of the kingdom ought to have the same customs, lest variations in their ways of observing the Rule should bring their way of life into disrepute.[88] It is clear, moreover, that the monasteries established and reformed in England during and after the late tenth century followed a curriculum similar to that set out by Charlemagne in the *Admonitio generalis*. The desire for linguistic accuracy is attested by recent work on the school that Bishop Æthelwold established at Winchester: grammar, metre, and the study of the liturgy seem to have been at the core of the curriculum.[89] Evidence for the attention to music is provided by the Winchester Tropers, two manuscripts which preserve numerous tropes, sequences, and *organa*

---

[86] *Epistola de litteris colendis*, ed. Alfred Boretius, *MGH CRF*, 1:79: "qui Deo placere appetunt recte vivendo, ei etiam placere non negligant recte loquendo."

[87] *King Alfred's West Saxon Version of Gregory's Pastoral Care*, ed. Henry Sweet, EETS o.s. 45, 50, 2 vols. (London: Oxford University Press, 1871–1872; repr. 1934), 1:2–3.

[88] *Regularis concordia Anglicae nationis monachorum sanctimonialiumque*, esp. §§ 4–6, ed. Thomas Symons (London: T. Nelson, 1953), 3–4. I say "Edgar was made," because this representation of his role in directing the reform movement is the work of Bishop Æthelwold: see Michael Lapidge, "Æthelwold as Scholar and Teacher," in *Bishop Æthelwold: His Career and Influence*, ed. Barbara Yorke (Woodbridge: Boydell Press, 1988), 89–117, at 98–100. Lapidge identifies Fleury as the source of many of the usages adopted by Æthelwold, but the ideology of the prologue takes up Louis the Pious's insistence that there should be *una regula et consuetudo*, for which see Joseph Semmler, "Benedictus II: Una regula—una consuetudo," in *Benedictine Culture 750–1050*, ed. Willem Lourdaux and Daniel Verhelst, Mediaevalia Lovaniensia, 1st ser., 11 (Leuven: Leuven University Press, 1983), 1–49.

[89] See Wulfstan of Winchester, *The Life of St Æthelwold*, ed. and trans. Michael Lapidge and Michael Winterbottom, OMT (Oxford: Clarendon Press, 1991), lxxxvi–xcii; Lapidge, "Æthelwold as Scholar and Teacher," 89–117; idem, "Ælfric's Schooldays," in *Early Medieval Texts and Interpretations: Studies Presented to Donald G. Scragg*, ed. Susan Rosser and Elaine M. Treharne, MRTS 252 (Tempe: Arizona Center for Medieval and Renaissance Studies, 2003), 301–9; Mechthild Gretsch, *The Intellectual Foundations of the English Benedictine Reform*, Cambridge Studies in Anglo-Saxon England 25 (Cambridge: Cambridge University Press, 1999), esp. 1–6, 226–60.

which were used in the tenth century.[90] Evidence for the place of computus in the curriculum is provided, not only by the compilation and copying of computistical collections,[91] but also by the efforts of Byrhtferth and Ælfric to make computistical learning available in the vernacular. Byrhtferth's *Enchiridion*, a manual produced between 1004 and 1016, offers some particularly useful insights.[92] Written primarily in Latin, it incorporates a translation which was intended, so the author's comments suggest, to make the text accessible to the young secular clerics who sat in on the monks' lessons,[93] but Byrhtferth refers to them with such sarcasm (*ic þe secge, la cleric, on þin eare . . .*) that taking his classes is likely to have been a unpleasant experience. Some of the novices may have been amused by their teacher's humiliation of their clerical counterparts, but the main effect of the contrast which he draws between the clerics' sloth and the monks' passion

---

90 *The Winchester Troper from MSS of the Xth and XIth Centuries*, ed. Walter H. Frere, HBS 8 (London: Henry Bradshaw Society, 1894). See also Elizabeth C. Teviotdale, "Troper," in *The Liturgical Books of Anglo-Saxon England*, ed. Richard W. Pfaff, Old English Newsletter Subsidia 23 (Kalamazoo: Medieval Institute Publications, 1995), 39–44.

91 For an outline of the collections known in later Anglo-Saxon England, see Byrhtferth, *Enchiridion*, esp. xlii–lii. Various computistical tracts, written in the vernacular and found chiefly in five eleventh-century English MSS, are also printed and discussed in Heinrich Henel, *Studien zum altenglischen Computus*, Beiträge zur englischen Philologie 26 (Leipzig: B. Tauchnitz, 1934).

92 For the dating, see Byrhtferth, *Enchiridion*, xxvi–xxviii. Ælfric's work is briefer and less informative as to the nature of its author's interest in computus: see *Ælfric's De temporibus anni*, ed. Heinrich Henel, EETS o.s. 213 (London: Oxford University Press, 1942; repr. 1970). On Abbo of Fleury's role in transmitting the Carolingian approach to computus to England, see Byrhtferth, *Enchiridion*, xx–xxii, xli–xlv; Harry Bober, "An Illustrated Medieval School Book of Bede's *De natura rerum*," *Journal of the Walters Art Gallery* 19–20 (1956–1957): 65–97, at 74–77; A. van der Vyver, "Les œuvres inédites d'Abbon de Fleury," *Revue bénédictine* 47 (1935): 125–69.

93 E.g. Byrhtferth, *Enchiridion*, 1.1.214–16; 1.4.13–15. Byrhtferth's comments at *Enchiridion*, 1.2.323–25, suggest that these men were junior clerics who had to acquire sufficient knowledge of computus to pass an oral examination conducted by their bishops. This "test" was perhaps similar to that which is recorded in *Capitula de quibus conuocati compotistae interrogati fuerint*, ed. Ernst Dümmler, *MGH Epp.*, 4:565–67. This fascinating document sets out a test of computistical knowledge which is said to have taken place in 809. It involved 23 questions of varying difficulty. The document records the examinees' answers and a number of these show that they were, alas, unable to explain topics which ought, if they had followed Bede carefully enough, to have been within their grasp: see Charles W. Jones, "An Early Medieval Licensing Examination," *History of Education Quarterly* 3 (1963): 19–29. For an alternative interpretation, one which does not explain why the test continued to be copied, see Arno Borst, "Alcuin und die Enzyklopädie von 809," in *Science in Western and Eastern Civilization in Carolingian Times*, ed. Paul L. Butzer and Dietrich Lohrmann (Basel: Birkhäuser, 1993), 53–78, at 70–72. On the manuscripts of this test, see now Wallis, lxxxix, n. 246.

for computus was to make acquiring competence in this discipline a necessity for any novice who wanted to be worthy of his office.[94] The consequence, in short, of Byrhtferth's comments was to make an enthusiasm for computus a defining trait of monastic identity.

The belief, in short, that divine support depended on rectitude in the performance of liturgical prayer made the teaching of computus a priority for every monastery. Indeed, it was so fundamental that its purpose and importance did not in the twelfth century require any explanation.[95] The decades immediately after the Norman Conquest comprised, moreover, a period when England's Benedictine houses were menaced by the threat of reform. It was a time when the new regime was looking for pretexts to legitimise and extend its takeover of the kingdom and its church—for signs of corruption and decline which could be used to justify the removal of Anglo-Saxon abbots and bishops.[96] The intensity of the scrutiny to which the liturgical customs of the English church were subjected is clear from the precision of some of the changes to the ecclesiastical calendar which were adopted at this time.[97] In many churches Norman prelates introduced liturgical customs which were close to those of the most fashionable Continental centres. In some cases the process of reform was arbitrary and violent;[98] but, since the new regime was anxious to preserve the legitimacy of its

---

[94] Byrhtferth, *Enchiridion*, 4.2.13–20, 26–28. See, likewise, 1.1.115–16, 172–73; 1.2.64–65; 1.3.3–11; 1.4.3–11; 2.1.420–23; 2.3.8–9; 3.3.330, and so on.

[95] On the continuing influence of Carolingian scholarship on the Black Monks' understanding of the liturgy, see Marjorie Chibnall, *The World of Orderic Vitalis* (Oxford: Clarendon Press, 1984), 87–89; on the continuing centrality of the liturgy to their spirituality, see John H. van Engen, *Rupert of Deutz* (Berkeley: University of California Press, 1983), esp. 360–68, and idem, "The 'Crisis of Cenobitism' Reconsidered: Benedictine Monasticism in the Years 1050–1150," *Speculum* 61 (1986): 269–304, at 295.

[96] The most recent discussion of the programme of reform begun by the papal legates and elaborated by Archbishop Lanfranc is that in Cowdrey, *Lanfranc*, esp. 83–86, 120–28, 149–74. For the gradual but systematic replacement of Anglo-Saxon clergy, see Williams, *English and the Conquest*, 45–46, 131–33, 168; Henry R. Loyn, "Abbots of English Monasteries in the Period following the Norman Conquest," in *England and Normandy in the Middle Ages*, ed. David Bates and Anne Curry (London: Hambledon Press, 1994), 95–103. These issues are discussed further in Paul A. Hayward, *The Politics of History in Anglo-Norman England* (Oxford, forthcoming).

[97] Note, for example, the reform of the feast of St Bartholomew, which was moved from 25 to 24 August: see *C&S I*, 2:607; Martin Brett, "A Collection of Anglo-Norman Councils," *Journal of Ecclesiastical History* 26 (1975): 301–8, at 303–5. For other reforms, see now T. A. Heslop, "The Canterbury Calendars and the Norman Conquest," in *Canterbury and the Norman Conquest: Churches, Saints and Scholars 1066–1109*, ed. R. G. Eales and Richard Sharpe (London: Hambledon Press, 1995), 53–85.

[98] For the violence which erupted when the monks of Glastonbury resisted the efforts of Abbot Turstin (1077/8–1096) to impose the form of chant used at Fécamp, see

position, effective resistance was possible. A community could protect itself by ensuring that it kept up with the prevailing notions of best practice—by ensuring that it maintained high standards in the performance of the liturgy. It is true that the emergence of the new monasticism was beginning to put other issues at the top of the agenda for reform during this period, but the divine office could hardly be neglected by those orders that professed an allegiance to the Rule of St Benedict. The Cistercians may have pruned the level of communal worship back to the programme specified in the Rule,[99] but that by no means removed the need for monks who understood how to use the tools that had been developed for the purpose of accurate time-keeping. It seems, moreover, to have been in the context of this discipline that novices and oblates were asked to read chronicles.

## (d) Breviate World Chronicles as Educational Texts

The various tools which had been developed by Dionysius and Bede simplified the tasks involved in working out the liturgical year, but to use them effectively the trainees will still have needed to master the principles that governed their construction. They will have found many explanations of the various cycles of time and of how to track their movement in Bede's *De temporum ratione*, but these concepts will have remained abstractions if they could not relate them to the nature of the world around them. It was chiefly by providing oblates and novices with a basic map of what had happened over the longer term that the annalistic chronicle supported the teaching of computus.

It is worth pausing to consider how a young person enclosed within a monastery will have gained a concrete sense of the shape of time. Having been imbued with the regular round of services from the moment of his entry as an oblate, a novice may have had a strong sense of how the shorter measures of time—the hour, the day, the week, and the year—related to one another. There will also have been many reminders of just how much time had passed since the Incarnation: one of the cantor's tasks, for example, was to inscribe this date on each

*Orderic*, 2:270–71, JW*CC* 1083, WM*GP*, ii.91, and *ASC* (E) 1083. For discussion, see D. Hiley, "Thurstan of Caen and Plainchant at Glastonbury: Musicological Reflections on the Norman Conquest," *Proceedings of the British Academy* 72 (1986): 57–90.

[99] For Benedict's version of the divine office, see *Regula monachorum*, §§ 9–10, 16–18, ed. and trans. Justin McCann, *The Rule of St Benedict in Latin and English* (London: Burns and Oates, 1952), 50–53, 60–67. On the origins of the Benedictine office, see Robert F. Taft, *The Liturgy of the Hours in East and West* (Collegeville, MN: Liturgical Press, 1986), 93–140; Paul F. Bradshaw, *Daily Prayer in the Early Church*, Alcuin Club Collections 63 (London: Published for the Alcuin Club by the Society for Promoting Christian Knowledge, 1981), 124–49.

year's paschal candle when it was set up on Holy Saturday.[100] But the implications of that number may well have meant nothing to most novices, since by reason of their youth they had yet to acquire direct experience of long-term historical change. The novice master will have needed to find a way of equipping his students with a concrete sense of the larger measures of time—or rather, he will have needed to find a way of identifying those among each new cohort who had a gift for understanding time. Introducing them to the example of how time has worked in the past will have been one solution, but for the purpose of setting out this example some historical texts will have provided more assistance than others. Bede had incorporated a chronicle in his *De temporum ratione*,[101] which had its uses as an overview of the six ages as a whole, but its use of the *Anno-mundi* dating system and of irregular dates to anchor its entries meant that it provided an imprecise impression of the Sixth Age itself and especially of the flow of time.[102] Breviate world chronicles of the kind exemplified by *Winchcombe* and *Coventry* were better suited for the latter task.

Chronicles of this kind were laid out, first of all, in ways which suggest that they were meant to provide diagrammatic representations of time. Although scribes often left out year-numbers through error, the inclusion of a number for every year of the Sixth Age of the World was the pattern towards which most examples of the genre aspired, and it is these numbers which are invariably the most prominent feature on the page. This was the result, in part, of the practice of failing to provide notices of events for every year-number, since the presence of spaces in the main text area has the effect of directing the eye towards the list(s) of numbers, making them the dominant textual element on the page. In some manuscripts, however, the design of the page highlights the year-numbers. The *Annals of Mont-St-Michel*, for example, are laid out in two columns on each page, and each column is itself subdivided by a list of year numbers running up its centre. The four text areas created in this way, to the right and to the left of the two lists of numbers, remain largely unfilled.[103] In the manuscript, likewise, of the E-text of the *Anglo-Saxon Chronicle* the annal numbers are given in red, whilst the text is almost uniformly written in black.[104] In *Winchcombe* and the early

---

[100] Lanfranc, *Decreta Cantuariensibus transmissa*, § 46.

[101] Bede, *DTR*, § 66, ed. Theodor Mommsen and Charles W. Jones under the title *Chronica maiora seu de sex aetatibus mundi* in CCSL 123B (Turnhout: Brepols, 1977), 463–535, hereafter Bede, *CM*.

[102] As will emerge below, the use of irregular dates seems to have been part of Bede's ideological strategy in *CM*. On the utility of *CM* in the classroom, see also Wallis, 364.

[103] MS. Avranches, Bibliothèque municipale, 211, fols. 67r–77v. Some idea of the effect is conveyed by the plate of *part* (!) of fol. 68r in Samaran and Marichal, *Catalogue des manuscrits en écriture latine*, vol. 7, pt. 2, plate xxxvi.

[104] They are discernible in Dorothy Whitelock's black-and-white facsimile: *The Peterborough Chronicle (The Bodleian Manuscript Laud Misc. 636)*, Early English Manuscripts

stages of *Coventry* there are fewer barren entries than in the various versions of the Norman Annals, but the columns housing the year-numbers are given extra prominence by being outlined in red ink in the manuscripts, a feature which was probably carried over from the common root. It is hard not to infer that these chronicles were laid out in order to achieve a diagrammatic effect. Certainly, scholars who have given close attention to annalistic chronicles in their manuscript contexts have often suggested that the intention was to provide a kind of visual representation of the passing of time,[105] and the use of diagrams to explain concepts is a feature of manuscripts of computistical texts.[106] Isidore's *De natura rerum* is the classic example—a work also known as the *Liber rotarum* because it was usually copied along with an extensive series of circular diagrams.[107]

A marked interest in computistical matters also emerges from the contents of these breviate world chronicles. They contain numerous references, for example, to the cycles of time that were the subject of computistical reckoning. The common root behind *Winchcombe* and *Coventry* contained, for example, notices for when, according to Dionysius Exiguus, the great paschal cycle began anew,[108]

---

in Facsimile 4 (Copenhagen: Rosenkilde and Bagger, 1954). For the inks, see Whitelock, *Peterborough Chronicle*, 19–20.

[105] E.g. Janet Bately, "Manuscript Layout and the Anglo-Saxon Chronicle," *Bulletin of the John Rylands University Library of Manchester* 70 (1988): 21–43 (esp. 41–42); Rosamond McKitterick, *Perceptions of the Past in the Early Middle Ages*, The Conway Lectures in Medieval Studies 2004 (Notre Dame: University of Notre Dame Press, 2006), 14–19 (on the MSS of the Chronicle of Eusebius and its continuations); and now A. Grafton and M. Williams, *Christianity and the Transformation of the Book: Origen, Eusebius, and the Library of Caesarea* (Cambridge, MA: Harvard University Press, 2006). See also Hans-Werner Goetz, "The Concept of Time in the Historiography of the Eleventh and the Twelfth Centuries," in *Medieval Concepts of the Past: Ritual, Memory, Historiography*, ed. Gerd Althoff, Johannes Fried, and Patrick J. Geary (Cambridge and Washington, DC: German Historical Institute and Cambridge University Press, 2002), 139–65, at 148–53.

[106] Among the many excellent contributions, see esp. Bober, "An Illustrated Medieval School Book," 81–86; Bianca Kühnel, *The End of Time in the Order of Things: Science and Eschatology in Early Medieval Art* (Turnhout: Brepols, 2003), esp. 65–83; Barbara Obrist, "Wind Diagrams and Medieval Cosmology," *Speculum* 72 (1997): 33–84; Bruce S. Eastwood, "Astronomy in Christian Latin Europe, c.500–c.1150," *Journal for the History of Astronomy* 28 (1997): 235–58; Evelyn Edson and E. Savage-Smith, *Medieval Views of the Cosmos: Picturing the Universe in the Christian and Islamic Middle Ages* (Oxford: Bodleian Library, 2004), esp. 26, 67–69 and figs. 8, 11, 34; Evelyn Edson, "World Maps and Easter Tables: Medieval Maps in Context," *Imago Mundi* 48 (1996): 25–42; Edson's article includes as fig. 1 a splendid reproduction of the wind diagram in Tiberius E.IV (fol. 30r). See also Bober, "An Illustrated Medieval School Book," fig. 6; Kühnel, *The End of Time*, plate 94.

[107] See, for example, the Malmesbury copy in MS. Oxford, Bod.L., Auct. F.3.14, fols. 1r–19v, where there are eleven diagrams of this kind.

[108] *Winchcombe* 532, 1064; *Coventry* 1062.

for when the great paschal cycles would have begun if Marianus's date for the creation of the world were taken as their starting point,[109] and for when the great paschal cycles would have begun if Marianus's date for the Passion of Christ were taken as their starting point.[110] To this array of notices *Winchcombe* added references to the moments where the great paschal cycles would have begun if Marianus's corrected date for the Incarnation were taken as the starting point.[111] This kind of attention to computistical detail is also be found in the other breviate world chronicles. It is clear, for example, that the root behind the Bermondsey-Reading-Winchester complex of chronicles listed the date of Easter for each of its years,[112] in much the same way as *Coventry*, in its final form, notes each year's dominical letter(s).[113] The various chronicles based on the Norman Annals provide fewer computistical references, but that is probably a reflection of the fact that the earliest versions of these annals were lodged alongside tables covering the great paschal cycle. Indeed, two of the English versions of these annals, those associated with Ely and Chichester, seem to preserve aspects of this arrangement on their opening leaves.[114] The upshot is that these chronicles integrate abstract notices of this kind with items referring to concrete historical incidents, with events that will have had a recognisable meaning for the novices—events such as storms, crop failures, and the deaths of famous men.

Some of these chronicles, most notably the common root behind *Winchcombe* and *Coventry*, also exhibit an interest in the shape, not just of time, but also of the world. Various notices reveal an interest in the geographical extent and chronological span of kingdoms and empires: the chronicle includes, for example, three notices which refer to the duration and extinction of the early

---

109 *Winchcombe* 53 (the beginning of the ninth cycle), 585 (the beginning of the tenth cycle), 1117 (the beginning of the eleventh cycle). See, likewise, *Coventry* 53, 585, 1117.

110 *Winchcombe* 544; *Coventry* 544.

111 *Winchcombe* 510.2, 1043.

112 The manuscript which preserves these notes in their clearest form is Faustina A.VIII, fols. 120v–146v, where the dates appear in red, typically at the beginning of the annals (e.g. s.aa. 1076, 1087, 1089, and so on). The scribe has sometimes misunderstood their purpose, however, taking them as dates for the events described in the annals, dislocating them into the body of the text itself. See Brett, "Annals of Bermondsey," esp. 283–84 (and n. 12), 289–92.

113 See chap. 4 below.

114 MS. London, B.L., Cotton Vespasian D.XIX, fol. 53r (AD 1–35); MS. London, B.L., Cotton Vitellius A.XVII, fol. 1r (AD 1–34). Both begin with five columns of computistical data on their opening pages: the first identifying the bissextile years, the second the AD-year number, the third the indictional number, the fourth the epacts, and the fifth the concurrent. From the second page onwards the chronological apparatus reduces two columns, the first for leap years, the second for the AD-year number. I am grateful to Julian Harrison for the suggestion that these leaves are evidence of derivation from an Easter table.

Anglo-Saxon kingdoms of Kent, Northumbria, and East Anglia.[115] In *Winchcombe*, furthermore, these items are also made to stand out through the use of capitals and red highlights. This interest in the chronological and geographical span of kingdoms is also reflected in the compiler's choices in selecting material concerned with the Franks, as can be seen from their coverage of subdivisions of the Frankish kingdoms which took place in 843, 855, and 876–879.[116] The political and military events that caught the compiler's attention were, in short, often those that resulted in the division or re-allocation of known lands among peoples and rulers. The significance of this emphasis lies in the fact that geography was an auxiliary discipline of computus, as can be seen from the way in which many computistical collections include maps of the world and geographical tracts.[117] Indeed, the importance of computus as a formative influence on the development of historical writing may explain why so many medieval chronicles, including much fuller texts than the breviate world chronicles, display an interest in topography.[118]

One advantage of seeing world chronicles as teaching tools is that it helps to make sense of the practice of adding brief continuations. These additions are sometimes so meagre and so incomplete as to make the idea that they were meant as serious records of events that future generations ought to remember quite ludicrous.[119] Was the fact that miracles—whose miracles is not stated—began

---

[115] *Winchcombe* 823.1, 867, 870.3; *Coventry* 823.1, 867, 871. The marginalia also include an attempt to define the geographical scope of the early Anglo-Saxon kingdoms in terms of the counties they comprised: see *Winchcombe* 738.2, the commentary, and chap. 3, § g, below.

[116] *Winchcombe* 842, 855, 878; *Coventry* 842, 855, 879.

[117] E.g MS. Oxford, St John's College, 17 (which includes five maps at fols. 5v, 6r, 8r, 40r, and 87v); MS. London, B.L., Harley 3667 (which includes a copy of the former manuscript's world map at fol. 8v). For discussion, see Edson, "World Maps and Easter Tables," esp. 27–30, 35–39; Faith E. Wallis, "Oxford, St John's College, MS 17: A Medieval Manuscript in its Context," 2 vols. (Ph.D. diss., University of Toronto, 1985), 219–23.

[118] On later medieval historians as topographers, see Given-Wilson, *Chronicles*, 127–36, and esp. his discussion of Ranulph Higden.

[119] It is true that the preface found at the head of the Reading and Worcester Annals (ed. Luard, *AM*, 4:355) calls for care to be taken of the updating of these chronicles: it asks for loose leaves be added to the end of the book on which memoranda are to be noted; these are then to be edited and added to the end of the text at the end of the year by someone especially appointed for the purpose. But the very nature of this plea for order together with its author's attempt to defend the *rudis et inculta latinitas* of the entries left by earlier continuators suggests that he was attempting to swim against the onrushing tide of actual practice. Cf. Clark, *Peterborough Chronicle*, xvi, n. 1; Gransden, *HWE*, 1:319–20; Michael T. Clanchy, *From Memory to Written Record: England, 1066–1307*, 2nd ed. (Oxford: Basil Blackwell, 1993), 100–1.

to take place in Burton in 1201 all that the continuator of *Coventry* could find worthy of record for that year? Were there no other memorable events that could have been recorded? Was the cathedral priory so cut off from the town beyond the walls of its precinct that this was all its monks could have come up with? This addition makes sense, however, if it is seen as part of the process of updating a practical teaching text that was to be used in the monastic classroom: the chronicle will have become increasingly irrelevant to the novice master's pupils if it were not kept up to date, but there was no need to go to great lengths over the matter. The addition of a few very recent events will have been sufficient to make it relevant to pupils whose memory of the past was confined to only the most recent events—the storm that levelled a parish church two years ago, the death of the local bishop, or the departure of the earl on crusade. Indeed, one might see the choice of addition as a reflection of the teacher's understanding of what would arouse the students' interest. The process of maintaining these briefer chronicles is aptly seen, then, as a pragmatic activity governed by the needs of the moment, with just enough new material being added to make the lesson work until it next had to be given.[120]

The need, furthermore, to make computus comprehensible for students also helps to explain the addition of annals to the margins of Easter tables. These tables were probably as baffling to many novices as the logarithmic tables which were once, before the advent of the calculator, a staple component of secondary-school mathematics lessons. The insertion of chronological material in their margins will have helped to make these abstract matrices of data seem more concrete—to show that the numbers actually referred to real phenomena. This point is well illustrated by the annals in the margins of the Easter tables which John of Worcester prefixed to his *Chronica chronicarum*. Based on those of Marianus Scotus, these tables cover the full 532-year great paschal cycle whilst the annals cover the period from the Incarnation through to the early 1130s: that is, three runs of "overlapping" notices occur in the margins. But the integration of the three series of events provides a clear illustration of the great paschal cycle's utility for working out the date of Easter in any given year—the point stressed by Bede in his treatment of the topic.[121] A pupil sitting, for example, on his bench in the monastic school at Worcester with the second nineteen-year table before him could see from a glance at the margins that when it was last applicable to the calculation of Easter (during AD 1083–1101) building-work began on his

[120] One might compare the way in which computistical *argumenta* (e.g. those found in Bede's *De temporum ratione*, §§ 49, 52, and 54) were sometimes updated when the text was copied anew so that the current year became the subject of the calculation. For a number of examples, see Alfred Cordoliani, "Les manuscrits de comput ecclésiastique de l'abbaye de Saint-Gall du VIII<sup>e</sup> au XII<sup>e</sup> siècle," *Zeitschrift für Schweizerische Kirchengeschichte / Revue d'histoire Ecclésiastique Suisse* 49 (1955): 161–200 (esp. 180).

[121] Bede, *DTR*, § 65.

very own monastery; that when it was applicable the time before that (during AD 551–569) Pelagius, the fifty-ninth pope, presided over the church in Rome for ten years and eleven months; and that when it had been applicable the time before that (during AD 19–37) the Emperor Gaius was killed in his palace.[122] Seeing annals of this type as teaching materials helps to resolve the mystery as to why they were so often added retrospectively to Easter tables.[123] Indeed, it is clear that some annalists, not only John of Worcester,[124] went to the trouble of extracting items from fuller chronicles—from texts in which the information was preserved in a far more detailed form—in order to insert them into the margins of Easter tables, a practice which can scarcely be explained by the assumption that these annals were intended to preserve historical data for the use of future generations.

All of this helps, finally, to make sense of the character of the manuscripts in which the briefer types of annalistic chronicle are to be found. The breviate world chronicles, for example, are often to be found in booklets or collections of a humble kind, but their format and their sometimes scruffy aspect is aptly explained by the hypothesis that they are teaching texts.[125] The process of producing annalistic chronicles is often discussed as though it was an immensely serious activity,[126] but this notion is contradicted by much of the manuscript evidence, since it often shows that the scribes left out year-numbers, miscopied them, or dislocated whole rafts of entries. Even more telling is the fact that these errors usually escaped correction. There were certainly some attempts to correct annal numbers; but, as can be seen from the text of *Coventry* below, these were often fitful and inconsistent. It is as though the authors of these chronicles were more

---

[122] Oxford, Corpus Christi College, MS 157 (hereafter C), 56. The relevant table is reproduced as plate I below. On John and the purpose of the *Chronica chronicarum*, see chap. 2, § a, below.

[123] Cf. Dumville, "What is a Chronicle?," 9.

[124] At Malmesbury, for example, additions to the second nineteen-year cycle included notices for the death of Malcolm, king of the Scots, for the start of the first crusade (*Peregrinatio in Ierusalem*), for the exile of Archbishop Anselm, and so on: see MS. Oxford, Bod.L., Auct. F.3.14, fols. 120r–132v, at 120v (ed. Stevenson, "Domesday Survey," 81).

[125] For a chronicle on the verge of shabbiness, see the facsimile of the F–text of the Anglo-Saxon Chronicle in *ASC Coll.*, vol. 1, esp. fols. 46–49. These MSS may be compared with some of the finer products of post-Conquest manuscript production, such as the deluxe copies of Augustine and Bede which were produced for Winchcombe Abbey in the 1130s and 40s: see Ker, *English Manuscripts*, plates 24–25.

[126] E.g. Sarah Foot, "Finding the Meaning of the Form: Narrative in Annals and Chronicles," in *Writing Medieval History*, ed. Nancy Partner (London: Hodder Arnold, 2005), 88–108, at 96: "The omission of even one year would be unthinkable: God's time is sacred and therefore irreducible." See, likewise, Goetz, "Concept of Time," esp. 147–48.

interested in their overall effect than with matters of detail. When the briefer types of annalistic chronicle are found in better-quality productions, these often turn out to be "computus manuscripts."

There survive for England and Normandy a number of collections of computistical texts which date from the eleventh and twelfth centuries. Manuscripts of this kind are never exactly alike in their contents or organisation, and all attempts to categorise them yield imperfect results, but it is useful to divide them into three groups. The first might be said to comprise those which follow the "classic pattern": to comprise books which contain copies of the usual tools for calculating dates — a calendar and various sets of tables — and Bede's manuals on how to use them, either *De temporum ratione* or *De temporibus*, together with various auxiliary texts such as the computistical works of Abbo of Fleury and Helperic of Grandval. English examples of books of this kind include:

1. Cambridge, Corpus Christi College, 291 (s. xi/xii, St Augustine's, Canterbury)[127]
2. Cambridge, St John's College, I.15 (s.xii², England)[128]
3. Glasgow, U.L., Hunterian 85 (T.4.2) (s.xii¹–s.xii^med, Durham)[129]
4. London, B.L., Cotton Nero C.VII, fols. 80–84 + Oxford, St John's College, 17 (s.xii^in, Thorney)[130]
5. London, B.L., Cotton Tiberius E.IV (s.xii^2/4–s.xii², Winchcombe)[131]
6. London, B.L., Cotton Vitellius A.XII, fols. 4–86 (s.xii¹, Salisbury)[132]
7. London, B.L., Royal 12.D. IV (s.xii¹, Christ Church, Canterbury)[133]

[127] For a recent description, see Mildred Budny, *Insular, Anglo-Saxon, and Early Anglo-Norman Manuscript Art at Corpus Christi College, Cambridge*, 2 vols. (Kalamazoo, MI: Medieval Institute Publications, 1997), 705–10 and plate XVIa. See also Borst, *Schriften zur Komputistik*, 1:222–3.

[128] M. R. James, *A Descriptive Catalogue of the Manuscripts in the Library of St John's College, Cambridge* (Cambridge: Cambridge University Press, 1913), 253–56.

[129] See John Young and P. Henderson Aitken, *A Catalogue of the Manuscripts in the Library of the Hunterian Museum in the University of Glasgow* (Glasgow: James Maclehose, 1908), 91–94; R. A. B. Mynors, *Durham Cathedral Manuscripts to the End of the Twelfth Century* (Durham: Dean and Chapter of Durham Cathedral, 1939), no. 71.

[130] See Ralph Hanna, *A Descriptive Catalogue of the Western Medieval Manuscripts of St John's College, Oxford* (Oxford: Oxford University Press, 2002), 27–34, and the references cited there. See also Hart, *Learning and Culture*, 2:309–45.

[131] See chap. 3, § a, below.

[132] Webber, *Scribes and Scholars*, esp. 41, 144–45, 159.

[133] It should be noted that both the calendar and computistical tables in Royal 12.D.IV remain unfinished (fols. 4v–16r); its contents match those of no. 91 in the late twelfth-century booklist of Christ Church Cathedral Priory: see M. R. James, *Ancient*

8. London, B.L., Royal 12.F.II (s.xii$^{2/4}$, St Albans)[134]
9. London, B.L., Royal 13.A.XI (s.xii$^{1/4}$, England, possibly Ramsey)[135]
10. Oxford, Bod.L., Auct. F.3.14 (s.xii$^{1}$, Malmesbury)

All but one have Bede's *De temporum ratione* at their centre, the exception being Vitellius A.XII which has Hrabanus Maurus's *Liber de computo.*[136] A second group of manuscripts might be said to comprise those which are probably fragments of larger collections that followed the classic pattern, or perhaps companion volumes to books containing the usual manuals. English examples of manuscripts of this kind include:

11. Baltimore, Walters Art Museum, W.73 (s.xii$^{ex}$, England, possibly the southwest)[137]
12. Cambridge, U.L., Kk.5.32, fols. 61r–76v (s.xii$^{1/4}$, England, possibly the southwest)
13. Durham, Cathedral Library, Hunter 100 (s.xii$^{1}$, Durham)
14. London, B.L., Cotton Tiberius C.I, fols. 1–42 + Harley 3667 (s.xii$^{1}$, Peterborough)[138]

The third group might be described as comprising "semi-computistical miscellanies": that is, manuscripts largely made up of tracts having a tangential relationship to the discipline, such as treatises on astronomy or the use of the abacus. English examples of books of this kind include:

---

*Libraries of Canterbury and Dover* (Cambridge: Cambridge University Press, 1903), 26, and for a description, see Warner and Gilson, *Royal and King's MSS*, 2:38.

134 Warner and Gilson, *Royal and King's MSS*, 2:61–62; Rodney M. Thomson, *The Manuscripts of St Albans Abbey, 1066–1235*, 2 vols. (Woodbridge: D. S. Brewer, 1982), 1:96.

135 Borst, *Schriften zur Komputistik*, 1:245–6, traces MS. Royal 13.A.XI to Ramsey, but includes the possibility that it was "developed" in Normandy or northwestern Frankia. Cf. Gneuss, *Handlist of Anglo-Saxon MSS*, no. 483; Warner and Gilson, *Royal and King's MSS*, 2:80–81; Kauffmann, *Romanesque Manuscripts*, 68.

136 Vitellius A.XII, fols. 10v–40v. Royal 12.F.II is also something of an exception, since it combines Bede's *De temporibus* (fols. 22–114v) with only two satellite texts.

137 For this MS and its relationship to Tiberius E.IV, see Bober, "An Illustrated Medieval School Book," esp. 77–78, 87–88; for the dating, see Borst, *Schriften zur Komputistik*, 1:211.

138 For descriptive matter, see Jonathan Wilcox, *Anglo-Saxon Manuscripts in Microfiche Facsimile*, vol. 8, *Wulfstan Texts and Other Homiletic Materials* (Tempe: Arizona Center for Medieval and Renaissance Studies, 2000), 30–45, 69–71; Borst, *Schriften zur Komputistik*, 1:242; Kauffmann, *Romanesque Manuscripts*, 86–87, and the works cited there.

15. Oxford, Bod.L., Auct. F.1.9 (s.xii$^{2/4}$, Worcester)[139]

The attentive reader will have noticed, moreover, that there is considerable overlap between this list and the list of Easter tables with annals in their margins set out above. Indeed, when they are to be found in these manuscripts (and here it has to be remembered that many of them do not survive entirely intact) their Easter tables almost invariably have annals referring to a range of historical events in their margins.[140] Such marginalia as can be found in the Easter tables of liturgical manuscripts tend, on the other hand, to be confined to obits and often to obits of the royal family and of monks or priests of the community for whom the book was made.[141]

Tiberius E.IV stands outside the usual pattern of these manuscripts in its inclusion of a chronicle as substantial as *Winchcombe*, but it might not be so exceptional as it seems. There is reason to think, for example, that others among the surviving codices of this kind may once have contained breviate world chronicles, for early modern book collectors often broke up manuscripts and reorganised their contents to form new books.[142] These collectors may well have failed to see the point of keeping history together with works on time-reckoning. It is possible, moreover, that the presence of *Winchcombe* in T is related to its want of a set of Easter tables. It contains a series of tables which would have allowed its owners to work out the date of Easter and the date of the various moveable feasts

139 The chief contents of the MS. are astronomical in character: see Charles Burnett, "Mathematics and Astronomy in Hereford and its Region in the Twelfth Century," in *Medieval Art, Architecture and Archaeology at Hereford*, ed. David Whitehead, British Archaeological Association Conference Transactions 15 (Leeds: British Archaeological Association, 1995), 50–59. MS. Auct. F.1.9 was copied mostly in the hand that has been identified as that of John of Worcester, and Alexander and Temple, *Illuminated MSS in Oxford*, 5, make the interesting suggestion, worthy of further investigation, that it and the holograph of John's *Chronica chronicarum* (i.e. MS. Oxford, Corpus Christi College, 157) were "companion volume[s]." See also Rodney M. Thomson, *A Descriptive Catalogue of the Medieval Manuscripts in Worcester Cathedral Library* (Woodbridge: Published for the Dean and Chapter of Worcester Cathedral by D. S. Brewer, 2001), xxiii, 163.

140 The MSS in this list which contain Easter tables with annals are nos. 3, 4, 10, 12, 13, and 14. These MSS correspond to nos. 5, 7, 11, 3, 4 and 9 in the list of Easter table chronicles given in § b above.

141 See, for example, the tables in MS. Rouen, Bibliothèque municipale, 274, fols. 15v–18v (ed. Henry A. Wilson, *The Missal of Robert of Jumièges*, HBS 11 [London: Henry Bradshaw Society, 1916], 27–33). There are, however, some manuscripts which combine substantial liturgical contents with small computistical collections: see n. 53 above.

142 See James P. Carley and Colin G. C. Tite, "Sir Robert Cotton as Collector of Manuscripts and the Question of Dismemberment: British Library MSS Royal 13 D. I and Cotton Otho D. VIII," *The Library*, 6th ser., 14 (1992): 94–99; N. R. Ker, "Membra Disjecta," *British Museum Quarterly* 12 (1937–1938): 130–35 (esp. 130–32).

across every year in the Great Paschal Cycle, but it is devoid of a conventional set of Easter tables which could be used to house a set of annals in its margins.[143] It is possible, therefore, that the monks of Winchcombe included a breviate world chronicle in their computus as an alternative to the usual kind of Easter table with annals.

The exact purpose for which the computus manuscripts of the "classic type" were created is something of a moot point. In his pastoral letters Ælfric of Eynsham numbered a computus among the books which every priest ought to own,[144] but the manuscripts which belong to the twelfth-century cluster of English examples can almost invariably be associated with major, established, monasteries or cathedral priories. It is probably a safe assumption that priests had much humbler versions of these books. Some scholars have written about the larger collections as though they were the guidebooks for the cantor himself, as though they were designed to provide him with the reference material he needed to carry out his work.[145] Others, most notably the art historian Harry Bober, have suggested that they were intended to be used as school-books, as textbooks for the teaching of computus. Bober builds his argument on the way in which the compilers of these books tended to revise their contents, replacing sections on particular topics with more informative and more concise alternatives when and where they could be found. This "critical selectivity" extended, he argues, to the picking out of illustrative diagrams, and to the way in which these figures were used to comment on and develop the contents of the text.[146] It is probably a mistake to attempt to define the purpose of these books too narrowly. Like most reference books, a monastery's computistical collection probably played a range of roles: the cantor might have consulted it at certain crucial moments in the year; the novice master might have consulted it in order to compare what the various authorities had to say when revising and illustrating his lessons; and a brighter novice might

143 The three tables on fols. 32r–33r are the closest items in T to an Easter table: see chap. 3, § a, below. There is some uncertainty as to the exact way in which T was originally compiled, but there is little reason to doubt that *Winchcombe* was bound with the "tabular" section of the surviving codex.

144 Ælfric, "Pastoral Letter for Wulfsige III, bishop of Sherborne (993–1002)," § 52, and his "First Old English Pastoral Letter for Wulfstan I, Archbishop of York (1002–23)," § 157, both printed in *C&S I*, 1:196–226 (at 206–7) and 260–302 (at 291–92).

145 E.g. Andrew J. Piper, "The Durham Cantor's Book (Durham, Dean and Chapter Library, MS B.IV.24)," in *Anglo-Norman Durham, 1093–1193*, ed. David W. Rollason, Margaret Harvey, and Michael Prestwich (Woodbridge: Boydell Press, 1994), 72–92.

146 See Bober, "An Illustrated Medieval School Book," esp. 73, 81–86. Cf. Edson, "World Maps and Easter Tables," esp. 27, 39, and Richard Corradini, "The Rhetoric of Crisis: *Computus* and *Liber annalis* in Early Ninth-Century Fulda," in *The Construction of Communities in the Early Middle Ages*, ed. idem, Max Diesenberger, and Helmut Reimitz, The Transformation of the Roman World 12 (Leiden: Brill, 2003), 269–321 (esp. 312–16, on Walahfrid Strabo's activities as a student and teacher of computus).

have found it being put before him when the cantor allocated the abbey's books at the annual book distribution on the first Sunday in Lent.[147] There is a lot to be said, however, for the theory that these books were devised, in part at least, for the purpose of teaching computus to novices, not least because it helps to explain the inclusion of annals among their satellite texts.

## (e) Breviate World Chronicles as Commemorative Texts

It is sometimes suggested that the production of annalistic chronicles owed much to a need to commemorate the dead. It cannot be denied that these texts record large numbers of obits (the verb *obeo* appears in *Winchcombe* no less than 322 times), and that the cantor was involved in organising prayer for the souls of the dead. He was responsible for scheduling the masses which were to be said for the souls of deceased monks during the anniversary period after their deaths.[148] But there are good reasons for doubting whether these chronicles were themselves intended as commemorative records in either a modern or a liturgical sense. The breviate world chronicles fail to fulfil this role in the former sense, because they rarely say enough about the deceased to serve as obituaries or as celebrations of their achievements.[149] They fail in the latter sense for two reasons: first, because they seldom record the obits of the monks of the house where they were produced—of the very souls, that is, for whom the community was most obliged to pray;[150] and second, because they often record obits without specifying the precise date on which the person died—that is, they typically provide only the year whilst omitting the month and the day. These chronicles do not, in short, provide enough information to allow the cantor to institute prayers or services for the souls of those whose deaths they record. Another type of book, the necrology or *Liber vitae*, served this purpose. The large numbers of obits recorded in these

147 For the practice of allocating books on the first Sunday in Lent, see Lanfranc, *Decreta Cantuariensibus transmissa*, § 20, and for the procedure followed at Peterborough, see *CBMLC*, 8:xxviii–xxix.

148 Lanfranc, *Decreta Cantuariensibus transmissa*, § 86, requires the cantor to keep count of the *tricenaria* and *septenaria*, that is, of the thirty masses which were to be said for the soul of a deceased brother and of the obituary mass which took place on the seventh day after his death.

149 The only exceptions in the chronicles edited here are the entries celebrating the life of England's apostle, St Gregory, and that of Winchcombe's founder, King Cenwulf of Mercia (798–821): see *Winchcombe* 575, 578, 591.2–4, 595, 597, 606.1, 795.1–4, 798, 811.1–5, 819.

150 A notable exception is JW's record of the obit of the monk Florence in *CC* 1118.

texts are better explained as a form of shorthand—as a way of conveying that crucial impression of the passage of time which did not involve the chronicler in having to narrate these persons' deeds.

## (f) Breviate World Chronicles as Political Texts

There is, in short, much to recommend the view that the briefer types of annalistic chronicle were conceived chiefly as teaching texts intended to be used by newcomers to the subject of computus. The hypothesis certainly helps to explain many of their features, but it should not be taken as implying that political and ideological factors did not influence the selection of material. On the contrary, it is clear that the choice of material reflected the preoccupations of the monastic world—that these chronicles were used to win converts for particular positions in ideological debates in much the same way as modern educators use textbooks to disseminate attitudes and ideas. In the case of the annalistic chronicle, however, the ideological burden seems to have been a matter not of insinuating a particular moral code or a social identity, but largely one of promoting theories concerned with the structure of time.

Bede, for example, developed a much shorter chronology for the first five ages of the world in order to confound millenarian expectations. The problem with which Bede was contending was the widespread belief that the Second Coming would take place in the 6000th year from the Creation. Eusebius of Caesarea (ca. 260–339) had challenged this notion in his chronicle by placing the Incarnation in the 5197th or 5198th year from the Creation, thus disrupting the idea that there would be seven ages in all, each lasting a thousand years.[151] Jerome adjusted that dating to 25 December in AM 5199, and it was this date which found widespread acceptance in the West.[152] This had helped to avert the problem, but millenarian thought remained deeply entrenched.[153] Bede's solution was to develop a

---

[151] For further discussion, see Richard Landes, "Lest the Millennium be Fulfilled: Apocalyptic Expectations and the Pattern of Western Chronography, 100–800 C.E.," in *The Use and Abuse of Eschatology in the Middle Ages*, ed. Werner Verbeke, Daniel Verhelst, and Andries Welkenhuysen, Mediaevalia Lovaniensia, 1st ser., 15 (Leuven: Leuven University Press, 1988), 137–209 (esp. 174–78); von den Brincken, *Studien zur lateinischen Weltchronistik*, esp. 50–60; Martin Haeusler, *Das Ende der Geschichte in der mittelalterlichen Weltchronistik*, Beihefte zum Archiv für Kulturgeschichte 13 (Cologne: Böhlau, 1980), 24–32; Allen, "Universal History," esp. 21, 32–34; Wallis, lxix–lxx, 353–69.

[152] E.g. Isidore of Seville, who dates Christ's birth to AM 5196, in his *Chronica majora*, §§ 235, 237, ed. Theodor Mommsen, *MGH AA*, 11:424–81, at 453–54.

[153] For the context, see Bede, *DTR*, §§ 67–69. The persistence of millenarian beliefs in England, even among the ecclesiastical elite, is illustrated by the circulation in the late tenth and early eleventh century of a set of notes on the six ages which specified the length of the period from the nativity of the Lord to the coming of the Antichrist as

new chronology which placed the Incarnation in the 3952nd year from the Creation, exploding the millennial conceit even more profoundly and rendering the timing of the Second Coming even more unpredictable.[154] The new chronology attracted fierce criticism. Bede was accused of heresy when he first articulated it in the earlier of his two computistical manuals, *De temporibus* of about 703.[155] His response was to strengthen his arguments in his later work, the *De temporum ratione* of 725, in which he included an expanded account of the six ages, the so-called *Chronica maiora*. He asserted that his revised chronology was grounded in "the Hebrew Truth" (that is, in the Vulgate translation of the Bible),[156] and he invested it with further allegorical and moral significance.[157] Bede also used his *Chronica maiora* to affirm his view of the true reckoning of Easter by celebrating the floruits of the authorities to whom he was indebted—those of Hippolytus, Theophilus, Paschasinus, Victorius, Dionysius, and Victor of Capua.[158] Many of these floruits were repeated in later chronicles, including *Winchcombe* and *Coventry*, but with the difference that they add Bede's name to those of the other great pioneers of sacred mathematics.[159]

Arguments of this kind seem to have comprised the typical ideological and rhetorical burden of the briefer types of annalistic chronicle. Indeed, it will be

999 years: see Cotton Titus D.XXVI, fol. 3r (ed. Günzel, *Ælfwine's Prayerbook*, 144), and Bodley 579, fol. 55v (ed. Orchard, *Leofric Missal*, ii, 94). Byrhtferth, furthermore, found it necessary to take issue with those who believed *þæt þes middaneard scyle standan on syx þusend wintrum* in his *Enchiridion* (iv.2.73–125). See also Aaron J. Kleist, "The Influence of Bede's *De temporum ratione* on Ælfric's Understanding of Time," in *Time and Eternity: The Medieval Discourse*, ed. Gerhard Jaritz and Gerson Moreno-Riano (Turnhout: Brepols, 2003), 81–97; and for the Frankish world, see Johannes Heil, "'Nos nescientes de hoc velle manere' – 'We Wish to Remain Ignorant about This': Timeless End, or Approaches to Reconceptualizing Eschatology after A.D. 800 (A.M. 6000)," *Traditio* 55 (2000): 73–103.

154 See Bede, *CM*, §§ 1–6, where the durations of the first five Ages are set at 1,656, 292, 942, 473, and 589 years respectively. For another approach to refuting millennial anxieties, one which involved arguing that over 6,000 had already passed since the Creation, see Jane B. Stevenson, *The "Laterculus Malalianus" and the School of Archbishop Theodore*, Cambridge Studies in Anglo-Saxon England 14 (Cambridge: Cambridge University Press, 1995), esp. 23–26. This approach was brought to England by Archbishop Theodore (668–690), but seems to have found no traction in the West.

155 Ed. Charles W. Jones, CCSL 123C (Turnhout: Brepols, 1975–1980), 585–611. *De temporibus*, §§ 16–22, comprise Bede's *Chronica minora*, the earlier version of *Chronica maiora*. For the opposition, see his *Epistula ad Pleguinam*, ed. Charles W. Jones, CCSL 123C, 617–26.

156 Bede, *DTR*, pref. and § 67.

157 Bede, *DTR*, §§ 10, 71; Bede, *CM*, §§ 1–9, 20, 38, 81, 143, 268.

158 Bede, *CM*, 355, 456, 481, 497, 518, 520.

159 E.g. *Winchcombe* 211, 468, 526, 703 and 725.2; *Coventry* 468, 526, 703, 725.2.

argued in chapter two below that the common root behind *Winchcombe* and *Coventry* is yet another example, since it may well have been produced in order to elicit acceptance for another contentious theory as to the chronology of the sixth age: that associated with Marianus Scotus. There was, of course, a political dimension to the role that chronicles played in promoting intellectual positions of this kind, in as much as the reputations of the ecclesiastical, and sometimes also the secular, authorities who were promoting these theories were also advanced by the dissemination and success of these chronicles.[160] It has recently become fashionable to argue, however, that annalistic chronicles were used to articulate claims to authority in a rather more direct sense—as a kind of semi-explicit propaganda for particular groups and communities. Sarah Foot, for example, has argued in a recent essay that annalistic chronicles worked on two levels: the layout of the chronicle and the listing of the dates provided, on one level, "a linear representation of all the years elapsed since the Incarnation, a line tracing the natural, divinely ordained progression of historical time from the birth of Christ, through the recorded past and on, beyond the present of the scribe, into an infinite future"; the annals provided, on the other level, a way of locating the community whose deeds they recorded "within the same divine temporal framework and thus within God's plan for redeemed humanity."[161] The genre's *raison d'être*, in short, was to provide particular groups with a means of legitimising their social position. Its defining trait, the dating of the years by reference to the Incarnation of the Lord, was "central to the entire enterprise": far from being merely a grid for arranging memoranda, the sequence of years was itself the narrative which could be used to locate the story of an ethnic group or religious community within a larger order which was invested with greater religious meaning and authority.

There is certainly something in this theory,[162] but it is doubtful whether disseminating propaganda of this kind was ever the *raison d'être* of the annalistic chronicle, especially where the briefer forms of the genre are concerned. Cultural and social biases certainly influenced the selection of items and the way in which events were reported in twelfth-century chronicles of this kind, but it is quite another thing to suggest that they were the products of systematic attempts

[160] It is a much-stressed point of recent scholarship that Charlemagne presided over the Carolingian reforms of the calendar and of computus (e.g. Kühnel, *The End of Time*, 101–15), but in the eleventh and twelfth centuries it seems to have been bishops, figures such as Wulfstan II of Worcester (d. 1095) and Robert de Losinga (d. 1095), who presided over the dissemination of these ideas: see chap. 2 below.

[161] Foot, "The Meaning of the Form," 96.

[162] White, "Narrativity in the Representation of Reality," 11, goes too far when he states that "what is lacking [in annals] . . . is a notion of a social center by which to locate [events] with respect to one another and to charge them with ethical or moral significance." A social centre of a Christian kind is always implicit even if it is nowhere expressly mentioned in any of the annals.

to fashion the identity of one group at the expense of others. The texts often include entries celebrating the achievements of or bemoaning the disasters which had befallen the leaders and peoples with whom the authors identified, but these items tend to form isolated outbursts within much larger complexes of material. Indeed, the scissors-and-paste methods of the compilers of these texts and the somewhat haphazard nature of their continuations often results in chronicles that are full of political contradictions: items that favour a Frankish perspective are brought together with items that favour an English perspective, items that favour a West-Saxon perspective are brought together with items that favour a Mercian perspective, and so on.[163] This phenomenon is so common that it makes one ask why, if their function was to nurture a particular sense of identity, did later editors fail to erase or re-write those annals which were biased in favour of their enemies? Why did they not do more to fashion the past to serve their politics? It is true that one often can, as Foot argues, discern larger narrative patterns among the items brought together in annalistic chronicles, but the strongest patterns usually relate to topics of general religious rather than of immediate political interest. The entries in the breviate world chronicles which refer, for example, to the acts of the popes could be said to provide an account of the development of the liturgy and its administration from its earliest days of the church, albeit one which usually peters out by the end of the sixth century.[164] The practice, likewise, of carefully recording the obits and successions of the holders of the imperial title is better explained as a way of tracing the fate of the empire rather than as a meaningful expression of political allegiances.[165] It is telling, moreover, that in the process of selecting material for the root behind *Winchcombe* and *Coventry*, the compiler draws more heavily on *Chronica chronicarum*'s reports of prodigies and astral phenomena than on its coverage of high politics.[166]

Where the breviate world chronicles *sometimes* provide more support for Foot's thesis is in their treatment of the history of their own houses. Thus the institution of the order of canons at Southwark is duly noted in the annals of

---

[163] E.g. Hughes, "Welsh Latin Chronicles," 67–85, at 79–81, which traces several 180-degree shifts of perspective in the B-text of *Annales Cambriae*, a work that favours sometimes the Welsh point of view, at other times that of the Norman settlers.

[164] This pattern reflects the fact that many of these items seem to have been derived from Pseudo-Isidore, whose coverage, as it were, of papal history ended at this point (see chap. 3, § c, below), but compilers often seem to have tried to extend the theme into the seventh and eighth centuries (e.g. *Winchcombe* 614.2, 686.5, 733.2).

[165] It is true that William of Malmesbury justifies the inclusion in WM*GR*, § i.67, of a digression on the kings of the Franks with the point that their *imperium* extends to the people of England, but this was a literary conceit rather than a comment about political realities.

[166] Consider, for example, its coverage of the first decade of the twelfth century, in which more attention is given to effusions of blood (1103), comets (1106.2), and unusual sights in the night sky (1106.3) than to the struggle over investitures (1107.1).

the house under 1106, and an annotator has even drawn a picture of the church in the margins of the Bodleian copy.[167] *Winchcombe* shows, likewise, some signs that it may have been adapted for the purposes of legitimising the social position of the abbey where it was produced, since the compiler of the first phase incorporated three documents and several passages celebrating its foundation.[168] But the first phase includes scarcely any entries about the subsequent history of the abbey: it has nothing, for example, to say about its refoundation as a Benedictine house by Bishop Oswald of Worcester and Abbot Germanus or about the way in which this reform was contested after the death of King Edgar in 975.[169] Some of these chronicles provide, moreover, only the most sketchy details about the histories of the institutions where they were made. *Coventry*, for example, is so reticent about the house for which it was produced that it is difficult to be confident about its provenance.[170] The authors and redactors of breviate world chronicles often fail to take up opportunities to mention their houses, their families, their kingdoms, and their nations.

There are signs, in short, that breviate world chronicles were sometimes adapted as a means of legitimising claims to power and property, but these efforts were so limited and spasmodic as to make it most unlikely that this was their *main* function—at least, not in twelfth-century England. That should not surprise, for there flourished at this time other types of history that could be used to make this type of argument in a far more powerful fashion: namely the rhetorical monograph as reworked by writers such as William of Malmesbury and, above all, hagiography.[171] It is true that there are more signs that annalistic chronicles were used to develop political arguments in the ninth century. Foot's hypothesis is certainly applicable to some prominent early examples of the genre such as the Royal Frankish Annals and the Alfredian phase of the *Anglo-Saxon*

[167] Rawlinson B.177, fol. 209r. The symbol is akin to those used by Diceto. In Faustina A.VIII, the entry is one of three concerning Southwark which are entered in red. The others are the obit of Prior Valerian (fol. 136r, s.a. 1190) and that of Prior William of Oxford (fol. 137v, s.a. 1203).

[168] See *Winchcombe* 787.2, 798, 811.1–3, 818.3, 819, and the commentary below. In this respect *Winchcombe* is similar to the E-text of the *Anglo-Saxon Chronicle*, since it represents a version of the latter chronicle which was adapted for the needs of Peterborough Abbey in much the same way as the former adapted the root on which it depends for the use of Winchcombe Abbey. The monks of Peterborough interpolated various passages and documents relating to foundation of their house which are not dissimilar to those in *Winchcombe* (e.g. *ASC* (E) 657, 675, 686, 777, 851), and they added continuations of their own devising for 1121–1154: see *Peterborough Chronicle, 1070–1154*, ed. Cecily Clark, 2nd ed. (Oxford: Clarendon Press, 1970), xxiv–xxviii.

[169] Cf. Byrhtferth, *Vita Oswaldi*, 4.4, 11–13. *Winchcombe*'s entry for the appointment of Abbot Germanus (s.a. 966) is a later addition.

[170] See chap. 4, §§ c-d, below.

[171] See Hayward, *The Politics of History*, forthcoming.

*Chronicle.*[172] These chronicles are best seen, however, as examples of a different annalistic sub-genre, that of the chronicle as an official record compiled at the royal court or on behalf of the state. The Royal Frankish Annals offer a discontinuous but fairly full record of events from 741 to 829 in which the Carolingians are presented as the legitimate rulers of the Franks, who are themselves defined as God's chosen people.[173] Ardo was thinking of this type of chronicle when he wrote in the preface to his *Life of St Benedict of Aniane* that it was "a very ancient custom, still used by kings, to have consigned to annals whatever was done or whatever happened that ought to be known to posterity."[174] Chronicles of this kind certainly exercised a wider influence. Copies were acquired by many cathedrals and monasteries where they were sometimes taken over and continued.[175] Moreover, their contents were often re-used in local productions. Indeed, many of the items in *Winchcombe* and *Coventry* can be traced back to the Royal Frankish Annals and to the first phase of the *Anglo-Saxon Chronicle.*[176] In England, furthermore, this type of chronicle underwent something of a revival in the late twelfth century, when Roger of Howden and Ralph de Diceto, both of whom were secular clerks, tried to produce an exhaustive, year-by-year, record of the events of their own time.[177]

---

172 Foot, "The Meaning of the Form," 97–101.

173 The Carolingian bias of *ARF* was first noted by Ranke (see Poole, *Chronicles and Annals*, 30), but the argument has recently been developed in detail in McKitterick, *History and Memory*, esp. 113–19. Further nuances are added in eadem, *Perceptions of the Past*, 64–89. See also Roger Collins, "The 'Reviser' Revisited: Another Look at the Alternative Version of the *Annales Regni Francorum*," in *After Rome's Fall: Narrators and Sources of Early Medieval History: Essays Presented to Walter Goffart*, ed. Alexander C. Murray (Toronto: University of Toronto Press, 1998), 191–213; Janet L. Nelson, "The Lord's Anointed and the People's Choice: The Carolingian Royal Ritual," in *Rituals of Royalty: Power and Ceremonial in Traditional Societies*, ed. David Cannadine and S. R. F. Price (Cambridge: Cambridge University Press, 1987), 137–80. As for *ASC*, there remains much of value in Ralph H. C. Davis, "Alfred the Great: Propaganda and Truth," *History* 56 (1971): 169–82, an article which suggested that many of the Alfredian annals were intended to convince the West-Saxon élite of the need to carry out his military programme properly and efficiently.

174 Ardo, *Vita Benedicti abbatis Anianensis et Indensis* (*BHL* 1096), ed. Georg Waitz, *MGH SS*, 15:200–220, at 201: "Perantiquam siquidem fore consuetudinem actenus regibus usitatam, quaeque geruntur acciduntve annalibus tradi posteris cognoscenda, nemo, ut reor, ambigit doctus."

175 See McKitterick, *History and Memory*, esp. 111–13.

176 For examples of derivation from *ARF*, see *Winchcombe* 742.3, 768.2; for examples of derivation from *ASC*, see *Winchcombe* 471, 508, 520.1, 527, 538, 540.1, 559.2, 560, and so on.

177 On the "official" character of these chronicles, see Bartlett, *England 1075–1225*, 627–28, 630–31; on the uses to which chronicles were put by the late medieval English state, see Given-Wilson, *Chronicles*, 65–78.

But none of this means that the use of chronicles for official purposes was the most influential form of annalistic activity—or that the ninth-century examples of this form of chronicle were the "ur-type" from which the various subgenres prevalent in later centuries were distilled. It is true that *Anno-Domini* dating seems first to have become widespread at the time when the Royal Frankish Annals were produced, but their example seems to have had much less influence on the motivations of chroniclers than that set by Isidore and Bede even though they had used *Anno-Mundi* dating. That is, monastic chroniclers may have recycled the material provided by the court-centred chronicles, but they did so in the pursuit of their own, local, needs. The brief world chronicle was probably always the most common form of chronicling, even in the Carolingian world. Chronicles of this kind do appear in Frankish codices of the eighth, ninth, and tenth centuries,[178] and it has to be admitted that many more examples of this sub-genre may have been produced during this period than the manuscript record now suggests, for world chronicles were often revised and improved, rendering earlier "editions" obsolete and vulnerable to destruction.

The historical culture of the twelfth-century monastery seems, moreover, to have been set against the composition of "political history", and increasingly so. In practice, it usually seems to have taken a serious crisis—a crisis affecting a community's survival or its status within the ecclesiastical order—before a monk was permitted to undertake an historical work of the kind akin to that commended by Cicero. This much can be seen from the fact that the only Benedictines to attempt such histories in the second half of the twelfth century were Gervase of Canterbury and Richard of Devizes, both of whom were writing in the midst of the attacks on Benedictine cathedral priories which took place in the late 1180s and 1190s.[179] Gervase, for example, was writing in the midst of the

[178] E.g. MS. Vatican City, Bibliotheca Apostolica Vaticana, Reg. lat. 226, in which a brief computistical collection (fols. 18r–32v) is followed by a *Chronicon mundi* that extends to the year 824 (fols. 32v–33v). On Carolingian world-chronicles, and especially the various elaborations of Bede's *Chronica majora* which have been discussed as witnesses to the so-called "Chronicle of 741," see von den Brincken, *Studien zur lateinischen Weltchronistik*, 113–15; McKitterick, *Perceptions of the Past*, 22–32.

[179] There are, of course, exceptions to the rule, of which Orderic's *Historia ecclesiastica* is perhaps the most outstanding. But even this work may be seen as a case in point, since it was first conceived as a short history celebrating the foundation of St-Évroult and recording the development of its endowment. It was Abbot Roger du Sap (1091–1123) who asked Orderic to produce the work, and his reign was a time when Norman monasteries were concerned with protecting the basis of their income. See Marjorie Chibnall's general introduction to *Orderic*, 1:29–34, and Véronique Gazeau, "The Effect of the Conquest of 1066 on Monasticism in Normandy: The Abbeys of the Risle Valley," in *England and Normandy in the Middle Ages*, ed. David Bates and Anne Curry (London: Hambledon Press, 1994), 131–42. It should also be noted that the present point excludes the secular clerks (e.g. John of Salisbury, Roger Howden, and Ralph de Diceto) whose

crisis that overtook Canterbury Cathedral Priory when Archbishop Baldwin set in motion his plan to found a college of secular canons at Hackington: the college was to receive half the offerings from the cathedral, a move which seemed to imply, not just a loss of income, but that the canons were to supplant the monks of the priory as the custodians of Becket's cult.[180] The cathedral priory at Winchester escaped any direct attack, but, as a monk of a priory which might well have been the next to suffer an assault on its status and privileges, Richard of Devizes leapt to the defence of his fellow Benedictines, denouncing the reforms of both Archbishop Baldwin and Hugh de Nonant, the bishop who suppressed the monastic chapter at Coventry.[181] The history, moreover, which Gervase wrote in defence of the monks' position is notable for the way in which it is presented as though it were not a work of rhetoric but merely a humble chronicle. The work is in fact a history masquerading as a chronicle and the disguise is established in the preface, a text which provides such important insights as to the attitudes and practices governing the production of chronicles and histories in the monastic context that it needs to be discussed in detail.[182]

Though the author's position turns out to be more ambiguous than first appears, this preface is ostensibly organised as an explanation as to why he has

---

output overtook that of the monastic writers in late twelfth-century England, as may be seen from the survey in Bartlett, *England 1075–1225*, 616–33 (esp. table 12). But for the thirteenth century see Given-Wilson, *Chronicles*, 16.

[180] See Margaret T. Gibson, "Normans and Angevins, 1070–1220," in *A History of Canterbury Cathedral*, ed. Patrick Collinson, Nigel Ramsay, and Margaret Sparks (Oxford: Oxford University Press, 1995), 38–68, at 66–67; Knowles, *MO*, 314–22, 325–27. *Chronica* was begun in 1188 and was presumably completed in or soon after the death of King Richard I (6 April 1199), the event with which it concludes: see Gransden, *HWE*, 1:253–60.

[181] For Richard's view of the conflict at Canterbury, see Devizes, *CTR*, 66; for his view of Hugh's character and of his actions at Coventry, see Devizes, *CTR*, 8, 13, 48, 51, 69–72, and Devizes, *AW*, s.a. 1198.

[182] The passage is often cited, but seldom with attention to its many nuances or to the political context in which Gervase was writing: e.g. Janet Coleman, *Ancient and Medieval Memories: Studies in the Reconstruction of the Past* (Cambridge: Cambridge University Press, 1992), 298–300. See, likewise, Bernard Guenée, "Histoire et chronique: Nouvelle réflexions sur les genres historiques au moyen âge," in *La chronique et l'histoire au moyen-âge*, ed. Daniel Poiron, Culture et Civilisations Médiévales 2 (Paris: Presses de l'Université de Paris-Sorbonne, 1984), 3–25; Vivian H. Galbraith, *Historical Research in Medieval England* (London: University of London, 1951), 1–3; Poole, *Chronicles and Annals*, 7–8, and so on. The most attentive discussion to date is that offered by Roger Ray, "Historiography," in *Medieval Latin: An Introduction and Bibliographical Guide*, ed. F. A. C. Mantello and A. G. Rigg (Washington, DC: Catholic University of America Press, 1996), 639–49 (esp. 640–41). The present author has in hand a fuller study of Gervase and his methods as an historian.

chosen to produce a chronicle rather than a history.[183] Gervase begins by defining the differences between the two forms. Both types of history have, he explains, the same purpose, because both provide examples of good living which help to dispel human ignorance, and the same subject matter, because both are directed towards the truth. Where they differ is in style and format: "The historian moves along diffusely and eloquently, yet the chronicler goes forward simply and briefly"; historians "caress their listeners or readers with sweet and elegant words," whereas chroniclers "compute the years and months and kalends of the years of the Incarnation of the Lord, note briefly the acts of kings and princes that happened in them, and record also events, portents, and wonders."[184] This typology is sufficiently similar to that set out in Cicero's *De oratore* as to suggest that Gervase may well have been thinking of the work;[185] but if so, the intention must have been to stand Cicero's scheme on its head, for Gervase goes on to adopt an entirely different posture. It is true that the words with which he begins suggest a moral equivalence between the two types of history, but the allusions with which he elaborates this typology imply that it is more appropriate for a monk to compile a chronicle than to write a history.

There are two pairs of contrasting allusions. In the first a phrase from Horace is set against another from Virgil: the historian, Gervase declares, "throws forth bombastic and extra-long words," whereas the chronicler "meditates on the woodland muse," or since the line has a double meaning, "practises his woodland music, with [a] thin [pipe of] oat stalks."[186] The former phrase derives from Horace's *Ars poetica* and is used in a way which implies that historians are pompous and overbearing.[187] The latter phrase is an allusion to the opening of Virgil's

---

[183] Gervase, 1:89: "quoniam aliqua gestorum præteriti temporis et futuri compilare potius quam scribere cupio."

[184] Gervase, 1:87: "Forma tractandi varia, quia historicus diffuse et eleganter incedit, cronicus vero simpliciter graditur et breviter . . . Proprium est historici veritati intendere, audientes vel legentes dulci sermone et eleganti demulcere . . . Cronicus autem annos Incarnationis Domini annorumque menses computat et kalendas, actus etiam regum et principum quæ in ipsis eveniunt breviter edocet, eventus etiam, portenta vel miracula commemorat."

[185] *Latin Historians*, ed. Thomas A. Dorey (London: Routledge, 1966), xii–xiii, considers the passage a "clear trace of Ciceronian influence." Cf. Gransden, *HWE*, 1:259–60. Gervase might also have been thinking of Cassiodorus, *Institutiones*, 1.17.1–2, ed. R. A. B. Mynors (Oxford: Clarendon Press, 1937), 55–57, who contrasts the works of Josephus and of the ecclesiastical historians with the Chronicle of Eusebius and its continuations. Cassiodorus treats both types of history in entirely positive terms.

[186] Gervase, 1:87: "'Proicit' historicus 'ampullas et sesquipedalia verba'; cronicus vero 'silvestrem musam tenui meditatur avena'."

[187] Horace, *Ars poetica*, line 97; ed. C. O. Brink, *Horace on Poetry: The 'Ars Poetica'* (Cambridge: Cambridge University Press, 1971), 58. It should be noted that Gervase has misunderstood Horace's meaning. At this point in his poem, Horace is using the example

first *Eclogue*, where the herdsman Tityrus is shown practising his simple songs while reclining under his beech tree.[188] In the second pair of allusions a phrase from John of Salisbury is set against an image from Lucan. The historian, writes Gervase, "sits among the weavers of grandiose words and pomposities," but the chronicler "rests within the covered hut of the pauper Amyclas lest there should be conflict for the sake of a humble shelter."[189] The former phrase is an allusion to a line in *Entheticus minor*, a poem that John of Salisbury composed as a preface to his *Policraticus*. The line is part of a longer passage in which John exhorts his book—*Entheticus minor* is constructed in Ovidian fashion as a set of instructions to a personified *Policraticus*—to resist the temptation to speak too much and too often whilst sitting among the weavers of grandiosities.[190] The allusion in the latter clause is to a passage in the *Pharsalia*, where the humble fisherman Amyclas is awoken by Julius Caesar banging on the door of his broken-down shack.[191] The significant point here is that Lucan endows Amyclas with a certain self-assurance born of extreme poverty. As Robert Graves puts it in his translation,[192]

> Amyclas was not frightened of the visitor, knowing that humble shelters like his own were not plundered even in times of civil war. Though poor, he lived a safe and peaceful life; and it is a comment on the lack of appreciation with which most people view the bounty of nature, that no temple and no fortified town could have said with Amyclas: "When Caesar knocks, why should I feel alarm?"

---

of the playwrights Sophocles and Euripides to explore the ways in which authors ought to moderate their style and tone. These great poets, he explains, made their characters Telephus and Peleus "give up" the pomposities of their usual dialogue when they really wanted their audiences to recognise the depth of the despair into which they had fallen (see Brink, *Horace on Poetry*, 174–75). That is, in Horace's line the verb *proicio* means "to put aside," whereas Gervase, missing the subtlety of the argument, reads it in its primary sense, as meaning "to throw forth." But this was how the line was usually understood in the twelfth century: cf. Guibert of Nogent, *Gesta Dei per Francos*, vii.32, ed. R. B. C. Huygens, CCCM 127A (Turnhout: Brepols, 1996), 77–352, at 329.

188 Virgil, *Ecloga*, 1.2; ed. Robert Coleman, *Virgil's Eclogues* (Cambridge: Cambridge University Press, 1977), 43. The line is meant to be read in both ways.

189 Gervase, 1:87: "Sedet historicus 'inter magniloquos et grandia verba serentes', at cronicus sub pauperis Amiclæ pausat tugurio ne sit pugna pro paupere tecto."

190 John of Salisbury, *Entheticus in Policraticum*, 231, ed. Jan van Laarhoven, *Entheticus maior et minor*, Studien und Texte zur Geistesgeschichte des Mittelalters 17, 3 vols. (Leiden: Brill, 1987), 1:230–47, at 245: "Inter multiloquos et grandia verba serentes / esto tardiloquus, estoque pauca loquens."

191 Lucan, *De bello civili libri X*, 5.515–535; ed. David R. Shackleton Bailey (Stuttgart: Teubner, 1988), 122–23.

192 Lucan, *Pharsalia: Dramatic Episodes of the Civil Wars*, trans. Robert Graves (Harmondsworth: Penguin, 1956), 121.

The implication of this dense cluster of allusions is that by writing history a monk will expose himself to the envy of the powerful and to the spiritual danger of pride, but by writing chronicles he will enjoy the contentments of a humble existence. This alignment of chronicle-writing with the monastic virtue of *humilitas* is made all but explicit when Gervase begins to criticise those chroniclers who introduce the rhetorical practices of the historian into their work. For he attributes their failings to their love of enlarging their *philacteria* and of magnifying their *fimbrias*, words which allude to Jesus's denunciation of the Pharisees and scribes of the Temple: "They do all their deeds to be seen by men; for they make their phylacteries broad and their fringes long, and they love the place of honour at feasts and the best seats in the synagogues, and salutations in the market places, and being called rabbi by men."[193] By alluding to this passage of scripture, Gervase is accusing these chroniclers of succumbing to vanity and pride.

However, Gervase is almost certainly being disingenuous with this line of argument, for his actual practices, especially in the later sections of his *Chronica*, are closer to those of his *historicus* than to those of his *chronicus*.[194] Indeed, the preface seems to develop three contradictory lines of thought: on a literal level it is saying that histories and chronicles are of equal merit; with his allusions it seems to be saying that the chronicle is to be preferred; but by its use of such allusions he shows himself to be a writer of rhetorical history. The aim was perhaps to make ready defensive measures which could be deployed if the writing of the book was questioned, or perhaps to a create a fog of ambiguity so dense that it would deter any attempt to criticise the author. Like many prefaces, this is a text the meaning of which cannot in the end be determined, but, whatever Gervase's actual rhetorical strategy, the line of thought which valorises the chronicle at the expense of history would seem to represent a point of view that was current in the intellectual milieu in which he was working.[195] It was perhaps an opinion which a would-be *historicus* had to overcome in some way, especially at a time when the claims of the Cistercians and the contemplative orders to spiritual supremacy had finally won out over those of the Benedictines.[196] After all, authors were advised

[193] Matthew 23:5–7.

[194] See Gransden, *HWE*, 1:253–59. Cf. Hay, *Annalists and Historians*, 59.

[195] Note, likewise, how *Orderic*, 2:104, invokes the demands of monastic life when resisting the temptation to write a history of the deeds of William the Conqueror: "Nos autem quia sæcularibus curiis non insistemus, sed in claustris monasterii degentes monasticis rebus incumbimus, ea quæ nobis competunt breuiter adnotantes ad inceptam materiam redeamus."

[196] Richard of Devizes may well have been taking action against this same line of thought with his satirical treatment of Abbot Robert of Witham's interest in history in the preface to his chronicle: see Devizes, *CTR*, 1–2. The Carthusian order is not known for the composition of historical works. Indeed, the only historical work which a monk of Witham is known to have produced is the Life of Adam of Dryburgh (ed.

by the rules of composition current in the twelfth century that the function of the preface was to make their audience receptive to the contents of what was to follow.[197]

## Conclusion

The upshot is that the writing of history within the monastic context was controlled by the needs of religious life (and of the institutions that supported it) rather than by those of history as a forensic discipline. The priorities of the religious life tended, moreover, to divert the energies of monastic authors away from rhetorical history towards the preparation of the simpler kinds of historical text such as the breviate world chronicles edited below. Annalistic chronicles of this kind can seem strangely naïve when compared to modern works of analytical history, but this does not mean that they should be seen as the expressions of an early stage in the development of historical consciousness—as the inchoate effusions of a primeval historical *mentalité*. When the occasion demanded it, the very same communities that produced these texts could supply from their own ranks authors who were adept at the art of writing rhetorical history—at the art of inventing speeches and of using literary allusions to point up their texts, as can be seen from the preface to Gervase of Canterbury's *Cronica*. Such extreme changes of gear would scarcely be possible if the communities that produced these chronicles were full of primitive minds.

The differences, moreover, in the character of the various types of historical writing attested in the manuscript record may be explained satisfactorily enough by the different purposes and audiences for which they were intended. Whereas rhetorical histories were addressed to a wider audience of learned readers, the briefer types of annalistic chronicle seem to have been produced for an internal audience of newcomers to the subject of history. These chronicles were not

---

André Wilmart, *Analecta Praemonstratensia* 9 [1933]: 209–32). E. Margaret Thompson, *The Carthusian Order in England* (London: Society for Promoting Christian Knowledge, 1930), 134, treats it as "the chronicle of the foundation of the House of the Salutation [London]," but as Wilmart saw, it is better seen as a saint's life. The question of whether the new monastic movements of the twelfth century were hostile to rhetorical history is, unfortunately, often treated as though it were a question of whether they were "anti-intellectual" (e.g. Freeman, *Narratives of the New Order*, 91–98), a subtle mis-configuration of the issue which betrays the influence of modern academic values. The problem is better understood as a question of *which kinds* of intellectual (and historical) activity were considered appropriate.

[197] See Antonia Gransden, "Prologues in the Historiography of Twelfth-Century England," in *England in the Twelfth Century*, ed. Daniel Williams (Woodbridge: Boydell Press, 1990), 55–81, repr. in eadem, *LTH*, 125–51 (esp. 125–26).

the product of a random process of accumulating memories. It is true that some chronicles of this kind were gradually enlarged by the addition of new entries, but these items usually continued the generic pattern which had been established when the chronicle was first compiled. Indeed, it seems almost certain that the briefer types of annalistic chronicle, the breviate world chronicles and Easter table annals, were used as aids to the teaching of computus, one of the fundamental disciplines of the monastic curriculum. It is true that some of the manuscripts in which these chronicles are preserved exhibit signs of poor production and rough treatment, but it is arguable that they tell us more about the actual practices and thinking of the religious communities which produced them than their unspoilt, deluxe copies of the works of the fathers. They are not, moreover, devoid of intellectual content, for they were used to disseminate ideas about the structure of the universe and the unfolding of God's scheme for the salvation of humanity. *Winchcombe* and *Coventry* need to be seen, in short, as witnesses to an important dimension of monastic culture.

# Chapter Two: John of Worcester and the Common Root

It has long been understood that the *Winchcombe Chronicle* was related in some way to John of Worcester's *Chronica chronicarum*. Darlington saw as much when he printed the annals for AD 1049 to 1181, and he also considered the possibility that the two works were related indirectly, through an abridgement, since annals as "brief as those compiled at Winchcombe would be more easily put together" from such a work than from *Chronica chronicarum* itself. He soon recognised, however, that *Winchcombe* could not have been based on *Chronicula*, the known breviate version of *Chronica chronicarum*, and did not pursue the question any further.[1] Thanks, however, to the discovery of the hitherto unknown *Coventry Chronicle* and the re-examination of other chronicles which are related to *Winchcombe*, it can now be shown that just such an abridgement did indeed exist.[2] For it is clear that *Winchcombe* and *Coventry* share a common root for their annals from the Incarnation as far as 1122, at which point they diverge.[3] Within this span there are some 718 items in *Coventry* for which there are strong textual echoes in *Winchcombe*, and the great majority of these items are reported in words which are all but identical. It is clear, however, that neither chronicle has been derived from the other, for each abbreviates a number of items that are to be found in a fuller form in the other text.[4] It follows that they depend on a common ancestor.

---

[1] Reginald R. Darlington, "The Winchcombe Annals, 1049–1181," in *A Medieval Miscellany for Doris Mary Stenton*, ed. Patricia M. Barnes and C. F. Slade, PPRS 76, n.s. 36 (London: J. W. Ruddock, 1962), 111–37, at 112; hereafter Darlington.

[2] For the sake of clarity this chapter will establish the existence of the common root using *Winchcombe* and *Coventry* alone. The evidence provided by the lesser witnesses will be examined in chap. 5 below.

[3] The last of the shared items is a report of the fire at Gloucester which is dated to Wednesday 8 March (*viii id' Martii, feria iiii*). See further the commentary on *Winchcombe* 1122.1.

[4] *Winchcombe* has fuller versions of some forty-five items: 195, 207.1, 220.2, 250, 350, 380, 415, 439, 468, 477.1, 485, 526.1, 526.2, 534.2, 559.1, 603, 609, 655.1, 715.1, 735, 793, 795.1, 807, 876.3, 968.1, 1004, 1014.2, 1016, 1017, 1020, 1052.2, 1054, 1074.1, 1075.1, 1088, 1091, 1096, 1098.1, 1099.1, 1100.1, 1100.2, 1100.3, 1103, 1104, 1110.2. *Coventry* has fuller versions of three items: 465.2, 773.3, and 1028.2. Note also *Coventry*

The present chapter will attempt to define the character of this common root. It will argue that the root was compiled at Worcester Cathedral Priory, in tandem with *Chronica chronicarum* and *Chronicula*, by John of Worcester himself. I hope, moreover, that it will show, not only that John was probably the author and that he devised the work as part of a larger project the aim of which was to disseminate the revised chronology of Marianus Scotus, but also that it represents an attempt to explore alternative approaches to some of the historical issues that intrigued him, not least of which was the problem of reconstructing the early history of the Franks. Given that John's project is central to what follows, it is necessary to begin by examining what is presently known about the man and his work.

## (a) John of Worcester and his Project

John of Worcester is known above all for his authorship of one of the major works of the efflorescence of historical writing that took place in England between the 1090s and the 1140s, the Worcester *Chronica chronicarum* (hereafter JWCC).[5] It used to be thought that the work was largely compiled by a monk called Florence whose contribution to the project is celebrated in his obit, which appears under the year 1118 in the same text. The theory was that he executed the work as far as 1117 or 1118, whilst the remainder, down to 1140, was the work of "a continuator," John. John was certainly the author of the final sections, since he names himself as such in a hexameter in the annal for 1138: *Corrigat ista legens offendit siqua Iohannes*. It is now recognised, however, that Florence was merely a helper whilst John was the orchestrator of the project as whole. This conclusion seems inescapable when the testimony of Orderic Vitalis is set alongside the evidence for how the chronicle was put together. For there are no alterations in style or method which might suggest that a new author took over in or shortly before

437.2, where it preserves a manifestly more accurate version of the common source. It must be kept in mind that the division into items that has been applied to the texts is necessarily somewhat misleading, since it reflects joins between the sections created by the compiler's scissors rather than the number of distinct events recorded. Editorial policies are explained further in chap. 6 below.

[5] This background chapter is chiefly indebted to Brett, "John," though his findings have been modified to take account of (1) the revisions signalled by Patrick McGurk in the introductions to volumes two and three of the new OMT edition (*The Chronicle of John of Worcester*, ed. and trans. Reginald R. Darlington, Patrick McGurk, and Jennifer Bray, OMT, 3 vols. [Oxford: Clarendon Press, 1995–], 2:xvii–lxxxi; 3:xv–l), and (2) study of the manuscripts, especially C and D. Much of the earlier scholarship is summarised in Gransden, *HWE*, 1:143–48. The introductory volume of the new OMT edition has still to appear.

1119; on the contrary, its main source for the period from the mid-1090s through to 1122 is the final edition of Eadmer's *Historia novorum*, a work which was not available until early 1123.[6] For his part, Orderic identifies a contemporary called John as the author of an elaboration of the Chronicle of Marianus Scotus: "Following him [Marianus] John wove together the deeds of around a hundred years and at the command of the venerable Wulfstan, bishop and monk, he inserted them into the aforesaid *Chronica*, in which are usefully and fully laid out in an estimable narrative much about the Romans, the Franks, the Germans, and other peoples that he knew about."[7] Given the reference to Wulfstan, this description can refer only to the Worcester version of Marianus's chronicle. It is true that the words *acta fere centum annorum* fail to do justice to the amount of new material that was inserted into this version of Marianus, but since the text is outshone when seen as an exercise in coherent and insightful narrative history by Orderic's own work, he might well have viewed it with some condescension in much the same way as many modern observers have done.[8] Orderic's comments provide, more importantly, a clue as to the nature of John's project in as much as they stress its debt to Marianus. They imply that if we are to comprehend his project we must first grasp the scope and purpose of the Chronicle of Marianus Scotus.

An Irishman who had undertaken a "pilgrimage for Christ," Marianus spent most of his career in the Rhineland, becoming an *inclusus* at the abbey of St Martin, Mainz. A radical attempt to provide a coherent solution to the chronological problems in the Christian theory of world history, his *Chronica* comprises a tract in three books with a prologue (and appendix) of auxiliary texts.[9] The first two books address problems involved in establishing the age of the world and in dating the events of the life of Jesus Christ.[10] A driving concern was the need to

---

6 See Brett, "John," 104, 111–12; McGurk in J*WCC*, 2:xvii–viii; WM*VW*, xi–xviii; Patrick McGurk, "Worcester, John of (fl. 1095–1140)," *ODNB*, 60: 292–93. But cf. Hollister, *Henry I*, 8, who suggests that "several Worcester monks, including Florence, contributed to the project up to 1118, and perhaps beyond."

7 *Orderic*, 2:186–8: "Quem [Marianum] prosecutus Iohannes acta fere centum annorum contexuit, iussuque uenerabilis Wlfstani pontificis et monachi supradictis cronicis inseruit—in quibus multa de Romanis et Francis et Alemannis aliisque gentibus quæ agnouit—utiliter et compendiose narratione digna reserauit."

8 However, Orderic, whose visit to Worcester can have taken place no later than 1124, may have seen the work at a primitive stage in its development: see J*WCC*, 2:xvii–xviii.

9 Peter Verbist, "Reconstructing the Past: The Chronicle of Marianus Scottus," *Peritia* 16 (2002): 284–334, provides an excellent overview of Marianus's project. See also Anna Dorothee von den Brincken, "Marianus Scottus als Universalhistoriker *iuxta veritatem Evangelii*," in *Die Iren und Europa im früheren Mittelalter*, ed. Heinz Löwe, 2 vols. (Stuttgart: Klett-Cotta, 1982), 2:970–1009.

10 The preface and book 1, §§ 1–8 were printed by Anna Dorothee von den Brincken, "Marianus Scottus: Unter besonderer Berücksichtigung der nicht veröffentlichen Teile

establish the correct date of the Incarnation. For Marianus was of the view that the birth of the Saviour had taken place some twenty-two years earlier than had been reckoned by Dionysius Exiguus—a position similar to that which Abbo of Fleury adopted at the end of his career.[11] The third book is a chronicle in which Marianus sets out a revised chronology from the birth of Christ to his own time in which he attempts to find the extra twenty-two years required to make his theories work.[12] This was achieved by comparing the chronologies of earlier historians and by evaluating them against the evidence provided by various "primary sources"—namely by consular tables, by the passions of Roman martyrs, and by the dating clauses of papal letters (as found in, among other collections the False Decretals of Pseudo-Isidore). As first completed, book three ended with 1076, but Marianus may himself have inserted the first continuation, which brought it down to 1082.[13] It was certainly added in the Rhineland. Events are dated in this chronicle according to a variety of chronological schemes: the Dionysian AD numbers are retained, but priority is given to a series of corrected numbers which are entered in red ink with the phrases *uerior assertio*, "the truer doctrine", sometimes abbreviated as "VA", and *secundum Euangelicam ueritatem*, or "according to the Gospel truth." The former phrase echoes that used by Abbo of Fleury;[14] both echo Bede's use of the tag *iuxta Hebraicam ueritatem* to validate his revised chronology. The third point of reference is the year of the reigning emperor. As left by Marianus, book three was somewhat lighter than the other books: it is books one and two that represent the heart of his project.[15] The prologue (and appendix) comprise a series of auxiliary texts which provide "evidence" for the arguments deployed in the treatise itself: that is, a set of consular tables organised according

---

seiner Chronik," *Deutsches Archiv für Erforschung des Mittelalters* 17 (1961): 191–238.

[11] On the flaws in the Dionysian reckoning with which Abbo and Marianus were grappling, see Georges Declercq, *Anno Domini: The Origins of the Christian Era* (Turnhout: Brepols, 2000), esp. 189–92; Wallis, lv, lxx–lxxi, 336–38. See also Peter Verbist, "Abbo of Fleury and the Computational Accuracy of the Christian Era," in *Time and Eternity: The Medieval Discourse*, ed. Gerhard Jaritz and Gerson Moreno-Riano (Turnhout: Brepols, 2003), 63–80 (esp. 71, n. 40, where he corrects some crucial errors in previous interpretations of Abbo's contribution). It should be noted that Abbo developed his ideas about the timing of the Incarnation after his sojourn at Ramsey in 987–988: there is, consequently, little sign of their reception in England (see Verbist, "Abbo and the Christian Era," 66).

[12] Book 3 was edited by Georg Waitz in *MGH SS*, 5:481–562.

[13] For these dates, see Verbist, "Reconstructing the Past," 285–87, 322–23, 325, 329.

[14] Verbist, "Abbo and the Christian Era," esp. 72, n. 42 (*secundum ueriorem assertionem*). But note also that Verbist expresses doubts as to whether Marianus was indebted to Abbo for his position in "Reconstructing the Past," 330 and n. 257.

[15] Book 3 takes up 50 folios (i.e. fols. 106vb–156vb), or 32 per cent, of the text in the London manuscript, Cotton Nero C.V, folios 3r–161v.

to three different systems, a list of popes, a full set of twenty-eight nineteen-year Easter tables, and a few other computistical texts.

Of the two surviving manuscripts, that preserved in the Cotton Collection (N) is the more significant for present purposes. It comprises evidence, first of all, for the reception of Marianus's ideas in England. The hands that copied the text have a Lotharingian or northern Frankish aspect, implying that the book was either made on the Continent or written by scribes trained there; but a continuation covering the years 1083 to 1087 has been entered by an English scribe. It includes an account of the Domesday survey, and its final entry records the consecration of William II as king of England (4 October 1087).[16] The hand of the mid-twelfth-century rubric *CRONICA* on folio 3r has been identified, moreover, as that of a scribe who executed titles in five other Hereford manuscripts.[17] All of this strongly suggests that this may be the same copy of Marianus which, according to William of Malmesbury, Robert de Losinga, bishop of Hereford (1079–1095), brought to England.[18] Robert was certainly an enthusiast for Marianus: he produced a treatise in support of his rejection of the Dionysian era, and this treatise, known rather misleadingly as *Excerptio de chronica Mariani*, includes a description of the Domesday survey which was the source of the entry under 1086 in N.[19] It is quite likely, finally, that John actually used this very manuscript in the making of his own version of Marianus, albeit perhaps only when he came to correct his work.[20] He certainly used a copy of Marianus in which the third

[16] N, fols. 158vb–159ra. See Stevenson, "Domesday Survey," esp. 77. For the other MS (Vatican City, B.A.V., Pal. lat. 830), see Verbist, "Reconstructing the Past," 285–87, 322–24 and the works cited there.

[17] JW*CC*, 3:xviii. See also Mynors and Thomson, *Hereford Cathedral Library*, xvi, xxvii, n. 105, and plate 24.

[18] WM*GP*, iv.164. On Robert, see Julia Barrow, "A Lotharingian in Hereford: Bishop Robert's Reorganisation of the Church at Hereford," in *Medieval Art, Architecture and Archaeology at Hereford*, ed. David Whitehead, British Archaeological Association Conference Transactions 15 (Leeds: British Archaeological Association, 1995), 29–49; eadem, *EEA*, 7:xxxiii–xxxiv.

[19] Alfred Cordoliani, "L'activité computistique de Robert, évêque de Hereford," in *Mélanges offerts à René Crozet à l'occasion de son 70e anniversaire*, ed. Pierre Gallais and Yves-Jean Riou, 2 vols. (Poitiers: Société d'Études Médiévales, 1966), 1:333–40; Stevenson, "Domesday Survey," 72–78.

[20] There is, as Valerie I. J. Flint, "The Date of the Chronicle of 'Florence' of Worcester," *Revue Bénédictine* 86 (1976): 115–19, argues, evidence that N was used in the final stages in the production of the Worcester *Chronica chronicarum* to correct its passages from Marianus, but it does not necessarily follow that the "errors" resulted, as she suggests, from the use of a different, defective, copy. They may well have crept in as a result of John's own editorial work and the repeated copying of his working text. See JW*CC*, 2:lxiv, n. 29.

book had been continued down to 1087 and one that contained the entry derived from Robert's account of Domesday.[21]

The influence of Marianus on the structure of JWCC is readily apparent when it is seen, not as it has thus far been printed, but in its manuscript context. The working copy, Corpus 157 (C), is organised in much the same way as the London manuscript. It begins with a "prologue" of auxiliary texts (pages 4–77), which includes, as in N, a set of consular tables (pages 5–29), a list of popes (pages 29–34), a full set of twenty-eight paschal tables with three series of annals (pages 56–69), and a few other short computistical texts (pages 55 and 70–71). However, the annals in the margins of these tables have been much expanded with additional entries, some relating to events in England, and a variety of other texts, many of English interest, have also been inserted. The auxiliary texts also include a history of the see of Worcester (fol. 1r to page 3), a set of tables listing the bishops of England's sees with notes on individual bishops and on the foundation and subdivision of the various dioceses (pages 39–45), and a series of tables setting out in brief the history of the various Anglo-Saxon kingdoms of the so-called heptarchy and the genealogies of their rulers (pages 47–54). This prologue is followed, as in N, by the text of Marianus's *Chronica* (pages 77–396), the preface and the first two books of which, comprising over a quarter of the book (pages 89 to 203), are reproduced without any major modification. The third book's annals for the first five centuries of the Christian era are also reproduced without substantial changes, but with the annal for 450 (page 242) John begins to introduce material from other sources, gradually transforming the work such that the narrative is dominated by English events from around the late sixth century onwards until its conclusion.

The survival of a working text (C) together with several manuscripts derived from it at diverse stages in its development means that it is possible, as Martin Brett has shown, to observe the final stages in the intrusion of this new material in some detail. In its existing state, C is mostly the work of three scribes: the first ($C^1$) is chiefly responsible for the tables and for most of the *Chronica* down to mid-1101 (pages 5–363); the second ($C^2$) is chiefly responsible for the annals from mid-1102 to 1128 (pages 364–379); the third scribe ($C^3$), John himself, is chiefly responsible for a continuation that begins with the annal for 1128 and which ends imperfectly in the middle of an episode in August 1140 (pages 379–396). I say "chiefly responsible" because *all* three scribes were also responsible for introducing many annotations and corrections in the margins and over erasures

[21] See further JW 1086 (esp. n. 2). John also knew the report of Pope Gregory VII's deathbed confession which is also found in N (fol. 1v). It is the only copy now extant: see JW 1084. The confession is printed in H. E. J. Cowdrey, *The Age of Abbot Desiderius: Monte Cassino, the Papacy, and the Normans in the Eleventh and Early Twelfth Centuries* (Oxford: Clarendon Press, 1983), 250.

in the text.[22] In addition to C, some six other medieval manuscripts of JW*CC* are known. Two—MS. Dublin, Trinity College, 502 (D), and MS. London, Lambeth Palace, 42 (L)—bear witness to the state of C around 1132, for they derive from a copy of C made at about this time. Most notably, they end with a different set of annals for the years 1128 to 1131. It is clear that C once contained this alternative ending only for it to be erased by $C^3$ when he added his continuation—that is, probably between 1140 and 1143. Two direct copies of C have also survived. One may well comprise the copy from which D and L derive, but of this only a single leaf survives. Used in the binding of a fourteenth-century Psalter, it is preserved at the Evesham Almonry Museum (E). The other direct copy—MS. Oxford, Bod.L., Bodley 297 (B)—was made at Bury St Edmunds at some point between 1133 and 1143:[23] it represents a somewhat later stage in the development of the chronicle than that attested by DL. Like them, B ends with the 1131 conclusion, but it also has a more extensive selection of the marginal annotations now present in C, allowing us to single out a layer of annotations that had been added to C after the copying of the ancestor of D and L. The fifth manuscript, MS. Cambridge, Corpus Christi College, 92 (P), is a hybrid copied at Abingdon after 1174. It derives from more than one exemplar: it is often close to L, but it also derives from a copy of C made not long after it was borrowed for the making of B.[24]

With the evidence provided by these manuscripts it is possible to distinguish some five stages in the finalisation of JW*CC*, and these may be briefly described as follows:

1. The first represents the text at the time when $C^1$ began copying it into C. By this time *Chronica chronicarum* was already a complex work that integrated annals concerned with Continental events drawn almost entirely from the world history of Marianus Scotus with annals concerned with English events drawn from several versions of the *Anglo-Saxon Chronicle*, from Bede, from Asser, and from a number of saint's lives.[25] This stage in the development of the text is represented in C by the surviving work of $C^1$.

[22] JW*CC*, 2:xxi–xxxv. See also Kauffmann, *Romanesque Manuscripts*, 87–88; Alexander and Temple, *Illuminated MSS in Oxford*, 5.

[23] JW*CC*, 2:lii–liii.

[24] For fuller descriptions of the five MSS, see JW*CC*, 2:xxxv–lix.

[25] On the earlier elements in the text, see McGurk's comments in JW*CC*, 2:xix–xx, lxxix–lxxxi; Reginald R. Darlington and Patrick McGurk, "The *Chronicon ex chronicis* of 'Florence' of Worcester and its Use of Sources for English History before 1066," *Anglo-Norman Studies* 5 (1982): 185–96; Flint, "'Florence' of Worcester," 115–19; and Brett, "John," 115, n. 4.

2. The second stage involved the introduction of material from Eadmer's *Historia novorum* which John knew in a version close to its final form.[26] This was achieved by rewriting the annal for 1095, by writing a new set of annals for the years 1102 to 1122 which were largely based on Eadmer, and by making some marginal annotations (e.g. 1091, 1098, 1099, 1108). The task of introducing these alterations into C was mostly carried out by C². C¹ makes some of the marginal annotations. This work cannot have been begun before October 1122 (where Eadmer's work ends), but it need not have been finished until about 1131 when C¹ and C² probably carried out their major stints of work on the manuscript.

3. The third stage saw the introduction of material drawn from diverse sources: that is, of material concerned with papal affairs drawn from documents in a collection compiled by William of Malmesbury, of material concerned with Norman affairs taken from the so-called Norman Annals, of material concerned with Frankish affairs taken from Hugh of Fleury's *Historia ecclesiastica*,[27] of material concerned with the north of England derived from Durham and shared with Symeon's *Libellus de exordio atque procursu istius, hoc est Dunhelmensis, ecclesie*, and of one or two items from Malmesbury's *Gesta pontificum*. These modifications were integrated into the body of the chronicle in the exemplar that lay behind H and L, and they comprised most of the alterations and additions made by C¹ and C² and a few of those made by C³.

4. The fourth stage saw the correction of many misplaced episcopal successions and the introduction of a text of the *Visio Eucherii* under 741, of material from the *Hadrianum* under 773, and of much more from William of Malmesbury's *Gesta regum* and *Gesta pontificum*. It also saw the reorganisation of the "prologue": a list of French kings and a list of the dukes of Normandy, but a text on bishoprics and councils was, for some reason, deleted. The results of this work can be measured in the differences between HL and BP, and they correspond to various additions in the margins, over erasures, and between the lines of earlier text mostly made by C³.

5. The final stage, apparently implemented by John alone, involved the erasure of the earlier annals for 1128 to 1131, the composition of an

---

[26] Eadmer, *Historia novorum in Anglia*, ed. M. Rule, RS 81 (London: Longman, 1884). Martin Brett, "A Note on the *Historia Novorum* of Eadmer," *Scriptorium* 33 (1979): 56–58, shows that John used a version of Eadmer that included books five and six, in which the author continued his narrative down to the death of Archbishop Ralph d'Escures on 19 or 20 October 1122, but one whose readings "predated" those of the version known from MS. Cambridge, Corpus Christi College, 452—the version most likely to represent the author's final thoughts. See also idem, "John," 111–12; JW*CC*, 2:lxxiii–lxxiv; 3:xxvi–xxvii.

[27] *Hugonis Floriacensis monachi Benedictini Chronicon*, ed. B. Rottendorf (Münster: Bernard Raesfeld, 1638), hereafter HF*Chron*.

> updated conclusion covering 1128 until at least mid-1141, and the rewriting of the list of popes in the preliminaries as a chronicle of papal *acta*—the "Papal Annals."

In the absence of a clear statement from John as to his aims as distinct from those of Marianus, the purpose of all this work remains a matter of some uncertainty. Since the main interest of the text for modern historians has been its account of events in England, it is often assumed that John was motivated by similar concerns: that his aim was to produce a work of English history whilst using Marianus as a scaffold on which to hang his material.[28] John's certainly provided extended treatment of English events, yet there are strong grounds for thinking that the Marianan element was far more than just scaffolding. One reason is the sheer quantity of Marianan material that survives in John's version of the Chronicle: it comprises around half the contents of the materials in C. The titles given to the text in the rubrics of C—*Mariani Scotti Chronica*[29]—and in the annal for 1118—*Chronica chronicarum*—are another. *Chronica* and *Chronica chronicarum* are the exact same names as are given to the Chronicle of Marianus Scotus in the rubrics of the London manuscript.[30] But perhaps the most telling evidence for taking the Marianan element seriously is that provided by a twelfth-century reader of John's work, Gervase of Canterbury.

Among the various kinds of chronicler with whom Gervase finds fault in his preface are those who have focused on finding an improved chronology for the Sixth Age. It is better, he argues, to stick to the Dionysian scheme even though it may be flawed, the reason being that the result of *cronici* having taken the revision of the *anni Domini* as their overriding aim has been the proliferation of diverse chronological structures and the rise of *dissensio* and *multa mendaciorum confusio* in the church.[31] In particular, he criticised chroniclers who used multiple dating schemes—that is, chroniclers who supported their annals with two or more alternative calculations of the *anni Domini*. John was certainly guilty of this practice and it would appear that Gervase had his work in mind, since he goes on

[28] E.g. Brett, "John," 110–11. See also Prologue, p. 6, n. 9, above; and Martin Brett, "The Use of Universal Chronicle at Worcester," in *L'Historiographie médiévale en Europe*, ed. Jean-Philippe Genet (Paris: Éditions du Centre national de la recherche scientifique, 1991), 277–85, where he makes the alternative suggestion that John intended the *Chronica chronicarum* to serve as a kind of index to Christian hagiology.

[29] JWCC (C), 79. See likewise, MS. H, page 75.

[30] Cf. the inscription in N, fol. 2v: "Meum nomen ut dignum cronica chronicarum, cum pre illis seruo, uerba euangelistarum. Nulla enim cronica conseruat diem mensis solaris resurrectionis Christi iuxta historiam euangelii nisi ista sola."

[31] Gervase, 1:88: "Nam cum omnium unica et præcipua sit intentio annos Domini eorumque continentias supputatione veraci enarrare, ipsos Domini annos diversis modis et terminis numerant, sicque in ecclesiam Dei multam mendaciorum confusionem inducunt." On Gervase and his preface, see chap. 1, § f, above.

to mention a *Cronica Mariani* "assembled from various authorities yet still made known under the name of the same Marianus" (*ex auctoribus diversis collecta nomini tamen ejusdem Mariani dicata*) that had covered the period from the beginning of the world up to the death of King Henry I and the reign of King Stephen.[32] Gervase's preface is, as was seen in chapter one above, a difficult text to interpret, but there seems to be no obvious reason for doubting that these comments report accurately the way in which John's work was received in the late twelfth century and the responses of some sections of the monastic establishment. Indeed, it is easy to see how the conservative element whom Gervase needed to appease might have been dismayed, not just by monks who indulged in the writing of rhetorical history,[33] but also by chroniclers whose work stirred up debate about fundamental problems, as when they drew attention to the church's inability to provide certainty as to the exact date of the Incarnation. In the eyes of Marianus and John, multiple series of dates were helpful reference points in the development of their arguments, but in the eyes of others they were a cause of disruption and a threat to the decorum of the monastic life.

It seems to the present author that John's version of the *Chronica chronicarum* is best understood in much the same way as it was seen by these contemporary observers—that is, as a project the overriding purpose of which was to promote the reformed chronology of Marianus Scotus. John may have been commended by Orderic for usefully and fully narrating the histories of peoples known to him, but his contribution should be seen as much more than an attempt to enlarge that work's coverage of the past. He clearly had considerable sympathy for the history of the English. Several scholars have shown, indeed, that John was so committed to their point of view that he silently corrected misrepresentations which had been perpetrated in Norman propaganda.[34] Yet by redating the events

32 Gervase, 1:89. Gervase is generally cited as a supporter of the Marianan chronology, but his view of John's work seems to have been that of a sceptic: it is true that he nowhere denies the validity of Marianus's arguments or chronology, but nor does he come out in favour of them. He opts for the Dionysian system and writes of the *anni Domini* which "are called," rather than "which are," *Secundum Evangelium*, and that the former chronicle "seems" to have covered its period "fully and lucidly enough" (*satis compendiose et lucide digessisse videtur*). Gervase also appears to have used a Gloucester chronicle derived from the *Chronicula*[2] (see chap. 3, §§ e-f, below).

33 See chap. 1, § f, above.

34 E.g. Hugh M. Thomas, *The English and the Normans: Ethnic Hostility, Assimilation and Identity 1066–c.1220* (Oxford: Oxford University Press, 2003), 245–46; Williams, *English and the Conquest*, 168–70. Note esp. JW*CC*'s treatment of the year 1066. John reports that Harold was Edward the Confessor's chosen successor, that he was properly elected king, that he was crowned, not by Archbishop Stigand, but by Archbishop Ealdred, and that he was a 'good' king. He nowhere questions the legitimacy of Harold's kingship. He nowhere mentions a visit to Normandy or that Harold made a promise to Duke William, nor does he treat the Battle of Hastings as a trial by combat.

of England's history and by creating a coherent narrative from the diverse and meagre materials that had survived to his own time—especially for the period between 731 and 1066, for which there was nothing similar in detail or coherence to Bede's *Historia ecclesiastica* or Eadmer's *Historia novorum*—John helped to make Marianus's scheme tangible for English readers. He created a vehicle for insinuating the new chronology into their thinking, and he saved them from having to figure out its implications for the histories of their communities. It is true that his devotion to the task was such that the work of expanding the preliminaries and book three was spun out over several decades—indeed, for well over four decades if the claim, reported by Orderic who probably had it from John himself, that the project was begun on the orders of St Wulfstan (d. 1095) is to be believed—but these materials were probably peripheral in John's mind to books one and two which remained the core of *Chronica chronicarum*. Indeed, the book's organisation and purpose is usefully compared to that of a computistical collection, for many books of this kind have at their core a copy of Bede's *De temporum ratione* the text of which was usually carefully preserved from alteration whilst great effort was invested in the elaboration and interpolation of the satellite texts and diagrams.[35] It is as though Bede's manual were sacrosanct whilst the remaining texts comprised a kind of commentary upon its contents.[36] John's version of the *Chronica chronicarum* of Marianus Scotus is aptly seen as the product of the same working method. His revisions to the prelims and to book three should probably be seen, in short, as an expression of his devotion to the Marianan cause—as a project with the overarching purpose of winning converts within the English church for the theories of the Irish monk.

John was certainly industrious. He was also the author of an abbreviated version of the reworked *Chronica*. It survives in a single manuscript, today MS. Dublin, Trinity College, 503 (G),[37] a book which was the product of two phases of production. The first phase saw the production of the greater part of the chronicle found in this manuscript (fols. 37r–151v), that is, of all the text from the description of Britain with which it opens down to the departure of Archbishop William of Corbeil for Rome to collect his pallium in March 1123 (folios 37r–113v23, hereafter designated "*Chronicula*[1]").[38] The remainder of the chronicle, a continuation which picks up where the former item ends and which continues down to the middle of 1141 where it ends imperfectly, the remainder of the manuscript having been lost, was inserted during phase two (folios 113v24–151v,

[35] See Jones's comments in CCSL 123B, 241–42; Wallis, lxxxvii.

[36] Cf. Bober, "An Illustrated Medieval School Book," 86.

[37] The description that follows summarises and builds on the descriptions in JW*CC*, 2:lix–lxiv; 3:xl–l; Colker, *TCD*, no. 503. See also *The Chronicle of John of Worcester, 1118–1140*, ed. J. R. H. Weaver, Anecdota Oxoniensia: Medieval and Modern Series 13 (Oxford: Clarendon Press, 1908), 4–7.

[38] See JW*CC* 1123 with notes d and 5.

hereafter "*Chronicula*²"). *Chronicula*¹ was copied by the hand of John himself, but *Chronicula*² is largely copied by a second scribe (G²),[39] who was also responsible for inserting a selection of the preliminary matter from the final version of John's *Chronica chronicarum* on fols. 1v–36r.

The word *chronicula*, "little chronicle," is the first-phase author's own term for his work. The author explains that this *chronicula* provides a more succinct version of the materials found in a larger *chronica chronicarum*, and that he has taken care to include "only the more useful matter in this little book."[40] The work is indeed largely comprised of material that echoes items in John's text. It appears to derive from a relatively advanced version, one close to that used in the making of B—that is, C as it stood in the mid- to late 1130s; but it also introduces additional material from new sources or rather sources not fully exploited in the making of the main chronicle. It begins, for example, with a description of the island of Britain and its peoples derived from that prefaced to the F-text of the *Anglo-Saxon Chronicle*. This gives the impression of greater emphasis on English history than is found in *Chronica chronicarum*, but the Frankish element also is enlarged through greater use of Hugh of Fleury and of several items from Rheims, including a forged letter of St Benedict (folio 47r–v)[41] and a record of the 868 Synod of Meaux (folios 58v–59v).[42] There can be little doubt that it was John himself who produced *Chronicula*¹, but its purpose is considerably more obscure than that of John's version of the *Chronica chronicarum*.[43] It is much less helpfully organised than the main chronicle, with the material lumped together in long entries and allocated to widely-spaced chronological anchors in something like the manner of Bede's *Chronica maiora*. It covers, for example, the first three hundred years of the Sixth Age whilst naming only thirty-eight of them. But in contrast to Bede, it often digresses to discuss topics at length—topics such as the organisation of the Anglo-Saxon kingdoms.

The answer may lie in its physical shape, for it has a highly portable format. As enlarged at Gloucester, it is a relatively thick volume of 151 folios, but the pages themselves are small, measuring 125 × 88 millimetres with a text area of 112 × 62.[44] It is nevertheless an attractive book, and it is not difficult to see how

39 That is, G² wrote folios 113v24–115r and 116v17–151v, G³ wrote 115v, and G⁴ wrote 116r–v17.

40 *Chronicula*¹ VA 918: "Horum [Deiorum regum] omnium acta pessima qui nosse uoluerit, seriatim pleniusque reperiet scripta in cronicarum chronica. Huic uero libello dumtaxat utiliora studuimus inserere."

41 *Chronicula*¹ VA 548, quoting *Epistula monachorum S. Remigii ad fratres Casinenses*, ed. Bruno Krusch, *MGH SS rer. Merov.*, 3:347–49.

42 *Chronicula*¹ AD 868, quoting the "Second Capitulary" of Bishop Hildegar of Meaux, ed. Peter Brommer, *MGH CE*, 1:198–99. See also Brett, "John," esp. 123–24.

43 Brett, "John," 124.

44 See Colker, *TCD*, no. 503.

it might have been conceived and prepared as a gift for someone whose work might involve frequent travel, someone who might well appreciate reading some edifying matter while on long journeys away from his own church. Such a purpose might well explain the presence of the many metrical entries and poems that figure in its later sections, and why the book travelled to Gloucester so soon after the first phase was completed. Indeed, it is tempting to suggest that the intended recipient was Gilbert Foliot, who was appointed abbot of Gloucester in 1139; but there is no evidence in the manuscript itself to support this suggestion.

*Chronicula*² also depends on JW*CC*, but the material derived from this source has been reworked and amplified by someone other than John. He typically reproduces many passages found in John's work almost verbatim, but he also suppresses details which manifest their author's presence, converting passages written in the first person into the third and excising John's portentous comments on the meaning of events. He used at least two exemplars: that is, for 1123–1131 he used an exemplar similar to DL rather than BP, but for 1128–1140 he used an exemplar which was close to but not exactly the same as C in the form in which John finally left it.[45] The use of this all-but-C-like exemplar also extended to the preliminary matter. For example, the "Papal List" in G (folios 16v–24v) reproduced the revised list with which John replaced the earlier papal list in C (pages 29–34). McGurk's analysis of the annals for 1123 to 1140 shows that the compiler attempted, with limited success, to synthesise the material provided by his exemplars and that he intruded much new material, almost all of it reflecting the interests and viewpoint of Gloucester Abbey.[46] It seems almost certain that G had travelled to St Peter's, that the continuation was assembled by one of the abbey's monks (possibly but not necessarily the scribe G²), and that it was copied into the manuscript there. Since the latest of the additions to the episcopal lists in its version of the prelims is William, bishop of Norwich, who was appointed in 1146/47, and since the lists fail to note the appointment of successors to Simon of Worcester and Richard of London, both of whom died in 1150, it seems likely that *Chronicula*² was compiled in the late 1140s and that it originally extended down to this point.

It is important to note that the Worcester-derived material in *Chronicula*² probably extended beyond August 1140 into the section of G which has no counterpart in C as it presently stands. Given that C ends imperfectly, there is no

---

[45] *Chronicula*²'s use of John is discussed in greater detail in JW*CC*, 3:xli–lviii, where McGurk attempts to explain G's inability to date accurately its material for 1131–1136 by suggesting that the material was delivered to the compiler in draft form without annal numbers.

[46] In the report, for example, of Gilbert Foliot's election as abbot of Gloucester he is described as *noster domnus* (*Chronicula*² 1139); he later reports the empress's own words to Miles, earl of Hereford, "as we heard them from his own mouth" (*Chronicula*² 1141 [3:298]).

sure way of telling exactly where the Gloucester material entirely supplanted that from John (if it ever did), and there are, as McGurk points out, events in this section (such as the storm on 15 May 1141 at Wellesborne) which are recounted from a Worcester rather than a Gloucester perspective.[47] It follows that John may have continued to develop his *Chronica chronicarum* well into the 1140s, C being incomplete. All that can be said about when John undertook the final stage of the *Chronica chronicarum* is that the annal for 1134 was written between 1139 and 1143, for it mentions Henry of Blois as *nunc Romane ecclesie legatus*.[48] One might contend that more manuscripts of the final stages of the work would have survived if he had continued to update the text well beyond 1141; but the absence of such books may be explained as an effect of the civil war, since the upheavals of King Stephen's reign may well have inhibited the lending of John's precious holograph to more remote centres. In the mid-1130s it had been possible to send C to Bury for the making of B,[49] but this is likely to have been a much riskier undertaking between 1139 and 1153. It is true that the fighting of 1139–1141, when the cities of Worcester and Gloucester were at war with each other,[50] will have made travel between the cathedral and St Peter's an activity that required careful timing, but it will at least have been possible to calculate the risks involved. However, the crucial point for the purposes of the present study is that *Chronicula*², as distinct from *Chronicula*¹, is in essence a "Gloucester reworking" of the final stages of John's text.

## (b) The Common Root and *Chronica Chronicarum*

Of John's two known works it is his *Chronica chronicarum* to which the common root seems most closely related. Matches can be found in this work for some 668 of the 718 items shared by both *Winchcombe* and *Coventry*—that is, for about ninety-three per cent of the known contents of the common root. Consider, for example, the following item, which *Winchcombe* and *Coventry* report in the same words under 1117:

> Apud Lumbardiam terremotus factus est Mediolani, turris magna subito cecidit, et omnes qui intus erant oppressit. Robertus Stefordensis episcopus obiit.

[47] JWCC, 3:lviii–l.

[48] Henry's reign as legate began in 1139 and ended with the death of Pope Innocent II in 1143: see JWCC, 2:lxix; Weaver, *Chronicle of John of Worcester*, 10–11.

[49] See Brett, "John," 107; JWCC, 2:lii–liii.

[50] See JWCC 1139–1141 (esp. 3:272–77).

The words of this item are all to be found in *Chronica chronicarum*'s annal for 1117:

> [1117] . . . *Apud Lumbardiam, magno terremotu facto*, et, ut testati sunt qui nouere, .xl. dierum spatio durante, plurima domorum edificia corruere, et, quod uisu dictuque constat mirabile, uilla quedam pergrandis mota est repente de statu proprio, iamque ab omnibus in longe remoti consistere cernitur loco. *Mediolani*, dum patricie dignitatis uiri, de republica tractantes, sub una residerent turri, auribus omnium uox foras insonuit, unum ex illis nomine uocans, et festinato exire rogans. Quo tardante, persona quedam coram apparuit, que uocatum uirum ut egrederetur prece optinuit. Exeunte illo, *turris* repente *cecidit et omnes qui* ibidem ad*erant* casu miserabili *oppressit. Robertus Stæffordensis episcopus obiit*, et Gilebertus abbas Westmonasterii .viii. idus Decembris.

The relationship between the annal for 1117 in *Winchcombe-Coventry* and that in *Chronica chronicarum* is most likely to have been one of abbreviation rather than expansion, and it is unlikely that two writers could have condensed such a long annal in exactly the same way while working independently of each other. Consider, likewise, the following item, which both *Winchcombe* and *Coventry* report in the same words under 842:

> Tres fratres regnum Francorum inter se diuiserunt, Karolus occidentem usque ad Mosam fluuium, Ludouuicus Germaniam usque Hreni fluenta, Lotharius imperator medium inter utrosque tenuit regnum, totam Prouinciam et omnia regna Italiæ cum ipsa Roma. Ab hoc Lothario Lotharingia hactenus *dicitur*.

Matching material for this annal is to be found in *Chronica chronicarum*'s annals for 841–842 and 844:

> [841] Ludouuicus uero et Karolus paterno regno priuati, apud Fontaniacum fratrem Lotharium bello superant.
>
> [842] Tres supradicti fratres regnum Francorum inter se diuiserunt, Karolus occidentem tenet a Brytannico oceano usque ad Mosam fluuium . . .
>
> [844] Ludouuicus suscepit orientem, id est Germaniam usque Hreni fluenta et aliquas ciuitates trans Hrenum cum adiacentibus plagis propter copiam uini. Lotharius primogenitus et imperator medium inter utrosque tenuit regnum, totam Prouinciam et omnia regna Italie cum ipsa Roma. Ab hoc Lothario regnum Lotharingia hactenus *dicitur*.

Here again it is most unlikely that two chroniclers could have combined and condensed these annals in exactly the same way if they were working independently of each other. It is true that all of this material is ultimately derived from the entries for VA 863 and 864 in Marianus Scotus, but the presence of the word *dicitur* (given in italics) as opposed to *nominatur*, the word used by Marianus, indicates that the material has been transmitted through *Chronica chronicarum*. This exercise can be repeated for most of the 668 shared entries that echo items in *Chronica chronicarum*, with similar results. Most are, of course, ultimately derived from some other source, but it is often clear that the notices have been transmitted through and abbreviated from *Chronica chronicarum*.

The shared entries do, however, modify John's treatment of certain themes, not least his organisation of the notices recording the holders of the imperial title. The series shares with *Chronica chronicarum* and *Chronicula* the adjustments which John made to Marianus's numbering of the later emperors,[51] implying that the sequence is more closely related to that found in John's chronicle than to the notices found in Marianus; but the common root rearranges these notices, presenting them in a slightly different way. That is, whereas *Chronica chronicarum*'s entries follow this model,

> [244] . . . Decius occiditur cum filio inhabito Tracie loco a Gothis in bello; Romanorum tricesimus Gallus cum filio Volusiano regnauit annis duobus, mensibus iiii$^{or}$, hoc est usque kl. Septembris in anno ducentesimo .xxx$^{o}$.iiii$^{o}$. post passionem . . .

the entries shared by *Winchcombe* and *Coventry* follow this model,

> [244] Romanorum xx$^{us}$ix$^{us}$ Decius in Tracia a Gothis occiditur in fine Aprilis. Cui Gallus cum filio Volusiano succedens, regnauit annis ii$^{bus}$, mensibus iiii$^{or}$.

Whereas *Chronica chronicarum* gives the numbers for each emperor at the moment of their appointment, the shared entries number them at the moment of their death, and whereas *Chronica chronicarum* gives the month in which their reign came to an end when specifying the length of their reign, the shared entries give the month in which they died when recording their obits, often by using the phrase *in fine [mensis]*. To rearrange *Chronica chronicarum*'s information in this way, the compiler of the annal will have needed to refer not just to its annal for 244 but also to its annal for 241 where the month of Decius's death is specified:

> [241] Romanorum xx$^{us}$viiii$^{us}$ Decius secundum Orosius regnauit annis .iii$^{bus}$. mensibus .iii$^{bus}$. . . hoc est usque kl. Maii in anno .cc$^{o}$.xxx$^{o}$.ii$^{o}$. post passionem. . .

[51] John renumbered the sequence so as to include Louis the Stammerer (877–879) as the eighty-fourth emperor: see the commentary on *Winchcombe* 878 below.

That is, the shared entry's *in fine aprilis* derives from *Chronica chronicarum*'s *usque kl. maii*. There are a few places where this alternative format for presenting these entries is not strictly enforced, invariably because information such as the month of the predecessor's death was lacking; but this arrangement is to be found throughout the shared entries — that is, from the annal which records the death of Octavian and the succession of Tiberius (VA 16) through to that which records the death of Henry V (AD 1106). This pattern might be thought to count against John's being the author of the common root, but the systematic re-arrangement of borrowings whilst preserving much of their vocabulary is one of the defining traits of John's compositional method. McGurk has observed that the annals in the margins of John's version of the nineteen-year cycles of Marianus were rewritten in a similar fashion.[52] These annals comprise a *selection* of the annals in the margins of Marianus's Easter Tables, to which have been added items from book three of Marianus, from the material which John added to his own version of book three, and from other books and items in his workshop. John had a propensity for playing with his material, transferring items from one place in his work to another, and the entries shared by *Winchcombe* and *Coventry* reveal a similar tendency in the way in which they rework their source material.

This is not, furthermore, the only way in which the material in *Chronica chronicarum* seems to have been rearranged in the making of the common root. For the shared entries were not drawn in a tidy sequence from the main chronicle; rather, the compiler seems to have mined every section of the work. To be sure, the bulk of the material relating to English and imperial events matches material in John's version of book three and was probably derived from it, but much also appears to have been taken from the preliminary texts and tables. There are at least four entries that seem to depend on items found in either the "Consular Annals" or the "Easter table annals", but not in the main chronicle of *Chronica chronicarum*.[53] There are, moreover, at least eight items that seem to depend on the so-called "accounts" — the texts that accompany the genealogies rather than the main chronicle itself. For example, the notices recording the extinction of the heptarchic kingdoms of Kent, Northumbria, and East Anglia under 823, 867, and 870 seem to derive from the accounts that accompany the Kentish, Northumbrian, and East Anglian royal genealogies.[54] The main chronicle has no items that could have supplied this material. The compiler was apparently so well acquainted with the organisation and contents of the *Chronica*

---

52 JW*CC*, 2:lxxviii.

53 See *Winchcombe* 9.1, 53.1, 65.1, 228, and the commentary below.

54 See *Winchcombe* 823.2, 867, 870.3, and the commentary below. Similar material to the notices under 823.2 and 870.3 appears in *Chronicula* VA 835 and 877, but it lacks the chronological references or the precise wording required to produce the Northumbrian notice (i.e. 867). For the other stronger examples, see *Winchcombe*, 672.2, 760, 794.2, 809.1, and 876.2.

*chronicarum* (or perhaps with his working notes) that he was able to pull together its diverse strands and pillage them at will. All of this begins to suggest that John was the author.

Another feature of the *Chronica-Chronicarum*-related items shared by *Winchcombe* and *Coventry* that points in this direction is that Worcester Cathedral, John's own church, figures much more prominently among them than any other English church or religious community. The shared entries include, for example, a long series of entries recording the successions of the bishops of Worcester, most of whom are numbered.[55] The shared entries begin with Bosel and conclude with Theulf. *Winchcombe* adds a single item of this kind, an entry for the appointment of Bishop Samson under 1096. If it added several entries that might weaken the case for a Worcester provenance, but a single addition suggests that this is a case of *Coventry* omitting an element of the root. *Chronica Chronicarum* has a similar series of notices, but they omit the numbering imperfectly executed among the shared entries. The shared items include several that concern Wulfstan II, including his appointment as abbot of Gloucester, his election to the see of Worcester, and his recovery of the church's estates.[56] The presence of these entries in both *Winchcombe* and *Coventry* suggests that the root was prepared at Worcester, and this impression is reinforced by the presence in the late medieval annals of Worcester, in the so-called *Annales prioratus de Wigornia*, of some sixty items that echo material shared by *Winchcombe* and *Coventry.*[57]

## (c) The Common Root and *Chronicula*[1]

It is natural to ask next whether the common root is related to *Chronicula*[1], not least because it too is an abbreviated version of *Chronica chronicarum*. That the first phase of *Chronicula* also concludes in the early 1120s (albeit in March 1123 rather than in March 1122) certainly seems significant; but as Darlington concluded, it is unlikely to have played a role in the making of *Winchcombe* and *Coventry*. That *Chronicula*[1] was not itself the common root is clear from its coverage of the Lombard earthquake, for it has *Chronica chronicarum*'s account in its entirety when it would need to provide a version identical to that found in both *Winchcombe* and *Coventry* to be the common source.[58] *Chronicula* is fuller in its

[55] See *Winchcombe* 680.1, 689, 692, 718.2, 743, 774.4, 778.1, 781.1, 802, 822.1, 846, 872.1, 915.2, 922, 929, 957, 959.2, 960, 1003.1–2, 1033, 1038, 1046, 1062, 1095.1, 1096, 1112, 1113. Neither chronicle numbers Bosel and Oftfor (the first two bishops), Wilfrid (the fourth), Dunstan (the sixteenth), Oswald (the eighteenth), or Wulfstan II (the twenty-fifth).

[56] See *Winchcombe* 1058, 1062, and 1070.

[57] See chap. 5, § a, below.

[58] *Chronicula*[1] VA 1128 (G, fol. 111r–v).

coverage of some events, and thinner in its treatment of others. Consider, for example, its treatment of the life of Origen. *Winchcombe* and *Coventry* both share some five entries relating to the theologian's life, dated in both texts to 177, 197, 222, 232, and 247 respectively. All match notices in *Chronica chronicarum*. For its part *Chronicula*[1] has a single item for the life of Origen, one which combines the material found under AD 222 and 232 in *Winchcombe* and *Coventry*, and which is dated along with other notices to VA 233—that is, to AD 211.[59] *Chronicula* lacks not just the required information, but also the chronological apparatus that would have sufficed for the production of *Winchcombe* and *Coventry*, for it lumps items together in long annals in something like the manner of Bede's *Chronica maiora*, whereas *Winchcombe* and *Coventry* organise their material into short annals tied to specific years. In the absence of precise information as to years in which events took place, it would not have been possible to create *Winchcombe* and *Coventry* using this source. *Chronicula*[1] also lacks the errors which are common to both *Winchcombe* and *Coventry*, such as the confusion of St Bartholomew with St Benedict under 839/840.[60] There is no sign, finally, in *Winchcombe* and *Coventry* of the material which is distinctive to *Chronicula*[1], such as the alleged letter of St Benedict to St Remigius or the poems which are its most distinctive feature. It is clear, in short, that *Chronicula*[1] was not itself the common root, nor is it likely to have played a significant role in the making of that chronicle.[61]

There is, however, an important way in which the entries shared by *Winchcombe* and *Coventry* resemble *Chronicula*[1], namely the way in which they too include a small set of items not otherwise reported by John. That there are no corresponding items in *Chronica chronicarum* for at least forty-eight of the 718 notices shared by *Winchcombe* and *Coventry* shows that the source material from which the common root was drawn differed to a small but significant extent from that used in making of the former chronicle, implying that it was more than just an abbreviation of *Chronica chronicarum*. These notices represent a mere seven per cent of the shared items, but their diversity is striking: thirty-three match items found in various versions of the Norman Annals,[62] four items in Bede's *Chronica maiora*,[63] four items found in Frankish chronicles,[64] three notices found in the calendar of the computus manuscript in which *Winchcombe* is preserved (Tiberius

---

59 See the commentary to *Winchcombe* 177, 197, 222, 232, and 247.1.

60 *Winchcombe* 840; *Coventry* 839.2. Cf. JW*CC* 809 and 840; *Chronicula*[1] VA 868.

61 But see *Winchcombe* 1102.2, where a shared entry is closer to *Chronicula*[1] VA 1088 than JW*CC* 1102.

62 *Winchcombe* 97, 102.2, 135.1, 183, 437.1, 446, 473.2, 507.1, 514.1, 567 (?), 584.1, 605, 627.1, 637, 657, 662.1, 666.1, 677.3, 742.2, 763, 773.1, 778.2, 782, 890, 928, 942, 950, 968.2, 974, 993, 1004, 1013.1; *Coventry* 773.3. For details as to the sources, see the commentaries below.

63 *Winchcombe* 309.2, 309.3, 357.2, 405.2.

64 *Winchcombe* 541, 645, 742.3, 768.2.

E.IV, fols. 35r–40v);[65] one matches an item found in Orosius, *Historiae aduersum paganos*,[66] one an entry found in the E-text of the *Anglo-Saxon Chronicle*,[67] and two are items of uncertain origin.[68] Since they provide significant clues as to the composition and origin of the common root, these departures from *Chronica chronicarum* need to be discussed in some detail.

The one-off items are particularly striking. The item from Orosius refers to the rise and death of the tyrant Gratian in the final days of Roman Britain, whilst the item from the *Anglo-Saxon Chronicle* is chiefly concerned with the help that William Rufus received from the English in putting down the revolt of various great Norman magnates in favour of Robert Curthose in 1088. It seems extraordinary that the compiler should have pulled these books out of the cupboard for such brief additions to the text, but both, as with some of the items unique to *Chronicula*[1], are items of special relevance to England. Consider, for example, the item for 1088 as found in *Winchcombe*:

> Primates Anglie regem Willelmum regno priuare et fratrem eius Robertum comitem Normannie regem constituere conati sunt. Sed rex maximo Anglorum adiutorio preualuit, quibus promisit legem Eaduuardi regis tenere multaque bona, nec tamen reddidit. Suum autem patruum Odonem episcopum Baiocensem nonnullosque alios Anglia expulit.

*Coventry* abbreviates this item, but enough remains of the original entry to show that it was indeed derived from the common root:

> Primates Anglie Uuillelmum regem regno priuare et fratrem eius Robertum comitem Normanni regem constituere conati sunt. Sed rex maximo Anglorum adiutorio preualuit, et patruum suum Odonem nonnullosque alios Anglia expulit.

*Chronicula* uses different words, but offers a similar interpretation, emphasising the promises which William Rufus gave to his English adherents and his failure to honour them:[69]

---

65 *Winchcombe* 13, 14.1, 992.1. These items will be discussed in chap. 5, § a, below.

66 *Winchcombe* 407.1.

67 *Winchcombe* 1088.

68 *Winchcombe* 622.2, 1106.2.

69 *Chronicula*[1] VA 1088: "But having heard about the treachery of the Normans, the king quickly assembled the English to himself. To anyone who wanted the better to be chosen, he promised law provided that they were for him in providing assistance against the enemy force. The English trusted these royal promises, and until the glory of victory they were more faithful to the king than those Normans who stuck to the royal side. At length the king obtained victory from his enemies with the utmost help from the English, but he cheated them in everything which he had promised them just a short time ago."

> Rex autem audita Normannorum traditione, Anglos ad se conuocat celerrime. Quibusquam uellent eligere meliorem, promittit legem dummodo sibi sint in auxilium contra impetum hostium. Regiis promissis fidem adhibent Angli et usque ad triumphi gloriam fideliores existunt regi quam illi qui regali adhesere lateri Normanni. Tandem rex Anglorum maxime auxilio potitus de inimicis uictoria que dudum illis promiserat mentitus est omnia.

The language is sufficiently different to rule out the existence of a direct relationship between the entry in *Winchcombe* and *Coventry* and that in *Chronicula*; but both seem to derive from a version of the *Anglo-Saxon Chronicle* related to the E-text, for it interprets the events of 1088 in relatively similar terms:[70]

> 7 beht heom þa betsta laga þæ æfre ær wæs on þisan lande, 7 ælc u<n>riht geold he forbead 7 geatte mannan heora wudas and slætinge; ac hit ne stod nane hwile. Ac englisce men swa þeah fengon to þam cynge heora hlaforde on fultume . . . Se biscop Odo mid þam mannum þe innan þam castele wæron ofer sæ ferdon, 7 se biscop swa forlet þone wurðscipe þe he on þis lande hæfde . . . Eac manige frencisce men forleton heora land 7 ferdon ofer sæ . . .

*Chronica chronicarum*, on the other hand, treats the episode in rather different terms. It contains no suggestion that William Rufus made a particular appeal to the English for their support; rather, William is simply said to have made laws and to have promised *omnia bona* to his supporters. In this text, moreover, John nowhere accuses him of failing to honour his promises; rather, he goes on to describe various engagements, and especially the support given to the king in Worcestershire by the bishop of Worcester, Wulfstan II. There are signs, however, that for this annal John also made use of a version of the *Anglo-Saxon Chronicle* related to the E-text.[71]

The upshot is that although the entry shared by *Winchcombe* and *Coventry* differs in its words from its counterparts in John's known works, it seems to share with both of them a dependence on the same source, and with *Chronicula* a certain sensitivity to the sufferings of the English under Norman rule. In other words, the surviving fragments of this chronicle share significant affinities of

[70] *ASC* (E) 1087: "[William promised the English] the best law that there had ever been in this country, and forbade every unjust tax and granted people their woods and hunting rights—but it did not last any time. But nevertheless, the Englishmen came to the help of their lord the king. . . . Bishop Odo, with the men who were in the castle, went overseas, and the bishop relinquished the dignity that he had in this country . . . Many Frenchmen also gave up their lands and went overseas."

[71] See JWCC 1088 (esp. 3:56, n. 16). For John's use of an ancestor of the E-text, see *Two of the Saxon Chronicles Parallel*, ed. Charles Plummer and John Earle, 2 vols. (Oxford: Clarendon Press, 1892–1899), 2:lxxxv.

method, purpose, and outlook with the known works of John of Worcester even when they deviate over matters of detail. This much may also be true of its use of the Norman Annals. I say "may" because there is some uncertainty as to the full extent of the root's Norman component.

## (d) The Common Root and its Norman Sources

The common root's Norman entries seem to be the product of the independent use of a source which was also used in the making of the *Chronica chronicarum*, although the matter is obscured by the fact that *Winchcombe* and *Coventry* differ in their use of the Norman Annals. The two chronicles share, to begin with, some fifty-four items: there are the thirty-five items for which there is no counterpart in *Chronica chronicarum*;[72] some six where material from both the Norman Annals and *Chronica chronicarum* has been combined to produce an annal;[73] and some thirteen that could derive from either the Norman Annals or *Chronica chronicarum*, because virtually identical information was also available through Marianus or the *Anglo-Saxon Chronicle*.[74] *Coventry*, for its part, contains nothing in addition to these fifty-three items that could derive from the Norman Annals, but *Winchcombe* adds some seventy-seven notices that echo entries in this source,[75] some three of which also match items in *Chronica chronicarum*.[76] Some of these entries represent, furthermore, thematic strands in the Norman Annals which are not exhibited in the other texts: there is, for example, no counterpart in *Chronica chronicarum*, *Chronicula*, or *Coventry* for a long series of notices concerned with the archbishops of Rouen.[77] Two explanations are possible. One is that the common root underwent a process of expansion similar to that attested in the manuscripts of *Chronica chronicarum*—that further entries from this source, reflecting the emergence of new interests, were added to the common root in the interim between the making of an exemplar behind *Coventry* and the

---

[72] See n. 62 above and the cross-references in the commentary to *Winchcombe*.

[73] See *Winchcombe* 413.3, 426, 608.2, 742.1, 753, 1099.1.

[74] *Winchcombe* 159.2, 224.3, 269.3, 433, 439, 490.1, 567, 786.1, 876.3, 898, 915.1, 917.1, 1060.

[75] *Winchcombe* 44, 65.5, 91.2, 102.5, 125.2, 150.1, 150.2, 204.2, 207.3, 242.2, 242.3, 245.2, 246.2, 246.3, 266.3, 296.1, 316.2, 325, 330.6, 341, 342.2, 349.2, 356.1, 365.2, 399.3, 455, 474.2, 482, 484, 487.4, 529.3, 529.4, 530.2, 582.2, 583, 584.2, 621, 635.3, 655.2, 674.3, 677.5, 713.2, 719.2, 722, 730, 756.2, 761, 767.2, 776.1, 778.3, 779, 780, 781.2, 800.2, 809.3, 812, 813.2, 815, 817.1, 817.2, 818.1, 822.2, 824.2, 824.3, 825.2, 835, 837, 849.2, 850.2, 859, 865, 869, 871.2, 885.1, 888.2, 895, 1044.2.

[76] *Winchcombe* 583, 677.5, 761.

[77] See *Winchcombe* 296.1, 316.2, 325, 341, 365.2, 399.3, 455, 474.2, 529.3, 582.2, 621, 719.2, 722, 730, 756.2, 767.2, 835, 849.2.

making of *Winchcombe*. The other possibility is that the additional entries were inserted when *Winchcombe* itself was produced. The palaeographical data are not conclusive, but favour the latter explanation. For the way in which some of these entries are fitted onto the pages of Tiberius E.IV suggests that they were inserted after the rest of the items in the relevant area of the chronicle had been copied by the scribe of the first phase, as he seems to have returned to the text to insert some, if not all, of these items.[78] That is, he was expanding the root's Norman component as he set about completing his work.

That *Coventry* shows no signs of independent use of the Norman Annals strongly suggests, to return to our main subject, that all of the shared items were components of the common root. There is little more to be gained by comparing the patterns of abbreviation found among these items, since they were so brief to begin with that there was little need to shorten them. There are, however, some striking affinities in the ways in which the two texts arrange their Norman material. Compare, for example, their annals for the year 773. *Coventry* has the fuller version of the annal for this year:

> (1) Karolus imperator Romam perrexit, inde reuersus Papiam cepit, et diuersis ciuitatibus direptibus, (2) totam Italiam subegit et omnia a Longobardorum regibus erepta, (3) et inde in Hispaniam intrauit et Saxoniam uenit, et Pampileniam uenit, et eam destruxit, atque Augustam exercitum suum coniu<n>xit, et acceptis obsidibus, subiugatisque Saracenis, per Narbonam et Wasconiam Franciam rediit.

*Winchcombe* is similar, but briefer where the third item is concerned:

> (1) Karolus imperator Romam perrexit, inde reuersus Papiam cepit, et direptis uniuersis ciuitatibus, (2) totam Italiam subegit et omnia a Longobardorum regibus erepta, (3) et inde in Hispania<m> intrauit et Saxoniam uenit, subiugatisque Sarracenis, per Narbonam et Wasconiam Franciam rediit.

Items one and three derive from the Norman Annals, but neither chronicle could have arrived at this arrangement by independent use of that source, for item two, the *totam. . .erepta* clause which both insert into the middle of this annal, is an echo of John of Worcester.[79] None of the known versions of the Norman Annals, furthermore, puts items one and three together under a single year. The *Annals of St-Évroult*, for example, arrange them as follows:[80]

---

[78] Note, for example, *Winchcombe* 756.2. The compiler's method is discussed further in chap. 3, § d, below.

[79] *JWCC* 773: ". . . atque Italiam totam subegit, et omnia a Longobardorum regibus erepta . . ."

[80] For the other versions, see the commentary on *Winchcombe* 773.1–3 and *Coventry* 773.3 below.

[774] Karolus Romam vadit; inde reversus, Papiam cepit cum rege Desiderio, captis civitatibus et direptis universis Italie.

[775]

[776] Conversio Saxonum.

[775]

[778] Karolus Pampiloniam urbem destruxit; apud Cesaraugustam exercitum suum conjunxit, et, acceptis obsidibus subjugatisque Sarracenis, per Narbonam et Vuasconiam Franciam rediit. Karolus in Yspanias intravit. Karolus Saxoniam venit.

It seems almost certain, even though *Winchcombe* is briefer in its treatment of the third item than *Coventry*, that the way in which they arrange this material derives from a common root. It follows, first, that the shared material of "Norman" origin seems to have been derived through a common root, and second, that *Winchcombe* preserves a much fuller range of Norman notices, perhaps partly because it reports this root in more detail than *Coventry*, but mostly (if not entirely) because its redactor made additional use of Norman Annals, inserting many items from this source that had been excluded during the making of the common root. The seventy-seven additional notices tend, indeed, to be concentrated in two periods, 200–400 and 750–900, suggesting that the redactor's efforts to beef up the common root were somewhat inconsistent.

As has been noted, John also used the Norman Annals in the *Chronica chronicarum*, but there are significant differences in the way in which he uses this source there. The items which he there draws from this source divide into two groups.[81] The first comprises a series of fifteen notices concerned with the successions of the early kings of the Franks and two concerned with the early eleventh-century dukes of Normandy.[82] These are embedded in the text of the holograph

[81] Some caution is necessary when discussing JW's use of the Norman Annals, for the various preliminary texts to JW*CC* also include some items from the Norman Annals, most notably among the annals in the margins of the Easter Tables (e.g. C 65, where there is a notice for Rollo's arrival in Normandy alongside the third year of the nineteenth cycle; cf. *Winchcombe* 876.3), and among the revised papal annals (see chap. 3, § d, below). The Bury St Edmund's interpolations in MS. B also include a number of additions which derive from the Norman Annals: see JW*CC* (B), 620, 636, 660, 684, 699, 701, 717, 718, 784, 893, 914, 916, 992, 993, 1031, 1047, 1054. As with the run of entries in the common stock, this run also represents a distinctive selection from this body of material, different from that found in *Coventry* and *Winchcombe*.

[82] JW*CC* 426, 431, 438, 451, 474, 493, 515, 528, 557, 580, 586, 590, 600, 634, 660, 1026, 1035. Images of C may be examined online at "Early Manuscripts at Oxford University" (http://image.ox.ac.uk/).

(C) and, except in the case of the last of the Merovingian items (that for Clothar III), they show no signs of being additions to the whole.[83] There are counterparts for some of these items among the Norman entries common to both *Winchcombe* and *Coventry*, but, as will be shown below, the latter chronicles cover the earliest Frankish kings in an entirely different way. The other group of Norman entries in *Chronica chronicarum* comprises some eight items which appear, from the way in which they are entered in the holograph, to have been added to *Chronica chronicarum* at a late stage in its development:[84] two appear, for example, as isolated notes at the end of long annals;[85] four appear in the margins;[86] and one appears at the end of an annal where the final line has been erased and rewritten so that it could be accommodated on an extra line.[87] It is true that one sits at the beginning of an annal, but in this instance the entire annal has been erased and rewritten in a compressed fashion so as to permit its insertion.[88] That they were late additions is *sometimes* confirmed, furthermore, by their absence from manuscripts D and L of the *Chronica chronicarum*. They are usually to be found in B and P.[89] John's use of the Norman Annals in *Chronica chronicarum* seems, in short, rather cautious when compared with that found in the common root. That text's series of Norman items is certainly less extensive than that found among the items shared by *Winchcombe* and *Coventry*.[90] Much the same findings emerge when these shared items are compared with the smattering of Norman entries which John included in *Chronicula*. He there includes most of the borrowings found in *Chronica*

---

[83] For the exception, see JW*CC* 660 (n. c).

[84] JW*CC* 433, 490, 588, 678, 876, 898, 914, 917.

[85] C 240, where an annal celebrating the sermons of Maximus of Turin (*AU* 432) appears at the end of the annal for 433; C 267, where the obit of St Ouen (*AU*, *ACad.*, *ASN*, RT*Access*. 677, *AG* 669) is placed at the end of the long annal for 677.

[86] C 246, where the institution of rogation services by Mamertus of Vienne (*AU*, *ASC* (E) 490, *AG* 488; cf. *Winchcombe* 490.1) is reported alongside the annals for 490 and 491; C 254, where the birth of St Ouen (*AU*, RT*Access*. 588; cf. *Winchcombe* 583) is reported alongside the beginning of the annal of 588; C 303, where Rollo's siege of Chartres (*AU*, *ACad.*, *AMSM*, *ASN* 898; *AG*, RT*Access*. 908; cf. *Winchcombe* 898) is reported in the margin and assigned to the year 898 by the red line surrounding it on three sides; C 246, where the obit of Rollo *primus dux Normannorum* and the succession of William Longsword (*AU*, *AG*, *ACad.*, *AMSM* 917, and so on; cf. *Winchcombe* 917.1) is noted in the margin alongside the beginning of the annal for 917.

[87] C, 306, where the return of the relics of St Ouen (*AU*, *AG*, *ACad.*, *AMSM*, RT*Access*. 915) has been inserted at the end of the annal for 914. Cf. *Winchcombe* 915.1.

[88] C, 240, where *Tertius rex Francorum Meroueus*, from the Norman Annals (*AU*, *ASN* 437, *AG* 436), is inserted at the beginning of the annal for 438. Cf. *Winchcombe* 898.

[89] See the apparatus to JW*CC* 588 (n. a), 677 (n. b), 876 (n. o), 898 (n. f), 914 (n. e), 917 (n. j). Note that MS. D is McGurk's MS. H.

[90] Cf. nn. 62, 82, and 84 above.

*chronicarum*, except that the items which appear in the margins in C are fully embedded in the text of *Chronicula.*[91]

## (e) The Common Root and its Frankish Sources

The significance of these differences in the use of the Norman Annals becomes clearer when they are considered alongside the material that has been taken from Frankish sources. These items comprise four notices that refer to several of the most sensational episodes in their early history: the assassination of the kings Sigibert and Chilperic, the fall and recovery of the mayor Ebroin, the *coup d'état* in which Pippin III overthrew the Merovingians, and the imperial coronation of Charlemagne.[92] The account of Ebroin is doubly striking because it deviates from the usual generic pattern in as much as it is unusually long:[93]

> Francorum xv^us Clotarius rex obiit. Cui Theodericus frater eius succedit, cuius maior domus erat Ebroinus nomine. Franci uero contra Theodericum regem surrexerunt, eumque a regno deiciunt, crinesque capitis eius totonderunt. Similiter et Ebroinum maiorem domus totonderunt atque Luxouio monasterio in Burgundia direxerunt. Mittentes legationem in Austrasios propter Childericum regem fratrem Theoderici eum super totum regnum constituunt. Contra quem etiam Franci consurgentes eo, quod crudelis esset, interfecerunt eum. Audiens autem predictus Ebroinus Theoderici regis quondam maior domus has dissensiones inter Francos, exiens a Luxouio monasterio comamque capitis sui crescere sinens, cum ualida manu Theodericum regem in regnum restituitur, ipseque principatum suum obtinuit. Eo tempore interfectis regibus Martinus et Pipinus iunior filius Ansigisili dominabantur in Austria. Qui dimicantes contra Theodericum et Ebroinum in fugam uersi sunt. Ceciditque ibi Martinus dux cum suis, Pipinus uero per fugam lapsus. Porro Theodericus regnauit annos xix. Regnauitque Clodoueus filius eius pro eo annis ii.

John of Worcester also recounts Ebroin's recovery of his position in his *Chronicula*, but there he notes a different dimension of these events, the martyrdom of St Leudegar (d. 675).[94] The ultimate and perhaps the direct source of the present

---

[91] E.g. *Chronicula*[1] VA 604 (birth of St Ouen), 896 (the arrival of Rollo in Normandy), 909 (the siege of Chartres and the return of Ouen's relics), 1046 (the death of Duke Richard II, the reign of Richard III, the reign of Robert, and the succession of William the Bastard).

[92] See *Winchcombe* 541, 645, 742.3, 768.2 and the commentary below. *Coventry* has all four items.

[93] *Winchcombe* 645; in *Coventry* the same material is split between 644.3 and 645.

[94] *Chronicula*[1] VA 706 (fol. 51v), using HF*Chron.*, 158: "Sanctus Leodegarius Eduensis episcopus ab Ebroino, qui monachili ueste qua induebatur, iam deposita maior regie domus effectus est, martyrizatur."

entry is a series of passages in the *Liber Historiae Francorum*, a non-annalistic chronicle produced at Soissons in the late 720s.[95] The other item related to this source is the entry covering the deaths of Sigibert and Chilperic under 541. It attributes the murder of Sigibert to Chilperic's wife Fredegund, and goes on to describe how Chilperic ruled for the following twenty-three years until she had him murdered as well. It mentions that the former was buried at Soissons and the latter at Paris. The language is much compressed, but all of these details are to be found in the *Liber Historiae Francorum*.[96] This entry differs greatly, moreover, from its counterpart in *Chronica chronicarum*, for the latter follows the Norman Annals in attributing the murder of Sigibert to Chilperic and in going on to say that Childebert, a *puerulus*, received the kingdom with his mother, Brunhild.[97]

The passages concerned with the coup of 751 and the imperial coronation of 800 are less unusual. *Winchcombe* and *Coventry* are by no means the only twelfth-century English chronicles to report these events,[98] but the language of their notices is much closer to that of *Annales Regni Francorum* than is the norm.[99] Moreover, they arrange and interpret this material in an unusual way. Both place the notice for the imperial coronation of Charlemagne not under or close to the

[95] *LHF*, § 45 (pp. 317–318): "In his diebus Chlotharius rex puer obiit regnavitque annis 4. Theudericus, frater eius, elevatus est rex Francorum . . . Eo tempore Franci adversus Ebroinum insidias preparant, super Theudericum consurgunt eumque de regno deiciunt, crinesque capitis amborum vi abstrahentes, incidunt. Ebroinum totundunt eumque Luxovio monasterio in Burgundia dirigunt. In Auster propter Childericum mittentes accommodant. Et una cum Vulfoaldo duce veniens, in regno Francorum elevatus est"; § 46 (pp. 319–320): "Eo quoque tempore, decedente Vulfoaldo de Auster, Martinus et Pippinus iunior, filius Anseghiselo quondam, decedentibus regibus, dominabantur in Austria, donec tandem aliquando hii duces in odium versi contra Ebroinum, exercitum plurimum Austrasiorum commotum, contra Theudericum regem et Ebroinum aciem dirigunt . . . Austrasii devicti, in fugam lapsi, terga verterunt . . . Martinus per fugam elapsus, Lauduno Clavato ingressus, illuc se reclusit; Pippinus autem altrinsecus evasit . . . [et Martinus] ibi cum sociis suis interfectus est"; and, § 49 (pp. 323–324), which states that Theuderic reigned for 19 years and that his son—here named not "Chlothar" but *Chlodoveus*, "Clovis"—reigned for two years. On the dating and the context in which *LHF* was produced, see Richard A. Gerberding, *The Rise of the Carolingians and the* Liber Historiae Francorum (Oxford: Clarendon Press, 1987), 150–58, with Janet L. Nelson, "Gender and Genre in Women Historians of the Early Middle Ages," in *L'Historiographie médiévale en Europe*, ed. Genet, 149–63.

[96] *LHF*, § 32 (pp. 295–297).

[97] JW*CC* 557. Cf. Norman Annals: *AU* 556.

[98] One of the earliest chronicles to record the imperial coronation is the so-called *York Annals*, a late eighth/ninth-century chronicle which was later elaborated at Ramsey Abbey: see SD*HR*, § 62 (pp. 63–64); cf. *Historia post Bedam*, as quoted in RH*Chron.*, 1:18. On the making of its annal for 800, see Story, *Carolingian Connections*, esp. 112–15, 123–26.

[99] See further the commentary on *Winchcombe* 742.3 and 768.2 below. Cf. *APW* 783.

year 800 when the event took place, but under 768, at the start of his reign. It is there reported in both chronicles that he was the first of the kings of the Franks to be called emperor: Pope Leo crowned him in St Peter's and he was acclaimed by the Roman people. The extract concerning the *coup d'état* against the Merovingians is joined, moreover, to the account of how Carloman and Pippin III succeeded Charles Martel, which precedes it with the eccentric claim that Theoderic IV first took the kingdom from Pippin by force: *Theodericus regnum a Pippino ui arripuit*. This supposition seems to be the product of an attempt to reconcile the conflicting accounts of these events provided by three different sources: the *Annales Regni Francorum*, the Norman Annals, and Marianus Scottus. It seems to have been Marianus who was responsible for leading the compiler astray, for he described Charles Martel as "the king of the Franks who was also called the mayor of the palace."[100] The same misunderstanding of the nature of the Pippinids' authority as mayors of the palace has also influenced other items shared by *Winchcombe* and *Coventry*, such as their annal for 687, where they have Pippin II succeeding Childebert, "the eighteenth king of the Franks," and that for 714, where they have Charles Martel succeeding Pippin, "the nineteenth king of the Franks." Having treated the Pippinids as kings for the previous half century, the compiler was faced with having to explain why Pippin III had needed papal permission to depose King Childeric in the 740s.

These items of Frankish origin need to be seen, moreover, as part of a long series of entries in which the compiler attempted to reconstruct the sequence of the earliest kings of the Franks. As can be seen from Fig. 1, a table in which they are compared with their counterparts in the *Chronica chronicarum*, the series is one of the most distinctive aspects of the common root. The differences are clear just from looking at the numbering of the kings. By leaving out several kings recognised by John (including Theuderic I), the common root ends up numbering Clovis II as the fourteenth king whereas John makes him the nineteenth. The relevant entries in *Winchcombe* and *Coventry* are, moreover, fuller in their treatment of these kings than their counterparts in *Chronica chronicarum*. As well as numbering the kings, they assign lengths to their reigns—lengths which do not always agree with the years to which the notices are allocated.[101] A similar contrast occurs in the common root's account of the dukes of Normandy, for the

[100] Marianus/JW*CC* 741: "Karolus, filius Pippini, qui et maior domus dictus, rex Francorum obiit." Confusion over this issue seems to have been widespread: cf. the continuation to the Moore Bede, s.a. 741 (printed in Bede, *HE*, 573–77), and *ALD*, s.a. 713.

[101] This might be taken as evidence that the compiler made use of a regnal list, such as the *Genealogia regum Francorum* from Faramund to Pippin II in MS. Bod.L., Lat. class. d. 39, fol. 125rv. This example provides a different sequence of kings and different lengths for their reigns, but it is conceivable that some such source may have been available to the compiler. On Malmesbury's use of the genealogy in Lat. class. d. 39, see Thomson, *William of Malmesbury*, 142–43.

four items in question were misdated by the compiler of the common root, who seems to have assigned them on the basis that the Norman Annals were using the Marianan rather than the Dionysian chronological system. The upshot is that the series ends by having William the Bastard appointed in 1013, and there follows the rather implausible suggestion, seemingly of the compiler's own making, that he reigned for fifty-two years before becoming a king with the conquest of England in 1066.[102] In contrast, *Chronica chronicarum* has just two entries for the dukes of Normandy: one is for the deaths of Richard II and Richard III, and the succession of his brother Robert; and the other is for the death of Robert and the succession of his bastard son, William. These items are placed with greater accuracy under 1026 and 1035.[103]

The common root seems, in short, to have been put together by a compiler who was wrestling with the problem of reconciling the conflicting evidence as to the early kings of the Franks and the dukes of the Normans provided by such accounts of their history as were available in twelfth-century England.[104] It might be inferred that the differences between the shared entries and *Chronica chronicarum* in their coverage of these rulers count against John's being the compiler of the common root, but they need not have a great influence over this question. For the alternative series which survives in *Winchcombe* and *Coventry* is aptly explained as the product of a first attempt to resolve the problem of plotting the sequence of Frankish kings—an attempt which was, for the most part, jettisoned when John returned to work on *Chronica chronicarum*. Both interpretations certainly seem to have been guided by the same aim, both depend heavily on the Norman evidence, and both make similar assumptions about the nature of the Merovingian regime—that the Pippinids succeeded to the throne in the time of Pippin II and that one king succeeded another in a linear sequence. Both might well, therefore, be the work of John of Worcester, the root's version being a "road-test" for that found in *Chronica chronicarum*.

---

102 *Winchcombe* 917.1, 974, 1004, 1013.1. *Coventry* has all of these entries.

103 JW*CC* 1026, 1035. Cf. *Chronicula* VA 1046.

104 Similar investigations seem to have been undertaken at Durham, since a number of manuscripts associated with the cathedral priory contain brief chronicles which are concerned with the early history of the Franks, such as the *Compendiosum cronicum de regibus Francorum* which occurs in MS. Cambridge, U.L., Ff.1.27, fols. 249–253. This text offers a more successful account of the Merovingians in so far as it recognises some of the sixth-century divisions of the kingdom, such as that on death of Clothar I in 664 (p. 249) and in so far as it rightly distinguishes those Carolingians, such as Charles Martel, who were mayors, from those, such as Pippin I, who were kings (p. 251). On the brief but different chronicle which Symeon of Durham entered in MS. Durham, Cathedral Library, B.IV.22, fols. 3r–5v, see J. E. Story, "Symeon as Annalist," in Rollason, *Symeon of Durham*, 202–13, at 203–7 and plates 32–37.

Fig. 1
The Sequence of Frankish Kings in the Common Root and John of Worcester's *Chronica chronicarum*

| Kings of the Franks | *Winchcombe / Coventry* | | | John of Worcester, *Chronica chronicarum* | | |
|---|---|---|---|---|---|---|
| | | | | In the Genealogy among the prelims* | In the main chronicle | |
| | Numbering | Regnal Years | Regnal-Dates | | Numbering | Dates |
| Faramund | 1 | 4 | 426–429/30 | | 1 | 426–431 |
| Chlodio | 2 | 7 | 429/30–437 | | 2 | 431–438 |
| Merovech | 3 | 9 | 437–446 | 1 | 3 | 438–451 |
| Childeric (d. c.481) | 4 | 27 | 446–473 | 2 | 4 | 451–474 |
| Clovis I (c.481–511) | 5 | 20 | 473–493 | 3 | [5] | 474-? |
| Theuderic I (511–534) | Missed or omitted by the compiler of the common root? | | | | 6 | appears s.a. 493 |
| Theudebert I (534–548) | 6 | 14 | 493–507/8 | | 7 | appears s.a. 515 |
| Theudebald (548–555) | 7 | 7 | 507/8–514 | | 8 | appears s.a. 528 |
| Chlothar I (511–561) | 8 | 13 | 514–528 [sic] | 4 | John does not mention but recognises in his numbering the reigns of Chlothar and his four sons (including Sigibert I) as mentioned in the Norman Annals (see *AU*, s.a. 527) | |
| Sigibert I (561–575) | 9 | 14 | 528–541 [sic] | | 13 | appears s.a. 557 |
| Chilperic I (561–584) | 10 | 23 | 541–567/8 [sic] | 5 | 15 | appears s.a. 580 |
| Chlothar II (584–629) | 11 | 23 | 567/8–584 | 6 | 17 | appears s.a. 590, 600 |
| Childebert II (575–595) | 12 | 20 | 584–605/6 | | 16 | appears, s.a. 586 |
| Theudebert II (595–612) | | | | | 18 | appears s.a. 600 |
| Dagobert I (623–639) | 13 | 22 | 605/6–626/7 | 7 | '4th after Clovis' | appears s.a. 555 |

| | | | | | | |
|---|---|---|---|---|---|---|
| Clovis II (639–657) | 14 | 13 | 627–637 [sic] | 8 | 20 | appears s.a. 634 |
| Chlothar III (657–673) | 15 | 4 | 637–645 [sic] | | | appears s.a. 660 |
| Theuderic III (673, 675–690/1) | 16 | 19 | 645–662/3 [sic] | 9 | | |
| Clovis III (690/1–694) | 17 | 2 | 662/3–666 [sic] | | | |
| Childebert III (694–711) | 18 | 17 | 666–687 [sic] | | | |
| Pippin II, the Elder (d. 714) | 19 | 27 | 687–714 | | 'who ruled' | 688–715 |
| Charles Martel (d. 741) | 20 | 27 | 714–741/2 [sic] | | both king and mayor | 715–741 |
| Pippin III and Carloman | | | appear s.a.741/2 | | | appear s.a. 715 |
| Theuderic IV (721–737) | | 6 | [741/2–748?] | | | |
| Pippin III [again] (751–768) | 77 of the Romans | | [748?]-768 | | first emperor of the Franks | 741–767 |
| Charlemagne (768–814) | 78 of the Romans | 46 + 4 months | 768–813/4 | | 78 of the Romans | 768–813 |
| Louis the Pious (814–840) | 79 of the Romans | 27 + 11 months | 813/4–839 | | 79 of the Romans | 813–840 |
| Lothar (817–855) | 80 of the Romans | 15 | 839–855 | | | 840–855 |

*In Corpus 157, p. 4: *Genealogia regum Francorum. Ex genere Priami fuit Meroueus. . . .* The sequence of kings runs: Merovech, Childeric, Clovis, Chlothar, Chilperic, Chlothar, Dagobert, Clovis, Theodoric, Childebert, Dagobert, Theodoric, Chlothar, then it proceeds into a genealogy of the Pippinids.

A careful reading of *Liber Historiae Francorum* and of *Annales Regni Francorum* ought to have provided the compiler of the common root with a fuller grasp of both the fundamental distinction between kings and mayors of the palace and of the crucial point that the Franks had been accustomed to dividing their territories among the surviving sons of the deceased king. That he failed to grasp these points might be taken as a sign that he knew these texts in fragments so incomplete that they could not be fully understood. This much is also suggested by the relative distance between the language of the entries derived from the *Liber Historiae Francorum* and that of the source itself. The words are sufficiently dissimilar to suggest that the material has been transmitted indirectly to the common root though some other chronicle. Evidence for the use of these chronicles in England during the twelfth century is also extremely scarce, especially in the case of *Liber Historiae Francorum*. A single copy of late twelfth-century date produced at Reading is all that otherwise exists to show that this chronicle was known in England.[105] So far, however, it has provided impossible to identify a plausible intermediary,[106] and there was probably more early Frankish material in English monastic libraries than first appears: various histories "of the Franks" are named in the known booklists;[107] William of Malmesbury also had access to a modified version of the *Annales Mettenses Priores*;[108] and the Bury St Edmunds

[105] MS. Cambridge, Gonville and Caius College, 177, pages 89–115. For the provenance, see Elisabeth M. C. van Houts, ed., *The Gesta Normannorum ducum of William of Jumièges, Orderic Vitalis and Robert of Torigni*, OMT, 2 vols. (Oxford: Clarendon Press, 1994–1995), 1:cxii–cxiii; Coates, *EMB*, 149; *CBMLC*, 4:433 (no. B71.84). Among his 50 manuscripts, Bruno Krusch, *MGH, SS rer. merov.*, 2:224, also lists MS. Oxford, Corpus Christi College, 82 (mislabelling it as MS. 73), a late twelfth-century manuscript which was certainly in England by the end of the fifteenth century, but it is thought to have been made in France. See Alexander and Temple, *Illuminated MSS in Oxford*, 65.

[106] The material could not, for example, have been obtained from either Hugh of Fleury or Ado of Vienne. Their chronicles were certainly known in early twelfth-century England, both cover similar ground to *Winchcombe* 541 and 645, and both contain echoes of *LHF* in the relevant sections; but variations of emphasis and language prevent either being the means by which this material was transmitted to the present chronicle. See HF*Chron.*, 157–58, and AV*Chron.*, 184 and 200–1.

[107] E.g. *CBMLC*, vol. 4, nos. B13.241, B37.23, B68.219, B79.136.

[108] See Rodney M. Thomson, *William of Malmesbury*, 2nd ed. (Woodbridge: Boydell Press, 2001), 68, 138–39 and 143–45, where it is argued that MS. Oxford, Bod.L., Lat. class. d. 39, is "a later copy of a copy of a collection of materials for Carolingian history compiled by William." It includes a copy of *Annales Mettenses Priores* on fols. 125v–136v. It is clear, furthermore, that the twelfth-century copy in Durham Cathedral Library (MS. C.IV.15), a manuscript which also contains a copy of Regino of Prum's *Chronica*, had reached the monastic priory there by the second half of the twelfth century: see Andrew J. Piper, "The Historical Interests of the Monks of Durham," in Rollason, *Symeon of Durham*, 301–32 (esp. 311–13, 328).

compiler of the *Annals of St Neots* also made use of the *Annales Regni Francorum*.[109] The compiler of the root might well, therefore, have had direct access to both *Liber Historiae Francorum* and *Annales Regni Francorum*. In that case, the crucial factor in his misreading of the Merovingian period may have been his high regard for the authority of Marianus—a regard so strong that he interpreted material derived directly from earlier, near-contemporary, accounts of the history of the Franks so as to make it agree with the Irish chronicler's view of events.[110] It is not difficult, however, to see how the growing realisation that this material was incompatible with the narrative provided by Marianus might have led John, if he were the compiler of the common root, to ignore or perhaps to excise this material when it came to revising the text of the *Chronica chronicarum*.

## (f) Dating the Common Root

One implication of these suggestions is that the common root was produced whilst John was still at work on his version of the *Chronica chronicarum*. This is a difficult point to prove, but it is not contradicted by the evidence of the shared entries. The root was certainly produced in John's lifetime or within a few years of his death. The *terminus a quo* for its composition depends on the final annal among the shared items which reports the destruction of Gloucester by fire in March 1122; the *terminus ad quem* depends on the relatively imprecise evidence provided by the palaeography of Tiberius E.IV, the manuscript in which *Winchcombe* is preserved, and it suggests that the principal scribe flourished in or close to the 1140s.[111] In theory it ought to be possible to refine this dating by observing which stages in the evolution of the *Chronica chronicarum* are represented among the shared entries which seem to have been abbreviated from this source.

It is certainly the case that the shared entries include none of the materials which were added during the fourth and the fifth stages in its development: that is, the shared items show no sign of the material which *Chronica chronicarum* shares with William of Malmesbury, nor any of that contained among the revised versions of the prelims, such as the set of "Papal Annals" which John added to his holograph and which a Gloucester scribe added to the *Chronicula*. The first

---

[109] See *ASN* 814 (the death of Charlemagne) and 823 (a miracle story). Their most recent editor, David N. Dumville (*ASC Coll.*, 17:lii–liii) asks whether this material was derived from *ARF* indirectly, perhaps through an expanded version of the Norman Annals; but there is, as he points out, no sign of this material (or of any other unadulterated quotations from *ARF*) in the known versions of these annals.

[110] There is evidence that John intervened to correct details in Marianus's text, but none of these interventions questioned the fundamental assumptions on which it depends. See the commentary on *Winchcombe* 878 below.

[111] See chap. 3, § b, below.

and second stages in the development of *Chronica chronicarum* are, on the other hand, well represented among the shared entries. The shared entries include, for example, items containing echoes of the extracts that John took from Eadmer's *Historia Novorum*.[112] But stage three is barely represented. There is little sign, for example, of the material which John obtained from a northern chronicle compiled at Durham,[113] or of the material which he took from Hugh of Fleury's *Historia Ecclesiastica*. In view of the attention that the shared entries give to St Benedict one might expect, for example, to find an echo of the notice that John derived from Hugh concerning the translation of his body from Monte Cassino to Fleury, but it is not to be found among them.[114] Moreover, the common root makes independent use, as has been shown above, of the Norman Annals. All of this suggests that the insertion of "stage-three" material into *Chronica chronicarum* was far from complete when the common root was produced—that it was made at some point between the mid-1120s and around 1130.

It is difficult, however, to be certain as to exactly how long the compiler may have spent developing the common root, for it follows from the likelihood that John was the author that this text was probably subject to a process of ongoing revision and refinement similar to that revealed by the manuscripts of *Chronica chronicarum*. The best that can be said is that the period in which the root was compiled coincides for the most part with John's own lifetime. The date of John's death is, as has been pointed out already, obscure, but he was alive until at least the middle of 1141, and may well have lived on into the mid-1140s.

## (g) The Context and Function of the Common Root

This chapter has demonstrated that *Winchcombe* and *Coventry* rest on a common root which covered the period from the Incarnation down to 1122, but perhaps the crucial point to emerge from it is that the surviving fragments of this

---

[112] E.g. *Winchcombe* 1107.1; *Coventry* 1109. Both items are reported in almost exactly the same words and both preserve a minor variant—the insertion of the preposition *de* before *episcopatu aut abbatia*—which shows that they derive from Eadmer, *HN*, iv (p. 186), indirectly through JW*CC* 1107. The other entries which appear to derive from Eadmer through JW*CC* are *Winchcombe* 1108.2, 1109.1, 1109.2, 1115.1, 1115.2, 1118.1, 1119–21, 1122.3.

[113] See JW*CC*, 635, 651, 664, 676, 687, 698, 707, 721, 802, 819, 828, 845, 900, 915, 928, 944, 995, 1020, 1048, 1070 (3:16). With the exception of the last item which now appears as part of a much longer passage of text rewritten by $C^3$, all of these additions were entered in the holograph by $C^2$. There is an echo of this material in *Winchcombe* under 819.2, but this item is not shared by *Coventry*, and it belongs to a section where the former chronicle deviates from the common root.

[114] Compare JW*CC* 674 and *Chronicula* VA 690, which derive from HF*Chron*., 153–55, with *Winchcombe* 526.2, 596 and 840 (sic). But see also *Winchcombe* 611 and 622.

chronicle share affinities of method, purpose, and outlook with the known works of John of Worcester even when they differ over matters of detail. Indeed, the contrasts between the shared entries and *Chronica chronicarum* seem no greater than those between the latter text and John's *Chronicula*. These contrasts need not prevent John's being the author of this chronicle, and there are, indeed, many reasons for thinking he was its author. One is that it was almost certainly produced at Worcester during the period he was its most active historian. Another is that he was a leading advocate of the revised chronology of Marianus Scotus, and the root almost certainly employed the Marianan chronological apparatus found in its descendants, *Winchcombe* and *Coventry*. A third reason for thinking that John might be the author is that the common root contains so much material relating to the history of Worcester Cathedral and its priory that it is difficult to avoid the conclusion that it was compiled there. A fourth reason is that the common root appears to exploit the contents of *Chronica chronicarum* in such a deft and complex fashion that it would seem to have been compiled by someone who had a thorough knowledge of its contents and organisation. The final and perhaps the most striking reason for thinking that John is the author is that many of the items that make up the common root show signs of having been reworked in ways that are typical of his compositional methods. The notices recording the holders of imperial title appear to have been reshaped almost as though the intention was to provide an aesthetic alternative—a mirror image of the pattern found in *Chronica chronicarum*. The intention was perhaps to hold the interest of those who might have occasion to consult both texts.

If John's authorship is accepted, then it needs to be asked why he compiled it. Given that it is, for the most part, an epitome of *Chronica chronicarum*, it cannot be argued that it was intended as a better or more comprehensive record of the events it covers. Rather, the aim seems to have been to reach out to a new and different audience from that which was likely to use *Chronica chronicarum* or *Chronicula*. It seems likely that John had a particular generic scheme in mind: that he was attempting, not only to traverse a particular body of information, but also to disseminate that material by occupying three different niches in the market for chronicles—that he was producing three different kinds of text, each designed to be used in a different way, or rather to meet the needs three different kinds of reader. *Chronica chronicarum* can be seen as the comprehensive version intended for the intellectual heavyweights. It combines Marianus's tract-like exposition of his ideas with, in its third book as expanded by John, an attempt to provide a careful and systematic chronicle of particular interest for English readers. It offers extended narrative treatment of events, especially political events but not to the exclusion of the matter often found in annalistic chronicles, such as wonders and portents; but its main aim seems to be to set out the intellectual foundations of the revised chronology of Marianus Scotus. The *Anglo-Saxon Chronicle* was, in some though certainly not all of its component parts, a narrative-chronicle of a relatively exhaustive kind, and it may well have served as the model for John's reworking of the third book. *Chronicula* seems to have been devised as a kind of diversion. It certainly provides a lighter treatment of the ground covered in book three of the *Chronica chronicarum*, adding a considerable amount of poetic content.[115] It arranges its notices by reference to irregular chronological anchors in the manner of Bede's *Chronica maiora*, but the years specified are those of Marianus alone. It omits the arguments which he developed in support of his chronology, but by robbing its readers of the Dionysian anchors to which they had become accustomed it forces them to use the Marianan system.

The shared entries in *Winchcombe* and *Coventry* cover much the same ground as the other two works: they present a mixture of material from Marianus, English, and Continental sources, and they cover the whole of the Sixth Age down to 1122, but they organise their material in a different way yet again, this time according to a pattern which is typical of the breviate world chronicle in annalistic format, a type of chronicle which flourished in England during the twelfth and thirteenth centuries.[116] The only shared items seriously at odds with the generic pattern are the long entries under 645 and 742 that cover the fall and return of the mayor Ebroin and the coup in which Pippin III deposed the last Merovingians. Apart from these exceptions, the common root, as revealed by the items shared by *Winchcombe* and *Coventry*, adheres to the pattern of annalistic chronicles of this type. If its chronological apparatus was similar to that found in its descendants, then it will have provided a required diagrammatic representation of the passage of time, but one which was indexed by giving the years of the Incarnation according to Marianus Scotus as well as those according to Dionysius Exiguus. It was argued in chapter one that this type of annalistic chronicle was devised as a kind of foundation text for newcomers to the subject of computus—that the genre was devised as a means of equipping newcomers to the religious life with a sense of the development of time over the longer term. For an historian who was attempting to win long-term acceptance for a new chronological scheme, this was perhaps the most crucial audience of them all.

---

[115] See esp. *Chronicula* VA 918, 1061, 1088.

[116] See chap. 1, esp. § a, above.

# Chapter Three: The *Winchcombe Chronicle*

## (a) The Manuscript

The *Winchcombe Chronicle* is preserved in a large computus manuscript—today MS. London, B.L., Cotton Tiberius E.IV (hereafter "T").[1] There is little reason to doubt that the manuscript represents a medieval compilation, but its exact construction can no longer be recovered owing to the damage inflicted by the fire which ravaged the Cotton Collection on 23 October 1731 when it was at Ashburnham House in London. Indeed, the catalogue of 1802 gives the impression that Tiberius E.IV had been ruined beyond repair.[2] The damage to the 187 remaining leaves of the manuscript is, however, mostly confined to the edges of the pages, and in 1845 they were mounted in cardboard frames and rebound, though not always in the right order.[3] As far as the chronicle is concerned, the most serious effects of the fire and the restoration process are that many of the marginalia

[1] The first two sections of this chapter rest in part on the work of Julian Harrison who has made a fine study of the present manuscript in 2004 in the process of preparing a new catalogue of the Cotton Collection. It is to be hoped that he will set out in print his theories as to the development of T and as to its relationship with the other major English computistical collections. A copy of the full description may be consulted on the open shelves of the Manuscripts Reading Room in the British Library. For another modern attempt to describe the book, see Byrhtferth, *Enchiridion*, lvii–lviii.

[2] Planta, *MSS in the Cottonian Library*, 40: "This once valuable and elegant MS. on vellum, consisting of historical tracts, the chief of which is 'Beda de temporibus,' is so much damaged as to be useless." Some idea of the original contents of Tiberius E.IV can be ascertained from the list recorded by Smith, *MSS Bibl. Cotton.*, 29–30. Smith's descriptions were usually based on the contents lists which are to found among the preliminary matter to many of Sir Robert Cotton's manuscripts. There is no such list among the surviving contents of T, but it may have been destroyed in the fire of 1731.

[3] The correct order of folios 103 to 116 is 104–112, 116, 103, 115, 114, 113. On the restoration process, see Andrew Prescott, "'Their present miserable state of cremation': The Restoration of the Cotton Library," in *Sir Robert Cotton as Collector: Essays on an Early Stuart Courtier and his Legacy*, ed. C. J. Wright (London: British Library, 1997), 391–454, at 405, n. 120; 411 n. 169; 426, n. 280. The "Winchcombe cartulary" cited by

are no longer legible and that at least one leaf—that which began with the second half of Pope Leo III's letter to King Cenwulf (811.5)—is no longer to be found among the surviving folios. But the main text area has survived largely unscathed, except on the first folio, though the damage there is perhaps as much a result of earlier wear and tear as of the fire itself. The twelfth-century contents of the book may be listed as follows:

| | | |
|---|---|---|
| 1. | *Winchcombe Chronicle* | fols. 1r–27v16 |
| 2. | A tract derived from Isidore of Seville, *Etymologiae*, 13.11, prefacing a rota of the twelve winds.[4] | 29vb–30r |
| 3. | Table arranged in 10 columns correlating ten different chronologies for the opening years of the 28 decennovenial cycles comprising the Great Paschal Cycle for VA 1086–1618/AD 1064–1596 (i.e. correlating the years AD 1064, 1083, 1102, and so on down to 1577 with other systems for counting years). | 30vb–31v |
| 4. | Three tables relating to the Great Paschal Cycle with explanatory matter: (i) a table of concurrents for AM 5268–5810 (*recte* 5800) / VA 1086–1618 (that is, for AD 1064–1596), arranged in 19 vertical and 28 horizontal columns; (ii) a table of lunar letters for the same period arranged in the same way, except that the chronological indices are placed at the top rather than at the side of the table; (iii) a table for finding the dates of moveable feasts using the former data.[5] | 32r–33r |
| 5. | Table with four formulas for finding Easter. | 33v |
| 6. | Table entitled *Hic sic descriptum lunarem noscito cyclum*.[6] | 34r |
| 7. | Rota of the months, accompanied by two sets of verses: the first is entitled *Legitima cunctorum iiii ieiunia Christianorum* and begins *Ebdomada prima Martis ieiunia prima*,[7] the second is entitled *De vii embolismis cicli xixnalis* and begins *[. . .] primus erit.* | 34v |

Prescott, "Restoration of the Cotton Library," 417, as having been inlaid in 1845 refers to Tiberius E.IV.

[4] See also Lynn Thorndike and Pearl Kibre, *A Catalogue of Incipits of Mediaeval Scientific Writings in Latin*, 2nd ed. (London: Mediaeval Academy of America, 1963), col. 1685.

[5] Similar tables to (i) and (ii) are printed in *PL* 90.735–736, 737–738, 745–746. Table (iii) is similar to that in *PL* 90.747B–750A, but the present tables use Marianan indices as opposed to the Dionysian ones found in *PL*. These tables and their affinities need further study. In the meantime, see Jones, *BP*, 59–64.

[6] Partly printed in the appendix to Byrhtferth, *Enchiridion*, 423 (no. 38: moveable feasts only).

[7] Walther, *Initia*, no. 5057.

| | | |
|---|---|---|
| 8. | Calendar adapted for the use of Winchcombe Abbey, with many festal entries given in verse form.[8] | 35r–40v |
| 9. | Table of lunar letters beginning *Hec tabula quadrata per xi. epactas.*[9] | 41r–v |
| 10. | A tract on the nones, ides, and kalends that comprise each month, headed *Ratio calculandi, de singulis mensibus quot nonis, idibus, kalendis et diebus consistunt.* | 42r1–6 |
| 11. | Tables with instructions concerning Roman ferial regulars, concurrents, lunar regulars, epacts, and the *claues terminorum.* | 42r |
| 12. | *Argumentum de regularibus mensium unde sumunt originem*, a note beginning *Meminisse debes quia secundum solarem cursum dies anni sunt ccclxv. . .* | 42r7–16 |
| 13. | Bede, *De temporum ratione*, with an interlinear gloss which extends to chapter 55. | 46r–95ra |
| 14. | Bede, *Epistola ad Wicthedum presbiterum.*[10] | 95ra–97va |
| 15. | Bede, *De temporum ratione* (continued). | 97va–125rb |
| 16. | Bede, *De natura rerum* with marginal and interlinear glosses.[11] | 125rb–131vb |
| 17. | Bede, *De temporibus*, §§ i–xv.[12] | 131vb–134va7 |
| 18. | Computistical text, beginning *Decennouenalis cycli fir-. . .* | 134va8–vb7 |
| 19. | Computistical text beginning *Unciarum quoque diuisionem nosse que non minus temporibus rebus ue aliis quam nummis est apta computandis.*[13] | 134vb8–135r |
| 20. | Dionysius Exiguus, computistical letter addressed to Bishop Petronius.[14] | 136r–138ra |

[8] All of the verse entries but one are printed as "The Metrical Calendar of Winchcombe," in Lapidge, "A Metrical Calendar," 383–86. The omitted entry is that under 7 August for the end of summer and the beginning of autumn: "Augusti solitus post estatem redit ortus."

[9] See Byrhtferth, *Enchiridion*, 419 (no. 25).

[10] Ed. Charles W. Jones, CCSL 123C (Turnhout: Brepols, 1980), 635–42.

[11] Ed. Charles W. Jones and Frances Lipp, CCSL 123A (Turnhout: Brepols, 1975), 189–234. Charles W. Jones, "Manuscripts of Bede's *De Natura Rerum*," *Isis* 37 (1937): 430–40, at 439–40, recovers and prints the text of one marginal annotation (from fols. 130v–131r) using MS. London, B.L., Egerton 3088, fol. 75r, the thirteenth-century computus of Dore Abbey. Jones recognised that Egerton 3088 was closely related to T, but the exact nature of that relationship needs further investigation.

[12] Ed. Charles W. Jones, CCSL 123C, 585–600.

[13] The text is akin to Bede, *De temporum ratione*, § 4, and the text edited as *De ratione unciarum* in *PL* 90.699–702, but with a different ending. See Jones, *BP*, 55.

[14] Ed. Bruno Krusch, *Studien zur christlich-mittelalterlichen Chronologie: die Entstehung unserer heutigen Zeitrechnung* (Berlin: Published by W. de Gruyter for Akademie der Wissenschaften, 1938), 63–67.

| | | |
|---|---|---|
| 21. | Dionysius Exiguus, computistical letter addressed to Boniface and Bonus.[15] | 138rb–140ra |
| 22. | Abbo of Fleury, *De differentia circuli et sphere.*[16] | 140ra–142vb5 |
| 23. | Five lines of verse, beginning *Sexies mxxix sunt vi$^{m}$clxxiii*, ending *Duodecies dxiiii sunt clxviii.* | 142vb6–10 |
| 24. | Map of Jerusalem. | 143r |
| 25. | Helperic of Grandval, *De computo.*[17] | 144r–161ra |
| 26. | Note on Jerusalem. | 161rb |
| 27. | Robert de Losinga, *Excerptio de chronica Mariani.* | 162r–176ra |
| 28. | Walcher of Great Malvern, *De lunationibus.* | 176rb–178v |
| 29. | Abbo of Fleury, *Computus*, incorporating (180r) a set of acrostic verses.[18] | 179r–180r |
| 30. | Computistical table. | 181r |
| 31. | Geographical compendium (imperfect), beginning *Maiores nostri orbem totius terre occeani limbo circumseptum triquadrum statuere.* | 182r–183v |

As this contents list shows, T is a computistical manual of the classic type:[19] at its core lie copies of Bede's manuals on time-keeping, around which have been amassed various diagrams and auxiliary texts, many of which connect T with the computistical tradition associated with Abbo of Fleury and Byrhtferth of Ramsey.[20] Items 2, 4–6, 8–11, and 29 in this list are related, for example, to texts which Byrhtferth is thought to have included in the computistical collection which he assembled between 988 and 996.[21] It needs to be stressed, however, that these texts were edited and modified in the process of producing the book. The three tables relating to the Great Paschal Cycle (item 4) seem, for example, to represent an attempt to provide a Marianan version of their Byrhtferthian counterparts in St John's 17 (fols. 30r–31v). Their Marianan chronological apparatus is

15 Ed. Krusch, *Studien zur christlich-mittelalterlichen Chronologie*, 82–86.

16 Ed. Ron B. Thomson, "Two Astronomical Tractates of Abbo of Fleury," in *The Light of Nature: Essays in the History and Philosophy of Science presented to A. C. Crombie*, ed. John D. North and J. J. Roche (Dordrecht: M. Nijhoff, 1985), 113–33, at 120–33.

17 *PL* 137.13–48.

18 *PL* 90.729–730 (acrostic verses only). See Jones, *BP*, 60–61.

19 On the various types of computus MS, see chap. 1, § d, above and the works cited there.

20 It has been shown, for example, that T's version of Helperic derives from the edition of the text which Abbo of Fleury brought to Ramsey in 987–988: see Patrick McGurk, "*Computus Helperici:* Its Transmission in England in the Eleventh and Twelfth Centuries," *Medium Ævum* 43 (1974): 1–5; A. Van de Vyver, "Les œuvres inédites d'Abbon de Fleury," *Revue Bénédictine* 47 (1935): 125–69, at 147–49.

21 They are identified and discussed in the appendix to Byrhtferth, *Enchiridion*, 373–427, where they are listed as nos. 53, 32, 37, 38 + 6 (items h and i), 15, 25, 5, 6 (items a, c, d, f, and h), and 23. For the dating, see Byrhtferth, *Enchiridion*, xxv–xxvi.

certainly their most distinctive feature.[22] The calendar (item 8) also seems to represent an overhaul of the Byrhtferthian alternative in St John's 17 (fols. 16r–21v). It is similar in conception and design, but almost every element shows signs of "revision" (or "deviation"):[23] both calendars use an Abbonian computistical apparatus, but they differ in their choice of letter- and numerical-series; both include in the feast-area a large number of entries in verse—there are 128 in the Thorney text as opposed to 114 in its Winchcombe counterpart—but these entries differ in their metres, in the set of saints they choose to celebrate, and in what they have to say about them;[24] both calendars are surrounded by a dense array of decorative verses and explanatory texts, but whilst they show some parallels they also differ over many points of detail such as the number of hours, points, minutes, and moments in each month. T's calendar is clearly the product of much creative editing.[25] This much is also clear from the attention it gives to the feasts of Winchcombe's patrons, the Virgin Mary and the royal martyr St Kenelm.[26]

---

[22] They share many of the same explanatory notes as the Thorney manuscript. Cf. Byrhtferth, *Enchiridion*, 421 (no. 32); Hart, *Learning and Culture*, 2:326–28; Jones, *BP*, 59–64.

[23] Lapidge and Baker discuss the affinities between the two calendars in Byrhtferth, *Enchiridion*, 390–91, but the differences are greater than they admit. It is not merely a case of T "drop[ping] some of the computistical notes" found in MS. St John's 17: there is, for example, only one month (March) where the notes at the foot of each page in T (fol. 36r) might have been wholly derived from those found in MS. St John's 17 (cf. Byrhtferth, *Enchiridion*, 398, lines 233–235, 242–244). Most of these notes seem to derive from other sources.

[24] For the Thorney version, see Byrhtferth, *Enchiridion*, 391–416. The entries in verse are also printed as "The Metrical Calendar of Ramsey," in Lapidge, "A Metrical Calendar," 380–83. Lapidge (377) points out that the verses in T employ leonine hexameters with bisyllabic rhyme, a form which was not used in England before the early twelfth century. Cf. Hart, *Learning and Culture*, 2:350–51.

[25] Elzbieta Temple, "The Calendar of the Douce Psalter," *Bodleian Library Record* 12 (1985–1988): 13–38, at 23–24, may well be right when she argues that another layer of material may have come from Mont-St-Michel. Arno Borst sees connections with, besides St John's 17, the Worcester calendar in MS. Cambridge, Corpus Christi College, 391, 3–14, and the Le Mans calendar, which also dates from the beginning of the twelfth century, in MS. Paris, B.n.F., lat. 13013, fols. 24r–26v (*Die karolingische Reichskalender und seine Überlieferung bis ins 12. Jahrhundert*, ed. Arno Borst, MGH Libri Memoriales 2, 3 vols. [Hannover: Hahn, 2001], 1:282–83, 290, 294–95 and 297–99). The present author has in hand an edition and study of the Winchcombe Calendars. See also chap. 5, § a, below.

[26] Kenelm's natal feast (17 June) is marked out by a single line of verse in capitals, and it is also given its octave (24 June). Four feasts of the Virgin are marked out with lines of verse in capitals: that is, the Annunciation (25 March, here given as *Conceptio Christi*), the Assumption (15 August), the Nativity with its octave (8 and 15 September), and the Immaculate Conception (8 December). But the last feast does not seem to have been

There can, indeed, be no doubt that the book as a whole was produced for the use of Winchcombe Abbey. There is no explicit *ex libris*, but many of the book's component parts display stylistic affinities with the various twelfth-century books that have been identified as having been produced for Winchcombe:[27]

1. Cambridge, U.L., Mm.3.31 (Bede, *In Cantica Canticorum*)[28]
2. Cambridge, U.L., Additional 3303 (19) (Jerome, *Epistulae*)
3. Dublin, Trinity College, 53 (New Testament, Psalter)[29]
4. Hereford, Cathedral Library, P.VIII.4 (Augustine, *Epistulae*)[30]
5. Hereford, Cathedral Library, P.IX.5 (Augustine, *In Euangelium Ioannis*)[31]
6. London, B.L., Royal 11.D.VIII (*Collectio Lanfranci*)[32]
7. Oxford, Bod.L., Douce 368 (Bede, *Historia Ecclesiastica*)
8. Oxford, Bod.L., Lat.th.d.46 (Augustine, *Soliloquia* and other tracts)[33]

---

actually celebrated at Winchcombe (see § b below). Some prominence is also given to the Translation of St Benedict (11 July), which is marked out by two lines of verse in capitals, and it is given its octave (18 July). This much might be put down to its connections with Ramsey, since that abbey was dedicated to St Benedict, but the verses used for this feast in T differ from those found in St John's 17. They are best seen as evidence of Winchcombe's sense of Benedictine identity.

[27] The present list updates *MLGB*, 198–99 and *MLGBS*, 68.

[28] *A Catalogue of the Manuscripts Preserved in the Library of the University of Cambridge*, 5 vols. (Cambridge: Cambridge University Press, 1856–1867), 4:208–9; Max L. W. Laistner and H. H. King, *A Hand-List of Bede Manuscripts* (Ithaca: Cornell University Press, 1943), 67.

[29] Colker, *TCD*, no. 53; Meehan, "MSS of James Ussher," esp. 102, 106, 107, with plates 68 and 71; Heimann, "Dublin, Trinity College, MS 53," 86–109; Kauffmann, *Romanesque Manuscripts*, 86–87.

[30] Mynors and Thomson, *Hereford Cathedral Library*, 115.

[31] Mynors and Thomson, *Hereford Cathedral Library*, 123–24.

[32] Gullick, "Manuscripts of the *Collectio Lanfranci*," 112–14; Rodney M. Thomson, "Books and Learning at Gloucester Abbey in the Twelfth and Thirteenth Centuries," in *Books and Collectors 1200–1700: Essays Presented to Andrew Watson*, ed. James P. Carley and Colin G. C. Tite (London: British Library, 1997), 3–26, at 19. It appears that MS. Royal 11.D.VIII had migrated to Gloucester by s.xv, when the *ex libris* of that abbey was added to fol. 1v.

[33] *A Catalogue of Western Manuscripts and Miniatures . . . sold . . . by Sotheby, Parke, Bernet and Co., Tuesday 11 November 1979* (London: Sotheby's, 1979), 48–50. I am grateful to Peter Kidd for drawing this MS to my attention.

9. Oxford, Bod.L., Rawlinson C.435 + Auckland, Public Library, G.132 (Gregory the Great, *Moralia in Iob*)[34]

10. Oxford, Jesus College, 102 (Augustine, *Enarrationes in Psalmos LI–C*)[35]

11. San Marino, Huntington Library, 52435 (Ambrosiaster, *Commentarius in XIII epistulas Paulinas*)[36]

12. Valenciennes, Bibliothèque municipale, 116 (Winchcombe Breviary)[37]

Several of these manuscripts are explicitly identified as the property of Winchcombe by a series of *ex libris* labels. These labels were produced when the abbey's books were rebound in the late fifteenth century by the so-called fish-tail binder, and on several the labels may have gone but nail-holes matching those of the horn covers used to hold them in place still remain.[38] The shared characteristics of this core group provide a basis for attributing other books to the abbey's collection. In many of these volumes, for example, the major initials have been executed by an artist (or artists) with a relatively distinctive approach. The traits of his work have been defined as follows:[39]

---

[34] Margaret M. Manion, Vera F. Hines, and Christopher de Hamel, *Medieval and Renaissance Manuscripts in New Zealand Collections* (Melbourne: Thames and Hudson, 1989), no. 12.

[35] Henry O. Coxe, *Catalogus codicum MSS. qui in collegiis aulisque Oxoniensibus hodie adservantur*, 2 pts. (Oxford: e Typographeo academico, 1852), 2:35; Alexander and Temple, *Illuminated MSS in Oxford*, 7 (no. 32).

[36] C. W. Dutschke, *Guide to Medieval and Renaissance Manuscripts in the Huntington Library*, 2 vols. (San Marino, CA: Huntington Library, 1989), 2:773–75. There are useful plates of the illuminations in *The Estelle Doheny Collection from the Edward Lawrence Doheny Memorial Library, St. John's Seminary, Camarillo, California Sold on Behalf of the Archdiocese of Los Angeles*, 7 vols. (New York: Christie, Manson and Woods, 1987–1989), 2:28–31.

[37] Victor Leroquais, *Les bréviaires manuscrits des bibliothèques publiques de France*, 5 vols. and plates (Paris: Mâcon, Protat frères, 1934), 4:283–85 (no. 883).

[38] MS. Oxford Lat.th.d.46 offers a well-preserved example of this binding with the horn cover and label in their proper positions on the back cover. In the cases of Trinity 53 and Douce 368, the labels have been removed and pasted inside their covers. Hereford P.IX.5, Huntingdon 52435, and Jesus 102 retain fifteenth-century bindings with nail-holes matching the points where the horn cover was fixed in place on Lat.th.d.46.

[39] Heimann, "Dublin, Trinity College, MS 53," 108. Heimann avoids dating these initials, opting simply to note their likeness to those found in other MSS which have been dated to the 1130s. For another attempt to define the style, see Rodney M. Thomson, "Minor Manuscript-Decoration from the West of England in the Twelfth Century", in *Reading Texts and Images: Essays on Medieval and Renaissance Art and Patronage in Honour of Margaret M. Manion*, ed. Bernard J. Muir (Exeter: Exeter University Press, 2002), 19–34, at 25 (Style 5). Thomson also makes important comments about secondary initials in these MSS: see Thomson, "Minor Manuscript-Decoration," 25–26 (Style 6).

> A certain linear quality, a smooth flow of movement, a preference for rounded contours and an aversion to spiky forms, a loose filling of the body of the initials, all these impart a special flavour which makes it possible to recognise the products of this workshop. The ever-recurring leaves twisting round slender stems seem here less formalized, imbued with more vigorous sap. The same applies to the large flowers which every school incorporates into its design at this time. They too seem a little less mechanically contrived, and the sparsely filled space in conjunction with a decidedly gay colour scheme—light blue grounds to offset bright green and red drawings—help to bestow a certain rhythmic elegance. New combinations of large flowers, scalloped leaves, lion masks, winged dragons, occasional birds and human profiles are attempted. Leaves or little side shoots often grow out of a kind of pouch made up of three concentric pads. There is a fair amount of hatching on the insides of leaves. The outside of foliage is quite often decorated with tiny regular dots either all over or within a decorative band. Even though most of these features may be found on initials from other centres, in accumulation they help to characterise this particular group.

Tiberius E.IV has two initials of this type, one for the preface and one for the opening chapter of Bede's *De temporum ratione* (fols. 46r, 47r).[40] There are many indications, in short, that T was made *for* and probably *at* Winchcombe.

This much is clear. Uncertainty begins to arise, however, when we turn to the dating of the book and the question of how it was put together, for its contents are the work of a large number of scribes who were active from the middle of the twelfth century through to the fourteenth century. The following table lists the scribes responsible for the components of the book which are relevant to the present study. It excludes those who were responsible for copying the various letters and bulls on fols. 27v17–29va, 30va, 43r–45v and those who made additions so brief that they are not easily grouped or analysed. The scribes are listed according to the order in which they make their appearance in the book as presently constructed:[41]

[40] Other Winchcombe MSS with initials of this kind include Cambridge Mm.3.31, fol. 1r; Trinity 53, fols. 1r, 7v, 24v, 36r, 54v, 55r, 69r, 88r, 151r, 164r, 178v; Hereford P.VIII.4, fol. 1v; Royal 11 D. VIII, fol. 1r; Douce 368, fols. 1r, 2r, 80r; Oxford Lat. th.d.46, fol. 1r. It should be noted that initials by the same artist(s) have also been identified in Oxford, Bod.L., MS. Bodley 269, fol. iiiv, a book which was at Eynsham by ca. 1300 (see Thomson, "Minor Manuscript-Decoration," 25), and in Oxford, St John's College, MS. 96, a book which was given to Pershore in the thirteenth century (see Alexander and Temple, *Illuminated MSS in Oxford*, 12 [no. 84]). Both may have been produced at or for Winchcombe.

[41] The following table is based on the analysis of Julian Harrison, but the dating and numbering of the scribes have been modified in keeping with the conventions of the present volume.

| | | |
|---|---|---|
| $T^{1}$ | *Winchcombe Chronicle* 1–1122.1 (fols. 1r–14rb11, 15r–22v8); calendar and computistical texts, diagrams and tables (29vb–30r, 30vb–42r); diagrams (62r, 64r–68r, 69r, 71r, 73v–74r, 75v, 77r, 141r–v, 176r, 180r, ?181r); glosses *uel inuestigatione*, *succurrente*, *locuturi* (47rb); marginalia (?49v, 98v, 126r, 129r, 130r, 133r); verse beginning *Sexies mxxix sunt vi*$^{m}$*clxxiii* (142vb6–10).[42] | s.xii$^{\text{med}}$ |
| $T^{2}$ | Marginalia in the *Winchcombe Chronicle*, 680.2 (11r). | s.xii$^{2}$ |
| $T^{3}$ | Marginalia and other additions in the *Winchcombe Chronicle*, 738.2, 966, 1046, 1047, 1049.2, 1059, 1066.2, 1074.3, 1077, 1099.2, 1107.2, 1108.3, 1117.2, 1128.2, 1136.2, 1147.2 (12r, 17v, 19r–20r, 21r–23v). | s.xiii$^{\text{med}}$ |
| $T^{4}$ | Marginalia in the *Winchcombe Chronicle*, 787.2 and 798, relating to the foundation of Winchcombe Abbey (13r). | s.xii/xiii |
| $T^{5}$ | Addition to the *Winchcombe Chronicle*, 795.4 (13r23–28); annotation of map of Jerusalem (143r). | s.xii$^{2}$ |
| $T^{6}$ | Extension of the *Winchcombe Chronicle*, 811.4–5 (14rb12–40). | s.xii$^{\text{med}}$ |
| $T^{7}$ | Extension of the *Winchcombe Chronicle*, 811.5 (14rb41–49). | s.xii$^{\text{med}}$ |
| $T^{8}$ | Extension of the *Winchcombe Chronicle*, 811.5–6 (14va1–vb40). | s.xii$^{2}$ |
| $T^{9}$ | Extension of the *Winchcombe Chronicle*, 811.6 (14vb41–47). | s.xii$^{2}$ |
| $T^{10}$ | Marginalia in the *Winchcombe Chronicle*, 857.3–6 (15v). | s.xii$^{\text{med}}$ |
| $T^{11}$ | *Winchcombe Chronicle* 1122.2 (22v9). | ?s.xii$^{2}$ |
| $T^{12}$ | *Winchcombe Chronicle* 1122.3–1172.2 (22v10–25v). | s.xii$^{2}$ |
| $T^{13}$ | Marginalia in the *Winchcombe Chronicle*, 1165.4 (25r). | s.xii$^{\text{ex}}$ |
| $T^{14}$ | *Winchcombe Chronicle* 1172.2–1181.7 (26r–27v16). | s.xii$^{\text{ex}}$ |
| $T^{15}$ | Bede, *De temporum ratione* and associated texts (46r–135r, 136r–142v, 144r–161ra, 162r–180r); glosses in the same part of the manuscript; annotation of diagrams (?71r, 72r). | s.xii$^{1}$ |
| $T^{16}$ | Marginalia in the computus (47v, 87r, 100r, 130v–131r). | s.xii$^{2}$ |
| $T^{17}$ | Note relating to Jerusalem (161rb). | s.xii$^{2}$ |
| $T^{18}$ | Geographical compendium (182r–183v). | s.xii$^{\text{ex}}$ |

It should be noted that the fundamental components of the book are largely the work of two scribes, $T^{1}$ and $T^{15}$. The former was responsible for the first phase of the chronicle, for many of the tables, and for the calendar (for items 2–12), while the latter was responsible for the majority of the computistical commentaries or manuals in the manuscript (for items 13–23, 25, and 27–29). It seems likely that these scribes were collaborators—that they were working together to produce a large, deluxe computus, one which would, in its undamaged state, have rivalled the Thorney Computus as a statement of Winchcombe's dedication to the discipline. This inference would certainly be helpful to the present study's argument that the production of breviate world chronicles was driven by the need to equip novices with a thorough understanding of time and its workings. But it has to

[42] For reproductions of fol. 30r, see Kühnel, *The End of Time*, pl. 94; Edson, "World Maps and Easter Tables," fig. 1; and Bober, "An Illustrated Medieval School Book," fig. 6.

be admitted that the data also permits an alternative explanation — namely, that the manuals and satellite tracts copied by $T^{15}$ were meant to form a book in their own right, while the annals, the calendar, and the satellite texts associated with scribe $T^{1}$ were added as afterthoughts.[43] There are considerable discrepancies in the way in which the two sections of the manuscript are laid out.[44] It is true that $T^{1}$ appears to have been responsible for adding many of the diagrams to the section copied by $T^{15}$;[45] but in the twelfth century decoration was often added to manuscripts some time after their texts were copied. It is often the case, indeed, that monasteries never got around to completing the illuminated initials, and this is true of T itself, for the space which was left at the beginning of the chronicle for the insertion of a large initial remains unfilled (fol. 1ra).[46] It is as though deluxe manuscripts of this kind were long-term projects to be continued as and when time and resources permitted. It might well have been possible to resolve this question had the evidence of earlier bindings not been destroyed by the Cottonian fire and the restoration of the book; but in the absence of such evidence some doubt will continue to hang over whether it was first conceived as a single volume.

There is no doubt, however, that folios 1–45 — the leaves which house the chronicle together with its late twelfth-century continuation and the computistical tables copied by $T^{1}$ — were bound together by the end of the thirteenth century, for at that time the blank leaves and spaces within these gatherings were used to house various letters and documents. These items may be listed as follows:[47]

---

[43] It is this uncertainty which leads Gameson, *Manuscripts*, nos. 408–409, to divide the manuscript into two parts.

[44] Harrison reports, for example, that the pages where the text has been copied by $T^{1}$ are usually ruled for 36–42 lines per page compared to the 33 lines on those where the text is the work of $T^{15}$. The main text area on the former pages is approximately 245–256 × 167–193 mm; that of the latter is 218–230 × 148–165 mm. These dimensions make it a somewhat smaller volume than the other known Winchcombe books, since most have a text area measuring some 300 × 190 (Ker, *English Manuscripts*, 40–41, 50n and pls. 24–25), but it is similar in size to St John's 17.

[45] $T^{1}$'s diagrams on fol. 62r (a chart tracing the course of the moon through the constellations of the zodiac) and fol. 75v (a zonal map based on Macrobius) are reproduced by Bober, "An Illustrated Medieval School-Book," fig. 23, and Edson, "World Maps and Easter-Tables," fig. 3.

[46] MS. Dublin, Trinity College, 53 is another Winchcombe MS. the decoration of which remains incomplete: the initial for the opening of Matthew's Gospel has not been attempted (fol. 6vb); those for Mark (24v), Luke (36r), and John (54r) have been started but remain unfinished.

[47] Some other late additions also appear on fols. 184r–187r, but these add nothing to the present discussion.

| | | |
|---|---|---|
| 1. | Bull of Pope Boniface VIII (1295–1303), Rome, 26 February 1296.[48] | 27v17–28r8 |
| 2. | Bull of Pope Boniface VIII, Rome, 21 April 1296. | 28r9–14 |
| 3. | Endorsement of the former bull, Paris, 10 October 1296. | 28r14–20 |
| 4. | Letter of Robert Winchelsey, archbishop of Canterbury (1294–1313), forwarding the former bull for publication, Croydon, 10 December 1296.[49] | 28r20–24 |
| 5. | Letter of King Edward I (1272–1307), 22 December 1300. | 28r24–30 |
| 6. | Award of Norham, 5–6 June 1291 (attested by William March, Treasurer, 9 July 1291), addressed to the abbot and convent of Winchcombe.[50] | 28v |
| 7. | Memorandum that Edward I adjudged the kingdom of Scotland to John Balliol, November 1292. | 29r1–8 |
| 8. | Bull of Pope Boniface VIII to Edward I, concerning the peace with the king of France, Lateran Palace, 19 February 1295.[51] | 29r9–32 |
| 9. | Letter of Edward I to the abbot of Winchcombe, expelling the alien religious, Westminster, 17 November 1295. | 29r33–48 |
| 10. | Abdication of John, king of Scots (1292–1296), to Edward I, Brechin, 10 July 1296 (French).[52] | 29va1–31 |
| 11. | Letter of Queen Margaret to the abbot of Winchcombe, announcing the birth of Thomas of Brotherton, 1 June 1300. | 29va32–39 |
| 12. | Account of how Henry of Lancaster did homage to King Edward II (1307–1327) at Berwick for the earldoms of Lancaster, Leicester, Derby (de Ferrers), Lincoln, and Salisbury, following the death of Henry de Lacy, earl of Lincoln (5 February 1311), dated 1310. | 30va |
| 13. | Account of the foundation of Gloucester College, Oxford, by a Benedictine General Chapter at Abingdon, 11 July 1290, confirmed at Salisbury, 11 September 1291.[53] | 43r–44r32 |

[48] Ed. David Wilkins, *Concilia magnae Britanniae et Hiberniae, a synodo Verolamiensi A.D. CCCCXLVI ad Londiniensem A.D. MDCCXVII*, 4 vols. (London: R. Gosling, 1737), 2:223.

[49] Ed. William W. Capes, *Registrum Ricardi de Swinfield, episcopi Herefordiensis, A.D. MCCLXXXIII–MCCCXVII*, Canterbury and York Series 6 (London: Wilson and Phillips, 1909), 342–43.

[50] Ed. Edward L. G. Stones and Grant G. Simpson, *Edward I and the Throne of Scotland, 1290–1296*, 2 vols. (Oxford: Oxford University Press, 1978), 2:120, 68, 74.

[51] Bartholomaeus de Cotton, *Historia Anglicana (A.D. 449–1298), necnon ejusdem liber de archiepiscopis et episcopis Angliæ*, ed. Henry R. Luard, RS 16 (London: Longman, 1859), 280–81. Cf. Jane E. Sayers, *Original Papal Documents in England and Wales from the Accession of Pope Innocent III to the Death of Pope Benedict XI (1198–1304)* (Oxford: Oxford University Press, 1999), no. 981.

[52] Ed. Edward L. G. Stones, *Anglo-Scottish Relations, 1174–1328: Some Selected Documents* (London: Nelson, 1965), 73–74 (no. 24).

[53] Ed. William A. Pantin, *Documents Illustrating the Activities of the General and Provincial Chapters of the English Black Monks 1215–1540*, Camden Society, 3rd ser., 45 (London: Royal Historical Society, 1931), 129–31, with Clement Reyner, *Apostolatus*

14. Account of the inception of William de Brok, monk of Gloucester Abbey, as a master of theology (5 June 1298).[54] 44r33–37
15. Papal bull concerning the clergy in France (undated). 44v–45r7
16. Letter of Archbishop Boniface of Canterbury (1245–1270), addressed to the Holy Church, concerning the vacancy in the see of Worcester (28 July 1268). 45r8–37
17. Letter of Archbishop Robert Winchelsey of Canterbury (1294–1313), addressed to the prior of Worcester, concerning the vacancy in the see of Worcester (13 March 1301/2). 45v1–8
18. Decree of Archbishop Robert Winchelsey of Canterbury, addressed to the vicar of the bishop of Worcester, concerning the archbishop of York (7 May 1309). 45v9–26

These documents are copied by a number of different hands and they do not conform to exact chronological order, but in as much as they show that the first forty-five folios of the book were being exploited as a register for a relatively brief period they help to prove that they were bound together at the time when they were inserted—that is, that *Winchcombe* was then bound with some, if perhaps not all, of the book's computistical components.

The palaeographical data have, more importantly, implications for our understanding of the development of the chronicle itself. They imply that *Winchcombe* was produced mainly in two phases, the first taking its coverage down to 1122, the second extending it until at least 1172 if not all the way to 1181.[55] It is clear, to begin with, that the chronicle was mostly the work of three scribes: the first ($T^1$) produced and corrected the text from the Incarnation to the first item

*Benedictinorum in Anglia* (Douai: Laurence Kellam, 1626), appendix 2, 54–57. Gloucester College was a collective enterprise started by the great Benedictine houses of the central and western parts of the province of Canterbury. Winchcombe participated in the foundation and owned rooms within its walls.

54 William de Brok was the first Benedictine to gain the degree of doctor in theology and his inception was attended by numerous Benedictine priors and monks. The present account is similar to that in *Cart. Gloc.*, 1:34–35, the account which is usually cited, but there are significant differences. It dates the inception to 5 June 1298 (*Anno domini m°cc° nonagesimo octauo, nonas Iunii, quinta uidelicet feria post festum Sancte Trinitatis . . .*), and it lists the abbots present as those of Gloucester, Abingdon, Eynsham, Winchcombe (*de Wynch.*), and Reading. The Gloucester account dates the inception to 12 June (*in crastino sancti Barnabæ*), and lists the abbots present as those of Westminster, Reading, Abingdon, Evesham, and Malmesbury. Cf. Alfred B. Emden, *A Biographical Register of the University of Oxford to A.D. 1500*, 3 vols. (Oxford: Clarendon Press, 1957–1959), 1:272.

55 When it is necessary to distinguish these phases they will be cited as *Winchcombe*[1] and *Winchcombe*[2] respectively.

under 1122,[56] whilst the second and third (T[12] and T[14]) entered the continuation which begins with the third item under that year. The two major contributions are separated by a brief note entered in a small hand (T[11]):

> Obiit domnus Girmundus abbas Wincelcumbensis, uir sincere religionis et ecclesie sue ditator egregius, iiii id' Iunii. Huic successit Godefridus eiusdem loci prior uenerandus.

As can be seen from plate III, this note sits in the middle of the annal: it is preceded by the final item of the first phase and a curious one-line gap, and is followed on the next line by the first item of the continuation, the obit for Archbishop Ralph (1122.3).[57] Further evidence for the existence of a break at this point is provided by the cessation of certain practices with this annal. A series of interlinear glosses ends at this point,[58] and there is a shift in the pattern of decoration, from the use of inks of diverse colours for the minor initials at the start of each annal to a much less time-consuming approach.[59] There is also, as will be explained in detail below, a fundamental change in textual strategy at this point: the annals down to 1122.1 represent an expanded version of the common root, those from 1122.3 onwards seem to have been largely derived from a single source produced outside the abbey—that is, a late twelfth-century Gloucester chronicle.

---

[56] The break was identified in Harrison, "New Discoveries," 26–27. See also Gullick, "Manuscripts of the *Collectio Lanfranci*," 113 and n. 44; Gameson, *Manuscripts*, no. 408.

[57] It is difficult to say when this brief note might have been added to the text. Given that no further annals were added by this scribe, it is tempting to suggest that he was at work during the reign of Girmund's successor Abbot Godfrey—that is, between 1122 and 6 March 1137 (see *Heads I*, 79). But the likelihood that the first phase was itself executed after 1137 makes that unlikely, and there are many different scenarios that might explain its presence in the text. It could, for example, have been added after the long continuation which follows as part of an attempt to repair an omission. This much is suggested by the way in which the scribe has made an effort to get the entire note onto a single line (fol. 22v9) with the words *eiusdem loci prior uenerandus* wrapping back around at its end. It might also have been the first of a number of historical notes that were added to the page, only for the rest of them to be removed when the continuation was added, since they would have clashed with its contents. The evidence is certainly ambiguous.

[58] The series begins with *Winchcombe* 17; the final items containing these glosses are *Winchcombe* 1036, 1052.2, 1086.2, 1087, 1093.1, 1093.3, 1100.2, 1100.3, 1105, 1107.1, 1108.2, 1109.1, 1114, 1115.2, 1118, 1121.

[59] In the first phase, these capitals are mainly in red or green, with purple and even less often blue being used in one portion alone (fols. 9r–17v). Brown, the ink of the text itself, is also used throughout. After the shift of hands under 1122, a different shade of red is used for 1123–1136; black is then used continuously as far as T[14]'s contribution, in which there are a few more red initials (s.aa. 1175, 1177, 1179, 1181).

The other major change of hand, that which takes place under 1172, is much more ambiguous. There is a continuity of textual strategy across this break which strongly suggests that the two scribes responsible for annals from 1122.3 to 1181.7 were collaborators, and the break itself also suggests this at first sight, for T[12]'s contribution ends at the foot of folio 25v in the middle of a sentence which T[14] seems to complete at the top of folio 26r. The problem, however, is that the sentence is incoherent, since the clause in question lacks the main verb which it requires. A corrector made an attempt to improve the sense by adding the syllable *ti* so as to render the connecting word as *adpe-ti-cionem*, but this by no means resolves all of the problems.[60] This is not, furthermore, the only discontinuity at this point. T[12]'s hand is, for example, different in aspect from that of T[14], which is somewhat more Gothic and angular in appearance, having a backward lean.[61] The layout also changes. Folio 25v is the last page, for example, on which vertical lines in red marked off the chronological apparatus from the main text area.[62] It could be argued that the changes in layout are of no consequence, since the ruling on folios 23 to 25 may have been executed when the first phase was produced and folio 26 may represent the point where it first became necessary to add new leaves in order to accommodate the continuation. But the way in which these discontinuities coincide with one another invites doubt as to whether T[12] and T[14] were collaborators. The probability that they were depends in the final analysis on the continuities in bias and textual affinity which bridge this break in the palaeography of the manuscript.

## (b) The Dating of the First Phase, *Winchcombe*[1]

In their efforts to maximise the significance of palaeographical evidence, some scholars have taken the changes of hand under 1122 as evidence that the first phase of the chronicle was executed in or soon after that year.[63] Some have even made the case for a much earlier date.[64] There is no denying that T[1]'s hand is of a type often found of the first half of the twelfth century: it is a well-rounded,

[60] See further the textual notes on *Winchcombe* 1172.2 below.

[61] See the reproduction of fol. 27r in Andrew G. Watson, *A Catalogue of Dated and Datable Manuscripts, c. 435–1600, in Oxford Libraries*, 2 vols. (Oxford: Clarendon Press, 1984), plate 106.

[62] Compare plates III and IV below.

[63] E.g. Gameson, *Manuscripts*, no. 408, who dates the first phase "s.xii$^{1-2/4}$ (?shortly after 1122)."

[64] Gullick, "Manuscripts of the *Collectio Lanfranci*," 113, n. 44, suggests that year-by-year annalistic activity began in 1106 on the grounds that the space left for a minor capital has been left unfilled at this point! There are many places, however, where T[1] has left a capital unfilled (e.g. *Winchcombe* 862, 1017, 1022, 1038, 1053, 1055, 1058, 1061,

Anglo-Norman script; but the reason why this scribe's contribution terminates with the opening item under 1122 is most likely to have been that the common root came to an end at this point rather than because he was writing in that year. The first phase of *Coventry* also concludes with this notice, and 1122–1123 was a significant *terminus* for the likely author of the root, John of Worcester, since his principal source for the first half of Henry I's reign, Eadmer's *Historia novorum*, also came to an end in 1122—with the death of Archbishop Ralph on 19 or 20 October of that year. *Chronicula*[1] ends in like fashion with the events of early 1123, but there are in its case good grounds for thinking that it was not composed before the late 1130s.[65] There is, moreover, clear evidence that T[1] was active well after 1122, for he was also responsible for copying a charter of King Stephen that was forged at Gloucester between 1146 and March 1148 (MS. London, B.L., Cotton Charters XVII.3).[66] That the first phase was copied after the late 1130s is also suggested by its use, as will be shown below, of John's "Papal Annals", a brief satellite text which was among the last of the works of this kind to be placed among the prelims to *Chronica chronicarum*. If, as seems almost certain, this source was composed in or perhaps after the late 1130s, then the first phase of *Winchcombe* cannot have been produced before that time.

For what it is worth (and that may not be very much), the abbey later claimed that *all* of its books were destroyed when its buildings were burnt down in 1149. A charter preserved in its thirteenth-century *Landboc* states that this fire "reduced the monastery to ashes along with all its caskets, vestments, books, charters, and all the buildings,"[67] and *Winchcombe* itself reports that the fire consumed

---

1064, 1066, 1071, 1075, 1118), so many that this omission cannot be considered a significant indication of a shift in scribal practice.

[65] See chap. 2, §§ a and c, above.

[66] *EGC*, no. 44. Part of the sheet is reproduced as plate II. The charter is dated to 1138, but it confirms four grants made to Gloucester between 1141 and 1146. The scribe has appended to the text an *inspeximus* by Simon, bishop of Worcester (1125–1150), which is addressed to the archbishop of Canterbury *totius Anglie primatus*. Brooke, *CWB*, 61–64, 67–70, has argued that it was concocted on behalf of Abbot Gilbert Foliot in the winter of 1147/8, for the purpose of persuading Archbishop Theobald to confirm the four grants. See also *RRAN*, 3: no. 344n. It is to Julian Harrison that we owe the identification of T[1] as the scribe of the charter. There have been various attempts to connect this same scribe with other manuscripts (e.g. MS. Cambridge, U.L., Kk.3.28), but these need not detain us, since they do not affect the dating of Tiberius E.IV. Cf. *The Original* Acta *of St. Peter's Abbey, Gloucester c.1122 to 1263*, ed. Robert B. Patterson, Gloucestershire Record Series 11 (Gloucester: Bristol and Gloucestershire Archaeological Society, 1998), xxxii–xxxiii (scribe 1), and the works cited there; Thomson, "Books and Learning at Gloucester Abbey," esp. 6, 15–16.

[67] *Landboc*, 1:83: ". . . hinc ecclesie culmina vorax flamma consumpsit. Monasterio, itaque, cum scriniis, vestimentis, libris, et cartis, ac edificiis omnibus, in cinerem redactis, suprascripta cartula [Willelmi de Solers de capella de Potteslep] eodem incendio conflagravit."

the entire abbey.[68] The former claim must be an exaggeration, for it can be shown that some documents survived the fire: the foundation charter attributed to King Cenwulf (S 167) was, for example, almost certainly in existence before 1126, since William of Malmesbury consulted a document whose contents all but match those of the text presently preserved in *Winchcombe* itself.[69] The author of the former charter also had reason to exaggerate the scale of the disaster, for he brings the fire in as a way of explaining the loss of an earlier charter which would have provided written title for the abbey's rights over the chapel at Postlip. If, however, the abbey's book cupboard was among the furniture destroyed at this time, then that would help to explain why so many of the known Winchcombe manuscripts seem to belong to a sustained campaign of production which took place in the middle of the twelfth century. A fire of this magnitude may have necessitated the replacement of many items in the abbey's library, and $T^1$'s contributions to Tiberius E.IV might have been one product of such a campaign. This suggestion would imply a date in the early 1150s, but such a dating would not be at odds with the discovery that $T^1$ was responsible for producing a forged Gloucester charter in about 1147.

At this point one might object that $T^1$ made his contribution to Tiberius E.IV at an earlier date, for the calendar on folios 35r–40v has been dated to between

68 *Winchcombe* 1151.2. For the dating of the fire, see the commentary and § f in the present chapter.

69 See the commentary on *Winchcombe* 811.3 below. There is one authentic early ninth-century charter that might conceivably come from the Winchcombe archive — that is, MS. London, B.L., Cotton Charters VIII.39 (S 1861). It comprises a four-line strip from a charter in which, according to its thirteenth-century endorsement on the reverse side, King Cenwulf granted Aldington near Evesham to a certain Wulfled. The surviving clauses, imperfect though they are, show that the king reserved, besides the three common dues and the right to try evil-doers on the third occasion of their arrest, a rent of four oxen and four jars of honey to the monastery *quæ sita est æt Wincelcumbe* (for this interpretation, see Finberg, *ECWM*, 98, 229; Levison, *EC*, 249, n. 1). The reservation of a rent will have given Winchcombe a reason for preserving a copy in its archive, but the estate at Aldington later passed into the possession of Evesham (see Domesday, 1.175d), and it will have been even more important for that abbey to preserve a copy in its archive. It seems likely that it was one of Wulfled's descendants who was responsible for granting the estate to Evesham, and it will have been important for the abbey to have had a record of what services were due from the estate. That the charter was recycled as binding material may be explained, furthermore, by the fabrication of S 80, a charter in which Evesham claimed that they had received this estate amid various royal benefactions which had accompanied the foundation of the abbey in 709. Once this manifest forgery had won acceptance, S 1861 will have become obsolete. The fragment is reproduced and transcribed in *Facsimiles of Ancient Charters in the British Museum*, ed. Edward A. Bond, 4 vols. (London: British Museum, 1873–1878), 4, no. 6.

1126 and 1138.[70] But the calendar does not represent an obstacle to a later dating, for the arguments for these *termini* are not secure. The supposed *terminus a quo* of 1126 depends on the presence of the feast of the Immaculate Conception (8 December), a feast whose adoption at the abbey has been dated to 1126 on the basis of an entry under that year in *Winchcombe* itself:

> Ipso anno primum cepit celebrari apud nos solennitas conceptionis sancte Marie.

The problem with this argument is that this entry belongs to a section of *Winchcombe* which appears to derive from a Gloucester source,[71] and there is indeed a slightly fuller version of this notice in another Gloucester chronicle, one which is also indebted to this source:

> Istius vero tempore coepit primum celebrari apud nos in Anglia solemnitas Conceptionis Beatæ Genitricis Mariæ.[72]

The presence of the words *in Anglia* clearly implies that this entry refers, not to the feast's adoption at Winchcombe, but to its wider dissemination in the English church. There are, moreover, grounds for thinking that the feast was not actually celebrated at Winchcombe, for it does not appear in the calendar of the abbey's breviary (Valenciennes 116, fols. 1r–6v), a manuscript datable to the mid-twelfth century. It needs to be remembered that whilst calendars in computus manuscripts typically tend towards an encyclopaedic record of feasts and anniversaries, the aim being to provide information about the practices of the church at large, those in liturgical books often confine themselves to recording the feasts that a given church actually observed. The feast was legitimised by a council which met in London in late September and early October of 1129;[73] but there was no attempt as yet to ensure that it was observed by every church. It may well have been too controversial for Winchcombe. The feast's presence in T's calendar is probably to be explained, furthermore, by the role which Ramsey seems to have played in its dissemination in England: the feast is recorded in a late twelfth-century liturgical calendar from that abbey (now MS. London, B.L., Cotton Galba E.X, fols. 2r–7v), and, according to a *miraculum* in circulation from the 1130s at the very latest, its observance had been introduced by Æthelsige, a former abbot of St

---

[70] Temple, "Calendar of the Douce Psalter," 24–26.

[71] See the present chapter, §§ d-e, below.

[72] *Cart. Gloc.*, 1:15.

[73] See *Chronicula*[2] 1129: "Inde in concilio apud Lundoniam congregato in presentia eiusdem regis Henrici ex auctoritate apostolica confirmata est festiuitas conceptionis sancte Dei genitricis Marie." This item is reproduced in *Winchcombe* 1129.2.

Augustine's who had custody of Ramsey from 1080 until 1087.[74] It follows that neither the entry in *Winchcombe* nor that in T's calendar can be taken as reliable evidence for the *terminus a quo* for T[1]'s work on the manuscript.

The alleged *terminus ad quem* of 1138 rests on the calendar's placement of an entry referring to the Transfiguration on 26 July as opposed to 6 August. The argument is that if the calendar had been copied after 1138, it would have specified the second date, for the abbey received in that year a Cluniac abbot (Robert, who ruled until 1152) and Cluny had adopted this date for the Transfiguration in 1132. The first problem with this argument is that it is by no means certain that Robert, who may have owed his appointment more to his kinship with the king rather than to his spiritual qualities,[75] would have insisted that the abbey follow the liturgical practices of his native congregation. Cluny was much admired, but it was not the only model of best practice, and the Transfiguration, a relatively novel festivity, was still far from being widely recognised as a legitimate observance in the English church.[76] The second problem is that the Transfiguration is not recorded in the calendar of the Winchcombe Breviary, implying again that the feast was not actually observed at the abbey. It is possible, indeed, that the line of verse in T (*Visio turbatis uirtusque patet deitatis*) does not actually refer to a feast at all, for this calendar has a number of entries that refer to events in the Gospel narrative which were not commemorated as formal liturgical festivities. It includes, for example, a notice for the Lord's flight to Egypt (7 February) and another for the resurrection of Lazarus (19 March).[77] If the entry as presented in the source-text was not familiar to the compiler or his readers as a regular liturgical observance, then the need to revise the placement of this entry might well

[74] Three twelfth-century versions of the story are printed in *Eadmeri monachi Cantuariensis tractatus de Conceptione sanctae Mariae . . . adiectis quibusdam documentis coaetaneis*, ed. Herbert Thurston and Thomas Slater (Freiburg: Herder, 1904). 88–92, 93–95, 96–98. On the origins of the feast of the Immaculate Conception and its hagiography, see Stephen J. P. Van Dijk, "The Origins of the Latin Feast of the Conception of the Blessed Virgin Mary," *Dublin Review* 118 (1954): 251–67, 428–42 (esp. 430–31), with Richard W. Southern, "The English Origins of the 'Miracles of the Virgin'," *Medieval and Renaissance Studies* 4 (1958): 176–216 (at 194–98). For Æthelsige's career and dates, see *Heads I*, 36, 62, 253.

[75] *JWCC* 1138 (3:240): "ut ferunt regis propinquus." On the wave of "Cluniac" appointments during Stephen's reign and their orchestration by Henry of Blois, bishop of Winchester (1129–1171), see David Crouch, *The Reign of King Stephen, 1135–54* (Harlow: Longman, 2000), 302–3.

[76] The Transfiguration celebrates the occasion in the Gospels when Christ took his disciples Peter, James, and John aside to a high place and was metamorphosed in their sight into a vision of radiance: see Matthew 17:1–6, Mark 9:1–8, Luke 9:28–36. On the introduction of the feast into England, see Richard W. Pfaff, *New Liturgical Feasts in Later Medieval England* (Oxford: Clarendon Press, 1970), 13–39.

[77] T, fols. 35r, 36r.

have been overlooked. It follows that the entry for the Transfiguration cannot be taken as a clue to the *terminus ad quem* for T[1]'s work on the manuscript, and since there is nothing in his other contributions to the manuscript to prevent them being dated to the 1140s or 1150s,[78] it seems best to conclude that the first phase of the chronicle was produced in or close to those decades.[79]

## (c) The Provenance of *Winchcombe*[1]

There is no reason to doubt, however, that the first phase was produced for Winchcombe Abbey. It is true that the abbey's own history is rather poorly reported in both the first phase and its continuation. It is not until 1093, for example, that an obit or succession of an abbot is recorded by the hand which produced the whole of the first phase (scribe T[1]): all the earlier obits are additions entered by later hands, mostly by scribe 6.[80] It is, moreover, the history of the church at Worcester which dominates the first phase and the history of St Peter's Abbey at Gloucester which bulks large in the second. But there are entries which provide indisputable evidence that the chronicle was produced for the consumption of Winchcombe Abbey. Foremost among these are the foundation documents under 811 and 818. They comprise a copy of a privilege attributed to Pope Leo III (795–816), a copy of the supposed foundation charter of King Cenwulf (796–821), and a copy of a privilege attributed to Pope Paschal I (817–824), and all three were inserted by T[1].[81] The chronicle also contains a number of annals celebrating the ancestry and achievements of the abbey's founder and the martyrdom of his son, St Kenelm, the abbey's patron saint.[82] That these documents and annals were grafted onto the common root as part of the process of adapting it for the abbey's needs seems clear. There are also numerous Winchcombe items

[78] Cf. also *The Miracles of St Æbbe of Coldingham and St Margaret of Scotland*, ed. Robert Bartlett, OMT (Oxford: Clarendon Press, 2003), xxvii, who dates T's calendar to ca. 1130–1160 on the basis of its script.

[79] This conclusion is, therefore, in agreement with that of Watson, *Catalogue of Dated and Datable MSS in Oxford Libraries*, 1:107, who writes that the annals up to 1172 "are written in several hands of s.xii$^{\text{med-ex}}$."

[80] *Winchcombe* 966, 1066.2, 1074.3, 1077, 1093.2. Whenever items are cited, readers should also refer to the relevant sections of the commentary that accompanies the text.

[81] See *Winchcombe* 811.2, 811.3 and 818.2, and plate II below. Their status as historical documents, origins, and implications for the history of Winchcombe Abbey are discussed in the commentary below. That commentary vindicates and develops the findings of Wilhelm Levison, *England and the Continent in the Eighth Century* (Oxford: Clarendon Press, 1946), 249–59, hereafter Levison, *EC*.

[82] See *Winchcombe* 795.1–3 and 819.1. There is also a long annal under 850 covering the martyrdom of Wigstan, a saint venerated at the nearby abbey of Evesham, but this item was part of the common root.

among the additions that were made to the chronicle, including a letter which King Cenwulf wrote to Pope Leo III and another which he received from him.[83] It is clear, furthermore, that the chronicle was available at Winchcombe in the mid-thirteenth century when it was used in the making of another set of annals, that imperfectly preserved in MS. London, B.L., Cotton Faustina B.I, fols. 12r–29v.[84] The main areas of uncertainty surrounding this chronicle concern the processes and purposes for which it was constructed.

## (d) The Making of *Winchcombe*[1]

The main problem raised by the first phase is that of accounting for the entries which do not figure among the items shared with *Coventry*—of ascertaining whether they were added at Worcester or at Winchcombe. That *Winchcombe*[1] is an enlarged version of the common root is clear. It omits a mere eight of the 726 items that comprise *Coventry*, possibly through carelessness rather than policy since all of them were probably part of the common root;[85] but it adds to the shared entries some 300 or so items. It is also clear, moreover, that some of this material was added at (or perhaps for) Winchcombe. The entries relating to the early history of the abbey were almost certainly added to the root in the process of producing the chronicle. This much is clear. What is not clear is how many of the remaining entries were added at or for Winchcombe. John was an inveterate elaborator of his own work, and it is possible that *Winchcombe* derives from a version of the root which was more "advanced" than that which underpins *Coventry*, the latter being derived from an exemplar which was produced at an early stage in its development.

The difficulties involved in resolving this problem are well illustrated by considering the series of items in *Winchcombe* that echo material in Bede's *Chronica maiora*. The *Chronica chronicarum* also includes many items which Marianus derived from this source, but there are some forty-nine entries in *Winchcombe* either for which there is no echo in the former work or which are significantly closer to the version in Bede.[86] There are, to make matters even more intriguing, at least

[83] See *Winchcombe* 787.2, 795.4, 798, 811.4–6.

[84] The provenance of F and its relationship to *Winchcombe* are discussed in chap. 5, § d, below. Darlington treated F as another manuscript of the *Winchcombe Chronicle*, but it seems better to treat it as a new chronicle in view of how substantial the additions to the text are. It is perhaps best designated the *Later Winchcombe Annals*.

[85] *Coventry* 42.1, 226, 317, 466, 607, 688, 747, 819. See also chap. 4,§ b, below.

[86] *Winchcombe* VA16.2, VA21.1, 1.1, 14.3, 17.2, 17.3, 37.2, 37.3, 37.4, 37.5, 37.6, 37.7, 46.2, 46.3, 53.4, 80.2, 82.3, 82.4, 102.3, 102.4, 125.1, 146.3, 179.2, 179.5, 180.2, 201, 202, 210.2, 211.1, 212.3, 224.2, 229, 263.2, 270.2, 276.2, 283.3, 297.2, 309.4, 330.3, 330.4, 330.4, 360.3, 360.4, 365.3, 382.2, 399.5, 400, 466, 476.

wo items in *Winchcombe* which seem to have been derived from Bede's *Chronica minora*.[87] The way, moreover, in which these items are arranged, especially at the beginning of the chronicle, is reminiscent of the way in which Bede organises his material. For the first 125 years are dominated by several relatively long annals which have been created through the piling up of material drawn chiefly from Bede. These annals occur under AD 17, 37, 46, 53, 82, and 102. In each of them an item or two shared with *Coventry* is followed by several drawn from Bede and sometimes from other sources as well. The annal for AD 37 is enlarged, for instance, with no less than five items from Bede's *Chronica maiora*.[88] Other sources have also been used to enlarge these annals, but the effect is reminiscent of the rambling and irregularly-spaced annals of Bede's *Chronica maiora*, and this begins to suggest that the common root had been enlarged by someone who had misunderstood the nature of the work—who had, that is, misunderstood the underlying generic model, having taken his ideas of how the text should be laid out from chapter 66 of *De temporibus ratione* as opposed to the Norman Annals. This can be interpreted as evidence that the Bedan material unique to Winchcombe was added there rather than at Worcester; but it should also be noted that *Winchcombe* shares with *Coventry* a small group of items which are closer to Bede than to *Chronica chronicarum*. These four entries imply that the compiler of the root was making direct use of Bede's *Chronica maiora*, perhaps even collating his material with it.[89] That encourages speculation as to whether the long rambling annals preserved under AD 17, 37, 46, 53, 82, and 102 in *Winchcombe* might be products of the first version of the root—as to whether *Winchcombe* might preserve evidence as to the presence of some generic confusion on the part of the original compiler, at least in the initial stages of his work. Similar ambiguities hang over many of the 300 or so additional entries in *Winchcombe*[1].

A way of resolving this problem emerges, however, when the items are grouped and analysed, not according to the sources whence they were derived, but according to the themes they cover, for there are grounds for thinking that some thematic strata were added as *Winchcombe*[1] was being produced. This much has already been suggested above with regard to the series of entries recording the successions and obits of the archbishops of Rouen—a series of entries which derive from the Norman Annals and which seem to have held no interest for the root's compiler.[90] But the clearest evidence for this phenomenon is that provided by the series of entries recording papal *acta*. Entries recording the

---

[87] See *Winchcombe* 360.2 and 361.2 which are almost certainly indebted to Bede's *Chronica minora*. *Winchcombe* 266.3 is another potential case in point, but it might also have been derived from the Norman Annals (*AU* 270, *AG* 270).

[88] See, likewise, *Winchcombe* 17 which adds at least one (maybe three); 46 adds two, 53 adds one, 82 adds three, 102 adds two.

[89] *Winchcombe* 309.2, 309.3, 357.2, 405.2.

[90] See chap. 2, § d, above.

legislative acts of the papacy, above all those concerned with the development of the liturgy, are often to be found in breviate world chronicles, but it is clear that the compiler of the common root was largely indifferent to entries of this kind. Just fifteen items among the 718 shared with *Coventry* might be said to fall under this heading,[91] and to locate this many examples requires stretching the category to include any item that relates to a pope. To this smattering of material the first phase of *Winchcombe* adds no fewer than ninety entries, the vast majority of which are typical of entries of this kind.[92] These items were added either in the process of producing *Winchcombe* itself or in the process of enhancing the common root after the exemplar of *Coventry* had been copied at Worcester. Many of these papal entries seem to derive from the recognised works of John. Matching material for eighty-one of them can be found in *Chronica chronicarum*, and sixty-seven are reported in more than one part of that work. Some occur, for example, in both the main chronicle and in the "Papal Annals," others in both the "Papal Annals" and the "Consular Annals." A version of all but one of these items can be found, moreover, in the "Papal Annals"[93]—that is, there are thirteen items for which matches are to be found in these annals alone.[94] Furthermore, where there are differences in the way in which the material is reported in several parts of *Chronica chronicarum*, it is almost invariably this preliminary text that provides the closest match for the corresponding entry in *Winchcombe*.[95]

These affinities are crucial because the "Papal Annals" belong to the final phase in the production of *Chronica chronicarum*. That is, they were among the final items to be added to the preliminary matter in the holograph: instead of this

[91] *Winchcombe* 128, 162, 291.1, 440, 445, 591.1, 591.2, 591.4, 597, 606.1, 608.2, 609.2, 782, 799, 883.2. As the commentary explains, there is similar material for most of these entries in John's "Papal Annals," but their language tends to be closer to material found in the main chronicle of JWCC, a pattern which contrasts with that of the *Winchcombe*'s additional "papal" entries (see below).

[92] *Winchcombe* 44, 69.2, 80.4, 82.5, 91.2, 102.5, 102.6, 111.2, 119, 141.2, 158.2, 180.2, 180.3, 190.2, 204.2, 204.3, 211.3, 218.2, 220.3, 242.2, 242.4, 247.3, 253.2, 261.3, 266.2, 267.2, 273.2, 291.3, 291.4, 299.2, 299.3, 303.3, 303.4, 338.2, 338.3, 353, 356.2, 363.2, 363.3, 363.4, 365.3, 394.3, 394.4, 399.3, 399.3, 413.3, 413.4, 417.3, 417.4, 418.2, 418.3, 434.2, 459.2, 459.3, 464, 487.2, 487.3, 487.4, 499.2, 499.3, 512.3, 512.4, 522.2, 522.3, 525.3, 529.2, 529.6, 539.3, 556.2, 556.3, 584.3, 591.3, 614.2, 614.3, 616.3, 623.2, 633.2, 633.3, 669.2, 686.5, 686.6, 707.2, 707.3, 710.2, 710.4, 715.4, 733.2, 733.3, 800.1, 891.1.

[93] The exception is *Winchcombe* 399.3.

[94] *Winchcombe* 69.2, 82.5, 119, 180.3, 211.3, 220.3, 242.4, 291.3, 399.2, 459.2, 487.2, 539.3, 591.3.

[95] See, for example, *Winchcombe* 111.2, 190.2, 204.3, 218.2, 247.3, 338.2, 356.2, 363.4, 417.4, 434.2, 616.3, 623.2, 710.2, 800.1, 891.1, and the commentaries below. The only exception to the pattern is 499.3, but this corresponding item in the "Papal Annals" has been modified by a later hand.

text the other copies have a numbered list of popes, and there are clear signs that it was this text which was erased on pages 29 to 30 of C so that the "Papal Annals" could be entered. An extra bifolium (pages 31 to 34) was also inserted so that they could be copied there, and the text was copied by C[3], the scribe thought to be John himself.[96] That means that the "Papal Annals" were almost certainly composed after the mid-1130s when C sent to Bury for the making of B. It is true that these annals are also to be found among the texts prefixed to *Chronicula* in G, but they were added to this manuscript around 1150 by the Gloucester scribe who was responsible for its auxiliary matter. Since these annals belong to the final phase of John's work on *Chronica chronicarum*, the affinities between them and *Winchcombe* would seem to be open to two interpretations: the first is that both texts depend for these items on a version of the common root that had been expanded by the addition of this strand of the material; the second is that the "Papal Annals" were used by the redactor of *Winchcombe* to supplement the papal material he had derived from the common root. Either interpretation is possible, but the latter is the simpler of the two and is supported by the palaeography of T. For a good many of these entries are inserted in a compressed fashion, in the margins, at the end of a line, and in the gaps left on the page after the other entries had been copied. That is, they were still copied in the hand of the original scribe (T[1]), but they have the appearance of having been added to the whole as he went back to revise his work.[97]

This is not the only noteworthy pattern in this group of entries. For *Winchcombe* has a further eight entries of this kind for which there are no matches in John's "Papal Annals" or elsewhere in his work;[98] rather, matches for these notices are to be found in Bede's *Chronica Maiora* and in the Norman Annals.[99] The presence of these items strongly suggests that it was a local redactor, probably T[1] himself, who was responsible for adding the papal entries to *Winchcombe*. If the further eight entries had been generated at Worcester, then some of them would almost certainly have found their way into the "Papal Annals," but John simply does not seem to have used Bede's *Chronica maiora* or the Norman Annals

[96] See chap. 2, § a, above.

[97] E.g. *Winchcombe* 80.4, 204.2–3, 211.3, 220.3, 242.2, 242.4, 247.3, 363.3–4, 459.2–3, 487.2–4, 512.3–4, and the notes in the textual apparatus.

[98] The reader may have noticed that 81 plus 8 falls one short of 90. There is one other item, a notice which may derive from an alleged letter of St Jerome although annals covering its contents can also be found in the works of contemporary chroniclers such as Sigebert of Gembloux (see *Winchcombe* 363.3 and the discussion in the commentary below). It is not, however, reported in the *Chronica chronicarum*, and may therefore have been added at Winchcombe.

[99] *Winchcombe* 44, 91.2, 102.5, 180.2, 204.2, 242.2, 365.3, 487.4. See also *Winchcombe* 111.2, where an item from JW*CC* has been modified under the influence of the Norman Annals. The same might also be said of 102.5–6.

when generating papal *acta*.[100] Rather, his items of this kind seem to have been derived largely from Marianus and, curiously, from his own investigations using documents such as the so-called Plegmund Narrative[101] and the *Collectio Lanfranci*, a condensed version of the False Decretals attributed to Isidore of Seville.[102] It had been introduced into England and disseminated there through the agency of Lanfranc, archbishop of Canterbury (1072–1089).[103] These primary sources supplied John with at least ten items for his "Papal Annals." It follows that he was more of an active researcher than is sometimes recognised.

---

[100] There are a few partial matches (e.g. JW*CC* (C) 123), but none of John's papal *acta* seem to derive from the Norman Annals. As far as Bede's *Chronica majora* is concerned, there are a few matches (e.g. JW*CC* 128 and 429, which echo Bede, *CM*, 322 and 485 respectively), but this seems to have come about because Marianus used *Chronica majora* (see Marianus VA 150 and 429), rather than because John went to Bede to obtain additional entries.

[101] See *Winchcombe* 891.1 and the discussion in the commentary below.

[102] See *Winchcombe* 69.2, 82.5, 180.3, 211.3, 220.3, 242.4, 291.3, 459.2, 487.1, and the discussion in the commentary below. A further possibility is the first half of 399.2, but it is open to doubt. Another potential source for entries of this kind was the *Liber pontificalis*, but it has material for only one of the items (i.e. 180.3; see the commentary below). It might also be contended that the version of Marianus used by John may have been amplified with these entries, but if so it is strange that these items do not appear elsewhere in John's version of the *Chronica chronicarum*—that they appear only in the final version of the papal annals. Still, it may have been Marianus who inspired John to investigate the contents of the *Collectio Lanfranci*, for he certainly made use of Pseudo-Isidore, albeit chiefly for the dating clauses of the alleged papal letters (see the commentary on *Winchcombe* 247.3 below). Another possibility which needs to be considered is that some of these items might have been generated at Winchcombe, since there survives a twelfth-century copy of the *Collectio Lanfranci* which has been identified as one of the abbey's books (today MS. London, B.L., Royal 11.D.VIII: see Gullick, "Manuscripts of the *Collectio Lanfranci*," 112–14). This magnificent manuscript could certainly have supplied the required entries, but if Winchcombe had a copy of this collection, Worcester will almost certainly have had one as well. On the *Collectio Lanfranci*, see also Lotte Kéry, *Canonical Collections of the Early Middle Ages, ca.400–1140* (Washington, DC: Catholic University of America Press, 1999), 239–40; Webber, *Scribes and Scholars*, 47–48. In the absence of an edition of the *Collectio Lanfranci*, the Royal manuscript (R) is cited in the commentary below.

[103] On the English reception of the collection, see Cowdrey, *Lanfranc*, 139–41; Mark Philpott, "Lanfranc's Canonical Collection and 'the Law of the Church'," in *Lanfranco di Pavia e l'Europa del secolo XI nel IX centenario della morte (1089–1989)*, ed. Giulio d'Onofrio, Italia sacra 51 (Rome: Herder, 1993), 131–47; Martin Brett, "The *Collectio Lanfranci* and its Competitors," in *Intellectual Life in the Middle Ages: Essays Presented to Margaret Gibson*, ed. Leslie Smith and Benedicta Ward (London: Hambledon Press, 1992), 157–74.

The implication of this analysis of the papal entries is that the common root was taken over by the makers of *Winchcombe* in much the same form as it was received by the makers of *Coventry*—that most if not all of the additional items in the first phase were inserted for the abbey as the chronicle was being produced. This analysis implies, more significantly, that the process of amplifying the root for Winchcombe was driven by critical assessment of its coverage of particular topics and themes. Records of the liturgical acts of popes seem to have been considered a desideratum in breviate world chronicles, and the common root's coverage of this theme was found wanting. John of Worcester had, however, compiled a convenient set of "Papal Annals" which made the process of strengthening the chronicle's coverage of this theme a relatively simple matter. A few more items of this kind were also to be found in Bede's *Chronica maiora* and in the Norman Annals.

It is not difficult, furthermore, to see how these materials may have been transmitted from Worcester to Winchcombe, for John seems to have spent some time there. It was at Winchcombe, so he says, that he acquired two of his most sensational stories, the first being the story of King Henry I's visions. The royal physician Grimbald had recounted them to Abbot Godfrey while John was present and listening.[104] The other sensational story acquired at the abbey was that of the two Christian knights who were captured and tortured by a Saracen in Apulia. The abbot of St Valéry-sur-Somme had told him this story, "once when he was in exile at Winchcombe."[105] If it actually took place, the occasion on which the first story was related would have happened before Godfrey's death on 6 March 1137,[106] and perhaps after 1 December 1135 since it is the kind of story a royal doctor is unlikely to have repeated while it might be reported back to his patient. But it needs to be stressed that John need not have heard both stories on the same visit—if, that is, he has not invented both or either episode. The abbey lies within the same diocese as Worcester, being some thirty-two kilometres from the cathedral—close enough for John to have made several visits. John's use, moreover, of the verb *exsulo* suggests that the stay at Winchcombe during which he heard the second story may have been a lengthy one, while the phase of *Chronica chronicarum* to which the two stories belong is, furthermore, the final

---

[104] JW*CC* 1131: "Erat itaque iste medicine artis peritus, Grimbaldus nomine, qui apud Wincelcumb, me presente et audiente, narrauit hec omnia domno Godefrido eiusdem ecclesie abbati."

[105] JW*CC* 1134: "Hec olim exulans Wincelcumbe, ab ore doctissimi uiri abbatis de Sancto Walarico audiui, et huic chronice nostre inserere curaui." A visit is plausible since St Valéry-sur-Somme possessed land in England: see Donald Matthew, *The Norman Monasteries and their English Possessions* (Oxford: Clarendon Press, 1962), 30, but note also Martin Brett, *The English Church under Henry I* (Oxford: Clarendon Press, 1975), 87. Interestingly also, the calendar in T, fols. 35r–40v, contains an entry in red for St Valéry (1 April).

[106] *Heads I*, 79.

one, "stage five," on which John had begun working before 1143 at the latest.[107] It is possible, therefore, that he may have learnt of the second story some time after 1137. But whatever their precise timing, his sojourns at the abbey will have provided John with ample opportunity to pass on the materials which were subsequently used in the development of *Winchcombe*[1].

## (e) The Textual Affinities of the Continuation, *Winchcombe*[2]

Close examination of the 156 items that comprise the annals for 1122.3 to 1181.7 (excluding the later additions) reveals a surprising range of textual connections. They contain parallels with Gervase of Canterbury's *Chronica*, with several annalistic chronicles from the west of England and Wales (the most telling being those with the *Annals of Tewkesbury*), and with three historical works produced at St Peter's, Gloucester: that is, they share parallels with *Chronicula*[2], with the fragments of the lost Chronicle by Gregory of Caerwent, and with the surviving version of that abbey's cartulary-chronicle. These affinities may be explained, however, by positing the existence of a lost common link between these texts: a late twelfth-century chronicle produced at Gloucester in the early 1180s. The hypothesis is that this chronicle was dependent upon *Chronicula*[2] and on a primitive version of the cartulary-chronicle for its coverage of events down to around 1150. Having been continued down to the 1180s, it was then exploited by the Winchcombe monks who added the annals for 1122.3 to 1181.7 in a single campaign, by Gervase of Canterbury, and by Gregory of Caerwent. It seems best to proceed by examining these annals' affinities with each of these chronicles in turn, before the present chapter goes on to consider the Gloucester characteristics of their contents.

### (i) *Winchcombe*[2] and *Chronicula*[2]

Given that *Chronicula*[2] ends imperfectly in the middle of 1141, analysis of its relationship with *Winchcombe* must confine itself to the forty items of information which comprise the annals for 1122.3 to 1141. *Chronicula*[2] is, however, the chronicle among the surviving corpus with which the annals for these years show the strongest affinities. There are some thirteen items which *could* conceiv-

[107] On the dating of the final phase of *Chronica chronicarum*, see chap. 2, § a, above; JW*CC*, 2:xxxv. One might go on at this point to ask whether John was also responsible for the production of *Winchcombe*[1] were it not for the way in which many of the additions, not least those drawn from Bede's *Chronica majora*, distort the generic pattern of the common root. The best that can be said is that the monks of Winchcombe are likely to have been familiar with John, his project, and its aims, from the mid-1130s at the latest.

ably have been derived from either the final section of *Chronica chronicarum* or *Chronicula*², but this is only to be expected given *Chronicula*²'s verbatim use of much material from the former.[108] There are, however, six entries which are significantly closer to *Chronicula*² than to *Chronica chronicarum*,[109] and a further seven entries which may be found in *Chronicula*² but nowhere in the other work.[110] Into the latter category fall, among other entries, items such as *Winchcombe*'s account of the discovery of the body of St Matthias the Apostle in Trier (1127.1), its account of Charles, count of Flanders (1127.2), and its coverage of the Welsh revolt in Ceredigion (1136.1, 1137.2). It is not the case, however, that all the entries among *Winchcombe*'s annals for 1123–1141 could have been derived from *Chronicula*². *Chronicula*² has no counterpart for some thirteen entries. Definitive parallels have yet to be found for most of these items.[111] A few could have been derived from *Chronica chronicarum:* these include the obit of Bishop Hervey of Ely (1131.4) and the detail that the Theobald of Bec was consecrated as archbishop of Canterbury at the 1138 Council of Westminster (1139.3). *Winchcombe*'s obit for Robert Curthose (1134.2) is also somewhat closer to that found in the Cartulary-Chronicle than that found in *Chronicula*². The upshot is that whilst *Winchcombe*'s annals for 1123 to 1141 are clearly related to *Chronicula*², they cannot have been derived from this source alone.

### (ii) *Winchcombe*² and the Later Gloucester Histories

Since they survive in fragments and in a much reworked form, the later Gloucester sources are problematic witnesses to the materials used in the making of *Winchcombe*'s annals for 1122.3 to 1181.7, but they provide some important clues. Gregory of Caerwent was a monk of St Peter's and the author of a chronicle which covered the period from the foundation of the abbey in 681 at the latest through to the year 1290.[112] The text is lost, the only surviving witness to its contents being a set of notes made by the antiquarian Lawrence Nowell (d. ca. 1570) which

[108] See further the commentary on *Winchcombe* 1123, 1125.1 (?), 1125.3, 1127.3, 1130.2, 1130.4, 1131.1, 1131.2, 1134.2, 1135.1, 1138.1 (?), 1139.2, and 1140.

[109] See *Winchcombe* 1128.1, 1130.1, 1135.2, 1137.1, 1138.2, 1139.4.

[110] See *Winchcombe* 1126.2, 1127.1, 1127.2, 1129.2, 1136.1, 1137.2, 1139.5.

[111] See *Winchcombe* 1125.2, 1126.1, 1129.1, 1130.3, 1131.3, 1132.1, 1132.2, 1133.1, 1133.2, 1134.1, 1139.1.

[112] For discussion, see Michael Hare, "The Chronicle of Gregory of Caerwent: A Preliminary Account," *Clevensis* 27 (1993): 42–44; Adrian Morey and Christopher N. L. Brooke, *Gilbert Foliot and his Letters*, Cambridge Studies in Medieval Life and Thought 11 (Cambridge: Cambridge University Press, 1965), 36, n. 1; Brooke, *CWB*, 52, n. 9; Sharpe, *HLW*, 154.

later passed into the Cotton collection.[113] These notes are brief and were probably collected with a view to discovering information not recorded elsewhere. Hence they are rather unhelpful for the purpose of establishing the full character and scope of Caerwent's work, but there is enough reference to events of national significance to suggest that it was a work of some ambition. The extant version of the Gloucester Cartulary-Chronicle was produced for Abbot Walter Frocester (1382–1412), and it survives in three manuscripts all of which date from the fifteenth century.[114] In contrast to Gregory's chronicle, this work is more strictly focused on the history of the abbey and its property rights from its foundation through to the late fourteenth century.

It depends, moreover, on earlier versions of that history which took the same generic form. The first stage in its development appears to have taken place in the ninth century when a crude foundation narrative was cobbled together from various charters.[115] The relative thinness of the existing text's coverage of the tenth and early eleventh centuries, as opposed to the density of its coverage of the period from 1072 to 1139, strongly suggests that a second phase in its development took place in the early to mid-twelfth century.[116] That at least one of the contributors to the cartulary-chronicle flourished in the 1130s is implied, indeed, by the lengthy account of Abbot Walter de Lacy's illness, for the author of this account claims to have himself heard Walter complaining about his illness.[117] That this period may, moreover, have seen more than one campaign of activity is implied by the work's complex relationship with *Chronica chronicarum* and *Chronicula*$^2$. McGurk has argued that the material generated in the second phase of writing

[113] MS. London, B.L., Cotton Vespasian A.V, fols. 195r–203v (hereafter V). On Nowell and his methods, see now Carl T. Berkhout, "Lawrence Nowell (1530–ca. 1570)," in *Medieval Scholarship: Biographical Studies in the Formation of a Discipline*, vol. 2, *Literature and Philology*, ed. Helen Damico et al. (New York: Garland, 1998), 3–17; Retha M. Warnicke, "The Laurence Nowell Manuscripts in the British Library," *British Library Journal* 5 (1979): 201–2; and Robin Flower, "Lawrence Nowell and the Discovery of England in Tudor Times," *Proceedings of the British Academy* 21 (1936): 47–73.

[114] *Historia et Cartularium Monasterii S. Petri Gloucestriae*, ed. W. H. Hart, RS 33, 3 vols. (London: Longman, 1863–1867) (hereafter *Cart. Gloc.*), 1:3–125. For the authorship, see Brooke, *CWB*, 51–52. On MS. Gloucester Cathedral Library 34, the most important copy of Frocester's Cartulary-Chronicle, see *MMBL*, 2:968–69.

[115] See Finberg, *ECWM*, 153–66, and the commentary on 680.2 below.

[116] See Brooke, *CWB*, 56–60, who demonstrates that the history was by this time a work of the same generic type as Frocester's Cartulary-Chronicle—that is, a history of benefactions and land transactions as well as of obits and of local events.

[117] *Cart. Gloc.*, 1:16: "Cum autem de hoc verbere sicut ex ipsius ore audivimus aliquamdiu vehementer gavisus fuisset in Domino." The final part of this long entry, the part which recounts Walter's death, was used in the making of *Chronicula*$^2$ 1139. See Brooke, *CWB*, esp. 56–58. Note also the similarity with the way in which *Chronicula*$^2$ 1140 (see n. 144 below) cites Milo as an authority.

found its way into *Chronica chronicarum* while it was still at a middling stage in its development, probably in the early 1130s.[118] This material was then transmitted back to Gloucester through an updated version of *Chronica chronicarum* and used in the making of *Chronicula*² and in the revision of the cartulary chronicle.[119] That there was a further campaign of updating in the mid-thirteenth-century stage is suggested, furthermore, by the relationship between the cartulary-chronicle and Gregory of Caerwent, since there are, as Michael Hare observes, down to but not beyond 1231 "many annals in Gregory which are phrased in similar or identical terms to equivalent records in Frocester's *Historia*."[120] It seems likely that Caerwent used a version of the cartulary-chronicle which ended soon after 1231, but it is also possible that Frocester may have used Caerwent, among other local sources, to fill in the gaps between, say, ca. 1150 and 1231, only to turn to other sources thereafter.

It would be wrong, given the way in which later redactors have edited the cartulary-chronicle and the very imperfect way in which Caerwent's history has been transmitted, to expect these sources to provide a continuous or comprehensive set of verbal echoes for the contents of *Winchcombe*; rather, it is all the more telling that they provide as many echoes as they do. In all there are some fifteen entries among the annals for 1122.3 to 1181.7 for which there are clear echoes, albeit usually in an abbreviated form, among Nowell's notes from Caerwent.[121] These textual reflections extend from 1130 to 1179—that is, they reach across the problematic change of hands which occurs in *Winchcombe* under 1172. The closeness of the connection is well illustrated by Nowell's notes from Caerwent's annal for 1148, for they echo much of the content of the corresponding annal in *Winchcombe*, and they do so in the same order whilst adding further information concerning the identity of the bishop responsible for blessing Abbot Hamelin and the date when the ceremony took place:

---

[118] For passages in *Cart. Gloc.* which are also found in both JW*CC* and *Chronicula*², see JW*CC* 1058 (the dedication and refoundation by Ealdred, bishop of Worcester), 1100 (the dedication of Abbot Serlo's church), 1101 (the burning of Gloucester), 1122 (the second fire), 1130 (the death of Abbot William and the appointment of Abbot Walter). The corresponding passages in *Cart. Gloc.* are 1:9, 12, 14–15. For analyses of the problem, see McGurk in JW*CC*, 2:xxx–xxxi; Brooke, *CWB*, 65–66.

[119] See *Cart. Gloc.*, 1:17–18 and *Chronicula*² 1139 (the death of Walter de Lacy, the calling of Gilbert Foliot, and the arrival of Gilbert Foliot).

[120] Hare, "Caerwent," 42. Note, for example, Gregory of Caerwent's entry for the death of Walter de Lacy as reported in V, fol. 198v: "Obiit abbas Walterus 6° idus Febr. cui procurante Milone Constabulario successit Gilebertus cognatus eique monachus Cluniacensis eximiæ sapientiæ."

[121] See further the commentary on *Winchcombe*²'s entries for 1130.4, 1131.1, 1131.2, 1134.2, 1136.1, 1139.4, 1139.5, 1143.1, 1148, 1149, 1150, 1171.4, 1179.3, 1180.3, 1181.6. Of these entries, five (1130.4, 1131.2, 1134.2, 1139.5, and 1179.3) are also echoed in the Cartulary-Chronicle.

*Winchcombe*

<U>chtredus Landauensis episcopus kl' Februarii decessit. Cui Nicholaus Gloecestrensis monachus successit. Robertus Herefordensis episcopus ad concilium Remis profectus ibidemque infirmatus uita decessit. Cuius corpus domno papa permittente ad sedem propriam relatum, et in ecclesia quam ipse anno eodem dedicauerat sepultum est. Cui successit Gillebertus abbas Gloecestrensis, a Teodbaldo archiepiscopo apud sanctum Audomarum in Flandria iubente domno papa consecratus. Preficit Gloecestrensi ecclesie uir uenerabilis Hamelinus.

Gregory of Caerwent

Nicholaus monachus vir religiosus ad episcopatum Landauensis est assumptus. Obiit ut creditur sanctus Robertus de Betun Herfordensis episcopus ad concilium Remis.

Cui successit abbas Gloecestrensis Gilebertus et in abbatia successit eiusdem loci prefectus Hamelinus qui ab Simone Wigornensis episcopo non decembris consecratus est'.

There are strong affinities here, but it is clear that Gregory could not have derived all of this information from *Winchcombe* itself. It might be contended that he has used *Winchcombe* and collated its material with another source—namely, a set of Worcester annals which could have provided information about the role the bishops of that see played in inaugurating abbatial appointments within the diocese[122]—but the simplest explanation is that the two versions represent differing approaches to the abbreviation of a common source: that the information about when and by whom Hamelin was blessed was omitted in the process of inserting the annal into *Winchcombe* because it was not considered worthy of note by the continuator of that chronicle. That this was indeed the process is all but demonstrated by the contents of Nowell's notes from Gregory's annal for 1130:

> Abbas Willelmus Gloc' infirmitate depressit, pastoralem curam deponens eam domno Waltero de Laci tradidit *qui a Symonem Wigornensis episcopo 3º non. Augusti consecratus est.*

[122] The existence of a twelfth-century chronicle of this kind ("Wig.dep.") was posited by Eric John in "A Critical Study," esp. 5, 9, 14–15. It is the present author's view that all of the pre-1181 items which John traces to "Wig.dep." are best seen as material which was derived from our lost Gloucester source. John was working from the items found in the margins of the later Winchcombe Annals (those in MS. London, B.L., Cotton Faustina B.I: see chap. 5, § d, below), but the items in question (see John, "A Critical Study," 26) can all be seen as extracts from *AT* which were derived from our Gloucester source. It is not unlikely, of course, that there were spasmodic efforts at Worcester to continue the 'common root' of *Winchcombe*[1] and *Coventry*[1]. The question at issue is the extent to which this material may have contributed to the development of chronicles such as that of Gregory of Caerwent, *AT*, and *APW* (see chap. 5, § a, below).

The significant point is that Gregory's reference to Simon's role in the appointment of Abbot William is missing from the corresponding annal in *Winchcombe* (1130.4):

> Domnus abbas Willelmus Gloecestrensis, infirmitate depressus, curam deponens pastoralem eam domno Galtero de Laci eiusdem ecclesie professo tradidit regendam.

It could be argued, again, that this was because Gregory had used *Winchcombe* along with some Worcester annals, but in this case there is good, if not entirely straightforward, evidence that both versions derive from a common source that included the information about Bishop Simon. I say "not entirely straightforward" because there are no less than three versions of an "earlier" form of this item:

| JW*CC* 1130 | *Chronicula*[2] 1130 | *Cart. Gloc.*, i, 15 |
|---|---|---|
| Willelmus Glaornensis abbas pre senectute pastorali cura sponte dimissa, eiusdem ecclesie religiosum cenobitam Walterum nomine cum consensu fratrum pro se abbatem elegit qui a Simone Wigornensi presule .iii. non. Aug. die dominica, abbas consecratur Wigornie. | Willelmus Glaornensis abbas pre infirmitate pastorali cura sponte absque tamen sui conuentus consensu dimissa, eiusdem ecclesie religiosum cenobitam Walterum nomine cum consensu fratrum pro se abbatem elegit qui a Simone Wigornensi presule .iii. non. Aug. die dominica, abbas consecratur Wigornie. | Domnus abbas Willelmus post tantas donationes factas ecclesiæ Sancti Petri, præ infirmitate, pastorali cura sponte absque cum sui conventus consensu dimissa, ejusdem ecclesiæ religiosum cœnobitam, Walterum nomine, cum consensu fratrum pro se abbatem elegit qui a Symone Wygorniensi presule tertias nonas Augusti, die dominica consecratur Wygorniæ. |

It is not entirely clear which of these "earlier" versions should have priority. It is possible, as McGurk would argue, that the item originated at Gloucester in an early version of the Cartulary-Chronicle whence it was transmitted to Worcester only for it to be included in the *Chronica chronicarum* whence it was returned to Gloucester.[123] But it matters not which of the three is earliest. The crucial points are, first, that all three earlier versions make reference to Bishop Simon and his role in consecrating Walter, and, second, that *Winchcombe* and Caerwent are clearly closer to each other than to the versions of the entry in these other sources: both use the verbs *deprimo*, *depono,* and *trado*, both assign the title *domnus* to Abbot Walter, and both supply his surname. Taken together, these points strongly suggest that *Winchcombe*[2] and Caerwent depend on a lost common source in which the item had been reworked in a slightly briefer form but

[123] See JW 2:xxx–xxxi.

one which retained the reference to Bishop Simon. The best way, then, of explaining the relations among *Winchcombe*, the Cartulary-Chronicle, and Gregory of Caerwent is to postulate the existence of a lost Gloucester chronicle—one which included some information about the bishops of Worcester and their role in consecrating abbots within the diocese.

### (iii) *Winchcombe*[2] and Gervase of Canterbury's *Chronica*

The parallels between *Winchcombe* and Gervase of Canterbury's *Chronica* cover the period from 1135, where he begins his narrative proper, to 1168, where they peter out.[124] That is, of the seventy-four items in *Winchcombe*[2]'s annals for 1135 to 1168, thirty-eight show *some* similarity of content with passages in Gervase's *Chronica*.[125] As that way of putting the matter implies, there is often some doubt as to the full extent of the relationship, as Gervase often combines two or more sources, sometimes rewriting them in his own words—indeed, he often seems to introduce an emphasis on Canterbury's lordship over the churches of its province. But there are within this group a number of cases where the existence of a textual relationship cannot be denied, such as the following:

| *Winchcombe*[2] | Gervase |
|---|---|
| [1160.2] Rex H. inauditam prius census exactionem per terras sibi subditas fecit, dehinc uersus Tolosam copiosum mouens exercitum, frustratis principalis intentionis nisibus est regressus, Ludouico Francorum rege urbem tuente. Hinc inter eos orta est discordia. | [i, 167] De aliis vero *terris sibi* subjectis inauditam similiter *census fecit exactionem, dehinc versus Tolosam copiosum valde movit exercitum*, obseditque urbem . . . Sed Francorum rege Ludouico civitatem prædictam tuente, *frustrata* est *intentio* regis Anglorum; nam obsidione soluta, post summam pacem et concordiam *inter eos* factam, *discordia* maxima post modicum est sub*orta*. |
| [1160.2] Fridericus in Papiniensi concilio cliii episcoporum Octouianum scisma fauore suo roborauit. Ludouicus rex Francorum et H. rex Anglorum partibus Alexandri pape cesserunt. | [i, 167] Romanorum imperator *Fridericus in Papiensi concilio cliii. episcoporum Octouiani scisma favore suo* et auctoritate *roborauit*. De cujus susceptione regi *Franciæ Ludouico*, et *Henrico* regi *Anglorum*, spectabiles legatos cum litteris suis misit. Sed reges prædicti parti et obedientiæ catholici *papæ cesserunt Alexandri*. |

[124] On Gervase, his methods and his aims, see chap. 1, § f, above.

[125] See *Winchcombe* 1137.2, 1138.2, 1139.1, 1139.2, 1139.3, 1139.4, 1140, 1141, 1142, 1143.1, 1145, 1147.1, 1152.1, 1153, 1154.1, 1154.2, 1155.1, 1155.2, 1157.1, 1157.2, 1158.2, 1159.2, 1159.3, 1160.2, 1160.4, 1162.1, 1162.2, 1163.1, 1163.3, 1163.4, 1164.1, 1164.2, 1164.4, 1165.2, 1165.3, 1167.2, 1168.2, 1168.4, and the commentary below.

In these instances Gervase may even preserve the annals which lie behind their counterparts in *Winchcombe*. That both were working from a shared source which has been more heavily abbreviated in *Winchcombe* than in Gervase's *Chronica* is all but put beyond doubt by close examination of the annals for 1135 to 1141, the period where the coverage offered by the latter overlaps with that provided by *Chronicula*$^{2}$. For there are many echoes of *Chronicula*$^{2}$ in Gervase's *Chronica*,[126] some of which show an overlap with the contents of *Winchcombe*$^{2}$. Compare, for example, the way in which the three chronicles cover the Battle of Cardigan in October 1136:

*Winchcombe*$^{2}$ 1137.2

Subsecutum est hoc anno bellum grauissimum apud Karadigan mense Octobrio, ebdomada ii, in quo tanta strages hominum facta est, ut de mulieribus in captiuitatem abductis decies centum decime remanerent, maritis earum cum paruulis innumeris partim aqua demersis, partim flamma consumptis, partim gladio trucidatis.

*Chronicula*$^{2}$ 1136

Subsecutum est hoc anno, bellum aliud grauissimum apud Karadigan mense Octobrio, ebdomada secunda, in quo tanta hominum strages facta est ut, exceptis uiris in captiuitatem abductis, de mulieribus in captiuitatis decies centum decime remanerent, maritis earum cum paruulis innumeris, partim aqua demersis, partim flamma consumptis, partim gladio trucidatis. Eratque ibi magnum uidere miseriam, cum fracto ponte super fluuium Teuwi, fieret huc illucque discursantibus pons humanorum corporum siue equorum inibi dimersorum horrenda congeries.

Gervase, i, 96

Eodem anno factum est grave prælium apud Karadigan mense Octobri, ebdomada secunda. In quo tanta hominum strages facta est, ut exceptis viris in captivitatem ductis, de mulieribus captiuitatis decies centum decimæ remanerent, maritis earum cum parvulis innumeris partim aqua demersis, partim flamma consumptis, partim gladio trucidatis. Eratque ibi magnum videre miseriam, cum fracto ponte super fluvium Tuidæ, fieret huc illucque discursantibus pons humanorum corporum siue equorum inibi demersorum congeries horrenda.

[126] For passages which echo *Chronicula*$^{2}$ but which could not have been derived from JW*CC*, see Gervase, 1:96 (Welsh revolt), 100 (the Anacletan schism—note especially the beginning), 101 (the end of the Anacletan schism), 103–4 (the arrest of the bishops), 105 (the invitation to the empress to come to England), 105 (the death of Roger of Salisbury), 110 (the arrival of the empress—note especially the references to the siege of Marlborough, the empress's passage to Bristol, and her visit to Gloucester), 112 (the obit of Archbishop Thurstan), 112 (solar eclipse), 112 (Robert's attack on Nottingham), 118 (the capture of King Stephen), 119 (the storm at Wellesborne), 119–21 (the collapse of the Empress's position), 121–22 (the capture of Robert of Gloucester). For passages which might have been derived from either *Chronicula*$^{2}$ or JW*CC*, see Gervase, 1:95 (the burial of Henry I, the revolt of Baldwin de Redvers), 99 (the miracles at Windsor), 101

Clearly Gervase did not derive this material from *Winchcombe*; he might, as is usually thought, have derived it from *Chronicula*², but the larger pattern of interdependence is more simply explained by arguing that there was a common source behind both *Winchcombe* and Gervase, one which was itself substantially indebted to *Chronicula*².

If so, the passages reproduced from *Chronicula*² in Gervase may be taken as evidence that the common source was a substantial text, one which offered a considerably fuller account of events than that now found in *Winchcombe*². Given that the parallels between *Winchcombe*² and Gervase peter out in the late 1160s it might be inferred that the common source also ended at this point—an inference which would lend support to the view that the change of hands under 1172 represents a significant turning point. It is certainly true that the textual parallels between *Winchcombe*² and Gervase dry up after 1168, even though they often report the same events.[127] There remain, however, a couple of minor but striking parallels under 1178.3 and 1179.4, and the general shift in the pattern of textual affinities is probably to be explained by the emergence of the Becket controversy as the focus of Gervase's narrative and the ready availability at Canterbury of alternative sources which spoke directly to this subject—sources such as the Lives of Becket. A Gloucester text biased in favour, as will emerge below, of Gilbert Foliot and his family is unlikely to have been a satisfactory source for these events.

---

(the French succession), 101 (Stephen's return to England), 102–3 (the miracles at Prüm), 101–2 (the visitation of the papal legate, Alberic of Ostia), 105 (King David's invasion), 112 (Stephen at Reading and Ely), 112 (the marriage of his son, Eustace). I have located nothing which could have been derived from JWCC that could not also have been derived from *Chronicula*².

[127] See, for example, *Winchcombe*²'s entry for 1177.2: "In uigilia sancti Andree uisa est una eademque hora cum marinis et transmarinis claritas quedam mirum in modum fulgurans, quasi finitima terre pertransiens, non citato transitu in modum fulguris sed morose et ut intuentium occulis pernotabilis esset." Gervase, 1:260, describes the same event but with entirely different words and metaphors: "Hoc anno, vigilia Sancti Andreæ apostoli, hora necdum prima, apparuit in Cantia rubor quidam quasi flamma ardens et volans impulsu venti qui veniebat. Quidam vero certissime affirmabant draconem flammeum crispo capite se manifeste eadem hora vidisse. Dixerunt plurimi signum hoc sive draconis seu flammæ ardentis vel ruboris per totam Angliam apparuisse." See, likewise, *Winchcombe* 1173.1 and 1175.4.

## (iv) *Winchcombe*² and the *Annals of Tewkesbury* (*AT*)

The so-called *Annals of Tewkesbury* comprise a far from straightforward chronicle. As preserved in MS. London, B.L., Cotton Cleopatra A.VII, fols. 9r–58r, they cover the period from 1066 to 1262.[128] Down to the end of 1253 or 1258 they represent a fair copy of an earlier text executed by two or perhaps three scribes. The first hand ends on folio 36v11 (in 1238); a second carries the text forward to the foot of folio 42v (in 1242), at which point the first returns to continue the text from the top of folio 43r to folio 54v18 (in 1253). A third scribe continues the text to 58r (the end of 1257), while leaving large spaces for the insertion of additional matter some of which have been filled by later scribes. The increasing untidiness of the entries from 1258 onwards suggests that from this point it is a near contemporary account of the events it describes. That there once existed, furthermore, a version of this chronicle covering the twelfth century somewhat more fully than what is presently preserved in Cleopatra A.VII is shown by the contents of another closely-related chronicle from Tewkesbury's daughter house at Cardiff. Known as the *Annals of Cardiff*, this chronicle is preserved in MS. London, B.L., Royal 6.B.XI, folios 105r–109r.[129] It is copied in a single hand and covers the period from 1066 to 1268. It is clear, moreover, that its annals as far as 1248 were abridged from a chronicle almost identical to that now found in Cleopatra A.VII, but sometimes more detailed and more accurate in aligning its entries to the right year.[130] All of this strongly suggests that there was once a fuller version of the *Annals of Tewkesbury*, one which probably ended in 1248 where its agreement with the *Annals of Cardiff* ceases.

This Tewkesbury chronicle is, more to the point, related, perhaps at somewhat greater distance than the other chronicles discussed so far, to *Winchcombe*². Their coverage of the period from 1122 to 1181 contains echoes, albeit sometimes relatively remote echoes, for some eighty-two of the 156 items that comprise *Winchcombe*².[131] A striking feature of these correspondences is that *Tewkesbury* often covers much the same events as *Winchcombe* and in much the same order—a point which sets it apart from Gervase, whose words are closer, but

[128] Gransden, *HWE*, 1:405, n. 13, distinguishes these annals (which she called "Tewkesbury I") from "a second chronicle" ("Tewkesbury II") which covers 1258–1263. They are preserved in the same MS (fols. 59r–69v), but are separated by a blank leaf (fol. 58v). Both are edited in Luard, *AM*, 1:43–174 and 174–80 respectively. The present foliation differs from that given in the margins of Luard's text.

[129] For a description, see Warner and Gilson, *Royal and King's MSS*, 1:139–40.

[130] Note, for example, *Annals of Cardiff*, s.a. 1147 (MS. Royal 6.B.XI, fol. 105r): "Obiit Robertus consul Gloucs' et sepultus est apud sanctum Jacobum Bristoli. cui successit Willelmus filius eius." Cf. *AT* 1147: "Illustris comes Gloucestriæ Robertus obiit."

[131] See the commentary on *Winchcombe* 1125.1 to 1181.7 below, and for evidence as to relative distance in *Winchcombe*²'s relationship to *AT*, see esp. the commentary on *Winchcombe* 1161.1.

who often rearranges the material. Compare, for example, their coverage of years 1163 and 1164:

| *Winchcombe*$^{2}$ | *AT* |
| --- | --- |
| [1163] (1) <H>enricus rex in Angliam est reuersus, (2) et papa Alexander Turonis generale concilium celebrauit. (3) Gillebertus Herefordensis episcopus ad sedem Lundonie transfertur, (4) et Robertus de Melum Herefordensis episcopus consecratur. | [1163] Rogerus filius comitis Gloecestriæ ad pontificatum eligitur, Wigorniæ, in mense Martii. Alexander Papa generale concilium tenuit Turonis. Gilebertus episcopus Herefordiæ permissu domini Papæ ad episcopatum Lundoniæ provehitur. |
| [1164.1] (1) <R>ogerius Roberti comitis Gloecestrensis filius Wigornensis consecratur episcopus. (2) Orta discordia inter H. regem et Th. archiepiscopum, archiepiscopus metu regis ad exilium compulsus est, et a rege Francorum honorifice susceptus est. (3) Obiit Octouianus, cui successit Wido Cremensis unus de scismaticis. (4) <L>udouico regi Francorum nascitur filius Philippus nomine toti Francie leticia expectata. | [1164] Rogerus consecratur in episcopum Wigorniæ, x. kal. Septembris. Robertus de Melun consecratur in episcopum Herefordiæ, xi. kal. Januarii. Thomas Cantuariæ archiepiscopus regi invisus effectus transfretavit. Octovianus schismaticus obiit, cui succedit Wido schismaticus de Crema. |

*Tewkesbury* leaves out some events—Henry II's transfretation in 1163 and the birth of Philip II—but the chronicle includes details that are overlooked by *Winchcombe:* the election of Roger of Worcester, the dates of his consecration and of that of Robert of Melun. It seems likely that the two chronicles are here providing a slightly divergent selection of material from a single common source. There is clear evidence, furthermore, that *Tewkesbury* was not using *Winchcombe* itself, for the former succeeds in avoiding the chronological dislocation that affects the latter's annals for 1156 to 1160.[132] The number of entries where *Tewkesbury* mentions relatively obscure Worcester events and has detailed information about when a bishop of Worcester was consecrated or died suggests that its compilers may have collated the source behind *Winchcombe*$^{2}$ with some annals originating from the Cathedral Priory,[133] but it is also possible that the common source had—as was suggested when considering this issue with regard to

[132] See esp. commentary to *Winchcombe* 1159.2 and 1159.3, where there are close parallels with Gervase and *AT*. Both Gervase and *AT* rightly assign these events to 1158.

[133] E.g. *AT* 1145 (the deposal of Prior David, the appointment of Prior Osbern), 1150 (the obit of Bishop Simon, the burning of Worcester), 1158 (the enthronement of Bishop Alfred on Palm Sunday), 1163 (the election of Bishop Roger), 1165 (Roger's enthronement on 2 February), 1180 (the day [10 August] on which Baldwin of Ford was consecrated as bishop). *Winchcombe* has none of these details, but it shares other Worcester items, such as the death of Bishop John of Pagham in Rome (1157.1) and the consecration of Bishop Roger (1164.1).

Gregory of Caerwent—more Worcester material than the contents of *Winchcombe*[2] presently suggest.

Furthermore, when we consider *Tewkesbury*'s coverage of the period before 1122, we find little to demonstrate dependence on *Winchcombe*, but some evidence to suggest that its compilers had access to a Gloucester chronicle. *Tewkesbury* notes, for example, the appointment of Abbot Serlo,[134] the beginning of work on his church,[135] the fires of 1101 and 1122,[136] Abbot Serlo's obit,[137] and the start of work on the great bridge over the Severn at Gloucester.[138] *Winchcombe* has only two of these events, the fires of 1101 and 1122.[139] In its coverage of these entries *Tewkesbury* uses, moreover, almost the same language as other "Gloucester" chronicles for this period—that is, Gregory of Caerwent and the Cartulary-Chronicle. As for the other end of the work, the parallels with *Winchcombe*[2] extend beyond the point where Gervase begins to part company (that is, 1168), petering out somewhat in the later 1170s. There are also fewer Gloucester items in *Tewkesbury*'s coverage of the decades immediately after 1181, and some significant absences such as the omission of the fire that damaged Gloucester Abbey in 1190.[140] Taken together these findings suggest that the source linking *Tewkesbury* and *Winchcombe*[2] began well before 1122, the point where it was taken up by *Winchcombe*'s continuators, perhaps even in 1066 where *Tewkesbury* begins, and that it came to an end in or soon after 1181, at the point where *Winchcombe* reached its conclusion. But whatever the full chronological extent of the common source, the cumulative weight of the textual evidence suggests that *Winchcombe*'s annals for 1122.3 to 1181.7 were largely if not entirely derived from a single source which was intimately related to a number of Gloucester chronicles. This impression that the continuation is in some sense a Gloucester text is further reinforced by close examination of the historical contents of the annals themselves.

---

134 *AT* 1072. Cf. *Cart. Gloc.*, 1:10; Gregory of Caerwent (V), fol. 195v.

135 *AT* 1089 ("et ecclesia Petri Gloecestriæ inchoata est"). Cf. Gregory of Caerwent (V), fol. 196r ("Serlo abbas inchoavit monasterium"); *Cart. Gloc.*, 1:11.

136 *AT* 1102, 1122. Cf. Gregory of Caerwent 1103 (V), fol. 196v; *Cart. Gloc.*, 1:12, 14–15.

137 *AT* 1102. Cf. Gregory of Caerwent 1103 (V), fol. 196v; *Cart. Gloc.*, 1:13.

138 *AT* 1119 ("Pons Glocestriæ inceptus fuit"). Cf. Gregory of Caerwent 1119 (V), fol. 197v ("Pons magnus Glocestriæ coepit exordium idibus Maii").

139 *Winchcombe* 1101.1 and 1122.1. But note that *Winchcombe* has other Gloucester events in this period, such as the dedication of the new church in 1100.

140 *Cart. Gloc.*, 1:22; Gregory of Caerwent 1183 (V), fol. 200r.

## (f) The Gloucester Perspective of *Winchcombe*²

Many of *Winchcombe*'s annals for 1122.3 to 1181.7 exhibit a Gloucester perspective. To begin with, they celebrate the achievements of Gloucester's abbots and those of its monks who went on to higher office elsewhere. They note, for example, how the abbey secured the appointment of Gilbert Foliot (1139.5), how he was appointed to the bishopric of Hereford (1148), and how he was later transferred to London (1163.3),[141] whilst suppressing any mention of his inglorious role in leading the opposition to Becket. They rejoice in the long reign of Hamelin, "a man venerable and of worthy memory, a commendable lord," who "entered upon the way of all flesh in the thirty-first year of his abbacy" (1179.3). They note likewise that in the case of four abbatial appointments elsewhere that the appointees were monks of Gloucester.[142] It is particularly striking that two of these monks were members of the Foliot family—Reginald Foliot who was appointed to the abbacy of Evesham in 1130 and Osbern Foliot who was appointed to the abbacy of Malmesbury in 1180—not least because these are the only entries (apart from Reginald's obit) for the monasteries of Evesham and Malmesbury in *Winchcombe*².[143] In the case of Osbern the annalist notes somewhat defensively that he "was elected by the common assent of the brothers of that place in accordance with canon law" (1180.3).

*Winchcombe*²'s treatment of secular events, likewise, displays an interest in the deeds of Gloucester's friends and allies. The continuation notes, for instance, the obit of another Foliot kinsman, Miles, the constable of Gloucester and earl of Hereford (1143.1). It was Miles, according to *Chronicula*², who had interceded with King Stephen to secure Gilbert Foliot's election as abbot.[144] Another family whose leaders figure prominently is that of Gilbert de Clare. Having passed away

---

141 This parochialism is more explicit in Gregory of Caerwent's version of this annal (as reported in V, fol. 199v): "Gilebertus episcopus Herefordensis, prius abbas Gloc', ad sedem Londinensem transfertur."

142 *Winchcombe*² 1130.2, 1148, 1171.4, and 1180.3. This feature is also typical of Caerwent, e.g. 1173 (as reported in V, fol. 199v): "Obiit Bernardus, abbas de Borouton, quondam prior Gloc'."

143 On Reginald, who was Gilbert's uncle, see Morey and Brooke, *Gilbert Foliot and his Letters*, 36–38, 51, and 78.

144 J*WCC* (G) 1139. In Gregory of Caerwent, as found in V, fol. 198v (s.a. 1139), Milo's intervention is recorded with the additional explanatory comment that Gilbert was his *cognatus*. A Winchcombe writer might well be less well disposed towards Milo given John of Worcester's report (C and G, s.a. 1140) that he had sacked the town and imprisoned many of its citizens. On Milo, see Katherine S. B. Keats-Rohan, *Domesday Descendants: A Prosopography of Persons Occurring in English Documents 1066–1166* (Woodbridge: Boydell Press, 2002), 480; D. G. Walker, "Miles of Gloucester, Earl of Hereford," *Transactions of the Bristol and Gloucestershire Archaeological Society* 77 (1958): 66–84; *Peerage*, 6:451–54.

in 1117, before the text commences, Gilbert does not himself figure in *Winchcombe*², but much feeling is shown in the treatment of two of his descendants. It is with some distress that the annalist reports the death of his son Richard during the Welsh rebellion of 1136: "Richard fitz Gilbert, was slain *for our anguish* and *to be mourned by everyone in the world*, done away on 15 April."[145] Richard had been a major benefactor of Gloucester, refounding as a monastic priory the *clas* church at Llanbadarn Fawr which his father had given to the abbey around 1111.[146] Since, furthermore, the Priory of St Padarn was lost along with Ceredigion, Richard's body was taken to Gloucester and buried in the chapter house there.[147] His was an obit of particular interest to the monastery of Gloucester. The other descendant of Gilbert de Clare to figure in the continuation is his grandson Richard, the second earl of Pembroke, better known as "Strongbow." The continuation reports his intervention in Ireland and marriage to Aífe, the daughter of Diarmait Mac Murchada, king of Leinster (1170.3), his reconciliation with Henry II (1171.3), and his death and burial at Dublin as tremendous successes. It even reports the miracle of a wondrous plant which grew out of his marble sarcophagus (1176.2). It is striking that both Richards had stormy relations with the crown: the former was in revolt against Stephen when he died in 1136; the latter was always the object of Henry II's suspicion.

*Winchcombe*² also views events from the perspective of the earls of Gloucester. Roger's consecration as bishop of Worcester is recorded, for example, as that of "Roger, the son of Robert, count of Gloucester" (1164.1). It fails to mention some significant incidents in the history of the earldom which appear in Gervase and other related texts,[148] yet it alone among chronicles of this period notes an event that had tremendous implications for the future of the earldom: the death of Robert, the infant son of Earl William (1147–1183), and his burial at Keynesham (1166.2).[149] Even more striking is *Winchcombe*²'s treatment of the Battle of Fornham, for the author credits Earl William with the capture of Robert of Leicester (1173.6). This interpretation is quite different from that advanced by the other late twelfth-century chroniclers. Jordan Fantosme, for example,

---

[145] *Winchcombe*² 1136.1. The italicised words do not appear in the "source," *Chronicula*², 1136.

[146] St Padarn was lost in the Welsh rebellion of 1136, never to be regained: see Brooke, *CWB*, 55–56. See also David Crouch, "Clare, Richard de (*d.* 1136)," *ODNB*, 11: 760–61.

[147] JW*CC* (G) 1136.

[148] Cf. Gervase, 1:131, on the death of Earl Robert (1121/2–1147) and the succession of his son, William (1147–1183).

[149] See further the commentary on *Winchcombe* 1166.2 below. *Annals of Cardiff*, s.a. 1169 (MS. Royal 6.B.XI, fol. 105r), likewise, record the inception of building work at Keynesham: "Et ecclesia de Keynesham inchoata est a Willelmo comite Gloucs'." This may well represent an otherwise unattested echo of the lost Gloucester source.

attributes the capture to Humphrey de Bohun and the earl of Arundel.[150] In the build-up to the battle, moreover, he casts Earl William's role in an ambiguous light by having Robert's wife offer the following advice: "The earl of Gloucester is much to be feared, but he is married to your sister and not for all the wealth in France would he start any extravagant action that would cause you trouble!"[151] The contrasts between these two approaches are to be explained by the rift between Earl William and King Henry II that emerged after the great rebellion was over. William soon found himself being cast as a potential traitor when, in 1175, the king had him arraigned for having expelled the royal garrison from the castle at Bristol and having held it in his own hands for the duration of the war.[152] The earl surrendered control of the castle and in 1176 he agreed to the betrothal of his daughter, Isabella, to Prince John, and to recognise John as his heir;[153] but this did not save him from imprisonment in 1183. He would die in custody on 23 November of that year. Thus Fantosme and other "public historians" of the great rebellion will have found it convenient to suppress any positive role that William might have played in the Battle of Fornham. This need not mean that *Winchcombe²*'s treatment was propaganda produced in defence of the earl—other historical genres will have fulfilled that purpose much more effectively.[154] Rather, it shows that the lost root was compiled or perhaps updated by a monk who was predisposed towards the earls' cause.

By comparison with its treatment of Gloucester and its great patrons, *Winchcombe²* is somewhat reticent about the history of Winchcombe. Altogether there are seven Winchcombe entries, six of which are concerned with the obits and successions of the abbey's rulers. One abbot, Godfrey, is noted as being "of good memory" (1138.1) and another, Gervase, as "venerable" (1157.4),[155] but none is accorded the effusive praise given to Abbot Hamelin of Gloucester. *Winchcombe²* briefly notes, for example, that "Robert succeeded to the abbacy of Winchcombe" in 1139 and that he "died on 15 January" in 1151 (actually 1152), whereas John of Worcester (and the Gloucester Continuator of the *Chronicula*) provide much more detail, recording that he was blessed on 22 May, being a monk of Cluny

[150] Jordan Fantosme, *The Chronicle*, ed. R. C. Johnston (Oxford: Clarendon Press, 1981), 78–79 (§ 107). See also RH*GHS*, 1:61; Gervase, 1:246; Diceto, 1:373–74.

[151] Fantosme, *Chronicle*, § 99 (pp. 72–73): "Li cuens de Glowecestre fet mult a redut-er, / Mes il ad vostre sorur a muillier e a per; / Put tut l'aveir de France ne volsist cumencier / De faire nul ultrage dunt eussiez desturbier."

[152] RH*GHS*, 1:92: "Interim rex implacavit comitem Gloucestriæ, eo quod tempore hostilitatis expulit custodes regis de turre Bristoldi, et eam in manu sua tenuit quamdiu werra duravit. Et comes inde volens regi satisfacere, reddidit ei turrim Bristoldi." On the context of the dispute over the castle, see *EGC*, 3–4.

[153] RH*GHS*, 1:124.

[154] See chap. 1, esp. § f, above.

[155] For the other notices of this type, see 1151.3, 1152.2, 1171.4, and 1181.6.

and reportedly (*ut ferunt*) a relative of King Stephen.[156] In this case, however, one could see this as a kind of *damnatio memoriae* since in the aftermath of the Angevin victory in the civil war Winchcombe may have wished to forget its former association with Stephen's family. The seventh Winchcombe entry is a somewhat cursory and perhaps inaccurate account of the fire which destroyed the abbey in the final years of the anarchy (1151.2). The continuator places this event in 1151 with the seemingly precise date of 28 September, but the year is at odds with that provided by an assured Winchcombe source. This is a *miraculum* of the abbey's patron, St Kenelm, which was appended to Goscelin's *Vita S. Kenelmi* in a manuscript with a certain Winchcombe provenance (today MS. Oxford, Bod.L., Douce 368, fol. 83v). It dates the fire to 1149.[157] The discrepancy cannot be resolved as the effect of a dislocation, for the other events reported in the annal for 1151 belong to that year and to 1152.

Taken together, the evidence assembled above suggests that the continuation derives from a Gloucester composition. It betrays, within the limits of the annalistic form, certain distinctive prejudices: *Winchcombe*² is proud of Gloucester Abbey's achievements, it mourns its losses, it defends the Angevin cause, but it also takes the side of its aristocratic patrons when they are in conflict with Henry II. Since these affections will have become imprudent once the earldom reverted to royal control with Earl William's death in 1183 and with Prince John's betrothal to his heiress, Isabella, their presence suggests that the chronicle arrived at Winchcombe soon after the latest events it records—that is, soon after 26 November 1181.[158] It follows, however, that the annals for 1122.3 to 1181—if indeed they were lifted from a single text which concluded at the very same point—may have been added to T some time after that final year. It follows, more importantly, that *Winchcombe*² should be seen as further evidence that St Peter's was a minor but significant centre of historical writing in the twelfth century, one which produced at least three historical works: a continuation to John of Worcester's *Chronicula*, an evolving Cartulary-Chronicle, and now also a lost annalistic chronicle covering, perhaps, 1066 to 1181. This lost chronicle was evidently a work not of great, but of some ambition which enjoyed sufficiently wide circulation that it became a major source for chronicles produced at Tewkesbury and Canterbury as well as at Winchcombe. Its reach extended to events throughout the Angevin empire as a whole, and to episodes in the history of the empire and the papacy, such as the papal schisms of 1130–1138 and 1160–1177. Places mentioned include Le Mans, Milan, Nantes, Rheims, Rome, St Omer, Thouars,

---

156 JWCC 1138. See *Heads I*, 79.

157 The *Miraculum* (*BHL* 4641t), ed. Love, *Three Lives*, 123–24. See the commentary for 1151.2 below.

158 See the commentary on *Winchcombe* 1181.7 below.

Tours, Toulouse, and Trier.[159] Gloucester seems, in short, to have become a modest but perhaps the most influential centre of annalistic activity in the West Midlands in the half century after the deaths of John of Worcester and William of Malmesbury. The stemma in figure two sets out the position of *Winchcombe*[2] and its relations to other texts produced in the twelfth and thirteenth centuries as suggested by the present analysis.

## (g) The Insertions and Marginal Annotations

Besides the long continuation, numerous comments and documents were also inserted into the margins of *Winchcombe*. Owing to the effects of the 1731 fire, it is no longer possible to recover all of the marginal material, but such material as can be reconstructed provides some useful clues to the reception of the text. These additions show that *Winchcombe* was being read and studied well into the thirteenth century even though the text itself was not updated beyond 1181. There is, however, no single pattern to these annotations: some strengthen the chronicle's coverage of the abbey's own history, others gloss or strengthen its coverage of themes relevant to the discipline of computus, such as its coverage of the historical geography of England. The diversity of interests driving the development of the chronicle is well illustrated by a stratigraphic analysis—that is, by an analysis which treats the major groups of annotations in the approximate order in which they were made:

1. It is important to begin by recognising that a number of the marginal entries were inserted by the original scribe ($T^1$). The most impressive of these is a version of an appendix to the *Gesta Silvestri* which recounts the vision that led Constantine to found the city of Constantinople (311). This extract is curious in as much as it seems to depend on a fuller version of this appendix than those known to modern scholarship.[160] $T^1$'s other marginalia include several of the papal entries discussed above (80.4, 204.3, 211.3, 220.3, 242.2, 242.4, 363.3–4, 487.2–4, 512.3–4, 616.3) and several of the Norman ones (514.2, 635.3, 677.5).[161]

2. The most substantial annotation after that for the foundation of Constantinople concerns the origins of Peter's Pence (857.3–6). It is entered by a mid-twelfth-century scribe ($T^{10}$), was badly damaged in the Cottonian fire, but is mostly comprised of the relevant material in Asser's

159 *Winchcombe* 1127.1, 1127.2, 1128.1, 1148, 1158.1, 1162.1, 1167.2, 1170.3, 1178.1, 1179.5.

160 See further the commentary on *Winchcombe* 311 below.

161 For further examples, see *Winchcombe* 360.2, 816.2, 817.2, 906.2–909, 1100.3, 1110.

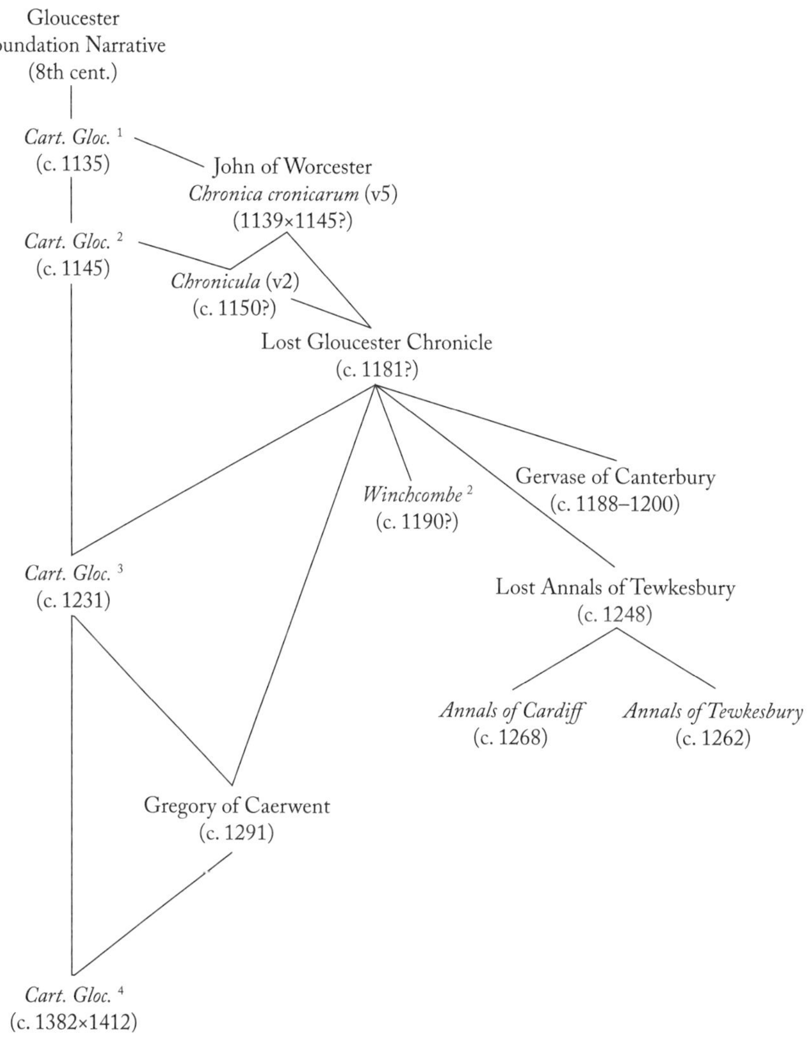


FIG. 2
The Textual Affinities of *Winchcombe*[2]

*De rebus gestis Ælfredi* as reported in John of Worcester's *Chronica chronicarum* and from William of Malmesbury's *Gesta regum Anglorum.*[162]

3. At some point in the middle of the twelfth century, a team of scribes ($T^{6-9}$) used material extracted from William of Malmesbury's *Gesta regum Anglorum* to extend the documents gathered under 811 (fols. 13va–14rb). This material is chiefly comprised of a letter from King Cenwulf to Pope Leo III in support of the restoration of Canterbury's rights as the metropolitan see for southern England (811.5) and a later letter of Pope Leo III to Cenwulf concerned with the same issue (811.6). These letters were quoted by William of Malmesbury and the extract begins with the very same signpost with which he introduces them in *Gesta regum* (811.4). Space seems to have been left for the insertion of additional material by the original scribe ($T^1$), for he copied the first part of folio 14ra–rb, leaving the remainder of the folio blank. A further leaf was probably inserted so that 811.6 (and perhaps some other documents as well) could be copied into the chronicle, but this is no longer extant and the item now ends imperfectly in mid-text. The chronicle resumes with its annal for 812 at the head of folio 15r. It follows that further information about the founder was almost certainly a *desideratum* for the original redactor(s). They seem to have been anxious to remedy gaps in their knowledge of the founder and his achievements, and their reliance on William of Malmesbury bears witness to the paucity of the archive at their disposal.

4. A late twelfth-century annotator ($T^5$) drew out the implications of these letters in a brief addition to the annal celebrating Cenwulf's life (795.4). What the documents demonstrated for him was that Cenwulf was a ruler who gave due respect to ancient custom and to churchmen of virtue, and a man who was himself held in high esteem by the Roman church.

5. Another late twelfth-century annotator ($T^2$) inserted an abbreviated version of the Gloucester foundation narrative (680.2), an account of how St Peter's was founded and endowed by various Hwiccan and Mercian kings which is otherwise principally attested in that abbey's late fourteenth-century cartularies.[163]

6. The most interesting of the additions is an account of the flying crucifix of Stanway, an item added in the margin alongside 1165 by a hand dating from the final decade of the twelfth century ($T^{13}$). It differs in language and emphasis from the version given by Gerald of Wales.[164]

[162] See the commentary on *Winchcombe* 857.3–5 below.

[163] See further the commentary on *Winchcombe* 680.2 below.

[164] *Gemma Ecclesiastica*, dist.1, § 35 (ed. John S. Brewer, *GCO*, 2:109–10). See further the commentary on *Winchcombe* 1165.4 below.

7. Two additions, both concerning the foundation of Winchcombe Abbey and both related to a compilation known as the *Quedam Chronica de Anglia* (787.2 and 798), were inserted around the turn of the twelfth century (T$^4$). The latter chronicle appears to date from the 1130s and was probably compiled in the west midlands even though it survives in a single mid-twelfth-century manuscript from Rievaulx (MS. London, B.L., Cotton Vitellius C.VIII, fols. 6r–21).[165]

8. The most extensive set of additions was entered by a mid-thirteenth-century scribe (T$^3$). His additions include a list of the counties of England and of how they were allocated to the Anglo-Saxon kingdoms which shows affinities with that found in Peter of Ickham's *Le livere de reis de Brittanie*, a historical tract in Anglo-Norman which dates from after 1274 (738.2).[166] Several notices concern two of the new orders which emerged in the twelfth century, the Cistercians (1099.2, 1136.2, 1147.2) and the Templars (1117.2, 1128.2). Two record the obits of important local figures, Robert fitz Haimo and Urse de Abbetot (1107.2, 1108.3), and another notes the accession of Ealdred as bishop of Worcester (1046). But the most significant of his additions are four notices concerned with the abbots of Winchcombe (966, 1066.2, 1074.3, 1077) and three recording grants to the abbey of churchscot (an annual levy of grain rendered to a church at Martinmas) from Halling, Diclesdon, and Aldrington and of half the profits from a fishery on the River Frome (1047, 1049.2, 1059).

9. Another thirteenth-century annotator added two brief Arthurian items: one records Arthur's withdrawal to Avalon to nurse his wounds (540.2), the other may refer to Carausius's usurpation of the British kingdom (281.3).

This list does not exhaust all of the insertions and marginal additions. There are many glosses and minor annotations, many of which provide clues as to the way in which the chronicle was used.[167] Some may well be products of the continuator's collation of *Winchcombe*$^1$ with the source of *Winchcombe*$^2$. Others elaborate the computistical element of the chronicle, noting for example where the great paschal cycles would have begun if Marianus's corrected date for the Incarnation were taken as their starting point.[168] Others extend its geographical element.

---

165 See the commentary on *Winchcombe* 787.2 below.

166 See the commentary on *Winchcombe* 738.2 below.

167 *Winchcombe* 24, 43, 121.2, 454.3, 465.3, 490.3, 510.2, 520.2, 529.7, 531, 547.2, 551, 571.2, 587.1, 587.2, 588.2, 610, 627.2, 646.3, 823.3, 875.2, 909.2, 913.2, 916.2, 926.2, 1017.2, 1035.2, 1042.2, 1043.2, 1054.2.

168 *Winchcombe*, 510.2, 1043.2.

One item notes, for example, the unification of Deira and Bernicia, another the elimination of the kingdom of Essex.[169]

## (h) The Context and Function of the Chronicle

The *Winchcombe Chronicle* was, in short the product of a complex process of development, one which raises many questions about the balance of priorities in its making. Though there are some deviations from the usual format, such as the lengthy annals which were created chiefly by the introduction of material from Bede's *Chronica maiora*, the prevailing generic pattern is that of the breviate world chronicle: one in which computistical observations mingle with historical data, one which attempts in *pointilliste* fashion to build up an overview of the development of the Christian world through space as well as time, albeit an overview constructed from an English and local perspective. There is, moreover, evidence that the compiler was concerned to strengthen the chronicle's coverage of some topics which were in keeping with the expected pattern of the breviate world chronicle, such as its coverage of the work of the papacy in building up and reforming the sacramental institutions of the church. Further evidence of the compiler's commitment to the creation of a universal narrative is provided by the introduction from the Norman Annals of a series of entries referring to the archbishops of Rouen—entries known to the compiler of the common root, but which he chose to omit.[170]

There is much evidence, however, that the compiler of the first phase was also interested in the history of his own abbey. The foundation charters incorporated into the chronicle under 811 and 818 represent a considerable portion of *Winchcombe*[1]—namely, some 1200 of the 18,000 or so words that comprise the first phase as a whole. The compiler has also incorporated material covering the life of the founder, Cenwulf (795.1–3), and the martyrdom of his son, Kenelm (819.1), but the coverage given to history of the house in the first phase is quite uneven. The concentration of items under the years 795, 811, 818, and 819 contrasts with the dearth of material for the later ninth, tenth, and eleventh centuries. It is not until 1093 that the reader finds an abbatial obit or succession entered by the original hand.[171] T[1] seems, however, to have anticipated the desire to add further material about the foundation of the abbey, for he seems to have left spaces under 795 and on folio 14rv so that more material could be entered about Cenwulf as and when it came to hand.

The long continuation covering the years 1122 to 1181 is somewhat at odds with both of these tendencies. It is neither particularly "universal" nor is

169 *Winchcombe* 588.2, 909. See, likewise, *Winchcombe* 823.3, 875.2.

170 See chap. 2, § d, above.

171 See *Winchcombe* 1093.2, Abbot Ralph's obit.

it Winchcombe-centred. Rather the authors' horizon seems to narrow a little to events in England and Wales and in the overseas dominions of the Angevin empire, though it still records some events of universal importance such as the Second Crusade. Events are viewed, moreover, from the perspective of Gloucester Abbey rather from that of Winchcombe itself. A record of the foundation of St Peter's Abbey, Gloucester, was also entered in the margins of T (680.2), but other additions to the chronicle continue to develop the emphases established by the first phase. There is, as has been shown above, much evidence for sporadic attempts to improve the chronicle's coverage of both its universal side and its Winchcombe-centred side. This much is well illustrated by scribe T³'s annotations as they develop both aspects: he entered an account of how the counties of England were divided among its Anglo-Saxon rulers and material relating to the emergence of the Cistercians and the Templars, as well as seven notices concerned with Winchcombe itself.

There are, however, grounds for thinking that the scribes and annotators might have had much more to say about the history of Winchcombe had better sources of information been available. The lacunae left by T¹ and the recourse to William of Malmesbury for material to fill those gaps certainly suggests that hardly any material was available in the abbey's archives to flesh out its early history. This much seems to be confirmed by the placement of T³'s entries concerning Abbots Germanus, Galandus, and Ralph. Of the four entries only the final one seems to have been placed under the right year.[172] T³ seems to have been working from speculation rather than a secure tradition. Later generations were to blame the fire of 1149 for the destruction of the abbey's archives, but it cannot be the only explanation for the thinness of their administrative records, for it is clear that some muniments survived this disaster.[173] Rather, it seems likely that previous efforts to maintain an archive were rather fitful. The chronicle's attempts to repair this deficiency are perhaps best interpreted as sign that the abbey was, like many other institutions in twelfth-century England,[174] becoming more serious about the need to create a fuller record; but if so, the results remained modest.

The upshot is that it is difficult to rank the priorities of *Winchcombe*'s compilers on the basis of internal evidence alone; rather, the decisive evidence—the evidence which puts the computistical side in the foreground—is that provided by the manuscript in which the chronicle is housed. Tiberius E.IV is a computistical manuscript of considerable substance. Whether its main contents were always intended to comprise a single volume—whether, that is, the components executed by the scribe T¹ were always bound together with those executed by T¹⁵—re-

[172] See the commentary on *Winchcombe* 966, 1066.2, 1074.3, and 1077 below.

[173] See chap. 3, § b, above and the commentary on *Winchcombe* 811.2–3 and 818.3 below.

[174] See further Clanchy, *Memory to Written Record*, esp. 92–109, 146–49, 154–62.

mains uncertain; but there is little reason to doubt that the section executed by T[1] included a group of computistical texts, devices, and tables (fols. 29v–42r) as well as the first phase of the chronicle (fols. 1r–22v). It seems likely, furthermore, that the presence of a breviate world chronicle in T is related in some way to the absence of a set of Easter tables. T is certainly unusual among English computus manuscripts of the classic type in having a chronicle as substantial as *Winchcombe*.[175] Most opt for a complete or fullish set of Easter tables with annals in their margins. There are tables among the items in folios 29v–42r which provide a basis for the reckoning of Easter, but none is of a type which would have provided a home for the insertion of annals in their margins. The explanation is perhaps that *Winchcombe* was incorporated into this computus manuscript so that its users could turn to it for an overview of the development of time that would otherwise have been provided by conventional set of tables-with-annals.

175 See chap. 1, § d, above, and also chap. 5 below where it is suggested that the major exemplar used in the making of T was a Worcester computus which contained the common root behind *Winchcombe* and *Coventry*.

# Chapter Four: The *Coventry Chronicle*

## (a) The Manuscript

The text here designated the *Coventry Chronicle* has hitherto gone almost entirely unnoticed, perhaps largely because the manuscript in which it is transmitted is complex and unattractive. MS. London, B.L., Harley 3775 (H) is a miscellany comprising some ten units which appear to have been taken from different books or which were once free-standing gatherings.[1] Most are clearly distinguished from one another by disparities in age, script, and content, and in the layout and size of their pages.[2] Exactly when the ten units were assembled in their present order is uncertain, but the hand of Lord William Howard (1563–1640) appears in several, suggesting that these units, perhaps all of them, were combined in, if not before, his time.[3] For present purposes, it is the fourth unit (comprising fols. 34 to 67 *and* 73) that concerns us, the rest being relevant only in so far as several have a connection with the Midlands.[4] Some attention must also be given, however, to the fifth (comprising fols. 68 to 72), because it has been inserted into the midst of the fourth and because their contents were confused in the

[1] The present editor distinguishes ten units as follows: I. Anglo-Norman Life of Becket (fols. 1r–14v); II. A version of the Anglo-Norman *Gui de Warewic* (fols. 15r–26v); III. Liturgical Verses (fols. 27r–33v); IV. *Coventry Chronicle* (fols. 34r–67v + 73rv); V. Derby Chronicle and annalistic summary from Bede, *HE*, 5.24 (fols. 68r–72v); VI. Life of Robert of Knaresborough (fols. 74r–77v); VII. Miscellaneous historical texts pertaining to London (fols. 72r–99v); VIII. Miscellaneous texts pertaining to St Albans (fols. 100r–139v); IX. Anglo-Norman verses on the Patriarchs Abraham, Isaac, and Jacob (fols. 140r–149v); X. Geoffrey of Vinsauf, *De artificio loquendi* (fols. 150r–178v).

[2] For example, unit III, comprising various liturgical texts, measures 225 × 152 with a text area of 165 × 90, ruled for 22 lines, whereas unit IV measures 240 × 165 with a text area of 190 × 155, ruled for 35/36 lines.

[3] C. E. Wright, *Fontes Harleiani: A Study of the Sources of the Harleian Collection of Manuscripts* (London: British Museum, 1972), 199 and 394, identifies Howard's hand as that which inscribes the title on folio 74, the opening leaf of unit VI. The same hand also appears in units IV and V (see n. 35 below). The manuscript was later in the possession of John Warburton of Bury (1682–1759) from whom it was bought for Lord Harley.

[4] For the St Alban's provenance of item VII, see *MLGB*, 167.

only published description of Harley 3775—that prepared by David Casley in the middle of the eighteenth century and published in the *Catalogue of Harleian Manuscripts.*[5] Casley conflated *Coventry* with the first chronicle of the fifth unit, defining them as a *Chronicon a Christo nato usque ad AD 1266*, when they are in fact two distinct texts.

To explain, folios 34 to 72 appear at first sight to constitute a sequence of five quires of eight leaves,[6] and this is how the folios were mounted on folds of cardboard when the manuscript was last rebound. But the "fifth quire" in this sequence (fols. 66 to 72) is rightly seen as comprising two gatherings of three and five folios: an "outer quire" comprising a singleton (fol. 66) and a bifolium (fols. 67/73), and an "inner quire" comprising two bifolia (fols. 68/72 and 69/71) and a singleton (fol. 70). The "outer quire" represents the tail-end of the fourth unit of Harley 3775: its first two folios contain *Coventry*'s annals for 1188 to 1197, and the recto of the final leaf (fol. 73) its annals for 1198 to 1202. The hand that executed the annals for 1197 ($H^{11}$) is, furthermore, the same as that which begins the annal for 1198. The dominical letters which appear in margins of *Coventry* are continued, likewise, on this page, but are lacking on the folios of the intervening "inner quire." The reverse side of folio 73 was originally blank, but a fourteenth-century scribe later added a nine-line poem on the medical properties of the scabious plant, *Vrbanus pro se nescit precium scabiose.*[7] The "inner quire" contains two short chronicles. The first, occupying folios 68r to 70v, opens with a genealogy from William the Bastard to the two eldest sons of Henry III (1216–1272), Edward, later king of England (1272–1307) and Edmund, later earl of Lancaster (d. 1296). Its annals commence with the death of Henry II in 1189, and as far as

[5] *A Catalogue of the Harleian Manuscripts in the British Museum*, 4 vols. (London: British Museum, 1808–1812), no. 3775. For the authorship of the description, see *Catalogue of the Harleian Manuscripts*, 1:28. Several of the other texts in H have been published, but rarely with extended discussion of the manuscript containing them: e.g. *Gui de Warewic, roman du XIIIe siècle*, ed. Alfred Ewert, 2 vols. (Paris: É. Champion, 1932–1933), 1:xii; J. Weiss, *Boeve de Hamtone and Gui de Warewic: Two Anglo-Norman Romances,* MRTS 332, FRETS 3 (Tempe: Arizona Center for Medieval and Renaissance Studies, 2008); Paul Grosjean, "Vitae S. Roberti Knaresburgensis," *Analecta Bollandiana* 57 (1939): 364–400, at 364.

[6] Four of these quires are numbered in Roman majuscules written in red ink, the first three on the final pages of the first three quires and the fourth on the first page of the fourth quire: H, fols. 41v ('I'), 49v ('II'), 57v ('III'), and 58r ('IIII'). Located at the bottom-middle of the page, all of these numbers have been damaged by the plough and it is likely that others have been lost—that is, that all the folios were once numbered in this way, both front and back.

[7] Walther, *Initia*, no. 19692. For a related but not identical text, see *Flos medicinae Scholae Salerni*, § 77, ed. Salvatore De Renzi, *Collectio Salernitana*, 5 vols. (Naples: Tip. del Filiatre-Sebezio, 1852–1859), 1:445–83, at 469.

1200 they are almost entirely derived from Roger of Howden's *Chronica*.[8] Thereafter they offer cursory coverage of the period from 1207 to 1266. There are no indications of provenance, apart from an interest in the acts of the earls of Derby.[9] The second chronicle, occupying folios 71r to 72r, is an abbreviated version of Bede's annalistic summary of his *Historia ecclesiastica*.[10] Most of folio 72 has been cut away, but it appears that its reverse side was originally blank, a heading and several lines of verse having been added in the fifteenth century. The hands of the late thirteenth-century scribes that entered these two chronicles are nowhere to be found in the folios that comprise the fourth unit. The layout of the historical texts in folios 66 to 73 is roughly similar,[11] and such are the many changes of hand in the latter stages of the *Coventry Chronicle* that it is easy to see how Casley leapt to the assumption that the first chronicle of the fifth unit was a continuation of the text that preceded it. There is, however, no genuine continuity between them, and they need to be considered as distinct texts.

## (b) The Development of the Chronicle

Having defined the external boundaries of our text, it is necessary to distinguish the various phases in its production. The first phase (*Coventry*$^1$), as has been indicated above, extends to 1122 and represents an abbreviated version of the lost Worcester chronicle described above in chapter three. Given that the common root no longer exists, it is difficult to assess the extent of the abbreviation, but this was probably not very great. The division into items that has been applied to the text below is necessarily somewhat arbitrary; but some comparisons and figures will help to illustrate the latter point. Of the 726 items that comprise *Coventry*$^1$, all but eight are echoed in *Winchcombe*$^1$,[12] but these eight are of the same character as the materials that comprise the common root. In other words, in sharp contrast to *Winchcombe*$^1$ nothing appears to have been added to the text in the

---

8 That for 1199 is, for example, substantially abbreviated from RH*Chron.*, 4:82–83; that for 1200 from RH*Chron.*, 4:114–15 and 148. For information about Richard I's wars, the reader is referred under 1189 to the *cronica magistri Hugonis de Houedene*.

9 Note esp. Harley 3775, fol. 70rv, s.a. 1190 (obit, on crusade, of William I de Ferrers), 1217 (the departure on crusade of Ranulf of Chester and William II de Ferrers), 1227 (obit of Ranulf of Chester), 1247 (obit of William II de Ferrers), 1254 (obit of William III de Ferrers), 1266 (the capture of Robert III de Ferrers in the church at Chesterfield).

10 Bede, *HE*, 5.24. The annals omitted include the entries for 597, 603, 626, 640, 668, 670, 673, 697, 698, and 731. It ends with the annal for 734 from the Moore Continuation of Bede (Bede, *HE*, 572).

11 The pages and text areas are roughly similar: the typical text area in unit IV is 190 × 155, ruled for 35 lines; that of the Derby chronicle is 180 × 125, ruled for 34 lines; and that of Bede's chronological summary 180 × 110, ruled for 37 lines.

12 *Coventry* 42.1, 226, 317, 466, 607, 688, 747, 819.

making of the first phase. Of the 718 items that echo material in *Winchcombe*[1], *Coventry*[1] appears to provide a fuller version of just three,[13] but briefer versions of some forty-six, though sometimes by only one or two words.[14] *Coventry*[1] lacks, moreover, three items in *Winchcombe*[1] that almost certainly derive from the common root,[15] and another nineteen that probably derive from that source.[16] The tendency, in short, of *Coventry*[1] was towards abbreviation, but its effects seem to have been quite mild. One of its virtues, indeed, is that it appears to provide an impression of the common root which is free from the layers of further annotation and elaboration found in *Winchcombe*[1]. However, it does not provide an error-free version of that text. It was copied by two mid-twelfth-century scribes ($H^1$ was responsible for folios 34r, 35r–40v, and 42r–61r34, $H^2$ for folios 34v and 41rv), and their work, especially that of $H^2$, contains many errors, especially in the copying of the Marianan series of annal numbers, and it has been subjected to extensive correction, perhaps by a third scribe, here designated $H^3$.

Given that there are scarcely any additions or alterations of substance, the first phase reveals little as to where or for whom the chronicle was copied. For answers to these questions, it is necessary to turn to the evidence of the later continuations. These are many and diverse, but they may be distinguished (and grouped) as follows:

1. The **first continuation** (fols. 61r34 to 64r) covers the years 1123 to 1150 and is copied by a single hand dating from the third quarter of the twelfth century ($H^4$). For the years 1123 to 1139, this text is an abbreviated version of John of Worcester's *Chronica chronicarum*, but one wholly distinct from that found in *Winchcombe*[2]. It incorporates material which is extant only in the holograph (C) and the Dublin (D) manuscripts.[17] Collation with these manuscripts suggests that the compiler made direct use of D itself. H often varies from both C and D. There are some variants which align the text with C, but none is of any great significance.[18] Where variants of substance rather than orthography are concerned, H invariably aligns with D. Under 1135,

[13] *Coventry* 465.2, 773.3, 1028.2.

[14] *Coventry* 195, 207, 220, 250, 350, 380, 415, 439, 468, 477, 485, 526.1, 526.2, 534.2, 559.1, 596.1, 603, 609, 655, 715, 735, 793, 795, 803, 876.3, 968.1, 1004, 1014.2, 1015.2, 1016, 1020, 1052.2, 1054, 1074, 1075, 1088, 1091, 1096, 1098, 1099, 1100.1, 1100.2, 1102.3, 1103, 1104, 1111.2.

[15] *Winchcombe* 653.2, 961, 1118.2.

[16] *Winchcombe* VA16.2, 62.1, 65.2, 65.4, 80.3, 135.2, 146.2, 179.4, 220.1, 281.2, 283.2, 373.2, 397, 421.1, 451, 592, 809.2, 810, 1086.2. This mostly comprises short, non-papal, items echoed in JW*CC*.

[17] See the commentary on *Coventry* 1135 and 1136 below.

[18] In 1128, for example, H and JW*CC* (C) have *ingrauescente*, where JW*CC* (D) has *ingrauascente*; in 1133 H and JW*CC* (C) have *eiusdem* where JW*CC* (D) has *eundem* in the clause *que tamen unius eiusdem quantitatis per totam Angliam non comparuit.*

for example, the length of Henry I's reign is given as thirty-six years and four months as was the case in D before the *i* of *xxxvi* was erased; C has *xxxv*. Under 1138, likewise, H agrees with D in having *in calce*, "under heel," where C has *ad ultimum*, "in the end," in the clause *deuictis tamen ad ultimum Flandrensibus*.[19] It seems all but certain that the first continuation was abbreviated from D. Indeed, the continuation's final entry from this source, 1139.2, corresponds to the penultimate sentence in H's version of the *Chronica chronicarum*.[20] For the period down to 1154, where H⁴'s annal numbers cease, the scribe could provide only four short annals under the years 1141, 1143, 1148, and 1150, each referring to the most famous events of the Anarchy. It appears that the first continuator was working after 1150 and that *Chronica chronicarum* was the only major work available to him for the history of this period.

2. The **annal** for 1154 (fol. 64r, lines 37–38) is entered by a single hand ($H^5$).

3. The **second extended continuation** (fols. 64v to 65r) covers the years 1155 to 1184, and is copied by a single late twelfth-century hand ($H^6$). These entries are mostly brief, the fullest being those which cover the events of 1171 to 1173. With this continuation the Marianan chronological apparatus is abandoned, the year being given according to the Dionysian reckoning alone.

4. The items under **1185** and **1186** (fol. 65v, lines 1–6) are entered by a single spiky hand distinguished from those that precede it by its greater regularity, the use of a heavier pen, and its vertical, proto-Gothic, aspect ($H^7$). This hand is similar to those responsible for the next continuation, and may belong with them. It should also be noted that with folio 65v the ruling changes from drypoint to plummet.

5. The **third extended continuation** covers 1187 to 1190. This continuation is the work of perhaps four scribes: $H^8$ (fols. 65r7 to 66r5), $H^9$ (fols. 66r6 to 66v14), $H^{10}$ (fols. 66v14 to 67r10), and $H^{11}$ (fols. 67r10 to 67v1, and 1190.4 in the margins of fol. 66v).[21] The character of the hands and of the material entered by these scribes is similar enough, however, that these entries may safely be treated, *for present purposes*, as belonging to a single phase in the production of the chronicle. By contrast with the continuations that precede and follow it, that for 1187 to 1190 offers fuller coverage of high politics. That coverage is not nearly as full as that found in the major chronicles of the period, but it includes some unique details[22] and some events seldom reported

---

19 See the apparatus to JW*CC* 1137 (3:228), note m.

20 See the apparatus to JW*CC* 1138 (3:234–6), notes b, h, and j.

21 But there is scope for doubt: see plate VI below.

22 See, for example, William des Barres's role in the felling of the great Elm of Gisors in *Coventry* 1188.4, and the commentary below.

by other English chroniclers of the period.[23] This continuator is better, albeit not always accurately, informed about events in France,[24] and he writes about these events from the perspective of King Richard I in the period when he was a close ally of Philip Augustus, prior to their falling out during the Third Crusade. He notes, for example, King Henry II's fury at Richard's submission to Philip's authority in November 1188, but without taking the side of either the father or the son.[25] His account of King Henry II's death makes, moreover, the remarkable suggestion that Richard had been genuinely forgiven by his father before his death. The continuator makes the claim, indeed, that father and son were reconciled by no less a person than the king of France. Philip is said to have hastened from Tours to Chinon with Richard when he heard that Henry was close to death and to have there interceded with Henry on Richard's behalf.[26] The usual sources imply, in contrast, that the settlement reached at Chinon on 4 July 1189 was entirely superficial and that Henry II remained implacably hostile towards Richard until death.[27] The continuator's other striking notice is his account of the meeting in Normandy at which Philip and Richard agreed to defer their departure on Crusade until 24 June: most chroniclers report Philip's excuse that he needed to mourn his first wife, Queen Isabel, who had just died, but the continuator adds the unique claim that Richard too needed to mourn, in his case for his brother-in-law, William II, king of Sicily. The two men are presented as equals in grief.[28] These emphases imply that the continuation was produced before news of the events at Messina in September 1190 had reached England—at a time, that is, when it was Richard's policy to present himself as Philip's man and ally.[29] $H^{11}$'s notices cover the departures on crusade of Earl Robert III of Leicester and of the armies of the kings of France and England. $H^{11}$ was also responsible for the annal numbers for 1191, 1192, and 1193, but nothing was entered alongside them.

6. The remainder of the chronicle, comprising the annals for 1194 to 1202, consists of a series of **short continuations** by some seven hands which are similar in character to one another and to $H^{6}$. With these entries

---

23 See, for example, the miracle at Châteauroux in *Coventry* 1187.2, and the commentary below.

24 See *Coventry* 1187.2–3, 1188.1, 1188.3 (but note that the continuator is mistaken here in his assumption that Raymond V had died), 1188.4–5, 1189.1, 1190.1.

25 *Coventry* 1188.5.

26 *Coventry* 1189.1.

27 Compare RH*GHS*, 2:71; RH*Chron.*, 2:367; Gerald of Wales, *De principis instructione*, 3.26 (ed. George F. Warner, *GCO*, 8:296), and the commentary on *Coventry* 1189.1 below.

28 See *Coventry* 1190.1 and the commentary below.

29 Compare the retrospective account of these wars in Devizes, *CTR*, 76–80, which was written after Philip Augustus had returned from the east, accusing Richard of having betrayed his cause.

the chronicle reverts to being a record of appointments, obits, and wondrous events. These scribes and their work may be listed as follows: H[12] enters the three annals for 1194 to 1196 (fol. 67v, lines 8–10, 13–15, 18–28); H[13] enters the items under 1197 and 1198.1–2 (fols. 67v, lines 30–33, and fol. 73r, lines 1–2); H[14] enters 1198.3 and 1198.5–6 (fol. 73r, lines 2–3); H[15] enters 1199.1–2 (lines 4–8); H[16] enters 1199.3 (lines 9–10); H[17] enters 1200.1 (lines 11–18); H[18] enters 1200.2 to 1202.3 (lines 19–21, 23–26) and the annal number for 1202. Spaces have been left for the addition of further material, and it follows that some of these entries may have been added retrospectively by continuators who were going back to fill gaps in the record and to correct omissions.

7. The **dominical letters** (folios 34r to 73r). When the chronicle was first drawn up, it was laid out in three columns, the first for the year "according to the Gospel truth," the second for the year according to Dionysius, and the third for the historical matter. In the first phase of the chronicle the vertical lines separating the columns were ruled in red. This structure was maintained by the continuators as far as 1156, where the author of the second extended continuation abandoned the Marianan years, reducing the layout from three to two columns. At perhaps the final stage in its evolution, however, the outer margins of the pages were "cleaned up" and a computistical apparatus comprising three columns of letters was added: in the outer one the symbol *B'* for *bissextilis* appears alongside the leap years, in the middle one the dominical letters that applied from 1 January until the first 24 February in a leap year, and the inner one the letter that applied from the second 24 February in a leap year or from 1 January to 31 December in an ordinary year.[30] Mostly this apparatus was inserted in the outer margins, but on folios 61v–63v it had to be fitted into the gaps in the columns of annal numbers, and from folio 64v it appears at the right-hand margin. It seems to be the work of a single scribe working soon after 1202,[31] whose eye was following the Marianan annal numbers. This much is clear from the way in which he skips over the year when the Marianan number has been left out, but continues to enter a letter when the Dionysian number is omitted. The reader has only to compare the correct statement in the opening annal that the dominical letter in VA1 was "B" with the "F" that appears alongside it in the margin to see that the results are not perfect, but the letters are accurate for 663–978 and 1096–1203. The pattern of error shows, moreover, that

[30] It was the practice of the church, inherited from the Romans, to insert the leap day by having two days for the sixth day before the kalends of March (i.e. 24 February), the second of which was designated *bis-sextus kal. mar.* See Bede, *DTR*, §§ 38, 40 (pp. 400, 404–5).

[31] With so few letter forms to examine it is difficult to reach a conclusion on this issue: a mix of minuscules and majuscules occurs throughout: the A, G, and F are quite consistent, but the B and D less so.

the scribe worked backwards from the end to the beginning.[32] It also needs to be noted that some, but not all, of H's marginal material was erased in the process of adding this structure: this much is implied by the insertion marks left in the text by the corrector (H³) alongside which only erasures are to be found in the margins.[33] More will be said about the significance of these letters below.

8. Besides these additions, various **marginal glosses** were inserted by hands ranging in date from the thirteenth to the seventeenth century. The early modern glosses have mostly been omitted from the edition below (the exception being one helpful occasion where a sentence has been completed),[34] but it should be noted that the latest additions include some thirty-seven glosses, mostly drawing attention to post-Conquest events, in the hand of William Howard (1563–1640).[35] The lower margins also contain a series of rough glosses in pencil, and this hand may be the same as that which scattered numerous crosses and asterisks in pencil throughout the text and which attempted to correct many of the leap years by entering a large lower-case "b" for *bissextilis* alongside the relevant year.

It can be seen from all this that the chronicle was updated at reasonably frequent intervals during the final third of the twelfth century, though perhaps in a rather irregular and sometimes quite rudimentary way. The house where this updating took place was almost certainly located in the central midlands.[36] This much is implied by the later continuations' coverage of the obits of lesser clergy—that is, of clerics below the rank of bishop.[37] Its obits of this kind comprise those of

[32] From VA1 to AD128 the leap-years and dominical letters have been displaced forward four years (that is, VA1 has the right letter for VA5, 2 the right letter for 6, and so on); from 131 to 168 they have been displaced forward six years, from 171 to 331 four years, from 333 to 373 three years, from 375 to 468 two years, from 470 to 482 one year, from the second 482 to 491 two years, from 493 to 596 one year, from the second 596 to 649 two years, from the second 649 to 659 three years, from 663 to 978 they are accurate, from 979 to 1094 they are displaced forward one year, and from 1096 to 1203 they are accurate.

[33] See, for example, *Coventry* 717.1 and 825 below.

[34] For the medieval glosses, see *Coventry* 281.2, 449.3, 592.3, 1159.2, 1160.2, 1176, 1181.3, 1190.6, and 1198.4.

[35] See H, fols. 48r, 56v, 57r, 57v (3x), 58r (3x), 59r (4x), 60r (4x), 60v, 61r, 61v (2x), 62r, 62v, 63r (2x), 63v (3x), 64r, 64v, 65r, 65v (2x), 66r (2x), 66v (2x). The "Derby Chronicle" on fols. 68r to 70v includes another six glosses in the same hand.

[36] Cf. *Liber Eliensis*, ed. Ernest O. Blake, Camden Society, 3rd ser., 92 (London: Royal Historical Society, 1962), xxix, n. 20, who, for some reason which I have not been able to discover, identified Harley 3775 as a chronicle associated with Bury St Edmunds.

[37] At the higher level a broader geographical awareness is apparent, the bishoprics represented comprising Canterbury, Coventry, Durham, Ely, Hereford, Lincoln,

two abbots of St Mary of the Meadows in Leicester, of one prior of Coventry Cathedral Priory, of an archdeacon of Coventry, of a dean of Lincoln Cathedral, and that of an archdeacon of Northampton.[38] When it comes to local prodigies the chronicle notices, in similar fashion, miracles which took place when the Church of St Mary in the Castle at Leicester was struck by lightning in 1196, when St Hugh of Avalon was buried at Lincoln in 1200, and at Burton-on-Trent in 1201.[39] The enshrinement of St Gilbert, the founder of Sempringham, is also noted under 1202. Below the level of events of national importance there is such a clear focus on events in the central midlands that there can be little doubt that the chronicle was produced there. Further indications of its provenance point to two different houses in this region: to the Abbey of St Mary of the Meadows, Leicester, and to Coventry Cathedral Priory.

## (c) The Leicester Connection

The existence of a Leicester connection is strongly suggested by the continuators' interest in the city and its earls. They note, for example, the obit of Earl Robert II (d. 1168). They note the misfortunes that resulted from Earl Robert III's participation in the great rebellion: the ravaging of the city of Leicester in 1173, his invasion of England and defeat at the Battle of Fornham, the destruction of the city's walls and castle in 1176, and his confinement in 1183.[40] Another item records his departure on crusade.[41] Other entries record Earl Robert IV's capture and imprisonment by the French in 1194, his release in March 1196, his return to England later that year, the election of his uncle, Roger Beaumont, as bishop of St Andrews in 1198, and the same kinsman's death in 1202.[42] The notice of Robert IV's release names his mother, Petronilla, as well as his father.[43] It is true that the text lacks an obit for Earl Robert III; but his death took place in mid-1190, at the beginning of the long lacuna which ends with 1194,[44] and the extent of the continuators' interest in the earls of Leicester is confirmed by the almost complete absence of items concerned with any of the other great English

Norwich, St Andrews, Worcester, and York. The chronicle does not provide a "complete" run of obits for any one bishopric in the late twelfth century, except for Coventry and Canterbury—if that is, certain omissions are deliberate (see below).

[38] *Coventry* 1168.2, 1177, 1179.1–2, 1195.2, and 1200.3.

[39] *Coventry* 1196.2, 1200, 1201.

[40] *Coventry* 1173.1–2, 1176, 1183.2.

[41] See *Coventry* 1190.4 and the commentary below.

[42] *Coventry* 1194.1, 1196.1, 1196.3, 1198.2, and 1202.2. See also the commentary on 1202.2 below.

[43] *Coventry* 1196.1.

[44] See *Coventry* 1168.1 and the commentary on *Coventry* 1190.4 below.

magnates of the twelfth century. For the other great magnates, there are just two notices: one for Richard fitz Gilbert, earl of Striguil (d. 1176), and one for Hugh II, earl of Chester (d. 1181).[45] This continuators' interest in the earls of Leicester can even be used to explain why the chronicle has a notice recording the exploits of a French magnate, William des Barres: William may have been a knight of Philip Augustus, but he was also the brother-in-law of Earl Robert III.[46] These details show that the chronicle was completed in the midlands, at a religious house close to if not within Leicestershire, perhaps at Earl Robert II's foundation and *Eigenkloster*, the Abbey of St Mary of the Meadows. It might even be considered relevant that the Church of St Mary in the Castle, which is recorded as the site of various prodigies under 1196, had been the former site of the community before Earl Robert II refounded it as an Augustinian house in 1143.[47]

There are, however, problems with assigning the chronicle to Leicester. Its coverage of the obits of the abbots of St Mary's is not, to begin with, quite as comprehensive as might be expected had it been composed there,[48] and the abbey's library catalogue contains no record of the manuscript. It is true that the catalogue contains one entry that might well describe H: *Cronica abbreuiata per magistrum Thomam de Ripley in quaternis, 2° fo. mar'*.[49] The present chronicle is indeed an abbreviated work and the physical description, *in quartos*, matches the appearance of H. The entry contains, however, one clear discrepancy that prevents it being taken as a record of our manuscript. That the name *Thomas de Ripley* appears nowhere in H need not be considered an issue, since any such inscription could easily have been cut away, but it is clearly problematic that *mar'* is not the first word on the second folio. The first sentence on the second folio (today fol. 35r) does contain the word *mar'* (for *Martii*), but it occurs as the last word in the first line.[50] Second folio references typically refer to the first *words* of the leaf (numerals being overlooked where they intervene), and this is the case with all the items in the Leicester Abbey catalogue that have been identified to

[45] *Coventry* 1172.1, 1182.1. Note also the muddled reference to Robert I of Gloucester under 1143.

[46] See *Coventry* 1188.4 and commentary. There are, as will emerge below, other ways of explaining the presence of this item, most notably by reference to the influence of Hugh de Nonant.

[47] See Dugdale, *Monasticon*, 6:463–64; Thomson, *St Mary of the Meadows*, 1–3.

[48] The chronicle has the obits of abbots Richard (1168) and William of Calwich (1177), but not that of Abbot William de Broke (1187): see *Heads I*, 171.

[49] MS. Oxford, Bod.L., Laud misc. 623, fol. 24v (ed. Teresa Webber and Andrew G. Watson, *CBMLC*, 6:109–399, at 237 [no. 643]). For the dating of the catalogue, see Maude V. Clarke, "Henry Knighton and the Library Catalogue of Leicester Abbey," *English Historical Review* 45 (1930): 103–7.

[50] See *Coventry* 37.

date.[51] Given that this register is one of the most substantial book lists to survive for any medieval English monastery, recording well over a thousand items, this discrepancy might well be taken as positive evidence that Leicester Abbey did not own H. Indeed, the entry quoted above might well be read as evidence that the abbey possessed a *different* copy of a closely related chronicle, a copy of similar size where the scribe had managed to include a little more of the text on the first folio putting *mar'* at the very beginning of the second. But in the absence of this manuscript suggestions of this kind are highly speculative, and the date of the library catalogue—it was compiled in the late fifteenth century—means that its evidence cannot rule out the possibility that H may have belonged to Leicester Abbey in the late twelfth century.

## (d) The Coventry Connection

The existence of a Coventry connection is implied by data of a somewhat different order. There is, to begin with, the evidence that D—the manuscript of John of Worcester's *Chronica chronicarum* from which the first continuation was derived—was almost certainly produced at and for the cathedral priory at Coventry. This much is clear from various adaptations made by D[1], the scribe who was responsible for much of the whole. To John's list of the bishops of Lichfield, for example, he has added the rubric *Nomina episcoporum Couentrensium* between Peter, bishop of Lichfield from 1072 to 1085, and Robert de Limsey, bishop from 1086 to 1117. Bishop Peter had moved the episcopal seat from Lichfield to Chester in 1075, but it was later relocated a second time by Bishop Robert, who moved it to Coventry in the late 1090s.[52] D[1] also continued John's list of the see's bishops adding Robert Peche (1121–1126) and Roger de Clinton (1129–1148), and it was later extended twice again, first, to include Walter Durdent (1149–1159), and then in the thirteenth century to include Richard Peche (1161–1182), Gerard Pucelle (1183–1184), and Geoffrey Muschamp (1198–1208).[53] A couple of the other

[51] Teresa Webber, "The Books of Leicester Abbey," in *Leicester Abbey: Medieval History, Archaeology and Manuscript Studies*, ed. Joanna Story with Jill Bourne and Richard Buckley (Leicester: Leicestershire Archaeological and Historical Society, 2006), 127–46, at 130 and nn. 41–42. For a slight exception to the usual pattern, see Michael Gullick and Teresa Webber, "Summary Catalogue of Surviving Manuscripts from Leicester Abbey," in *Leicester Abbey*, ed. Story et al., 173–92, at 186–87 and n. 35. I am most grateful to Teresa Webber for allowing me to read both essays in advance of publication. On the library of Leicester Abbey, see also *CBMLC*, 6:104; *MLGB*, 113.

[52] WM*GP*, 4.173. The move was legitimised by a privilege of Pope Paschal II dated to 18 April 1102 (JL 5912; ed. *PL* 163.95).

[53] D, fol. 7r: "Nomina episcoporum Couentrensium: i. Rodbertus de Linisig, ii. Rodbertus Peket, iii. Rogerus de Clintun, iv. Walterus, Ricardus peccatum, Gerardus

lists (those for Worcester and Canterbury) have also been updated, but none has been maintained so intensively. Earl Leofric's name has also been entered in capitals on fols. 212v, 216v, and 219v. There are many marginal references that imply Coventry's ongoing ownership of the book, including a rough note on fol. 219v describing Earl Leofric as *huius ecclesie fundator*; a twelfth-century note on fol. 227r recording Leofwine's demotion from the episcopal see of Lichfield and his retirement to the abbey of Coventry whence he had come; a thirteenth-century note on fol. 245v which dates the translation of the see from Chester to Coventry to 18 April, in the tenth indiction and the third year of the pontificate of Pope Paschal II; and a note highlighting the obit of Robert Peche beside the annal containing it on fol. 258v.[54] It is clear, then, that the exemplar used in the making of the first extended continuation was a Coventry manuscript.

Having established this connection, it is natural to go on to look for codicological links between the two books, but although there is a certain similarity in the general appearance of D and the earlier, mid-twelfth-century, sections of H (that is, those executed by scribes $H^1$–$H^6$),[55] the two manuscripts do not seem to have any scribes in common, and there are a number of contrasting features. D is ruled, for example, in drypoint, whereas H is ruled in plummet. None of these divergences is so great as to prevent H and D being the products of the same scriptorium, but, alas, their palaeography does not provide any substantial grounds for associating H with the priory.[56] The best that can be said on the basis of their history as books is that H and D had a similar afterlife, since both passed through the hands of Lord William Howard. Howard, as has already been noted, owned H, making extensive annotations in the margins of the text. D, meanwhile, was the manuscript which Howard took as the basis of his 1592 edition of the *Chronicarum Chronica*.[57] He wrote his name on fol. 1r, and the lion-emblem which appears in many Howard manuscripts is to be found on fols. 1r and 266v. It is tempting to suggest, therefore, that Howard may have acquired H at the same time as he obtained D, but this is not an especially convincing reason for associating H with Coventry.

Pucelle, Gatfridus de Muscham."

54 For other indications, see Brett, "John," 106 n. 1; McGurk in JW*CC*, 2:xl–xli; Colker, *TCD*, no. 502.

55 For the general aspect of D, see Meehan, "MSS of James Ussher," pl. 70 (fol. 10r).

56 The same points apply to the one other Coventry MS of twelfth-century date which is presently known: MS. Cambridge, Trinity College, O.1.64. On the library of Coventry Cathedral Priory, see *MLGB*, 24; *MLGBS*, 15; *CBMLC*, 2:297–98, and 4:108.

57 Howard also made use of G, which was then in the possession of William Lambard, to supply material lacking in D: see *Chronicon ex chronicis ab initio mundi usque ad annum Domini 1118 deductum, auctore Florentio Wigorniensi monacho*, ed. Lord William Howard (London: Thomas Dauson, 1592), pref., and McGurk in JW*CC*, 2:xxxvi–xli.

Much stronger grounds for doing so are, however, provided by a curious pattern of omission which is common to the additions to both H and D, for both sets of additions record the successions and obits of all the bishops of Coventry in the late twelfth century except for those of Hugh de Nonant, the infamous bishop who expelled the monks from the cathedral priory in late 1189.[58] Hugh, it should be recalled, was one of the leaders of a movement that was attempting to bring about the replacement of England's monastic chapters with colleges of secular canons.[59] The rise of this movement is to be explained by reference on the one hand to the emergence of new monastic movements such as the Carthusians whose prestige diminished the authority of the Benedictines and their ability to defend their privileges, and on the other hand to the emergence of an ambitious and better-educated secular clergy. As Michael Franklin puts it, "the new generation of bishops, trained in canon law, of which Bishop Hugh and Archbishop Baldwin were a part, could see no place for the monastic chapter, which markedly restrained their freedom of action, at least when compared with the patronage available to their brothers with secular chapters."[60] But from the perspective of those who stood to lose out if they had their way, this movement was an outrage and a threat to the very survival of monasticism itself. Thus Gervase of Canterbury has Hugh declare before the king that if he had his way, "within a brief period not one monk would remain in England—to the Devil with monks!"[61] For Gervase, Hugh is a *monachorum persecutor specialis*,[62] who was "intruded" rather than "elected" to the see.[63]

[58] See *Coventry*, 1129 (election of Roger de Clinton), 1161 (consecration of Richard Peche), 1182.2 (obit of Richard Peche), 1183.4 (consecration of Gerard Pucelle), 1184.2 (obit of Gerard Pucelle), 1198.3 (consecration of Geoffrey Muschamp).

[59] See chap. 1, § f, above. On Hugh and his career, see Michael J. Franklin, "Nonant, Hugh de (d. 1198)," *ODNB*, 40: 991–93; idem, *EEA*, 17:xxvi–xlvii; D. E. Desborough, "Politics and Prelacy in the Late Twelfth Century: The Career of Hugh de Nonant, Bishop of Coventry," *Historical Research* 64 (1991): 1–14 (esp. 3–6). On the great crises that afflicted the priory in the twelfth century, see also Everett U. Crosby, *Bishop and Chapter in Twelfth-Century England: A Study of the 'Mensa Episcopalis'*, Cambridge Studies in Medieval Life and Thought, 4th ser., 23 (Cambridge: Cambridge University Press, 1994), 113–32; Ralph H. C. Davis and R. Bearman, "An Unknown Coventry Charter," *EHR* 86 (1971): 533–47; Richard Goddard, *Lordship and Medieval Urbanisation: Coventry, 1043–1355* (Woodbridge: Boydell Press for the Royal Historical Society, 2004), 51–56.

[60] Michael J. Franklin, "The Bishops of Coventry and Lichfield, c. 1072–1208," in *Coventry's First Cathedral: The Cathedral and Priory of Saint Mary*, ed. George Demidowicz (Stamford: Paul Watkins, 1994), 118–38, at 135. On this movement in the late twelfth-century English church, see Knowles, *MO*, 313–30.

[61] Gervase, 1:470. Cf. Devizes, *CTR*, 69–73, who states that Hugh expelled the monks *ex odio religionis*.

[62] Gervase, 1:550. See also Gervase, 1:488.

[63] Gervase, 1:326.

The chronology of Hugh's actions at Coventry may be reconstructed as follows.[64] He initiated his reform in September 1189: on 17 September he obtained a royal confirmation of his right to appoint the prior and to regulate all the affairs of the priory in return for 300 marks;[65] on 9 October there was a violent confrontation of some kind within the priory itself;[66] and on 22 October Hugh laid a complaint against the monks before his fellow bishops who were then meeting at Westminster for the consecration of Godfrey de Luci. He accused the monks of having assaulted him, but he had already, according to Richard of Devizes, ejected the greater part of the community before bringing the case.[67] The rest of the monks are said to have been expelled in December 1190, after Hugh obtained a ruling in favour of his reform from Pope Clement III which was promulgated at a council in Westminster on 16 October.[68] The secular clerks whom Hugh had assembled were installed, but their college survived for only six years.[69] The course of events turned against Hugh in early 1194, when King Richard was released from captivity and began to take action against those who had colluded with Prince John during his absence. Hugh had at least spent several months in Germany with the king and he managed to avoid giving himself away as greviously as his brother, Richard de Nonant (who had openly declared himself to be John's man when asked to stand hostage for his king),[70] but charges were still brought against him after the king's return. He was able to obtain a pardon and the restoration of his temporalities by

[64] The dispute is discussed in detail in Knowles, *MO*, 322–24, and Crosby, *Bishop and Chapter*, 126–30. See also *C&S I*, no. 175, and for the possibility that Hugh was responding to the monks' usurpation of the bishop's right to appoint the prior, see Desborough, "Politics and Prelacy," 7; Franklin in *EEA*, 17:xxxi.

[65] For the confirmation, see *The Great Register of Lichfield Cathedral known as Magnum registrum album*, ed. H. E. Savage, Collections for the History of Staffordshire 1924 (Kendal: Titus Wilson, 1926), 78 (no. 168). For the sum of 300 marks, see Gervase, 1:461, and for the occasion of the grant, RH*Chron.*, 3:15.

[66] Gervase, 1:461, reports an "armed invasion" of the priory: "the prior fled, the monks fleeing into the church were beaten with sticks, others returned wounded and useless, others were put in chains and in prison, others fled naked and in ignominy"; the record-cupboard of the church was broken open and the monks' charters were incinerated. For the destruction of records, see also the Memorandum of ca. 1226 (in Dugdale, *Monasticon*, 8:1242), and for the incursion, Newburgh, 2:394.

[67] Devizes, *CTR*, 8. See also Gerald of Wales, *Speculum ecclesiae*, ed. John S. Brewer, *GCO*, 4:64–67.

[68] In Gervase, 1:488–89, the monks are dispersed *per diversa vagantes*. See also Devizes, *CTR*, 13.

[69] Devizes, *CTR*, 69–73, goes on to claim that Hugh demolished the priory, building a new church and canons' houses in its place. See also Newburgh, 2:393–94; Diceto, *YH*, 2:159; RH*Chron.*, 3:168.

[70] RH*Chron.*, 3:232–33, 287. Hugh's stay in Germany began before 30 September 1193 and ended after 21 or 22 January 1194: see *EEA*, 17:xliii.

submitting to a fine of 2000 marks,[71] but the political climate was now far more receptive to the monks' cause. The prior whom Hugh had ejected, Moses, duly brought a case for novel disseisin before the royal court in September 1194, and, having countered the canons' offer of 600 marks by offering a sum just as great, he succeeded in persuading the king to confirm a charter which assigned the barony and the priorate to the prior.[72] Moses was now able, in addition, to find the financial backing to put the monks' side of the dispute before the papal court—something he had been unable to do in 1189–1190.[73] The outcome was that Pope Celestine III issued a bull in their favour in 1197, and although Moses was not himself reinstalled as prior, his monks were formally restored on 18 January 1198.[74] By this time an ailing Hugh had retired to the monastery of Bec, where he became a monk and died on Good Friday 1198.[75]

Almost all the major chroniclers of the period cover these sensational events, the monastic writers such as Richard of Devizes deploring Hugh's actions, the seculars such as Gerald of Wales defending them.[76] In contrast, our chronicle records the restoration of the monks in 1198, but makes no mention of their expulsion. There is, moreover, no mention whatsoever of Hugh, but this is in keeping with the policy found in the one other surviving historical work maintained at Coventry at this time.[77] For Nonant's name is conspicuous by its absence from the list of the see's bishops on folio 7v of the Dublin manuscript of John of Worcester's *Chronica chronicarum*, its thirteenth-century continuator having moved, as was pointed out above, straight from Gerard Pucelle (1183–1184) to

[71] RI I*Chron.*, 3:233, 241–42, 287. Howden puts the level of the fine at 5000 marks, but a fine of 2000 marks was recorded by the exchequer and remained on Hugh's account: see *Pipe Roll 7 Richard I*, 191; *EEA*, 17:xliii. Might one surmise that Hugh had already paid the difference?

[72] *Rotuli curiae regis: Rolls and Records of the Court Held before the King's Justiciars or Justices*, ed. Francis Palgrave, 2 vols. (London: Eyre and Spottiswoode, 1835), 1:3, 66–67. On these proceedings, see Crosby, *Bishop and Chapter*, 128–29.

[73] See Newburgh, 1:393–95.

[74] RH*Chron.*, 4:35–37, but note also Jocelin of Brakelond, 94–95, who makes Abbot Samson of Bury instrumental in seeing through the fulfilment of the papal mandate in spite of further obstruction from the king and Archbishop Hubert Walter. For the date of the restoration, see the commentary on *Coventry* 1198.1 below.

[75] RH*Chron.*, 4:45; Gervase, 1:552. For contrasting attempts to explain the significance of date on which Hugh died, see Devizes, *AW*, s.a. 1198; Roger of Wendover, *Liber qui dicitur flores historiarum*, ed. H. G. Hewlett, RS 84, 3 vols. (London: Eyre & Spottiswoode, 1886–1889), 1:273–74; Gerald of Wales, *Speculum ecclesie*, in *GCO*, 4:68–71.

[76] See *GCO*, 4:394–95. In addition to the works already cited, compare also other local, "midland," records such as the "Derby" Chronicle in H, fol. 68v: "mcxxi . . . Hugo de Nonant expulit monachos de Couentre et posuit ibi canonicos seculares"; *Annales monasterii de Burton*, s.a. 1186 (ed. Luard, *AM*, 1:183–500, at 188).

[77] For the lost "Chronicle of Prior Geoffrey," see n. 92 below.

Geoffrey Muschamp (1198–1208). It is true that Hugh's name appears in a later Coventry list of the bishops of the see which seems to originate from the priory, but this list dates from around 1300 and the historical notes which accompany it cover Hugh's attempted secularisation as though it were still an open wound.[78] It seems, in short, to have been the policy of Coventry's monks around 1200 to damn Hugh's memory,[79] and the presence of this pattern in H points to the cathedral priory as almost the only place where our chronicle could have been maintained. Had it been produced at any other monastic centre in the midlands, Hugh's actions would almost certainly have attracted some kind of attention.[80] This is, furthermore, not the only feature of the chronicle which is tidily explained by reference to the history of the cathedral priory in the late 1180s and 1190s. For Hugh's appointment helps to make sense of shifts in the general character of the chronicle during this period and of the third extended continuation's somewhat denser coverage of political events, since he was exceptionally well placed to provide information on the affairs of the kingdom.

Having begun his career as a clerk of Thomas Becket in the 1160s, Hugh had gone on to become a royal servant and one of Henry II's closest allies. It was to this that he owed his election as bishop of Coventry, but his involvement in royal affairs seems to have kept him at court, except when he was carrying out important missions for the king. Indeed, his involvement in royal business seems to have been so intense that it prevented him being consecrated until some three

---

[78] The list is to be found in MS. Oxford, Bod.L., Douce 139, fol. 2r, and names thirteen bishops from Robert de Limsey (1086–1117) through to Roger de Meyland (1258–1296), including *vii hugo de nunant.* Mostly comprised of the texts of royal laws and statutes, Douce 139 shows its association with the priory clearly from the various agreements concerning the priory and acts of homage to its priors inserted s.xiv on spaces and spare leaves towards the end of the volume (e.g. fols. 141v, 177v–178v). Two historical notes next to the list of popes on fol. 2r treat the suppression of the priory in a curious fashion: *xix Clemens. Tempore istius papa ex[pulsus] sunt monachi couen[trie.]; xx Celestinus. Tempore istius papa re[uersus] sunt monaci Couentrie.* They minimise the scandal by using the passive voice and by detaching the episode from Hugh. The coverage of the bishops of Coventry in the brief chronicle on fol. 1v concludes, unfortunately, with the obit of Walter Durdent (1149–1159).

[79] It is true that Prior Geoffrey's testimony during the investigation of the monks' electoral rights does cover the suppression of the priory and Hugh's death (see the Memorandum of ca. 1226 in Dugdale, *Monasticon*, 6:1242–44, and below), but then he could scarcely avoid doing so in a record of this nature.

[80] It is possible that the policy of *damnatio memoriae* in H may even have extended to Archbishop Baldwin, who attempted a less extreme kind of secularisation at Canterbury (see Knowles, *MO*, 314–22, 325–27). For H has notices for the obits and successions of Baldwin's predecessors Thomas Becket and Richard (see 1162, 1171.2, 1175, 1184.1 below), but nothing for Baldwin himself. However, he died at Tyre on 19 November 1190, within the period between late 1190 and 1194 when work on the chronicle was in abeyance.

years after his election in January 1185.[81] In 1186 he was sent to Rome to obtain papal permission for John to become king of Ireland, and returned with a papal commission to carry out the planned coronation.[82] But having spent a little over one month in England, he departed again for Normandy with the king in February 1187, not returning again until late January 1188.[83] He was finally consecrated by Archbishop Baldwin at Lambeth on 31 January, but he appears to have spent almost all of his time during this visit to England with either the king or the archbishop. Henry returned to Normandy on 10 July 1188. Hugh appears to have headed there in advance of the king, remaining on the Continent from June 1188 until August 1189.[84] It is only after Richard I's coronation on 3 September 1189 that the historical record finds Hugh within his diocese and reforming his cathedral. Indeed, one interpretation might be that he turned his energies to this project because with Henry's death he was deprived of the intimacy he had once enjoyed with royal affairs. Yet he was again with the royal court in Normandy in March 1190, when Richard summoned his brother John and compelled him to swear that he would not enter England within the three-year period following his departure for the Third Crusade, an event reported by *Coventry* with some circumstantial detail.[85] He seems to have remained with the king until the end of June when he once again returned to England.[86] Hugh de Nonant appears, in short, to have been in France with Henry's court and then with Richard's court when many of the events covered in the third extended continuation took place.

Given that the third extended continuation seems to have been added in or soon after the final months of 1190—that is, after the initial incursion of October 1189, but possibly before the final expulsions of December 1190—we are left with three possibilities. The first is that there were some exchanges of letters, if only for the sake of politeness, between Hugh and the monks in the period between his appointment and the final expulsions and that by this channel news of the court and of events in France, spun by Hugh for the benefit of Richard I, reached the community. This material might then have given rise to the third continuation. A second possibility is that the chronicle was briefly taken to another house where it was maintained in a different fashion. A third and perhaps the most likely possibility is that the chronicle was briefly taken over by the clerks

[81] Gervase, 1:326.

[82] RH*Chron.*, 2:317.

[83] RH*Chron.*, 2:337 names Hugh as one of the bishops who were with Henry II at Le Mans on 21 January.

[84] RH*GHS*, 2:66 lists Hugh among those on Henry's side at La Ferté Bernard on 28 May 1189, when a peace conference was held under the aegis of Cardinal John of Anagni. For other movements during this period, see RH*Chron.*, 2:317, 337, 338; 3:5, 8, 14–15, 24, 26; RH*GHS*, 2:73, 75, 79.

[85] RH*Chron.*, 3:32. Compare *Coventry* 1190.3.

[86] See *EEA*, 17:xli.

of Hugh's household during the only period when he is known to have resided at Coventry for an extended length of time.[87] If we were to add the annals for 1185 and 1186 to the work they carried out, this hypothesis would have the great virtue of explaining why the script employed by $H^7$ to $H^{11}$ is so different in aspect from those of the scribes that precede and follow them. The lacuna that follows these annals may be explained, furthermore, by reference to the neglect of the chronicle following the monks' expulsion: that is, it may be supposed that occasional updates resumed after the monks were restored in 1198 and that there was a fitful attempt to fill the gap between 1190 and 1198, one which yielded some material for 1194 onwards.

There are, then, many features of the present chronicle which can be explained by the hypothesis that it was continued at Coventry during the second half of the twelfth century.[88] But it must be acknowledged that there are problems with this argument. There remains, for example, the considerable evidence for an interest in Leicester and its earls, though this may be explained by the close proximity of the two cities and the great political importance of its ruling family. One might have expected a Coventry chronicle to have shown more interest in the deeds of the earls of Chester. Yet only two of the earls died within the period covered by the later continuations, Ranulf II (d. 1153) and Hugh II (d. 1181), and the chronicle has the latter's obit,[89] and the former's took place within the period where the first continuation petered out, evidently because it was added some time after the events it records.[90] A more serious problem for the present argument is that the continuations lack a complete set of dates for the priors of Coventry in the late twelfth century. It has an obit for Prior Laurence (d. 1179), but lacks those of Priors Thomas (d. 1180×1182) and Moses (d. 1198). In this respect the chronicle needs to be compared with another historical source from Coventry, the *lost* "Chronicle of Prior Geoffrey."

To explain, William Dugdale in his *Antiquities of Warwickshire* cited as one of his sources for the history of the cathedral in this period a text which he identified as *Chron. MS. Galfr. Pr. de Cov.* The *Galfr.* in question is evidently Prior Geoffrey who ruled from 1216 to 1235,[91] and the information that Dugdale

---

[87] It appears that some texts were destroyed when the monks were ejected from the cathedral priory (see above), but the memorandum of c.1226 (Dugdale, *Monasticon*, 8:1242) refers only to the loss of the monks' *instrumenta*. Their books may have survived unscathed.

[88] This hypothesis may also help to explain the presence of a notice under 1195 recording the obit of Haimo, dean of Lincoln, and the consequent appointment of Master Roger de Rolleston to that position: see the commentary on *Coventry* 1195.2 below.

[89] *Coventry* 1182.1.

[90] *Peerage*, 3:166–67; 14:170. It might also be significant that Hugh de Nonant had recruited Earl Ranulf III to his cause: see M. J. Franklin in *EEA*, 17:xxxviii–xl.

[91] *The Heads of Religious Houses, England and Wales*, vol. 2, *1216–1377*, ed. D. M. Smith and V. C. M. London (Cambridge: Cambridge University Press, 2001), 35.

took from his chronicle represents all that is now known of it.[92] Dugdale cited it on just two occasions, the first time when quoting an account of the priory's foundation by Earl Leofric and his wife, Godgifu, and its consecration by Archbishop Eadsige,[93] the second time when listing the dates of four of the house's priors: Laurence, who died on 29 January 1179; Moses, who died on 16 July 1198; Joybert, who died on 14 June 1216; and Geoffrey, who was elected on 17 July in the same year.[94] As far as present purposes are concerned, the key point is that for the period down to 1202 Geoffrey recorded the obit of Moses as well as that of Lawrence. It follows that the absence of the obit of Prior Thomas, whose brief

[92] The chronicle is usually identified as a document of about 1226—today MS. London, B.L., Cotton Charters XIII.26—which was printed in part in Dugdale, *Monasticon*, 6:1242–44, under the title *De electione episcopi*, and it is certainly true that this document reports the same man's words, but it takes the form not of an annalistic text, but of a memorandum or transcript of a legal process, being a series of sworn depositions concerning the priory's rights in elections to the bishopric of Coventry, the most substantial being that provided by Geoffrey. In addition, it lacks information that Dugdale attributes to Geoffrey's chronicle. The account of the priory's foundation is nowhere to be found in Cotton Charters XIII.26, and whilst it names the priors mentioned by Dugdale, it lacks the dates which he obtained from Geoffrey's chronicle. Michael Franklin may well be right, therefore, when he argues in *EEA*, 17:120–23, that Geoffrey was, in addition to being the major contributor to the memorandum, the author of another work, a chronicle that survived until the mid-seventeenth century when it was consulted by Dugdale but which is long since lost. It is worth stressing, therefore, that there is no possibility that the present chronicle is that of Prior Geoffrey, for it peters out in 1202, whereas Geoffrey's chronicle extended until at least 1216, and it lacks information such as the precise date of Prior Laurence's obit which Dugdale found in Geoffrey's chronicle (see below). It should also be noted that Dugdale's collaborator, the antiquarian Roger Dodsworth (1585–1654), made use of a *Registrum Galfridi Prioris Coventrensis temp. Henry III and Edward I* (see MS. Oxford, Bod.L., Dodsworth 39, fol. 103r). The cartulary in question may have been the bundle of 20 folios which Francis Douce (1757–1834) detached from MS. Oxford, Bod.L., Douce 139, and gave to Thomas Sharpe (1770–1841): see J. C. Lancaster, "The Coventry Forged Charters: A Reconsideration," *Bulletin of the Institute of Historical Research* 27 (1954): 113–39, at 116–17. If so, then it has certainly been destroyed, for Sharpe's folios passed into the Staunton Collection at Longbridge House, and from there to the Free Reference Library of Birmingham where they perished in the fire of 1879: see Ker, *MLGB*, 54, n. 7. It is worth asking whether Prior Geoffrey's chronicle was actually part of this cartulary, for short histories of monastic houses were often prefixed to cartularies, especially in the thirteenth century. Cf. Sharpe, *HLW*, 123; *Heads I*, 41, n. 1.

[93] Dugdale, *Antiquities*, 1:100: "Anno domini MXLIII, constructum fuit monasterium Coventrense a memorandæ recordationis duce Leurico, et uxore ejus Godiva, dedicatumque eodem anno ab archiepisc. Dorobernensi Edzio, quarto Non. Octob. post Pascha, Abbate Lefwino cum XXIIII monachis in eodem instituto."

[94] Dugdale, *Antiquities*, 1:105.

priorate is scarcely attested in the documentary record,[95] is a much less serious matter than the omission of Moses' obit. It is the latter omission and the comparative lack of detail that need to be explained.

It is not hard, however, to find reasons why a Coventry chronicler writing in the years immediately after Moses's death might have omitted his obit. It is just possible, first of all, that there was some kind of resentment against Moses on the part of the recently restored monks that prevented them commemorating him—a resentment that had been forgotten by the time of Prior Geoffrey. This much is suggested by the words of William of Newburgh, who reports that Hugh de Nonant had prepared the way for his reforms by sowing discord between the prior and the monks,[96] and by the actions of the prelates who re-established the priory in January 1198. For when the priory was restored it was not Moses who was made prior, but Joybert, who was also the head of the Cluniac priory at Much Wenlock. One would, however, prefer to think that the monks were not ingrates, for it was Moses who had led the campaign for their restoration. The omission of his obit is perhaps better explained by his refusal to accept Joybert's appointment. For Moses appealed to the papacy and succeeded in obtaining from Pope Innocent III on 3 June 1198 a mandate requiring his restoration and Joybert's removal,[97] but he died on 16 July before he could have it implemented.[98] The very fact that at the time of his death Moses was challenging the authority of the incumbent, Joybert, may have been enough to make the newly restored monks hesitate before recording his obit. A sense of what was proper at this moment may well have held the continuators back, but the need for such sensitivity would have passed by the time of Prior Geoffrey. The omission of Moses' obit need not, in short, be seen as a problem. It remains an issue that the Coventry obits recorded by the present work are not as detailed as those that Dugdale found in Geoffrey's chronicle, but a certain haste in the continuators' addition of data can perhaps be explained by examining the intended purpose of the chronicle.

## (e) The Context and Function of the Chronicle

The evidence for the provenance of the chronicle is not, then, entirely satisfactory, but there are still many reasons for thinking that it was produced and maintained at Coventry Cathedral Priory. Indeed, the presence of references to all the bishops of Coventry except the infamous Hugh de Nonant is a particularly

[95] His priorate may have ended in ignominy: see Michael J. Franklin in *EEA*, 17:xxiv–xxv, xxix. For a Prior Nicholas who may also belong to this period, see *Heads I*, 41.

[96] Newburgh, 2:394; *EEA*, 17:xxxi.

[97] *Selected Letters of Pope Innocent III Concerning England (1198–1216)*, ed. Christopher R. Cheney and William H. Semple (London: T. Nelson, 1953), no. 28.

[98] *EEA*, 17:xxxiv; *Heads I*, 41.

strong reason. It is not sufficient on its own to prove that H was produced there, but when combined with the rest a case emerges which is significantly stronger than that for its production at Leicester, and it is on this basis that the text has been designated the *Coventry Chronicle*. Where the manuscript and text allow us to reach rather more secure conclusions is with regard to the issue of the chronicle's context and function. To be sure, the shifts in the character of the entries suggest that some of the contributors differed in their ideas as to the value and purpose of the chronicle, but the addition of the dominical letters to the outer margins of the manuscript provides an unusually forthright clue as to one of the contexts in which the chronicle was used.

To explain: the dominical letter was a device usually found in a liturgical calendar. A typical twelfth- or thirteenth-century liturgical calendar would have within its chronological apparatus a column in which the first seven letters of the alphabet (A, B, C, D, E, F, and G) were repeated in a regular sequence, one letter for each day of the year beginning with an "A" on 1 January and ending with another "A" on 31 December. The function of these letters was to allow the practiced user to see at a glance which dates in a given year would be Sundays, hence the name "dominical" from *dominica dies*, "the Lord's day." In an "A" year the dates on which Sunday fell would be those marked with the letter "A", in a "B" year it would be those marked with the letter "B", and so on. With each change of year, the letter of the next year would necessarily be one step up the scale, since there are fifty-two weeks and one day in a common year: that is, if the dominical letter for one year were "E", the dominical letter of the next common year would be a "D"; if it were "D", then the letter of the next common year would be a "C", and so on. In a leap year, however, an additional change of letter would be required, for in these years two letters would apply, the first being that of period from 1 January to the first 24 February, the second being that of the period between the second 24 February (the *bissextus*) and 31 December. The change, as at the end of the year, always involved a single step up the scale: that is, if the dominical letter were "C" for the first part of the year, it would be "B" from the *bissextus*; if it were "E" for the first part of the year, it would be "D" from the *bissextus*, and so on. In practice, there were seven kinds of leap year, and their dominical letters followed a regular pattern, as follows:

A → G, C → B, E → D, G → F, B → A, D → C, F → E

The upshot, moreover, is that the dominical letter would change over time according to a regular twenty-eight-year pattern, there being one change for each common year and two changes for each leap year. Thus the sequence from one "AG" leap year to the next would be as follows:

AG → F → E → D → CB → A → G → F → ED → C → B → A → GF → E → D →
C → BA → G → F → E → DC → B → A → G → FE → D → C → B → AG

Now the main reason for having dominical letters in a liturgical calendar was in order to help the cantor work out how the temporal and sanctoral cycles (that is, the cycle of Sunday services and the cycle of feasts with fixed dates) would interact over the coming year.[99] By correlating the saints' days and anniversaries listed on the right-hand side of the page with the dominical letters, he could determine which feasts would fall on Sundays and which on weekdays and thus work out the appropriate combination of services and prayers for each day. For this purpose, the cantor would need to know what the coming year's dominical letter(s) would be. There was in the normal course of religious life no need to work out which days were Sundays in the past, so it is something of a mystery as to why someone would add dominical letters to a chronicle like *Coventry*. It is not difficult to come up with some rather specialised reasons for inserting them. One can imagine, for example, how the dominical letters in H might have been used to help a forger to fabricate the date of a charter where the intention was to specify, among other chronological data, the day of the week when it was drawn up. Having worked out the dominical letter for a given year, the forger could then consult a calendar to work out the day of the week on the date he had in mind—to discover, say, that 11 June 1145 was a Monday. This would, however, be a most unlikely reason for going back over the entire text of *Coventry* and indicating the dominical letters that applied in all the 1225 years of its coverage of the sixth age of the world, in part because of the work involved but also because the use of elaborate dating clauses in royal and episcopal *acta* had largely been abandoned by the end of the twelfth century. Few specified the year, let alone the month or the day of their issue, and a forger would not normally have needed data of this kind.

The only mundane reasons for going to such lengths would seem to be pedagogical ones: that is, the main reason for adding dominical letters to a chronicle such as *Coventry* would seem to have been to provide a tool a teacher might use in conjunction with a liturgical calendar to explain how dominical letters work—to explain how the dominical letter changed over the course of time, reversing its way up its seven-point scale in a slightly irregular, twenty-eight-year, cycle. The presence of this device in the margins of H implies, in short, that *Coventry* was used in the teaching of computus, and it adds to the body of evidence that annalistic chronicles were intended to be read by novices who were being trained in the hope that at least one or two of them might succeed to the all-important office of cantor.

---

[99] On the cantor's role in organising the liturgy, see chap. 1, § c, above; and for a fuller discussion of dominical letters, see Frederick P. Pickering, *The Calendar Pages of Medieval Service Books* (Reading: Graduate Centre for Medieval Studies, University of Reading, 1980), esp. 6–10. See also *HDSBH*, 7.

# Chapter Five: Other Descendants of the Common Root

Several minor chronicles must also be discussed in the present introduction. One, the annals preserved in MS. London, B.L., Cotton Faustina B.I, fols. 12r–29v, needs to be examined, if only because it must explained why the present editor has chosen not to treat it as another witness to the *Winchcombe Chronicle*. The others demand discussion because they provide additional evidence for the existence and character of the common root. That is, they contain annals which echo the shared items in *Winchcombe* or *Coventry*, but none of the three appears to depend on these witnesses for this material; rather, they appear to derive either from the common root itself or from other descendants now unknown. They also add a few annals which are unattested in *Winchcombe* and *Coventry*, and they help to show that the root was produced at Worcester Cathedral Priory. The four chronicles in question will be examined in the order of their importance for the present study.

## (a) *Annales prioratus de Wigornia*

The so-called *Annales prioratus de Wigornia* are to be found in MS. London, B.L., Cotton Caligula A.X, fols. 65r–193r (hereafter Cg).[1] These annals cover the period from the Incarnation to the year 1377, but their coverage from 1308 onwards is extremely thin: the text to this point is the work of a single late fourteenth-century Gothic hand; thereafter it is the work of two scribes who contribute a mere eighteen items of information.[2] The annals copied by the main hand consist, moreover, of two elements. At their core lies a series of annals which belongs to the Bermondsey-Reading-Winchester cluster of chronicles. Indeed, Luard

[1] Ed. Luard, *AM*, 4:356–564, hereafter *APW.*

[2] The main scribe enters the text down to 1308 (fol. 191v11); then another scribe adds 8 notes (from fol. 191v12) to 1346 (fol. 192r foot); another 10 notes covering 1346 to 1377 (fol. 192v). The main scribe also inserted some notes on the bishops of Worcester on fols. 195r–196r; and the *Brevis annotatio regum tam Anglorum quam Normannorum* (fols. 197r–204r), then some biblical exempla, *De Sancto Sallomone rege filio Davidis regis* (fols. 204v–206v).

showed that this series of annals was derived, except for those for the years 1202 to 1262, from the chronicle preserved in MS. London, B.L., Cotton Vespasian E.IV, folios 153r–201v, which is now thought to have belonged to Reading Abbey.[3] For our purposes, however, it is not this layer of material in *Annales de Wigornia* that concerns us, but rather the series of additions which Luard printed in larger type in his edition of the chronicle.[4] The great majority of these annals were inserted by the main hand who seems to have used a number of different sources, the most important of which was the common root which lies behind *Winchcombe* and *Coventry*.

The root appears to have supplied the compiler with some sixty-eight items, covering the period from 51 to 1121.[5] There are close textual matches for some sixty-four of these items in the entries found in *Winchcombe* and *Coventry*.[6] This group includes, moreover, identical matches for items such as their account of the Lombard earthquake (1117.1), items that derive from extended passages in John of Worcester's *Chronica chronicarum* but which could not have been condensed in such a similar way by several different authors working independently of one another.[7] But as the commentary below also demonstrates, these sixty-eight items also include twenty-three for which there are clear echoes among the English materials in the C-text of *Annales Cambriae*, another chronicle which, as will emerge shortly, appears to have derived material from the common root. Three of these twenty-three items are not attested in either *Winchcombe* or *Coventry*, but matches for all of them can be found in John's *Chronica chronicarum* and its auxiliary materials.[8] That helps to show that the compiler of *Annales de Wigornia* did

[3] On this chronicle, see also chap. 1, § a, above. Luard printed these annals in smaller type in *APW*.

[4] The relevant items have been printed in appendix A below together with a commentary.

[5] *APW* 51, 52, 654.1, 654.2, 656, 678, 680, 689, 692, 693, 714, 717, 742, 785, 787.1, 787.2, 775, 778, 781, 850, 855, 858, 859, 860, 862, 863, 864, 866, 868, 871, 873, 878, 879, 881, 917, 919, 922, 932, 961, 992, 993, 1058, 1084, 1104, 1105, 1106.1, 1106.2, 1107, 1108.1, 1108.2, 1109.1, 1109.2, 1110, 1111.1, 1111.2, 1112, 1113, 1114, 1115.1, 1115.2, 1116, 1117.1, 1117.2, 1118, 1119.1, 1119.2, 1120, 1121. This list excludes all items for which there is no clear match in one of the other witnesses to the root. The excluded items include, therefore, four of the metrical entries (*APW* 71, 220, 261, 953) and the six entries (680, 780, 732, 832, and 855) which appear to derive directly from one of the satellite texts in Corpus 157 (see below). It should be noted that the items are cited in the order in which they appear in Cg, where they do not always follow strict chronological order. Before people begin counting the number of entries, it should be noted that the texts of several of disconnected entries in *APW* appear as one item in *Winchcombe*[1] and vice versa.

[6] All of the 62 items appear in *Winchcombe*. *Coventry* omits 4, i.e. *APW* 654.1, 961, 1111.2, and 1118.2.

[7] Cf. chap. 2, § b, above.

[8] *APW* 1084, 1107, and 1119.2.

not derive these materials from *Winchcombe* or one of the other known descendants of the common root. Rather, it seems likely that he derived all sixty-five of these items from an alternative version of the root—one which was probably very similar to that lying behind *Winchcombe* and *Coventry*.

That the compiler of the *Annales de Wigornia* did not make use of *Winchcombe* is confirmed by the weakness of the parallels between the former chronicle and the additional material in the latter: its continuations and marginalia. There is, for example, no sign of the interlinear glosses added in *Winchcombe* to a number of the items which it shares with the former chronicle.[9] There is, likewise, no sign that the compiler made direct use of the continuation for the additional matter added to the core text of the *Annales de Wigornia* for the period covering 1122 to 1181. It is true that there are some entries in the relevant section of the latter chronicle which seem to be related to *Winchcombe*$^2$, but the language of the items in question is different enough to suggest that the relationship was not particularly close. Indeed, these additions seem, especially from around 1141 onwards, to be more closely related to the *Annals of Tewkesbury*,[10] a chronicle which, it was argued above, was distantly related to *Winchcombe*$^2$ through a shared dependence on a lost Gloucester chronicle.[11] The shift of allegiance which takes place after 1121 is towards the *Annals of Tewkesbury*, and it is tempting to argue that the additions to the *Annales de Wigornia* depend upon a version of the common root which had itself been continued with material drawn from a version of the former set of annals. This much is also suggested, as will be shown below, by the series of English annals which was added to *Annales Cambriae*.

The sixty-six entries exhibit, moreover, an interest in Worcester cathedral priory and its history sufficiently strong to suggest that they derive from a chronicle that belonged to that house. Material relevant to the cathedral is reported in no fewer than twenty-five items, twenty-one of which concern the obits and successions of its bishops.[12] They are more consistent in numbering the bishops than are their counterparts in *Winchcombe* and *Coventry*, but they do not provide as complete coverage of this series of entries. The pre-1122 Worcester-related additions to the core text in the *Annales de Wigornia* include, however, three items

[9] *APW* 1105, 1108.2, 1109.1, 1114, 1115.2, 1117.2, 1121.

[10] E.g. *APW* 1141: "Stephanus rex capitur in bello apud Lincolniam. Robertus comes Gloucestriæ captus apud Wintoniam, et alter pro altero redditur." *AT* has the same entry except for the words *in bello* and *Gloucestriæ*. *Winchcombe*$^2$ 1141 is significantly fuller: "<S>tephanus rex capitur die purificationis sancte Marie. Comes Gloecestrensis Robertus eodem anno in exaltatione sancte Crucis cum aliis multis capitur, sed postea ambo in festiuitate omnium sanctorum liberantur." See, likewise, *APW* 1162, 1164, 1165, 1166, and so on.

[11] See chap. 3, § e, above.

[12] *APW* 680, 689, 692, 693, 717, 742, 775, 778, 781, 859, 860, 864, 871, 917, 922, 992, 993, 1058, 1112, 1113, 1115.1. The other four items are *APW* 873, 879, 1084, 1118.

not otherwise attested in *Winchcombe* and *Coventry*. These items record the gifts which various Mercian kings bestowed on the cathedral, but the places named in these grants do not match those assigned to these kings in the history of its endowments which was prefixed to the Worcester manuscript of the *Chronica chronicarum*.[13] It seems almost certain that the compiler obtained these items from some other source as yet unknown, one which probably post-dated the work of John of Worcester.

Further clues as to the character of the sources the compiler used for the additions to the core text of the *Annales de Wigornia* are provided by the seven hagiological entries in hexameter verse. These entries commemorate the "birthdays" of the saints, their obits or rather their entrances into heaven. Three of them are also reported in both *Winchcombe* and *Coventry*.[14] Notices of this type are normally to be found in metrical calendars—that is, in computistical calendars which included a line in verse for all or most of the feasts falling on the various days of the year.[15] Indeed, five of the seven entries appear in the calendar of this kind found in Tiberius E.IV, fols. 35r–40v (T)—that is, in the computistical collection in which *Winchcombe* is preserved.[16] There is one overlapping entry which appears both among the shared items in *Winchcombe* and *Coventry* and in the calendar in T.[17] It is possible that the common root once contained all seven of these metrical items, but if so, it is a little strange that *Winchcombe* and *Coventry* report only three of them, the exact same three. A more likely explanation is that for the four additional items the compiler made use of a calendar akin to that found in T.

Indeed, it is tempting to suggest, albeit tentatively, that the compiler had access to a computistical collection very similar to that found in Tiberius E.IV, but one oriented to the needs of Worcester Cathedral Priory—that is, a "Worcester computus," a computus manuscript of the "classic type" with Bede's *De temporum ratione* at its core, but one containing a chronicle virtually the same as the common root and a metrical calendar very similar to that found in T. No trace has survived, unfortunately, of the book of this type which was used at Worcester in

---

[13] *APW* 780, 732, 832. See also *APW* 855. Cf. JW*CC* (C), fol. 1–p.3 (ed. Dugdale, *Monasticon*, 1:607–9).

[14] See *APW* 51, 52, and 992. Cf. *Winchcombe* 13, 14.1, 992.1.

[15] On the development of the metrical calendars in England, see Lapidge, "A Metrical Calendar," 343–86. See also André Wilmart, "Un témoin anglo-saxon du calendrier métrique d'York," *Revue Bénédictine* 46 (1934): 41–66; Patrick McGurk, "The Metrical Calendar of Hampson," *Analecta Bollandiana* 104 (1986): 79–125; David N. Dumville, *Liturgy and the Ecclesiastical History of Late Anglo-Saxon England: Four Studies*, Studies in Anglo-Saxon History 5 (Woodbridge: Boydell Press, 1992), 1–37.

[16] *APW* 52, 71, 220, 261, 953. On Tiberius E.IV's calendar and its metrical entries, see chap. 3, § a, above.

[17] See *APW* 52. Cf. *Winchcombe* 14.1; *Coventry* 14.

the early twelfth century. In its absence it has been argued that the Winchcombe computus is another version of the surviving Thorney computus (today MS. Oxford, St John's College, 17), which has a metrical calendar similar to that found in T (fols. 16r–21v).[18] It is thought that both collections derive from an earlier collection assembled at the beginning of the eleventh century by Byrhtferth of Ramsey.[19] It seems likely, however, that Worcester and perhaps John himself may have played a part in the redaction of this material prior to its arrival at Winchcombe. This view of the matter receives some support from a curious connection between the calendar in T and the annals in the paschal tables in John's *Chronica chronicarum*, in that both commemorate St Oswald with the same hexameter couplet:[20]

> Aula Dei patuit Oswaldo pridie Martis
> Summo pontifici celsa petendo poli.

There is a similar couplet in the calendar of St John's 17 (fol. 16v), but the final line differs in its word order and in its use of *altus* for *celsus:*[21]

> Aula Dei patuit Oswaldo pridie Martis
> Pontifici summo alta petendo poli.

The problem needs further investigation, but these clues, taken together, begin to suggest that the common root may once have been a component of a collection of computistical materials similar in contents and organisation to that which has survived for Winchcombe Abbey and connected with Worcester in some way.

## (b) The Annals of St David's Cathedral

The annals in MS. London, B.L., Cotton Domitian A.I, folios 138r–155r (hereafter Dm), comprise a chronicle which was produced in the late thirteenth century at St David's Cathedral.[22] The association with this church is clear from the

---

[18] Ed. Byrhtferth, *Enchiridion*, 390–416. The metrical entries are also printed in Lapidge, "A Metrical Calendar," 380–83.

[19] See the introduction to Byrhtferth, *Enchiridion*, esp. lvii–lviii.

[20] JW*CC* (C) 68 (in cycle 25, year 5 = 992); the calendar in T, fol. 35v (28 February). Cf. *Winchcombe* 992, a leonine: "Presul transiuit sanctus Oswaldus et astra petiuit." The connection between these items was first observed by P. McGurk: see Lapidge, *Anglo-Latin Literature, 900–1066*, 489.

[21] Ed. Byrhtferth, *Enchiridion*, 395. This version of the couplet is also quoted by Byrhtferth in his *Vita Oswaldi*, vi (p. 472): it has hiatus instead of the more classical elision.

[22] The C-text of *Annales Cambriae* has yet to be edited in full. There have been two attempts to produce a critical edition based on the three main versions, the first being that in *Monumenta historica Britannica*, ed. Henry Petrie, John Sharpe, and Thomas D. Hardy

many annals that refer to the cathedral and its bishops and from the manuscript context. The larger book of which the annals are a part—that is, Domitian A.I, folios 56–160—is dominated by the works of Gerald of Wales (1146–1223), who was a canon of the cathedral, and it certainly remained at St David's until the 1530s when it was sent by the cathedral's treasurer, John Lewis, to Sir John Prise (d. 1555).[23] The "core-text" is a version of the *Annales Cambriae* in which the traditional stock of those annals has been grafted onto the world history compiled by Isidore of Seville (d. 636) and combined with material from Geoffrey of Monmouth's *Historia regum Britanniae* (d. 1155). It covers the period from the creation of the world down to 1288,[24] but it does so without reference to AD dates for large stretches of time. In the section down to 641 the material is grouped under the reigns of the Roman emperors; thereafter the years are distinguished by the word *Ann'*. The core text and its contents need not detain us, however, for the present study is concerned with the contents of two bifolia and a single leaf which were inserted into the manuscript so that additional material could be added to the chronicle, almost all of it concerned with English history between 1016 and 1199.

The entries on the five leaves in question (that is, folios 142, 144, 146, 148, and 150) are linked to the C-text with a complex series of *signes-de-renvoi*, but without much regard for chronological accuracy or historical consistency. An entry that has William II returning to England from Normandy is aligned, for example, with an annal in the host text that has the same king going to Normandy.[25] The former item seems to refer to 1097, the latter to 1092. Indeed, these additions seem on the whole to have been dislocated forwards by between six and four years; but this issue will be precisely resolved only when the C-text has been edited properly and in full—when, that is, all the dislocations in the underlying

(London: Eyre and Spottiswoode, 1848), 1:830–40, the second that in *Annales Cambriae*, ed. J. Williams 'ab Ithel', RS 20 (London: Longman, 1860). But the former covers only 445 to 1066 whilst the latter is quite inaccurate. Both exclude, moreover, the English material in the C-text with which our study is concerned. A large part of the annals is printed in *Annales Cambriae, A.D. 682–954: Texts A-C in Parallel*, ed. and trans. David N. Dumville, Basic Texts for Brittonic History 1 (Cambridge: Department of Anglo-Saxon, Norse and Celtic, University of Cambridge, 2002), 1–19, but this edition does not cover the period with which we are concerned. The annals in question have, therefore, been printed in appendix B below. It will be cited as "*AC* (C)," and by reference to the "interim annal numbers" which have been assigned to the entries in the absence of a clear chronological apparatus in the manuscript itself.

[23] Neil R. Ker, "Sir John Prise," *The Library*, 5th ser., 10 (1955): 1–24; repr. in idem, *Books, Collectors and Libraries*, 471–95, at 473, 492–93.

[24] On the C-text and its relationship to the other versions of the *Annales Cambriae*, see Hughes, "Welsh Latin Chronicles," esp. 73–76, 85; Dumville, *Annales Cambriae 682–954*, v–xii, and the works cited there.

[25] *AC* (C) 1097.

chronological apparatus have been identified and resolved, a complex task which lies beyond the scope of the present study.[26] The hand that copied these annals was the same as that which copied the C-text, implying that the bifolia were added at much the same time as the main set of annals was produced—perhaps as an afterthought.

It has long been recognised that much of this additional material is concerned with Worcester Cathedral, and it has been assumed that it derives from a chronicle that was related in some way to the *Annales prioratus de Wigornia*.[27] This much can now be confirmed. It can now be shown, moreover, that the annals probably derive from a version of the common root. As can be seen from the commentary that accompanies the text in Appendix B below, the first seventy-eight items, those covering 1016 to 1121, include seventy-five for which there are echoes in *Winchcombe*, seventy-three for which there are echoes in *Coventry*, and twenty-six for which there are echoes in *Annales de Wigornia*. Especially striking are the twenty items in *Annales Cambriae* for which echoes are to be found in all of these witnesses.[28] In all there are six items among those for 1016 to 1121 for which there are no parallels in *Winchcombe* or *Coventry*. There are parallels for three of the six in *Annales de Wigornia*,[29] leaving three items which do not appear in any of the other major witnesses to the common root;[30] but all three match material that occurs either in the main chronicle of John's *Chronica chronicarum* or in one of its auxiliary texts. It is a fairly safe assumption, therefore, that they too represent items which were once part of the common root. It is possible that they were added to it soon after it was used in the making of the exemplars behind *Winchcombe* and *Coventry*. It follows that the English additions to the C-text of the *Annales Cambriae* were, down to 1121, almost certainly derived from the common root.

As for the rest of these additions, comprising some eighty items that cover the period from 1122 to 1199, these follow a pattern similar to that found in the additions to the core text of the *Annales de Wigornia*. That is, there is a shift of allegiance which becomes stronger from the late 1130s onwards towards the *Annals of Tewkesbury*, suggesting that the St David's annalist made use of the same extended version of the common root which was used by the compiler of the *Annales de Wigornia*—a version of the common root which had been augmented with material drawn from a version of the *Annals of Tewkesbury*. Among the more striking items which support this conclusion are the item for 1178 reporting the destruction of Tewkesbury Abbey by fire in that year, and the curious pair of

[26] On the nature of the problem, see Dumville, *Annales Cambriae 682–954*, xiii–xiv.

[27] Hughes, "Welsh Latin Chronicles," 76, n. 58.

[28] *AC* (C) 1058, 1104, 1105, 1106.1, 1106.3, 1108.1, 1108.2, 1109.1, 1109.2, 1110.2, 1111, 1112, 1113, 1114, 1115.1, 1115.2, 1116, 1119.1, 1120, 1121.

[29] *AC* (C) 1083, 1107, 1119.2. Cf. *APW* 1084, 1107, 1119.2.

[30] *AC* (C) 1022, 1084, 1106.2.

entries recording Master Simon Luvel's appointment as archdeacon of Worcester in 1167 and his death in 1188. It is true that the *Annals of Tewkesbury* are related to *Winchcombe²* for this period, but at some remove, and the present series of Anglo-Welsh annals has stronger affinities with the Tewkesbury text than with that from Winchcombe. The series extends some eighteen years beyond 1181, where *Winchcombe²* comes to an end, and it contains items not preserved in the latter chronicle, items such as that recording the deaths of Nigel of Ely and Hilary of Chester (1169). This item occurs both in *Tewkesbury* and among the additions to the core text in the *Annales de Wigornia*. It is nowhere to be found in *Winchcombe*. These annals cannot, therefore, have been derived from *Winchcombe* itself.

## (c) The "Worcester" Version of the Norman Annals

The chronicle in MS. London, B.L., Cotton Claudius C.IX, fols. 12v–17v (hereafter Cs), is one of the eight English versions of the so-called "Norman Annals."[31] It covers the period from AD 1 to 438 and 629 to 1171, the lacuna being the consequence of the loss of one leaf between folios 14 and 15.[32] It is closely related to that found in MS. London, B.L., Royal 4.B.VII, fols. 211r–218v, which also concludes in 1171. The annal numbers extend as far as 1178; the hand belongs to the second half of the twelfth century; and it seems likely that the annals were copied in or soon after the late 1170s. The Royal manuscript has been assigned, like most of the English versions of these annals, to a monastery in southeastern England—in this case, Rochester Cathedral Priory. The Claudius C.IX version may also have been produced in that region, but it contains a series of additions which show that it had reached Worcester by the end of the twelfth century. The entries in question record the succession of Bishop Bosel (680), that of Bishop Oftfor (689), the consecration of Bishop Ecgwine (693), and the consecration and obit of Bishop Wulfstan II (1062, 1095).[33] The final two items were added by a hand dating from around 1200,[34] but they are so terse that it is hard to show

---

31 For the "Norman Annals," see chap. 1, § a, above.

32 Liebermann, *ANG*, 35–49, prints the annals in a slightly abridged form, collating them with those in MS. Royal 4.B.VII, fols. 211r–218v. Cotton Claudius C.IX is a composite manuscript, and the section to which the present manuscript belongs comprises fols. 4r–17v. For a detailed description of this unit and a plate of fol. 17v (that is, of the leaf on which are copied the annals for 1075 to 1178), see Julian P. Harrison, "The English Reception of Hugh of St Victor's *Chronicle*," *The Electronic British Library Journal* 1 (2002), article 1, 12–15. This article may be obtained from http://www.bl.uk/collections/eblj/2002/article1.html. See also Harrison, "New Discoveries," 27–28.

33 Ed. Liebermann, *ANG*, 36, 46–47.

34 Cotton Claudius C.IX, fol. 17r–v. Cf. *Winchcombe* 1062, 1095.1; *Coventry* 1062.1, 1095; *AC* (C) 1062, 1095. The additions to *APW* do not cover these years.

that they are related to the common root. The other three items are more promising, but also rather ambiguous. Entered by a late fourteenth-century bookhand, these entries are almost identical to their counterparts among the "additions" to the core text of *Annales de Wigorniae*. The corresponding items in *Winchcombe* and *Coventry* are not quite as close, suggesting that they derive from the former chronicle, *Annales de Wigorniae*, rather than the common root itself.[35] In any case, their presence suggests the beginnings of an attempt to collate these annals with a series of entries derived from the common root. That this part of Claudius C.IX remained at Worcester until the end of the Middle Ages is confirmed, finally, by the presence in the top margin of folio 12v of John Musart's signature. Musart was one of the priory's monks between 1504 and 1538.[36]

## (d) The Later Winchcombe Annals

MS. London, B.L., Cotton Faustina B.I, fols. 12r–29v (hereafter F), is a fragment of what may once have been a much larger book.[37] In its present form it contains only one text: a set of annals which, owing to the loss of folios at either end of the text, begins imperfectly in 1049 and ends imperfectly in 1232. The peculiar history of the Cotton collection, the way in which so many of its historical texts were dismembered and rebound in new formations, means that the lost portions may yet be rediscovered; but this is all that is now known of this book. The annals are, moreover, laid out in a complex fashion.[38] The folios, as cut down by the plough, now measure around 170 × 245 millimetres. Each page is laid out in plummet as follows: at the centre is a broad text area measuring 75–90 × 145–165 millimetres and ruled with between 26 and 32 lines. It is the sequence of annals in this central text area which begins in mid-sentence in the year 1049 and ends in mid-sentence in 1232. In the present cut-down state of the folios, this text area sits relatively high on the page with a margin at the top of just 20

[35] See Cotton Claudius C.IX, fol. 15r; *APW* 680, 689, 693, which may be used to complete the first and the third item. Cf. *Winchcombe* 680.1, 689.2, 692; *Coventry* 680, 690.2, 692.

[36] Greatrex, *BR*, 853–54; Harrison, "Hugh of St Victor's *Chronicle*," 15. See also Liebermann, *ANG*, 32; *MLGB*, 207.

[37] These folios are not related to the other sections of this composite manuscript, for which see Smith, *MSS Bibl. Cotton.*, 150–51; Planta, *MSS in the Cottonian Library*, 605.

[38] Parts of the text have been edited. Twenty-two annals, most of which are concerned with Continental affairs, were printed by Georg H. Pertz in *MGH SS*, 16:481–82. Darlington, 114–37, reports the variants in F for those items which were derived from *Winchcombe*. The core text and marginalia for 1181–1232 were also edited along with some of the marginalia for 1049 to 1181 at John, "Sources," 27–89 and 91 respectively; but the copy of this thesis which the present author has seen in the John Rylands Library wants a number of pages.

millimetres and one at the bottom of 60 to 70. On the outer side of this central panel is a broad margin some 45 to 55 millimetres wide. On the inner side of the central panel a another text area has been defined, one 15 to 25 millimetres wide (often but not always separated from the main text area by a defined space some six millimetres wide), and this was filled with a single set of annal numbers in red ink. That is, this second text area sits on the left-hand side on the recto and on the right-hand side on the verso of each folio. Many lengthy annotations and additions, some linked to the central panel by *signes-de-renvoi*, have been inserted into this second text area, into the margins, in the gaps between the annal numbers, and in the spaces that were left between the annals themselves. Many are written in minute scripts.[39] The density of annotation also varies from leaf to leaf. Some leaves, most notably folios 17 to 20, are relatively lightly annotated, but the fact that the outer margin is seldom less than two-thirds of the width of the central panel suggests that the plan was always to add further material in the margins. From 1182 onwards, furthermore, the scribes have also left gaps in the central panel, at the conclusion of each annal, and these have also been used to accommodate additions.

The layout suggests, at first sight, that it was put together in two stages, the first involving the production of the central column of text, the second involving the insertion of the additions. Source analysis suggests, however, that the process was more complex than that.[40] The annals down to the year 1181 depend, first of all, on *Winchcombe*. The borrowings cross over the 1122 break in that text and incorporate various interlinear additions, implying that the compilers were working directly from Tiberius E.IV, but the text is not reproduced in its entirety. It is a fairly full transcript, but there are some omissions. From the point in late 1181 where *Winchcombe* comes to an end the central panel is closely related to the *Annals of Tewkesbury*, and it probably depends on a slightly earlier version of those annals—perhaps the lost version which ended in 1248. *Tewkesbury* also supplied, however, some of the marginal material in the annals down to 1181, and it seems likely that these items were fed into the margins of the earlier section before or perhaps at the same time as the source was used for the purpose of extending the central panel. The collation of this source in the pre-1181 section could hardly be said to enhance the value of the text, for the latter's annals for this period seem to comprise a much abbreviated version of the same source as

[39] For a useful reproduction of fol. 13r, which covers AD 1074–1088, see Antonia Gransden, "The Chronicles of Medieval England and Scotland," *Journal of Medieval Studies* 16 (1990): 129–50, and 17 (1991): 217–43; repr. in eadem, *LTH*, 199–238 (pl. 24).

[40] John, "Sources," 2–26, attempts to identify a number of these sources, giving particular attention to the annals for 1181–1232. His posited connection with a lost set of Cirencester Annals seems plausible enough, but John's "Wig.dep.," a supposed lost set of Worcester Annals is better seen—at least for the period before 1182—as the Gloucester source the existence of which is posited in chap. 3, §§ e-f, above.

lies behind *Winchcombe*².[41] That is, these items represent distorted duplications of the material in the central panel rather than independent annals with a different perspective on the major events of the period.

The nature of the layout also invites speculation as to the purpose of the chronicle. It has been suggested that manuscripts of this kind were produced as working texts, as exercises in assembling material prior to the production of a fair copy in which the marginal material would be integrated into the whole.[42] But if such a copy was undertaken, it is not known to have survived. The presence of decoration suggests, moreover, that the existing copy may always have been regarded as the final version—that there was never an intention to integrate the marginal material into the main panel or to resolve the contradictions between the additions and the items in the central panel.

It is clear that the chronicle was produced after 1232, but since the text breaks off before it reaches its final annal its precise date remains a mystery. The palaeography of the hands suggests, however, that it was not written long after 1232. All of the scribes, including those responsible for the marginalia, were writing cursive bookhands of the type current in the middle of the thirteenth century—that is, between about 1225 and about 1275. I say "scribes", moreover, because the chronicle seems to have been the work of a number of them. At least three were responsible for the central panel: $F^1$ executed the section covering 1049–1170 (fols. 12r–18v), $F^2$ that covering 1170–1181 (fols. 19r–20v) *and* 1230–1232 (fols. 29r–v), and $F^3$ that covering 1182–1230 (fols. 21r–28v). Each hand seems to have been responsible for drawing up the pages in their section, for entering the text in its central panel, and for decorating that text.[43] Each probably also added some of the marginalia. A further sign that the manuscript was not produced after the mid-thirteenth century is that text is written above the top line of the central panel on a number of pages (fols. 12r–22r, 23r–v, 25v,

41 See chap. 3, § e, above.

42 See Darlington, 111–12; Christopher R. Cheney, "Notes on the Making of the Dunstable Annals, A.D. 33 to 1242," in *Essays in Medieval History Presented to Bertie Wilkinson*, ed. T. A. Sandquist and Michael R. Powicke (Toronto: University of Toronto Press, 1969), 79–98; repr. in idem, *Medieval Texts and Studies* (Oxford: Clarendon Press, 1973), 209–30, at 226–27; and Gransden, "Chronicles of England and Scotland," 233.

43 I follow here the identifications made by Julian P. Harrison, who is preparing a description of Cotton Faustina B.I for a new catalogue of the Cotton manuscripts. One indicator of changes comprises shifts in the decoration: $F^1$ used an orange-red ink for his minor capitals, for annal numbers, for some run-over marks, and for the notices marking the beginning of new paschal cycles under 1061 and 1117; $F^2$ also used orange-red ink for his minor capitals (but much less frequently), for his annal numbers, for paragraph marks, and occasionally for highlights; $F^3$ emphasises similar features, but he uses a darker shade of red ink for his annal numbers and paragraph marks; he does not use this ink for his capitals, but often highlights letters. Cf. John, "Sources," 2, who posited a single hand.

28v–29v). This practice, as Ker showed long ago, became increasingly unfashionable from around 1230 onwards.[44]

The question of provenance is not entirely straightforward. The marginalia contain numerous entries which imply a connection with the house of Augustinian canons at Cirencester,[45] and it has been suggested that the chronicle was compiled there.[46] However, the compilers' use of Tiberius E.IV for the central text as far as 1181 implies that they had access to this chronicle, and there are two marginal entries, one on folio 23v, the other on folio 24r, which show that some if not all of the annotations were made at Winchcombe. The first appears adjacent to the annal for 1206 along with a pointing hand in the margin:

> Hoc anno emit abbas Robertus Halling' et Haseltone et Ianewihe secundum tenorem qui scribitur in parua cedula.

The other appears adjacent to the annal for 1208:

> Hoc anno dedit abbas R. ix$^{xx}$ marcas pro remissione x librarum que debebantur annuatim pro Halling' et cetera.

Its importance for the readers of the chronicle is clear from the gloss *Nota Halling'* which appears in the lower margin with a *signe-de-renvoi*. These entries refer to the series of transactions by which Robert de Hazleton, abbot of Winchcombe (1196–1221), acquired the manors of Halling, Hazleton, and Yanworth from William de Bethune. The first item apparently refers to the original transaction, usually thought to have occurred in about 1200. Under its terms the abbey purchased the manors for £558 whilst promising to pay a fee-farm rent of £20 per annum. The second item refers to the renegotiation of the terms which took place in 1208. Under the new agreement the abbey was to pay £10 per annum for the three manors.[47] The rental was further reduced in 1217 when Daniel de Bethune

---

[44] See Neil R. Ker, "From 'Above Top Line' to 'Below Top Line': A Change in Scribal Practice," *Celtica* 5 (1960): 13–16; repr. in idem, *Books, Collectors and Libraries*, 70–74. He cites, among other examples, that of the Hyde Abbey Chronicle in MS. Oxford, Bod.L., Bodley 91, fols. 103r–127v, where the switch from above to below the top takes place amid the annal for 1265.

[45] E.g. MS. Faustina B.I, fol. 21r (s.a. 1183): "Adam abbas Cirencestr' obiit, cui successit Robertus eiusdem ecclesie canonicus, magis nummi fultus auxilio quam conventus electione." Many of the relevant items are transcribed in John, "Sources," 91–94.

[46] Clifford H. Lawrence, *St Edmund of Abingdon: A Study in Hagiography and History* (Oxford: Clarendon Press, 1960), 174 and n. 2.

[47] For this grant, see *Landboc*, 2:311–12 (no. 248). The original transaction was confirmed in a privilege issued by Pope Innocent III (1198–1216) on 11 May 1206: see *Landboc*, 1:110–11.

gave up another £1. It was finally remitted altogether in 1251.[48] The financial implications of these transactions will have made them a matter of great import for the monks of Winchcombe, but they will have been of little significance for any other community. These notes record the transactions without bothering, furthermore, to name Winchcombe as their beneficiary. This much must have been common knowledge to the intended audience, and it is hard not to conclude that they were entered while the chronicle was at the abbey.

## (e) Conclusion

The *Later Winchcombe Annals* are of considerable interest in their own right, but for present purposes their value is rather limited, since the contents of the central spine for 1049 to 1122 were taken from a descendant of the lost annalistic chronicle with which this study is chiefly concerned rather than from the "original" text. Indeed, their readings are often inferior. The other three chronicles discussed in the present chapter have greater value for present purposes, chiefly because they help to show that Worcester Cathedral Priory was the centre responsible for disseminating the lost annalistic chronicle which lies behind *Winchcombe* and *Coventry*. The *Annales prioratus de Wigornia* are also important in that they provide a tantalising clue as to the character of the book in which the root was housed: for although they do not depend on Tiberius E.IV, they were nevertheless compiled by someone who seems to have had access to a calendar which seems to have been closely related to that found in the Winchcombe computus. It is tempting to suggest, indeed, that the exemplar used in the making of the latter manuscript was a version of the lost computus of Byrhtferth of Ramsey which had been redacted at Worcester Cathedral Priory during the lifetime of John of Worcester. In the absence of any such manuscript this theory must be considered highly speculative, but it is one that has much to commend it since it would help to explain the peculiar mixture of materials in Tiberius E.IV—that is, its mix of Byrhtferthian and Marianan items, and its inclusion of items such as Abbo's version of Helperic's *De computo* (fols. 144r–161ra) alongside items such as Robert of Hereford's *Excerptio de chronica Mariani* (fols. 162r–176ra). In any case, it will be useful to conclude the present chapter with, for what it is worth, a stemma which defines the relationships between the common root and its descendants.

[48] See *Landboc*, 2:110–12, 313–14.

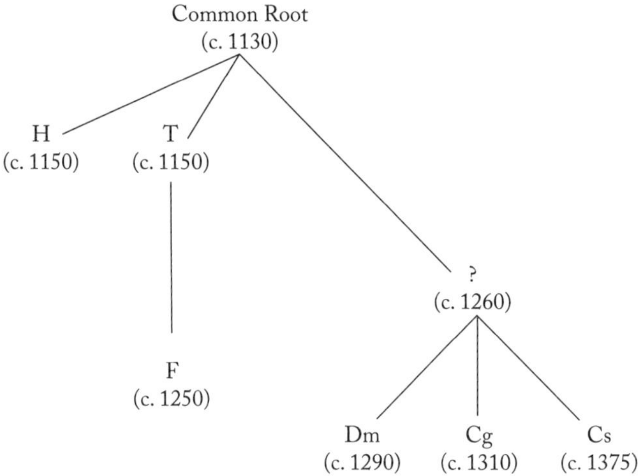


FIG. 3
John of Worcester's Lost Breviate World Chronicle and its Descendants

# Chapter Six: Editorial Policies

The chronicles discussed in this volume have suffered a mixed fate in the hands of previous editors. *Coventry* has gone unprinted in its entirety, but several extracts from *Winchcombe* were printed in the nineteenth and mid-twentieth centuries. The three charters quoted in the chronicle were printed in the nineteenth century,[1] and in 1962 R. R. Darlington produced a critical edition of *Winchcombe*'s annals for the years 1049 to 1181, which he collated with the matching elements of later annals in Faustina B.I (F).[2] Darlington's reading of Tiberius E.IV was, for the most part, accurate, although he sometimes misreported the modifications found in F. More seriously, his edition rests on different premises from those set out in the present study. He failed to pick up the changes of hand within the annal for 1122, and regarded the whole as the work of a single scribe as far as the middle of the annal for 1172 who was collaborating with a second scribe who continued the text to the year 1181. He failed, moreover, to identify the principles guiding the construction of the chronicle, and declared that the chronicle's compiler was a man of "little intelligence" and a "high degree of incompetence."[3] In his estimation its contents—with the exception of a few statements in the most recent annals, those covering the 1160s and 1170s—were suspect unless corroborated by another source.

There is, as has been admitted in the prologue above, no denying *Winchcombe*'s modest value as a source for traditional history, but Darlington's commentary and especially his failure to print the text as a whole has meant that a full appreciation of the chronicle's historiographical significance and a proper sense of the reliability of the data it contains has eluded modern scholarship.[4] If the textual strategies and the view of the world that governed the making of a medieval historical text are to be fully understood, then it is not sufficient simply to print the unique items which a chronicle may contain or those which were added by its continuators. It is necessary to print the entire text, warts and all. This is the fundamental policy on which the present edition is founded.

---

[1] B*CS*, nos. 337, 338, and 363.

[2] Darlington, 114–37.

[3] Darlington, 113.

[4] See the prologue to the Introduction above.

It might be contended that the best policy would be to attempt a reconstruction of the root from which *Winchcombe* and *Coventry* are descended, but there are a number of reasons why such an exercise is best avoided. There are, to begin with, discrepancies in the numbering of the annals, not all of which can be resolved with certainty; but, more seriously, each of the major witnesses mangles the root's chronological apparatus in its own peculiar way, and each contains additional matter which has been organised in accordance with its own peculiar structure. If one were to construct a "perfect" chronological apparatus of the kind to which Marianus Scotus and John of Worcester aspired, and if one were to assign the annals of the common root as they probably intended, it would become impossible to allocate the items unique to each witness and the various marginal materials (above all, the dominical letters as found in *Coventry*) in a way that gave a clear and consistent impression of their role in the descendants. It seems best, therefore, to print the texts in a form as close to that found in the manuscripts themselves as clarity permits, and to allow readers to assess for themselves the likely position and status of the shared items in the common root. The other editorial policies may be briefly described as follows.

## (i) Reconstructing the Texts

Both chronicles, especially *Winchcombe*, have necessarily required much reconstruction. The following conventions have been employed: the restoration of text the loss of which has been caused by damage to a manuscript has been indicated by square brackets (e.g. "mitt[it]"); additions to the manuscript readings made in order to produce a coherent text have been indicated with angle brackets (e.g. "Nichefor<us>"); deletions required to produce a coherent text are signalled with round brackets (e.g. "(cui) Heathoredus"); erasures are indicated with asterisks ("***") and changes of page with a forward slash ("/"). In both chronicles, especially *Coventry*, correctors have marked letters and words as errors to be ignored with subscripted points, and it has been the policy to implement these corrections, even when they are themselves mistaken, indicating what has been omitted in the footnotes. Redundancies and manifest errors that have not been marked as errors have, where necessary, been left in the text and enclosed in round brackets, "( )". In general, however, the tendency has been to preserve errors that have been inherited from the chronicle's sources, not least because these errors often preserve important clues as to the identity of those sources.

## (ii) Glosses and Later Interlinear Additions

Contemporary interlinear additions and glosses have been distinguished with the following punctuation: *glosses* and *interlinear* additions which are contemporary (or nearly so) to the scribe responsible for the original version of a section of text are marked with curly brackets (e.g. "{magnus}"), insertions made by hands which are *clearly* later than the original are given in italics (e.g. "*Germanus uir religiosus*").

## (iii) Other Punctuation

The text has been edited with full use of modern punctuation.

## (iv) Orthography

Since the orthography often varies in accordance with the source material being used by the compiler, there has been no attempt to impose standardised spellings on the text, with some exceptions. Capital "U/V" has been rendered as "V". It could be argued that scribe $T^1$ uses both capital "U" and "V", but his letter "U" is better seen as an uncial variation for V. $T^1$ often varies the appearance of his capitals using uncial forms, most of which cannot be represented using the present range of unicode letter-forms. It seems best, therefore, to suppress this distinction. Lower-case "u" has been converted, however, to "v" in the case of the numeral *quinque* so that the reader may distinguish numerals more easily. No distinction has been retained, furthermore, between *e*-caudata and tailed-*e* or between the various forms of *et*, since the scribes are inconsistent in their use of these forms. The edition preserves the scribes' inconsistencies in the use of the historic present and perfect tenses; but abbreviations such as *succ'*, *ob'*, and *regn'*, which may be expanded in various ways—as say *succedit*, *succedens* or *successit*, and so on—have been rendered using the form most appropriate for the sentence in which they appear.

## (v) Personal Names

In the Latin text personal names have been rendered as found in the manuscripts. In the English translation the forms that have become standard in modern usage have been adopted, except in the case of Anglo-Saxon names where standard Old English forms have been used.

## (vii) Place Names

Where placenames have been given in a contracted form which could be expanded in more than one way, the abbreviated form has been retained (e.g. *Eborac'*).

## (viii) Dates

The abbreviations *kl'*, *id'*, and *non'* have not been expanded. Dates have been given according to modern calendrical practice in the translation.

## (ix) The Chronological Apparatus

In the manuscripts two columns of year-numbers are given, the first comprising the years according to the corrected chronology of Marianus Scotus, the second the years according to the now widely accepted chronology of Dionysius Exiguus. The manuscripts give precedence to the first column, where the numbers are listed in red, an emphasis which if retained would cause confusion for many readers. For the sake of clarity, therefore, the second series of numbers is given in **bold** in both the text and the translation, but the numbers are given in the same order as in the manuscript. It should be noted that this solution differs from that adopted in the OMT edition of John of Worcester's *Chronica chronicarum* where the order of the numbers has been reversed. The Dionysian numbers also provide the basis for the reference system, except in the period before AD 1 where the Marianan numbering (VA 1–21) is used. That is, readers should focus on the numbers in bold when following up references. Bold has also been used to highlight the numbers for each entry in the commentaries.

## (x) The Facing-Page Translation

The policy has been to provide a rendering which is as close to the sense of the Latin as possible with the intention of making the texts accessible to the widest possible audience. That aim is sometimes at odds, however, with the general policies of editing the text with a light hand and of preserving inherited errors.[5] In general these issues have been resolved on a case-by-case basis, the need to provide a sensible and coherent translation being balanced against the desire to render the Latin as accurately as possible. The options adopted are sometimes explained in the commentaries. Both the square and the angle brackets used in producing the text are omitted in the translation, but sometimes further additions are made here in angle brackets (e.g. "<of Nero>") where such insertions will make the meaning explicit whilst avoiding the need for a footnote. Paragraphing and itemisation are consistent between text and translation.

## (xi) The Division of the Text into "Items"

In order to facilitate analysis of the text, the annals have been divided into items and entries. There are two ways in which this division might be implemented: one is by distinguishing "events" or episodes in the text, the other is by distinguishing the "borrowings"—the units of text at the points where one source is abandoned in favour of another. The former approach would support analysis of the chronicle's coverage of events and issues, but it complicates the commentary in as much as it necessitates further explanation of how different sources have

---

[5] E.g. *Winchcombe* 339, 811.2, 818.3.

been combined to produce a particular report whilst also requiring the repetition of information where the same source has been used for several events in succession. The latter approach facilitates analysis of a compiler's exploitation of his sources and has, on the whole, the advantage of greater brevity, but it also obscures the full extent of the compilers' dependence on particular sources, since it often involves treating several reports as a single unit. Neither approach is perfect, but in the end the overriding need for brevity has won out over the desire for precision. That is, the policy has been to divide the longer annals at the points where the compilers appear (or may) have switched from one source to another.

## (xii) The Commentaries

The commentaries emphasise source-criticism and problems of interpretation rather than the identification of persons and events mentioned in the text, except in the few places where the text preserves new information unattested elsewhere. The notes on those items which belong to the common root follow a standard format: they begin by identifying the other witnesses which contain a version of this item; they then proceed, in the commentary on the text which contains the fullest version of the item, to discuss the textual echoes which bear upon the question of its origins. It follows that the sources are usually discussed in the commentary on *Winchcombe*, because it is this chronicle which usually preserves the fullest version of the item in question. There are, however, a few items which are preserved in a fuller form in *Coventry*. If, moreover, the source has not been indicated, the reader should use the cross-references to identify the commentary where the source has been discussed. Possible sources that have been considered but rejected are typically signalled with the usual abbreviation for *conferre* ("cf."). The aim throughout has been to identify the source of every passage and, given their importance for the arguments developed in the introduction, the "indirect" sources of those passages which were taken directly from John of Worcester's *Chronica chronicarum*. It is not, however, always possible to identify the direct or indirect source. In a few cases this difficulty arises because the text preserves information that is likely to have belonged to one of the usual source texts (John of Worcester and the Norman Annals), but which has not been retained in the witnesses that have come down to us. In other cases it is because the entry is so brief and so lacking in distinguishing detail that there are simply too many possibilities. This is especially true of those entries which simply name the reigning pope, because the Norman Annals, the Worcester Chronicle, and other potential sources all provide information for the generation of entries of this type. The phrase "indeterminate source" is used to indicate such cases.

Since the preliminary matter and the annals of the main chronicle for 22 BC to AD 450 in JW*CC* have still to be printed, the principal witness, MS. Oxford, Corpus Christi College, 157 (C), has been cited for these years. For the sake of continuity with the OMT edition which serves for the period after 450, the manuscript is cited by reference to its Dionysian AD annal numbers (given in bold in that edition and below) rather than to its primary chronological apparatus—the Marianan annal numbers—except, that is, for the years before AD 1. In this section reference is made to the Marianan numbers (cited as "VA" for *uerior assertio*). The Norman Annals are cited mainly by reference to Continental witnesses (i.e. *ACad.*, *AG*, *AMSM*, *ASBD*, *AU*, RT*Access.*); only some of the English witnesses (chiefly *ASN*, *ASC* (F) and (E)) have been cited.

## (xiii) Abbreviations and Sigla

Texts and secondary sources cited in more than one chapter or on repeated occasions in the commentary are invariably cited by reference to an abbreviation in the list provided in the front matter. The initial intention was to emulate the sigla and practices used in the OMT edition of John of Worcester's *Chronica chronicarum*, so as to reduce potential sources of confusion for scholars consulting both texts, but the development of the project has necessitated some departures from this policy. It needs to be noted, therefore, that the siglum "H", traditionally used for the Dublin MS of *Chronica chronicarum*, refers here to Harley 3775. The Dublin MS will be cited as "D". The siglum "C" is a potential source of confusion, since it has traditionally been used of both Corpus 157 and Cotton Domitian A.I, the "C-text" of *Annales Cambriae*. It is here reserved for the former manuscript. The sigla employed may be listed as follows:

*Winchcombe Chronicle*

| | |
|---|---|
| T | MS. London, B.L., Cotton Tiberius E.IV |
| $T^1$, $T^2$, $T^3$, etc. | The scribes of the manuscript. |

*Coventry Chronicle*

| | |
|---|---|
| H | MS. London, B.L., Harley 3775 |
| $H^1$, $H^2$, $H^3$, etc. | The scribes of the manuscript. |

Other Witnesses to the Common Root

| | |
|---|---|
| Cg | MS. London, B.L., Cotton Caligula A.X |
| Cs | MS. London, B.L., Cotton Claudius C.IX |
| Dm | MS. London, B.L., Cotton Domitian A.I |
| F | MS. London, B.L., Cotton Faustina B.I |

John of Worcester, *Chronica chronicarum*

| | |
|---|---|
| B | MS. Oxford, Bod.L., Bodley 297 |
| C | MS. Oxford, Corpus Christi College, 157 |
| $C^1$ | The scribe chiefly responsible for pages 5–363. |
| $C^2$ | The scribe chiefly responsible for pages 364–379. |
| $C^3$ | The scribe chiefly responsible for pages 379–396. |

| | |
|---|---|
| D | MS. Dublin, Trinity College, 502 |
| $D^{1}$, $D^{2}$ | The scribes of the manuscript. |
| E | MS. Evesham, Almonry Museum, s.n. |
| L | MS. London, Lambeth Palace, 42 |
| P | MS. Cambridge, Corpus Christi College, 92 |

John of Worcester, *Chronicula*$^{1}$, and its continuation, *Chronicula*$^{2}$

| | |
|---|---|
| G | MS. Dublin, Trinity College, 503 |

Marianus Scotus, *Chronica chronicarum*

| | |
|---|---|
| N | MS. London, B.L., Cotton Nero C.V, fols. 3r–161v |

Lawrence Nowell's Notes from the Chronicle of Gregory of Caerwent

| | |
|---|---|
| V | MS. London, B.L., Cotton Vespasian A.V |

*Collectio Lanfranci*

| | |
|---|---|
| R | MS. London, B.L., Royal 11.D.VIII |

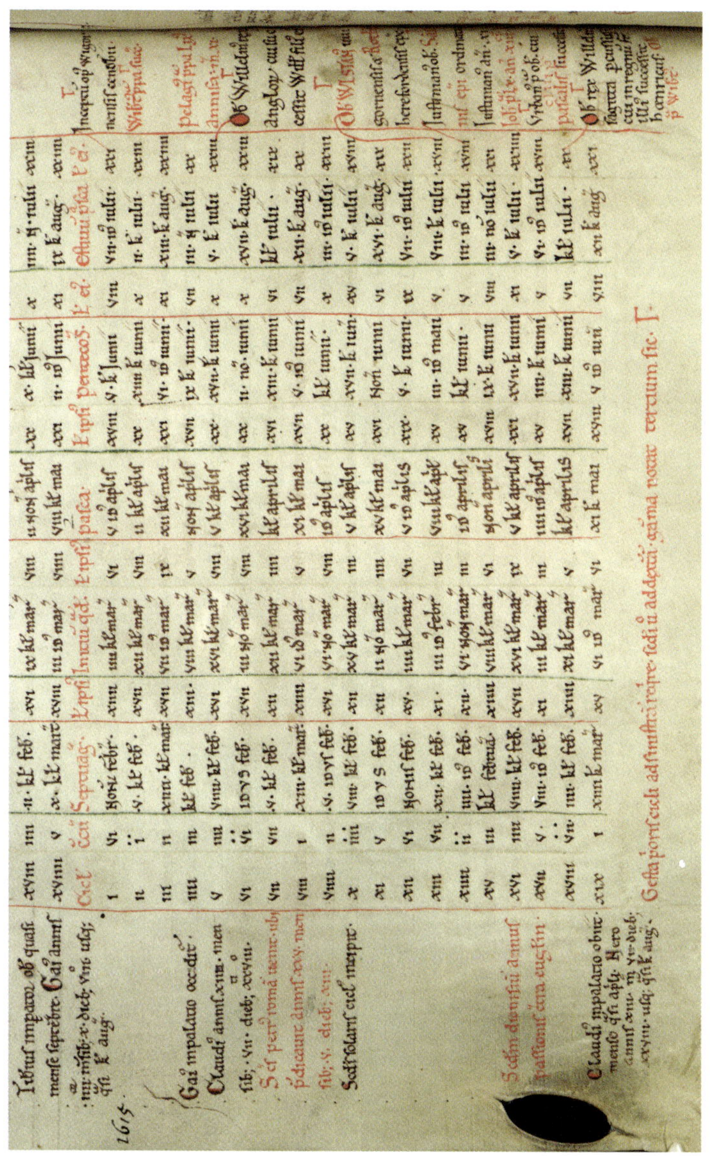

**I. MS. Oxford, Corpus Christi College, 157, p. 56 (lower half).** This plate reproduces the second nineteen-year cycle in the Easter tables among the prelims to the holograph MS of John of Worcester's *Chronica chronicarum*. As the inscription in red at the foot of the page explains, the first series of annals (covering AD 19–37) is placed on the left-hand side, the second (covering AD 551–569) is on the right, while the entries which make up the third (covering AD 1083–1101) are distinguished with a gamma, "Γ". This approach is the same as that used in the Easter tables of the Hereford MS of Marianus Scotus's *Chronica chronicarum* (that is, MS. London, B.L., Cotton Nero C.V, fols. 19v–26r). They also offer precisely the same explanation at the foot of folio 19v. The same system is used in other versions of Marianus's tables (e.g. MS. Cambridge, U.L., Kk.5.32, fols. 61r–74v).

**II. MS. London, B.L., Cotton Tiberius E.IV, fol. 13r.** *Winchcombe Chronicle*: annals for AD 809–811, and the Winchcombe foundation charter, all of which is the work of scribe T[1].

**III. MS. London, B.L., Cotton Tiberius E.IV, fol. 22v.** *Winchcombe Chronicle*: annals for AD 1121–30, illustrating the changeover between scribes T[1], T[11], and T[12]. The first phase ends with the first item under AD 1122; the second begins with the final item under that year.

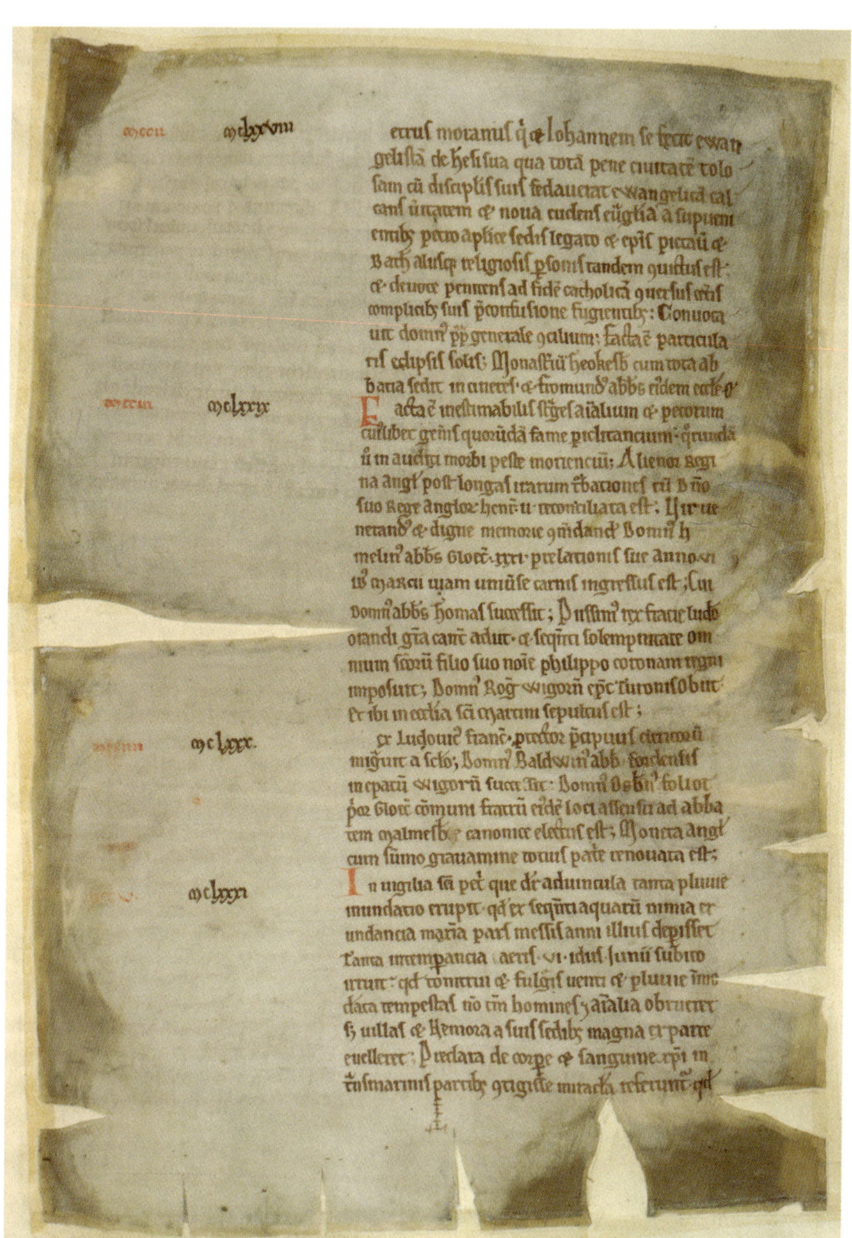

**IV. MS. London, B.L., Cotton Tiberius E.IV, fol. 27r.** *Winchcombe Chronicle*: annals for AD 1178–1181, illustrating the work of scribe T[14].

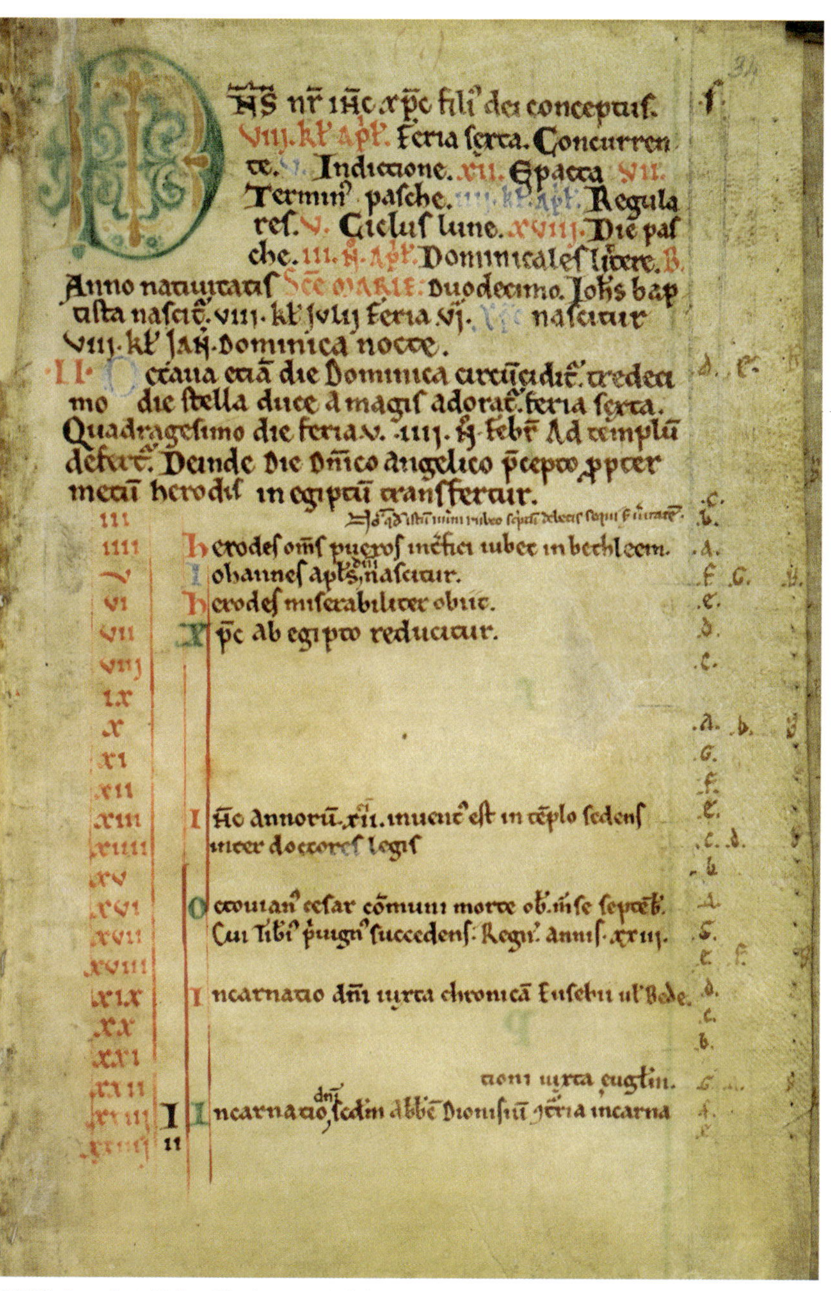

**V. MS. London, B.L., Harley 3775, fol. 34r.** *Coventry Chronicle*: opening leaf with annals for VA 1 to VA24/AD 2, illustrating the work of scribe H[1]. Note also the dominical letters in the right-hand margin.

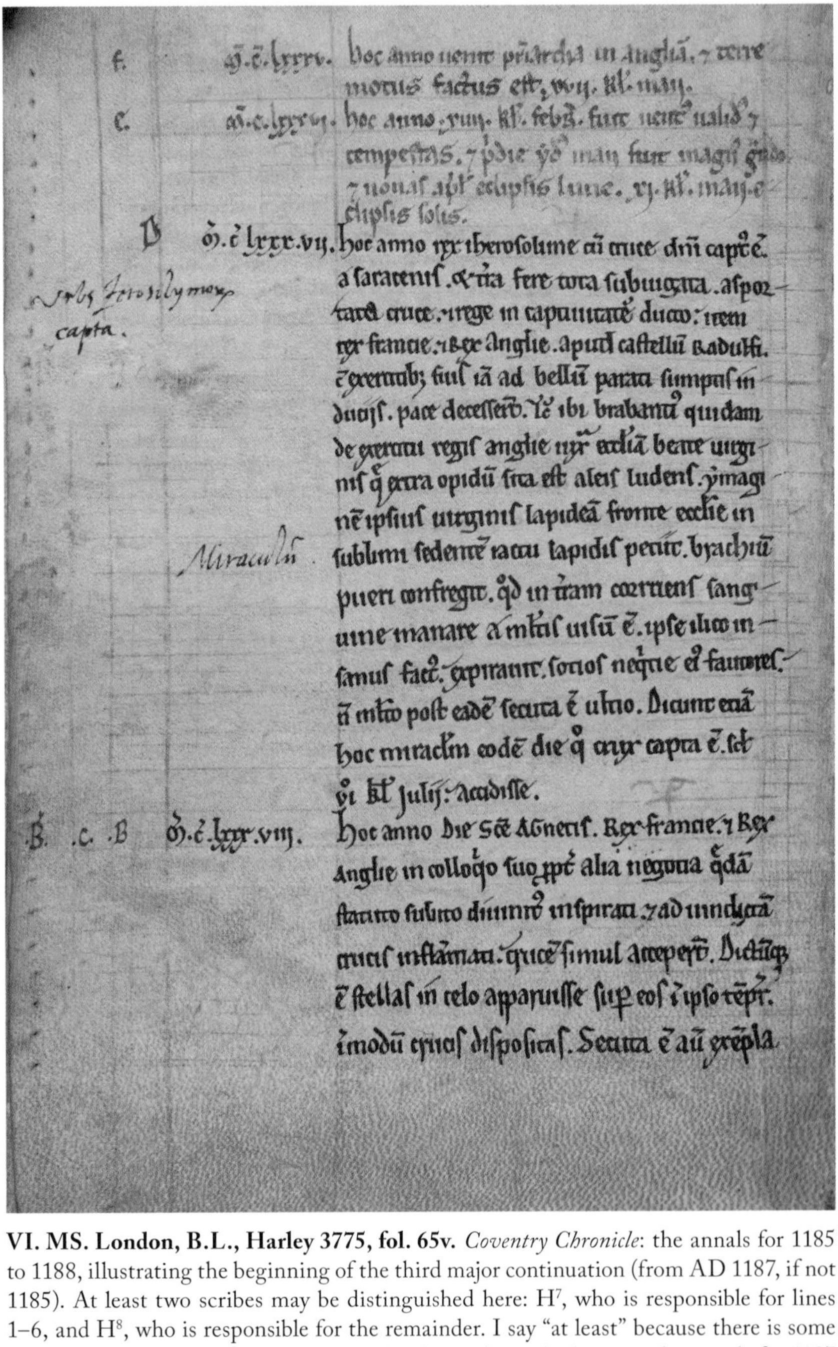

**VI. MS. London, B.L., Harley 3775, fol. 65v.** *Coventry Chronicle*: the annals for 1185 to 1188, illustrating the beginning of the third major continuation (from AD 1187, if not 1185). At least two scribes may be distinguished here: $H^7$, who is responsible for lines 1–6, and $H^8$, who is responsible for the remainder. I say "at least" because there is some variation in letter forms—in, for example, the *h* of *hoc* which opens the annals for 1187 and 1188—which gives a little cause for doubt as to whether these annals were written by a single scribe.

# The *Winchcombe Chronicle* Commentary

**VA1** Common root: *Coventry*[1] VA1. Perhaps an elaboration of Marianus via JWCC (C, p. 203) VA1: "Dominus noster Ihesus Christus filius Dei conceptus viii° kl. Aprilis, feria vi[a], indictione xii[a], anno etatis sancte Marie duodecimo, Iohanne Baptista, viii° k. Julii in presentia eiusdem uirginis nato, his consulibus Cassiodoro teste in Bethleem Jude, viii° kl Ianuarii, indictione xiii, dominica nocte nascitur." Cf. Norman Annals: *AMSM* Annus mundi 5198 and AD 1 (p. 214).

**VA2** Common root: *Coventry*[1] VA2. Marianus via JW*CC* (C) VA1: "Octaua etiam dominica circumciditur, xiii° die stella duce a magis adoratur, quadragesimo die, feria v, iiii. non' Feb. a sancto sene Symeone et Anna uidua agnoscitur, deinde precepto dominico in Egyptum propter metum Herodis indictione xiii[a] transfertur."

**VA4** Common root: *Coventry*[1] VA4. Marianus via JW*CC* (C) VA4.

**VA5** Common root: *Coventry*[1] VA5. Marianus via JW*CC* (C) VA5.

**VA6** Common root: *Coventry*[1] VA6. Marianus via JW*CC* (C) VA6.

**VA7** Common root: *Coventry*[1] VA7. Marianus via JW*CC* (C) VA7.

**VA12** Common root: *Coventry*[1] VA13. Marianus via JW*CC* (C) VA 13. Cf. Norman Annals: *AU*, *AG* 12, *AMSM* 15; *ASC* (F) 12.

**VA16.1** Common root: *Coventry*[1] VA16. Marianus via JW*CC* (C) VA 17. Cf. Bede, *CM*, 270; Norman Annals: *AU*, *AG* 15; *ASC* (F) 15.

**VA16.2** Bede, *CM*, 271: "Huius anno XII Pilatus Iudeae procurator ab eodem dirigitur." Cf. Marianus via JW*CC* (C) 7: "Pilatus procurator Iudeae a Tiberio mittitur." See also Norman Annals: *AU*, *AG*, *AMSM* 27; *ASC* (F) 26.

**VA21.1** Bede, *CM*, 272. Cf. Marianus via JW*CC* (C) AD 8.

**VA21.2** Common root: *Coventry*[1] 19. Marianus via JW*CC* (C) VA 19.

**1.1** Bede, *CM*, 268.

**1.2** Common root: *Coventry*[1] 1.2. Marianus via JW*CC* (C) AD 1.

**9.1** Common root: *Coventry*[1] 9.1. This entry matches that in the Easter Table Annals in JW*CC* (C), p. 56 (in cycle 1, year 10), but it has no counterpart in the Chronicle itself.

**9.2** Common root: *Coventry*[1] 9.2. Marianus via JW*CC* (C) 9. Cf. Norman Annals: *AU*, *AG*, *AMSM* 30; *ASC* (F) 30.

**12** Common root: *Coventry*[1] 12. Marianus via JW*CC* (C) 12. Cf. also Norman Annals: *AU* 33. It was Abbo of Fleury who identified AD 12 as the date of Christ's passion on the basis of the longstanding tradition that it took place on Friday 25 March, at the solar equinox, and of John 13:1, where it is indicated that the Last Supper took place on the day before the passover. In the Alexandrian Easter tables used by Dionysius, Easter Sunday falls on 27 March in AD 12. See further chap. 2, § a, above.

**13** Common root: *Coventry*[1] 13; *APW* 51. An entry in leonine hexameter verse which seems to derive from a calendrical source: see further chap. 5, § a above.

**14.1** Common root: *Coventry*[1] 14.1; *APW* 52, and **13** above.

**14.2** Common root: *Coventry*[1] 14.2. Marianus via JW*CC* (C) 13, possibly modified under the influence of Bede (see **14.3** below).

**14.3** Bede, *CM*, 274: "Et praedicaturi per Iudeae regiones apostoli Iacobum fratrem domini Hierosolimis ordinant episcopum; ordinant et VII diaconos, et lapidato Stephano ecclesia per regiones Iudeae et Samariae dispergitur."

**17.1** Common root: *Coventry*[1] 17. Marianus via JW*CC* (C) 17. Cf. Norman Annals: *AU*, *AG* 37; *ASC* (F) 34.

**17.2** Bede, *CM*, 279. Cf. Marianus via JW*CC* (C) 20: "Pilatus multas incidens calamitates, et irrogante Gaio coactus est ut sua manu qua Christum crudelissime flagellauit ipsa semet perimeret."

**17.3** Either Bede, *CM*, 282 or Marianus via JW*CC* (C) 22. Cf. Norman Annals: *AU* 38, *AG* 37; *ASC* (F) 38.

**17.4** Perhaps something from Bede, *CM*, 277–78: "Hic [Caligula] Herodem Agrippam amicum suum uinculis liberatum regem Iudeae facit, qui permanet in regno an. VII, id est usque ad quartum Claudii annum. Quo ab angelo percusso successit in regnum filius eius Agrippa, et usque ad exterminium Iudaeorum XXVI annos perseuerat. Herodes tetrarcha et ipse Gai amicitiam petens cogente Herodiade Romam uenit, sed accusatus ab Agrippa etiam tetrarchiam perdidit, fugiensque in Hispaniam cum Herodiade merore periit." Or Marianus via JW*CC* (C) 19: "Herodes tetrarcha et ipse amicitiam Gaii petens agente Herodiade uxore sua Romam uenit. Sed accusatus ab Agrippa tetrarcham perdidit, fugiensque Hyspania cum Herodiade merore periit, pro letitia decollationis Sancti Johannis." Another possibility is Norman Annals: *AU* 37, 39: "Hic Herodem Agrippa a vinculis liberatum regem Judee facit . . . Herodes tetrarcha Romam ueniens accusatur ab Agrippa; tetrarchiam perdit, fugiensque in Hispaniam cum Herodiade merore periit." Cf. likewise *ASC* (F) 39.

22 Common root: *Coventry*[1] 22. Marianus via JW*CC* (C) 22. Cf. Bede, *CM*, 283; Norman Annals: *AU* 43, *AG* 42; *ASC* (F) 45.

24 Source unknown.

30 Common root: *Coventry*[1] 30. Marianus via JW*CC* (C) 29.

34 Common root: *Coventry*[1] 33. Marianus via JW*CC* (C) 34. Cf. Norman Annals: *AU* 33.

**37.1** Common root: *Coventry*[1] 37. Marianus via JW*CC* (C) 36. Cf. Bede, *CM*, 289; Norman Annals: *AU*, *AG* 56.

**37.2** Bede, *CM*, 283 has identical material. Cf. Marianus via JW*CC* (C) 24: "Petrus apostolus cum primus Antiochenam ecclesiam fundasset,

Romam mittitur, ubi euangelium predicans $xx^{ti}v^{e}$ annis, mensibus $v^{e}$, diebus $xiii^{ci}$, episcopus eiusdem urbis preseuerat."

37.3 Bede, *CM*, 284. The same material could have been derived from Marianus via JW*CC* (C) 33, but the sequence of material suggests that our compiler is following Bede, *CM*, at this point. Cf. also JW*CC* (C) 25, and Norman Annals: *AU*, *AG* 47; *ASC* (F) 48.

37.4 Bede, *CM*, 285. Cf. Marianus via JW*CC* (C) 26: "Quarto anno Claudii fames grauissima, cuius Lucas meminit, facta est. Hec Beda." Likewise, Norman Annals: *ASC* (F) 47.

37.5 Bede, *CM*, 286, but reading *in deditionem* instead of T's *inditionem*. Cf. Marianus via JW*CC* (C) 26: "Claudius de Britaniis triumphauit, et Orcades insulas Romano adiecit imperio."

37.6 Bede, *CM*, 288. Cf. Marianus via JW*CC* (C) 33: "Magna fames Rome"; Norman Annals: *AU* 47 and 53.

37.7 Bede, *CM*, 290: "Huius [Neronis] secundo anno Festus Iudeae procurator successit Felici, a quo Paulus Romam uinctus mittitur." Cf. Marianus via JW*CC* (C) 38; Norman Annals: *ASC* (F) 58.

41 Common root: *Coventry*[1] 41. Marianus via JW*CC* (C) 41.

42 Common root: *Coventry*[1] 42.2. Marianus via JW*CC* (C) 42. Cf. Bede, *CM*, 291; Norman Annals: *ASC* (F) 62, 63.

43 Source unknown.

44 Norman Annals: *AU*, *AG*, *ASC* (F) 68. Cf. Marianus via JW*CC* (C) 38, 50.

45 Common root: *Coventry*[1] 45. Marianus via JW*CC* (C) 45: "Marcus euangelista carne exuitur, sancto die Pasche, $vii^{o}$ kl' Maii, ut legitur in martirologio . . ." Cf. Norman Annals: *AU*, *AG*, *ASC* (F) 63.

46.1 Common root: *Coventry*[1] 46. Marianus via JW*CC* (C) 46. Cf. *Chronicula*[1] VA 64: "Nero retibus aureis piscabatur et ut similitudinem Troie ardentis inspiceret Romam incendit." The final verb in JW*CC* (C) is *accendit*.

46.2 Bede, *CM*, 292. Cf. Marianus via JW*CC* (C) 42, 46: "Festo procuratori Iudee successit . . . Albino successit Florus, sub quo Iudei contra Romanos rebellauerunt."

46.3 Bede, *CM*, 294, referring to Nero.

50 Common root: *Coventry*[1] 50. Marianus via JW*CC* (C, pp. 210–11) 50. Cf. Bede, *CM*, 293; Norman Annals: *AU*, 70–71, *AG* 71–72; *ASC* (F) 70.

51.1 Common root: *Coventry*[1] 51.1. Marianus via JW*CC* (C) 50.

51.2 Common root: *Coventry*[1] 51.2. Marianus via JW*CC* (C) 51. Note, however, that the length of Otho's reign is here put at ninety days ($xc^{simo}$).

52 Common root: *Coventry*[1] 52.1. JW*CC* (C) 51 (for the month), 52 (for the method of Vitellius's end).

53.1 Common root: *Coventry*[1] 53. This entry echoes the Easter Table Annals in JW*CC* (C), p. 57 where the words *Caput mundi* appear alongside

53/585/1117 (i.e. in cycle 3, year 16 = 53/585/1117). This entry indicates that this is the first year of the ninth 532-year interval since the creation of the world—that is, in 53 AD the world was entering its 4257th year. JW*CC* is here following Marianus Scotus who recalculated the length of the pre-Christian era, placing Christ's birth in *Anno mundi* 4183, some 22 years earlier than Dionysius Exiguus. Moreover, in a passage which JW*CC* faithfully reproduces in C at p. 97, Marianus explicitly states that there are 4203 years from the creation to the first year of the standard Dionysian 532-cycle (that is, our 1 BC): "Usque autem ad magnum ciclum pascalem in cuius secundo anno iuxta Dionisium natus est Dominus hoc est in anno xx$^{o}$iii$^{o}$ dominice natiuitatis secundum hystoriam euangelii, sunt anni īīīī cc$^{ti}$ iii$^{es}$" (*Chronica chronicarum*, ii.1). It follows that *Anno mundi* 4204 = 1 BC. If we subtract 4256 (the sum of 8 times 532) from 4204 we arrive at AD 52. Compare also the related entries under **585** and **1117** below.

**53.2** Common root: *Coventry*[1] 52.2. Marianus via JW*CC* (C) 52. Cf. Bede, *CM*, 295.

**53.3** Common root: *Coventry*[1] 54.1. Marianus via JW*CC* (C) 54. Cf. JW*CC* (C) 52, where the same material is given in a similar form: "Titus uero ab exercitu pronuntiatus est imperator, captaque urbe, muros uniuersos solo coequauit . . . [Iosephus] scribit undecies centena milia gladio et fame perisse, reliquos autem toto orbe dispersos dcccc$^{m}$ narrat." Cf. also Bede, *CM*, 296; Norman Annals: *AU* 72, *AG* 74, *ASC* (F) 74.

**53.4** Bede, *CM*, 296–7. Cf. Marianus via JW*CC* (C) 52: "Hic [Vespasianus] imperante Claudio ab eodem in Britanniam missus, etiam Uectam insulam Britannie proximam a meridie Romanorum dicioni subegit."

**53.5** Common root: *Coventry*[1] 54.2. Marianus via JW*CC* (C) 58. Cf. Bede, *CM*, 298. The colossus in question was begun as a bronze image of Nero, but dedicated by Vespasian as a statue of the sun (see Samuel B. Platner and Thomas Ashby, *A Topographical Dictionary of Ancient Rome* [London: Oxford University Press, 1929], 130–31, and **179.5** below).

**61** Common root: *Coventry*[1] 61. Marianus via JW*CC* (C) 61: "Tres ciuitates Cipri terre motu corruerunt. Lues ingens Rome facta, ita ut post non multos dies in Ephemeridem decem ferme milia mortuorum hominum efferentur."

**62.1** Marianus via JW*CC* (C) 62.

**62.2** Common root: *Coventry*[1] 62. Marianus via JW*CC* (C) 62. Cf. Bede, *CM*, 299; Norman Annals: *AU*, *AG* 80.

**65.1** Common root: *Coventry*[1] 65. Marianus via the Consular Annals in JW*CC* (C, p. 8) 65. The month of Titus' death is not spelt out in the main chronicle of JW*CC*.

**65.2** Marianus via JW*CC* (C) 64: "Titus . . . theatrum Rome edificans in dedicatione eius v̄ ferarum occidit . . . . Titus uir fuit omnium uirtutum genere mirabilis, adeo ut amor et delicie humani generis diceretur . . . ." Cf. Bede, *CM*, 299–300.

65.3 Common root: *Coventry*[1] 65. Marianus via JW*CC* (C) 64: "Cui successit frater suus iunior Domitianus . . . regnauit annis xv[ci] mensibus v[e]."

65.4 Marianus via JW*CC* (C) 78. Cf. Bede, *CM*, 302.

65.5 Norman Annals: *AU* 83, *AG* 82.

69.1 Indeterminate source.

69.2 There is enough detail to suggest that the original entry may have been almost identical to that now found among the "Papal Annals" in JW*CC* (C) p. 29: "Hic constituit ut altaris pallia, cathedra, candelabrum, et uelum si fuerint uetustate consumpta incendio dentur, quoniam non licet ea que in sanctuario fuerint male tractari, sed incendio omnia dentur." The ultimate source of this page is a forged letter of Pope Clement to Bishop Jacob of Jerusalem (Pseudo-Isidore, II Clemens p. 45) as quoted in *Collectio Lanfranci* (R, fol. 8v): "De uasis sane sacris ita gerundum est. Altaris palla, cathedra, candelabrum et uelum si fuerint uetustate consumpta, incendio dentur, quam non licet ea que in sanctuario fuerunt male tractari, sed incendio uniuersa tradantur. Cineres quoque eorum in baptisterio inferantur, ubi nullus transitum habeat, aut in pariete aut in fossis pauimentorum iactentur, ne introeuntium pedibus inquinentur." The same letter is also quoted in Marianus (N, fol. 112vb), but with *incendentur* for *incendio dentur* and omitting the clause *quam non licet ea que in sanctuario fuerunt male tractari, sed incendio uniuersa tradantur.*

78 Common root: *Coventry*[1] 77. Marianus via JW*CC* (C) 78: "Et sub eo [Domitiano] apostolus Iohannes in feruentis olei dolium ante portam Latinam Rome missus sed nichil lesus, sicut a corruptione carnis fuit immunis. Deinde Pathmos insulam religatus apocalipsin uidit." Cf. Bede, *CM*, 302–3; Norman Annals: *AU*, *AG* 83.

80.1 Common root: *Coventry*[1] 79. Marianus via JW*CC* (C) 80. Cf. Bede, *CM*, 304.

80.2 Bede, *CM*, 305. Cf. JW*CC* (C) 81: "Itaque multi quos iniuste eiecerat de exilio reuersi, nonnulli propria bona receperunt. Aiunt et apostolum Iohannem inter reuersos de exilio solutum Ephesum reuersum fuisse, ubi et hospitiolum et amicos amantissimos sui habebat. Euangelium quoque contra hereticos conscripsit." Cf. Norman Annals: *ASC* (F) 98.

80.3 Marianus via JW*CC* (C) 77. Cf. *Chronicula*[1] VA 104; Norman Annals: *AU*, *ASC* (F) 99.

80.4 Marianus via JW*CC* (C) 79. Cf. Norman Annals: *AG* 97.

82.1 Common root: *Coventry*[1] 81. Marianus via JW*CC* (C) 82. Cf. Bede, *CM*, 306; Norman Annals: *AU*, *AG* 98, *ASC* (F) 100.

82.2 Bede, *CM*, 308. Cf. Norman Annals: *AG* 98.

82.3 Bede, *CM*, 312. Cf. JW*CC* (C) 95.

82.4 Bede, *CM*, 313.

82.5 There is enough detail to suggest that the original entry may have been almost identical to that now found among John's "Papal Annals" (C) p. 29: "Euaristus . . . Hic constituit ut diaconi .vii$^{em}$. sint qui custodiant episcopum, ne ipse ab insidiatoribus quoquomodo infestetur aut a suis ledatur aut uerba diuina detrahendo aut insidiando polluantur uel despiciantur." The ultimate source of the enty is a forged letter of Pope Evaristus (Pseudo-Isidore, I Evaristus p. 138), as quoted in *Collectio Lanfranci* (R, fol. 17v): § 1, "Diaconi qui quasi oc(c)uli uidentur esse episcopi in unaquoque ciuitate iuxta apostolorum constituta septem debent esse qui custodiant predicantem episcopum, ne . . . ." Marianus via JW*CC* (C) 89 mentions this letter in passing, but without specifying its contents. Cf. *LPont.* 6: "Hic titulos in urbe Roma dividit presbiteris et VII diaconos ordinavit qui custodirent episcopum praedicantem propter stilum veritatis."

84 Common root: *Coventry*[1] 83. Marianus via JW*CC* (C) 89: "Hoc anno dominicus dies vi kl. ianuarii contigit, quo forte sanctus Iohannes obiit." Cf. Bede, *CM*, 307: "Iohannes apostolus lxviii anno post passionem Domini, etatis autem suae xc et viii, Ephesi placida morte quieuit."

91.1 Indeterminate source.

91.2 Norman Annals: *AU*, *ASC* (EF) 114; *AG* 104 (where this entry is transferred to Pope Evaristus). Cf. the material derived from Marianus in JW*CC* (C) 101, and John's "Papal Annals" in JW*CC* (C) p. 29: "Hic constituit aquam sparsionis cum sale benedicto in habitaculos hominum spargi."

92 Common root: *Coventry*[1] 91. Marianus via JW*CC* (C) 92: "Traiano Christianos persequente, Simon qui et Simeon filius Cleophe, qui post Iacobum Ierosolimis tenebat episcopatum crucifigitur, omnibus mirantibus, et ipso iudice, ut centum uiginti annorum senex crucis supplicium pertulisset." Cf. Bede, *CM*, 308 (who omits Simon's age); Norman Annals: *AU*, *ASC* (F) 115, *AG* 101.

93 Common root: *Coventry*[1] 92. Marianus via JW*CC* (C) 93. Cf. Bede, *CM*, 309.

94 Common root: *Coventry*[1] 93.1. Marianus via JW*CC* (C) 94. Cf. Bede, *CM*, 311.

95 Common root: *Coventry*[1] 93.2. Marianus via JW*CC* (C) 95.

97 Common root: *Coventry*[1] 97. Norman Annals: *AU* 119: "Aquila interpres habetur." Cf. JW*CC* (C) 123: "Hoc tempore erat Aquila Ponticus secundus interpres post lxx$^{ta}$ interpretes, qui scripturam de Hebreo transtulit." Cf., likewise, *Chronicula*[1] VA 124.

101 Common root: *Coventry*[1] 100. Marianus via JW*CC* (C) 101: "Alexandri pape passio v$^{o}$ non' mai Rome uia Numentana, ab urbe miliario vii$^{o}$, cum Euentio et Theodolo presbiteris, sub Traiano imperatore, iudice autem Aureliano, decollatus." Cf. Bede, *CM*, 310: "Alexander quoque

Romanae urbis episcopus martyrio coronatur, et VII ab urbe miliario uia Numentana ubi decollatus est, sepelitur."

**102.1** Common root: *Coventry*[1] 101.1. Marianus via JW*CC* (C) 102 or the Consular Annals in JW*CC* (C, p. 9) 100. Cf. Bede, *CM*, 315.

**102.2** Common root: *Coventry*[1] 101.2. Norman Annals: *AU* 117: "Hadrianus Helius imperator Jerosolimam murorum extructione reparavit . . . Idem Judeos secundo rebelles perdomuit ultima cede, ablata licentia Jerusalem introeundi." *AG* 117 is almost identical. Cf. JW*CC* (C) 120: "Bellum Iudaicum quod in Palestina gerebatur finem accepit, rebus Iudeorum penitus oppressis, ex quo tempore etiam introeundi eis Ierosolimam licentia ablata est primum Dei nutu sicut prophete uaticinati sunt, deinde Romanis interdictionibus." Cf. Bede, *CM*, 317: "Idem [Hadrianus] . . . etiam introeundi eis Hierosolymam licentia ablata, quam ipse in optimum statum murorum extructione reparauit."

**102.3** Bede, *CM*, 316.

**102.4** Bede, *CM*, 318. Cf. Marianus via JW*CC* (C) 117; the "Consular Annals" in (C, p. 9) 100: "Adrianus Athenis . . . agonem edidit bibliothecamque exstruxit." The two languages are, of course, Latin and Greek.

**102.5** Norman Annals: *AU*, *AG*, *ASC* (EF) 124: "Hic constituit ymnum decantare *Sanctus*, *sanctus*, *sanctus*, in officio misse."

**102.6** Matching material, derived from Marianus, occurs in JW*CC* (C) 101: "Sixtus papa quintus . . . constituit in decretis suis ut sacra misteria non tractarentur nisi a sacris ministris, et ut intra actionem missarum 'Sanctus, sanctus, sanctus' cantaretur." See also John's "Papal Annals" (C) p. 29, and in his "Consular Annals" (C, p. 9) 100.

**111.1** Indeterminate source.

**111.2** The closest parallel is to be found in the "Papal Annals" in JW*CC* (C) p. 29: "Hic decreuit ut per .vii$^{em}$. epdomadas plenas ante pasca ieiunium celebretur, omnesque clerici a carne ieiunent, et in nocte natalis domini misse celebrentur, et ad missam 'Gloria in excelsis Deo' cantetur. Passus est nonas Ianuarii." Similar entries appear in the main chronicle, JW*CC* (C) 123, and in the Consular Annals in JW*CC* (C, p. 10) 113. All three items seem to depend on Marianus's consular annals (N, fol. 7v): "Thelesphorus papa passus non. ianuarii. Hic decreuit ut per vii$^{em}$ ebdomadas plenas ante pasca ieiunium celebrent, et omnes clerici a carne ieiunent, et in nocte natalis Domini misse celebrarentur, et ad missam 'Gloria in excelsis Deo' cantaretur." The entry also shows the influence of Norman Annals: *AU* 134 ("Hic constituit ymnum angelicum cantari *Gloria in excelsis Deo* diebus festis"), *ASC* (EF), *AG* 134.

**118** Common root: *Coventry*[1] 117. Marianus via JW*CC* (C) 118: "Iudei ad arma uersi, Palestinam depopulati sunt."

**119** The item could have been generated by combining the entries in JW*CC* (C) 123 and the "Consular Annals" in JW*CC* (C, p. 10) 123; but there is a single entry which provides all the information given here in the "Papal Annals" (C) p. 29: "Yginus papa natione graecus de athenis sedit annis iiii[or] mensibus iii[bus] diebus xxi[o]. Hic constituit clerum et distribuit ecclesiasticos gradus."

**121.1** Common root: *Coventry*[1] 120.1. Marianus via JW*CC* (C) 121. Cf. Bede, *CM*, 319.

**121.2** Source unknown.

**122** Common root: *Coventry*[1] 120.2. Marianus via JW*CC* (C) 122. Cf. Bede, *CM*, 317; Norman Annals: *AU* 117, *AG* 117.

**123.1** Common root: *Coventry*[1] 122.1. Marianus via JW*CC* (C) 123. However, Marianus and JW*CC* opt for a reign of twenty-three years and three months rather than one of twenty-four years and three months. See, likewise, the Consular Annals in JW*CC* (C, p. 10) 126. Cf. Bede, *CM*, 320; Norman Annals: *AU*, *AG* 138, *ASC* (F) 137.

**123.2** Common root: *Coventry*[1] 122.2. Marianus via JW*CC* (C) 124: "Iste Antoninus dictus ideo Pius est, quia in omni Romano regno hominibus debita relaxauit."

**125.1** Bede, *CM*, 321. Marianus via JW*CC* (C) 127 omits the clause "benignumque . . . fecit." Cf. Norman Annals: *AU* and *AG* 139.

**125.2** Norman Annals: *AU* and *AG* 139: "Valentinus et Marcion heretici." Cf. Marianus via JW*CC* (C) 131 and 133.

**127** Indeterminate source.

**128** Common root: *Coventry*[1] 126. Matching material occurs in JW*CC* (C) 128, the "Papal Annals" (C) p. 29, and Bede, *CM*, 322. Cf. Norman Annals: *AU*, *AG* 149, *ASC* (F) 158.

**135.1** Common root: *Coventry*[1] 135. Norman Annals: *AU*, *AG*, *ASC* (F) 157 ("Policarpus Romam ueniens multos ab heresi liberauit").

**135.2** Marianus via JW*CC* (C) 143: "Sub Aniceto papa Policarpus Romam ueniens, multos ab heretica labe castigauit, qui Valentini et Cerdonis fuerant nuper doctrina corrupti." The same material also appears in Bede, *CM*, 323.

**141.1** Indeterminate source.

**141.2** Matching material, derived from Marianus, appears in JW*CC* (C) 142, in the "Consular Annals" (C, p. 10) 143, and in the "Papal Annals" (C) p. 29. The allusion is to the apostle Paul's precept in 1 Corinthians 11:14.

**146.1** Common root: *Coventry*[1] 146. Marianus via JW*CC* (C) 146, or the Consular Annals in JW*CC* (C, p. 10) 146. Cf. Bede, *CM*, 324; Norman Annals: *AU*, *AG* 160. "Marcus Antoninus Verus" is the emperor Marcus Aurelius.

**146.2** Marianus via JW*CC* (C) 147. Cf. Bede, *CM*, 325.

**146.3** Bede, *CM*, 326. Cf. Marianus via JW*CC* (C) 151.

**150.1** Norman Annals: *AU*, *AG* 162.

**150.2** Norman Annals: *AU* 163 and *AG* 162: "Catafrigarum heresis exorta est." Cf. JW*CC* (C) 157: "Pseudoprophetia que catafrigarum nominatur accepit exordium."

**158.1** Indeterminate source.

**158.2** Matching material, derived from Marianus, occurs in JW*CC* (C) 154, in the "Consular Annals" (C, p. 11) 153, and in the "Papal Annals" (C) p. 30.

**159.1** Common root: *Coventry*[1] 161.1. Marianus via JW*CC* (C) 159.

**159.2** This item echoes both Marianus via JW*CC* (C) 174 and Norman Annals: *AU*, *AG* 183; *AMSM* 184.

**159.3** Indeterminate source.

**162** Common root: *Coventry*[1] 161.2. Matching material appears in JW*CC* (C) 162: "Lucius Brittanniorum rex ab Eleutherio papa per epistolam Christianum se fieri impetrat, et mox effectum pie petitionis consecutus est, susceptamque fidem Britanni usque in tempora Dioclitiani principis inuiolatam integramque quieta pace seruabant." John's "Papal Annals" (C), p. 30, are somewhat more remote in their treatment: "Ab hoc Lucius Brittanniorum rex per epistolam Christianum se cum gente sua fieri impetrauit. quod .cc$^{tis}$xvi$^{cim}$. annis usque Dioclitiani principis tempora durauit." Cf. Bede, *CM*, 331; Norman Annals: *AU*, *AG* 188; *AMSM* 186; *ASC* (F) 167. The annotator has confused King Lucius with the adopted son of Antoninus Pius of the same name.

**165** Common root: *Coventry*[1] 165. Marianus via JW*CC* (C) 165, possibly with the month inferred from JW*CC* (C) 146. Cf. Bede, *CM*, 333; Norman Annals: *AU*, *AG* 180.

**171** Common root: *Coventry*[1] 171. Marianus via JW*CC* (C) 171.

**177** Common root: *Coventry*[1] 177; JW*CC* (C, p. 218) 177, where there is a tiny marginal addition *O. nascitur.*

**179.1** Common root: *Coventry*[1] 179.1. Marianus via JW*CC* (C) 179: "Commodus strangulatur . . . Pertinax secundum omnes regnauit mensibus vi hoc est usque kl. Feb. in anno centesimo lx$^{o}$viii$^{o}$." The month was inferred from JW*CC* (C) 165. Cf. Norman Annals: *AU*, *AG* 193.

**179.2** Bede, *CM*, 334. Cf. Marianus via JW*CC* (C) 166.

**179.3** Common root: *Coventry*[1] 179.2. Marianus via JW*CC* (C) 179. Cf. Bede, *CM*, 337.

**179.4** Marianus via JW*CC* (C) 168. Cf. Norman Annals: *AU* 181, *AG* 180; Bede, *CM*, 335.

**179.5** Bede, *CM*, 336. Cf. Marianus via JW*CC* (C) 175, which has everything but the pronoun *ei*. The giant statue in question is that of Nero mentioned in **53.5** above: Commodus converted it into a statue of himself as Hercules, but it was turned back into an image of the sun after his death. See Platner and Ashby, *Topographical Dictionary of Ancient Rome*, 130–31.

**180.1** Common root: *Coventry*[1] 180. Marianus via JW*CC* (C) 180. The month of Pertinax's death has been inferred from JW*CC* (C) 179. Cf. Bede, *CM*, 338; Norman Annals: *AU* 193–94, *AG* 193.

**180.2** Bede, *CM*, 339 is almost identical: "Victor XIII Romae episcopus datis late libellis constituit pascha die dominico celebrari, sicut et predecessor eius Eleuter a XIIII luna primi mensis usque in XXI." Marianus via JW*CC* (C) 180, is similar but with more variants. Cf. also Norman Annals: *AU*, *ASC* (E) 202, *AG* 203.

**180.3** The original entry almost certainly matched that now found among the "Papal Annals" in JW*CC* (C) p. 30: "Hic [Victor papa] constituit ut si necesse fuerit aut mortis periculum ingruerit, gentiles ad fidem uenientes quocumque loco uel momento ubicunque euenerit siue in flumine, siue in mari, siue in fontibus, tantum Christiane confessione credulitatis clarificata, baptizentur." John's source may have been a forged letter of Pope Victor (Pseudo-Isidore, I Victor pp. 228–29) as quoted in *Collectio Lanfranci* (R, fol. 24r): § 1, "Sed tamen si necesse fuerit aut mortis periculum ingruerit, gentiles ad fidem uenientes quocumque loco uel momento ubicunque euenerit siue in flumine siue in mari siue in fontibus tantum Christiane confessione credulitatis clarificata, bapti<za>rentur." But cf. *LPont.* 15: "Hic constituit ut, necessitate faciente, ut ubiubi inventus fuisset sive in flumine, sive in mari, sive in fontibus, tantum christiano confessione credulitatis clarificata, quicumque hominum ex gentile veniens ut baptizaretur." It needs to be kept in mind that John had access to William of Malmesbury's version of *Liber pontificalis* (today MS. Cambridge, U.L., Kk.4.6, fols. 224r–80r; see the discussion under **891.1** below), which retains the passage in question (fol. 225v).

**182** Common root: *Coventry*[1] 182. Either Marianus via JW*CC* (C) 181 or Bede, *CM*, 342, who both read: "Clemens Alexandrine ecclesie presbyter et Panthenus stoicus philosophus in disputatione dogmatis nostri dissertissimi habentur."

**183** Common root: *Coventry*[1] 183. Norman Annals: *AU* 196. Cf. JW*CC* (C) 183; Bede, *CM*, 343.

**185** Common root: *Coventry*[1] 185. Marianus via JW*CC* (C) 185 (omitting *populum*).

**188** Common root: *Coventry*[1] 189. Marianus via JW*CC* (C) 189. Cf. Bede, *CM*, 344; Norman Annals: *AU* 196, *AG* 193.

**190.1** Indeterminate source.

**190.2** Almost identical material, derived from Marianus, occurs in JW*CC* (C) 188, the "Consular Annals" (C, p. 11) 188, and in the "Papal Annals" (C) p. 30, where the word order is closest to the present item: "Hic [Zepherinus] constituit ut presentibus omnibus clericis et laicis fidelibus diaconus siue presbiter ordinetur, et astantibus sacerdotibus misse celebrentur."

**191** Common root: *Coventry*[1] 190. Either Marianus via JW*CC* (C) 190 or Bede, *CM*, 344.

**192** Common root: *Coventry*[1] 192. Marianus via JW*CC* (C) 192.

**195** Common root: *Coventry*[1] 195. Marianus via JW*CC* (C) 194–5: "Clodium Albinum qui se in Gallia cesarem fecerat, apud Lugdunum Seuerus interfecit. Seuerus in Britannos bellum transiecit." But cf. Bede, *CM*, 345 to whom the annalist is just as close as to JW*CC*.

**197** Common root: *Coventry*[1] 197. Marianus via JW*CC* (C) 197. Cf. Norman Annals: *AU* 227, *AG* 226.

**198.1** Common root: *Coventry*[1] 198.1. This item echoes JW*CC* (C) 195, 198: "Seuerus imperator in Britannos bellum transiecit, ubi ut receptas prouincias ab incursione barbarica faceret securiores, uallum per c$^{tum}$xxx$^{ta}$ duorum passuum milia a mari ad mare deduxit . . . Seuerus obiit Eboraci in Britannia." It derives not from Marianus, but from Bede, *CM*, 345.

**198.2** Common root: *Coventry*[1] 198.2. Marianus via JW*CC* (C) 198. Cf. Bede, *CM*, 347; Norman Annals: *AU*, *AG* 212.

**201** Bede, *CM*, 348.

**202** Bede, *CM*, 349.

**203** Common root: *Coventry*[1] 203. Marianus via JW*CC* (C) 203. Cf. Bede, *CM*, 346.

**204.1** Indeterminate source.

**204.2** The closest match is provided by Norman Annals: *AU*, *AG* 226; *AMSM* 224, where this constitutional ruling is attributed to Pope Urban I. There is nothing comparable in Marianus or JW*CC*.

**204.3** There is enough detail to suggest that the original entry may have matched that now found among the "Papal Annals" in JW*CC* (C) p. 30: "Hic [Calixtus] constituit .iiii$^{or}$. temporum ieiunium in anno fieri. propter abundantiam frumenti. uini 7 olei iuxta prophetiam. 7 in sabbato .xii$^{em}$. lectiones." Cf. the main chronicle in JW*CC* (C) 207.

**205** Common root: *Coventry*[1] 206. Marianus via JW*CC* (C) 205.

**207.1** Common root: *Coventry*[1] 207. Marianus via JW*CC* (C) 206–7. Cf. Bede, *CM*, 352–3.

**207.2** Indeterminate source.

**207.3** Norman Annals: *AU* 218, with either Marianus via JW*CC* (C) 207 or Bede, *CM*, 351.

**210.1** Common root: *Coventry*[1] 210.1. Marianus via JW*CC* (C) 210.

**210.2** Bede, *CM*, 354. The allusion is to Luke 24:13–35.

**211.1** Bede, *CM*, 355.

**211.2** Indeterminate source.

**211.3** There is enough detail to suggest that the original entry may have matched that now found among the "Papal Annals" in JW*CC* (C) p. 30: "Hic [Anterus] constituit {et decreuit} episcopos communi utilitate atque necessitate sed non libito cuiusquam aut dominatione de ciuitate qua ordinantur in aliam ciuitatem posse transferri." The ultimate source of this entry is a forged letter of Pope Anterus (Pseudo-Isidore, Anterus p. 285) as quoted in *Collectio Lanfranci* (R, fol. 28va): "De mutatione episcoporum unde sanctam sedem apostolicam consulere uoluistis, scitote eam communi utilitate atque necessitate fieri licere sed non libito cuiusquam aut dominatione ...." Marianus (N fol. 120v) cites the dating clause of a decretal of Pope Anterus, but does not quote its contents.

**212.1** Common root: *Coventry*$^{1}$ 211. Marianus via JW*CC* (C) 211: "His consulibus Cassio teste Antoninus Rome occiditur tumultu militari cum matre. Romanorum xx$^{us}$v$^{us}$. Alexander Mamee filius secundum omnes regnauit annis xiii$^{cim}$ et aliquibus diebus, hoc est usque kl. ianuarii in anno cc$^{o}$ xii$^{o}$ sub quo hi consules fuerunt."

**212.2** Either Bede, *CM*, 357 or Marianus via JW*CC* (C) 220.

**212.3** Bede, *CM*, 359. The pronoun *eum* refers not to Alexander but to "Origen of Alexandria," information having been lost in the process of abbreviation.

**218.1** Indeterminate source.

**218.2** Matching material, derived from Marianus, occurs in JW*CC* (C) 225 and in the "Papal Annals" (C), p. 30: "Hic .vii$^{em}$. diaconos ordinauit, qui .vii$^{em}$. imminerent notariis, gestaque martyrum in integro colligerent."

**220.1** Marianus via JW*CC* (C) 220.

**220.2** Common root: *Coventry*$^{1}$ 220. Marianus via JW*CC* (C) 223. Cf. Bede, *CM*, 358.

**220.3** There is enough detail to suggest that the original entry may have matched that now found among the "Papal Annals" in JW*CC* (C) p. 30: "Hic [Urbanus] constituit ut fidelium oblationes non in alios usus quam ecclesiasticos et Christianorum fratrum uel indigentium conuertantur quia uota sunt fidelium et pretia peccatorum." The ultimate source is probably a forged letter of Pope Urban, § 1 (Pseudo-Isidore, Urbanus p. 266) as quoted in *Collectio Lanfranci* (R, fol. 28ra): "Non ergo debent in alios usus quam ecclesiasticos et praedictorum christianorum fratrum uel indigentium conuerti, quia uota sunt fidelium et pretia peccatorum atque ad praedictum opus explendum domino tradite." Marianus (N fol. 119r) cites the dating clause of a decretal of Pope Urban but does not quote its contents.

**222** Common root: *Coventry*$^{1}$ 222. Marianus via JW*CC* (C) 222; *Chronicula*$^{1}$ VA 233. Cf. Bede, *CM*, 359; Norman Annals: *AU* 227, *AMSM* 226.

**224.1** Common root: *Coventry*$^{1}$ 224. Marianus via JW*CC* (C) 224.

**224.2** Bede, *CM*, 361.

**224.3** Marianus via JW*CC* (C) 226, or Norman Annals: *AU* 238.

**228** Common root: *Coventry*$^{1}$ 228. Marianus via JW*CC* (C) 228 gives Gordian a reign of ten years, but in the consular annals, JW*CC* (C, p. 13)

228, and in the Easter Table Annals, JW*CC* (C, p. 62) 228, he is given a reign of six years.

229 Bede, *CM*, 364. Cf. Norman Annals: *AU* 241, *AG* 240 ("Africanus inter scriptores nobilis habetur").

232 Common root: *Coventry*[1] 232. Marianus via JW*CC* (C) 232. Cf. *Chronicula*[1] VA 233; Bede, *CM*, 368.

234.1 Common root: *Coventry*[1] 234.1. Marianus via JW*CC* (C) 234.

234.2 Common root: *Coventry*[1] 234.2. Marianus via JW*CC* (C) 235. Cf. Norman Annals: *AU* 247; *ASN* 246.

237 Common root: *Coventry*[1] 238. Marianus via JW*CC* (C) 238. Two ancient cities called Philippopolis have been confused in the present entry: modern-day Plovdiv in Thrace, which was founded by Philip of Macedon, and Shahba, in Syria which was founded by the emperor Philip the Arab. The error was inherited from Marianus.

241 Common root: *Coventry*[1] 241. Marianus via JW*CC* (C) 241.

242.1 Indeterminate source.

242.2 Norman Annals: *AU*, *ASC* (E) 254 (identical), *AG* 254 (with variations in word order and some additional detail). Cf. Bede, *CM*, 376; JW*CC* (C) 241.

242.3 Norman Annals: *AU* 256, *AG* 244.

242.4 There is enough detail to suggest that the original entry may have matched that now found among the "Papal Annals" in JW*CC* (C) p. 30: "Hic [Cornelius] constituit ut sacramentum a summis sacerdotibus uel reliquis nisi pro fide recta minime exigatur, et ut nullus sacerdotum causam suam alieno committat iudicio nisi ad sedem apostolicam fuerit appellatum." The ultimate source is probably a forged letter of Pope Cornelius, §§ 1–2 (Pseudo-Isidore, II Cornelius) as quoted in *Collectio Lanfranci* (R, fol. 30v): "Sacramentum ergo hactenus a summis sacerdotibus, uel reliquis exigi nisi pro fide recta minime cognouimus nec sponte eos iurasse repperimus"; "Nullus uero sacerdotum causam suam alieno committat iudicio, nisi ad sedem apostolicam fuerit appellatum." Marianus VA 242 (N fol. 121rv) covers the pontificate of Cornelius without mentioning this decree.

243 Common root: *Coventry*[1] 243. Marianus via JW*CC* (C) 243.

244 Common root: *Coventry*[1] 244. Marianus via JW*CC* (C) 244 with the month of Decius's death inferred from 241.

245.1 Common root: *Coventry*[1] 245. Marianus via JW*CC* (C) 245.

245.2 Norman Annals: *AU* 256, *AG* 254.

246.1 Common root: *Coventry*[1] 246. Marianus via JW*CC* (C) 246 with the month of Gallus's death inferred from 244.

246.2 Norman Annals: *AU* 257, *AG* 267.

246.3 Norman Annals: *AU* 259, *AG* 267.

**247.1** Common root: *Coventry*[1] 247. Marianus via JW*CC* (C) 246. Cf. Bede, *CM*, 375.
**247.2** Indeterminate source.
**247.3** Marianus via JW*CC* (C) 245: "In hac sancta sede apostolica constituimus ut duo presbyteri et tres diaconi in omni loco episcopum non deserant, propter testimonium ecclesiasticum." John's "Papal Annals" (C) p. 30, is closer but has seven deacons instead of three: "Hic [Lucius] constituit ut .ii°. presbyteri 7 .vii$^{em}$. diaconi episcopum in omni loco non deserant, propter ecclesiasticum testimonium." The ultimate source is a forged letter of Pope Lucius, § 1 (Pseudo-Isidore, Lucius), as quoted in *Collectio Lanfranci* (R, fol. 30v): "Quam et in hac sancta sede constitutum habemus, ut duo presbiteri et tres diaconi in omni loco episcopum non deserant propter testimonium ecclesiasticum."
**249** Common root: *Coventry*[1] 249. Marianus via JW*CC* (C) 249.
**250** Common root: *Coventry*[1] 250. Marianus via JW*CC* (C) 250.
**252** Common root: *Coventry*[1] 252. JW*CC* (C) 252. Cf. Bede, *CM*, 379.
**253.1** Indeterminate source.
**253.2** Matching material, derived from Marianus's consular annals (N, fol. 9r–v), is to be found in JW*CC* (C) 241, in John's "Consular Annals" (C, p. 13) 248, and in his "Papal Annals" (C) p. 30.
**256** Common root: *Coventry*[1] 256. Marianus via JW*CC* (C) 255.
**259** Common root: *Coventry*[1] 259. Marianus via JW*CC* (C) 259.
**261.1** Common root: *Coventry*[1] 260. Marianus via JW*CC* (C) 261.
**261.2** Indeterminate source.
**261.3** Matching material, derived from Marianus, occurs in JW*CC* (C) 253, in John's "Consular Annals" (C, p. 13) 253, and in his "Papal Annals" (C) p. 30: "Hic [Dionisius] constituit ecclesias presbiteris et parrochias diocesis dedit et constituit." Cf. *LPont.* 26.
**263.1** Common root: *Coventry*[1] 262. Marianus via JW*CC* (C) 263.
**263.2** Bede, *CM*, 385.
**266.1** Indeterminate source.
**266.2** Matching material, derived from Marianus, occurs in JW*CC* (C) 263 and in John's "Papal Annals" (C) p. 30.
**266.3** Norman Annals: *AU* 270, *AG* 270. Or perhaps Bede, *DTemp.*, § 22 (p. 609). See also **360.2** above and **361.2** below.
**267.1** Indeterminate source.
**267.2** Matching material, derived from Marianus, occurs in JW*CC* (C) 263, in John's "Consular Annals" (C, p. 13) 267, and in his "Papal Annals" (C) p. 30.
**269.1** Common root: *Coventry*[1] 268.1. Marianus via JW*CC* (C) 269 (p. 224).
**269.2** Common root: *Coventry*[1] 268.2. Marianus via JW*CC* (C) 269 (p. 225). Cf. Bede, *CM*, 388.

**269.3** Either Marianus via JW*CC* (C) 269 (p. 244), or Norman Annals: *AU* 279, *AG* 280. Cf. Bede, *CM*, 390.

**270.1** Common root: *Coventry*[1] 270. Marianus via JW*CC* (C) 270.

**270.2** Bede, *CM*, 392. Cf. JW*CC* (C) 270.

**273.1** Indeterminate source.

**273.2** Matching material, derived from Marianus (N fol. 123v), occurs in JW*CC* (C) 287 and in John's "Papal Annals" (C) p. 30.

**276.1** Common root: *Coventry*[1] 276. Marianus via JW*CC* (C) 276.

**276.2** Bede, *CM*, 397.

**277** Common root: *Coventry*[1] 277. Marianus via JW*CC* (C) 277.

**278** Common root: *Coventry*[1] 278. Marianus via JW*CC* (C) 278.

**279** Indeterminate source.

**280** Common root: *Coventry*[1] 280. Marianus via JW*CC* (C) 280.

**281.1** Common root: *Coventry*[1] 281.1. Marianus via JW*CC* (C) 281.

**281.2** Marianus via JW*CC* (C) 282–3. Cf. Bede, *CM*, 399. Possibly common root.

**281.3** Possibly a reference to Geoffrey of Monmouth's account of Carausius's usurpation: GM, §§ 75–76 (p. 48).

**283.1** Common root: *Coventry*[1] 282. Marianus via JW*CC* (C) 283. Cf. Bede, *CM*, 399.

**283.2** Marianus via JW*CC* (C) 284. Cf. Bede, *CM*, 400.

**283.3** Bede, *CM*, 401.

**287** Indeterminate source.

**291.1** Common root: *Coventry*[1] 292. Marianus via JW*CC* (C) 294. Cf. JW*CC* (C) 287, and the "Papal Annals" (C), p. 30.

**291.2** Indeterminate source.

**291.3** The source is evidently the "Papal Annals" in JW*CC* (C) p. 30: "Hic [Marcellus] constituit ut laici aut suspecti episcopos non debeant accusare, neque accusatoribus de inimici domo prodeuntibus credendum sit." John seems to have derived the item from a forged decretal of Pope Marcellus (Pseudo-Isidore, II Marcellus) as quoted in *Collectio Lanfranci* (R, fol. 36v): § 3, "Quod laici aut suspecti episcopos non debeant accusare, neque accusatoribus, de inimici domo prodeuntibus credendum sit. . . ." See Marianus VA 320, which is reproduced in JW*CC* (C) 298, cites *epistolae decretales Marcelli pape*, but for the evidence provided by their dating clauses as opposed to their dispositive content.

**291.4** Matching material, derived from Marianus, occurs in JW*CC* (C) 298, and in John's "Papal Annals" (C), p. 30.

**296.1** Norman Annals: *AU* 306, *AG* 356 (*recte* 306); RT*Access.* 306.

**296.2** Indeterminate source.

**297.1** Common root: *Coventry*[1] 297. Marianus via JW*CC* (C) 297.

**297.2** Bede, *CM*, 402, 405, 406, 407.

**298** Common root: *Coventry*[1] 298. Marianus via JW*CC* (C), 297–98 and 299.

**299.1** Indeterminate source.

**299.2** Matching material, derived from Marianus VA 320 (N fol. 124v), occurs in JW*CC* (C) 298, in John's "Consular Annals" (C, p. 13) 299, and in his "Papal Annals" (C) p. 31.

**299.3** Matching material, derived from Marianus VA 325, occurs in JW*CC* (C) 303 and in John's "Papal Annals" (C), p. 31.

**299.4** Common root: *Coventry*[1] 299. Marianus via JW*CC* (C, pp. 228–9) 299. *Winchcombe*[1] adds *summe mansuetudinis et ciuilitatis uir* from Bede, *CM*, 404, and the words *ex concubina Helena in Britannia creatus imperator* from Bede, *CM*, 411. Cf. *Chronicula*[1] VA 300.

**300** Common root: *Coventry*[1] 300. Marianus via JW*CC* (C) 300: "Maxentius Herculii Maximiani filius a pretorianis militibus Rome Augustus appellatur. Severus cesar a Galerio Maximiano contra Maxentium missus Rauenne interficitur."

**301** Common root: *Coventry*[1] 301. Marianus via JW*CC* (C) 301.

**302** Common root: *Coventry*[1] 302. Marianus via JW*CC* (C) 302.

**303.1** Common root: *Coventry*[1] 302. Marianus via JW*CC* (C) 303.

**303.2** Indeterminate source.

**303.3** Matching material, derived from Marianus VA 338, occurs in JW*CC* (C) 316, in John's "Consular Annals" (C, pp. 13–14) 303, and with greater similarity in his "Papal Annals" (C), p. 31.

**303.4** Matching material, derived from Marianus VA 349, occurs in JW*CC* (C) 327, and in John's "Papal Annals" (C), p. 31.

**305** Common root: *Coventry*[1] 305. Marianus via JW*CC* (C) 305.

**306** Common root: *Coventry*[1] 306. Marianus via JW*CC* (C) 306.

**307** Common root: *Coventry*[1] 309. Marianus via JW*CC* (C) 309–10.

**308** Common root: *Coventry*[1] 308. Marianus via JW*CC* (C) 308.

**309.1** Common root: *Coventry*[1] 325.1. Marianus via JW*CC* (C) 325: "Edicto Constantini gentilium templa subuersa sunt." This item appears under 325 in *Coventry*, and it seems likely that this was its position in the common source.

**309.2** Common root: *Coventry*[1] 325.2. Bede, *CM*, 416.

**309.3** Common root: *Coventry*[1] 325.3. Bede, *CM*, 424. Cf. Marianus via JW*CC* (C) 324.

**309.4** Bede, *CM*, 416, 417.

**311** In spite of the damage to the margins of T, it is clear that the source of this item was an appendix to the *Gesta Silvestri* that credited Pope Sylvester with an important role in the foundation of Constantinople. This appendix was probably added to the A-version of *Gesta Silvestri* (which was in existence by the end of the fifth century) before the beginning of the seventh. Certainly, it was the principal source for Aldhelm's account of Pope Sylvester in his *De virginitate prosa*, § 25 (ed. Rudolf Ehwald, *MGH AA*, 15:211–323, at 257–60). Unfortunately, only two of the many variant versions of this text have been printed: (1) *BHL* 7733, published in *Catalogus codicum hagiographicorum Bibliothecæ Regiæ Bruxellensis*, SH 1, 2 vols. (Brussels: Socii Bollandiani, 1886–1889), 1:119–20; and (2) *BHL* 7742e, ed. C. Narbey, *Supplément aux Acta Sanctorum de Saints de l'époque mérovingienne*, 3 vols. (Paris: Le Soudier, 1899–1912), 2:175–76. This appendix is absent, furthermore, from the version of the Sylvester Legend which is to be found in the so-called "Cotton-Corpus Legendary," a large passional with a certain Worcester provenance (see **622.2** below). Of the various manuscripts of the *Gesta Silvestri* which contain this appendix, only seven are accessible to the present editor. The upshot is that it has proved impossible to provide a definitive reconstruction of this item. For neither of the printed texts, nor any of the versions in manuscript that we have been able to examine, provides an exact match. This much can be ascertained by comparing the text of *BHL* 7742e, as found in an eleventh-century manuscript from Luxeuil which is an early witness to the appendix in question (today MS. London, B.L., Additional 21917, fols. 130r–131v):

> Et dicta de ciuitate Constantinopolim. Post hec Constantinus habuit bellum Scitarum. Et uictoria celebrata, cum esset in partibus Traciarum, in ciuitate que Byzantium uocabatur, uidit uisionem magnificam dormiens, in qua oblata ei fuerat mulier anicula a beato Siluestro papa iam mortuo, et dicebat ei Siluester episcopus: "Fac orationem, et suscitabis eam." Orante autem Constantino imperatore, illa anicula surrexit et facta est iubencula pulcherrima et placuit oculis Constantini casta contemplatione, et induit eam chlamydem suam et diadema quod optimum habebat posuit super caput eius. Helena autem mater eius, dicebat ei, "Hec tua erit, et non morietur nisi in fine mundi." Euigilans autem narrauit omnibus amicis suis uisionem, et omnia excogitabant non erant accepta auribus eius. Tunc posuit se Constantinus in oratione et ieiunio, dicens Domino: "Non cessabo ieiunare et orare, Christe, fili Dei, donec in uisionem quam ostendisti mihi per famulum tuum Siluestrum, aperias." Septima autem die ieiunii sui, adest iterum in uisione sanctus Siluester dicens: "Anus decrepita, hec est ciuitas in qua tua moraris, nomine Byzantium; cuius et muri pre uetustate consumpti sunt et pene omnia eius menia corruerunt. Ascende itaque illum equum tuum in quo baptizatus in albis sedisti in urbe Romana et per apostolorum et martyrum limina circuisti, et hunc sedens tene labarum tuum, quod signo crucis ex gemmis et auro est pictum. Hoc labarum tenens in dextera tua, dimitte frenum equi tui, et quo eum duxerit angelus, illuc eat. Tu autem fixo cuspite labari in terram, sic trahe illum ut semitam faciat transitus

> sui, per quam semitam extrui facies muros, et hanc ciuitatem ueteranam et pene mortuam in iuuenculam suscitabis, et tui nominis uocabulo decorabis, ita ut reginam illam facias omnium urbium. Erit enim in illa nomen Domini nostri Ihesu Christi magnificum, et erunt in ea templi Dei ad honorem omnium sanctorum instructa, et filii tuorum filiorum regnabunt in ea." Euigilans autem Constantinus, statim ad ecclesiam pergit indicatque episcopo ciuitatis, uiro sancto nomine Sis[sinni]o, somnium quod prius uiderat, et offerens Domino munera, et communicans sacramento Dominico, ascendit equum et perrexit quo eum duxit angelus Domini, usque ad que per semitam labari fundamenta exstructa sunt. Appellata est autem ciuitas Constantini, quod greco sermone dicitur eiusdemque interpretatur Constantinopolim usque in hodiernum diem.

This version is somewhat briefer than the present fragment, but the two texts are sufficiently close to allow us to make some plausible, though admittedly far from secure, guesses as to what the shorter lacunae might once have contained. For the sake of offering a partial reconstruction, then, a few suggestions have been included in the edition and have been used in the making of the translation. It needs to be stressed, however, that for this entry (**311**) the material in the square brackets comprises *guesses*, some of which may well be wrong.

It is worth noting that William of Malmesbury included the story in WM*GR*, 4.354, but in his case the story is derived indirectly from the *Gesta Silvestri* through Aldhelm. William reworked Aldhelm's version, and his version was used in turn by Ralph de Diceto in *AChron.*, 74–75. On the development of the Constantine legend in the West, see Wilhelm Pohlkamp, "Textfassungen, literarische Formen und geschichtliche Funktionen der römischen Silvester-Akten," *Francia* 19 (1992): 115–96 (esp. 142–43, 184–87); Wilhelm Levison, "Konstantinische Schenkung und Siluester-Legende," in *Miscellanea Francesco Ehrle: Scritti di storia e paleografia*, Studi e Testi 38, 2 vols. (Vatican City: Biblioteca Apostolica Vaticana, 1924), 2:159–247; repr. in idem, *Aus rheinischer und fränkischer Frühzeit: Ausgewählte Aufsätze* (Düsseldorf: L. Schwann, 1948), 390–465; Samuel N. C. Lieu, "From History to Legend and Legend to History: The Medieval and Byzantine Transformation of Constantine's *Vita*," in *Constantine: History, Historiography and Legend*, ed. idem and D. Montserrat (London: Routledge, 1998), 136–76 (esp. 136–52).

**316.1** Common root: *Coventry*[1] 316.1. Marianus via JW*CC* (C) 316.

**316.2** Norman Annals: *AU* 312, *AG* 311; RT*Access.* 311.

**316.3** Common root: *Coventry*[1] 316.2. Marianus via JW*CC* (C) 316, with the order in which the information is given reversed.

**317** Common root: *Coventry*[1] 318. Marianus via JW*CC* (C) 317.

**318** Common root: *Coventry*[1] 319. Marianus via JW*CC* (C) 319.
**325** Norman Annals: *AU* 325, *AG* 325; RT*Access.* 326.
**327** Indeterminate source.
**329** Common root: *Coventry*[1] 329. Marianus via JW*CC* (C) 329.
**330.1** Common root: *Coventry*[1] 330.1. Marianus via JW*CC* (C) 329. Cf. Bede, *CM*, 426.
**330.2** Common root: *Coventry*[1] 330.2. Marianus via JW*CC* (C), p. 231 (a marginal entry in a red box adjacent to the annal for 330), or via the Easter Table Annals in JW*CC* (C), p. 64 (in cycle 18, year 8 = 330).
**330.3** Bede, *CM*, 428.
**330.4** Bede, *CM*, 429.
**330.4** Bede, *CM*, 427.
**330.6** Norman Annals: *AU* 340: "Hilarius Pictavensis ad ecclesiam rediit." Cf. Bede, *CM*, 433.
**331** Common root: *Coventry*[1] 331. Marianus via JW*CC* (C) 331.
**332** Indeterminate source.
**333** Common root: *Coventry*[1] 333. Marianus via JW*CC* (C) 333.
**338.1** Indeterminate source.
**338.2** Matching material occurs in John's "Papal Annals" (C), p. 31: "Hic [Julius] angelico iussu Cersonam perrexit et transtulit corpus sancti Clementis, mari in occursu eius partito." A fuller version, with some verbal parallels, occurs as a marginal addition in JW*CC* (C) p. 231. Cf. *Chronicula* VA 353 (G, fol. 44r).
**338.3** Matching material, derived from Marianus VA 366, occurs in JW*CC* (C) 344, in John's "Consular Annals" (C, p. 16) 344, and in John's "Papal Annals" (C), p. 31.
**339** Common root: *Coventry*[1] 339. This entry echoes Marianus via JW*CC* (C) 339: "Dirrachius terremotu corruit, et tribus diebus ac noctibus Roma natauit, plurimeque urbes Campanie uexate." This entry is ultimately derived from Jerome's continuation of the Chronicle of Eusebius, s.a. 346 (ed. Rudolf Helm, *Eusebius Werke*, vol. 7, *Die Chronik des Hieronymus*, 2 pts., GCS [Leipzig: Hinrich, 1913–1926], 236), who has *nutauit* for *natauit.* Since the inherited error occurs in both *Winchcombe* and *Coventry* it is retained in the present edition, but Jerome's version is followed in the present translation.
**341** Norman Annals: *AU*, RT*Access.* 341.
**342.1** Common root: *Coventry*[1] 342. Marianus via JW*CC* (C) 342.
**342.2** Norman Annals: *AU* 341, *AG* 309: "Transitus sancti Nicholai."
**343** Common root: *Coventry*[1] 343. Marianus via JW*CC* (C) 343.
**346** Common root: *Coventry*[1] 346. Marianus via JW*CC* (C) 346.
**348** Common root: *Coventry*[1] 348. Marianus via JW*CC* (C) 348.
**349.1** Common root: *Coventry*[1] 349. Marianus via JW*CC* (C) 349 or the Consular Annals in JW*CC* (C, p. 16) 348. Cf. Bede, *CM*, 430.

**349.2** Norman Annals: *AU* 365: "Tunc Cesarauguste Petrus *orator* insignis habetur" (emphasis added)!

**350** Common root: *Coventry*[1] 350. Marinus via JW*CC* (C) 350, but *Winchcombe*[1] adds the reference to the relics of Timothy from Bede, *CM*, 431. The epithet *apostoli Pauli* appears to be the author's own addition: cf. Acts 16:1–4.

**351** Common root: *Coventry*[1] 351. Marianus via JW*CC* (C) 351.

**353** Liberius's obit is given as 24 April (*viii kl. Maii*) in JW*CC* (C) 363 and in John's "Papal Annals" (C), p. 31; but that of Pope Felix is specified as 29 July (*iiii kl. Augusti*) in his "Consular Annals" (C, p. 16) 349, and in his "Papal Annals" (C), p. 31. It follows that the present entry is probably the product of eye-skip. Cf. **356.2** below.

**354** Common root: *Coventry*[1] 354. Marianus via JW*CC* (C), p. 233 (a marginal entry in a red box adjacent to the annal for 354), or via the Easter Table Annals in JW*CC* (C), p. 65 (in cycle 19, year 13 = 354), or or the Consular Annals in JW*CC* (C, p. 16) 354.

**356.1** Norman Annals: *AU* 360. Cf. Bede, *CM*, 436.

**356.2** Felix's obit is given as as 29 July (*iiii kl. Augusti*) in John's "Consular Annals" (C, p. 16) 349, and in his "Papal Annals" (C), p. 31. As with **353**, the present entry is probably the product of error, the numeral having been combined with the month from the entry for Liberius in John's "Papal Annals" (C), p. 31.

**357.1** Common root: *Coventry*[1] 357.1. Marianus via JW*CC* (C) 357. Cf. Bede, *CM*, 434.

**357.2** Common root: *Coventry*[1] 357.2. Bede, *CM*, 435. Cf. Marianus via JW*CC* (C) 358.

**360.1** Common root: *Coventry*[1] 360.1. Marianus via JW*CC* (C) 360.

**360.2** A marginal addition which seems to derive from Bede, *DTemp.*, § 22 (pp. 609–10). See also **266.3** above and **361.2** below.

**360.3** Bede, *CM*, 439.

**360.4** Bede, *CM*, 438. The terms at issue in this doctrinal dispute are muddled in the present entry: it should be read in comparison with Bede's version. Cf. Marianus via JW*CC* (C) 360.

**361.1** Common root: *Coventry*[1] 361.1. Marianus via JW*CC* (C) 361.

**361.2** An addition which seems to derive from Bede, *DTemp.*, § 22 (pp. 609–10). See also **266.3** above and **360.2** below.

**363.1** Indeterminate source.

**363.2** Matching material, derived from Marianus VA 380, occurs in JW*CC* (C) 363 and in John's "Papal Annals" (C), p. 31: "Hic [Damasus] constituit ut in die nocteque cantarentur psalmi per omnes ecclesias."

**363.3** There is no mention of the *Gloria Patri* in the passages relating to Damasus in Marianus (N), JW*CC* (C), or in JW's "Papal Annals." There is a note on Hilary of Poitiers' contributions to the hymn *Gloria in excelsis Deo* in

*Chronicula*[1] VA 383 and on Jerome's role in translating the minor doxology at ibid. VA 430; but the present item almost certainly refers to the tradition that it was Damasus who prescribed the singing of the *Gloria Patri* at the end of a psalm. This tradition seems to have originated in a letter attributed to St Jerome: *Epistola ad Damasum*, § 1 (ed. *PL* 30.294–296), which is widely attested from the eighth century onwards. There are, as it happens, two MSS which may imply knowledge of this letter at Winchcombe. One is a binding strip containing a letter of St Jerome (*Ep.* 22) which is very similar in appearance, date, and layout to the other large MSS of patristic texts associated with the abbey—today MS. Cambridge, U.L., Additional 3303 (19). Its survival implies the presence of a collection of Jerome's letters in the abbey's *armarium*. The other is an especially fine New Testament and Psalter with a certain Winchcombe provenance—today MS. Dublin, Trinity College, 53. Like other biblical MSS from this period, it incorporates various prefatory texts produced chiefly by Jerome including, on fol. 144r, a version of the present letter: "Precans ergo cliens tuus, ut uox ista psallentium in sede Romana die noctuque canatur, ut in fine psalmi cuiuslibet, siue uel uespertinis coniungi precipiat apostolatus ordo finiri. Hoc est 'Gloria Patri, et Filio, et Spiritui Sancto, sicut erat in principio, et nunc, et semper, et in secula seculorum. Amen.' Istud carmen laudis omni psalmo coniungi precipias, ut fides trecentorum decem et octo <episcoporum> Niceni concilii, etiam nostro ore pari consortio declaretur. . . ." It is possible that the compiler enhanced the annal with information from this letter, but note also Sigibert of Gembloux, *Chronica*, s.a. 382 (ed. Ludwig Bethmann, *MGH SS*, 6:300–74, at 302): "Damasus papa rogatu Hieronimi instituit dicere in aecclesia in fine psalmorum 'Gloria patri et filio et spiritui sancto sicut erat'." For the letter and its transmission, see Bernhard Lambert, *Bibliotheca Hieronymiana manuscripta: La tradition manuscrite des oeuvres de Saint Jérôme*, Instrumenta Patristica et Mediaevalia, 4 vols. in 7 pts. (Steenbrugge: Martinus Nijhoff, 1969–1972), 3: no. 347. On MS. Dublin, Trinity College 53 (which should be added to Lambert's list of witnesses), see Colker, *TCD*, no. 53, and Heimann, "Dublin, Trinity College, MS 53," 86–109.

**363.4** The present item matches that in John's "Papal Annals" (C), p. 31, where Damasus's obit is given as *.iiii. id' Decembris*. Marianus VA 380 gives the date as *.iii. idus Dec*, which is the date specified in JW*CC* (C) 381.

**364** Common root: *Coventry*[1] 364. Marianus via JW*CC* (C) 364. Cf. Bede, *CM*, 444.

**365.1** Common root: *Coventry*[1] 365. Marianus via JW*CC* (C) 365. Cf. Norman Annals: *AU*, *ASN* 366; Bede, *CM*, 447.

**365.2** Norman Annals: *AG*, RT*Access*. 366.

**365.3** Bede, *CM*, 442.

**365.4** Either Marianus via JW*CC* (C) 367 or Bede, *CM*, 445.

**370** Common root: *Coventry*[1] 370. Marianus via JW*CC* (C) 370.

**372.1** Common root: *Coventry*[1] 372.1. Marianus via JW*CC* (C) 372. Cf. Bede, *CM*, 446; Norman Annals: *AU* 368; *AG*, *ASN* 369.

**372.2** Common root: *Coventry*[1] 372.2. Marianus via JW*CC* (C) 372: "Sanctus Patricius nascitur in Britannia ex patre Calprun nomine . . . Mater autem erat Patricii Conches soror Sancti Martini de Gallia."

**373.1** Common root: *Coventry*[1] 373.1. Marianus via JW*CC* (C) 373.

**373.2** Marianus via JW*CC* (C) 374. Cf. Bede, *CM*, 449.

**376** Common root: *Coventry*[1] 376. Marianus via JW*CC* (C) , 375–76.

**377** Common root: *Coventry*[1] 377. Marianus via JW*CC* (C) 377.

**380** Common root: *Coventry*[1] 380. Marianus via JW*CC* (C) 380. Cf. Bede, *CM*, 454; Norman Annals: *ASC* (E) 379. The synod in question is the First Council of Constantinople (AD 381) to which Damasus sent his legates.

**381** Common root: *Coventry*[1] 381. Marianus via JW*CC* (C) 381.

**382.1** Common root: *Coventry*[1] 382.1. Marianus via JW*CC* (C) 382 with 376 for the month of Gratian's death. Cf. Bede, *CM*, 457–58.

**382.2** Bede, *CM*, 458.

**382.3** Common root: *Coventry*[1] 382.2. Marianus via JW*CC* (C) 382.

**386** Either Bede, *CM*, 458 or Norman Annals: *AU*, *ASN* 375.

**387** Common root: *Coventry*[1] 386. Marianus via JW*CC* (C) 386.

**388** Common root: *Coventry*[1] 388. Marianus via JW*CC* (C) 388.

**390** Common root: *Coventry*[1] 390. Marianus via JW*CC* (C) 390.

**393** Common root: *Coventry*[1] 393. Marianus via JW*CC* (C) 393.

**394.1** Common root: *Coventry*[1] 394. Marianus via JW*CC* (C) 394.

**394.2** Indeterminate source.

**394.3** Matching material, derived from Marianus VA 419, occurs in JW*CC* (C) 396, in John's "Consular Annals" (C, p. 17) 397, and in his "Papal Annals" (C), p. 31.

**394.4** Matching material, derived from Marianus VA 424, occurs in JW*CC* (C) 402, in John's "Papal Annals" (C), p. 31.

**395** Common root: *Coventry*[1] 396. Marianus via JW*CC* (C) 395. Cf. Norman Annals: *AU*, *ASN* 412.

**396** This item does not seem to derive from any of the usual sources (i.e. JW*CC*, Bede, *CM*, and the Norman Annals). One possible source is Gregory of Tours, *Libri historiarum X*, 2.1 (ed. Bruno Krusch and Wilhelm Levison, *MGH SS. rer. Merov.* 1:37).

**397** Marianus via JW*CC* (C) 395.

**399.1** Indeterminate source.

**399.2** This item may be found in John's "Papal Annals" (C) p. 31: "Hic [Innocentius] constituit pacem dari post confectionem sacramentorum." This item may have been suggested by the forged decretal of Pope

Innocent which reports the ruling that lies behind **399.3** (see Pseudo-Isidore, I Innocent, quoted in *Collectio Lanfranci* [R, fol. 60r]), for its first section is indexed as *De pace danda post confecta sacramenta*.

**399.3** There is matching material, derived from Marianus VA 424, for the second half of this item in JW*CC* (C) 412: "Innocentius papa constituit sabbato ieiunium celebrari, quia in eo sepulcro iacuit [Marianus reads *erat*] Dominus, et discipuli ieiunauerunt." Cf. *LPont.* 42.

**399.4** Norman Annals: *AU*, *ASC* (E) 403, *AG* 404; RT*Access.* 405.

**399.5** Bede, *CM*, 466.

**399.6** Common root: *Coventry*[1] 399. Marianus via JW*CC* (C) 399.

**400** Bede, *CM*, 467.

**404** Common root: *Coventry*[1] 404. Marianus via JW*CC* (C) 404.

**405.1** Common root: *Coventry*[1] 405.1. Marianus via JW*CC* (C) 405.

**405.2** Common root: *Coventry*[1] 405.2. Bede, *CM*, 480.

**407.1** Common root: *Coventry*[1] 407.1. Orosius, *Historiarum aduersum paganos libri VII*, 7.40.4, ed. Carl Zangemeister (Leipzig: Teubner, 1889), pp. 294–95: "Apud Britannias Gratianus municeps eiusdem insulae, tyrannus creatur et occiditur, huius loco Constantinus . . . eligitur, qui continuo, ut inuasit imperium, in Gallias transiit." Cf. Marianus via JW*CC* (C) 406: "Constantinus in Britannia tirannus exoritur, et ad Gallias transit"; Bede, *CM*, 457–58.

**407.2** Common root: *Coventry*[1] 407.2. Marianus via JW*CC* (C) 406.

**408** Common root: *Coventry*[1] 408. Marianus via JW*CC* (C) 407.

**410** Common root: *Coventry*[1] 410. Marianus via JW*CC* (C) 410. Cf. Bede, *CM*, 469.

**411** Common root: *Coventry*[1] 411. Marianus via JW*CC* (C) 411 is similar but lacks some details: "Constantinus apud Arelatense oppidum uictus est et captus. Cuius filium Constantem, in Hispaniis regnare orsus, Geruntius comes in Maximum quendam tirannidem transferens, interimit."

**412** Common root: *Coventry*[1] 414.2. Marianus via JW*CC* (C) 412.

**413.1** Common root: *Coventry*[1] 413. Marianus via JW*CC* (C) 413.

**413.2** Indeterminate source.

**413.3** Identical material appears in John's "Papal Annals" (C) p. 31, and in the main chronicle, JW*CC* (C) 416, but there the material has the appearance of a later addition perhaps by C[3], with *paschalis* having been written over an erasure by a much later hand. Similar material also appears in the Norman Annals: *AU* 418, *AG* 408.

**413.4** Matching material, derived from Marianus VA 440, occurs in JW*CC* (C) 418, and in John's "Papal Annals" (C), p. 31.

**414** Common root: *Coventry*[1] 414.1. Marianus via JW*CC* (C) 414.

**415** Common root: *Coventry*[1] 415. Marianus via JW*CC* (C) 415. Cf. Bede, *CM*, 470.

**417.1** Common root: *Coventry*[1] 417. Marianus via J*WCC* (C) 417.

**417.2** Indeterminate source.

**417.3** Matching material, derived from Marianus VA 443, occurs in J*WCC* (C) 421, and in John's "Papal Annals" (C), p. 31.

**417.4** Matching material occurs in John's "Papal Annals" (C), p. 31. Marianus VA 444, and the main chronicle in J*WCC* (C) 422, have *viii kl. Nouembris* as the date of Boniface's obit.

**418.1** Indeterminate source.

**418.2** Matching material, derived from Marianus VA 451, occurs in J*WCC* (C) 429, in John's "Consular Annals" (C, p. 18) 422, and in his "Papal Annals" (C), p. 31. Cf. Bede, *CM*, 485. See also Peter Jeffery, "The Introduction of Psalmody into the Roman Mass by Pope Celestine I (422–432)," *Archiv für Liturgiewissenschaft* 26 (1984): 147–65.

**418.3** Matching material, derived from Marianus VA 454, occurs in J*WCC* (C) 432, and in John's 'Papal Annals' (C), p. 31.

**421.1** Marianus via J*WCC* (C) 420.

**421.2** Common root: *Coventry*[1] 421.1. Marianus via J*WCC* (C) 420, and also in the Easter Table Annals in J*WCC* (C), p. 67 (in cycle 23, year 3 = 420). Cf. Norman Annals: *AU* 420; *AG*, *ASN* 421.

**422** Common root: *Coventry*[1] 421.2. Marianus via J*WCC* (C) 421.

**423** Common root: *Coventry*[1] 423. Marianus via J*WCC* (C) 423.

**424** Common root: *Coventry*[1] 424. Marianus via J*WCC* (C) 424.

**425** Common root: *Coventry*[1] 425. Marianus via J*WCC* (C) 425.

**426** Common root: *Coventry*[1] 426. The *exordium regni Francorum* is also noted in the Easter Table Annals in J*WCC* (C), p. 67 (in cycle 23, year 8 = 425), following Marianus 415. But for Faramund, the source is apparently the Norman Annals: *AU*, *AG*, *ASN*, *ASC* (E) 425. J*WCC* (C) 426 lacks the length of Faramund's reign.

**429** Common root: *Coventry*[1] 428. Marianus via J*WCC* (C) 429. Cf. Bede, *CM*, 491.

**430.1** Common root: *Coventry*[1] 429.1. J*WCC* (C) 431, but lacking the length of Chlodio's reign. Cf. Norman Annals: *AU*, *ASN* 430.

**430.2** Common root: *Coventry*[1] 429.2. Marianus via J*WCC* (C) 430. Augustine's death is also noted in the Easter Table Annals in J*WCC* (C), p. 67 (in cycle 23, year 12 = 429). Cf. Norman Annals: *AU* 423; *ASN* 424.

**431** Common root: *Coventry*[1] 430. Marianus via J*WCC* (C) 431. Cf. Norman Annals: *ASC* (E) 433.

**432** Common root: *Coventry*[1] 431. Marianus via J*WCC* (C) 432. Patrick's conversion of Ireland is also noted in the Easter Table Annals in J*WCC* (C), p. 67 (in cycle 23, year 16 = 433).

**433** Common root: *Coventry*[1] 433. Norman Annals: *AU* 432. JW*CC* (C) 432, reports the same material but probably through independent use of the same source.

**434.1** Indeterminate source.

**434.2** Similar material, derived from Marianus VA 456, occurs in JW*CC* (C) 434, but virtually identical material, to the extent that it also fails to specify the date of Sixtus's obit appears in John's "Papal Annals" (C), p. 31. Cf. Bede, *CM*, 485.

**437.1** Common root: *Coventry*[1] 437.1. Norman Annals: *AU*, *ASN* 437, *AG* 436. Cf. JW*CC* (C) 438, which lacks the length of Merovech's reign. Furthermore, the heavy use of abbreviations and the compression suggests that the entire annal has been rewritten here to permit the insertion of this notice.

**437.2** Common root: *Coventry*[1] 437.2. Both *Coventry* and the source, Marianus via JW*CC* (C) 437, have a cycle of 95 years, but *Winchcombe* has a cycle of 153, the scribe's eye having picked up the numeral from the Diocletianic year that follows in the present entry.

**439** Common root: *Coventry*[1] 439. Exact parallels for this item are found in Marianus, JW*CC* (C) 438 and the Norman Annals: *AU* 431 (where the text is identical), *ASC* (E) 431 (with variations in word order), *AG* 435.

**440** Common root: *Coventry*[1] 442. Marianus via JW*CC* (C) 440: "Leo . . . quadragesimus quartus papa Romane ecclesie consecratur."

**445** Common root: *Coventry*[1] 445. Identical material, derived from Marianus VA 467, occurs in JW*CC* (C) 445 and in John's "Consular Annals" (C, p. 18) 440. The "Papal Annals" (C), p. 31, have a fuller entry: "Hic [Leo] constituit infra actionem misse dicere 'sanctum sacrificium immaculatam hostiam'."

**446** Common root: *Coventry*[1] 446. Norman Annals: *AU*, *AG*, *ASN* 450. Not present in JW*CC* as it stands, but C[3] has re-written the annals for 447–449 and it may once have contained this material.

**450** Common root: *Coventry*[1] 449.1. Marianus via JW*CC* 450.

**451** JW*CC* 450, adapting Marianus after Bede, *CM*, 489.

**452** Common root: *Coventry*[1] 451. Marianus via JW*CC* 452, after Bede, *CM*, 490.

**453** Common root: *Coventry*[1] 452. Marianus via JW*CC* 453. Cf. Norman Annals: *ASC* (E) 439.

**454.1** Common root: *Coventry*[1] 453.1. Marianus via JW*CC* 455. The compiler has misread JW*CC*'s *Ethius patricius*, "Aetius the patrician."

**454.2** Common root: *Coventry*[1] 453.2. JW*CC* 455 and also the Kentish Royal Genealogy in JW*CC* (C), p. 48.

**454.3** A marginal gloss.

**455** Norman Annals: *AU*, *AG*, RT*Access.* 459.

**456** Common root: *Coventry*[1] 456.1. Marianus via JWCC 456. *Winchcombe*[1] rearranges the sequence of items under 456 and 457, introducing the misleading suggestion that Leo succeeded Avitus. **457.2** should come after **456**, so that Avitus succeeds Maximus in the West and Leo Martian in the East. Cf. *Coventry*[1] **456–457**. The *Winchcombe*[1] compiler also transfers from Martian to Avitus the words *in fine Iunii*, which the author of the common root derived from JWCC 450, where Martian is said to have reigned for seven years *usque kalend. Julii.*

**457.1** Common root: *Coventry*[1] 457.1. Marianus via JWCC 457.

**457.2** Common root: *Coventry*[1] 456.2. Marianus via JWCC 456.

**457.3** Common root: *Coventry*[1] 457.2. Marianus via JWCC 457 with Bede, *CM*, 494.

**459.1** Indeterminate source.

**459.2** Matching material for this item occurs in John's "Papal Annals" (C) p. 31: "Hic [Hilarius] constituit ut penitentes, uel inscii litterarum aut aliqua membrorum dampna perpessi, uel ii qui expenitentes sunt, ad sacros ordines aspirare non audeant." John seems to have derived the item from a forged decretal of Pope Hilary (Pseudo-Isidore, I Hilary) as quoted in *Collectio Lanfranci* (R, fol. 99v): "Ut penitentes uel inscii litterarum aut aliqua membrorum dampna perpessi, uel ii qui expenitentes sunt ad sacros ordines aspirare non audeant." Marianus (N fol. 139v) nowhere mentions this decree.

**459.3** Matching material, derived from Marianus VA 492, occurs in JWCC (C) 470, and in John's "Papal Annals" (C), p. 31.

**461** Common root: *Coventry*[1] 460. Marianus via JWCC 461.

**464** Matching material, derived from Marianus VA 506, occurs in JWCC (C) 484, and in John's "Papal Annals" (C), p. 31.

**465.1** Common root: *Coventry*[1] 465.1. Marianus via JWCC 465.

**465.2** Common root: *Coventry*[1] 465.2. JWCC 465.

**465.3** A marginal gloss.

**466** Bede, *CM*, 496. Note, however, that the version of this annal in *Coventry* 466 is echoed by both Marianus via JWCC 466 and the Consular Annals in JWCC (C, p. 19) 463. In this instance, *Coventry* would appear to represent the shared source.

**467** Common root: *Coventry*[1] 467. Marianus via JWCC 467.

**468** Common root: *Coventry*[1] 468. Marianus via JWCC 468 or Bede, *CM*, 497.

**471** Common root: *Coventry*[1] 471. *ASC* via JWCC 473. The information that the British took refuge in London is not found in JWCC or in *Coventry* 471 and would appear to be the author's own addition to the text.

**473.1** Common root: *Coventry*[1] 472. Marianus via JWCC 472.

**473.2** Common root: *Coventry*[1] 473.1. Norman Annals: *AU*, *ASN* 473; *AG* 472.

**473.3** Common root: *Coventry*[1] 473.2. Marianus via JW*CC* 473.

**474.1** Common root: *Coventry*[1] 474. Marianus via JW*CC* 474.

**474.2** Norman Annals: *AU*, *AG*, RT*Access*. 473. Cf. Marianus via JW*CC* 474.

**475** Common root: *Coventry*[1] 475. Marianus via JW*CC* 475.

**476** Bede, *CM*, 504.

**477.1** Common root: *Coventry*[1] 476. Marianus via JW*CC* 476.

**477.2** Common root: *Coventry*[1] 477. JW*CC* 477, but JW*CC* lacks the reference to the descent of the English peoples to the north of the River Humber.

**482** Possibly a mistake: JW*CC* 484 implies that Pope Felix died in 492, but Norman Annals: *AU* 482 places his name in the appropriate year.

**483** Common root: *Coventry*[1] 483. Though Bede, *CM*, 483 is almost identical, the source seems to be Marianus via JW*CC* 483. It was claimed that the relics of St Barnabas were found in Cyprus under a cherry tree with a Gospel of St Matthew on his chest copied by Barnabas' own hand: see Alexander, *Acta S. Barnabe apostoli* (*BHG* 226), §§ 40–41 (ed. Godfrey Henschen, *Acta sanctorum Junii*, 7 vols., 3rd ed. [Paris: V. Palmé, 1866–1867], 2:431–47, at 445).

**484** Norman Annals: *AU*, *ASN* 488, *AG* 487. Cf. Marianus via JW*CC* 474; *Chronicula*[1] VA 479.

**485** Common root: *Coventry*[1] 485. Echoes: Marianus via JW*CC* 485; Bede, *CM*, 503.

**487.1** Indeterminate source.

**487.2** Matching material appears in the "Papal Annals" in JW*CC* (C) p. 31: "Hic [Gelasius] constituit ut ordinationes presbiterorum, siue diaconorum, nonnisi certis temporibus fiant, et ut in sabbatis .iiii[or]. temporum ordinationes circa uesperam celebrentur." The ultimate source is a forged decretal of Pope Gelasius (Pseudo-Isidore, I Gelasius), which is quoted in *Collectio Lanfranci* (R, fol. 105v), § 8: "Ordinationes etiam presbiterorum et diaconorum nisi certis temporibus et diebus exerceri non debeant, id est, quarti mensis ieiunio septimi et decimi, sed etiam quadragesimalis initii, ac mediane quadragesime die sabbati. Ieiunia circa uesperam nouerint celebranda. Nec cuiuslibet utilitatis seu presbiterum seu diaconum iis preferri qui ante ipsos fuerint ordinati." There is nothing similar in Marianus (N fol. 140r).

**487.3** Matching material, derived from Marianus VA 518, occurs in JW*CC* (C) 496, and in John's "Papal Annals" (C), p. 31.

**487.4** Norman Annals: *AG* 491 ("Gelasius papa fecit tractatus et ymnos et libros aduersus Nestorium et Euticen"); *AU* 491. Cf. Marianus VA 518 via JW*CC* 496. There is nothing similar in John's "Papal Annals" (C) p. 31.

**488** Common root: *Coventry*[1] 488. Marianus via JW*CC* 488.

**489** Common root: *Coventry*[1] 489. JW*CC* 488.

**490.1** Common root: *Coventry*[1] 490.1. Norman Annals: *AU*, *ASC* (E) 490, *AG* 488. Cf. JW*CC* 490: this material is inserted in the margins of C by C[1].

**490.2** Common root: *Coventry*[1] 490.2. JW*CC* 491.

**490.3** A marginal gloss.

**490.4** Indeterminate source.

**491** Common root: *Coventry*[1] 491.1. Marianus via JW*CC* 491.

**492** Common root: *Coventry*[1] 491.2. Marianus via JW*CC* 491.

**493** Common root: *Coventry*[1] 493. JW*CC* 493 and Norman Annals: *AU*, *AG*, *ASN* 492, refer to the accession of Theuderic rather than Theodebert.

**494** Common root: *Coventry*[1] 494. Marianus via JW*CC* 494.

**495.1** Common root: *Coventry*[1] 495. JW*CC* 495.

**495.2** This much might have been inferred by a glance at the stemma of the West-Saxon Royal Genealogy in JW*CC* (C) p. 53.

**498** Common root: *Coventry*[1] 498. Marianus via JW*CC* 498.

**499.1** Indeterminate source.

**499.2** Matching material, derived from Marianus VA 526, occurs in JW*CC* (C) 504, and in John's "Papal Annals" (C), p. 31. Cf. Bede, *CM*, 507.

**499.3** Marianus VA 515, via JW*CC* 513. John's "Papal Annals" (C), p. 31, omit the obit, but may once have contained one, for the final word of the previous item has been stretched out over an erasure by a later hand.

**500** Common root: *Coventry*[1] 499. Marianus via JW*CC* 499.

**507.1** Common root: *Coventry*[1] 508.1. Norman Annals: *AU*, *AG* 514.

**507.2** Common root: *Coventry*[1] 508.2. Marianus via JW*CC* 507.

**508** Common root: *Coventry*[1] 508.3. *ASC* via JW*CC* 508.

**509** Common root: *Coventry*[1] 509. Marianus via JW*CC* 509.

**510.1** Common root: *Coventry*[1] 510. Marianus via JW*CC* 510.

**510.2** Compare the entry for **1043.2** below.

**512.1** Common root: *Coventry*[1] 512. Marianus via JW*CC* 512. Cf. also Marianus's source, Isidore of Seville, *Chronica*, ed. Theodor Mommsen, *MGH AA*, 11:424–81, at 474 (§ 393): "Barbas quoque quidam Arrianus episcopus, dum contra regulam fidei quendam baptizans dixisset: 'Baptizat te Barbas in nomine patris per filium in spiritu sancto'." The joke has been lost in transmission.

**512.2** Indeterminate source.

**512.3** Matching material, derived from Marianus VA 539, occurs in JW*CC* (C) 517, and in John's "Papal Annals" (C), p. 31.

**512.4** Matching material, derived from Marianus VA 543, occurs in JW*CC* (C) 521, and in John's "Papal Annals" (C), p. 31.

**513** Common root: *Coventry*[1] 513. Oisc figures in the Kentish Royal Genealogy in JW*CC* (C), p. 48, but the date of his accession is not given in the accompanying accounts. Cf. Bede, *HE*, 2.5, via JW*CC* 616.

**514.1** Common root: *Coventry*[1] 514.1. Compare Norman Annals: *AU*, *ASN* 527: "Teodoberto successit Teobaldus i anno. Cui successit Clotharius, post quem iiii^or filii: Parisius, Aurelianum, Suessionis, Haribertus; Guntrannus, Hilpericus; Sigibertus, Metis." See also *AG* 527.

**514.2** This marginal entry was presumably introduced to repair the deficiencies of 514.1. Both entries, not least because the capitals have been inserted only at the third attempt, show that the compiler was baffled by the problem of the Merovingian succession. JW*CC* was no less confused, but provided a quite different reconstruction. Compare, for example, JW*CC* 528, who provides a different selection from the Norman Annals: *AU* 527: "Teodebaldus rex Francorum .viii. regnauit anno uno." See further the comments on **528** below.

**515** Common root: *Coventry*[1] 514.2. JW*CC* 514 probably represents the original version, to which *Winchcombe*[1] adds material about "Port" and "Portsmouth" drawn from JW*CC* 501.

**518** Common root: *Coventry*[1] 518. Marianus via JW*CC* 518.

**519** Common root: *Coventry*[1] 519.1. Marianus via JW*CC* 519.

**520.1** Common root: *Coventry*[1] 519.2. *ASC* via JW*CC* 519 or, more likely, the West-Saxon Royal Genealogy in JW*CC* (C) p. 53: "Anno dominice incarnationis secundum Dionisium dxix Cerdic 7 Cynric filius eius secundum Anglicam Cronicam in Westsaxonia regnare ceperunt. . . ."

**520.2** A marginal gloss.

**521** Common root: *Coventry*[1] 521. Marianus via JW*CC* 521.

**522.1** Indeterminate source.

**522.2** Matching material, derived from Marianus VA 545, occurs in JW*CC* (C) 523, and in John's "Papal Annals" (C), pp. 31–32.

**522.3** Matching material, derived from Marianus VA 546, occurs in JW*CC* (C) 524, and in John's "Papal Annals" (C), pp. 31–32.

**524** Common root: *Coventry*[1] 524. Marianus via JW*CC* 523.

**525.1** Common root: *Coventry*[1] 525. Marianus via JW*CC* 524.

**525.2** Indeterminate source.

**525.3** Matching material, derived from Marianus VA 551, occurs in JW*CC* (C) 529, and in John's "Papal Annals" (C), p. 32.

**526.1** Common root: *Coventry*[1] 526.1. Either Marianus via JW*CC* 526 or Bede, *CM*, 518. Cf. Norman Annals: *AU* 527, *ASC* (E) 528.

**526.2** Common root: *Coventry*[1] 526.2. Either Marianus via JW*CC* 526 or Bede, *CM*, 514. Cf. Norman Annals: *AU*, *AG*, *ASN* 509.

**526.3** Indeterminate source.

**526.4** Marianus via JW*CC* 531.

**527** Common root: *Coventry*[1] 527. *ASC* via JW*CC* 526.

**528** Common root: *Coventry*[1] 528. There is nothing quite like this in the Norman Annals. The compiler may have inferred from his material on Sigibert (see **541** below) that he was the principal successor of Clothar (see **514** above): that is, he may have inferred from the two Norman entries that Sigibert was the principal successor of "Clothar" in an attempt to preserve a tidy linear sequence of Frankish kings.

**529.1** Indeterminate source. Marianus via JW*CC* 533.

**529.2** Matching material, derived from Marianus VA 553, occurs in JW*CC* (C) 533, and in John's "Papal Annals" (C), p. 32.

**529.3** Norman Annals: *AU*, *AG*, RT*Access*. 534.

**529.4** Norman Annals: *AU* 530; *AG*, *ASN* 528.

**529.5** Indeterminate source.

**529.6** Matching material, derived from Marianus VA 556, occurs in JW*CC* (C) 533, and in John's "Papal Annals" (C), p. 32.

**529.7** For what it is worth, "Octa's" predecessor in the Kentish Royal Genealogy in JW*CC* (C), p. 48, is Hengist; but this notice is at such odds with the other notices for the Kentish kings that it is impossible to determine whose obit is being recorded here.

**530.1** Common root: *Coventry*[1] 530. Marianus via JW*CC* 530. Cf. Bede, *CM*, 517.

**530.2** Norman Annals: *AU* 527; *AG*, *ASN*, *ASC* (E) 528. Cf. JW*CC* 564.

**531** King Æscwine's name appears in the stemma of the East-Saxon Royal Genealogy in JW*CC* (C) p. 49, but his reign is not discussed nor is it dated in the accompanying accounts.

**532** Marianus as elaborated in JW*CC* 532.

**533** Common root: *Coventry*[1] 533. Marianus via JW*CC* 533.

**534.1** Common root: *Coventry*[1] 534.1. Marianus via JW*CC* 534.

**534.2** Common root: *Coventry*[1] 534.2. JW*CC* 534.

**538** Common root: *Coventry*[1] 538. *ASC* via JW*CC* 538.

**539.1** Indeterminate source.

**539.2** Indeterminate source.

**539.3** Matching material occurs in John's "Papal Annals" (C), p. 32.

**540.1** Common root: *Coventry*[1] 540. *ASC* via JW*CC* 540.

**540.2** Only faintly discernable in the manuscript, this addition has been tentatively reconstructed, but it is clearly, though perhaps not directly, derived from GM, § 178 (p. 132): "Set et inclitus ille rex Arturus letaliter uulneratus est; qui illinc ad sananda uulnera sua in insulam Auallonis euectus Constantino cognato suo et filio Cadoris ducis Cornubie diadema Britannie concessit anno ab incarnatione Domini .dxliii."

**541** Common root: *Coventry*[1] 541. The ultimate source of this item is, apparently, *Liber Historiae Francorum*, §§ 32 and 35 (ed. Bruno Krusch, *MGH, SS rer. merov.* 2:215–328, at 295–97 and 303–4). § 32 describes at greater length how Sigibert was murdered by Fredegund, mentioning that he was buried at Lambres and later reburied next to his father Chlothar in the basilica of St Medard at Soissons, whilst § 35 describes how Chilperic was assassinated by his wife Fredegund and how he was buried in the basilica of St Vincent in Paris. But whilst there is no doubt as to the ultimate source, it seems likely, as with the Frankish material under **645** below, that there is an intervening text lying between *Liber Historiae Francorum* and the present item. That medium does not, however, appear to be Hugh of Fleury or Ado of Vienne, neither of whom provides the present item's information about the resting places of Sigibert and Chilperic: see HF*Chron.*, 157–58, and AV*Chron.*, 184. The Norman Annals also have a different version of events: "Hoc tempore Sigibertus rex Francorum occisus est fraude Hilperici germani sui cum quo bellum inierat, regnumque ejus Childebertus filius ejus adhuc puerulus cum Brunnichilde matre regendum suscepit" (*AU* 556; cf. likewise, *AG* 556, *ASN* 534). Comparison may also be made with the *Compendiosum cronicum de regibus Francorum*, a short chronicle preserved in what is now thought to be a Durham production, MS. Cambridge, U.L., Ff.1.27, pp. 249–53. Its coverage of the two murders at p. 249 is closer to that of *Liber Historiae Francorum*, § 32, not least in that it rightly identifies Chilperic's resting place as the church of St Vincent in Paris. Cf. also JW*CC* 557, which reproduces the version of events found in the Norman Annals.

**544** Common root: *Coventry*[1] 544. Marianus via JW*CC* 544.

**547.1** Common root: *Coventry*[1] 548. The Northumbrian Royal Genealogy in JW*CC* (C), p. 51; JW*CC* 547, following Bede, *HE*, 5.24 (s.a. 547).

**547.2** A marginal gloss echoing 547.1.

**551** A marginal gloss. Octa figures as the father of Eormenric in JW*CC* 618, but as his grandfather in the Kentish Royal Genealogy in JW*CC* (C), p. 48.

**556.1** Indeterminate source.

**556.2** Matching material, derived from Marianus VA 580, occurs in JW*CC* (C) 554, and in John's "Papal Annals" (C), p. 32.

**556.3** Matching material, derived from Marianus VA 586, occurs in JW*CC* (C) 564, and in John's "Papal Annals" (C), p. 32.

**559.1** Common root: *Coventry*[1] 559.1. Marianus via JW*CC* 559.

**559.2** Common root: *Coventry*[1] 559.2. The Northumbrian Royal Genealogies in JW*CC* (C), p. 51; JW*CC* 559, following *ASC*.

**560** Common root: *Coventry*[1] 560. *ASC* via JW*CC* 560.

**561** Common root: *Coventry*[1] 561. Marianus via JW*CC* 561.

**564** Common root: *Coventry*[1] 564.1. Marianus via JW*CC* 564.

**565** Common root: *Coventry*[1] 564.2. Marianus via JW*CC* 564.

**566.1** Common root: *Coventry*[1] 565. Marianus via JW*CC* 565.

**566.2** Common root: *Coventry*[1] 566.1. Marianus via JW*CC* 566.

**566.3** Common root: *Coventry*[1] 566.2. The date of Adda's death and Clappa's accession could have been deduced from JW*CC* 559 and from the Northumbrian Royal Genealogies in JW*CC* (C), p. 51, since this gives

559 as the date of Adda's accession and seven years as the length of his reign.

**567** Common root: *Coventry*[1] 568. This item's provenance is rather obscure. It may represent an attempt to locate the undated information which was derived, "ultimately," from *Liber Historiae Francorum*, § 35, and used at **541** above; or, it may simply represent mis-allocated material from the Norman Annals. Cf. *AU*, *AG*, *ASN* 579, which record the death of Chilperic.

**568** Indeterminate source.

**571.1** Common root: *Coventry*[1] 571. The source is likely to have been either JW*CC* 559 or the list of Bernician and Deiran kings in JW*CC* (C), p. 51 which puts the length of Clappa's reign at five years.

**571.2** A marginal gloss of unknown origin. The accounts which accompany the East Anglian Royal Genealogy in JW*CC* (C) p. 49 do not date the foundation of the East Anglian kingdom, but the ruler intended here may be King Rædwald.

**572.1** Common root: *Coventry*[1] 572.1. Marianus via JW*CC* 572.

**572.2** Common root: *Coventry*[1] 572.2. The source is likely to have been either JW*CC* 559 or the list of Bernician and Deiran kings in JW*CC* (C), p. 51 which puts the length of Theodwulf's reign at one year.

**573** Common root: *Coventry*[1] 573. Marianus via JW*CC* 573.

**574** Common root: *Coventry*[1] 574. Marianus via JW*CC* 575. Cf. Norman Annals: *AU* 576, *AG* 574.

**575** Common root: *Coventry*[1] 575. Marianus via JW*CC* 576.

**578** Common root: *Coventry*[1] 578. Marianus via JW*CC* 578.

**579.1** Common root: *Coventry*[1] 579.1. Marianus via JW*CC* 579.

**579.2** Common root: *Coventry*[1] 579.2. The source is likely to have been either JW*CC* 559 or the list of Bernician and Deiran kings in JW*CC* (C), p. 51 which puts the length of Freothwulf's reign at seven years.

**581** Indeterminate source.

**582.1** Common root: *Coventry*[1] 582. Marianus via JW*CC* 582.

**582.2** Norman Annals: *AU*, *AG*, RT*Access.* 582.

**583** Norman Annals: *AU*, RT*Access.* 588. Also found in the margin of JW (C) 588.

**584.1** Common root: *Coventry*[1] 584. Norman Annals: *AU*, *AG* (though converting the entry into an obit), *ASN* 585.

**584.2** Norman Annals: *AU* 580 (virtually identical), *AG* 589 (abbreviated). Cf. Marianus via JW*CC* 585, Bede, *CM*, 529.

**584.3** Matching material, derived from Marianus VA 614, occurs in JW*CC* (C) 592, and in John's "Papal Annals" (C), p. 32. Bubonic plague was known as *lues* or *pestis inguinaria* because the buboes frequently emerged in the groin.

**585.1** Common root: *Coventry*[1] 585.1. See **53.1** above.

**585.2** Common root: *Coventry*[1] 585.2. Marianus via JW*CC* 585. Cf. *Chronicula*[1] VA 604; Bede, *CM*, 529.

**586** Common root: *Coventry*[1] 586. The source is likely to have been either JW*CC* 559 or the list of Bernician and Deiran kings in JW*CC* (C), p. 51 which puts the length of Theodoric's reign at seven years.

**587.1** A near-contemporary addition of unknown origin. This information may have been inferred from *ASC* via JW*CC* 627, or from the stemma of the Mercian Royal Genealogy in JW*CC* (C) p. 50, since Creoda is identified as an ancestor of King Penda in both places. The accounts which accompany the Genealogy make no attempt, however, to date the foundation of the Mercian kingdom nor do they associate it with Creoda. See also **600** and **610** below.

**587.2** A marginal gloss.

**588.1** Common root: *Coventry*[1] 588. The Northumbrian Royal Genealogies in JW*CC* (C), p. 51; JW*CC* 588, following *ASC*.

**588.2** A marginal gloss.

**589** Common root: *Coventry*[1] 589. Marianus via JW*CC* 589.

**590** Common root: *Coventry*[1] 591. Possibly related to JW*CC* 591 though it presents the information in a slightly different fashion, as does the West-Saxon Royal Genealogy in JW*CC* (C) p. 53.

**591.1** Common root: *Coventry*[1] 592.1. Marianus via JW*CC* 592.

**591.2** Common root: *Coventry*[1] 592.2. John's "Papal Annals" in JW*CC* (C) p. 32, describe Gregory as *dialogus romanus*, and there is much reference to what he wrote in the Dialogues in Marianus and JW*CC* 594, 595 and so on. Cf. *Chronicula* VA 604 (G, fol. 21r).

**591.3** An almost identical entry appears in the "Papal Annals" in JW*CC* (C) p. 32: "Hic [Gregorius] ita ecclesiastica ordinauit officia, ut prima oratio in missa officio, lectioni et euangelio semper concordet, sicut in omnibus solennitatibus deprehendi potest." It is not clear, however, whence JW*CC* derived this entry, which is quite atypical of the notices concerning Gregory the Great's liturgical innovations (cf., for example, the Annals of Southwark in Faustina A.VIII, fol. 127rv; Annals of Reading in Vespasian E.IV fol. 163rv). It is not to be found in the corresponding part of Marianus (N fol. 145rv), but one possibility is John the Deacon, *Vita S. Gregorii magni* (*BHL* 3641–2), 2.17 (ed. Daniel van Papenbroeck, *PL* 75.59–242, at 94): "Sed, et Gelasianum Codicem de missarum solemniis, multa subtrahens, pauca convertens, nonnulla vero superadjiciens, pro exponendis evangelicis lectionibus in unius libri volumine coartavit." On the origins of the tradition that attributed key features of western liturgical practice to Gregory the Great, see James W. McKinnon, "Gregorius presul composuit hunc libellum musicae artis," in *The Liturgy of the Medieval Church*, ed. Thomas J. Heffernan and E. Ann Matter (Kalamazoo: Medieval Institute Publications, 2001), 673–94.

**591.4** Common root: *Coventry*[1] 596.2. Matching material, derived from Marianus VA 619, occurs in JW*CC* (C) 597, and in John's "Papal Annals" (C), p. 32. Cf. Norman Annals: *ASC* (E) 591.

**592** *ASC* via JW*CC* 592.

**593** Common root: *Coventry*[1] 593. *ASC* via JW*CC* 593.

**595** Marianus via JW*CC* 595. Cf. Bede, *CM*, 530.

**596.1** Common root: *Coventry*[1] 596.1. JWCC (C) 596: "Cenobium sancti Benedicti abbatis a Longobardis noctu inuaditur."

**596.2** Norman Annals: *AU* 596: "Post sanctum Benedictum Constantinus, post Simplicius, post Vitalis, post Bonitus, sub quo destructio facta est." Cf. *AG* 597.

**597** Common root: *Coventry*[1] 597.3. JW*CC* 596 (from Marianus) and 597 (from Bede).

**599** Common root: *Coventry*[1] 599. From either JW*CC* 597 or the West-Saxon Royal Genealogy in JW*CC* (C) p. 53: "Cui [Ceol] post decessum, Ceoluulfus filius Cuthe regimen regni accepit."

**600** This entry may derive from *ASC* via JW*CC* 627, or the stemma of the Mercian Royal Genealogy in JW*CC* (C) p. 50, since Creoda and Pybba are named in both places as ancestors of Penda and "Wilba" might well be a misreading for Pybba. See also **587** above and **610** below.

**603** Common root: *Coventry*[1] 603. Either Marianus via JW*CC* 603 or Norman Annals: *AU* 603, *AG* 603; but all these accounts lack the detail that Phocas was *magister militum*.

**604** Common root: *Coventry*[1] 604. Marianus as adapted by JW*CC* 604.

**605** Common root: *Coventry*[1] 606. The accession of Dagobert is recorded in the Norman Annals: *AU*, *AG*, *ASN*, 620. Cf. JW*CC* 586.

**606.1** Common root: *Coventry*[1] 605.1. Marianus VA 626 via JW*CC* 605, who lacks the words *Anglorum apostolus*.

**606.2** Common root: *Coventry*[1] 605.2. Sabinian figures briefly in JW*CC* 606.

**608.1** Indeterminate source.

**608.2** Common root: *Coventry*[1] 608. Matching material, derived from Marianus VA 630, occurs in JW*CC* (C) 608, and in John's "Papal Annals" (C), p. 32.

**609.1** Indeterminate source.

**609.2** Common root: *Coventry*[1] 609. Matching material, derived from Marianus VA 632, occurs in JW*CC* (C) 609, and in John's "Papal Annals" (C), p. 32. Cf. Norman Annals: *AG* 608.

**610** This addition is at odds with JW*CC* 627 and the stemma of the Mercian Royal Genealogy in JW*CC* (C) p. 50, for though "Wilba" here might conceivably be identifed as "Pybba," JW*CC* nowhere mentions a king of Mercia called "Ceorl." See also **587** and **600** above.

**611** Common root: *Coventry*[1] 611. Marianus, via JW*CC* 611, has everything but the name of the Persian ruler. Given that **622.2** below appears to depend on the work of Hugh of Fleury, it seems likely that his chronicle was also used in the making of this item. Compare, for example, the following passage as found in a twelfth-century English MS. of the work (today MS. Dublin, Trinity College, 320, fol. 92v): "Hic [Heraclius] inuenit ualde dissolutam rem publicam et attritam. Siquidem Europam uehementer Auares uastauerant, et Asiam Perse. Huius etiam in diebus rex Persarum Cosrohes cepit Damascum, et deuastauit Iherosolimam, et uenerabilia loca que erant in ea conflagrauit, et populorum copias captiuauit, una cum patriarcha eiusdem urbis Zacharia et pretiosum crucis et lignum secum imperfidem asportauit. . . ." On this manuscript, see Colker, *TCD*, no. 320, and the works cited there. For a printed version, see HF*Chron.*, 147. Cf. also Bede, *CM*, 537.

**612.1** Common root: *Coventry*[1] 612. Marianus via JW*CC* 611.

**612.2** Common root: *Coventry*[1] 613. *ASC* via JW*CC* 611.

**614.1** Indeterminate source.

**614.2** Matching material, derived from Marianus VA 640, occurs in JW*CC* (C) 615, and in John's "Papal Annals" (C), p. 32.

**614.3** This date is at odds with the 8 November (*vi id. Nov.*) given in Marianus VA 640, and reproduced in JW*CC* (C) 619 and in John's "Papal Annals" (C), p. 32.

**616.1** Common root: *Coventry*[1] 616 and 617. Marianus via JW*CC* 616.

**616.2** Indeterminate source.

**616.3** Matching material, derived from Marianus VA 645, occurs in JW*CC* (C) 620, and in John's "Papal Annals" (C), p. 32. JW*CC* 620 omits the obit.

**618** Common root: *Coventry*[1] 618. Bede, *HE*, 2.6, as elaborated by JW*CC* 616.

**620** Common root: *Coventry*[1] 620. Bede, *HE*, 2.7, as elaborated by JW*CC* 620.

**621** Norman Annals: *AU*, *AG* 622, RT*Access.* 623.

**622.1** Indeterminate source.

**622.2** Common root: *Coventry*[1] 622. The source of this item remains somewhat uncertain. Marianus and JW*CC* 625 leave out the return of the cross: "Superueniens Heraclius imperator cum exercitu, superatis Persis, Christianos qui erant captiuitati reduxit." A possible source for the additional information about the cross may be *Exaltatio Sanctæ Crucis* (*BHL* 4178), ed. *PL* 110.131–134, which incorporates among other matter the story of Chosroes' removal of the cross, its recovery by an, alas, unnamed *Christianissimus imperator*, and its restoration to the city of Jerusalem. This text is preserved in the so-called Cotton-Corpus Legendary, a passional copied at Worcester Cathedral in the early part of Wulfstan's pontificate (1062–1095), the relevant section being MS. London, B.L., Cotton Nero E.I, pt. ii, fols. 167r–168v, at 168v. That this text may well have been studied by John of Worcester is strongly suggested by the item that follows on fols. 168r–180r. This is a copy of the *Gesta S. Siluestri* (*BHL* 7725, 7726, 7739), to which extensive alterations have been made "by a hand of the second quarter of the twelfth century, probably that of John of Worcester" (see Peter Jackson and Michael Lapidge, "The Contents of the Cotton-Corpus Legendary," in *Holy Men and Holy Women: Old English Prose Saints' Lives and Their Contexts*, ed. Paul E. Szarmach [Albany: State University of New York Press, 1996], 131–46, at 144). Alternatively, the passage can also be seen as a much abbreviated version of the lengthy account in the Chronicle of Hugh of Fleury. Compare, for example, MS. Dublin, Trinity College, 320, fol. 93v (for which MS, see **611** above): "Quod ut Chosdrues comperit fugere temptauit, sed comprehensus est cum Merdasan, quem coronauerat et ergastulum missus, ubi est mortuus est. Tunc Syrois pepigit cum Heraclio pacem uigere, reddens omnes Christianos qui in omni perfide tenebantur captiui, cum preciosissimis et uiuificis lignis que fuerant ex Ierosolimis asportata." Heraclius returns to Constantinople in triumph, rests, and then restores the timber of the Lord's cross to Jerusalem. For a printed version, see HF*Chron.*, 149. Cf. *Chronicula*[1] VA 633: "Hic [Heraclius] occiso rege Persarum Cosdrue, uexillum dominice crucis, quod a Persis Ierosolimam uastantibus abducta est, Ierosolimam reduxit." Cf. also Adémar of Chabannes, *Chronicon*, 1.41 (ed. P. Bourgain-Hemeryck, R. Landes, and G. Pon, CCCM 129 [Turnhout: Brepols, 1999], 57): "Tunc Heraclius imperator crucem Domini de fano Cosroe, quod erat in Perside, victor detulit in Jerusalem, et exaltacio sancte Crucis in sanctam civitatem tunc facta est."

**623.1** Indeterminate source.

**623.2** Similar material, derived from Marianus VA 657 and 659, occurs in JW*CC* (C) 637, but an exact match is provided by John's "Papal Annals" (C), p. 32: "Hoc papante, Iudei in Hispania Christiani efficiuntur. Obiit iiii no' Augusti."

**625** Common root: *Coventry*[1] 625. Bede, *HE*, 2.7–8, via JW*CC* 625.

**626** Common root: *Coventry*[1] 626.1. Bede, *HE*, 2.9, via JW*CC* 626.

**627.1** Common root: *Coventry*[1] 626.2. Norman Annals: *AU*, *AG*, *ASN* 633, record the accession of Clovis, the son of Dagobert.

**627.2** A marginal gloss of unknown origin.

**627.3** Common root: *Coventry*[1] 627.1. *ASC* via JW*CC* 627. Cf. the Mercian Royal Genealogy in JW*CC* (C) p. 50.

**627.4** Common root: *Coventry*[1] 627.2. Bede, *HE*, 2.5, via JW*CC* 628.

**632** Common root: *Coventry*[1] 632. Bede, *HE*, 2.15, via JW*CC* 632.

**633.1** Common root: *Coventry*[1] 633. Bede, *HE*, 2.20, via JW*CC* 633.

**633.2** Matching material, derived from Marianus VA 660, occurs in JW*CC* (C) 639, and in John's "Papal Annals" (C), p. 32.

**633.3** Matching material, derived from Marianus VA 666, occurs in JW*CC* (C) 644, and in John's "Papal Annals" (C), p. 32.

**634** Common root: *Coventry*[1] 634. Bede, *HE*, 3.6, via JW*CC* 634.

**635.1** Indeterminate source.

**635.2** Common root: *Coventry*[1] 635. Bede, *HE*, 3.1, 6, via JW*CC* 635.

**635.3** Norman Annals: *AU*, *AG*, RT*Access.* 635; *ACad.* 633.

**636** Common root: *Coventry*[1] 636. *ASC* via JW*CC* 636.

**637** Common root: *Coventry*[1] 637. Norman Annals: *AU*, *AG*, *ASN* 659, record the death of Clovis and the accession of his son Clothar.

**638** Common root: *Coventry*[1] 638. Marianus via JW*CC* 638.

**639** Common root: *Coventry*[1] 639. *ASC* via JW*CC* 640.

**640.1** Common root: *Coventry*[1] 640. Marianus via JW*CC* 638, 640. Cf. Norman Annals: *AU*, *AG* 640.

**640.2** Common root: *Coventry*[1] 641. Bede, *HE*, 3.8, via JW*CC* 640.

**642** Common root: *Coventry*[1] 642.1. Bede, *HE*, 3.6, 9, via JW*CC* 642.

**643** Common root: *Coventry*[1] 642.2. JW*CC* 642.

**644.1** Common root: *Coventry*[1] 644.1. Bede, *HE*, 3.14, via JW*CC* 644. Cf. *Chronicula*[1] VA 633.

**644.2** Common root: *Coventry*[1] 644.2. Bede, *HE*, 3.14, via JW*CC* 645.

**645** Common root: *Coventry*[1] 644.3 and 645. The ultimate and perhaps the direct source of this entry would seem to be *Liber Historiae Francorum*, § 45 (pp. 317–19), which records the revolt against Theuderic and Ebroin and their recovery at much greater length; § 46 (pp. 319–20), which records the war between Ebroin and the Austrasian *duces*, Martin and Pippin; and § 49 (pp. 323–24), which states that Theuderic reigned for 19 years and that his son—here named not "Chlothar" but *Chlodoveus*, "Clovis"—reigned for two years. The present material is, however, sufficiently distant in language and arrangement from *Liber Historiae Francorum* as to suggest that some other work lies between them. Possibilities that have been eliminated include HF*Chron.*, 157–58, and AV*Chron.*, 200–1: both cover similar ground and both contain echoes of *Liber Historiae Francorum*, but variations of emphasis and language prevent either being the means by which the material was transmitted to the present chronicle. *Chronicula*[1] VA 706 offers contrasting information on Ebroin drawn from HF*Chron.*, 158: "Sanctus Leodegarius Eduensis episcopus ab Ebroino, qui monachili ueste qua induebatur, iam deposita maior regie domus effectus est, martyrizatur." The account found in *Compendiosum cronicum de regibus Francorum*, a text preserved in a late twelfth-century Durham production (MS. Cambridge, U.L., Ff.1.27, pp. 249–53, at 250), also focuses on Ebroin's murder of St

Ledger and that of his brother Gerinus. The Norman Annals contain only brief allusions to these events: "Clothario successit Teodericus, et Childericus regnum invaserunt [sic] . . . Mortuo Childerico, regnat Teodoricus" (*AU* 679, 682; cf., likewise, *AG*, *ASN* 679, 682).

**646.1** Common root: *Coventry*[1] 646.1. *ASC* via JW*CC* 646.

**646.2** Common root: *Coventry*[1] 646.2. JW*CC* 642.

**646.3** A marginal gloss.

**647.1** Common root: *Coventry*[1] 648. Bede, *HE*, 3.20, via JW*CC* 647.

**647.2** Indeterminate source.

**649** Indeterminate source.

**651** Common root: *Coventry*[1] 651.1. Bede, *HE*, 3.14, via JW*CC* 651.

**652** Common root: *Coventry*[1] 651.2. Bede, *HE*, 3.14, via JW*CC* 651.

**653.1** Common root: *Coventry*[1] 653.1. Bede, *HE*, 3.21, 24, via JW*CC* 653.

**653.2** Common root: *APW* 654. Bede, *Historia Abbatum* (*BHL* 8968), §§ 1–2 (ed. Charles Plummer, *Venerabilis Baedae opera historica*, 2 vols. [Oxford: Clarendon Press, 1896], 1:364–87, at pp. 364–66), via JW*CC* 653.

**653.3** Common root: *Coventry*[1] 653.2 and 654.2; *APW* 656. Bede, *HE*, 3.20, via JW*CC* 653.

**654** Common root: *Coventry*[1] 654.1. *ASC* via JW*CC* 654.

**655.1** Common root: *Coventry*[1] 655. Bede, *HE*, 3.24, via JW*CC* 655.

**655.2** Norman Annals: *AU* 655, *AG* 649.

**656** Common root: *Coventry*[1] 656. Bede, *HE*, 3.24, via JW*CC* 656.

**657** Common root: *Coventry*[1] 657. Norman Annals: *AU* 657, *AG* 651, RT*Access*. 665.

**658** Common root: *Coventry*[1] 658. Bede, *HE*, 3.24, via JW*CC* 658.

**659** Common root: *Coventry*[1] 659. Bede, *HE*, 3.24, via JW*CC* 659.

**662.1** Common root: *Coventry*[1] 663. Norman Annals: *AU*, *AG*, *ASN* 698, record the death of Theuderic and the accession of Clovis.

**662.2** Common root: *Coventry*[1] 664.1. Bede, *HE*, 4.1, via JW*CC* 664.

**664** Common root: *Coventry*[1] 664.2. Bede, *HE*, 3.28; 4.1, 8; and idem, *Vita S. Cuthberti prosa* (*BHL* 2021), § 8 (ed. Bertram Colgrave, *Two Lives of Saint Cuthbert* [Cambridge: Cambridge University Press, 1940], pp. 142–306, at 182–85), via JW*CC* 664.

**666.1** Common root: *Coventry*[1] 666. Norman Annals: *AU*, *AG*, *ASN* 700, record the death of Clovis and the accession of his brother Childebert.

**666.2** Common root: *Coventry*[1] 667. JW*CC* 666.

**668** Common root: *Coventry*[1] 668. Marianus via JW*CC* 668.

**669.1** Common root: *Coventry*[1] 669. Bede, *HE*, 4.2–3, via JW*CC* 669. Cf. *Chronicula*[1] VA 662, which is much fuller on Theodore, with material derived from HF*Chron.*, 153.

**669.2** Matching material, derived from Marianus VA 691, occurs in JW*CC* (C) 669, and in John's "Papal Annals" (C), p. 32.

**670** Common root: *Coventry*[1] 670. Bede, *HE*, 4.5, via JW*CC* 670.

672.1 Common root: *Coventry*[1] 671. Marianus via JW*CC* 672.

672.2 Common root: *Coventry*[1] 672.1. JW*CC* 672, following Bede, *HE*, 4.12; but for the names of the *sub-reguli* the compiler will have needed to turn to another source, perhaps the West-Saxon Royal Genealogy in JW*CC* (C) p. 53. Neither Æscwine nor Centwine is designated *sub-regulus* there, but they follow Cenwealh in the sequence of kings.

673.1 Common root: *Coventry*[1] 672.2. Bede, *HE*, 4.3, via JW*CC* 672.

673.2 Common root: *Coventry*[1] 673.1. Bede, *HE*, 4.1, via JW*CC* 673.

673.3 Common root: *Coventry*[1] 673.2. Bede, *HE*, 4.19, via JW*CC* 673.

673.4 Indeterminate source.

674.1 Indeterminate source.

674.2 Common root: *Coventry*[1] 674. Bede, *Historia abbatum*, § 4 (pp. 367–8), via JW*CC* 674.

674.3 Norman Annals: *AU* 669; *AG* 669.

675.1 Common root: *Coventry*[1] 675.1. *ASC* via JW*CC* 675.

675.2 Common root: *Coventry*[1] 675.2. Bede, *HE*, 4.6, via JW*CC* 675.

676 Common root: *Coventry*[1] 676. *ASC* via JW*CC* 676.

677.1 Indeterminate source.

677.2 Common root: *Coventry*[1] 677. Bede, *HE*, 4.12, via JW*CC* 677.

677.3 Common root: *Coventry*[1] 678. Norman Annals: *AU, ACad.*, *ASN*, RT*Access*. 677, *AG* 669.

677.4 Indeterminate source.

677.5 Norman Annals: *AU, ACad.*, *ASN*, RT*Access*. 677, *AG* 669. Also found in JW 677.

679 Common root: *Coventry*[1] 679; *APW* 679. Bede, *HE*, 4.19, via JW*CC* 679.

680.1 Common root: *Coventry*[1] 680. Compare JW*CC* ($C^3BP^3$) 679. Similar material was entered in the margin of C by $C^3$ and in the margins of P by $P^3$, but it differs from the common root in as much as it suggests that Æthelred and Theodore acted together to effect the changes rather than that the initiative came from the latter alone. A somewhat different entry appears in *APW* 680.

680.2 Verbal echoes show that the present entry is related to the "Gloucester foundation narratives," but the exact relationship is far from clear. Of the other versions now extant, the earliest to provide a seemingly "complete" text survive from the time of Abbot Walter Frocester (1382–1412): there is a fullish text preserved in Gloucester Cathedral Library, Register A, and a briefer text in the extant, late fourteenth-century, version of the abbey's Cartulary-Chronicle. Both were printed by Hart in *Cart. Gloc.*, 1:lxxi–lxxiii and 3–5. In general, the verbal echoes in the present text seem closest to the text found in Register A. Consider, for example, the following passage, where the parallels have been underlined:

> Huiccorum Aldred dedisset suam hæreditatem illic, hoc est, æt Enneglan lx. manentes illius terræ; x. cassatorum æt Faganforda dedisset Burgredus pro libertate equorum ejus tributariorum; æt Hwicca wuda Idgut hæres nominatur; et æt Weapcaurtane xv. cassatorum, et in alio loco æt Ceddanwryde in terra montana xv. cassatorum; et in Nymdesfelda iii. manentes; istas terras dedit Aldred subregulus Huiccorum omnes pro se dedisset. Similiter etiam postea Æelmund in Geldinge xxx. tributariorum Æeoport dedit, xxxv. Lecche familiæ illæ ad suam mensam (*Cart. Gloc.* 1:lxxii–lxxiii).

However, the text in the abbey's Cartulary-Chronicle is sometimes closer, not least in its use of terms such as *hidas* for *cassates* and in the distribution of the words relative to the spaces left by the burning of T:

> Adelred, subregulus Wicciorum, dedit hæreditatem suam eidem ecclesiæ; hoc est in Culne Sancti Aeylwyny .lx. manentes illius terræ; Burgred rex Merciorum in Faireford, x hidas in Wyarkeston, xv. hidas in Geddanwyrda, in terra montana xv. hidas. Item Adelred dedit extra civitatem Gloucestriæ cxx. hidas, ubi nunc Bertona est in Numedesfeld iii. manentes. Edelmund subregulus dedit .xxx. manentes in Overe et .xxxviii. in Northleche' (*Cart. Gloc.* 1:3–4).

Neither of these texts provides an exact match, pointing to the dependence of the present fragment on a version more primitive than any of those now exant.

Working chiefly with the text in Register A, H. P. R. Finberg (*ECWM*, 162–63), provided reasons for thinking that the foundation narrative was first cobbled together in the ninth century from "oral tradition, the obits in their liturgical calendar, and perhaps monumental inscriptions in St Peter's church . . . and . . . authentic written materials dating from a much earlier period, writings perhaps already tattered and only in part legible." It can equally well be argued, however, that the narrative was first put together when the abbey was refounded after the Norman Conquest, when there would have been a need to demonstrate how St Peter's had acquired its property rights. The existing texts certainly contain later embellishments: see further Baker and Holt, *Gloucester and Worcester*, 15–20. In any case, the present entry shows that such a narrative must have existed by the late twelfth century.

Indeed, it is not unlikely that the exemplar may have formed part of the beginning of the lost late twelfth-century Gloucester Chronicle which lies, it is argued in the Introduction above (chap. 3, §§ e–f), behind the continuation to the Winchcombe Chronicle. Certainly there is ample evidence in the notes made by Lawrence Nowell in the sixteenth century that the late thirteenth-century Gloucester Chronicle produced by Gregory of Caerwent also contained a version of the foundation narrative. Nowell has an extended series of notes for 680 containing a number of clear echoes of the text (V, fol. 195r). Compare, for example, the following passage:

> Et postea subregulus Hwicciorum Aldredus dedit hæreditatem suam ecclesiae; hoc est in Culna 60 manentes. Et Burgreda dedit in Faireford 10. hid. in Wiarchanstona 15. hid. in Chendeswurtha in terra montana. 15 hidas. In Numesdesfelda 3 manentes. Omnes istas terras dedit et concessit Aldredus subregulus Hwicciorum. Item Ethelmundus de Geldinges dedit 30 hid. in Overe et 35 in Lethe.

Though fuller than normal for Nowell, these notes are unfortunately too brief to add anything to the textual comparisons made above. Indeed, the implication of these comparisons for present purposes is that whilst it is possible to make some reasonable guesses as to what has been lost from the present entry, it is impossible to provide a definitive reconstruction. This much is reflected in our presentation of the text. Cf. also *Quedam Chronica de Anglia*, in MS. London, B.L., Cotton Vitellius C.VIII, fol. 8vb (ed. Liebermann, *ANG*, 16–24, at 18). On the foundation and pre-Conquest history of St Peter's, see also Michael Hare, *The Two Anglo-Saxon Minsters of Gloucester*, Deerhurst Lecture 1992 (Deerhurst: Friends of Deerhurst Church, 1993), esp. 1–3.

**684** Indeterminate source, perhaps Norman Annals: *AU* 686, *AG* 682.

**685.1** Common root: *Coventry*[1] 685.1. Marianus via JW*CC* 685.

**685.2** Common root: *Coventry*[1] 685.2. Bede, *HE*, 4.26, via JW*CC* 685.

**685.3** Common root: *Coventry*[1] 686.1. Bede, *HE*, 4.28, via JW*CC* 685.

**686.1** Common root: *Coventry*[1] 686.2. Bede, *HE*, 4.26, via JW*CC* 685.

**686.2** Common root: *Coventry*[1] 686.3. *ASC* via JW*CC* 685.

**686.3** Common root: *Coventry*[1] 686.4. Bede, *HE*, 5.3, via JW*CC* 686.

**686.4** Indeterminate source.

**686.5** Matching material, derived from Marianus VA 712, occurs in JW*CC* (C) 691, and in John's "Papal Annals" (C), p. 33.

**686.6** Matching material, derived from Marianus VA 723, occurs in JW*CC* (C) 701, and in John's "Papal Annals" (C), p. 33.

**687** Common root: *Coventry*[1] 687. Marianus via JW*CC* 688: "Pippinus Ansgisi filii sancti Arnulfi filius regit Francos annis .xxuii." Cf. Norman Annals: *AU*, *AG*, *ASN* 687: "Pipinus primus major domus efficitur." The claim that Pippin succeeded on the death of Childebert seems to be the compiler's own inference. If so, it betrays considerable misunderstanding of Frankish history, even though the author appears to have had access to the *Liber Historiae Francorum* (see **541** and **645** above) that might well have provided him with a fuller grasp of the distinction between kings and mayors of the palace, and also to the Norman Annals which provided a radically different chronology (since the Childebert in question is apparently the one whose death is recorded in Norman Annals: *AU*, *AG* 716). But it is not difficult to see how the language which Marianus uses to define the authority of the Pippinids might have given rise to this confusion (see also **714** and **742.1** below).

**688** Common root: *Coventry*[1] 689. Bede, *HE*, 5.7, via JW*CC* 689: "Pontificatum agente Sergio, Ceaduualla Westsaxonum rex baptizatus est die sancto sabbati pascalis."

**689.1** Common root: *Coventry*[1] 690.1. Bede, *HE*, 5.8, via JW*CC* 690 and, for Brihtwald's succession, JW*CC* 693.

**689.2** Common root: *Coventry*[1] 690.2; *APW* 689. Marianus via JW*CC* 691.

**691** Common root: *Coventry*[1] 691. Bede, *HE*, 4.23, via JW*CC* 691.

**692** Common root: *Coventry*[1] 692; *APW* 692–3. Either JW*CC* 692 or the Easter Table Annals in JW*CC* (C), p. 60 (in cycle 9, year 10 = 693).

**693.1** Common root: *Coventry*[1] 693.1. Bede, *HE*, 5.8, via JW*CC* 693.

**693.2** Common root: *Coventry*[1] 693.1. Bede, *HE*, 5.24, via JW*CC* 693.

**694** Common root: *Coventry*[1] 695.1. Marianus via JW*CC* 695.

**695** Common root: *Coventry*[1] 695.2. Bede, *HE*, 4.19, via JW*CC* 695.

**696** Common root: *Coventry*[1] 696. Bede, *HE*, 5.11, via JW*CC* 696.

**697.1** Common root: *Coventry*[1] 697.1. Felix, *Vita S. Guthlaci* (*BHL* 3723), §§ 19–20 (ed. Bertram Colgrave, *Felix's Life of St Guthlac* [Cambridge: Cambridge University Press, 1956], 60–170, at 82–84), via JW*CC* 697.

**697.2** Common root: *Coventry*[1] 697.2. Marianus via JW*CC* 698, which is ultimately derived from Bede, *CM*, 570.

**698** Common root: *Coventry*[1] 698. Marianus via JW*CC* 698.

**699** Common root: *Coventry*[1] 699. Felix, *Vita S. Guthlaci*, § 27, via JW*CC* 699. Cf. *Chronicula* VA 720 (G, fol. 55v).

**701** Indeterminate source.

**703** Common root: *Coventry*[1] 703. Marianus via JW*CC* 703.

**704.1** Common root: *Coventry*[1] 704.1. Either *ASC* or Bede, *HE*, 5.24 (s.a. 704), via JW*CC* 704.

**704.2** Common root: *Coventry*[1] 704.2. Bede, *HE*, 5.24, via JW*CC* 704.

**705** Common root: *Coventry*[1] 705. Marianus via JW*CC* 705.

**706.1** Common root: *Coventry*[1] 706.1. *ASC* via JW*CC* 705.

**706.2** Common root: *Coventry*[1] 706.1. Bede, *HE*, 5.18, via JW*CC* 705.

**707.1** Indeterminate source.

**707.2** Matching material, derived from Marianus VA 727, occurs in JW*CC* (C) 705 (p. 162), and in John's "Papal Annals" (C), p. 33.

**707.3** Matching material, derived from Marianus VA 728, occurs in JW*CC* (C) 705 (p. 164), and in John's "Papal Annals" (C), p. 33.

**707.4** Common root: *Coventry*[1] 706.3. *ASC* via JW*CC* 705, but note that John calls Seaxwulf "bishop of the Mercians."

**708.1** Common root: *Coventry*[1] 708.1. Bede, *HE*, 5.19, via JW*CC* 708.

**708.2** Byrhtferth of Ramsey, *Vita S. Ecgwini Wigorniensis episcopi* (*BHL* 2432), ed. John A. Giles, *Vita quorundum Anglo-Saxonum* (London: Caxton Society, 1854), pp. 349–96, at 387, via JW*CC* 708.

**708.3** Common root: *Coventry*[1] 708.2. Bede, *HE*, 5.19, via JW*CC* 709.

**709** Common root: *Coventry*[1] 708.3. Bede, *HE*, 5.18–19, via JW*CC* 709.

**710.1** Indeterminate source.

**710.2** Matching material, derived from Marianus VA 729, occurs in John's "Papal Annals" (C), p. 33. JW*CC* 707, following Marianus, writes *Sisinnius .lxxxui. papa mense .i.*, but fails to include the obit.

**710.3** Indeterminate source.

**710.4** Matching material, derived from Marianus VA 736, occurs in JW*CC* (C) 715, and in John's "Papal Annals" (C), p. 33.

**711** Common root: *Coventry*[1] 711. Marianus via JW*CC* 711. Cf. Norman Annals: *AU* 711; *AG* 710.

**713.1** Common root: *Coventry*[1] 713. Marianus via JW*CC* 712, 713.

**713.2** Norman Annals: *AU* 713, RT*Access.* 720 (obit).

**714** Common root: *Coventry*[1] 714.1. Marianus via JW*CC* 715: "Pippinus filius Ansgisi apud Gallias Francorum regnans obiit. Cui Karolus qui et maior domus filius eius in regnum successit per annos uiginti septem." Cf. Norman Annals: *AU*, *AG*, *ASN* 717.

**715.1** Common root: *Coventry*[1] 714.2; *APW* 714. Felix, *Vita S. Guthlaci*, § 50 (pp. 152, 158), via JW*CC* 714.

**715.2** Indeterminate source.

**715.3** Common root: *Coventry*[1] 715. Marianus via JW*CC* 715.

**715.4** Matching material, derived from Marianus VA 738, occurs in JW*CC* (C) 716, and in John's "Papal Annals" (C), p. 33, but the latter is closer in as much as it also begins but fails to complete the obit.

**716.1** Common root: *Coventry*[1] 716. Marianus via JW*CC* 717.

**716.2** Common root: *Coventry*[1] 717.1. *ASC* via JW*CC* 716.

**717** Common root: *Coventry*[1] 717.2. *ASC* via JW*CC* 716.

**718.1** Common root: *Coventry*[1] 718.1. Marianus via JW*CC* 717, but giving the length of Leo's reign as nine years.

**718.2** Common root: *Coventry*[1] 718.2; *APW* 717. JW*CC* 717.

**719.1** Common root: *Coventry*[1] 718.3. *ASC* via JW*CC* 718.

**719.2** Norman Annals: *AU*, *AG*, RT*Access.* 719.

**721** Common root: *Coventry*[1] 721. Bede, *HE*, 5.6, via JW*CC* 721.

**722** Norman Annals: *AU*, *ACad.*, *AG* 722; RT*Access.* 721.

**725.1** Common root: *Coventry*[1] 725.1. Bede, *HE*, 5.23, via JW*CC* 725.

**725.2** Common root: *Coventry*[1] 725.2. Marianus via JW*CC* 725.
**728** Common root: *Coventry*[1] 728. Bede, *HE*, 5.7, via JW*CC* 728.
**729** Common root: *Coventry*[1] 729. Bede, *HE*, pref., 5.22, 23, via JW*CC* 716 and 729.
**730** Norman Annals: *AU*, *ACad.*, RT*Access.* 730.
**731** Common root: *Coventry*[1] 731. Bede, *HE*, 5.23, via JW*CC* 731.
**733.1** Indeterminate source.
**733.2** Matching material, derived from Marianus VA 760, occurs in JW*CC* (C) 738, and in John's "Papal Annals" (C), p. 33. In the Commemoration of the Departed.
**733.3** Matching material, derived from Marianus VA 764, occurs in JW*CC* (C) 742, and in John's "Papal Annals" (C), p. 33.
**734** Common root: *Coventry*[1] 734. *Continuatio Bedae* in Bede, *HE*, pp. 572–77, via JW*CC* 734.
**735** Common root: *Coventry*[1] 735. *ASC* via JW*CC* 734.
**738.1** Common root: *Coventry*[1] 738. *ASC* via JW*CC* 738.
**738.2** A number of twelfth- and thirteenth-century chronicles have explanatory accounts of how the counties and regions of England were divided into kingdoms during the earlier Anglo-Saxon period. The order in which this entry presents its material shows that it belongs to the tradition first attested in WM*GR*, 1.99–104, and among the preliminary matter in several but not all of the witnesses to JW*CC*, namely MSS L, P, and D, where this material is an addition dating from the very end of the twelfth or the early thirteenth century. The version found in JW*CC* (D) is printed in *Florentii Wigorniensis Monachi Chronicon ex Chronicis*, ed. Benjamin Thorpe, 2 vols. (London: English Historical Society, 1848–1849), 2:277–79. Conventionally given the rubric *De partitione regnorum et pagis et episcopatibus Anglie*, these items are thought to derive from a bundle of shared documents which were used by both William of Malmesbury and John of Worcester (see McGurk's comments in JW*CC*, 2:xxxix, xliv, lvi, and lxvi–lxvii; Rodney M. Thomson's comments in WM*GR*, 2:72–73; and Brett, "John," 113–17). For a relatively pure version, see Ralph Niger, *Chronicon a Christo nato ad regnum Henrici Secundi regis Angliae*, ed. Robert Anstruther, *The Chronicles of Ralph Niger* (London: Caxton Society, 1851), 136–37.

The present entry is significantly closer, however, to a late thirteenth-century version of this material, that found in a genealogical tract attributed to the Christ Church monk Peter of Ickham: *Le livere de reis de Brittanie e le livere de reis de Engleterre*, ed. John Glover, RS 42 (London: Longman, 1865), 8–10. Compare the following:

> Engleterre fust departe en cinc a cinc roys. Ly un aveit Kent. Lautre Westsex. Ly terce Marchenериche. Li quarte Northumberlond.

> Li quinte aveit Estangle. Ly rey de Kent, si regna soulement en Kent. Si aveit en sa terre li arceveske de Canturburi, e le eveske de Roucestre. Li rey de Westsex aveit Wilteschire, Barrocschire, Dorsetechire, Souþsex, Souþhamptechire, Souþþereiȝe, Somersete, Devenisschire, e Cornwaile . . . Li reis de Merchenericheaveit Gloucestreschire, Wirecestreschire, Warewicschire, Chesterschire, Dorbischire, Staffordschire, Schropschire, Herefordschire, Huntindoneschire, demi Bedefordschire, Norhamptechire, [Oxonefordschire, Bokinghamschire,] Leicestrechire, Lincolneschire, Notinghamschire. Si aveit quarte eveskes en sa terre: Cele de Nicole, de Cestre, de Hereforde, e de Wirecestre. Ly reys de Estangle aveit Grantebruggechire, Nortfolc, Souþfolc, Estsex, e demi Bedefordeschire . . . Ly reis de Northumberlond si aveit totes les terre outre Humbre, deskes en Escoce.

*Le livere de reis de Brittanie* is written in Anglo-Norman and, ending originally in 1274, it is perhaps somewhat later than the present entry, but they share a division of England into five kingdoms, whereas JWCC and WM, separating Essex from East Anglia, have six. There is indeed a minor historiographical tradition of a "quintarchic" as opposed to the more usual "hept-" or "sextarchic" division. Examples of the fivefold partition are to be found in several Middle English chronicles (e.g. *An Anonymous Short English Metrical Chronicle*, ed. Ewald Zettl, EETS, o.s. 196 [London: Oxford University Press, 1935], lxxiii–lxxiv, 14–17), but *Le livere de reis de Brittanie* is significantly closer to the present entry than any other example discovered thus far. It contains some striking linguistic echoes (e.g. *Marchenericbe* for "Mercia"; *Nicole* for "Lincoln"), and parts of either item might well have been translated word for word from the other. *Le livere de reis de Brittanie* is much fuller, however, in its treatment of the bishoprics of England, and the text as a whole is clearly a compilation of earlier material. The present entry is also fuller in its first sentence, and the remains of its final sentence (that dealing with the extent of Northumbria) suggest that its conclusion resembled that found in the version of this material in the St Alban's chronicles (e.g. Paris, *CM*, 1:252–53: "a magno flumine Humbrae usque ad mare Scotiae"). All of this tends to suggest that there is a shared source lying directly (or perhaps not far behind) both the partition narrative in *Le livere de reis* and the present entry, though perhaps one in a vernacular language rather than in Latin. The suggestions made above as to the contents of the gaps in the text are based, therefore, on *Le livere de reis de Brittanie*, but for the final sentence on Matthew Paris. On the dating of *Le livere de reis de Brittanie* and its companion tract *Le livere de reis de Engleterre* and their attribution to Peter of Ickham, see *Le livere de reis*, ed. Glover, ix–xiii; M.

Dominica Legge, *Anglo-Norman Literature and its Background* (Oxford: Clarendon Press, 1963), 291; Greatrex, *BR*, 207.

740 Common root: *Coventry*[1] 740. *ASC* via JW*CC* 741.

741.1 Common root: *Coventry*[1] 741.1. Marianus via JW*CC* 741.

741.2 Indeterminate source.

742.1 Common root: *Coventry*[1] 741.2. Possibly derived from a combination of Marianus via JW*CC* 741 ("Karolus, filius Pippini, qui et maior domus dictus, rex Francorum obiit") and Norman Annals: *AU*, *AG*, *ASN* 741; *ACad.* 738 (which record that Charles having died, his sons Carloman and Pippin attained the *maioratum domnus*). In JW*CC* (C), C[3] adds also much new material about the eternal damnation of Charles Martel in the margins alongside 741, from which apparently derives the statement that he was buried at St Denis; but this information may once have been found in the main body of the text where there is a lengthy erasure following its initial entry concerning Charles.

742.2 Common root: *Coventry*[1] 741.3. Norman Annals: *AU* 746 ("Karlomagnus Romam perrexit et monachus factus est in monte Sarepte, ubi ecclesiam in honore sancti Silvestri construxit, et inde in Cassinum monasterium sancti Benedicti transiit"); *ACad.*, *AG*, *ASN* 746. Cf. Marianus via JW*CC* 745.

742.3 Common root: *Coventry*[1] 741.4. The ultimate source is *ARF* 749–750: "Burghardus Wirzeburgensis episcopus et Folradus capellanus missi fuerunt ad Zachariam papam, interrogando de regibus in Francia, qui illis temporibus non habentes regalem potestatem, si bene fuisset an non. Et Zacharias papa mandauit Pippino ut melius esset illum regem uocari, qui potestatem haberet, quam illum, qui sine regali potestate manebat; ut non conturbaretur ordo, per auctoritatem apostolicam iussit Pippinum regem fieri. Pippinus secundum morem Francorum electus est ad regem et unctus per manum sanctae memoriae Bonifacii archiepiscopi et elevatus a Francis in regno in Suessionis ciuitate." The one major discrepancy is the eccentric statement that "Theuderic took the kingdom from Pippin by force, and he reigned for six years," which was presumably invented by the compiler in order to make the material agree with the statements derived from Marianus to the effect that the Carolingians were not mayors of the palace but kings of the Franks. It would have made more sense if the author had cast Childeric III (743–751) in this role. Cf. Marianus via JW*CC* 750/*Chronicula*[1] 764; Norman Annals: *AU*, *ACad.*, *ASN* 752 ("Pipinus rex efficitur").

743 Common root: *Coventry*[1] 743; *APW* 742. JW*CC* 743 and the Easter Table Annals in JW*CC* (C), p. 61 (in cycle 12, year 3 = 743).

744 Common root: *Coventry*[1] 744. Marianus via JW*CC* 744.

745 Common root: *Coventry*[1] 745. *ASC* via JW*CC* 744.

748 Common root: *Coventry*[1] 748. *ASC* via JW*CC* 744.

**751** Common root: *Coventry*[1] 750. Marianus via JW*CC* 751. Note the contradiction with the annal for 742.

**752** Indeterminate source.

**753** Marianus via JW*CC* 754, which appears to have been expanded using Norman Annals (*AU* 756; *ACad.*, 752 and 755; *AG* 752; *ASN* 757; *ASBD* 753), the effect being an enlarged version of the common root as found in *Coventry*[1] 752.

**754** Common root: *Coventry*[1] 754. *ASC* via JW*CC* 754.

**755.1** Common root: *Coventry*[1] 755.1. Marianus via JW*CC* 755. Cf. Norman Annals: *AU*, *AG* 757.

**755.2** Common root: *Coventry*[1] 755.2. *ASC* via JW*CC* 755.

**756.1** Common root: *Coventry*[1] 756. *ASC* via JW*CC* 755.

**756.2** An entry begun in a space left at the top of the page, but never completed. There is nothing in the relevant section of the main chronicle of JW*CC* that begins this way; the intention, therefore, was probably to added the following item from the Norman Annals: "In hoc anno domnus Remigius adeptus est sedem ecclesie Rotomagensis, ejecto ab episcopatu Ragenfrido" (*AU* 755).

**757.1** Common root: *Coventry*[1] 757.1. Marianus via JW*CC* 757.

**757.2** Common root: *Coventry*[1] 757.1. *ASC* via JW*CC* 757.

**758.1** Common root: *Coventry*[1] 758.1. *ASC* via JW*CC* 757.

**758.2** Common root: *Coventry*[1] 758.2. *ASC* via JW*CC* 758.

**758.3** Indeterminate source, but here probably Marianus via JW*CC 758.*

**759** Common root: *Coventry*[1] 759. *ASC* via JW*CC* 759.

**760** Common root: *Coventry*[1] 760. *ASC* via JW*CC* 760, but not for the details as to who succeeded Æthelberht, which may be a guess based on the Kentish Royal Genealogy in JW*CC* (C), p. 48. In the chronicle itself JW*CC* places the accession of Eadberht Præn under 794, an entry which is itself reproduced in **794.3** below.

**761** Marianus via JW 757, or Norman Annals: *AU*, *ACad.*, *AG* 761.

**762** Common root: *Coventry*[1] 762. *ASC* via JW*CC* 762–3.

**763** Common root: *Coventry*[1] 763. Norman Annals: *AU*, *AG*, *ASN* 763.

**765** Common root: *Coventry*[1] 765. JW*CC* 765.

**766** Indeterminate source.

**767.1** Indeterminate source.

**767.2** Norman Annals: *AU*, *AG*, RT*Access*. 772.

**767.3** *ASC* via JW*CC* 768.

**768.1** Common root: *Coventry*[1] 768.1. Marianus via JW*CC* 768.

**768.2** Common root: *Coventry*[1] 768.2. The ultimate source of this information is *ARF* 801, which uses the same words to describe both the pope's role and the acclamations: "Leo papa coronam capiti eius imposuit, et a cuncto Romanorum populo adclamatum est, 'Carolo augusto a Deo coronato magno et pacifico imperatori uita et uictoria!'." Cf. *Chronicula*[1]

VA 868, which is derived from HF*Chron.*, 172–3; Norman Annals: *ACad.* 768 and 800.

**773.1** Common root: *Coventry*[1] 773.1. Norman Annals: *AU*, *ACad.*, *AG*, *ASN* 774.

**773.2** Common root: *Coventry*[1] 773.2. Marianus via JW*CC* 773.

**773.3** Common root: *Coventry*[1] 773.3, which gives a fuller version of this item. For the source, see the commentary on *Coventry*.

**774.1** Common root: *Coventry*[1] 774.1. *ASC* via JW*CC* 774. Cf. Norman Annals: *AU*, *AG* 786.

**774.2** Common root: *Coventry*[1] 774.2. Source unknown.

**774.3** Common root: *Coventry*[1] 774.3. *ASC* via JW*CC* 774.

**774.4** Common root: *Coventry*[1] 775; *APW* 775. *ASC* via JW*CC* 775.

**776.1** Norman Annals: *AU*, *AG*, *ASN* 786; *ACad.*, 785; *ASC* (E) 788.

**776.2** Indeterminate source.

**778.1** Common root: *Coventry*[1] 778.1; *APW* 778. This succession is noted in JW*CC* 778 and the Easter Table Annals in JW*CC* (C), p. 62 (in cycle 13, year 18 = 778), but without mentioning that *abbas Tilherus* had been abbot of *Berclea*. This entry needs to be considered alongside that under **915** below which states that Bishop Æthelhun was also an abbot of Berkeley. The latter entry corresponds with similar information in JW*CC*, but there the words *abbas de Beorclea* have been interlined "probably by scribe C[3]" (JW*CC*, 2:369, n. 10). McGurk suggests that John may well have deduced Æthelhun's connection with the abbey from a grant of Ealdorman Æthelred to Berkeley which is preserved in Heming's cartulary, for this settlement is attested by a certain *Æthelhun abbas* (ibid., citing *S* 218, which is printed in *SEHD*, no. 12). Given the date (A.D. 883) this document might well have supported such a deduction, but this explanation still leaves the reference to Tilhere unexplained, and there is no good reason to doubt that both men were former abbots of Berkeley. Indeed, Tilhere was certainly an abbot before he became bishop of Worcester, for he attests two charters of 759 and 760 as such (S 56 and 63; B*CS*, nos. 187 and 218), whilst Berkeley itself might well have been a route to preferment in the Hwiccan church. Its importance is now obscured by Earl Godwine's having suppressed its existence at some point between 1019 and 1053, but the estates and rights that comprised its *hyrnesse* ("its lordship") were evidently substantial (see Brian R. Kemp, "The Churches of Berkeley Hernesse," *Transactions of the Bristol and Gloucestershire Archaeological Society* 87 [1968]: 96–110; C. S. Taylor, "Berkeley Minster," *Transactions of the Bristol and Gloucestershire Archaeological Society* 19 [1894–1895]: 70–84). Berkeley was at other times ruled by women: for Abbess Ælfthryth, see *Heads I*, 208; for Abbess Ceolburg, see JW*CC* 805 together with the discussion in Foot, *Veiled Women*, 2:39–42. Houses of this kind were usually ruled by women in the Anglo-Saxon period, but there is little difficulty in Berkeley's having been ruled by abbots as well as abbesses, for men are occasionally attested elsewhere as heads of monasteries containing nuns as well as monks: see Taylor, "Berkeley Minster," 74; Foot, *Veiled Women*, 1:52, 153–54.

**778.2** Common root: *Coventry*[1] 778.2. Norman Annals: *AU*, *AG* 799.

**778.3** Norman Annals: *AU*, *AG*, *ACad.*, *ASN*, *ASBD* 790.

**779** Norman Annals: *AU*, *ASN* 792, *AG*, *ASBD* 791. Cf. Marianus via JW*CC* 789.

**780** Norman Annals: *AU*, *AG*, *ASN*, *ASBD* 793. Cf. Marianus via JW*CC* 792.

**781.1** Common root: *Coventry*[1] 781; *APW* 781. JW*CC* 781.

**781.2** Norman Annals: *AU*, *AG* 792.

**782** Common root: *Coventry*[1] 782. Norman Annals: *AU*, *ACad.*, *AG* 804.

**784** Common root: *Coventry*[1] 784; *APW* under both 785 and 850. *ASC* via JW*CC* 784, but inferring the succession of Brihtric.

**786.1** Common root: *Coventry*[1] 786. Either Marianus via JW*CC* 786 or Norman Annals: *AU*, *AG*, *ASN*, *ASBD* 786.

**786.2** Common root: *Coventry*[1] 787.1; *APW* 787.1. Marianus via JW*CC* 786.

**787.1** Common root: *Coventry*[1] 787.2; *APW* 787.2. Marianus via JW*CC* 786.

**787.2** This addition has been damaged by fire, but the text can be reconstructed using Dugdale, *Monasticon*, 2:300, since Dodsworth and Dugdale transcribed the text in the mid-seventeenth century when T had yet to suffer the damage inflicted by the fire of 1731. The entry also appears in *Quedam Chronica de Anglia*, a collection of extracts from chronicles and similar sources preserved in MS. London, B.L., Cotton Vitellius C.VIII, fols. 6r–21v, at 9vb (ed. Liebermann, *ANG*, 16–24, at 19): "Anno Domini .dcc.lxxx.vii. rex Merciorum Offa in Glaornensi pago in loco qui Winchelcumbe dicitur, monasterium construxit, in quo sanctimoniales constituit." Copied in a good mid-twelfth-century hand, the manuscript has been identified as belonging to the northern monastery of Rievaulx (see *CBMLC*, 3:107, no. Z19.119; *MLGB*, p. 159, n. 8). It has been assumed that the text itself was compiled there (e.g. Freeman, *Narratives of the New Order*, 116–17), but its exact origin is quite uncertain. It is largely comprised of material derived from WM*GP* and JW*CC*, and seems to have been compiled soon after the early editions of these works appeared, since William, bishop of Exeter (1107–1137), is mentioned as being elderly but not yet deceased in a sentence added to an extract (fol. 11vb) from Malmesbury's account of the bishops of Exeter (WM*GP*, 2.95). It follows that *Quedam Chronica de Anglia* was produced c.1130×1137, a decade or so before *Winchcombe*.

**787.2** has generally been accepted by historians as providing reliable evidence that Winchcombe was founded in two stages, that King

Cenwulf (798–821), far from creating the house from scratch, took over and enlarged a project begun by King Offa in 787 (e.g. Blair, *Church*, 122, 288; Foot, *Veiled Women*, 2:239). Levison, *EC*, 31, 257–59, and Sims-Williams, *RLWE*, 165–66, found support for this argument in the presence of a church dedicated to St Peter within the town and in the presence of an emphasis on the cult of St Peter in the Winchcombe Sacramentary, a missal produced in the late tenth century for Abbot Germanus but later given to Fleury (see Lapidge, "Germanus," 103–6), since it is known that Offa had a policy of establishing monasteries dedicated to St Peter. It is certainly true that the church that is to be found serving the town's parishioners in the later Middle Ages was dedicated to Peter, and it is not unlikely that it was originally part of a minster complex. The church was certainly owned by the abbey in the later Middle Ages, and it was situated almost immediately to its west (see Goscelin's *Vita S. Kenelmi*, § 16; Stephen R. Bassett, "A Probable Mercian Royal Mausoleum at Winchcombe, Gloucestershire," *Antiquaries Journal* 65 [1985]: 82–100, esp. fig. 1). Early Anglo-Saxon minster complexes usually had two or more churches, often loosely aligned on an east-west axis (see Blair, *Church*, 199–201). It was a common pattern that in the wake of the late tenth-century monastic reforms churches dedicated to St Peter were supplanted in importance by those dedicated to St Mary. The classic case in point is Worcester where the church of St Mary built by Bishop Oswald gradually eclipsed the older cathedral church of St Peter (see Baker and Holt, *Gloucester and Worcester*, 134–35, and the works cited there). It follows that St Peter's at Winchcombe may well have been the major ecclesiastical centre in the town before the late tenth century, only for it to be handed over to the townspeople for their use, as it were, while the reformed community kept or perhaps built St Mary's for themselves. It is also true that the apostle is treated as though he were a patron of the abbey in the litany of the Winchcombe Sacramentary: his name is written in majuscules and a threefold invocation is specified; of the other saints listed only Benedict figures so prominently, while the names of the saints identified as the abbey's patrons in twelfth-century documents, Kenelm and Mary, are merely written in majuscules (ed. Anselme Davril, *The Winchcombe Sacramentary*, HBS 109 [Woodbridge: Boydell Press, 1995], 261). Offa's policy of assembling a network of monasteries dedicated to St Peter is revealed, finally, by a privilege of Pope Hadrian I (772–795) which is preserved in *Liber diurnus* (Vat. 93, which is quoted under **818.3** below). This privilege gives orders that the monasteries which the king had built or acquired and had dedicated to his patron, the blessed Peter, were to remain under his authority, that of his wife Cynethryth, and that of their descendants. Bath and Cookham, both located at the southern limits of Mercian territory, are two monasteries known to have been assimilated under this policy (Levison, *EC*, 30; Sims-Williams, *RLWE*, 159–65). It follows that **787.2** can be made to fit neatly into the little that is known about King Offa's monastic strategy and an entirely plausible scenario for the history of Winchcombe.

It needs to be stressed, however, that the annal on which these speculations rest does not carry the same weight as the three charters which imply that the abbey was founded by Cenwulf alone. It is true that the texts of all three charters are problematic, but all appear to have a genuine basis of some kind (see **811.1–3** and **818.3** below). The argument for Offa's role hangs, meanwhile, on the evidence of a marginal addition which, given its presence in *Quedam Chronica de Anglia*, might well originate from non-Winchcombe sources. Moreover, the status of this addition needs to be considered alongside **798**, the other item inserted by T[4]. **798** is a brief account of Cenwulf's role in the foundation which, like **787.2**, is echoed in almost the same words in *Quedam Chronica de Anglia* (see below). The item clearly derives, however, from WM*GP*, 4.156, an account of the foundation which predates the present chronicle and which is itself derived from Cenwulf's foundation charter (see **811.3** below). But **798** differs in one crucial detail: whereas William states that Cenwulf built the abbey with *ingens et nostris temporibus incredibilis munificentia*, it states that "he assembled in [Winchcombe] monks three hundred in number." This variant may be an embellishment of William's version, since it replaces vague praise with a precise but fanciful claim. It follows that if the author of these two items could invent this kind of detail he might also have fabricated the claims made for Offa in **787.2**.

**789** Common root: *Coventry*[1] 789. *ASC* via JW*CC* 789.

**790** Common root: *Coventry*[1] 790.1. *ASC* via JW*CC* 790.

**791** Common root: *Coventry*[1] 790.2. *ASC* via JW*CC* 790.

**792** Common root: *Coventry*[1] 792. *ASC* via JW*CC* 792.

**793** Common root: *Coventry*[1] 793. *ASC* via JW*CC* 793.

**794.1** Common root: *Coventry*[1] 794.1. *ASC* via JW*CC* 794.

**794.2** Common root: *Coventry*[1] 794.2. For this information the compiler may have used the list of Bernician and Deiran kings in JW*CC* (C), p. 51: "Quo [Æthelberhto] a suis interfecto, Osbaldus regnum suscepit, et paucis diebus tenuit, cui Eardulfus successit."

**794.3** Common root: *Coventry*[1] 794.3. *ASC* via JW*CC* 794.

**795.1** Common root: *Coventry*[1] 795. *ASC* via JW*CC* 794.

**795.2** Cenwulf is also recorded as the founder of Winchcombe in Goscelin of St Bertin, *Vita S. Kenelmi, regis et martyris* (*BHL* 4641n + p + r), § 12 (ed. Love, *Three Lives*, 50–88, at 66).

**795.3** From the accounts accompanying the Mercian Royal Genealogy in JW*CC* (C) p. 50: "Cui uir magnificus Coenulfus filius Cuthberhti trinepotis Pybbe regis successit. Huic regina sua Ælfthrytha filias duas Quendrytham et Burgenhildam sanctumque Kenelmum genuit. Decedens autem anno regni sui uicesimo quarto, Wincelcumbe sepultus requiescit, et heredem regni filium suum sanctum Kenelmum reliquit. . . ." The names of the ancestors connecting Cenwulf to Pybba, meanwhile, could have been supplied from the stemma itself which reads in reverse order: "Coenwulf, Cuthberht, Bassa, Cynreou, Centuuine, Cunduualh, Cenuualh, Pybba."

**795.4** This addition derives from WM*GR*, 1.87–89, and was probably inserted at the same time as the documents quoted by William were inserted under **811.3–5** below.

**798** Though substantially damaged by fire, the text of this entry can be recovered from the transcript made by Dodsworth and Dugdale (*Monasticon*, 2:300). It is also quoted in *Quedam Chronica de Anglia*, Cotton Vitellius C.VIII, fols. 9vb–10va: "Anno dccxcviii rex Merciorum Kenulfus Winchelcumbense monasterium construxit, et in eo monachos numero ccc collocauit. Ecclesia eiusdem monasterii dedicata est a .xiii. episcopis, quorum princeps erat Wulfredus Cantuarie archiepiscopus" (cf. Liebermann, *ANG*, 19). On the status of this passage and its derivation from WM*GP*, 4.156, see **787.2** above.

**798** is very distantly related to an entry in the "Anglo-Irish Annals" which has inspired the dubious theory—suggested by Robin Flower, "Manuscripts of Irish Interest in the British Museum," *Analecta Hibernica* 2 (1931): 292–340, at 319, and later developed by Aubrey Gwynn, "Some Unpublished Texts from the Black Book of Christ Church, Dublin," *Analecta Hibernica* 16 (1946): 281–337, at 313—that they were derived from a chronicle maintained at Winchcombe Abbey. To explain, the earliest surviving versions of these annals—the so-called *Annals of Multifernan* (MS. Dublin, Trinity College, 347, fols. 394r–403v) and the Annals of Christ Church, Dublin (ed. Gwynn, "Black Book," 324–29)—record the foundation of *Wycumbe* under 797, and the thinness of their coverage of events before 1050—there are just seven entries for the eighth century in the *Annals of Multifernan*—gives the entry a certain prominence. Its chronological location shows that the entry is an echo of the present item, albeit a very distant one, but there is little likelihood that this item reached the Anglo-Irish Annals *through* the *Winchcombe Chronicle*, where it is a late addition in the margins of the text. There are, as Martin Brett, "Canterbury's Perspective on Church Reform and Ireland, 1070–1115," in *Ireland and Europe in the Twelfth Century: Reform and Renewal*, ed. Damien Bracken and Dagmar Ó Riain-Raedel [Dublin: Four Courts Press, 2006], 13–35, at 34–35, points out, no other distinctive points of contact with the "Anglo-Irish Annals." The item's appearance in *Quedam Chronica de Anglia* suggests, moreover, that it may have been transmitted through Cistercian channels, for this work is preserved in a manuscript from Rievaulx (i.e. MS. Cotton Vitellius C.VIII: see **787.2** above) whilst the substantial number of items referring to signal events in the history of the Cistercian movement in the "Anglo-Irish Annals" suggests that the underlying English (or Scottish) text may have been of Cistercian origin. Other arguments to this effect are marshalled by Bernadette Williams, "The Dominican Annals of Dublin," in *Medieval Dublin II*, ed. Seán Duffy (Dublin: Four Courts Press, 2001), 142–68 (esp. 145–50). The present editor is grateful to Dr Nicholas Evans for having drawn our attention to this issue.

**799** Marianus via JW*CC* 795.

**800.1** The only place where JW*CC* has all the information found here is in John's "Papal Annals" (C) p. 33: "Leo . . . Hunc Romani in letania maiori captum excecauerunt et radicitus linguam eius amputauerunt, sed ex diuina gratia reddita sibi est loquela sine lingua." The entry in the main chronicle, JW*CC* 796 (following Marianus, VA 819), lacks the final clause, though there is similar information in MS. B where the words *sed Deo iuuante uisum recepit et loquelam* have been added in the margin presumably because B's editors recognised that this entry was incomplete. Marianus, 818–819/796–797, also lacks the final clause. Cf. also *Chronicula*[1] VA 868, which reflects the influence of HF*Chron.*, 173: "Romani captum Leonem papam excecauerunt et linguam eius absciderunt, sed Dei gratia postmodum reddita sibi pristina loquela locutus est et a Karolo imperatore ulciscente illum in sede sua restitutus est." *Coventry*[1] 796.1 would appear to represent the version of the annal found in the common root, the present one having been influenced by the "Papal Annals."

**800.2** Norman Annals: *AU*, *ACad.*, *AG*, *ASN*, *ASBD* 800. Cf. JW*CC* 800.

**801** Common root: *Coventry*[1] 797. *ASC* via JW*CC* 797.

**802** Common root: *Coventry*[1] 798. JW*CC* 798.

**803** Common root: *Coventry*[1] 799. Marianus via JW*CC* 799.

**804** Common root: *Coventry*[1] 800. *ASC* via JW*CC* 800.

**805** JW*CC* 800, but JW*CC* has *occiditur* rather than *martyrizatur*.

**807** Common root: *Coventry*[1] 803. *ASC* via JW*CC* 803–4.

**809.1** Common root: *Coventry*[1] 805. Following *ASC*, JW*CC* 805 reports the death of Cuthred, but not the accession of Baldred, who ruled in Kent from 823 until 824. He is briefly mentioned s.a. 823. The inference that he succeeded immediately may derive from the accounts accompanying the Kentish Royal Genealogy in JW*CC* (C), p. 48: "Cuthredus . . . decessit. Cui Baldredus successit, et anno dominice incarnationis iuxta Dionisium dcccxxiii. a rege Westsaxonum Ecgbrihto expulsus est regno."

**809.2** *ASC* via JW*CC* 805. The absence of reference to Ceolburg as abbess of Berkeley means that the compiler may have used the earlier version of JW*CC* 805 (attested in H and L) rather than the later version (inserted in C by $C^3$ and attested in B and P).

**809.3** Norman Annals: *AU*, *ACad.*, *AG* 808; *ASBD* 809.

**810** Marianus via JW*CC* 808.

**811.1** This sentence introduces the three foundation documents—a privilege of Pope Leo III (795–816), a foundation charter of Cenwulf, king of Mercia (797–821), and a privilege of Pope Paschal I (817–824)—which were inserted into the common root at or for Winchcombe. The three documents all present difficulties and the charter has certainly been forged to some extent, but as Levison argued in *EC*, 255–57, there are reasons to think that all three contain genuine elements. The notes that follow will revise these arguments, but it will be useful to begin by examining the ninth-century evidence for the origins and status of the minster at Winchcombe. For it is clear from the contents of two charters the authenticity of which is not in doubt that Cenwulf did indeed set up this minster to be the centre of a network of dependent monasteries and estates.

The earlier of the two charters (S 1436; B*CS*, no. 384) is a record dating from about 827 of the resolution of a dispute between *Cwoenðryð*, abbess of *Suthmynstre* (apparently, Minister-in-Thanet), and Wulfred, archbishop of Canterbury (805–832). Its contents include three details that are helpful for present purposes. The first is that Cwenthryth is named as the daughter and heiress of King Cenwulf. The second detail is that for the meeting which brought about the final reconciliation Wulfred is said to have travelled to the *prouincia Hwicciorum* to meet Cwenthryth at a place called *Oslafeshlau*. This detail implies that she was then residing in a region corresponding to the diocese of Worcester and containing Winchcombe rather than in Kent. The third detail is that it was a condition of this settlement that the names of the lands given to Wulfred were to be erased *de antiquis priuilegiis quae sunt aet Wincelcumbe*. It follows that Southminster was in some sense a dependency of an *Eigenkloster* at Winchcombe, where there were records of its properties and dependencies. On S 1436, its authenticity, Cwenthryth, and the causes of her dispute with Wulfred, see Brooks, *Canterbury*, 133–36, 180–97, and 322–23; Simon D. Keynes, "The Control of Kent in the Ninth Century," *Early Medieval Europe* 2 (1993): 111–31 (esp. 117–20, 125 n. 68); Keynes, *Councils of* Clofesho, 12, n. 56. See also S 165, a charter issued in 811 which she attests has *Quoenðryð filia regis*, and S 1423, for the settlement of another dispute between Archbishop Wulfred and Abbess Cwenthryth.

The later of the two charters (S 1442; B*CS*, no. 1088) is the record of another dispute settlement, one which involved an investigation into the status of five hides at Upton-on-Severn which were then in the possession of a certain Wullaf. The estate had once belonged to Winchcombe, but it had been leased by Abbess *Cyneðryð* to Wullaf's father for three lives, and that lease had been renewed for another three lives by Abbess Ælfflæd. In 897, however, the Mercian ealdorman Æthelwulf (d. 901) investigated the *hereditarii libri* of King Cenwulf and found in their texts that the heirs who came after him did not have the freedom to make grants from the *hereditas Cenuulfi quae pertinet ad Wincelcumbe* for longer than a single lifetime. Æthelwulf duly annulled *Cyneðryð*'s and Ælfflæd's grants to Wullaf and demanded that he return the original charters. The land was granted to Wullaf once again, but for his lifetime only, and it was not to revert to Winchcombe after his death; rather, it was to be given to the church of Worcester in order to renew the peace between the *familiae* of Worcester and Winchcombe. The charter is attested, finally, by three women (Æthelswyth, Wigswith, and Lulla), who may have been members of the community (see Foot, *Veiled Women*, 2:240). On S 1442, its authenticity, and the origins of the dispute between Winchcombe and Worcester, see Finberg, *ECWM*, no. 86.

These two ninth-century charters confirm, in short, that Cenwulf had bequeathed to Winchcombe a *hereditas* which was administered from this minster and which comprised both local properties and at least one other minster (and one located as far away as Kent) which was itself the owner of further properties. They would provide still more confirmation for this point if it were accepted that the *Cyneðryð* of S 1442 was an error for *Cwoenðryð*, allowing us to infer that the abbess of Winchcombe was the daughter of Cenwulf who was also abbess of Southminster and heir to the king's *hereditas*. Levison, *EC*, 252, opts for this identification, but Sims-Williams, *RLWE*, 165–66 and n. 107, would question it: having developed Levison's suggestion that Winchcombe was one of the monasteries "founded" by King Offa, he goes on to suggest that this *Cyneðryð* was Offa's queen, Cynethryth, who was the abbess of Cookham in 798 (S 1258).

It has been shown under **787.2** above, however, that the evidential basis for Offa's having founded Winchcombe is actually quite weak. It is true, as Sims-Williams points out, that records explicitly identifying the daughter of Cenwulf called Cwenthryth as the abbess of Winchcombe are lacking, but it is not hard to explain why such information may have been suppressed. For in the late eleventh century, Cenwulf's daughter was remembered as the villain in the legend of Winchcombe's patron, St

Kenelm. According to the version that was current after the Conquest, it was this Cwenthryth who brought about his murder and who then attempted to prevent the discovery of the body with an oppressive edict: see Goscelin, *Vita S. Kenelmi*, ed. Love, *Three Lives*, 50–88 (esp. §§ 1–2, 10, 16), and **819** below. In the absence of a contemporary record of what happened she cannot be proven innocent of these claims, but it seems likely that her posthumous reputation has, as in the case of many other powerful Anglo-Saxon women, been transmogrified by hagiological legerdemain and monastic misogyny (see Paul Hayward, *Kingship, Childhood and Martyrdom in Anglo-Saxon England*, forthcoming). But regardless of whether she was or was not guilty, it will have complicated matters for the monks of the post-Conquest abbey if their archive recorded that she had been their abbess. Indeed, as will emerge under **811.2** and **818.3** below, some of the linguistic wobbles in the three foundation documents can be explained as the result of the deletion of words naming her as the founding *abbatissa*. It is surely best, then, to follow Levison and to accept the natural inference that Cenwulf chose Cwenthryth to be the abbess of the chief *Eigenkloster* of his branch of the Mercian royal house. Indeed, that appointment is so likely that it probably happened even if the *Cyneðryð* of S 1442 refers to a different woman. As for S 1442's Ælfflæd, it is natural—as Sims-Williams, *RLWE*, 167, admits—to identify her with another member of the family, the *Alfleda* who is said in the various versions of the legend of St Wigstan (see **850** below) to have been the daughter of Cenwulf's brother and successor, King Ceolwulf I (821–823). Cf. Alan T. Thacker, "Kings, Saints and Monasteries in Pre-Viking Mercia," *Midland History* 10 (1985): 1–25, at 8–12; Brooks, *Canterbury*, 182.

**811.2** This privilege of Pope Leo III (795–816) presents considerable problems, but most seem to have been inherited from an earlier attempt to repair the text. To explain: there are two medieval copies, that in T and that preserved in the abbey's thirteenth-century cartulary (*Landboc*, 1:21–22). They are almost identical, but the latter cannot derive from T, for it has two variants which are clearly better (*impensius* for *impentius* and *in piis* for *impiis*) and one which makes no difference to the sense but is closer to formulas which underpin the text (*ausu* for *auso*). Its other variant, *iuxta* where T has *iuxta ordinem*, is an obvious mistake. If the later copy does not derive from T, it follows that they depend on a common ancestor and that *impentius* and *impiis* are errors introduced in the process of entering the "received text" of the privilege into *Winchcombe*. By referring to the text in *Landboc* these two minor errors may be resolved, but that still leaves the many problems of the "received text." A way of clarifying its contents is provided, however, by the models preserved in the so-called *Liber diurnus*, a collection of formulas which, though not the actual formulary of the papal chancery, contains many formulas which were used in the eighth and ninth centuries to make papal documents. (The three manuscripts of *Liber diurnus* are of northern Italian origin: see the introduction to Foerster's edition, *Liber diurnus*, esp. 36–68; Thomas F. X. Noble, "Literacy and the Papal Government in Late Antiquity and the Early Middle Ages," in *The Uses of Literacy in Early Medieval Europe*, ed. Rosamond McKitterick [Cambridge: Cambridge University Press, 1990], 82–108, esp. 95–96.) The present privilege does not exactly match any of the models known through *Liber diurnus*, but contains extensive echoes of, among others, number 86, a formula devised for the abbot of Piumarola.

The arenga, the elaborate preamble in which the pope is made to explain why it is right that the apostolic see should favour the petition, is almost identical, for example, with the opening sentences of number 86. The only significant change is the substitution of *ad stabilitatem nobilitatemque tue hereditatis* for number 86's *ad stabilitatem piorum*. The sanction, the final section of the document in which punishments and rewards in the next life are promised according to whether people have contravened or observed the injunctions contained in the privilege, contains echoes of several different formulas. There is, for instance, a further echo of formula 86 in the second sentence of the anathema: *Si quis autem quod non optamus nefario ausu presumpserit . . .* (cf. also *Liber diurnus*, Vat. 96). But the anathema continues with a clause closer to formula 89: *Sciat se anathematis uinculo esse innodatum, et a regno Dei alienum* (cf. also *Liber diurnus*, Vat. 86, 96). The blessing is also closer to formula 89: *At uero qui obseruator precepti gratiam atque misericordiam uitamque aeternam a misericordissimo Domino Deo nostro consequi mereatur* (cf. also *Liber diurnus*, Vat. 86). There are also, finally, echoes for the phrase *cuius uel immeriti uicem gerimus* in formulas 90 (*cuius nos etsi impares meritis . . . uices gerimus*), 96 (*cuius meritis impares . . . uices gerimus*) and 97 (*cuius meritis impares uices tamen gerimus*).

The intervening, dispositive, section of the privilege also presents a complex pattern. The second of its two sentences is relatively straightforward: it frees the monastery where the petitioner's body will rest from all forms of secular service and, in the manner of other Mercian royal charters of this period (cf. S 193, King Berhtwulf's charter for Eanmund, abbot of Breedon), it associates that freedom with the performance of prayer for the donor's soul. But some essential element is missing or has been corrupted in the first of the two sentences. Indeed, that sentence seems to represent a conflation of two distinct ideas. It uses, on the one hand, words drawn from a provision of the Piumarola privilege which placed that house under the jurisdiction of the pope's own holy church:

> Igitur quia postulasti a nobis quatenus monasterium sanctae Dei genetricis semper uirginis Mariae domine nostrae situm in locum qui uocatur plumbariolo territorio aquinense priuilegiis sedis apostolicae infulis decoretur, ut sub iurisdicione sanctae nostrae cui deo auctore deseruimus ecclesiae constitutum, nullius alterius ecclesiae iurisdicionibus submittatur (cf. also *Liber Diurnus*, Vat. 32, 77).
>
> Therefore, since you have asked us that the monastery of the holy mother of God, the ever-virgin, our lady Mary, sited in the place which is called Piumarola in the region of Abruzzi, shall be adorned with the privileges, the emblems, of the apostolic see so that, constituted under the jurisdiction of our holy church in which we serve God the Creator, it shall be subjected to the jurisdiction of no other church.

The present privilege retains a number of verbal echoes of this sentence, but the only remaining echo of its legal substance is a prepositional phrase which places the monastery under Cenwulf's authority (*sub iure ditionis tue*). For the sentence has been taken over by material similar to that found in number 93, a formula which was devised in order to legitimise Offa's creation of an extended network of monasteries and estates and to ensure its survival in perpetuity under his own, his wife's, and his descendants' authority (see **818.3** below). In the present version, however, these ideas are developed further than in number 93: there is more emphasis on the grand scale of the monastic network which has been assembled (e.g. *omnia monasteria uel uaria loca sita in ipsa insula Saxonia*), and the privilege also provides for an unrestricted power to bestow his minsters and lands "along with everything that pertains to them upon whomever he prefers, either upon pious places or upon any persons whatsoever." The recipient of this prerogative is undefined, but it is probably the monastery at the centre of this lordship or its head, since the phrase *sub iure ditionis tue* implies that the subject of the *uti*-clause is someone other than Cenwulf himself. The usual intention of such clauses was not, however, to allow the abbess the freedom to dispose of the endowment (cf. S 1442 and **811.1** above), but to protect it from resentful kinsmen. Earlier Anglo-Saxon founders usually sought rights of this kind when their grants included estates they had received from their ancestors, for the tenure of such lands was often restricted by rules which prevented them being bequeathed outside the family. It was necessary to legitimise the abrogation of these restrictions in order to avert the danger that kinsmen would attempt to reclaim them after the founder's death.

In his edition, Holtzmann, *PUE*, 3:124–25 (no. 1), attempts to resolve the problems with this sentence by repairing the text with the help of the Piumarola privilege. He edits it as follows. The parallels with formula 86 are underlined and his emendations are *italicised:*

> Et quoniam tua summa excellentia postulauit a nobis, *quatenus Wincecumba* pre omnibus monasteriis uel uariis locis que *iuste* conquisiuit, uel pre manibus detinere *uidetur*, iustitia parentum tuorum, *queque* de adquisito iuste et rationabiliter tibi allata sunt, hec omnia monasteria uel uaria loca sita in ipsa insula Saxonia *priuilegiis* sedis apostolice infulis *decorentur*, uti sub iure *dictionis* tue, *cui* cum omnibus sibi pertinentibus largiri maluerit, siue in piis locis uel quibuslibet personis, liberam habeat potestatem.

> And since your high Excellency has requested of us *that Winchcombe* before all the monasteries and diverse places which it procured *justly* or which it is known to have held beforehand by the judicial rulings of your parents, *and which* have been conveyed to you justly and reasonably by purchase—all of these monasteries and diverse places sited in the same Saxon island shall be adorned with the privileges, emblems, of the apostolic see, so that, by the right *of your authority*, it should have a free capacity to bestow <them> on whomever it prefers together with everything belonging to it, either on pious places or on any persons whatsoever.

As a way of bringing readers closer to the original texts of damaged diplomas, this approach has something to be said for it, but in this case it has produced dubious results. The replacement of *quamuis multa* with *quatenus Wincecumba* and the transformation of the ablative participle *uirente* into the verb *decorentur* are plausible enough, but much stronger intervention is required before the sentence will make proper sense. *Wincecumba* has been left as a hanging subject when the topic changes to *hec omnia monasteria uel uaria loca*, since all the verbs in the *quatenus-sunt* clause govern its sub-clauses—none governs *Wincecumba*. The *hec-decorentur* clause, meanwhile, needs to be coordinated with the rest of the sentence. The text preserved in the manuscripts is simply too far away from formula 86 for it to be taken as the basis of a convincing reconstruction.

It may well be the case, moreover, that any attempt to reconstruct a coherent text on the basis of the existing material is entirely wrongheaded, for the presence of echoes from several different formulae, the conflation of different legal ideas, and the grammatical incongruities suggest that two or perhaps even three privileges may lie behind the present text. This suggestion might be thought to lend support to

Chaplais' theory that the document was concocted with the help of the *Liber diurnus* ("Some Diplomas," 335–36), but if anything it favours the elaboration of Levison's theory that its many imperfections are the product, not of outright forgery, but of the effects of dampness and rough handling on the papyrus on which papal documents were issued before the eleventh century (*EC*, 255). The suggestion, in short, is that the scribe was making an earnest attempt to piece together a viable text without realising that he was dealing with the fragments of more than one privilege. The intention of one of them may have been similar to that of the Piumarola privilege which prohibits any bishop of any church whatsoever exercising authority over the monastery. If so, it may have been addressed to the head of the minster. The purpose of another may have been to permit the abrogation of the customary rules of inheritance which pertained to the various minsters and estates which Cenwulf wished to grant to Winchcombe. It remains possible, of course, that we are simply dealing with a single original that was put together in an unusual fashion or based on a more complex but otherwise unknown formula; but the separate existence of a privilege placing constraints of some kind on the ability of the episcopate to exercise jurisdiction over the churches of Cenwulf's *hereditas* has something to be said for it, since it would help to explain the origins of his struggle with Archbishop Wulfred. For two of the latter's complaints against the king and his daughter, Abbess Cwenthryth, were that they had defrauded the archiepiscopal see of the obedience due to it in respect of Southminster, and that he had been "dishonoured" in a great many places within his *porochia* (S 1436; B*CS*, no. 384). The reassertion of episcopal authority over monasteries was also a central theme of the canons of the synod which Wulfred convened at Chelsea in 816 (see H&S, 3:579–84), the synod at which he asserted his ideological position of the eve of the dispute (see Brooks, *Canterbury*, 175–91). Cf. Cubitt, *Church Councils*, 198–99.

In any case, if the privilege were an outright forgery then it would be natural to expect that its text would show much greater coherence, that it would clearly name Winchcombe as the minster that was to preside over Cenwulf's *hereditas*, and that it would include a dating clause of the kind normally found at the end of a papal privilege. The rights sought and granted are in keeping, moreover, with an early ninth-century context where the need to prevent their own kinsmen attempting to usurp their endowments by invoking the traditional rules of inheritance associated with folkland was a major issue confronting founders of monasteries.

Papal privileges issued or forged in the twelfth century for monasteries typically emphasise clauses designed to protect them from dangers of a quite different order, chiefly the efforts of bishops to use their rights of visitation and especially their sacramental powers, their monopoly on the performance of ordinations and consecrations, to assert their authority over the monasteries within their dioceses, and to exploit their resources. Thus privileges of this date often have clauses allowing the abbot to ask a bishop of his own choosing to perform consecrations when required, or prohibiting the bishop of a diocese to enter a monastery to say masses, and so on. Papal privileges issued for monasteries in or close to the eighth century often show an awareness of the threat represented by diocesan authority, but they are much more restrained when it comes to circumscribing the bishop's rights. Thus the privilege which Pope Constantine (708–715) granted for Bermondsey and Woking requires the bishop of the diocese to ordain as priests and deacons those persons whomever the "congregation" chooses for these roles, but he may still inquire into "those matters which canonically belong to such an ordination"; the congregation is to elect its abbot, but the right to consecrate the abbot belongs to the bishop. The emphasis here is on a just division of roles as opposed to a complete assertion of monastic independence: "And that our intention may be shown in brief, let the bishop inquire into those matters which belong to canonical care, and let the abbot with his *praepositus* and the elders of the congregation take order in regard to the goods and expenditure of the monastery as they may see fit" (JL 2148; B*CS* 133). The authenticity of this privilege is defended and its dispositive section is translated by Frank M. Stenton in "Medeshamstede and its Colonies," in *Historical Essays in Honour of James Tait*, ed. John G. Edwards et al. (Manchester: Printed for the Subscribers, 1933), 313–26, at 319–21; repr. in idem, *Preparatory to 'Anglo-Saxon England': Being the Collected Papers of Frank Merry Stenton*, ed. Doris M. Stenton (Oxford: Clarendon Press, 1970), 179–92, at 185–88. See also Keynes, *Councils of* Clofesho, 42–43.

A papal privilege forged in the twelfth century might well contain archaic clauses of the kind found in the present document, but one would also expect a strong and rather clumsy attempt to intrude a claim to an exemption of the later type. It seems likely, therefore, that this entry preserves the remains of one, if not several, genuine early ninth-century papal privileges. On the *Liber diurnus*, papal privileges, and ecclesiastical jurisdiction, see Hans H. Anton, *Studien zu den Klosterprivilegien der Päpste im frühen Mittelalter*, Beiträge zur Geschichte und Quellenkunde des Mittelalters 4 (Berlin: de Gruyter, 1975), esp. 89–92; Barbara H. Rosenwein, *Negotiating Space: Power, Restraint and Privileges of Immunity in Early Medieval Europe* (Manchester: Manchester University Press, 1999), esp. 106–9, 171–72, and the works cited there.

**811.3** The present document (S 167) purports to be a charter of Cenwulf, king of Mercia (797–821), issued on the occasion of the dedication of his foundation at Winchcombe Abbey in AD 811. T provides the only medieval copy now extant, and it has been printed several times: e.g. B*CS*, no. 338, and *Landboc*, 1:18–21. There can be no doubt that the document is in part, if not entirely, a forgery. It contains numerous chronological inconsistencies. The dating clause is internally consistent—9 November 811 falls in the fourth indiction and in the sixteenth year of King Cenwulf's reign—but it is at odds with the reference to the confirmation of Cenwulf's scheme by Pope Paschal I (817–824) as well as Pope Leo III (797–821): *hereditas quam domnus Leo papa primus affirmabat cum suo priuilegio, et postea Paschalis summus pontifex cum preceptis sue auctoritatis*. The dating clause is also incompatible with the witness list, since it includes Cuthred, who died in 807 (see *ASC* (BC) 807). Cuthred is said, moreover, to have been present when the church was dedicated in 811. As for its provisions, perhaps the most problematic is the sanctuary clause. It is true that there were in the later Middle Ages a number of churches in England which claimed the right to provide a form of asylum that went beyond the usual forms defined in law, and that most of these churches claimed that they had received this right by the gift of an Anglo-Saxon king. The problem is that in almost every case these claims depend on documents or narrative texts of relatively late date and doubtful reliability.

King Edgar is supposed, for example, to have granted to Ramsey rights of asylum for people accused of treason against the king and of any other offence (S 798; B*CS*, no. 1310); but the charter is a manifest forgery which has been attributed to Osbert of Clare (Chaplais, "Original Charters," 92–95). Edgar is supposed to have granted to the abbot and monks of Glastonbury the right to liberate those condemned to death wherever they encountered them (S 783), but this charter is also a forgery, one which may be the work of William of Malmesbury since it appears in the C-version of WM*GR*, 2.150C.4, as well as in his *De antiquitate Glastonie ecclesie*, § 60 (ed. John Scott, *The Early History of Glastonbury* [Woodbridge: Boydell Press, 1981], 124–25). See also Lesley Abrams, *Anglo-Saxon Glastonbury: Church and Endowment* (Woodbridge: Boydell Press, 1996), 128–30. King Æthelstan is supposed to have granted to the minster at Beverley the right to provide sanctuary for thirty days and to have defined its boundaries, but these claims are first recorded in Alfred of Beverley, *Libertates ecclesiæ sancti Johannis de Beverlik cum privilegiis apostolicis et episcopalibus*, §§ 4–8 (ed. James Raine, *Sanctuarium Dunelmense et Sanctuarium Beverlacense*, Surtees Society Publications 5 [London: J. B. Nichols, 1837], 97–108, at 98–101). The charter purporting to be a record of the grant (S 451; B*CS* 645) is a fourteenth-century forgery (see Hart, *ECNE*, no. 120a). The late medieval sanctuary at Abingdon's peculiar of Culham is supposed to have been established by King Cenwulf, but his charters concerning this estate are manifest forgeries and do not, in any case, make an explicit grant of such rights (S 166, 183–84; *Charters of Abingdon Abbey*, ed. Susan E. Kelly, 2 pts., Anglo-Saxon Charters 7–8 [Oxford: Oxford University Press for the British Academy, 2000–2001], nos. 8–10). There is no sign, furthermore, that Culham was regarded as a chartered sanctuary in the twelfth century. It was then held to be free from all forms of secular jurisdiction, but the estate figures in the *Hist. Abbend.*, 2.27, 303, a work datable to between 1164 and 1170, not as a place of refuge for thieves but as a property which suffered from their depredations.

The great age of the chartered sanctuary seems to have been the thirteenth to fifteenth centuries: see John C. Cox, *Sanctuaries and Sanctuary Seekers of Mediaeval England* (London: G. Allen, 1911), 48–226, and now Gervase Rosser, "Sanctuary and Social Negotiation in Medieval England," in *The Cloister and the World: Essays in Medieval History in Honour of Barbara Harvey*, ed. John Blair and Brian Golding (Oxford: Clarendon Press, 1996), 57–79 (esp. 70–71, 75–76), who provides an excellent survey with many references to recent literature. But the pattern of the evidence assembled above—the dating of these forgeries and of the historical texts in which these claims first make their appearance—suggests that a minor fashion for claiming rights of this kind took hold after the Conquest. See, likewise, *RRAN Will.*, no. 22, a forgery which Eleanor Searle dates to around 1166–1167 in *The Chronicle of Battle Abbey*, OMT (Oxford: Clarendon Press, 1980), 70, n. 1. To be sure, there is a single "early" instance of an alleged royal grant of sanctuary rights in the *Historia de Sancto Cuthberto* (*BHL* 2024–2025), § 13 (ed. Ted Johnson-South, *Historia de Sancto Cuthberto: A History of Saint Cuthbert and a Record of his Patrimony* [Woodbridge: Boydell Press, 2002], 52–53), where Cuthbert is said to have extracted from the viking king Guthred the right of asylum for thirty-seven days for anyone fleeing to his shrine. But the most recent editor of this text has argued against the usual theory that it was begun in the mid-tenth century, dating it instead to the mid- or late-eleventh century (see Johnson-South, *Historia de Sancto Cuthberto*, 25–36; cf. R. F. Hall, "The Sanctuary of St Cuthbert," in *St Cuthbert, His Cult and His Community to AD 1200*, ed. Gerald Bonner, David W. Rollason, and Clare Stancliffe [Woodbridge: Boydell Press, 1989], 425–36). The pattern suggests, in short, that the present document's sanctuary clause is likely to have been invented in the late eleventh or early twelfth century.

There are, however, aspects of the charter which suggest that some genuine or near-genuine material lies behind the existing text. Its insistence, for example, that the properties of the *hereditas* were not to be granted or leased without an agreement on reversion at the end of the leaseholder's lifetime matches the provision that Ealdorman Æthelwulf is said to have found in the *hereditarii libri* of King Cenwulf when he annulled Abbess Cynethryth's grant to Wullaf in 897 (S 1442; see **811.1** above). This stipulation also reflects ideas about how to protect monastic properties which were current in the early part of the ninth century: see the 816 Synod of Chelsea, § 7 (H&S, 3:582). Brooks, *Canterbury*, 175–80, sees the synod's ruling to this effect as part of a general movement intended to rescue *Eigenklöster* from exploitation by their lay owners, but it is possible to see how lay lords might also welcome this provision. Cf. H&S, 3:575.

Levison, *EC*, 253–54, demonstrated, furthermore, that many of the text's distinctive usages were typical of the language employed in genuine early ninth-century diplomas. To take a selection of the more compelling examples, the phrase *pro . . . expiatione piaculorum meorum* is echoed in a grant that Cenwulf issued on 1 August 811, preserved in a contemporary copy (S 168; B*CS*, no. 335). The same charter also provides an echo for the use of *imperium* for *regnum* when referring to the year of the king's reign in which it was issued. (For further examples from two genuine and two alleged charters of Cenwulf, see S 153, 155, 157, and 183.) Echoes can also be found in three charters of Cenwulf for Worcester, all dating from 816 and 817, for the idea that Cenwulf was king of the Mercians *Dei arridenti gratia*, "by the smiling grace of God": see S 180 (*cuius melliflua gratia adridenti*), 181 (*cuius melliflua gratia arridenti*) and 182 (*eius arridenti gratia*). Levison also found an echo for the phrase *in loco quem solicoli antiquo nomine Wincelcumbam appellare suescunt*, "in a place which its cultivators are accustomed to call by the ancient name Winchcombe," in a genuine charter of Deneberht, bishop of Worcester (798×800–822): *in . . . loco . . . ubi solicoli suescunt appellare æt Collesburnan* (S 1262; B*CS*, 304). But his other example belongs to a charter of King Offa for Westminster Abbey which is clearly a post-Conquest forgery (S 124; B*CS*, 245). The language of the sanction also contains echoes of those found in authentic royal charters of the period: e.g. S 188 (*Sciat se . . . anathematis vinculis esse nodatum, nisi ante ea digna satisfactione emendare voluerit*), S 171 (*nisi antea hic cum satisfactione emendaverit*).

The witness list also appears to have been copied from the authentic record of a synod which took place, given the presence of both Archbishop Wulfred (805–832) and King Cuthred (798–807), between 805 and 807. Some of the names are problematic, but if *Tilferthus* is identified as the bishop of Dunwich called Tidfrith, *Alchbertus* as the bishop of Elmham called Ealhheard, and *Wignothus* as the bishop of Winchester called Wigthegn, then it follows that all the Southumbrian sees in existence at this time are covered by the bishops named in the witness list, as the following table indicates:

| Form in T | Probable Identity | See | Dates |
|---|---|---|---|
| Wlfredus | Wulfred | Canterbury | 805–832 |
| Aldulfus | Ealdwulf | Lichfield | 799×801–814×816 |
| Denebertus | Deneberht | Worcester | 798×800–822 |
| Werenbrihtus | Werenberht | Leicester | 801×803–814×816 |
| Wlfhardus | Wulfheard | Hereford | 799×801–822×824 |
| Tilferthus | Tidfrith | Dunwich | 798–816×824 |
| Ætheluulfus | Æthelwulf | Selsey | 805×811–816×824 |
| Eadulfus | Eadwulf | Lindsey | 796–836×839 |
| Alchbertus | Ealhheard | Elmham | 781×785–805×814 |
| Æthelnothus | Æthelnoth | London | 805×811–816×824 |
| Wibertus | Wigberht | Sherborne | 793×801–816×824 |
| Beormonus | Beornmod | Rochester | 804–842×844 |
| Wignothus | Wigthegn | Winchester | 805×814–836 |

These identifications differ, of course, from those of the annotator who inserted names for each of the sees. He appears to have confused *Tilferthus* with the Tidfrith who was bishop of Hexham (813–821), *Ætheluulfus* with Æthelwulf, bishop of Elmham (758×781–781×785), *Eadulfus* with Eadwulf, bishop of Crediton (ca.909–934), *Alchbertus* with Aluberht, bishop of Selsey (747×765–772×780). His identification of Wignoth as a bishop of Exeter was pure invention, driven no doubt by the absence any record of a bishop with that exact name. The bishopric of Crediton/Exeter did not, of course, come into existence until about 909. As for Sigered, "king of the East Saxons," and the eleven *duces* who appear in the witness list, all of their names are to be found in two or more authentic charters whose dates either encompass 805 to 807 or fall within ten years of that date: see S 39, 40, 153, 155, 157, 161, 163–165, 168–173, 175, 178, 180–182, 186–187, 1186a, 1187, 1259, and 1260. All of these names appear, in other words, to refer to actual magnates or satellite rulers of King Cenwulf. There is, then, every reason to think that the witness list derives from a genuine charter, one issued at a synod which met between 805 and 807. Cf. H&S, 3:574. Cubitt, *Church Councils*, 284, implies that the document as a whole was reworked from a charter issued at a synod held in 811, but the text merely purports to recount a dedication ceremony—it does not imply, as she suggests, that an actual synod took place at Winchcombe.

Another factor that needs to be kept in view is that William of Malmesbury appears to have known a document almost identical to the present charter during the early 1120s, when he produced the first drafts of his *Gesta regum* and *Gesta pontificum*. For in WM*GR*, 1.95, and WM*GP*, 4.156, he describes the dedication of Winchcombe in such similar terms that he must have been using a version of the same charter. He refers, for example, to the gifts that Cenwulf disbursed at the ceremony: "Besides his gifts to the magnates, of inestimable number and value—dishes, raiment, horses of the choicest breeds—each landless man received a pound of silver, each priest a *mancus* of gold, each monk a shilling, and many presents were given to the whole people." The version that William knew may have differed in some details, for he states that thirteen bishops and ten thegns were present, whereas the charter lists eleven thegns. In WM*GR*, 1.95, William also mentions that it was on the actual dedication-day and before the high altar that Cenwulf freed Eadberht Præn, the leader of the Kentish rebellion of 796–798, with his brother, Cuthred, and the congregration applauding his act of mercy; but this scene is probably best explained as a product of his penchant for inventing arresting detail. Other versions of what happened imply that Cenwulf treated Eadberht with all the usual cruelty of Anglo-Saxon politics (see *ASC* (F) 796). The upshot is that a version of the charter, one which was probably almost identical to that found in *Winchcombe*, was in existence some fifteen to twenty years before the present chronicle was produced in the 1140s.

All of this tends to suggest that the existing text was produced between ca.1075 and 1125 by someone who had access to an archive containing some genuine charters of King Cenwulf. Worcester certainly had documents of the right type, as can be seen from the foregoing discussion of the formulas found in the charter. It is, however, worth considering the alternative possibility that the existing text was an attempt to adapt or improve the charter actually issued on the occasion of the abbey's dedication. For the text of the existing charter does not seem to provide enough gains to justify the difficulties that would have been involved in forging it. The gains it seems to offer consist chiefly of the right to offer an extended but vaguely defined form of asylum, and some colourful information as to the relative antiquity and distinction of the monastery itself.

With the exception of these desiderata, the document has the character of a charter which a ninth-century king might well have issued for his *Eigenkloster*, not least in its celebratory account of the vast riches that were disbursed on the occasion of its foundation. As James Campbell notes, "it is not easy to find a motive for forgery of the passage in question, which may be compared with the one in the (admittedly genuine) will of the Kentish reeve Abba (833 or 836) leaving to every priest in Kent a mancus of gold and to every servant of God a penny" ("The

Sale of Land and the Economics of Power in Early England: Problems and Possibilities," *Haskins Society Journal* 1 [1989]: 23–37, at 35, citing S 1482, which is printed in *SEHD*, no. 2). The present charter confers little, furthermore, that would have been of special value in the Anglo-Norman world: for example, it does not specify in detail the nature of the secular burdens from which the abbey was exempt (there is no mention, for example, of exemption from bridge- or castle-work), nor does it claim rights of exemption from diocesan control of the kind that monasteries such as Ramsey, Westminster, and Battle were intruding into their royal charters from the 1120s onwards. See Julia Crick, "St Albans, Westminster and Some Twelfth-Century Views of the Anglo-Saxon Past," *Anglo-Norman Studies* 25 (2002): 65–83 (esp. 71–72, 83); Eleanor Searle, "Battle Abbey and Exemption: The Forged Charters," *EHR* 83 (1968): 449–80 (esp. 452). It may well be the case, therefore, that **811.3** represents the remains of a genuine charter that has been retouched in much the same fashion as appears to have happened with Winchcombe's papal privileges. The claim made for rights of asylum is certainly suspicious, but the reference to these rights is brief and the clause could easily have been interpolated into the text. The same can also be said for the brief reference to the privilege of Pope Paschal I. Finally, the witness list might well have been imported to replace one that had been damaged in some way. In short, the charter has undoubtedly been tampered with, but a genuine charter of King Cenwulf for Winchcombe might well lie behind it.

**811.4** The text from *nulli ante* to *seriem uidear* is derived from WM*GR*, 1.87.4, which passage incorporates a long quotation from Alcuin, *Epistle* 255 (ed. Ernst Dümmler, *MGH Epp.*, 4:412, lines 16–22). The only variant of note is *recessus* for WM*GR*'s *reuersionis*. With the final sentence the compiler reproduces William's signpost even though it represents a reflexive apology for having inserted the following documents outside their natural place in the order of events—that is, whilst still covering the reign of Offa (757–797). As the presence of the signpost implies, the ensuing cluster of material is derived from WM*GR*, 1.87–89, rather than from the archives of Winchcombe Abbey.

**811.5** WM*GR*, 1.88, quoting King Cenwulf's only extant letter to Pope Leo III. This letter is also printed along with the pope's answer in H&S, 3:521–25. The readings in the present text—in so far as there are any significant variants—suggest that the text was derived from a B-group manuscript of *GR*. For example, T has *scinditur* in agreement with WM*GR* (B), where the other versions provide the subjunctive *scindatur.* The B-group was the latest of the four, and is thought to represent the state of *GR* in the late 1130s, when William had completed his editorial revisions: see Thomson and Winterbottom in WM*GR*, 1:xxii–xxiv.

The letter itself, which is otherwise known only through *GR*, provides precious information about the origins and fate of King Offa's scheme for the creation of a new archbishopric encompassing the Mercian sees of the province of Canterbury and subject to the authority of the bishop of Lichfield. It dates from around 799, and suggests that Offa was motivated by hostility towards the kingdom of Kent and Archbishop Jænberht. Cenwulf, in asking for the suppression of this archbishopric, suggests that London, not Canterbury, should be the seat of the southern metropolitan. The final paragraph also provides a rare insight into the workings of diplomacy in the early ninth century, not least in its reference to the incompetence of his previous messenger, Abbot Wada. For discussion, see Brooks, *Canterbury*, 123–25; Story, *Carolingian Connections*, 199–201.

**811.6** WM*GR*, 1.89.1–3, quoting a later letter of Pope Leo III to Cenwulf (JL 2511). This letter was not a reply to **811.5** (for which see H&S, 3:523–25), but was sent three years later, in 802, after Archbishop Æthelheard had himself gone to Rome. For the remainder of this letter, see WM*GR*, 1.89.3–6. The letter is also printed along with Leo's privilege for Æthelheard and Canterbury in H&S, 3:536–39.

**812** Norman Annals: *AU*, *ACad.*, *ASC* (E) 810; *AG*, 809.

**813.1** Common root: *Coventry*[1] 811. Marianus via JW*CC* 811.

**813.2** Norman Annals: *AU* 811; *ASC* (E) 812; *AG* 809.

**814** Common root: *Coventry*[1] 813. Marianus 813–14 via JW*CC* 813. Cf. Norman Annals: *ACad.*, *ASBD*, *ASN* 814.

**815** Norman Annals: *AU*, *AG* 815. Cf. *ASN* 815.

**816.1** Common root: *Coventry*[1] 817. Marianus via JW*CC* 817.

**816.2** *ASC* via JW*CC* 816.

**817.1** Norman Annals: *AU* 813.

**817.2** Norman Annals: *AU* 820.

**818.1** This item is significantly closer to Norman Annals: *AU*, *AG* 819, than to JW*CC* 820, where the account of Louis' campaign in Brittany is derived from Marianus. Morman is described by *ARF* 818 as having usurped royal authority in Brittany.

**818.2** Indeterminate source.

**818.3** This privilege of Pope Paschal I (817–824) for Winchcombe Abbey is the last of the three foundation documents which were incorporated into the chronicle by the scribe of the first phase. As in the case of the alleged privilege of Pope Leo III (see **811.2** above), the text presents a number of problems, yet these seem to be indications, not of outright forgery, but that the document has been revised, mostly in order to repair the effects of decay on the original, but perhaps also in order to erase references to Cenwulf's daughter Cwenthryth. The privilege is certainly closely related to formula 93 in the *Liber diurnus*, a formula which was devised by Pope Hadrian I (772–795) for Offa, king of Mercia (757–796). It will be helpful to quote formula 93 in full, with the points of difference marked in *italics*:

> Cum piae desideri*um* uoluntatis et laudande deuotionis intenti*o* apostolicis sit semper studiis adiuuand*a*, cura *est* sollicitudinis adhibenda, ut ea quae legaliter geruntur et equitatis forma conueniunt nulla ualeant refragatione perturbari, sed inrefragabili iure Deo auctore debeant permanere. *Et ob* hoc apostolicis promulgatis sanctionibus propria unicuique que rationis <rationes?> suppetunt, fas exigit possidenda confirmari. Et ideo quoniam constat excellentiam uestram plurima monasteria *construxisse, quamque iuste adquisisse et cuncta in honore et nomine fautoris uestri beati Petri constituisse ac dedicasse, quibus et diuersa* agrorum predia *ac* possessiones, et famulorum multitudinem *uidemini* con*tulisse*. Quae *omnia* sub *tuae excellentiae* dicione *uel coniugi tuae Cynedridae regine et natorum uestrorum genealogie* in perpetuum eadem monasteria et agrorum possessiones, cum omnibus originalibus fam*ulis*, ac manentibus, uel uniuersis sibi pertinentibus, apostolicae sedis priuilegi*is* poposcistis confirmari detinend*a*. Sicuti inferius adscripta eadem loca atque agrorum predi*c*a <predia?> continere monstratur.
>
> Since the desire of a pious will and the aim of praiseworthy devotion is always to be assisted by apostolic efforts, care must be taken in the allaying of anxiety, so that those things which are conducted legally and which are in accordance with the ideal of fairness cannot be disturbed by any opposition but ought to endure by irresistible right under God's authority. And on account of this, since apostolic sanctions were promulgated that peculiar to each <are those things> which reasons show to be theirs, right demands that what they possess should be confirmed. And so, because it is well known that your Excellency has constructed many monasteries, how justly you acquired them, that you have established and dedicated them in honour and in the name of your patron, the blessed Peter, and that you are seen to have handed over to them many rural estates and possessions and a multitude of servants, you have asked for the same monasteries and rural possessions with all their original servants and hides and everything which pertains to them to be confirmed in your possession by privileges of the apostolic see under the authority of your Excellency or of your wife, Queen Cynethryth, and of the lineage of your descendants in perpetuity, just as it is demonstrated that the same places and rural estates are included in what is listed below.

Offa is not named, but the original privilege was clearly intended for a king, and Offa was the only king with a wife whose name was close to *Cynedrida* in the period when the formulas in the *Liber diurnus* were being assembled. The dispositive section confirms their and their heirs' ownership of the monasteries which he had founded or acquired and had placed under the protection of his patron, St Peter. The naming of Cynethryth suggests, moreover, that Offa's reason for obtaining the diploma was to ensure that she would inherit full control of his monasteries after he was gone. That she struggled to retain ownership of some of these monasteries after his death is clear from S 1258 (ed. H&S, 3:512–13), a charter recording the settlement in 798 of a dispute over Cookham in Berkshire. It was found that this minster had not been Offa's to grant to his heirs, for it rightly belonged to Canterbury, and Abbess *Cynedritha* was forced to exchange substantial estates in Kent amounting to some 110 hides in order to retain it. Interestingly, Archbishop Æthelheard "conceded" as part of this exchange another monastery at *Pectanege* which had been given to Canterbury by Offa's son, King Ecgfrith (797–798). The charter is written from Canterbury's point of view and admits no claim to the estate on Cynethryth's part, but it is tempting to ask whether this side of the bargain represented the restoration to her of an estate that her son had wrongly alienated in contravention of her inheritance rights.

The present text's version of the arenga has been distorted by a couple of omissions and several grammatical aberrations, but it clearly depends on that found in number 93. The dispositive section differs in so far as it omits the clause referring to St Peter and in so far as it replaces the long prepositional phrase *sub tuae excellentiae dicione . . . genealogie* with *sub uestre confirmationis dictione, posteris heredibus inferius asscripta loca cum omnibus sibi pertinentibus largire maluerit*, complicating the flow of the text. The altered phrase echoes the language of the *libera potestas* clause in **811.2** (cf. *sub iure dictionis tue, cui cum omnibus sibi pertinentibus largiri maluerit*), suggesting that the former privilege's concern with the right to transfer estates may have contaminated the present text. It is not difficult to explain why the clause may have been altered, for in a document modelled on formula 93, it would be natural to refer at this point to the female relative who was to share or inherit the founder's authority over the monasteries and estates comprising the *hereditas*, and there are reasons, set out under **811.1** above, for thinking that the monks of the post-reform or post-Conquest monastery might have suppressed her name if, as is extremely likely, that abbess were Cenwulf's daughter. A further difficulty with this section of the text is the absence of the list of estates which ought to follow at the end, a fault which Levison put down to the decayed state of the original. The anathema and blessing which would come next in a typical privilege are also missing, but they are lacking in the underlying formula 93 as well.

A more serious issue is the failure of the "great date" to follow the usual pattern of ninth-century papal documents, but Levison, who thought the privilege a product of an essentially honest attempt to make sense of an obscure and decaying original, has shown how the existing text could have been produced by a scribe unfamiliar with both the cursive script and the abbreviations employed by the papal chancery. Here it is also necessary to note that the other copy of the privilege, that found in the thirteenth-century cartulary (*Landboc*, 1:23, corrected against the MS., which is presently held among the Muniments of the Dutton Family of Sherborne at the Gloucestershire County Record Office, Gloucester; cf. B*CS*, no. 363), has a fuller version of the dating clause:

> Hanc cartam scripsit Januasius presbiter anno Theodosii *summi* imperatoris Constantinopolis. Signum uero Lodouici Romanorum piissimi Augusti a Deo coronati in magni imperii iure, anno uero regni sui XI°. *Signum etiam Lotharii nouo imperatore eius filio. Anno primo* indictione XI.

As in the case of the privilege of Pope Leo (see **811.2** above), the copy in *Landboc* appears to represent a better witness to the "repaired text" of the present privilege than that found in T. The maker of the repaired text, Levison suggests, misread *s* for *r* and *u* for open *a*, failed to recognise the title *nomenclator*, which was unknown outside of Rome, was confused by the abbreviations for *datum* and *postconsulatus*, and so on. In Levison's view the dating probably ran as follows in its original form:

> [D]a[t*um*. . .] Ka[lenda]s Ianua[r]i[a]s p[e]r [m]an[um] Theodo[r]i [n]um[encl]atoris [s*anct*ae] s[edis a]po[stolicae, imp*erante* d*omino* n*ostro* H]ludouuic[o] piiss*imo* [p*er*p*etuo*] august[o] a Deo coronat[o] magn[o] imper[ato]re anno [q]u[a]r[t]o [et p*ostconsulatus* eius anno quarto] s[ed] et [H]lothari[o] novo imperatore eius filio anno primo, indictione XI[a].

For Levison's arguments in full, see *EC*, 255–57; for the history of *curialis* script, see Bernhard Bischoff, *Latin Palaeography: Antiquity and the Middle Ages*, trans. Daíbhí Ó Cróinin and David Ganz (Cambridge: Cambridge University Press, 1990), 101, and the works cited there.

This reconstruction has not gone unchallenged. Chaplais asked, for example, why the putative transcriber found the rest of the original privilege so much more readable than the dating clause. He suggested that the text was a forgery: "for the text the forger used the formula of no. 93 of the *Liber diurnus*, and for the date he used an original which he could not read" ("Some Diplomas," 336). There are, however, obvious ways of explaining how the dating clause may have become so much more corrupt than the rest of the text: namely, that sitting at the bottom of the large papyrus sheet on which the privilege was written and separated from its upper half by a list of properties, the *scriptum* formula, and the *Bene valete* monograph, all of which are omitted in the existing copies, it may well have been exposed to a quite different level of damage. It will all have depended on how the papyrus was folded and stored. The errors in the transcription of the arenga are difficult to explain, moreover, if the scribe did indeed have access to the *Liber diurnus*. The mistakes are not those of a forger. Indeed, the text is, in the forms in which it is preserved, a most improbable forgery, since it fails not only to supply the names of the estates which belonged to Cenwulf and his heirs, but also to say anything about Winchcombe itself and the rights the abbey was to enjoy. It seems best, therefore, to adopt a position similar to that of Levison.

One problem remains. Nicholas Brooks, *Canterbury*, 185–86, has suggested that the granting of this privilege requires a special explanation since it offers nothing in addition to what Cenwulf had already obtained from Pope Leo III (see **811.2** above). His explanation is that the king needed a re-affirmation of the rights which had already been granted, because of the emergence in 817 of his quarrel with Archbishop Wulfred over the minsters at Reculver and Thanet. It is known, he explains, that Wulfred had earlier returned from Rome in 815 "with the blessing of Pope Leo," and that Cenwulf later received papal support in the dispute. There was, he implies, a change in the papacy's position which will have been brought about by Cenwulf in some way. Brooks suggests, moreover, that the present privilege, which was issued—according to Levison's reconstruction—between 14 December 817 and 1 January 818, was the actual expression of this policy reversal: with this affirmation of Cenwulf's rights the papacy opted to help the king to check Wulfred's "interference."

This theory may well be right: it certainly provides a neat and pleasing fit with the little that is known about political life in this period—perhaps a little too neat. It may not be true, moreover, that the present privilege simply reiterated what had already been granted by Leo III. For if, as has been suggested above, the wording of the dispositive section was originally much closer to that of formula 93, then the emphasis may not have been on confirming Cenwulf's rights in respect of his monastic *hereditas*, but upon ensuring that his heirs, including probably his daughter Cwenthryth, succeeded to those rights. In other words, Cenwulf's reasons for obtaining the charter may well been closer to those which seem to have motivated King Offa when he wrote to Hadrian I: a concern to ensure the smooth succession of a close female relative to a monastic lordship. The timing of the grant certainly supports this interpretation since, if Levison's reconstruction of the dating clause is correct, the privilege was issued some twenty years into a long reign that began in 796 and just four years before Cenwulf died in 821. This hypothesis would also help to explain why Paschal's clerks chose to base their text on option 93 as opposed to others which would have provided Cenwulf with more support in his struggle with Wulfred.

**819.1** This annal seems to derive directly from JW*CC* 819, where the same passage appears in its entirety except that *Winchcombe* adds *patruus eius* in the penultimate sentence. The Worcester provenance is clear from the way in which it continues with JW*CC* 819's items concerning the succession of Ceolwulf and Ecgberht's obit (see **819.2** below). Some words from this entry are also echoed in *APW* 832, but in combination with a record of Cenwulf's gifts to Worcester. Cf. also *Coventry*[1] 819, and the genealogical data and verses about Kenelm entered in *Chronicula*[1] VA 918 ("De regibus Merciorum"). The ultimate source of the annal is one of the two accounts of St Kenelm, either Goscelin's *Vita S. Kenelmi, regis et martyris* (*BHL* 4641n + p + r), ed. Love, *Three Lives*, 50–88, or the *Lectiones S. Kenelmi* (*BHL* 4641m), ed. Love, *Three Lives*, 126–29, which is probably also attributable to Goscelin of St Bertin. It is the latter text, however, which provides stronger verbal parallels (see Love, *Three Lives*, 126–29, nn. 16, 18, 24, 26, and 28), and it may be significant that they survive in a single manuscript (MS. Cambridge, Corpus Christi College, 367, pt. 2, fols. 45r–48r) which has a clear Worcester provenance.

**819.2** This item echoes JW*CC* 819, and it is significant because it implies that the present annal was derived from a relatively advanced version of that chronicle. For this item was one of a number of entries relating to Northumbria which John seems to have obtained through an exchange of materials with the monks of Durham and which were inserted during the final stages of the development of the text. It was entered in C by scribe $C^2$ who rewrote the end of this annal from *suscepit Merciorum* onwards so that it could be accommodated. Similar material certainly appears in *LDE*, 2.5, where, having earlier placed the succession of Ecgberht in 802, Symeon reports that Heathured succeeded Ecgberht who had held the bishopric for eighteen years. Similar information would have allowed JW to place Ecgberht's death and Heathured's succession under AD 819. None of the other sources which John used when covering the north provides enough information to produce this result. *ASC* (DE), s.a. 803, for example, merely reports the succession of Ecgberht and the death of his predecessor. Cf. SD*LDE*, 92, n. 32; JW, 2:240, nn. a, b, and 2.

**821** Common root: *Coventry*[1] 822.1. *ASC* via JW*CC* 821.

**822.1** Common root: *Coventry*[1] 822.2. JW*CC* 822.

**822.2** Norman Annals: *AU*, *AG*, *ASBD*, *ASN* 822.

**823.1** Common root: *Coventry*[1] 823.1. *ASC* via JW*CC* 823.

**823.2** Common root: *Coventry*[1] 823.2. From the Kentish Royal Genealogy in JW*CC* (C), p. 48: "Huc usque regnum Cantuuariorum per .ccc[tos].lxviii. annos stetit, postea uero Westsaxonice dicioni cessit." The same material appears in *Chronicula*[1] VA 835.

**823.3** A marginal gloss which probably referred to the extinction of the kingdom of Kent.

**824.1** Common root: *Coventry*[1] 824. *ASC* via JW*CC* 823.

**824.2** Norman Annals: *AU*, *AG*, *ASBD*, *ASN* 823.

**824.3** Norman Annals: *AU*, *AG*, *ASN* 823; *ASBD* 824, where the material is very muddled. The annal appears to refer to the events of 822 and 823 when Louis wintered at Frankfurt while his eldest son Lothar, having dispensed justice in Italy, went to Rome (at Easter 823). In Rome Lothar was crowned by Pope Paschal and received the title of Emperor and Augustus (see *ARF* 823).

**825.1** Common root: *Coventry*[1] 825. *ASC* via JW*CC* 825.

**825.2** Norman Annals: *AU*, *AG* 825. Cf. Marianus via JW*CC* 825

**829** Common root: *Coventry*[1] 829. *ASC* via JW*CC* 829, 830.

**833** Indeterminate source.

**834** Indeterminate source.

**835** Norman Annals: *AU*, *AG* 838; RT*Access.* 837.

**836** Common root: *Coventry*[1] 836. *ASC* via JW*CC* 836.

**837** Norman Annals: *AU*, *AG*, RT*Access.* 836 (*vii idus Junii*), *ACad.* 836 (without specifying the day).

**838** Common root: *Coventry*[1] 838. JW*CC* 838 or perhaps the Mercian Royal Genealogy in JW*CC* (C) p. 50.

**839** Common root: *Coventry*[1] 839.1. Marianus via JW*CC* 840. Cf. Norman Annals: *AU*, *ACad.*, *ASN*, *ASBD*, *ASC* (F) 840; *AG* 839.

**840** Common root: *Coventry*[1] 839.2. Though *Winchcombe*[1] and *Coventry*[1] 839.2 identify Benedict as the subject of this translation, this entry probably represents a misreading of JW*CC* 809 or 840: "<C>orpus sancti Bartholomei de insula Lipparitana transuectum delatum est Beneuentum." Bartholomew's relics were indeed translated from Lipari to Benevento in 838: see *Annales Beneventani monasterii Sanctae Sophiae*, s.a. 838 (ed. Ottorino Bertolini, *Bullettino dell' Istituto Storico Italiano per il Medio Evo* 42 [1923]: 100–59, at 114). The Convent of St Sophia was then a dependency of Monte Cassino, but there is no tradition that Benedict's relics were ever translated there: see *Le culte et les reliques de Saint Benoît et de Sainte Scholastique*, ed. Anselme Davril, Studia Monastica 21 (Barcelona: Abadia de Montserrat, 1979); Graham A. Loud, "The Medieval Records of the Monastery of St Sophia,

Benevento," *Archives: The Journal of the British Records Association* 19 (1991): 364–73 (esp. 365). If indeed this is a reference to the translation of Bartholomew to Benevento, the passage may represent a clue to the original form of JW*CC*. The record of Bartholomew's translation is repeated in DL under 809 and at the conclusion of the annal for 840, but in the other manuscripts it appears solely around 809: C[1] inserts the entry in the margins of C alongside 809–810; in P it appears as part of a consolidated annal for 808–810; in G it appears as part of the consolidated entry for 800–814 (see JW*CC*, 2:232, n. h, and 2:258, n. d). It is natural to assume that C[1]'s marginal note was the "original entry," but the combined evidence of *Winchcombe*[1] and DL suggests that this material may first have been entered under 840 and that C[1]'s marginal note represents a *second attempt* to enter the material. Certainly this note is more accurately entered under 840, and it is odd that John should have placed it under 809. Cf. also *Chronicula* AD 868 (G, fol. 60r). However, the source whence John derived the information remains unclear: neither Marianus nor the Norman Annals (as attested in other chronicles) have it, but it is widely noted in Franco-Latin chronicles from the eleventh century onwards: e.g. *Annales Leodienses*, s.a. 831 (ed. Georg H. Pertz, *MGH SS*, 4:9–20, at 13); Sigibert of Gembloux, *Chronica*, s.a. 831 (ed. Ludwig Bethmann, *MGH SS*, 6:300–74, at 338); Hugh of Flavigny, *Chronicon*, a.d. 839 (ed. Georg H. Pertz, *MGH SS*, 8:288–502, at 353); *Annales Nivernenses*, s.a. 839 (ed. Georg Waitz, *MGH SS*, 13:89–91, at 89).

**842** Common root: *Coventry*[1] 842. The present item amalgamates JW*CC* 841, 842, and 844, items which derive from Marianus 842–843, 845. Cf. *ASN* 841.

**845** Indeterminate source.

**846** Common root: *Coventry*[1] 846. Either JW*CC* 847 or the Easter Table Annals in JW*CC* (C), p. 64 (in cycle 17, year 11 = 846).

**849.1** Common root: *Coventry*[1] 849. Asser, *De rebus gestis Ælfredi*, § 1 (ed. William H. Stevenson, *Asser's Life of King Alfred*, rev. Dorothy Whitelock [Oxford: Clarendon Press, 1959], 1–96, at 1), via JW*CC* 849.

**849.2** Norman Annals: *AU*, *AG*, RT*Access*. 849.

**850.1** Common root: *Coventry*[1] 850. Slightly abbreviated from JW*CC* 849: in C it is added in the margin by C[1] with *signe-de-renvoi*. The same material also appears in a somewhat different order in the Mercian Royal Genealogy in JW*CC* (C) p. 50. See JW*CC* 2:lxxv–vi. It is ultimately derived from the Life of Wigstan which was later reworked by Thomas of Marlborough to produce *Vita et miracula S. Wistani martyris* (*BHL* 8975–8977), ed. William D. Macray, *Chronicon Abbatiae de Evesham ad Annum 1418*, RS 29 (London: Longman, 1863), 325–37.

**850.2** Norman Annals: *AU*, *AG*, RT*Access*. 842; *ACad.*, 842 (but without specifying the day); *ASN* 842.

**852.1** Common root: *Coventry*[1] 852. JW*CC* 852. Cf. the Mercian Royal Genealogy in JW*CC* (C) p. 50.

**852.2** Common root: *Coventry*[1] 853. Asser, *De rebus gestis Ælfredi*, § 8, via JW*CC* 853.

**855** Common root: *Coventry*[1] 855.1. Marianus via JW*CC* 855 (2:268, 274). The idea that Louis "was also called Lothar" derives from Marianus VA 877: having correctly described the partition of Lothar's kingdom, he goes on to confuse Louis II, the king of Italy (855–875), with his brother Lothar II, the king of Lotharingia (855–869) when discussing the transmission of the imperial title.

**857.1** Common root: *Coventry*[1] 855.2. Asser, *De rebus gestis Ælfredi*, § 17, via JW*CC* 855.

**857.2** Common root: *Coventry*[1] 858. Abbo of Fleury, *Passio S. Eadmundi* (*BHL* 2392), §§ 3–4 (ed. Michael Winterbottom, *Three Lives of English Saints* [Toronto: University of Toronto Press, 1972], 67–87, at 71), via JW*CC* 855. Cf. *ASN* 855.

**857.3** Asser, *De rebus gestis Ælfredi*, § 11, via JW*CC* 855 (2:268). Written in a near-contemporary hand in the outer and lower margins, this marginal addition ultimately derives for the most part from Asser, §§ 11, 16, but via JW*CC* 855, as indicated by the notes that follow. It is, however, much damaged.

**857.4** WM*GR*, 2.109.

**857.5** Asser, *De rebus gestis Ælfredi*, § 16, via JW*CC* 855 (2:272–4).

**857.6** This query as to the financial implications of the foregoing items probably represents the annotator's own contribution to the present annal. It seems to have become standard practice during the twelfth century to interpret the 300 mancuses of the "original grant" as implying a payment of 300 marks — that is, of 48,000 pennies or of 200 pounds (see William E. Lunt, *Financial Relations of the Papacy with England to 1327*, Studies in Anglo-Papal Relations during the Middle Ages 1 [Cambridge, MA: Medieval Academy of America, 1939], 10). The *mancus* was a gold coin equal in weight to three silver pence, but the term refers here to a measure comprising thirty pence (see C. S. S. Lyon, "Historical Problems of Anglo-Saxon Coinage: 3. Denominations and Weights," *British Numismatic Journal* 38 [1969]: 204–22). But, as the annotator points out, if the 300 mancuses meant 300 *mancae* then the sum amounts to 9,000 pence — that is, £37 10s. On the uncertainties surrounding Peter's pence in the twelfth century, see Martin Brett, *The English Church under Henry I* (Oxford: Clarendon Press, 1975), 168–73.

**859** Norman Annals: *AU*, *AG* 859, but in *AG* October is given instead of December; *ASN* 859.

**860** Common root: *Coventry*[1] 860. Asser, *De rebus gestis Ælfredi*, § 18, via JW*CC* 860.

**861** Indeterminate source.

**862** Common root: *Coventry*[1] 862. *Vita S. Swithuni* (*BHL* 7943), § 8 (ed. Michael Lapidge, *The Anglo-Saxon Minsters of Winchester*, pt. 2, *The Cult of St Swithun*, Winchester Studies 4 [Oxford: Clarendon Press, 2003], 630–39, at 638), via JW*CC* 862.

**865** Norman Annals: *AU*, *AG*, *ACad.*, RT*Access.* 865; *ASN* 865.

**866** Common root: *Coventry*[1] 866. Asser, *De rebus gestis Ælfredi*, § 21, via JW*CC* 866.

**867** Common root: *Coventry*[1] 867. Northumbrian Royal Genealogy in JW*CC* (C), p. 51: "Osbryht et Ealle . . . anno dominice incarnationis iuxta Dionisium octingentesimo sexagesimo septimo in Eboraca cum flore Northymbrorum perempti sunt a paganis, uidelicet Danis, Norreganis . . . Quo anno Anglici reges qui annis .ccc.xxi. regnauere per annos quinquaginta et unum imperare in Northymbria desiere." Cf. Asser, *De rebus gestis Ælfredi*, § 27, via JW*CC* 867; *Chronicula*[1] VA 877.

**869** Norman Annals: *AU*, *AG*, *ASN*, *ASBD* 868–9; *ACad.* 868 (omits *fames ualida*).

**870.1** Common root: *Coventry*[1] 870.1. Marianus via JW*CC* 870.

**870.2** Common root: *Coventry*[1] 870.2. Asser, *De rebus gestis Ælfredi*, §§ 33–34, via JW*CC* 870.

**870.3** Common root: *Coventry*[1] 871. The East Anglian Royal Genealogy in JW*CC* (C) p. 49: "Quem anno regni sui [Eadmundi] .xvi. rex paganus Hinguar martirizauit. Ex quo tempore Anglisaxones in East Anglia regnare desiere annis fere .l." The same material appears in *Chronicula*[1] VA 877.

**871.1** Common root: *Coventry*[1] 873. Asser, *De rebus gestis Ælfredi*, § 42, via JW*CC* 871.

**871.2** Norman Annals: *AU*, *AG*, *ASBD* 871.

**872.1** Common root: *Coventry*[1] 872.1. JW*CC* 872.

**872.2** Common root: *Coventry*[1] 872.2. Asser, *De rebus gestis Ælfredi*, § 77, via JW*CC* 872.

**872.3** Indeterminate source.

**874** Common root: *Coventry*[1] 874.1. Marianus via JW*CC* 874.

**875.1** Common root: *Coventry*[1] 874.2. Asser, *De rebus gestis Ælfredi*, § 46, via JW*CC* 874. Cf. Mercian Royal Genealogy in JW*CC* (C) p. 50, which uses rather different words.

**875.2** A marginal gloss.

**876.1** Common root: *Coventry*[1] 876.1. Marianus via JW*CC* 875.

**876.2** Common root: *Coventry*[1] 876.2. Northumbrian Royal Genealogy in JW*CC* (C), p. 51: "Anno uero nono interfectionis regum Osbryht<i> et Ealle, pagani reges Halfdene et Eouuils in Northymbria regnare cepere." The deaths of Osberht and Ælle were entered under 867. Cf. Asser, *De rebus gestis Ælfredi*, § 47, via JWCC 875.

**876.3** Common root: *Coventry*[1] 876.3. The source may be the Norman Annals: *AU*, *AG*, *ASN*, *ASC* (EF) 876; *AMSM* 875. But JWCC 876, incorporates the same material over what was probably an erasure and in the Easter Table Annals in JWCC (C), p. 65 (in cycle 19, year 3 = 876): "Rollo cum suis Normanniam penetrauit xv k. Dec." Cf. also *Chronicula*[1] VA 896.

**877** Common root: *Coventry*[1] 876.4. *ASC* via JWCC 877.

**878** Common root: *Coventry*[1] 879. Marianus via JWCC 878–9 (2:308, 312). With this annal the common root diverges from Marianus Scotus in its numbering of the emperors. That numbering is identical as far as the eighty-third emperor Charles the Bald (see **876.1**), but Louis the Stammerer (877–879) is omitted by Marianus from his sequence, and he continues with Charles the Younger, whom he numbers as the eighty-fourth (VA 900). Thus his sequence concludes with Henry IV whom he numbers as the ninety-fifth. In the present text Louis is the eighty-fourth whilst the last of the emperors to be numbered is Henry IV, who is given as the ninety-sixth (see **1106.1** below). This dislocation in the numbering reflects the influence of a variant found in the London Marianus (N) and John of Worcester's efforts to correct his text in the light of it. For where the Vatican MS has *Post Carolum regnauit filius eius Ludowicus . . . annis duobus*, N adds *Romanorum* to the beginning of this clause, implying that he succeeded not as king of the Franks but as emperor of the Romans. John reproduces the variant in JWCC 876, and although he does not there number Louis as an emperor of the Romans he counts him in his sequence when he subsequently goes on to number Charles the Younger as the eighty-fifth under 878. His numbering subsequently remains one ahead of Marianus until he concludes the series with his ninety-sixth emperor, Henry IV (see JWCC 1056). Similar modifications to the numbering are to be found in *Chronicula*[1], except that Louis the Stammerer is there explicitly named under VA 898 as the eighty-fourth emperor. Charles the Bald is also numbered under VA 896 as the eighty-fourth, but this is clearly an unintended error for the previous holder of the title Louis II (855–875) is numbered under VA 893 as the eighty-second holder of the title.

**880** Common root: *Coventry*[1] 881. East Anglian Royal Genealogy in JWCC (C) p. 49, for the date of Guthrum's accession to the throne, and Asser, *De rebus gestis Ælfredi*, § 56, via JWCC 878, for Guthrum's baptism.

**882** Common root: *Coventry*[1] 883. Marianus via JWCC 882.

**883.1** Indeterminate source.

**883.2** Common root: *Coventry*[1] 885. Matching material, derived from Asser, *De rebus gestis Ælfredi*, § 71, occurs in JWCC (C) 884. Similar material occurs in John's "Papal Annals" (C), p. 33: "Hic [Marinus] scolam Saxonum Rome commorantium amore 7 deprecatione Alfredi Angulsaxonum regis ab omni tributo et telone benigne liberauit." Cf. *Chronicula*[1] VA 900.

**885.1** Norman Annals: *AU, AG, ASBD, ASN* 884; *ACad.* 883.

**885.2** Indeterminate source.

**886.1** Common root: *Coventry*[1] 886. Marianus via JW*CC* 885.

**886.2** Common root: *Coventry*[1] 887. Asser, *De rebus gestis Ælfredi*, § 83, via JW*CC* 886.

**888.1** Common root: *Coventry*[1] 888. Marianus via JW*CC* 887–88 (2:335).

**888.2** Norman Annals: *AU, AG, ASN*, RT*Access.* 893; *ACad.*, 892.

**889** Common root: *Coventry*[1] 889. *ASC* via JW*CC* 889.

**890** Common root: *Coventry*[1] 890. Norman Annals: *AG*, 912, *ACad.*, 913; *AU*, 911 (baptism), 914 (treaty), and 917 (Gisla). *AU* lacks the reference to the count of Senlis. See, likewise, *ASN* 912, 914; RT*Access.* 876, 912.

**891.1** The likely source for this item occurs in John's "Papal Annals" (C) p. 33: "Formosus . . . Huius iussu Plegmundus Dorubernensis archiepiscopus destitutas parrochias episcoporum per Angliam episcopis instituit, 7 in urbe Dorubernia .vii. episcopos, .vii. æcclesiis in una die consecrauit: Frithestanum ad æcclesiam Wintoniensem, Æthelstanum ad Coruinensem, Werstanum ad Scireburnensem, Æthelelmum ad Fontanensem, Eadulfum ad Cridiatunensem, Bernechun australibus Saxonibus et Merciis australibus, Cenulfum ad Dorkeceaster." A nearly identical version of the event appears in *Chronicula*[1] VA 933 (G, fol. 23v), and a somewhat fuller version, one which attributes the reform to King Edward the Elder, appears as an insert in the table of West-Saxon bishops in JW*CC* (C p. 41). The main chronicle in JW*CC* has a somewhat different account of these events, one which is derived from WM*GP*, 2.80, and which John himself inserted into the margins of C alongside the year 909: see JW*CC* (C[3]BP; not HL) 909. John here reproduces William of Malmesbury's mistaken substitution of *Cornubiensem* ("Cornwall") for *Coruinensem*. William evidently failed to see that *Coruinensem* was an attempt to Latinise "Ramsbury" by using *coruus* ("raven") to render "*Hraefn*'s [Raven's] burh," and this confusion caused William to have "Æthelstan" ordained twice, first to Cornwall and then again to Ramsbury. See also WM*GR*, 2.129 (s.a. 904), and R. Thomson's comments in WM*GR*, 2:112–13.

The ultimate source of all the different versions is the so-called "Plegmund Narrative," a forged document dated to the year 905 which makes Pope Formosus (891–896) the prime mover behind the division of the West-Saxon sees which took place at about that time. For the full text, see *C&S I*, 1:167–69; for further commentary, see *C&S I*, 1:165–67, and Alexander R. Rumble, "Edward the Elder and the

Churches of Winchester and Wessex," in *Edward the Elder, 899–924*, ed. N. J. Higham and D. H. Hill (London and New York, 2001), 230–47. John certainly knew this document, for it is to be found in his copy of William of Malmesbury's version of the *Liber pontificalis* (today MS. Cambridge, U.L., Kk.4.6, fols. 224r–280r, at 277v). The manuscript contains marginal annotations in the hand thought to be that of John of Worcester (e.g. fols. 233r, 244v, 268v). See Wilhelm Levison, "Aus Englischen Bibliotheken II," *Neues Archiv für ältere deutsche Geschichtskunde* 35 (1910): 333–431, with Rodney M. Thomson, *William of Malmesbury* (Woodbridge: Boydell Press, 1987), 119–38. On the various manuscripts, see also Rumble, "Edward the Elder," 241–42, and Patrick W. Conner, *Anglo-Saxon Exeter: A Tenth-Century Cultural History*, Studies in Anglo-Saxon History 4 (Woodbridge: Boydell Press, 1992), app. IV. The copy which appears in the Leofric Missal (MS. Oxford, Bod.L., Bodley 579, fol. 2) has also been printed by Nicholas A. Orchard, *The Leofric Missal*, HBS 113–114, 2 vols. (Woodbridge: Boydell Press, 2001–2002), 2:2–3.

**891.2** Common root: *Coventry*[1] 891.1. *ASC* via JW*CC* 891.

**891.3** Common root: *Coventry*[1] 891.2. Deduced from JW*CC* 905?

**893** Common root: *Coventry*[1] 893. *ASC* via JW*CC* 892.

**895** Norman Annals: *AU*, *AG* 898; *ACad.* 897; *ASBD* 895.

**896** Common root: *Coventry*[1] 895. Marianus via JW*CC* 896 (2:348).

**898** Common root: *Coventry*[1] 897. Norman Annals: *AU*, *ACad.*, *AMSM*, *ASN* 898; *AG*, RT*Access.* 908. *AMSM* is somewhat abbreviated: "Rollo cum exercitu suo Carnotensem urbem obsedit, sed episcopus eiusdem urbis, Waltelmus nomine, vir religiosissimus, tunicam sanctæ Mariæ in manibus ferens, Rollonem ducem divino nutu fugavit et civitatem liberavit." *ACad.* is somewhat abbreviated: "Rollo Carnotis civitatem obsedit. Sed religiosus Episcopus Waltelmus, Ricardum Burgundiæ ducem, et Ebalum comitem Pictaviensem in auxilio advocans, tunicam beatæ Mariæ in manibus ferens, Rollonem fugavit, civitatem liberavit, sex milia Normannorum interemit." *AG* differs from the Winchcombe text by having Richard as *Robertum ducem*, with *camisam* instead of *tunicam*, and with *in suum auxilium aduocans* instead of *in suo auxilio prouocans*. JW*CC* 898 is similar to T, but lacks the words *nomine uir religiosissimus*, adds the epithet *primus Normannorum dux* to Rollo, and arranges *in suo auxilio prouocans* as *in suum prouocans auxilium*. In JW*CC* (C) this material appears as a marginal addition assigned to the year 898 by the red line surrounding it. The same material appears in *Chronicula*[1] VA 909.

**900** Common root: *Coventry*[1] 899. Marianus via JW*CC* 899.

**901** Common root: *Coventry*[1] 901. *ASC* via JW*CC* 901.

**903** Common root: *Coventry*[1] 903. *ASC* via JW*CC* 903.
**904** Indeterminate source.
**905** Common root: *Coventry*[1] 904. *ASC* via JW*CC* 905.
**906.1** Common root: *Coventry*[1] 906. *ASC* via JW*CC* 906.
**906.2** Indeterminate source.
**907** Indeterminate source.
**908** Indeterminate source.
**909.1** Indeterminate source.
**909.2** A marginal gloss.
**910** Common root: *Coventry*[1] 910. *ASC* via JW*CC* 910.
**911.1** Common root: *Coventry*[1] 911.1. Marianus via JW*CC* 911. Cf. Norman Annals: *AU*, *ASN*, *AMSM*, *ACad.*, *ASBD* 911.
**911.2** Common root: *Coventry*[1] 911.2. *ASC* via JW*CC* 911.
**911.3** An entry which might belong to the common root, albeit only because it appears to derive from the Northumbrian Royal Genealogy in JW*CC* (C), p. 51, a text exploited elsewhere in the shared source: "Eouuils et Halfdene . . . annis . . . uiginti sex regnauere. Quibus ab Anglis interfectis, Reignaldus plusquam decem, dein Sihtricus annis regnauit paucis."
**912.1** Common root: *Coventry*[1] 912. *ASC* via JW*CC* 912.
**912.2** Indeterminate source.
**913.1** Common root: *Coventry*[1] 913; *APW* 919. *ASC* via JW*CC* 913. The compiler of *Winchcombe* appears to have added the claim, absent from *Coventry*[1], that Æthelflæd was the wife of King Burgred. Clearly, he was not using JW*CC* directly at this point, for she is explicitly identified there (s.a. 912) as the widow of the *dux et patricius dominus et subregulus Merciorum Ætheredus*.
**913.2** A marginal gloss.
**915.1** Common root: *Coventry*[1] 915.1. Norman Annals: *AU*, *AG*, *ACad.*, *AMSM*, RT*Access*. 915. The same material appears in JW*CC* (C[3]BP) 914, where it has the appearance of being a later addition. Cf., likewise, *Chronicula*[1] VA 909.
**915.2** Common root: *Coventry*[1] 915.2; *APW* 917. JW*CC* 915, but see also the discussion under **778.1** above.
**916.1** Common root: *Coventry*[1] 916.1; *APW* 919. *ASC* via JW*CC* 915.
**916.2** A marginal gloss.
**917.1** Common root: *Coventry*[1] 916.2. Norman Annals: *AU*, *AG*, *ACad.*, *AMSM*, RT*Access*. 917. *ASC* (EF) 928: "Willelm suscepit regnum et .xv. annis regnauit." Cf. JW*CC* 917.
**917.2** Indeterminate source.
**918** Common root: *Coventry*[1] 917. Marianus via JW*CC* 918. Cf. Norman Annals: *AU*, *AMSM* 919; *ASBD* 920.
**919.1** Common root: *Coventry*[1] 918. *ASC* via JW*CC* 919.
**919.2** Indeterminate source.

**921** Indeterminate source.

**922** Common root: *Coventry*[1] 921; *APW* 922. JW*CC* 922.

**923.1** Common root: *Coventry*[1] 922; *APW* 932. Marianus via JW*CC* 923. On the cult of the Holy Blood at Reichenau, see Helmut Binder, "Das Heilige Blut der Reichenau," in *900 Jahre Heilig-Blut-Verehrung in Weingarten 1094–1994*, ed. Norbert Kruse and Hans Ulrich Rudolf, 2 vols. (Sigmaringen: Jan Thorbecke, 1994), 1:337–47.

**923.2** Indeterminate source.

**924.1** Common root: *Coventry*[1] 924. *ASC* via JW*CC* 924.

**924.2** Indeterminate source.

**925** Common root: *Coventry*[1] 925. *ASC* via JW*CC* 925.

**926.1** Common root: *Coventry*[1] 926. *ASC* via JW*CC* 926.

**926.2** A marginal gloss.

**927** Indeterminate source.

**928** Common root: *Coventry*[1] 927. Norman Annals: *AU*, *AG* 927; *AMSM* 926; RT*Access.* 934; *ACad.* 935.

**929** Common root: *Coventry*[1] 930. Either JW*CC* 929 or the Easter Table Annals in JW*CC* (C), p. 66 (in cycle 21, year 17 = 928).

**933** Common root: *Coventry*[1] 934. *ASC* via JW*CC* 932.

**934** Common root: *Coventry*[1] 935. *ASC* via JW*CC* 934, 935.

**936.1** Common root: *Coventry*[1] 937.1. Marianus via JW*CC* 936. Cf. Norman Annals: *AU*, *AG*, *AMSM* 934; *ASBD* 935.

**936.2** Common root: *Coventry*[1] 937.2. *ASC* via JW*CC* 936.

**937** Common root: *Coventry*[1] 938. *ASC* via JW*CC* 937.

**940** Common root: *Coventry*[1] 940. *ASC* via JW*CC* 940.

**942** Common root: *Coventry*[1] 943. Norman Annals: *AU*, *AG*, *AMSM*, RT*Access.* 934. *ASC* (EF) 942: "Et Ricardus uetus suscepit et regnauit annos .lii." Cf. JW*CC* 942, who offers contrasting material.

**944** Common root: *Coventry*[1] 945. Adelard, *Vita S. Dunstani* (*BHL* 2343), § 3 (ed. William Stubbs, *Memorials of St Dunstan, Archbishop of Canterbury*, RS 63 [London: Longman, 1874], 53–68, at 56), via JW*CC* 943.

**946.1** Common root: *Coventry*[1] 946.1. *ASC* via JW*CC* 946.

**946.2** Common root: *Coventry*[1] 946.2. B., *Vita S. Dunstani* (*BHL* 2342), § 19 (ed. Stubbs, *Memorials of St Dunstan*, 3–52, at 29), via JW*CC* 946.

**950** Common root: *Coventry*[1] 950. Norman Annals: *AU*, *AG*, *AMSM*, RT*Access.* 972. The bishops mentioned here are Hilduin, bishop of Beauvais (c.933–972), and Guy, bishop of Soissons (c.937–970).

**951** Common root: *APW* 961. *ASC* via JW*CC* 951.

**955** Common root: *Coventry*[1] 955; *APW* 855. *ASC* via JW*CC* 955, whose text has been misread. As JW*CC* rightly reports, Eadred, king of England (946–955), was succeeded by Eadwig (955–959).

**956** Common root: *Coventry*[1] 956. *ASC* via JW*CC* 956. The same entry appears in *APW* 858.

**957** Common root: *Coventry*[1] 957; *APW* 859 and 860. *ASC* and Adelard, *Vita S. Dunstani*, § 7 (60), via JWCC 957.

**958** Common root: *Coventry*[1] 958; *APW* 862. *ASC* via JWCC 958.

**959.1** Common root: *Coventry*[1] 959.1; *APW* 863. *ASC* via JWCC 959.

**959.2** Common root: *Coventry*[1] 959.2. Osbern, *Vita S. Dunstani* (*BHL* 2344), § 33 (ed. Stubbs, *Memorials of St Dunstan*, 69–128, at 108), via JWCC 959.

**960** Common root: *Coventry*[1] 960; *APW* 864. Matching material for this item is to be found in JWCC 960, who appears to have derived it from *either* Byrhtferth, *Vita Oswaldi*, 3.5 (420), *or* perhaps, as is argued in Michael Lapidge, "Byrhtferth and Oswald," in *St Oswald of Worcester: Life and Influence*, ed. Nicholas P. Brooks and Catherine Cubitt, Studies in the Early History of Britain / The Makers of England 2 (London: Leicester University Press, 1996), 64–83 (esp. 76–78), from a lost Ramsey chronicle which was a common source for the material shared by JWCC and Byrhtferth's *Vita Oswaldi*.

**961** Common root: *Coventry*[1] 961. Marianus via JWCC 961.

**963** Common root: *Coventry*[1] 963; *APW* 866. JWCC 963, possibly derived from Byrhtferth, *Vita Oswaldi*, 3.11 (p. 427), or a lost Ramsey chronicle (see **960** above).

**964** Common root: *Coventry*[1] 964. *ASC* via JWCC 964.

**966** As with other successions entered by this thirteenth-century annotator (see **1066.2**, **1074.3**, and **1077** below), the chronological placement of this notice should be considered approximate rather than authoritative. Germanus's reign as abbot of Winchcombe actually seems to have begun in about 969 (Lapidge, "Germanus," 117–19).

**967** Common root: *Coventry*[1] 966; *APW* 868. JWCC 967.

**968.1** Common root: *Coventry*[1] 968.1. JWCC 968.

**968.2** Common root: *Coventry*[1] 968.2. Norman Annals: *AG*, *ACad.* 988; *AMSM* 989: "Hoc tempore Lotharius rex Francorum terram Arnulfi invasit, quia sibi servire noluit. Atrepatensem urbem et munitiones plures cepit. Sed Richardus eum regi pacavit." *ACad.* is rather abbreviated: "Lotharius terram Arnulfi, nolentis sibi servire, invadit. Atrebatum et plures munitiones capit. Sed Ricardus eum Regi pacificavit." Flodoard, *Annales*, s.a. 962, ed. Philippe Lauer, *Les Annales de Flodoard* (Paris: A. Picard, 1905), 152–53), and Richer of Reims, *Historiae*, 3.21 (ed. Hartmut Hoffmann, *MGH SS* 38:181), report an invasion of the *terra Arnulfi* by Lothar, king of the Franks (954–986), soon after the death of Arnulf I, count of Flanders (d. 965), but this annal probably refers to the episode reported by Dudo of St Quentin, *De moribus et actis primorum Normanniæ ducum*, ed. Jules Lair, Société des Antiquaires de Normandie (Caen: F. Le Blanc-Hardel, 1865–1872), 294, in which Lothar is said to have attacked Artois because Arnulf II, count of Flanders (d. 988), had refused to perform military service for him. It was through the intervention of Richard I, count of Normandy (942–996), that peace was achieved. Dudo fails to date the episode, but there are grounds for placing it in the mid 970s: see Jean Dunbabin, "The Reign of Arnulf II, Count of Flanders, and its Aftermath," *Francia* 16 (1989): 52–65 (esp. 60–61).

**969** Common root: *Coventry*[1] 969. Matching material appears in JW*CC* 969, possibly derived from Byrhtferth, *Vita Oswaldi*, 4.12 (435), or a lost Ramsey chronicle (see **960** above). Wynsige and his status has recently been the subject of much debate. That there was a significant historical figure of this name is strongly implied by Byrhtferth's *Vita Oswaldi*, 4.12 (435), where "Wynsige" is described, not only as a monk of Ramsey but also as *reuerendus presbyter*, a status which, the text seems to imply, he acquired prior to his monastic profession. This much would seem to be confirmed by the record of a synod supposedly held in 1092 (*Cart. Worcs.*, no. 52), which states that this Wynsige had previously been the priest of St Helen's (an ancient and important church within the walls of the burh at Worcester), that he gave up this vicarage to become a monk at Ramsey, and that he spent three years there before becoming the first prior of the cathedral priory in the process of its reform by Bishop Oswald. It has recently been argued, however, that this document was forged between the early 1130s and the 1150s and that everything it adds about Wynsige must be viewed with scepticism: see Julia S. Barrow, "How the Twelfth-Century Monks of Worcester Perceived Their Past," in *The Perception of the Past in Twelfth-Century Europe*, ed. Paul Magdalino (London: Hambledon, 1992), 53–74 (esp. 68); eadem, "The Chronology of Forgery Production at Worcester from c. 1000 to the Early Twelfth Century," in *St Wulfstan and His World*, ed. eadem and Nicholas P. Brooks (Aldershot: Ashgate, 2005), 105–22 (esp. 116–18). Barrow's arguments against the authenticity of the alleged synodal record are indeed strong: the reference, for example, to Wynsige as a "dean" of the cathedral priory (also found in the present entry) is certainly anachronistic, but the underlying assumption that JW*CC* 969 embodies Worcester's traditions concerning him *in their entirety* is unsafe. That different material on a variety of issues appears in *Chronicula*[1] shows that *Chronica chronicarum* is by no means a statement of everything that John "knew" about the past. Given Byrhtferth's description of Wynsige as *reuerendus presbyter*, it seems entirely plausible that he was indeed the priest of St Helen's. Cf. Eric John, "The Church of Worcester and St Oswald," in *Belief and Culture in the Middle Ages: Studies Presented to Henry Mayr-Harting*, ed. Richard Gameson and Henrietta Leyser (Oxford: Oxford University Press, 2001), 142–57.

**970** Common root: *Coventry*[1] 970. JW*CC* 970. Cf. *Miracula S. Swithuni*, § 4, ed. Lapidge, *The Cult of St Swithun*, 648–96, at 652, where the translation is dated to 971, but also, as in JW*CC*, to the 110th year after the death of Swithun.

**972.1** Common root: *Coventry*[1] 972.1; *APW* 878. JW*CC* 972.

**972.2** Common root: *Coventry*[1] 972.2; *APW* 879. JW*CC* 972, possibly derived from Byrhtferth, *Vita Oswaldi*, 4.5 (435), or a lost Ramsey chronicle (see **960** above).

**973.1** Common root: *Coventry*[1] 973.1. Marianus via JW*CC* 973.

**973.2** Common root: *Coventry*[1] 973.2; *APW* 881. *ASC* via JW*CC* 973.

**974** Common root: *Coventry*[1] 974. Norman Annals: *AU*, *AG*, *ACad.*, *AMSM*, RT*Access.* 996. Cf. *ASC* (EF) 996.

**975** Common root: *Coventry*[1] 975. JW*CC* 975, possibly derived from Byrhtferth, *Vita Oswaldi*, 4.11, 17–18 (443, 448–49), or a lost Ramsey chronicle (see **960** above).

**978** Common root: *Coventry*[1] 978. JW*CC* 978, possibly derived from *ASC* and Byrhtferth, *Vita Oswaldi*, 4.18, 5.4 (449, 455), or a lost Ramsey chronicle (see **960** above).

**979** Common root: *Coventry*[1] 979. JW*CC* 979, possibly derived from *ASC* and Byrhtferth, *Vita Oswaldi*, 4.19 (450), or a lost Ramsey chronicle (see **960** above).

**984.1** Common root: *Coventry*[1] 984.1. Marianus via JW*CC* 984. Cf. Norman Annals: *AU*, *AG*, *AMSM*, *ASBD* 983.

**984.2** Common root: *Coventry*[1] 984.2. *ASC* via JW*CC* 984.

**987** Common root: *Coventry*[1] 987. *ASC* via JW*CC* 987.

**988** Common root: *Coventry*[1] 988. *ASC* via JW*CC* (DLP) 988.

**989** Common root: *Coventry*[1] 989. *ASC* via JW*CC* (DL) 990.

**991** Common root: *Coventry*[1] 991. JW*CC* 991, possibly derived from Byrhtferth, *Vita Oswaldi*, 5.11 (463), or a lost Ramsey chronicle (see **960** above).

**992.1** Common root: *Coventry*[1] 992.1; *APW* 992. An entry in hexameter verse which seems to derive from a calendrical source: see further chap. 5, § a above.

**992.2** Common root: *Coventry*[1] 992.2; *APW* 993. *ASC* via JW*CC* 992.

**993** Common root: *Coventry*[1] 992.3. Of the various witnesses to the Norman Annals, *AG* 992 is the closest: "Obiit Lotharius rex Francorum, in quo progenies Karoli Magni a regno funditus destituitur. Filii enim regis Lotharii capiuntur, et Hugo magnus <filius> Roberti ducis in regnum eleuatur." A fuller version is to be found in *AMSM* 972, 982. Cf. also *AU* 986, *ACad.* 991.

**995** Common root: *Coventry*[1] 996. *ASC* via JW*CC* (DL) 995.

**1002** Common root: *Coventry*[1] 1002.1. Marianus via JW*CC* 1002.

**1003.1** Common root: *Coventry*[1] 1002.2. JW*CC* 1002, possibly following Eadmer's account of the translation of Oswald: *Miracula S. Oswaldi archiepiscopi Eboracensis* (*BHL* 6376), ed. James Raine, *Historians of the Church at York and its Archbishops*, RS 71, 3 vols. (London: Longman, 1879–1894), 2:41–59, at 45–46.

**1003.2** Common root: *Coventry*[1] 1002.3. JW*CC* 1002, but John calls Wulfstan an abbot.

**1004** Common root: *Coventry*[1] 1004. Norman Annals: *AU*, *ACad.*, *AMSM*, *AG*, RT*Access.* 1026; *ASC* (E) 1024, *ASC* (F) 1023: "Hic Ricardus secundus obiit. Ricardus filius eius regnauit prope uno anno, et post eum regnauit Rodbertus frater eius .viii. annos."

**1006** Common root: *Coventry*[1] 1006. *ASC* via JW*CC* 1006.

**1008** Common root: *Coventry*[1] 1008. *ASC* via JW*CC* 1008: "Rex Anglorum Ægelredus de trecentis et decem cassatis unam trierem, de nouem uero loricam et cassidem fieri, et per totam Angliam naues intente precepit fabricari."

**1011** Common root: *Coventry*[1] 1010. Abbreviated from JW*CC* 1011, following Osbern, *Vita S. Elphegi, archiepiscopi Cantuariensis* (*BHL* 2518), ed. Henry Wharton, *Anglia Sacra*, 2 vols. (London: Richard Chiswel, 1691), 2:122–42, at 136–37.

**1012** Common root: *Coventry*[1] 1012. JW*CC* 1012, following both *ASC* and Osbern, *Vita S. Elphegi*, 139–41.

**1013.1** Common root: *Coventry*[1] 1013.1. Norman Annals: *AU*, *ACad.*, *AMSM*, RT*Access.* 1035; *AG* 1037; *ASC* (E, expanded in F) 1031: "Rodbertus comes obiit in peregrinatione, et successit rex Willelmus in puerili etate." The statement that William reigned for 52 years is original to the present text and follows from its use of the Marianan chronological scheme for the placement of its Norman material.

**1013.2** Common root: *Coventry*[1] 1013.2. *ASC* via JW*CC* 1013.

**1014.1** Common root: *Coventry*[1] 1014.1. *ASC* via JW*CC* 1013.

**1014.2** Common root: *Coventry*[1] 1014.2. JW*CC* 1014, following *ASC* and a lost miracle story associated with the cult of St Edmund, king and martyr.

**1015** Common root: *Coventry*[1] 1015.1. *ASC* via JW*CC* 1015.

**1016** Common root: *Coventry*[1] 1015.2; *AC* (C) 1016. *ASC* via JW*CC* 1016 (484–92). In *Chronicula*[1] AD 1002, John, correcting his narrative, reckons the number of battles at five rather than four: "Hinc inter ambos reges atrocissima pugna quinquies bellatum est."

**1017.1** Common root: *Coventry*[1] 1016; *AC* (C) 1017. JW*CC* 1017, expanding *ASC*. The compiler adds the detail that Leofric's earldom was that of Chester.

**1017.2** A marginal gloss.

**1018** Common root: *Coventry*[1] 1018. JW*CC* 1018, following *ASC*.

**1019** Common root: *Coventry*[1] 1019. *ASC* via JW*CC* 1019.

**1020** Common root: *Coventry*[1] 1020; *AC* (C) 1020. *ASC* via JW*CC* 1020.
**1022** Common root: *Coventry*[1] 1022. *ASC* via JW*CC* 1022.
**1023** Common root: *Coventry*[1] 1023; *AC* (C) 1023. *ASC* via JW*CC* 1023.
**1024** Common root: *Coventry*[1] 1024. Marianus via JW*CC* 1024.
**1026** Common root: *Coventry*[1] 1026. *ASC* via JW*CC* 1026.
**1028.1** Common root: *Coventry*[1] 1028.1; *AC* (C) 1028. *ASC* via JW*CC* 1028.
**1028.2** Common root: *Coventry*[1] 1028.2. Marianus via JW*CC* 1028.
**1029** Common root: *Coventry*[1] 1029; *AC* (C) 1029. *ASC* via JW*CC* 1029.
**1030** Common root: *Coventry*[1] 1030; *AC* (C) 1030. *ASC* via JW*CC* 1030.
**1031** Common root: *Coventry*[1] 1031; *AC* (C) 1031. *ASC* via JW*CC* 1031.
**1033** Common root: *Coventry*[1] 1033; *AC* (C) 1033. JW*CC* 1033, expanding *ASC*.
**1035.1** Common root: *Coventry*[1] 1035; *AC* (C) 1035. JW*CC* 1035, expanding *ASC*.
**1035.2** A marginal gloss.
**1036** Common root: *Coventry*[1] 1036. JW*CC* 1036, developing *ASC*.
**1037** Common root: *Coventry*[1] 1037. JW*CC* 1036, expanding *ASC*.
**1038** Common root: *Coventry*[1] 1038; *AC* (C) 1038. *ASC* via JW*CC* 1038.
**1039** Common root: *Coventry*[1] 1039; *AC* (C) 1039. Marianus via JW*CC* 1039.
**1040** Common root: *Coventry*[1] 1040; *AC* (C) 1040. *ASC* via JW*CC* 1040.
**1041** Common root: *Coventry*[1] 1041. JW*CC* 1041, expanding *ASC*.
**1042.1** Common root: *Coventry*[1] 1042; *AC* (C) 1042. *ASC* via JW*CC* 1042.
**1042.2** A marginal gloss.
**1043.1** Common root: *Coventry*[1] 1043; *AC* (C) 1043. *ASC* via JW*CC* 1043.
**1043.2** See **510.2** above.
**1044.1** Common root: *Coventry*[1] 1044; *AC* (C) 1044. Marianus via JW*CC* 1044.
**1044.2** Norman Annals: *AU* 1047; *ACad.*, RT*Access.* 1046; *AMSM* 1048; *AG*, *ASC* (E) 1042.
**1046** Common root: *Coventry*[1] 1046; *AC* (C) 1046. JW*CC* 1046, following *ASC*, but with a thirteenth-century annotation.
**1047** The source was presumably the charter reported in *Landboc*, 1:219–221 (fol. 198v): "De Churchseat de Hallinga. Notandum, in primis, quod tempore Sancti Edwardi regis et confessoris, Goda þe Wode, domina de Hallinga, de Haseltona, de Janeworth, et de Rawelle, divina inspirante gratia, annuum redditum suum et villenagio suo in Hallinga, scilicet de xxv. virgatis terre, quem nos Churchesead appellamus, elemosinarie de Winchecumba dedit et concessit, in puram et perpetuam elemosinam . . . ." Churchscot was grain (and later other rent in kind) paid to the priest, as first fruits, at Martinmas (11 November). A daughter of King Æthelred II who was forced into exile 1016, Goda or Godgifu appears to have acquired or resumed extensive lands and rights in Gloucestershire (among other counties) soon after her brother, Edward

the Confessor, returned to England in 1041: see Domesday Book, fols. 166c and 170b; Ann Williams, "The King's Nephew: The Family, Career and Connections of Ralph, Earl of Hereford," in *Studies in Medieval History Presented to R. Allen Brown*, ed. Christopher Harper-Bill, C. J. Holdsworth, and Janet L. Nelson (Woodbridge: Boydell Press, 1989), 327–43 (esp. 327 and 331–32). It is clear that she was dead by 1049 because her second husband, Eustace II, count of Boulogne, was condemned at the 1049 Council of Reims for having contracted an incestuous marriage which can only have been that to his second wife, Ida of Bouillon. Her marriage to Eustace is now thought to have been contracted in about 1036 and her death to have taken place c.1047. See Heather J. Tanner, *Families, Friends and Allies: Boulogne and Politics in Northern France and England, c.879–1160* (Leiden: Brill, 2004), 113–14, 296; Frank Barlow, *Edward the Confessor* (London: Eyre Methuen, 1970), 307–8; David Bates, "Lord Sudeley's Ancestors: The Family of the Counts of Amiens, Valois and the Vexin in France and England during the Eleventh Century," in *The Sudeleys, Lords of Toddington* (London: Manorial Society of Great Britain, 1987), 34–48, at 36, 38. It follows that the grant, if genuine, is probably to be dated to between 1042 and c.1047.

**1049.1** Common root: *Coventry*[1] 1049. JW*CC* 1049 following *ASC* (D).

**1049.2** A note confirmed by or perhaps even derived from the Latin version of a writ preserved in *Landboc*, 1:226 (fol. 207): "Gloriossimus rex et sanctus Edwardus, devotus cenobiorum edificator, et fratrum in ipsis Deo servientium munificus provisor, beati Petri de Gloucestrie et innocentis regis et martiris Kenelmi de Winchecumba, divine caritatis intuitu, contulit totam piscariam suam de Fremelade, dividendam, equaliter, inter fratres dictorum monasteriorum, in omnibus capturis. Convenit, denique, inter rectores dictorum cenobiorum, quod labores piscarie, ut lucrum, communicarent, ita, videlicet, ut monasterium de Gloucestria totum mairemium inveniret; monachi, vero, de Winchecumba, totam virgam ad eandem necessarium. Cetera, vero, ad piscarie conservationem necessaria, communicatis, equaliter, invenient sumptibus." That is, the fishery at Framilode, on the River Frome, is to be held by both Gloucester and Winchcombe: the yield of fish is to be divided equally; the abbots will share the work and profits, Gloucester having the job of finding the large timbers, Winchcombe all the branches that are required; all other burdens are to be shared equally. The same charter, as far as the word *communicarent*, also appears in *Cart. Gloc.*, 3:276.

**1050** Common root: *Coventry*[1] 1050; *AC* (C) 1050. JW*CC* 1050 expanding *ASC* (D).

**1051** Common root: *Coventry*[1] 1051; *AC* (C) 1051. JW*CC* 1051 following *ASC*.

**1052.1** Common root: *Coventry*[1] 1052.1. Marianus via JW*CC* 1052.

**1052.2** Common root: *Coventry*[1] 1052.2. JW*CC* 1052 following *ASC*.

**1053** Common root: *Coventry*[1] 1053; *AC* (C) 1053. JW*CC* 1053 following *ASC* (D).

**1054.1** Common root: *Coventry*[1] 1054. JW*CC* 1054 expanding *ASC*. Curiously, the compiler has not reproduced JW*CC*'s notice that Godric was "constituted" (consecrated?) abbot of Winchcombe on 17 July, which was the festival of St Kenelm and a Sunday in 1054.

**1054.2** A marginal gloss.

**1055** Common root: *Coventry*[1] 1055. JW*CC* 1055 expanding *ASC*.

**1056** Common root: *Coventry*[1] 1057.1; *AC* (C) 1056. Either Marianus via JW*CC* 1056. Cf. *ASC* (E) 1056, following the Norman Annals: "Hic Henricus Romanorum imperator obiit cui successit filius eius Henricus."

**1057** Common root: *Coventry*[1] 1057.2. JW*CC* 1057 following *ASC*.

**1058** Common root: *Coventry*[1] 1058; *APW* 1058; *AC* (C) 1058. JW*CC* 1058 expanding *ASC* (D).

**1059** Winchcombe's ownership of the chapels in Diclesdon and Aldrington is confirmed in the bull the abbey obtained from Pope Alexander III (*Landboc*, 1:26–27), but this grant of churchscot is not recorded among the abbey's muniments. For burial rights in these locations, see also *Landboc*, 1:74.

**1060** Common root: *Coventry*[1] 1060. Perhaps *ASC* via JWCC 1060 *or* the Norman Annals: "Hic Henricus rex Francorum obiit cui successit Phylippus filius eius" (*AU* 1060).

**1061** Common root: *Coventry*[1] 1061. *ASC* (D) via JW*CC* 1061.

**1062** Common root: *Coventry*[1] 1062.1; *AC* (C) 1062. JW*CC* 1062, following Coleman's lost Old English *Life of Wulfstan* (see WM*VW*, xi–xvi).

**1064.1** Common root: *Coventry*[1] 1062.2. Marianus via JW*CC* 1064: "Cyclus magnus paschalis hic incipit indictione .ii."

**1064.2** Common root: *Coventry*[1] 1063.1. JW*CC* 1064 following *ASC* (D).

**1065.1** Common root: *Coventry*[1] 1063.2. JW*CC* 1065.

**1065.2** Common root: *Coventry*[1] 1063.3. JW*CC* 1065 following *ASC*.

**1066.1** Common root: *Coventry*[1] 1066; *AC* (C) 1066. JW*CC* 1066 revising *ASC*. Manuscript C gives the date of the battle of Hastings as *.xi. kalend. Nouembris*, but BP have *.ii. idus Octobris* as here. Cf. Norman Annals: *AU*, *ACad.*, *AG*, *AMSM* 1066.

**1066.2** The data provided by this thirteenth-century addition and the other related entries (see **1074.3** and **1077** below) need to be considered alongside those provided by Thomas of Marlborough's *History of the Abbey of Evesham* (TM*Chron.*). Now it is true Thomas was writing in the early thirteenth century, in much the same period as the present annotator; but there are good grounds for thinking that the relevant section—his account of Æthelwig, abbot of Evesham (1058–1077)—was extracted without significant emendation from a *gesta abbatum* compiled by Dominic, an Evesham writer who flourished in the 1120s (see J. C. Jennings, "The Writings of Prior Dominic of Evesham," *EHR* 77 [1962]: 298–304). What Dominic/Thomas reports (TM*Chron.*, § 158) is that Abbot Godric of Winchcombe was removed by King William and imprisoned at Gloucester while Æthelwig administered the abbey "as though it were his own for almost three years" (*fere per tres annos quasi propriam*); that the king then gave the abbey to a Norman called Galandus who died "after a brief time" (*post modicum tempus*); and that the abbey was then entrusted to Abbot Æthelwig once again, this time for "a long period" (*longo tempore postea*).

None of these temporal references is precisely anchored by reference to AD dates, but they may be aligned with the evidence provided by other records. The deposition of Godric would appear, first, to have taken place around or soon after 1072, for Dominic's notice to this effect follows his discussion of the assistance which Æthelwig gave to Serlo after he became abbot of Gloucester, an event which took place in 1072 (see *Heads I*, 52; Edward A. Freeman, *The History of the Norman Conquest of England*, 6 vols. [Oxford: Clarendon Press, 1867–1879], 4 [1st ed., 1871]: 177). If Æthelwig administered the abbey for almost three years from this point, it follows that Galandus was not appointed before late 1074. The "short period" when Galandus was abbot must, second, have overlapped with or fallen within the period between Christmas 1074 and 28 August 1075, for Galandus was listed among the abbots present at the Council of London which took place between these termini (see *C&S I*, 2:615). The "long period" when the abbey was again in Æthelwig's hands cannot, third, have comprised more than twenty-six months at the most, for he died on 16 February 1077 (see TM*Chron.*, 166, n. 1, and *Heads I*, 47, which notes the obit recorded in MS. London, B.L., Cotton Nero C.IX, fol. 5v) and the next abbot of Winchcombe, Ralph, was in place before his death. The latter point is evident from Bishop Wulfstan's confraternity agreement with the abbots and brethren of Evesham, Chertsey, Bath, Pershore, Winchcombe, and Gloucester, and the Dean of Worcester (ed. Benjamin Thorpe, *Diplomatarium Anglicum aevi Saxonici* [London: Macmillan, 1865], 615–17). The document is undated, but Ralph is listed in the preamble as the abbot of Winchcombe and the other named heads include Æthelwig as abbot of Evesham. This agreement must date, therefore, from the seemingly brief window between Ralph's consecration and Æthelwig's death, a period that was over by 16 February 1077. If Dominic's *longo tempore postea* means not more than about two years, then *post modicum* *tempus* would seem to mean six months or perhaps one year at the most. It is also worth noting that Godric was still alive at the time when the latter document was drawn up, for he is listed among the monks "at Evesham," immediately after Æthelwig (that is, as being second in rank to the monastery's abbot). Godric had been transferred to Æthelwig's custody at Evesham and his prominence in this record may well indicate, as Darlington inferred, that the abbot of Evesham treated him with some kindness (see Reginald R. Darlington, "Æthelwig, Abbot of Evesham," *EHR* 48 [1933]: 1–22, 177–98, at 11).

The upshot of all of this is (1) that Galandus appears to have been appointed abbot of Winchcombe not in 1066, but in late 1074 or early 1075, and (2) that his reign lasted, not eight years as is implied by the additions to the present chronicle (see **1074.3** below), but less, probably much less, than one year. Indeed, his abbacy was probably over before the middle of 1075 at the latest. The present editor has been reassured to find that Bernard Meehan reached much the same conclusions in an unpublished paper presented at the International Medieval Congress at Leeds in 1998, and we are grateful to him for sharing his work to the benefit of the present note.

**1067** Common root: *Coventry*[1] 1067; *AC* (C) 1067. JW*CC* 1067 following *ASC*.

**1068.1** Common root: *Coventry*[1] 1068.1; *AC* (C) 1068.1. JW*CC* 1068 following *ASC* (D).

**1068.2** Common root: *Coventry*[1] 1068.2; *AC* (C) 1068.2. The date of Henry's birth may well have been an important detail for historians writing after 1100, since it could be used to make the argument that he was, in contrast to his older brother Robert Curthose, *porphyrogenitus* or "born to the purple", and therefore more entitled to rule the kingdom. See Christopher N. L. Brooke, *The Saxon and Norman Kings* (London: Batsford, 1963), 171–72; Hollister, *Henry I*, 105. The source of the notice is unknown: Henry I's birth is also noted in Devizes, *AW*, 1068, but there is no relationship between the two reports. Cf. also the notes on the English succession in the eleventh century in JW*CC* (C), p. 54.

**1069** Common root: *Coventry*[1] 1069; *AC* (C) 1069. JW*CC* 1069 expanding *ASC*.

**1070** Common root: *Coventry*[1] 1070; *AC* (C) 1070. JW*CC* 1070, developing a record of the 1070 Legatine Council of Winchester. For the extant records, see *C&S I*, 2:565–70.

**1071** Common root: *Coventry*[1] 1071; *AC* (C) 1071. JW*CC* 1071 following *ASC*.

**1072** Common root: *Coventry*[1] 1072; *AC* (C) 1072. JW*CC* 1072 following *ASC*.

**1073** Common root: *Coventry*[1] 1073; *AC* (C) 1073. JW*CC* 1073 following *ASC*.

**1074.1** Common root: *Coventry*[1] 1074. JW*CC* 1074 expanding *ASC*. The annotator has confused Roger de Breteuil, earl of Hereford (1071–1075), with Roger de Pîtres, sheriff of Gloucester (d. 1086).

**1074.2** The corresponding item in JW*CC* 1074 refers to Edward the Confessor's queen: "Edgitha, regis Haroldi germana, quondam Anglorum regina . . ." But the present item refers to Ealdgyth, the daughter of Ælfgar, earl of Mercia (1057–1063), and the queen of King Harold II. Her fate is quite obscure: see Williams, *English and the Conquest*, 51–53. The item is unique to *Winchcombe*[1] and it is possible that the confusion was introduced by its compiler rather than the author of the common root.

**1074.3** An addition which presumably draws on Winchcombe traditions, but this obit may belong to 1075 rather than to 1074 for reasons set out above under **1066.2**.

**1075.1** Common root: *Coventry*[1] 1075. JW*CC* 1075 following *ASC*.

**1075.2** Common root: *Coventry*[1] 1076. JW*CC* 1076 expanding *ASC*, which does not mention Swein's learning.

**1077** As the discussion under **966**, **1066.2**, and **1074.3** above indicates, the chronological accuracy of this sequence of additions is at best haphazard, but this is perhaps the most accurate of the four items. Ralph's appointment is not reported elsewhere, but must have taken place before 16 February 1077, for he is mentioned in Bishop Wulfstan's confraternity agreement (ed. Thorpe, *Diplomatarium Anglicum aevi Saxonici*, 615–17) as abbot of Winchcombe along with Abbot Æthelwig of Evesham, who died on that date. It is just possible, therefore, that Ralph was appointed in 1077, but an election during 1076 is also a possibility, since the *terminus a quo* for the present event comprises the Evesham tradition (TM*Chron.*, § 158) that Æthelwig had custody of the abbey for "a long time" after the death of Abbot Galandus. See further the discussion under **1066.2** above.

**1079** Common root: *Coventry*[1] 1077; *AC* (C) 1079. This consecration is reported in JW*CC* 1079.

**1080** Common root: *Coventry*[1] 1078; *AC* (C) 1080. JW*CC* 1080. Cf. *HDE*, 3.23–24.

**1081** Common root: *Coventry*[1] 1081; *AC* (C) 1081. Marianus via JW*CC* 1080, 1083.

**1085.1** Common root: *Coventry*[1] 1085.1; *AC* (C) 1085. JW*CC* 1085 expanding *ASC*.

**1085.2** Common root: *Coventry*[1] 1085.2. JW*CC* 1083 following *ASC*. Cf. Norman Annals: *AU* 1084; *ACad.*, *AMSM* 1083.

**1086.1** Common root: *Coventry*[1] 1086. JW*CC* 1086, whose account of the Domesday Survey shares words with that added to the Hereford manuscript of Marianus Scotus (N, fol. 158v): see Stevenson, "Domesday Survey," 73–74.

**1086.2** JW*CC* 1086 echoing *ASC*. But JW*CC* lacks the information that Christina was the sister of Queen Margaret.

**1087** Common root: *Coventry*[1] 1087; *AC* (C) 1087. JW*CC* 1087 echoing *ASC*. Cf. Devizes, *AW*, 1087.

**1088** Common root: *Coventry*[1] 1088; *AC* (C) 1088. There are a few verbal parallels with JW*CC* 1088 (*Primates Anglie . . . regno priuare . . . maxime Anglorum . . . bona*), but this entry seems to have more in common with *ASC* (E) than JW*CC* in its present form. See further the Introduction, chap. 2, § c, above.

**1089** Common root: *Coventry*[1] 1089; *AC* (C) 1089. JW*CC* 1089, who expands *ASC* by supplying the dates for Lanfranc's death and the earthquake which are reported here.

**1090** Common root: *Coventry*[1] 1090. Derived wholly from JW*CC* 1091. Cf. WM*GR*, 4.323, where the storms are also reported, but with somewhat different details as to the number and size of the beams involved in the London incident.

**1091** Common root: *Coventry*[1] 1091; *AC* (C) 1091. All the information in this annal is present in JW*CC* 1091, whose account differs in substance from that found in *ASC*.

**1092** Common root: *Coventry*[1] 1092; *AC* (C) 1092. This fire is otherwise reported only in JW*CC* 1092.

**1093.1** Common root: *Coventry*[1] 1093.1; *AC* (C) 1093.1. JW*CC* 1093 expanding *ASC*.

**1093.2** This obit is not reported elsewhere: see *Heads I*, 79.

**1093.3** Common root: *Coventry*[1] 1093.2; *AC* (C) 1093.2. JW*CC* 1093 reports both obits.

**1094** Common root: *Coventry*[1] 1094. JW*CC* 1094. There is insufficient detail as to whether the compiler was following the earlier version of this annal (attested in HLP) or the later one (attested in C[3]BP). The expedition to Wales is otherwise reported only in JW*CC*.

**1095.1** Common root: *Coventry*[1] 1095; *AC* (C) 1095. JW*CC* 1095 reports both obits in much greater detail.

**1095.2** The name of the abbot has been lost in the fire damage, but this is presumably a reference to the appointment of Girmund, whose obit is recorded in **1122.2**. His abbacy is otherwise attested in *Hist. Abbend.*, 2.151, where he is said to have witnessed a quitclaim in the fourteenth year of King Henry I (that is, between 5 August 1113 and 4 August 1114), and in a forged Gloucester *pancarta* of 1114 (*RRAN*, 2: no. 1041; printed in W. St. C. Baddeley, "Fresh Material Evidence Relating to Norman Gloucester," *Transactions of the Bristol and Gloucestershire Archaeological Society* 41 [1918–1919]: 87–92, at 87–90), where he again figures as a witness (see Brooke, *CWB*, 60, n. 38). The present entry implies that his reign was preceded by a vacancy of two years, which is not implausible given that the practice of exploiting vacancies took off during the reign of William II: see Lauren H. Jared, "English Ecclesiastical Vacancies during the Reigns of William II and Henry I," *Journal of Ecclesiastical History* 42 (1991): 362–93 (esp. 370–75). See also *Heads I*, 79.

**1096** Common root: *Coventry*[1] 1096; *AC* (C) 1096. JW*CC* 1096, variously expanding and revising *ASC*.

**1097** Common root: *Coventry*[1] 1097; *AC* (C) 1097. All these incidents are reported in JW*CC* 1097.

**1098.1** Common root: *Coventry*[1] 1098; *AC* (C) 1098. All these incidents are reported in JW*CC* 1098.

**1098.2** William II's transfretation is reported in JW*CC* 1099.

**1099.1** Common root: *Coventry*[1] 1099; *AC* (C) 1099. Derived from JW*CC* 1099. JW*CC* lacks, however, the statement that Pope Paschal II was a monk of Monte Cassino—an error which may have arisen from a misreading of the Norman Annals. For *AMSM* mentions under 1087 that an unnamed monk of that abbey was elected to the papacy and reigned for one month. He then moves on to record the succession of Urban II (1088–1099). That monk was, of course, Abbot Desiderius who reigned for one year as Pope Victor III (1086–1087).

**1099.2** Indeterminate source.

**1100.1** Common root: *Coventry*[1] 1100.1. JW*CC* 1100. Cf. *Cart. Gloc.*, 1:12; Gregory of Caerwent (V), fol. 196v.

**1100.2** Common root: *Coventry*[1] 1100.2; *AC* (C) 1100. JW*CC* 1100 reports these obits and appointments.

**1100.3** Common root: *Coventry*[1] 1102.3. JW*CC* 1100 states that Henry recalled Anselm from France, but continues with the marriage of Henry to Queen Matilda as here.

**1101.1** Common root: *Coventry*[1] 1101.1. JW*CC* 1101. Other chronicles date the fire to 1102: e.g. *Cart. Gloc.*, 1:12; Gregory of Caerwent (V), fol. 196v.

**1101.2** Common root: *Coventry*[1] 1101.2; *AC* (C) 1101. From JW*CC* 1101, who has misdated Godfrey's death. Cf. WM*GR* 4.373–74, who rightly places the obit under 1100.

**1102.1** Common root: *Coventry*[1] 1102.1. JW*CC* 1101, but JW*CC* does not make explicit Duke Robert's return to Normandy.

**1102.2** Common root: *Coventry*[1] 1102.2. JW*CC* 1102, following Eadmer, *HN*, 3 (144); but note that JW*CC* 1102 lacks the *tam. . . quam* construction used in the present item, while it is used in the account of the council in *Chronicula*[1] VA 1088, which is otherwise an exact echo of JW*CC* 1102.

**1103** Common root: *Coventry*[1] 1103. JW*CC* 1103. *de quodam fonte* appears to be a Winchcombe addition. See *Coventry* 1103.

**1104** Common root: *Coventry*[1] 1104; *APW* 1104; *AC* (C) 1104. The source is probably JW*CC* 1104, but this effusion of blood is widely reported (e.g. Liebermann, *ANG*, 47, 131), whilst JW*CC*'s account of the storm may derive from *ASC*.

**1105** Common root: *Coventry*[1] 1105; *APW* 1105; *AC* (C) 1105. Matching material occurs in JW*CC* 1105, but the source of his account is unclear: see McGurk's comments in 3:107, n. 2.

**1106.1** Common root: *Coventry*[1] 1106.1; *APW* 1106.2; *AC* (C) 1106.3. JW*CC* 1106, following *ASC*.

**1106.2** Common root: *Coventry*[1] 1106.2; *APW* 1106.1; *AC* (C) 1106.1. Source unknown.

**1106.3** Common root: *Coventry*[1] 1106.3. JW*CC* 1106. Cf. Norman Annals: *AU*, *ACad.*, *AMSM* 1106.

**1107.1** Common root: *Coventry*[1] 1109. JW*CC* 1107, following Eadmer, *HN*, 4 (186).

**1107.2** JW*CC* 1107 notes Robert fitz Haimo's obit, but John treats his role as *fundator Theokesberie* in a borrowing from WM*GP*, 4.157, which he himself inserted into the margins of C, p. 360 ($C^3$). Cf. *AT* 1107.

**1108.1** Common root: *Coventry*[1] 1108.1; *APW* 1108.1; *AC* (C) 1108.1. JW*CC* 1108.

**1108.2** Common root: *Coventry*[1] 1108.2; *APW* 1108.2; *AC* (C) 1108.2. From JW*CC* 1108, following Eadmer, *HN*, 4 (196–98).

**1108.3** This obituary does not appear in JW*CC* nor is it reported elsewhere: see Judith A. Green, *English Sheriffs to 1154* (London: Public Record Office, 1990), 87. He cannot have died before the middle of 1108, for there exists a writ of King Henry I directed to himself and Bishop Samson which is witnessed by Richard de Belmeis, bishop of London (*RRAN*, 2: no. 892; William Farrer, "An Outline Itinerary of King Henry I," *EHR* 39 (1919): 303–82, 505–79, at 353). Richard was elected to his see on 24 May and consecrated on 26 July 1108: see Eadmer, *HN*, 4 (196–97). On Urse de Abbetot, see also Katherine S. B. Keats-Rohan, *Domesday People: A Prosopography of Persons Occurring in English Documents, 1066–1166*, vol. 1, *Domesday Book* (Woodbridge: Boydell Press, 1999), 439.

**1109.1** Common root: *Coventry*[1] 1110.1; *APW* 1109.1; *AC* (C) 1109.1. JW*CC* 1109, following Eadmer, *HN*, 4 (206, 210).

**1109.2** Common root: *Coventry*[1] 1110.2; *APW* 1109.2; *AC* (C) 1109.2. JW*CC* 1109, modifying Eadmer, *HN*, 4 (195–96). See McGurk's comments in JW*CC* 1109, n. 4.

**1109.3** Possibly an original contribution. Cf. *AT* 1109.

**1110.1** Common root: *Coventry*[1] 1111.1; *AC* (C) 1110.1. JW*CC* 1110.

**1110.2** Common root: *Coventry*[1] 1111.2; *APW* 1110; *AC* (C) 1110.2. JW*CC* 1110. The drying up of the River Trent is also reported in *AT* 1108.

**1110.3** JW*CC* 1111 (p. 126).

**1111.1** Common root: *Coventry*[1] 1112.1; *APW* 1111; *AC* (C) 1111. From JW*CC* 1111 (p. 120).

**1111.2** Common root: *APW* 1111. The figures in question are Bohemond, prince of Antioch (1099–1111), Roger I Borsa, duke of Apulia (1085–1111), Robert II, count of Flanders (1093–1111), and Baldwin VII, count of Flanders (1111–1119). Cf. Norman Annals: *AU* 1111: "Boamundus dux obiit."

**1111.3** Common root: *Coventry*[1] 1112.3. JW*CC* 1112, expanding *ASC*.

**1112** Common root: *Coventry*[1] 1113.1; *APW* 1112; *AC* (C) 1112. JW*CC* 1112.

**1113** Common root: *Coventry*[1] 1113.2; *APW* 1113; *AC* (C) 1113. JW*CC* 1113 is the earliest source for these obits. Cf. Devizes, *AW*, 1113.

**1114** Common root: *Coventry*[1] 1114; *APW* 1114; *AC* (C) 1114. JW*CC* 1114.

**1115.1** Common root: *Coventry*[1] 1115.1; *APW* 1115.1; *AC* (C) 1115.1. JW*CC* 1115, following Eadmer, *HN*, 5 (229–30).

**1115.2** Common root: *Coventry*[1] 1115.2; *APW* 1115.2; *AC* (C) 1115.2. JW*CC* 1115, following Eadmer, *HN*, 5 (235–37).

**1116** Common root: *Coventry*[1] 1116; *APW* 1116; *AC* (C) 1116. JW*CC* 1116, following *ASC* and Eadmer, *HN*, 5 (237–38).

**1117.1** Common root: *Coventry*[1] 1117.1. A reference to the number of 532-year cycles since the creation of the world: see **53.1** above.

**1117.2** No obvious parallels, but the date is accurate. Writing after 1169/73, William of Tyre, *Historia rerum in partibus transmarinis gestarum*, 12.7 (ed. R. B. C. Huygens, CCCM 63 [Turnhout: Brepols, 1986]: 553–55), assigns the foundation of the Order of the Temple to the year 1118. See also Malcolm Barber, "The Origins of the Order of the Temple," *Studia Monastica* 12 (1970): 219–40.

**1117.3** Common root: *Coventry*[1] 1117; *APW* 1117. JW*CC* 1117. McGurk comments (JW*CC* 3:142, n. 3) that JW*CC*'s account of this earthquake in Lombardy is fuller than that in *ASC* and that "it does not seem to be paralleled in any other known source."

**1118.1** Common root: *Coventry*[1] 1118. JW*CC* 1118, following Eadmer, *HN*, 5 (246, 248).

**1118.2** Common root: *APW* 1118. JW*CC* 1118.

**1118.3** Common root: *Coventry*[1] 1119.2. JW*CC* 1119. Cf. *ASC* (E) 1119.

**1119** Common root: *Coventry*[1] 1119.1; *APW* 1119.1; *AC* (C) 1119.1. JW*CC* 1119, following *ASC* and Eadmer, *HN*, 5 (249, 255–58).

**1120** Common root: *Coventry*[1] 1120; *APW* 1120; *AC* (C) 1120. JW*CC* 1120, following Eadmer, *HN*, 5 (259–60, 288–89).

**1121** Common root: *Coventry*[1] 1121; *APW* 1121; *AC* (C) 1121. JW*CC* 1121, following Eadmer, *HN*, 5 (290–98). The interlined words in the Winchcombe version, *de Sigillo capellani regis* and *Peceth*, also appear in

*Chronicula*[2] 1121's version of this material and were perhaps transmitted to Winchcombe through the Gloucester source of the continuation: that is, these annotations would appear to be products of an attempt to collate the two chronicles.

**1122.1** Common root: *Coventry*[1] 1122.1. JW*CC* 1122, but dating the fire to *.vii. idus Mar.* (which was a Thursday in 1122). The root also differs in giving 13 June rather than 22 May as the date of the first fire. *Cart. Gloc.*, 1:15, recounts the event in the same words as JW*CC* but, like the present entry, dates the fire to 8 March which was a Wednesday in 1122. *Chronicula*[2] 1122 also has *.vii. idus Mar.* but it does not provide any date for the earlier fire.

**1122.2** This obit is not reported elsewhere: see *Heads I*, 79.

**1122.3** The present item agrees with the earlier versions of JW*CC* (DL) and Eadmer, *HN*, 5 (302) in dating Ralph's death to 20 October, whereas later versions (CBP) date it to 19 October (i.e. *.xiiii. kal. Novembris*). This is the first item of the continuation which seems to derive, largely if not entirely, from a chronicle produced at St Peter's Abbey, Gloucester, in the early 1180s. See the Introduction, chap. 3, §§ e-f, above.

**1123** Matching material appears in both JW*CC* 1123 and *Chronicula*[2] 1123.

**1125.1** The present entry lies somewhere between *Chronicula*[2] 1125 and *AT* 1125, which uses the phrase *ultio facta est*.

**1125.2** No obvious parallels. Cf. *Chronicula*[2] 1125 and JW*CC* 1125, which both date the council to 9 rather than 8 September.

**1125.3** Matching material appears in both *Chronicula*[2] 1125 and JW*CC* 1125. The item in *AT* 1125 is probably more distantly related.

**1126.1** No obvious parallels.

**1126.2** Similar entries appear in *Chronicula*[2] 1129, in *Cart. Gloc.*, 1:15, and in *APW* 1125. Cf. JW*CC* 1126. On this item, see the discussion in the Introduction, chap. 3, § b, above.

**1127.1** *Chronicula*[2] 1127 is identical except that it has *pristine restituuntur* where the present text had *ubi creberrima fiunt miracula mortui etiam pristine uite restituuntur*. Cf. JW*CC* 1127.

**1127.2** Matching material appears in*Chronicula*[2] 1127. Cf. JW*CC* 1127.

**1127.3** Matching material appears in both JW*CC* 1127 and *Chronicula*[2] 1127.

**1128.1** Matching material appears in *Chronicula*[2] 1128. Cf. JW*CC* 1128. Posthumously enrolled as a monk, William Clito was buried at St-Bertin.

**1128.2** This enigmatic entry probably refers to granting of a rule to the Templars by Pope Honorius II (1124–1130) and Stephen, the Latin patriarch of Jerusalem (1128–1130), at the Council of Troyes (1129): see William of Tyre, *Historia*, 12.7 (1:553–55) and **1117.2** above.

**1129.1** JW*CC* 1129 proper and *Chronicula*[2] 1129 give the date of Bishop William's obit as *viii. kal. Feb.* and provide a date for the consecration (17 November) rather than for the election of Henry of Blois. Contrary to the impression given here, Henry did not give up the abbacy of Glastonbury.

**1129.2** Matching material occurs in *Chronicula*[2] 1129. JW*CC* lacks this material. A related entry occurs in *AT* 1129. The council was in session from 30 September to 4 October 1129: see *C&S I*, 2:750–54.

**1130.1** Matching material occurs in *Chronicula*[2] 1129. JW*CC* lacks the appointment of Innocent.

**1130.2** Matching material occurs in *Chronicula*[2] or JW*CC* (HLBP, but not C) 1130. It is significant that the records of Reginald Foliot's appointment as abbot of Evesham and that of his obit (see **1149** below) are the only Evesham obits recorded in the chronicle. They reflect the continuation's interest in the affairs of the Foliot family. See also *Heads I*, 47.

**1130.3** The ultimate source of this item remains obscure. Neither JW*CC* proper nor *Chronicula*[2] 1130 specifies the number of abbots present; JW*CC* proper lists thirteen bishops, *Chronicula*[2] twelve.

**1130.4** Matching material occurs in Gregory of Caerwent, s.a. 1130 (as reported in V, fol. 198r): "Abbas Willelmus Gloc' infirmitate depressit pastoralem curam deponens eam domno Waltero de Laci tradidit qui a Symone Wigornensis episcopo 3° non. Augusti consecratus est." *Cart. Gloc.*, 1:15, has almost the same entry. The language of JW*CC* and *Chronicula*[2] 1130 (p. 194) is significantly further away. See also *Heads I*, 52–53.

**1131.1** Matching material occurs in JW*CC* 1131, *Chronicula*[2] 1130, and Gregory of Caerwent, s.a. 1131 (as reported in V, fol. 198v): "Robertus de Betun prior Lantonensis in Wallia fit episcopus Hereford." More distantly related material occurs in *AT* 1131.

**1131.2** Matching material occurs in JW*CC* 1131, *Chronicula*[2] 1130, *Cart. Gloc.*, 1:15, and Gregory of Caerwent, s.a. 1131 (as reported in V, fol. 198r): "Obiit Willelmus quondam abbas Gloc' apud S. Paternum in Wallia 3° non. Febr."

**1131.3** No obvious parallels.

**1131.4** Matching material occurs in JW*CC* (HBP) 1131. This material is not in *Chronicula*[2], nor is it in JW*CC* (C). Cf. *Heads I*, 52–53.

**1132.1** No obvious parallels.

**1132.2** No obvious parallels. In JW*CC* (C) and *Chronicula*[2] 1132 the comet appears *fere per .v. diebus* but MS. D has *.vii.*

**1133.1** No obvious parallels.

**1133.2** The source of this item is perhaps JW*CC* 1133 (3:210, n. 3), but the present entry omits the distinguishing features of JW*CC*'s account, and the eclipse and ensuing earthquake are so widely reported in English chronicles (see Newton, 160–63, 615) that the present item might derive from a number of sources, if not from local observations at Gloucester. *Chronicula*², however, lacks this item.

**1134.1** No obvious parallels.

**1134.2** The echoes for this entry in *Cart. Gloc.*, 1:15, or Gregory of Caerwent 1133 (V, fol. 198v: "Obiit Robertus Curta ocrea regis 3° non' Feb' apud Caerdif et in ecclesiam Sancti Petri ante altare principali honore sepultus est"), are significantly closer that those found in JWCC 1134 and *Chronicula*² 1133. More distantly related material occurs in *AT* 1133, and *APW* 1134.

**1135.1** Matching material occurs in JWCC *Chronicula*² 1133 and 1135, and JWCC (C) 1134.

**1135.2** Matching material occurs in JWCC *Chronicula*² 1133 and 1134, and JWCC (C) 1135 and 1136. *Chronicula*² gives the date of Stephen's coronation as *.xiii. kal. Jan.* In JWCC (C) this reading has been corrected to *ix kal. Jan.* More distantly related material occurs in *AT* 1135.

**1136.1** Matching material occurs in *Chronicula*² 1135. Related material occurs in Gregory of Caerwent, s.a. 1136, 1137 (as reported in V, fol. 198v), and *AT* 1136. The item could not have been derived from JWCC. The circumstances in which Richard fitz Gilbert was ambushed and killed are reported more fully in *Gesta Stephani regis Anglorum et ducis Normannorum*, 1.9 (ed. K. R. Potter and Ralph H. C. Davis, OMT [Oxford: Clarendon Press, 1976], 16–19).

**1136.2** The Cistercian Abbey of Bordesley (Worcestershire) was founded on 22 November 1138 by the newly created earl of Worcester, Count Waleran of Meulan: see David Crouch, *The Reign of King Stephen, 1135–54* (Harlow: Longman, 2000), 86 and n. 6.

**1137.1** Matching material occurs in *Chronicula*² 1136 (p. 222), but with the obit falling on *.xii°. kl. Decembr.* JWCC (C) covers William's death without specifying the day of his death.

**1137.2** Matching material occurs in *Chronicula*² 1136 (p. 220), and Gervase, 1:96 (s.a. 1136). This material is not in JWCC (C).

**1138.1** Matching material occurs in *Chronicula*² 1137 (p. 222). Godfrey's death is not in JWCC (C), but it does appear among the late additions to JWCC (D) 1136. Cf. *AT* 1137.

**1138.2** Matching material occurs in *Chronicula*² 1137 (p. 228), but it has a different date, *.ii. non. Iunii*, for the fire at St Peter's. See, likewise, Gervase, 1:100. JWCC (CD) reports these fires in significantly different words. Compare also the Canterbury-Winchester version of the Norman Annals as attested in MS. London, B.L., Cotton Nero A.VIII, fols. 2r–41r, and MS. London, B.L., Cotton Nero C.VII, fols. 216r–223v (ed. Liebermann, *ANG*, 61–83, at 80).

1139.1 No obvious parallels. Cf. *Chronicula*[2] 1138, JW*CC* (C) 1138 (p. 236), Gervase, 1:101. All share the same material, but none specify the month of Anacletus's death.

1139.2 Matching material occurs in both *Chronicula*[2] 1138 and JW*CC* (C) 1138. Cf. Gervase 1:100 (s.a. 1138). *AT* 1139. Robert seems to have been appointed in 1138 rather than 1139: see *Heads I*, 79.

1139.3 Matching material occurs in JW*CC* (C) 1138. *Chronicula*[2] 1138 covers the council without mentioning Theobald's election to the archbishopric of Canterbury. Cf. *AT* 1139; Gervase, 1:105–9.

1139.4 Related material occurs in *Chronicula*[2] 1138 (p. 258), 1139 (p. 278); Gervase, 1:105 (s.a. 1138); and Gregory of Caerwent, s.a. 1139 (as reported in V, fol. 198v): "Obiit Rogerus episcopus Sars. castellorum fundator precipuus." Cf. JW*CC* (C) 1139 (p. 276). Roger died in 1139: see WM*HN*, 37.

1139.5 Related material occurs in *Chronicula*[2] 1139 (p. 262); *Cart. Gloc.*, 1:18; Gregory of Caerwent, s.a. 1139 (as reported in V, fol. 198v): "Obiit abbas Walterus 6° idus Febr. cui procurante Milone Constabulario successit Gilebertus cognatus eique monachus Cluniacensis eximiæ sapientiæ." See also *Heads I*, 53.

1140 Matching material occurs in JW*CC* (C) 1140, *Chronicula*[2] 1140, and Gervase, 1:112 (s.a. 1140). More distantly related: *AT* 1140.

1141 Much of this information appears in *Chronicula*[2] 1141, but it is at this point that the text of *Chronicula*[2] ends imperfectly before reaching the exchange of prisoners. However, Gervase, 1:118–22, has everything, including the use of the feasts to date the captures and the exchange of prisoners. *AT* 1141 is much briefer. Cf. also *APW* 1141, 1142.

1142 Cf. Gervase, 1:122: "Multis et maxime pauperibus ingratus effectus est, quia fere totus in ædificatione castellorum, combustione villarum, viola tione ecclesiarum, maxime completus est in pauperum deprædatione."

1143.1 Related material occurs in Gregory of Caerwent, s.a. 1143 (as reported in V, fol. 198v): "Milo Constabularius comes Hereford. venandi causam Devie/Deire adiens a quodam milite suo sagitte corde percussus idibus Jan. obiit. . . ." Related material also occurs in Gervase, 1:126, and *AT* 1143.

1143.2 *AT* 1143 is much briefer, but seems to be distantly related to the present item. Gervase, 1:127–28, also reports the death of Pope Stephen and the succession of Pope Lucius but in different words.

1145 Gervase, 1:129, also begins his annal for 1145 by reporting the death of Pope Lucius, the succession of Eugenius *ordinis Cisterciensis monachus*, and mentions Bernard, *qui tunc temporis domini papæ dominus et magister videbatur*. *AT* 1145 is much briefer, but seems to be distantly related to the present item.

1147.1 Gervase, 1:137, and *AT* 1147 may be related to the present item.

**1147.2** Bruern was founded on 10 July 1147: see H. E. Salter, *VCH Oxfordshire*, 2:81.

**1148** Remarkably similar material occurs in Gregory of Caerwent, s.a. 1148 (as reported in V, fol. 199r): "Nicholaus monachus vir religiosus ad episcopatum Landauensis est assumptus. Obiit ut creditur sanctus Robertus de Betun Herford. episcopus ad concilium Remis. Cui successit abbas Gloc. Gilebertus et in abbatia successit eiusdem loci prefectus Hamelinus qui ab S. Wigorn. episcopo non. decemb. consecratus est." More distantly related material occurs in *AT* 1148 and *APW* 1147. The circumstances of Foliot's election to the bishopric of Hereford are discussed by Adrian Morey and Christopher N. L. Brooke, *Gilbert Foliot and his Letters*, Cambridge Studies in Medieval Life and Thought 11 (Cambridge: Cambridge University Press, 1965), 96. Theobald was then living in exile at St Omer and Gilbert was consecrated there by Theobald and a group of French bishops, on the pope's authority, on 5 September 1148. See also *Heads I*, 53.

**1149** Similar material occurs in Gregory of Caerwent, s.a. 1149 (as reported in V, fol. 199r); Gervase, 1:141; and *AT* 1149. However, Gervase and *AT* differ in that they identify Reginald as the prior of St Martin's, Dover. See also **1130.2** above.

**1150** Gregory of Caerwent, s.a. 1150 (as reported in V, fol. 199r), has the same number of years, but uses a very striking verb: "Obiit Simon Wigornensis episcopus cum sordescet [?] annis 26." More distantly related material occurs in *AT* 1150.

**1151.1** Gervase, 1:142 (s.a. 1150), records the consecration of John, but not his surname. Related material also occurs in *AT* 1151.

**1151.2** The destruction of the abbey is also described in a miracle story which was appended to Goscelin's *Vita S. Kenelmi, regis et martyris* (*BHL* 4641t), in the Winchcombe copy, today MS. Oxford, Bod.L., Douce 368, fol. 83v (ed. Love, *Three Lives*, 123–24), and in a charter preserved in *Landboc*, 1:83. For discussion, see also E. Gee, "A Miracle of Saint Kenelm in MS Douce 368," *Notes and Queries* 231 (1986): 149–54. The hagiographical account and the present record differ, however, over the dating of the event, which the former places in the year 1149. The charter merely refers to *dies regis Stephani*, but it tends to confirm the extent of the destruction stating that the abbey's "shrines, vestments, books and charters, and all its buildings [were] reduced to ashes." Since the present annal is probably a Gloucester record, dating from the 1170s or early 1180s, it is the dating in the *miraculum* which is to be preferred.

**1151.3** This obit is not reported elsewhere: see *Heads I*, 79.

**1151.4** Related material occurs in *AT* 1151.

1152.1 Gervase, 1:149, also begins his annal for 1152 with Eleanor's divorce and her marriage to Duke Henry of Normandy. More distantly related material occurs in *AT* 1152.

1152.2 This appointment is not reported elsewhere: see *Heads I*, 79.

1152.3 Strictly speaking, Stephen besieged the castle at Wallingford by building another castle at the entrance to the bridge: Henry of Huntingdon, 10.32 (758–60).

1153 The present item is probably related to Gervase, 1:155–56, and also *AT* 1153: "Obiit piæ memoriæ Eugenius Papa. Anastasius successit. Obiit Henricus archiepiscopus Eboraci, et Bernaldus abbas Clarevalensis. Dux Normanniæ Henricus ante Purificationem in Angliam veniens, cepit castra de Malmesburia et de Staunforde. Sed eodem anno circa festum Sancti Martini, rex Stephanus cepit pacem. Obiit Eustachius filius regis Stephani, et comes de Clare, et comes de Norhamptone." For the sieges, compare also Henry of Huntingdon, 10.34 (Malmesbury), 10.36 (Stamford).

1154.1 Probably related to Gervase, 1:157–58, and *AT* 1154.

1154.2 That Henry's wife returned with him is not widely noted: cf. Gervase, 1:159–60. *AT* 1154 is probably distantly related to the present item.

1155.1 Cf. Gervase, 1:161.

1155.2 Prince Henry's birth is also noted in Gervase, 1:161, and *AT* 1155. Cf. Diceto, *YH*, 301.

1155.3 Cf. *AT* 1154.

1156 A chronological dislocation of one year begins after this blank annal. The correct dating is restored with the double entry for 1160.

1157.1 Related material occurs in Gervase, 1:162 (s.a. 1156): "Rex Henricus transfretavit et . . . castra Gaufridi fratris sui, qui rebellare temptabat, valide optinuit." And also in *AT* 1156: "Rex Henricus transfretatur, et castra Gaufridi fratris sui obtinuit."

1157.2 Prince William's death is also reported in Gervase, 1:162 (s.a. 1156), and in *AT* 1156.

1157.3 Matilda's birth is not widely reported, but see John Brompton, *Chronicon*, s.a. 1157 (ed. Roger Twysden, *Historiæ Anglicanæ scriptores X* [London: James Flesher, 1652], cols. 725–1283, at 1047).

1157.4 This appointment probably belongs to 1157: see *Heads I*, 79, 257.

1158.1 Related material occurs in *AT* 1158.

1158.2 Related material occurs in Gervase, 1:165–66 (s.a. 1157–1158) and *AT* 1157: "Rex Angliam reversus cum multa cæde suorum [Walliam] expugnavit." The expedition took place in July and August 1157 (Eyton, 28–29).

1158.3 Related material occurs in *AT* 1158. The birth took place on 11 September 1157 (Eyton, 30; Diceto, *YH*, 302).

**1159.1** *AT* 1158 has additional material as to the date of Alfred's enthronement: "Eluredus factus est episcopus Wigorniæ in Ramis Palmarum intronizatur."

**1159.2** Though he appears to have reorganised the material, Gervase, 1:166, provides strong parallels for this item, which he rightly places in 1158: "Rex Henricus transfretavit et Parisius profectus a rege Franciæ Ludovico in magna gloria et honore susceptus est; filiam eius filio suo Henrico petiit et accepit. . . . Hic fuit primus ingressus ejus super Britones edomandos, et sic civitatem de Nantes ad jus suæ dominationis inflexit. Dehinc expugnato Toarco, regem Franciæ a Cenomannica urbe ad Montem Sancti Michaelis, et exinde per Bajocas, Cadomum, Rotomagum, non inpari quam ille eum per Franciam gloriæ et honoris magnificentia in Franciam deduxit." See, likewise, *AT* 1158: "Rex, facta pace cum Reso, transfretavit, et mortuo Gaufrido fratre suo, Britanniam obtinuit. Regis Henrici filius Henricus duxit filiam Ludovici regis Franciæ." Henry crossed to Normandy in August 1158 and held a conference with Louis VII on the River Epte where the marriage of Prince Henry to Princess Margaret was arranged; the surrender of Nantes took place in late September; the siege of Thouars and the royal passage through Normandy took place in October to November: see RT*Chron.*, 196; Eyton, 41.

**1159.3** Persuasive parallels for this item occur under 1158 in Gregory of Caerwent (as reported in V), fol. 199v: "Thamesii Lundini actio exsiccata est ut siccis pedibus transferetur"); in *AT* 1158: "Terræmotus factus est magnus in pluribus locis per Angliam. Fluvius Tamesis apud [blank] desiccatus est, ut siccis pedibus transiretur"; and in Gervase, 1:166: "Eodem anno terræ motus factus est in pluribus locis per Angliam, et fluvius Tamisia apud Londoniam desiccata est, ut siccis pedibus transiretur."

**1160.1** Possibly related to *AT* 1159. Gervase, 1:166–67 (s.a. 1159), also covers the origins of the schism but at greater length and in different words.

**1160.2** Related material occurs in Gervase, 1:167 (s.a. 1159): "De aliis vero terris sibi subjectis inauditam similiter census fecit exactionem. Dehinc versus Tolosam copiosum valde movit exercitum, obseditque urbem . . . Sed Francorum rege Ludovico civitatem prædictam tuente, frustrata est intentio regis Anglorum; nam obsidione soluta, post summam pacem et concordiam inter eos factam, discordia maxima post modicum est suborta." Cf. also *AT* 1159. The siege took place in July to September 1159, whilst Henry's dispute with Louis VII lasted until May 1160 (Eyton, 47–49).

**1160.3** Possibly related to *AT* 1160.

**1160.4** Related material occurs in Gervase, 1:167 (s.a. 1160): "Romanorum imperator Fridericus in Papiensi concilio cliii. episcoporum Octoviani scisma favore suo et auctoritate roboravit. De cujus susceptione regi Franciæ Ludovico, et Henrico regi Anglorum, spectabiles legatos cum litteris suis misit. Sed reges prædicti parti et obedientiæ catholici papæ cesserunt Alexandri."

**1161.1** Gisors was taken in November 1160 and the rebuilding of the castle began soon afterwards: see RT*Chron.*, 208–9; Eyton, 52.

**1161.2** Possibly related to *AT* 1161. Theobald died on 18 April 1161: see Gervase, 1:168.

**1162.1** Related material occurs in Gervase, 1:171: "Hoc anno Frethericus imperator inclitam Italiæ urbem subvertit Mediolanum. Alexander vero papa . . . navibus advectus . . . deinde venit in Galliam. . . ." There is a distorted version of this item in *AT* 1162: "Alexander navigio venit in Angliam."

**1162.2** A fuller version appears in Gervase, 1:170–71, a briefer one in *AT* 1162.

**1163.1** Gervase, 1:172, places this transfretation in December 1162.

**1163.2** The council met on 19–21 May 1163. This item may be related to *AT* 1163.

**1163.3** Related material occurs in Gregory of Caerwent 1163 (as reported in V, fol. 199v): "Gilebertus episcopus Herefordensis, prius abbas Gloc', ad sedem Londinensem transfertur." The language used in Gervase, 1:173, and *AT* 1163, is somewhat more remote.

**1163.4** Probably related to Gervase, 1:176, and *AT* 1164, but on the possibility that *AT* also depends on a set of Worcester Annals at this point, see the introduction, chap. 3, § e, above. Cf. *APW* 1164.

**1163.5** Probably an allusion to the council held in London in October 1163 at which Thomas Becket, supported by the majority of bishops, protested against various royal customs: see Gervase, 1:174–75.

**1164.1** Probably related to Gervase, 1:182, and *AT* 1164, but on the possibility that *AT* also depends on a set of Worcester Annals at this point, see the introduction, chap. 3, § e, above. Roger's consecration took place on 23 August 1164: see *AT*, *APW* 1164.

**1164.2** Becket left England on 2 November. Cf. *AT*, *APW* 1164.

**1164.3** Probably related to *AT* 1164.

**1164.4** Gervase, 1:197–98 (s.a. 1165), is much fuller, but uses similar language: "Hoc quoque anno mense Augusto natus est filius Lodovico regi Franciæ Christianissimo, quem peperit ei filia comitis Theodbaldi senioris. Ex cujus ortu tota Francia lætificata est eo quod hucusque masculum non habuit hæredem. Puer autem baptizatus ad nomen comitis Flandriæ Philippus appellatus est." The item is probably distantly related to *AT* 1165.

**1165.1** The item is probably distantly related to *AT* 1164 and *APW* 1164. Cf. Gervase, 1:197.

**1165.2** Related material occurs in Gervase, 1:196: "Mense Januario terræ motus magnus factus est in Anglia nocte media Conversionis Sancti Pauli apostoli."

**1165.3** A much fuller report but one which contains a few verbal echoes occurs in Gervase, 1:197. Henry led two Welsh expeditions in 1165, one in May and one in August (Eyton, 79–82).

**1165.4** This account of the "flying crucifix of Stanway" differs in language and detail from that found in Gerald of Wales, *Gemma Ecclesiastica*, dist.1, § 35 (ed. John S. Brewer, *GCO*, 2:109–10), and probably represents an entirely independent report of the story. Gerald, who was writing in the 1190s, also dates the miracle to the Vigil of the Ascension, but he moves the event forward to 1169/1170 and turns it into a portent of the impending martyrdom of Thomas Becket; he also provides more circumstantial detail, stating that the parish priest sent news of the event to Bishop Roger of Worcester and that Roger sent "Master Silvester" to investigate. Silvester was a member of Roger's household (see Mary G. Chaney, *Roger, Bishop of Worcester, 1164–1179* [Oxford: Clarendon Press, 1980], 102). Stanway, as Gerald points out, is a little over two miles from the monastery of Winchcombe. Reports of miracles involving animate crucifixes are a striking feature of this period: cf. JW*CC* 1137 (p. 230); *Coventry* 1138.2; and RH*Chron.*, 4:17 (s.a. 1197).

**1166.1** Cf. Gervase, 1:198, who prints the entire edict, and Diceto, *YH*, 1:329.

**1166.2** In response to the death of his son and heir, Earl William founded a house of regular canons on his manor at Keynesham. The scheme was put into motion in 1167 with the support of his brother Roger, bishop of Worcester. On the circumstances of the foundation, see Nicholas Vincent, "The Early Years of Keynesham Abbey," *Transactions of the Bristol and Gloucestershire Archaeological Society* 111 (1993): 95–113, who prints the recently rediscovered foundation charters at 106–8. Cf. *EGC*, no. 99.

**1167.1** Probably distantly related to *AT* 1167 and *APW* 1167.

**1167.2** Related to *AT* 1167: "Fretherricus imperator cum exercitu copioso Romam veniens, Widonem Cirenensem in ecclesia Sancti Petri violenter intrusit, qui et altare destruxit, et aliud erexit, missas celebravit, imperatorem coronavit; etiam pro hoc facto magna pars exercitus sui divina ultione percussa est." Cf. also Gervase, 1:205.

**1168.1** This report of a lunar eclipse for September 1168 seems to be unique among English chronicles (see Newton, 654–66), but the missing numeral—either an "x" or "v" for the xiii or the viii kalends of October—can be deduced from the other chronological information. 1168 was indeed the tenth year of the sixth nineteen-year cycle within the Great Paschal Cycle for 1064–1595, and the moon was 13 days old on 19 September according to the system of reckoning set out in Bede, *DTR*, § 20 (346–49).

**1168.2** Perhaps distantly related to *AT* 1168. Cf. Gervase, 1:205.

**1168.3** Perhaps distantly related to *AT* 1168.

**1168.4** Probably distantly related to *AT* 1168. Cf. Gervase, 1:207.

**1169** These agreements took place at Montmiral in Maine, 6 January 1167. Gervase, 1:207–8, describes these events in rather different words.

**1170.1** Distantly related material occurs in *AT* 1170. Gervase, 1:219, describes these events in rather different words. Prince Henry was crowned on 14 June 1170: see RH*Chron.*, 2:4.

**1170.2** Council of Windsor, 5 April 1170. Gervase, 1:216, describes these events in rather different words.

**1170.3** No obvious parallels. Richard "Strongbow," the second earl of Pembroke, went to Ireland at the invitation of Diarmait Mac Murchada, the exiled king of Leinster (d. 1171), in August 1170 and married his daughter Aífe soon afterwards: see Orphen, *Ireland*, 1:179–202; Marie T. Flanagan, *Irish Society, Anglo-Norman Settlers, Angevin Kingship* (Oxford: Clarendon Press, 1989), 79–136.

**1170.4** The reconciliation took place on 22 July 1170. Perhaps distantly related to *AT* 1170. Cf. Gervase, 1:220–27.

**1171.1** Probably distantly related to *AT* 1172 and *APW* 1172. Cf. Gervase, 1:229–30.

**1171.2** Probably distantly related to *AT* 1171.

**1171.3** Probably distantly related to *AT* 1171. Strongbow met Henry II at Newnham in Gloucestershire.

**1171.4** Related material occurs in Gregory of Caerwent 1171 (as reported in V, fol. 199v): "Henricus prior factus est abbas Winchicumbae." See also *AT* 1171.

**1171.5** There are no obvious parallels for this item.

**1172.1** A summary of the meetings at Savigny and Avranches on 17 and 22 May 1172: cf. Gervase, 1:237–40. Probably distantly related to *AT* 1172.

**1172.2** Evidently an account of the negotiations at Montferrand in the Auvergne, January-February 1173: see RH*Chron.*, 2:41–45; Gervase, 1:237.

**1172.3** Probably distantly related to *AT* 1172. Prince Henry and his wife Margaret landed at Southampton and he was crowned soon afterwards, on 27 August, at Winchester, by Archbishop Rotrou with the assistance of Giles, bishop of Evreux, and Roger, bishop of Worcester. Meanwhile, Henry II went to Brittany. See Eyton, 168.

**1173.1** The report of this eclipse in Gervase, 1:241, is probably independent: "IIII$^{to}$ idus Februarii apparuit in cælo signum mirabile nocte plusquam media. Nam rubor quidam videbatur in aere inter orientem et occidentem in parte aquilonali." But that in *AT* 1173 is probably distantly related: "Circa mediam noctem visum est cælum rubere."

**1173.2** Probably distantly related to *AT* 1173. The rebellion began on 15 April: RH*GHS*, 1:41–42, 47.

**1173.3** The siege of Verneuil began around 9 July; Louis succeeded in taking the town on 9 August, before Henry came upon his army: see RT*Chron.*, 257, 259; RH*GHS*, 1:49–51, 54.

**1173.4** The sees of Winchester, Ely, Hereford, and Bath were filled in May, and the archbishopric of Canterbury on 3 June; but it is not clear exactly when Richard was appointed abbot of Glastonbury: see RT*Chron.*, 257; Gervase, 1:243–44; Devizes, *AW*, 1173. *Nicholaus filius regis* refers to Geoffrey Plantagenet, the bastard son of Henry II who was elected to the see of Lincoln in May 1173: see Devizes, *CTR*, 87–88, and *EEA*, 1:xxxvi–xxxviii.

**1173.5** No obvious parallels. Gervase, 1:245, uses different words.

**1173.6** Robert, the young earl of Leicester, landed at Walton, Suffolk, on 29 September 1173, with his force of Flemings. He was defeated at Fornham on 17 October. No other source credits William, earl of Gloucester, with Earl Robert's capture. Cf. Gervase, 1:246; Diceto, *YH*, 1:373–74; RH*GHS*, 1:61.

**1173.7** Matthew of Flanders, count of Boulogne, died of a wound received at the siege of Driencourt in July 1173: cf. Gervase, 1:246; RT*Chron.*, 258.

**1173.8** The earl of Chester and Ralph de Fougères were captured at Dol on 26 August: see RH*GHS*, 1:57–58; RT*Chron.*, 251–61; Diceto, *YH*, 1:373–74; Eyton, 176.

**1174.1** The words *Ob uenerationem beati Thome martiris Cantuariensis properante* have probably been abbreviated from a somewhat fuller account of Henry II's pilgrimage to Canterbury on 12 July. William the Lion, king of the Scots, was captured on 13 July: see Gervase, 1:248–49, who uses different words; RH*GHS*, 1:72; Diceto, *YH*, 1:382–84.

**1174.2** Henry returned to France on 8 August: see RH*GHS*, 1:74; Eyton, 183.

**1174.3** Distantly related material occurs in *AT* 1174. Louis VII withdrew from Rouen on 21 August, a truce was reached at Gisors on 8 September, and a settlement among Henry, Louis, and his sons at Mont Louis on 30 September: see Gervase, 1:250; Diceto, *YH*, 1:386–87; RH*GHS*, 1:74–76.

**1174.4** Distantly related material occurs in *AT* 1174; *APW* 1172. Cf. Gervase, 1:247, 251; RH*GHS*, 1:80, 83–84. For Nicholas—that is, Geoffrey Plantagenet—and the papal objections to his consecration, see Diceto, *YH*, 1:392–93.

**1175.1** Distantly related material occurs in *AT* 1175. Henry returned to England in early May. Cf. Gervase, 1:251.

**1175.2** Related material occurs in *AT* 1175: "Ricardus archiepiscopus Cantuariæ convocato concilio apud Lundoniam interdixit omnes præfationes præter decem quas Roma mater ecclesiæ inter missarum decantat solemnia." See, likewise, *APW* 1175. The council is that which met at Westminster on 18 May 1175. Its decrees are recorded by RH*GHS*, 1:80–90, the canon singled out for special mention being no. 14. Cf. Gervase, 1:251–55, and see further *C&S I*, 2:965–93.

**1175.3** Distantly related material occurs in *AT* 1175; *APW* 1175. John was elected at Eynsham on 26 November.

**1175.4** Cf. Gervase, 1:257: "Circuivit igitur legatus Angliam, considerans omnia proviso et constituendo concilio corrigenda. Et quia eradicare venerat et plantare, a dextris et a sinistris donantium manus donis exoneravit allatis, quæ in suis co<n>finis complanavit" (alluding to Jeremiah 1:10).

**1176.1** The council convened on 14 March: see Gervase, 1:258–59; RH*GHS*, 1:112–13.

**1176.2** This report of a miraculous tree at Strongbow's tomb seems to be unique. Gerald of Wales briefly describes his burial at Dublin in *Expugnatio Hibernica*, 2.14 (ed. James F. Dimock in *GCO*, 5:334), and he discusses the miracles associated with the cathedral's great cross in *Topographia Hibernensis*, dist. 1, §§ 44–45 (ed. James F. Dimock in *GCO*, 5:128–29), but he nowhere mentions this miracle. Cf. also Newburgh, 2.26. Later legends concerning the tomb are discussed in Orphen, *Ireland*, 1:359–60. Strongbow's obit was entered under 20 April in the calendar of Holy Trinity, Dublin: see *The Book of Obits and Martyrology of the Cathedral Church of the Holy Trinity Commonly called Christ Church, Dublin*, ed. John C. Crosthwaite (Dublin: Irish Archaeological Society, 1844), 21, 57.

**1176.3** Probably distantly related to *AT* 1176; *APW* 1175. The marriage was agreed at Westminster on 25 May: see Gervase, 1:260; RH*GHS*, 1:116–17; Eyton, 202.

**1176.4** Probably distantly related to *AT* 1176. Cf. Gervase, 1:260; Diceto, *YH*, 1:415; RH*GHS*, 1:125.

**1177.1** Probably distantly related to *AT* 1177.

**1177.2** Cf. Gervase 1:274 (s.a. 1177): "Hoc anno, vigilia Sancti Andreæ apostoli, hora necdum prima, apparuit in Cantia rubor quidam quasi flamma ardens et volans impulsu venti qui veniebat. Quidam vero certissime affirmabant draconem flammeum crispo capite se manifeste eadem hora vidisse. Dixerunt plurimi signum hoc sive draconis seu flammæ ardentis vel ruboris per totam Angliam apparuisse."

**1178.1** This entry is based ultimately, if not directly, on Abbot Henry of Clairvaux's Letter 29, "Audite cœli" (ed. *PL* 204.235–240), which provides an account of the anti-Cathar mission headed by Peter, cardinal-bishop of St Chrysogonus and papal legate. The letter circulated widely, and it is quoted in full in another English chronicle, RH*GHS*, 1:214–20. On the letter, see Beverly M. Kienzle, *Cistercians, Heresy and Crusade in Occitania, 1145–1229: Preaching in the Lord's Vineyard* (Woodbridge: York Medieval Press and Boydell Press, 2001), esp. 121–27; on Peter Maurand and his family, see John H. Mundy, *Liberty and Political Power in Toulouse, 1050–1230* (New York: Columbia University Press, 1954), 60–62.

**1178.2** Probably distantly related to *AT* 1179; *APW* 1179. Cf. Gervase, 1:276; RH*GHS*, 1:221–38.

**1178.3** There seems to be echo of this item in Gervase, 1:277: " . . . facta est eclipsis solis in Cantia, non universaliter sed particulariter." Cf. Newton, 168, 615.

**1178.4** Perhaps distantly related to *AT* 1178: "Monasterium Theokesberiæ incendio cum officinis conflagratur. Fromundus abbas Theokesberiæ obiit."

**1179.1** No obvious parallels.

**1179.2** No obvious parallels.

**1179.3** Similar material occurs in Gregory of Caerwent, s.a. 1179 (as reported in V, fol. 199v): "Obiit abbas Hamelinus postquam 6. idus Mart. cui successit Thomas Carbonet, tunc prior Hereford. ii. kl. octob. installatus." Note, likewise, *Cart. Gloc.*, 1:22: "Domnus Hamelinus abbas postquam ecclesiam istam annis xxxi. inter mundi turbines nimium crebrescentes strenue rexerat, vi. idus Martii vita discessit . . . Successit Hamelino abbati venerabilis Thomas prior Herefordiæ." More distantly related material occurs in *AT* 1179; *APW* 1179.

**1179.4** Perhaps related to Gervase, 1:293: "[Ludovicus] ad Sanctum Thomam *orandi gratia* veniebat ob spem recuperandæ salutis." Both texts share the phrase *orandi gratia*, but this is standard pilgrimage vocabulary for this period. The item may also be distantly related to *AT* 1179. Cf. RH*GHS*, 1:240–41.

**1179.5** Probably distantly related to *AT* 1179. There survives in a Pershore manuscript (MS. Oxford, St John's College, 96, fol. 151) a letter from the monks of Marmoutier protesting against King Henry II's attempt to make them give up the *celitus thesaurus* of Roger's body. In these protests they were successful. See Cheney, *Roger of Worcester*, 224–25.

**1180.1** Louis VII died on 18 September. Perhaps distantly related to *AT* 1180.

**1180.2** Probably distantly related to *AT* 1180; *APW* 1179. Cf. *Annales monasterii de Waverleia*, ed. Luard, *AM*, 2:129–411, at 281; Gervase, 1:294.

**1180.3** Related material occurs in Gregory of Caerwent, s.a. 1180 (as reported in V, fol. 200r): "Osbernus prior s.p. factus est Abbas Malmesburie."

**1180.4** Cf. Gervase, 1:294–95; *AT* 1180; *APW* 1180.

**1181.1** No obvious parallels.

**1181.2** This item seems to be an alternative version of the story of the woman from Arras in Gerald of Wales, *Gemma Ecclesiastica*, dist.1, § 11 (ed. John S. Brewer, *GCO*, 2:39); trans. John J. Hagen, *The Jewel of the Church: A Translation of* Gemma ecclesiastica *by Giraldus Cambrensis* (Leiden: Brill, 1979), 33 (modified):

> In the kingdom of France, in the city of Arras, which is the capital of Flanders, on a certain Easter Sunday a woman placed a consecrated host (given to her through the careless neglect of a priest to carry to the sick) in a locket tied in a knot in a silk wimple for her head. When a long period of time had passed and it had been completely forgotten, the woman lay awake one night and saw the same locket surrounded with a great light and, extremely frightened, she showed it to her husband. They saw the same thing the following night, and the third night. At length the woman, appearing very much concerned and thoroughly frightened over this matter, recalled that the host was placed inside the locket. First thing in the morning she opened the locket with her husband and everyone standing around and found the wimple and the knot where the host had been tied bloody with fresh blood. Without delay they showed it to their priest with tears and with great terror and then carried it in procession with due honor to the church. The priest opened the knot and locket in front of all the people, and the host appeared like bleeding flesh on one half and bread on the other. The letters impressed upon the host stood out legibly both in the flesh and in the form of bread (for the manifestation of a greater and more obvious miracle). Having heard about the miracle, a great crowd of people gathered together, not only from the city itself but from neighbouring villages, people who either had doubts or had completely turned aside [from the teaching] concerning the body of Christ. They saw with their own eyes and touched with their hands and, after seeing also the many other signs and miracles which God deigned to work there at that time, returned to the certitude of faith and the true way which they had left.

Gerald then claims to have investigated the incident himself when passing through Arras eight days after the event, and goes on to quote a letter of Pope Alexander III which mentions the incident in connection with a dispute over who should receive offerings made at a shrine which was set up to house the Eucharist. On the use of *miracula* to teach Eucharistic doctrine, see Miri Rubin, *Corpus Christi: The Eucharist in Late Medieval Culture* (Cambridge: Cambridge University Press, 1991), 108–29.

**1181.3** No obvious parallels.

**1181.4** No obvious parallels. The Count of Flanders invaded French territory in April; a reconciliation was achieved at Gisors in July (Eyton, 240).

**1181.5** Probably distantly related to *AT* 1181; *APW* 1181. Alexander died on 30 August and Lucius was elected on 1 September.

**1181.6** Possibly related to Gregory of Caerwent, s.a. 1181 (as reported in V, fol. 200r): "Obiit Henricus prior Winchecumb. quondam prior Gloc. 6 idus Novemb. et Osbernus abbas Malmesburie 16 kl. April." Cf. also *AT* 1181: "Henricus abbas Winchecumbe obiit, cui successit Crispinus ejusdem loci prior." *APW* 1181 reproduces *AT*, adding "et benedicitur Wigorniæ in translatione Sancti Wulstani [7 June]"; but this last detail is difficult to reconcile with Caerwent's date for the death of Prior Henry. Crispin's abbacy lasted for less than one year: *Landboc*, 1:45, 68–69; *Heads I*, 79.

**1181.7** Roger died at York on 22 November. Cf. *AT* 1181; Gervase, 1:297.

# The *Coventry Chronicle* Commentary

**VA1** Common root: *Winchcombe*[1] VA1.
**VA2** Common root: *Winchcombe*[1] VA2.
**VA3** A brief note intended to explain the distinction between the two series of numbers that constitute the chronicle's chronological apparatus.
**VA4** Common root: *Winchcombe*[1] VA4.
**VA5** Common root: *Winchcombe*[1] VA5.
**VA6** Common root: *Winchcombe*[1] VA6.
**VA7** Common root: *Winchcombe*[1] VA7.
**VA13** Common root: *Winchcombe*[1] VA12.
**VA16** Common root: *Winchcombe*[1] VA16.1.
**VA19** Common root: *Winchcombe*[1] VA21.2.
**1** Common root: *Winchcombe*[1] 1.2.
**9.1** Common root: *Winchcombe*[1] 9.1.
**9.2** Common root: *Winchcombe*[1] 9.2. *Coventry*[1] appears to give a fuller version of this entry.
**12** Common root: *Winchcombe*[1] 12.
**13** Common root: *Winchcombe*[1] 13; *APW* 51.
**14.1** Common root: *Winchcombe*[1] 14.1; *APW* 52.
**14.2** Common root: *Winchcombe*[1] 14.2.
**17** Common root: *Winchcombe*[1] 17.1.
**22** Common root: *Winchcombe*[1] 22.
**30** Common root: *Winchcombe*[1] 30.
**33** Common root: *Winchcombe*[1] 34.
**37** Common root: *Winchcombe*[1] 37.1.
**41** Common root: *Winchcombe*[1] 41.
**42.1** *Winchcombe*[1] lacks this item, but it almost certainly derives from the common root: cf. Marianus via the Easter Table Annals in JW*CC* (C) p. 57 (in cycle 3, year 7 = 44).
**42.2** Common root: *Winchcombe*[1] 42.
**45** Common root: *Winchcombe*[1] 45.
**46** Common root: *Winchcombe*[1] 46.1.
**50** Common root: *Winchcombe*[1] 50.
**51.1** Common root: *Winchcombe*[1] 51.1.
**51.2** Common root: *Winchcombe*[1] 51.2.
**52.1** Common root: *Winchcombe*[1] 52.
**52.2** Common root: *Winchcombe*[1] 53.2.
**53** Common root: *Winchcombe*[1] 53.1.
**54.1** Common root: *Winchcombe*[1] 53.3.
**54.2** Common root: *Winchcombe*[1] 53.5.
**61** Common root: *Winchcombe*[1] 61.
**62** Common root: *Winchcombe*[1] 62.2.
**65** Common root: *Winchcombe*[1] 65.1 and 65.3.
**77** Common root: *Winchcombe*[1] 78.

**79** Common root: *Winchcombe*[1] 80.1.
**81** Common root: *Winchcombe*[1] 82.1.
**83** Common root: *Winchcombe*[1] 84.
**91** Common root: *Winchcombe*[1] 92.
**92** Common root: *Winchcombe*[1] 93.
**93.1** Common root: *Winchcombe*[1] 94.
**93.2** Common root: *Winchcombe*[1] 95.
**97** Common root: *Winchcombe*[1] 97.
**100** Common root: *Winchcombe*[1] 101.
**101.1** Common root: *Winchcombe*[1] 102.1.
**101.2** Common root: *Winchcombe*[1] 102.2.
**117** Common root: *Winchcombe*[1] 118.
**120.1** Common root: *Winchcombe*[1] 121.1.
**120.2** Common root: *Winchcombe*[1] 122.
**122.1** Common root: *Winchcombe*[1] 123.1.
**122.2** Common root: *Winchcombe*[1] 123.2.
**126** Common root: *Winchcombe*[1] 128.
**135** Common root: *Winchcombe*[1] 135.1.
**146** Common root: *Winchcombe*[1] 146.1.
**161.1** Common root: *Winchcombe*[1] 159.1.
**161.2** Common root: *Winchcombe*[1] 162.
**165** Common root: *Winchcombe*[1] 165.
**168** Common root: *Winchcombe*[1] 179.4.
**171** Common root: *Winchcombe*[1] 171.
**177** Common root: *Winchcombe*[1] 177.
**179** Common root: *Winchcombe*[1] 179.1 and 179.3.
**180** Common root: *Winchcombe*[1] 180.1.
**182** Common root: *Winchcombe*[1] 182.
**183** Common root: *Winchcombe*[1] 183.
**185** Common root: *Winchcombe*[1] 185.
**189** Common root: *Winchcombe*[1] 188.
**190** Common root: *Winchcombe*[1] 191.
**192** Common root: *Winchcombe*[1] 192.
**195** Common root: *Winchcombe*[1] 195. *Coventry*[1] abbreviates this item.
**197** Common root: *Winchcombe*[1] 197.
**198.1** Common root: *Winchcombe*[1] 198.1.
**198.2** Common root: *Winchcombe*[1] 198.2.
**203** Common root: *Winchcombe*[1] 203.
**206** Common root: *Winchcombe*[1] 205.
**207** Common root: *Winchcombe*[1] 207.1. *Coventry*[1] abbreviates this item.
**210** Common root: *Winchcombe*[1] 210.1.
**211** Common root: *Winchcombe*[1] 212.1.
**220** Common root: *Winchcombe*[1] 220.2. *Coventry*[1] abbreviates this item.

222 Common root: *Winchcombe*[1] 222.
224 Common root: *Winchcombe*[1] 224.1.
226 Common root: Marianus via JW*CC* (C) 226: "Maximinus .iv[a]. persecutionem facit aduersus sacerdotes Christianos." Cf. *Winchcombe*[1] 224.3.
228 Common root: *Winchcombe*[1] 228.
232 Common root: *Winchcombe*[1] 232.
234.1 Common root: *Winchcombe*[1] 234.1.
234.2 Common root: *Winchcombe*[1] 234.2.
238 Common root: *Winchcombe*[1] 237.
241 Common root: *Winchcombe*[1] 241.
243 Common root: *Winchcombe*[1] 243.
244 Common root: *Winchcombe*[1] 244.
245 Common root: *Winchcombe*[1] 245.1.
246 Common root: *Winchcombe*[1] 246.1.
247 Common root: *Winchcombe*[1] 247.1.
249 Common root: *Winchcombe*[1] 249.
250 Common root: *Winchcombe*[1] 250. *Coventry*[1] abbreviates this item.
252 Common root: *Winchcombe*[1] 252.
256 Common root: *Winchcombe*[1] 256.
259 Common root: *Winchcombe*[1] 259.
260 Common root: *Winchcombe*[1] 261.1.
262 Common root: *Winchcombe*[1] 263.1.
268.1 Common root: *Winchcombe*[1] 269.1.
268.2 Common root: *Winchcombe*[1] 269.2.
270 Common root: *Winchcombe*[1] 270.1.
276 Common root: *Winchcombe*[1] 276.1.
277 Common root: *Winchcombe*[1] 277.
278 Common root: *Winchcombe*[1] 278.
280 Common root: *Winchcombe*[1] 280.
281.1 Common root: *Winchcombe*[1] 281.1.
281.2 A later addition drawn from Bede, *HE*, 1.6.
282 Common root: *Winchcombe*[1] 283.1.
292 Common root: *Winchcombe*[1] 291.1.
297 Common root: *Winchcombe*[1] 297.1.
298 Common root: *Winchcombe*[1] 298.
299 Common root: *Winchcombe*[1] 299.3, but *Coventry*[1] lacks *Winchcombe*[1]'s additions from Bede, *CM*, 404 and 411.
300 Common root: *Winchcombe*[1] 300.
301 Common root: *Winchcombe*[1] 301.
302 Common root: *Winchcombe*[1] 302.
303 Common root: *Winchcombe*[1] 303.1.
305 Common root: *Winchcombe*[1] 305.
306 Common root: *Winchcombe*[1] 306.

**308** Common root: *Winchcombe*[1] 308.
**309** Common root: *Winchcombe*[1] 307.
**316.1** Common root: *Winchcombe*[1] 316.1.
**316.2** Common root: *Winchcombe*[1] 316.3.
**317** Common root: Marianus via JW*CC* (C) 317: "Licinius Thessalonice contrarius sacramenti priuatus occiditur." There is no parallel for this item in *Winchcombe*[1], but it seems almost certain that it derives from the common source.
**318** Common root: *Winchcombe*[1] 317.
**319** Common root: *Winchcombe*[1] 318.
**325.1** Common root: *Winchcombe*[1] 309.1.
**325.2** Common root: *Winchcombe*[1] 309.2.
**325.3** Common root: *Winchcombe*[1] 309.3.
**329** Common root: *Winchcombe*[1] 329.
**330.1** Common root: *Winchcombe*[1] 330.1.
**330.2** Common root: *Winchcombe*[1] 330.2.
**331** Common root: *Winchcombe*[1] 331.
**333** Common root: *Winchcombe*[1] 333.
**339** Common root: *Winchcombe*[1] 339.
**342** Common root: *Winchcombe*[1] 342.1.
**343** Common root: *Winchcombe*[1] 343.
**346** Common root: *Winchcombe*[1] 346.
**348** Common root: *Winchcombe*[1] 348.
**349** Common root: *Winchcombe*[1] 349.1.
**350** Common root: *Winchcombe*[1] 350. *Coventry*[1] abbreviates this item, and lacks the additional material from Bede, *CM*, 431–32.
**351** Common root: *Winchcombe*[1] 351.
**354** Common root: *Winchcombe*[1] 354.
**357.1** Common root: *Winchcombe*[1] 357.1.
**357.2** Common root: *Winchcombe*[1] 357.2.
**360** Common root: *Winchcombe*[1] 360.1.
**361** Common root: *Winchcombe*[1] 361.1.
**364** Common root: *Winchcombe*[1] 364.
**365** Common root: *Winchcombe*[1] 365.1.
**370** Common root: *Winchcombe*[1] 370.
**372.1** Common root: *Winchcombe*[1] 372.1.
**372.2** Common root: *Winchcombe*[1] 372.2.
**373** Common root: *Winchcombe*[1] 373.1.
**376** Common root: *Winchcombe*[1] 376.
**377** Common root: *Winchcombe*[1] 377.
**380** Common root: *Winchcombe*[1] 380. *Coventry*[1] abbreviates this item.
**381** Common root: *Winchcombe*[1] 381.
**382.1** Common root: *Winchcombe*[1] 382.1.

382.2 Common root: *Winchcombe*[1] 382.3.
386 Common root: *Winchcombe*[1] 387.
388 Common root: *Winchcombe*[1] 388.
390 Common root: *Winchcombe*[1] 390.
393 Common root: *Winchcombe*[1] 393.
394 Common root: *Winchcombe*[1] 394.1.
396 Common root: *Winchcombe*[1] 395.
399 Common root: *Winchcombe*[1] 399.6.
404 Common root: *Winchcombe*[1] 404.
405.1 Common root: *Winchcombe*[1] 405.1.
405.2 Common root: *Winchcombe*[1] 405.2.
407.1 Common root: *Winchcombe*[1] 407.1.
407.2 Common root: *Winchcombe*[1] 407.2.
408 Common root: *Winchcombe*[1] 408.
410 Common root: *Winchcombe*[1] 410.
411 Common root: *Winchcombe*[1] 411.
413 Common root: *Winchcombe*[1] 413.1.
414.1 Common root: *Winchcombe*[1] 414.
414.2 Common root: *Winchcombe*[1] 412.
415 Common root: *Winchcombe*[1] 415. *Coventry*[1] slightly abbreviates this item.
417 Common root: *Winchcombe*[1] 417.1.
421.1 Common root: *Winchcombe*[1] 421.2.
421.2 Common root: *Winchcombe*[1] 422.
423 Common root: *Winchcombe*[1] 423.
424 Common root: *Winchcombe*[1] 424.
425 Common root: *Winchcombe*[1] 425.
426 Common root: *Winchcombe*[1] 426.
428 Common root: *Winchcombe*[1] 429.
429.1 Common root: *Winchcombe*[1] 430.1.
429.2 Common root: *Winchcombe*[1] 430.2.
430 Common root: *Winchcombe*[1] 431.
431 Common root: *Winchcombe*[1] 432.
433 Common root: *Winchcombe*[1] 433.
437.1 Common root: *Winchcombe*[1] 437.1.
437.2 Common root: *Winchcombe*[1] 437.2.
439 Common root: *Winchcombe*[1] 439. *Coventry*[1] slightly abbreviates this item.
442 Common root: *Winchcombe*[1] 440.
445 Common root: *Winchcombe*[1] 445.
446 Common root: *Winchcombe*[1] 446.
449.1 Common root: *Winchcombe*[1] 450.
449.2 Common root: *Winchcombe*[1] 451.
449.3 A later addition drawn from Bede, *HE*, 1.15.
451 Common root: *Winchcombe*[1] 452.

452 Common root: *Winchcombe*[1] 453.
453.1 Common root: *Winchcombe*[1] 454.1.
453.2 Common root: *Winchcombe*[1] 454.2.
456.1 Common root: *Winchcombe*[1] 456. *Coventry*[1] preserves the true sequence of items under 456 and 457, which is mangled in *Winchcombe*[1].
456.2 Common root: *Winchcombe*[1] 457.2.
457.1 Common root: *Winchcombe*[1] 457.1.
457.2 Common root: *Winchcombe*[1] 457.3.
460 Common root: *Winchcombe*[1] 461.
465.1 Common root: *Winchcombe*[1] 465.1.
465.2 Common root: *Winchcombe*[1] 465.2. *Winchcombe*[1] lacks *filius eius.*
466 Common root: Marianus via JW*CC* 466, or the Consular Annals in JW*CC* (C, p. 19) 463. Compare *Winchcombe*[1] 466, where a fuller account of Theodoret is derived from Bede, *CM*, 496.
467 Common root: *Winchcombe*[1] 467.
468 Common root: *Winchcombe*[1] 468. *Coventry*[1] abbreviates this item.
471 Common root: *Winchcombe*[1] 471.
472 Common root: *Winchcombe*[1] 473.1.
473.1 Common root: *Winchcombe*[1] 473.2.
473.2 Common root: *Winchcombe*[1] 473.3.
474 Common root: *Winchcombe*[1] 474.1.
475 Common root: *Winchcombe*[1] 475.
476 Common root: *Winchcombe*[1] 477.1.
477 Common root: *Winchcombe*[1] 477.2. *Coventry*[1] abbreviates this item.
483 Common root: *Winchcombe*[1] 483.
485 Common root: *Winchcombe*[1] 485. *Coventry*[1] abbreviates this item relatively severely.
488 Common root: *Winchcombe*[1] 488.
489 Common root: *Winchcombe*[1] 489.
490.1 Common root: *Winchcombe*[1] 490.1.
490.2 Common root: *Winchcombe*[1] 490.2.
491.1 Common root: *Winchcombe*[1] 491.
491.2 Common root: *Winchcombe*[1] 492.
493 Common root: *Winchcombe*[1] 493.
494 Common root: *Winchcombe*[1] 494.
495 Common root: *Winchcombe*[1] 495.1.
498 Common root: *Winchcombe*[1] 498.
499 Common root: *Winchcombe*[1] 500.
508.1 Common root: *Winchcombe*[1] 507.1.
508.2 Common root: *Winchcombe*[1] 507.2.
508.3 Common root: *Winchcombe*[1] 508.
509 Common root: *Winchcombe*[1] 509.
510 Common root: *Winchcombe*[1] 510.1.

512 Common root: *Winchcombe*[1] 512.1.
513 Common root: *Winchcombe*[1] 513.
514.1 Common root: *Winchcombe*[1] 514.1.
514.2 Common root: *Winchcombe*[1] 515. *Coventry*[1] omits the matter that *Winchcombe*[1] derives from from JWCC 501.
518 Common root: *Winchcombe*[1] 518.
519.1 Common root: *Winchcombe*[1] 519.
519.2 Common root: *Winchcombe*[1] 520.1.
521 Common root: *Winchcombe*[1] 521.
524 Common root: *Winchcombe*[1] 524.
525 Common root: *Winchcombe*[1] 525.1.
526.1 Common root: *Winchcombe*[1] 526.1. *Coventry*[1] abbreviates this item.
526.2 Common root: *Winchcombe*[1] 526.2. *Coventry*[1] abbreviates this item.
527 Common root: *Winchcombe*[1] 527.
528 Common root: *Winchcombe*[1] 528.
530 Common root: *Winchcombe*[1] 530.1.
533 Common root: *Winchcombe*[1] 533.
534.1 Common root: *Winchcombe*[1] 534.1.
534.2 Common root: *Winchcombe*[1] 534.2. *Coventry*[1] abbreviates this item.
538 Common root: *Winchcombe*[1] 538.
540 Common root: *Winchcombe*[1] 540.1.
541 Common root: *Winchcombe*[1] 541.
544 Common root: *Winchcombe*[1] 544.
548 Common root: *Winchcombe*[1] 547.1.
559.1 Common root: *Winchcombe*[1] 559.1. *Coventry*[1]'s version of this item is briefer.
559.2 Common root: *Winchcombe*[1] 559.2.
560 Common root: *Winchcombe*[1] 560.
561 Common root: *Winchcombe*[1] 561.
564.1 Common root: *Winchcombe*[1] 564.
564.2 Common root: *Winchcombe*[1] 565.
565 Common root: *Winchcombe*[1] 566.1.
566.1 Common root: *Winchcombe*[1] 566.2.
566.2 Common root: *Winchcombe*[1] 566.3.
568 Common root: *Winchcombe*[1] 567.
571 Common root: *Winchcombe*[1] 571.1.
572.1 Common root: *Winchcombe*[1] 572.1.
572.2 Common root: *Winchcombe*[1] 572.2.
573 Common root: *Winchcombe*[1] 573.
574 Common root: *Winchcombe*[1] 574.
575 Common root: *Winchcombe*[1] 575.
578 Common root: *Winchcombe*[1] 578.
579.1 Common root: *Winchcombe*[1] 579.1.

579.2 Common root: *Winchcombe*[1] 579.2.

582 Common root: *Winchcombe*[1] 582.1.

584 Common root: *Winchcombe*[1] 584.1.

585.1 Common root: *Winchcombe*[1] 585.1.

585.2 Common root: *Winchcombe*[1] 585.2.

586 Common root: *Winchcombe*[1] 586.

588 Common root: *Winchcombe*[1] 588.1.

589 Common root: *Winchcombe*[1] 589.

591 Common root: *Winchcombe*[1] 590.

592.1 Common root: *Winchcombe*[1] 591.1.

592.2 Common root: *Winchcombe*[1] 591.2.

592.3 An addition drawn from Bede, *HE*, 1.23, but note that Bede dates Gregory's appointment to 592.

593 Common root: *Winchcombe*[1] 593.

596.1 Common root: *Winchcombe*[1] 596. *Coventry*[1] reproduces the source more accurately than *Winchcombe*[1].

596.2 Common root: *Winchcombe*[1] 591.3.

596.3 Common root: *Winchcombe*[1] 597.

599 Common root: *Winchcombe*[1] 599.

603 Common root: *Winchcombe*[1] 603. *Coventry*[1] abbreviates this item.

604 Common root: *Winchcombe*[1] 604.

605.1 Common root: *Winchcombe*[1] 606.1.

605.2 Common root: *Winchcombe*[1] 606.2.

606 Common root: *Winchcombe*[1] 605.

607 Common root: Marianus via JW*CC* 608. *Winchcombe*[1] lacks this item.

608 Common root: *Winchcombe*[1] 608.

609 Common root: *Winchcombe*[1] 609. *Coventry*[1] abbreviates this item.

611 Common root: *Winchcombe*[1] 611.

612 Common root: *Winchcombe*[1] 612.1.

613 Common root: *Winchcombe*[1] 612.2.

616 Common root: *Winchcombe*[1] 616.1 (first half).

617 Common root: *Winchcombe*[1] 616.1 (second half).

618 Common root: *Winchcombe*[1] 618.

620 Common root: *Winchcombe*[1] 620.

622 Common root: *Winchcombe*[1] 622.2.

625 Common root: *Winchcombe*[1] 625.

626.1 Common root: *Winchcombe*[1] 626.

626.2 Common root: *Winchcombe*[1] 627.1.

627.1 Common root: *Winchcombe*[1] 627.3.

627.2 Common root: *Winchcombe*[1] 627.4.

632 Common root: *Winchcombe*[1] 632.

633 Common root: *Winchcombe*[1] 633.1.

634 Common root: *Winchcombe*[1] 634.

635 Common root: *Winchcombe*[1] 635.2.
636 Common root: *Winchcombe*[1] 636.
637 Common root: *Winchcombe*[1] 637.
638 Common root: *Winchcombe*[1] 638.
639 Common root: *Winchcombe*[1] 639.
640 Common root: *Winchcombe*[1] 640.1.
641 Common root: *Winchcombe*[1] 640.2.
642.1 Common root: *Winchcombe*[1] 642.
642.2 Common root: *Winchcombe*[1] 643.
644.1 Common root: *Winchcombe*[1] 645 (first sentence).
644.2 Common root: *Winchcombe*[1] 644.1.
644.3 Common root: *Winchcombe*[1] 644.2.
645 Common root: *Winchcombe*[1] 645 (the remainder apart from the first sentence).
646.1 Common root: *Winchcombe*[1] 646.1.
646.2 Common root: *Winchcombe*[1] 646.2.
648 Common root: *Winchcombe*[1] 647.1.
651.1 Common root: *Winchcombe*[1] 651.
651.2 Common root: *Winchcombe*[1] 652.
653.1 Common root: *Winchcombe*[1] 653.1.
653.2 Common root: *Winchcombe*[1] 653.3 (first half); *APW* 654 (second half).
654.1 Common root: *Winchcombe*[1] 654.
654.2 Common root: *Winchcombe*[1] 653.3 (second half); *APW* 656.
655 Common root: *Winchcombe*[1] 655.1. *Coventry*[1] abbreviates this item.
656 Common root: *Winchcombe*[1] 656.
657 Common root: *Winchcombe*[1] 657.
658 Common root: *Winchcombe*[1] 658.
659 Common root: *Winchcombe*[1] 659.
663 Common root: *Winchcombe*[1] 662.1.
664.1 Common root: *Winchcombe*[1] 662.2.
664.2 Common root: *Winchcombe*[1] 664.
666 Common root: *Winchcombe*[1] 666.1.
667 Common root: *Winchcombe*[1] 666.2.
668 Common root: *Winchcombe*[1] 668.
669 Common root: *Winchcombe*[1] 669.1.
670 Common root: *Winchcombe*[1] 670.
671 Common root: *Winchcombe*[1] 672.1.
672.1 Common root: *Winchcombe*[1] 672.2.
672.2 Common root: *Winchcombe*[1] 673.1.
673.1 Common root: *Winchcombe*[1] 673.2.
673.2 Common root: *Winchcombe*[1] 673.2.
674 Common root: *Winchcombe*[1] 674.2.
675.1 Common root: *Winchcombe*[1] 675.1.

**675.2** Common root: *Winchcombe*[1] 675.2.
**676** Common root: *Winchcombe*[1] 676.
**677** Common root: *Winchcombe*[1] 677.2.
**678** Common root: *Winchcombe*[1] 677.3.
**679** Common root: *Winchcombe*[1] 679; *APW* 679.
**680** Common root: *Winchcombe*[1] 680.1; *APW* 680.
**685.1** Common root: *Winchcombe*[1] 685.1.
**685.2** Common root: *Winchcombe*[1] 685.2 (first half).
**686.1** Common root: *Winchcombe*[1] 685.2 (second half).
**686.2** Common root: *Winchcombe*[1] 686.1.
**686.3** Common root: *Winchcombe*[1] 686.2.
**686.4** Common root: *Winchcombe*[1] 686.3.
**687** Common root: *Winchcombe*[1] 687.
**688** Common root: Bede, *HE*, 5.7, and *ASC* via JW*CC* 688: "Abeunte Ceadwalla Romam suscepit imperium Ini de stirpe regia, qui . . . monasterium quod Glæstingebyrig dicitur construxit." Though almost certainly an element of the common source, this item is not echoed in *Winchcombe*, probably as a result of eyeskip. Cædwalla is also the subject of **689** below.
**689** Common root: *Winchcombe*[1] 688.
**690.1** Common root: *Winchcombe*[1] 689.1.
**690.2** Common root: *Winchcombe*[1] 689.2; *APW* 689.
**691** Common root: *Winchcombe*[1] 691.
**692** Common root: *Winchcombe*[1] 692; *APW* 692–693.
**693.1** Common root: *Winchcombe*[1] 693.1.
**693.2** Common root: *Winchcombe*[1] 693.2.
**695.1** Common root: *Winchcombe*[1] 694.
**695.2** Common root: *Winchcombe*[1] 695.
**696** Common root: *Winchcombe*[1] 696.
**697.1** Common root: *Winchcombe*[1] 697.1.
**697.2** Common root: *Winchcombe*[1] 697.2.
**698** Common root: *Winchcombe*[1] 698.
**699** Common root: *Winchcombe*[1] 699.
**703** Common root: *Winchcombe*[1] 703.
**704.1** Common root: *Winchcombe*[1] 704.1.
**704.2** Common root: *Winchcombe*[1] 704.2.
**705** Common root: *Winchcombe*[1] 705.
**706.1** Common root: *Winchcombe*[1] 706.1.
**706.2** Common root: *Winchcombe*[1] 706.2.
**706.3** Common root: *Winchcombe*[1] 707.3.
**708.1** Common root: *Winchcombe*[1] 708.1.
**708.2** Common root: *Winchcombe*[1] 708.3.
**708.3** Common root: *Winchcombe*[1] 709.

711 Common root: *Winchcombe*[1] 711.
713 Common root: *Winchcombe*[1] 713.1.
714.1 Common root: *Winchcombe*[1] 714.
714.2 Common root: *Winchcombe*[1] 715.1; *APW* 714.
715 Common root: *Winchcombe*[1] 715.3. *Coventry*[1] has a somewhat briefer version of this item.
716 Common root: *Winchcombe*[1] 716.1.
717.1 Common root: *Winchcombe*[1] 716.2.
717.2 Common root: *Winchcombe*[1] 717.
718.1 Common root: *Winchcombe*[1] 718.1.
718.2 Common root: *Winchcombe*[1] 718.2; *APW* 717.
718.3 Common root: *Winchcombe*[1] 719.1.
721 Common root: *Winchcombe*[1] 721.
725.1 Common root: *Winchcombe*[1] 725.1.
725.2 Common root: *Winchcombe*[1] 725.2.
728 Common root: *Winchcombe*[1] 728.
729 Common root: *Winchcombe*[1] 729. *Coventry*[1] adds *Ii* but omits *presbiter*.
731 Common root: *Winchcombe*[1] 731.
734 Common root: *Winchcombe*[1] 734.
735 Common root: *Winchcombe*[1] 735. *Coventry*[1] abbreviates this item.
738 Common root: *Winchcombe*[1] 738.1.
740 Common root: *Winchcombe*[1] 740.
741.1 Common root: *Winchcombe*[1] 741.1.
741.2 Common root: *Winchcombe*[1] 742.1.
741.3 Common root: *Winchcombe*[1] 742.2.
741.4 Common root: *Winchcombe*[1] 742.3.
743 Common root: *Winchcombe*[1] 743; *APW* 742.
744 Common root: *Winchcombe*[1] 744.
745 Common root: *Winchcombe*[1] 745.
747 Common root: J*WCC* 745. There is no parallel for this item in *Winchcombe*[1], but it is almost certainly derived from the common source.
748 Common root: *Winchcombe*[1] 748.
750 Common root: *Winchcombe*[1] 751.
752 Common root: Marianus via J*WCC* 754. Cf. *Winchcombe*[1] 753.
754 Common root: *Winchcombe*[1] 754.
755.1 Common root: *Winchcombe*[1] 755.1.
755.2 Common root: *Winchcombe*[1] 755.2.
756 Common root: *Winchcombe*[1] 756.1.
757.1 Common root: *Winchcombe*[1] 757.1.
757.2 Common root: *Winchcombe*[1] 757.2.
758.1 Common root: *Winchcombe*[1] 758.1.
758.2 Common root: *Winchcombe*[1] 758.2.

759 Common root: *Winchcombe*[1] 759.

760 Common root: *Winchcombe*[1] 760.

762 Common root: *Winchcombe*[1] 762 (first half).

763 Common root: *Winchcombe*[1] 763 (second half).

765 Common root: *Winchcombe*[1] 765.

768.1 Common root: *Winchcombe*[1] 768.1.

768.2 Common root: *Winchcombe*[1] 768.2.

773.1 Common root: *Winchcombe*[1] 773.1.

773.2 Common root: *Winchcombe*[1] 773.2.

773.3 Common root: Norman Annals: *AU* 778 ("Karolus Pampiloniam urbem destruxit; apud Cesaraugustam exercitum suum conjunxit, et, acceptis obsidibus subjugatisque Sarracenis, per Narbonam et Vuasconiam Franciam rediit. Karolus in Yspanias intravit. Karolus Saxoniam venit."). *ACad.* 774, 779; *AG* 778, 779; *ASC* (E) 778 and *ASN* 778–80 are similar. See also *ASBD* 778, 779. The words *et Pampileniam … obsidibus* are absent in *Winchcombe*[1] 773.3, but evidently belong to the common source.

774.1 Common root: *Winchcombe*[1] 774.1.

774.2 Common root: *Winchcombe*[1] 774.2.

774.3 Common root: *Winchcombe*[1] 774.3.

775 Common root: *Winchcombe*[1] 774.4; *APW* 775.

778.1 Common root: *Winchcombe*[1] 778.1; *APW* 778.

778.2 Common root: *Winchcombe*[1] 778.2.

781 Common root: *Winchcombe*[1] 781.1; *APW* 781.

782 Common root: *Winchcombe*[1] 782.

784 Common root: *Winchcombe*[1] 784.

786 Common root: *Winchcombe*[1] 786.1.

787.1 Common root: *Winchcombe*[1] 786.2; *APW* 787.1.

787.2 Common root: *Winchcombe*[1] 787.1; *APW* 787.2.

789 Common root: *Winchcombe*[1] 789.

790.1 Common root: *Winchcombe*[1] 790.

790.2 Common root: *Winchcombe*[1] 791 (first half).

792 Common root: *Winchcombe*[1] 792.

793 Common root: *Winchcombe*[1] 793. *Coventry*[1] abbreviates this item.

794.1 Common root: *Winchcombe*[1] 794.1.

794.2 Common root: *Winchcombe*[1] 794.2.

794.3 Common root: *Winchcombe*[1] 794.3.

795 Common root: *Winchcombe*[1] 795.1. *Coventry*[1] offers a briefer version of this item.

796 Common root: Marianus via J*WCC* 796: "Quem [Leonem papam] Romani in letania maiori captam excecauerunt, et radicitus linguam eius absciderunt." Cf. *Winchcombe*[1] 800.1, where the item has been expanded using material also found in John's "Papal Annals" (C, p. 33).

797 Common root: *Winchcombe*[1] 801.
798 Common root: *Winchcombe*[1] 802.
799 Common root: *Winchcombe*[1] 803.
800 Common root: *Winchcombe*[1] 804.
803 Common root: *Winchcombe*[1] 807. *Coventry*[1] abbreviates this item.
805 Common root: *Winchcombe*[1] 809.1.
811 Common root: *Winchcombe*[1] 813.1.
813 Common root: *Winchcombe*[1] 814. *Coventry* adds Leo's ordinal.
817 Common root: *Winchcombe*[1] 816.1.
819 Common root: *ASC* via JW*CC* 819. *Winchcombe*[1]'s entry for 819 is also derived from JW*CC* 819, but its version comprises a far more elaborate account of Cenwulf's death and of Kenelm's martyrdom. The latter's treatment is what one expects from a chronicle written in a monastery founded by Cenwulf and for which Kenelm was the patron saint. The version in *Coventry*[1] probably represents, therefore, that which was found in John's lost annalistic chronicle, that in *Winchcombe*[1] 819 being derived directly from main chronicle in JW*CC*. See also *APW* 832.
822.1 Common root: *Winchcombe*[1] 821.
822.2 Common root: *Winchcombe*[1] 822.1.
823.1 Common root: *Winchcombe*[1] 823.1.
823.2 Common root: *Winchcombe*[1] 823.2.
824 Common root: *Winchcombe*[1] 824.1.
825 Common root: *Winchcombe*[1] 825.1.
829 Common root: *Winchcombe*[1] 829.
836 Common root: *Winchcombe*[1] 836.
838 Common root: *Winchcombe*[1] 838.
839.1 Common root: *Winchcombe*[1] 839.
839.2 Common root: *Winchcombe*[1] 840.
842 Common root: *Winchcombe*[1] 842.
846 Common root: *Winchcombe*[1] 846.
849 Common root: *Winchcombe*[1] 849.1.
850 Common root: *Winchcombe*[1] 850.1.
852 Common root: *Winchcombe*[1] 852.1.
853 Common root: *Winchcombe*[1] 852.2.
855.1 Common root: *Winchcombe*[1] 855.
855.2 Common root: *Winchcombe*[1] 857.1.
858 Common root: *Winchcombe*[1] 857.2.
860 Common root: *Winchcombe*[1] 860.
862 Common root: *Winchcombe*[1] 862.
866 Common root: *Winchcombe*[1] 866.
867 Common root: *Winchcombe*[1] 867.
870.1 Common root: *Winchcombe*[1] 870.1.
870.2 Common root: *Winchcombe*[1] 870.2.

871 Common root: *Winchcombe*[1] 870.3.
872.1 Common root: *Winchcombe*[1] 872.1.
872.2 Common root: *Winchcombe*[1] 872.2.
873 Common root: *Winchcombe*[1] 871.1.
874.1 Common root: *Winchcombe*[1] 874.
874.2 Common root: *Winchcombe*[1] 875.1.
876.1 Common root: *Winchcombe*[1] 876.1.
876.2 Common root: *Winchcombe*[1] 876.2.
876.3 Common root: *Winchcombe*[1] 876.3. *Coventry*[1] abbreviates this item.
876.4 Common root: *Winchcombe*[1] 877.
879 Common root: *Winchcombe*[1] 878.
881 Common root: *Winchcombe*[1] 880.
883 Common root: *Winchcombe*[1] 882.
885 Common root: *Winchcombe*[1] 883.2.
886 Common root: *Winchcombe*[1] 886.1.
887 Common root: *Winchcombe*[1] 886.2.
888 Common root: *Winchcombe*[1] 888.1.
889 Common root: *Winchcombe*[1] 889.
890 Common root: *Winchcombe*[1] 890.
891.1 Common root: *Winchcombe*[1] 891.2.
891.2 Common root: *Winchcombe*[1] 891.3.
893 Common root: *Winchcombe*[1] 893.
895 Common root: *Winchcombe*[1] 896.
897 Common root: *Winchcombe*[1] 898.
899 Common root: *Winchcombe*[1] 900.
901 Common root: *Winchcombe*[1] 901.
903 Common root: *Winchcombe*[1] 903.
904 Common root: *Winchcombe*[1] 905.
906 Common root: *Winchcombe*[1] 906.1.
910 Common root: *Winchcombe*[1] 910.
911.1 Common root: *Winchcombe*[1] 911.1.
911.2 Common root: *Winchcombe*[1] 911.2.
912 Common root: *Winchcombe*[1] 912.1.
913 Common root: *Winchcombe*[1] 913.1.
915.1 Common root: *Winchcombe*[1] 915.1.
915.2 Common root: *Winchcombe*[1] 915.2; *APW* 917.
916.1 Common root: *Winchcombe*[1] 916.1; *APW* 919.
916.2 Common root: *Winchcombe*[1] 917.1.
917 Common root: *Winchcombe*[1] 918.
918 Common root: *Winchcombe*[1] 919.1.
921 Common root: *Winchcombe*[1] 922; *APW* 922.
922 Common root: *Winchcombe*[1] 923.1; *APW* 932.
924 Common root: *Winchcombe*[1] 924.1.

925 Common root: *Winchcombe*[1] 925.
926 Common root: *Winchcombe*[1] 926.1.
927 Common root: *Winchcombe*[1] 928.
930 Common root: *Winchcombe*[1] 929.
934 Common root: *Winchcombe*[1] 933.
935 Common root: *Winchcombe*[1] 934.
937.1 Common root: *Winchcombe*[1] 936.1.
937.2 Common root: *Winchcombe*[1] 936.2.
938 Common root: *Winchcombe*[1] 937.
940 Common root: *Winchcombe*[1] 940.
943 Common root: *Winchcombe*[1] 942.
945 Common root: *Winchcombe*[1] 944.
946.1 Common root: *Winchcombe*[1] 946.1.
946.2 Common root: *Winchcombe*[1] 946.2.
950 Common root: *Winchcombe*[1] 950.
955 Common root: *Winchcombe*[1] 955; *APW* 855.
956 Common root: *Winchcombe*[1] 956; *APW* 858.
957 Common root: *Winchcombe*[1] 957; *APW* 859 and 860.
958 Common root: *Winchcombe*[1] 958; *APW* 862.
959.1 Common root: *Winchcombe*[1] 959.1; *APW* 863.
959.2 Common root: *Winchcombe*[1] 959.2.
960 Common root: *Winchcombe*[1] 960; *APW* 864.
961 Common root: *Winchcombe*[1] 961.
963 Common root: *Winchcombe*[1] 963; *APW* 866.
964 Common root: *Winchcombe*[1] 964.
966 Common root: *Winchcombe*[1] 967; *APW* 868.
968.1 Common root: *Winchcombe*[1] 968.1. *Coventry*[1] omits *Edgarus.*
968.2 Common root: *Winchcombe*[1] 968.2.
969 Common root: *Winchcombe*[1] 969. Cf. *APW* 873.
970 Common root: *Winchcombe*[1] 970.
972.1 Common root: *Winchcombe*[1] 972.1; *APW* 878.
972.2 Common root: *Winchcombe*[1] 972.2; *APW* 879.
973.1 Common root: *Winchcombe*[1] 973.1.
973.2 Common root: *Winchcombe*[1] 973.2; *APW* 881.
974 Common root: *Winchcombe*[1] 974.
975 Common root: *Winchcombe*[1] 975.
978 Common root: *Winchcombe*[1] 978.
979 Common root: *Winchcombe*[1] 979.
984.1 Common root: *Winchcombe*[1] 984.1.
984.2 Common root: *Winchcombe*[1] 984.2.
987 Common root: *Winchcombe*[1] 987.
988 Common root: *Winchcombe*[1] 988.
989 Common root: *Winchcombe*[1] 989.

**991** Common root: *Winchcombe*[1] 991.
**992.1** Common root: *Winchcombe*[1] 992.1; *APW* 992.
**992.2** Common root: *Winchcombe*[1] 992.2; *APW* 993.
**992.3** Common root: *Winchcombe*[1] 993.
**996** Common root: *Winchcombe*[1] 995.
**1002.1** Common root: *Winchcombe*[1] 1002.
**1002.2** Common root: *Winchcombe*[1] 1003.1.
**1002.3** Common root: *Winchcombe*[1] 1003.2.
**1004** Common root: *Winchcombe*[1] 1004. *Coventry*[1] omits *Ricardus.*
**1006** Common root: *Winchcombe*[1] 1006.
**1008** Common root: *Winchcombe*[1] 1008.
**1010** Common root: *Winchcombe*[1] 1011.
**1012** Common root: *Winchcombe*[1] 1012.
**1013.1** Common root: *Winchcombe*[1] 1013.1.
**1013.2** Common root: *Winchcombe*[1] 1013.2.
**1014.1** Common root: *Winchcombe*[1] 1014.1.
**1014.2** Common root: *Winchcombe*[1] 1014.2. *Coventry*[1]'s version is briefer.
**1015.1** Common root: *Winchcombe*[1] 1015.
**1015.2** Common root: *Winchcombe*[1] 1016; *AC* (C) 1016. *Coventry*[1]'s version is briefer.
**1016** Common root: *Winchcombe*[1] 1017.1; *AC* (C) 1017. *Coventry*[1]'s version is briefer.
**1018** Common root: *Winchcombe*[1] 1018.
**1019** Common root: *Winchcombe*[1] 1019.
**1020** Common root: *Winchcombe*[1] 1020; *AC* (C) 1020. *Coventry*[1] omits the succession of Æthelnoth.
**1022** Common root: *Winchcombe*[1] 1022.
**1023** Common root: *Winchcombe*[1] 1023; *AC* (C) 1023.
**1024** Common root: *Winchcombe*[1] 1024; *AC* (C) 1024.
**1026** Common root: *Winchcombe*[1] 1026.
**1028.1** Common root: *Winchcombe*[1] 1028.1; *AC* (C) 1028.
**1028.2** Common root: *Winchcombe*[1] 1028.2. *Coventry*[1] adds *probabilis.*
**1029** Common root: *Winchcombe*[1] 1029; *AC* (C) 1029.
**1030** Common root: *Winchcombe*[1] 1030; *AC* (C) 1030.
**1031** Common root: *Winchcombe*[1] 1031; *AC* (C) 1031.
**1033** Common root: *Winchcombe*[1] 1033; *AC* (C) 1033.
**1035** Common root: *Winchcombe*[1] 1035.1; *AC* (C) 1035.
**1036** Common root: *Winchcombe*[1] 1036.
**1037** Common root: *Winchcombe*[1] 1037.
**1038** Common root: *Winchcombe*[1] 1038; *AC* (C) 1038.
**1039** Common root: *Winchcombe*[1] 1039; *AC* (C) 1039.
**1040** Common root: *Winchcombe*[1] 1040; *AC* (C) 1040.
**1041** Common root: *Winchcombe*[1] 1041.

1042 Common root: *Winchcombe*[1] 1042.1; *AC* (C) 1042.
1043 Common root: *Winchcombe*[1] 1043.1; *AC* (C) 1043.
1044 Common root: *Winchcombe*[1] 1044.1; *AC* (C) 1044.
1046 Common root: *Winchcombe*[1] 1046; *AC* (C) 1046.
1049 Common root: *Winchcombe*[1] 1049.1.
1050 Common root: *Winchcombe*[1] 1050; *AC* (C) 1050.
1051 Common root: *Winchcombe*[1] 1051; *AC* (C) 1051.
1052.1 Common root: *Winchcombe*[1] 1052.1.
1052.2 Common root: *Winchcombe*[1] 1052.2. *Coventry*[1] abbreviates this item.
1053 Common root: *Winchcombe*[1] 1053; *AC* (C) 1053.
1054 Common root: *Winchcombe*[1] 1054.1. *Coventry*[1] lacks *filium regis de Cumbarlande.*
1055 Common root: *Winchcombe*[1] 1055.
1057.1 Common root: *Winchcombe*[1] 1056; *AC* (C) 1056.
1057.2 Common root: *Winchcombe*[1] 1057.
1058 Common root: *Winchcombe*[1] 1058; *APW* 1058; *AC* (C) 1058.
1060 Common root: *Winchcombe*[1] 1060.
1061 Common root: *Winchcombe*[1] 1061.
1062.1 Common root: *Winchcombe*[1] 1062; *AC* (C) 1062.
1062.2 Common root: *Winchcombe*[1] 1064.1.
1063.1 Common root: *Winchcombe*[1] 1064.2.
1063.2 Common root: *Winchcombe*[1] 1065.1.
1063.3 Common root: *Winchcombe*[1] 1065.2.
1066 Common root: *Winchcombe*[1] 1066.1; *AC* (C) 1066.
1067 Common root: *Winchcombe*[1] 1067; *AC* (C) 1067.
1068.1 Common root: *Winchcombe*[1] 1068.1; *AC* (C) 1068.1.
1068.2 Common root: *Winchcombe*[1] 1068.2; *AC* (C) 1068.2.
1069 Common root: *Winchcombe*[1] 1069; *AC* (C) 1069.
1070 Common root: *Winchcombe*[1] 1070; *AC* (C) 1070.
1071 Common root: *Winchcombe*[1] 1071; *AC* (C) 1071.
1072 Common root: *Winchcombe*[1] 1072; *AC* (C) 1072.
1073 Common root: *Winchcombe*[1] 1073; *AC* (C) 1073.
1074 Common root: *Winchcombe*[1] 1074.1. *Coventry*[1] omits the final sentence.
1075 Common root: *Winchcombe*[1] 1075.1. *Coventry*[1] omits the final two clauses.
1076 Common root: *Winchcombe*[1] 1075.2.
1077 Common root: *Winchcombe*[1] 1079; *AC* (C) 1079.
1078 Common root: *Winchcombe*[1] 1080; *AC* (C) 1080.
1081 Common root: *Winchcombe*[1] 1081; *AC* (C) 1081.
1085.1 Common root: *Winchcombe*[1] 1085.1; *AC* (C) 1085.
1085.2 Common root: *Winchcombe*[1] 1085.2.
1086 Common root: *Winchcombe*[1] 1086.1; *AC* (C) 1086.
1087 Common root: *Winchcombe*[1] 1087; *AC* (C) 1087.

**1088** Common root: *Winchcombe*[1] 1088; *AC* (C) 1088. *Coventry*[1] abbreviates this item, but evidence that *ASC* (E) 1087 was used in the making of this annal remains in the reference to the assistance provided by the English, suggesting that the *Winchcombe*[1] version was that found in the root text.
**1089** Common root: *Winchcombe*[1] 1089; *AC* (C) 1089.
**1090** Common root: *Winchcombe*[1] 1090.
**1091** Common root: *Winchcombe*[1] 1091; *AC* (C) 1091. Both *AC* (C) and *Coventry*[1] omit *et Eadgarus.*
**1092** Common root: *Winchcombe*[1] 1092; *AC* (C) 1092.
**1093.1** Common root: *Winchcombe*[1] 1093.1; *AC* (C) 1093.1.
**1093.2** Common root: *Winchcombe*[1] 1093.3; *AC* (C) 1093.2.
**1094** Common root: *Winchcombe*[1] 1094.
**1095** Common root: *Winchcombe*[1] 1095.1; *AC* (C) 1095.
**1096** Common root: *Winchcombe*[1] 1096; *AC* (C) 1096. *Coventry*[1] omits the consecration of Samson and William II's transfretation.
**1097** Common root: *Winchcombe*[1] 1097; *AC* (C) 1097.
**1098** Common root: *Winchcombe*[1] 1098.1; *AC* (C) 1098. *Coventry*[1] omits the date of Walkelin's obit.
**1099** Common root: *Winchcombe*[1] 1099.1; *AC* (C) 1099. *Coventry*[1] omits the date of Urban II's obit and the erroneous statement that Paschal was a monk of Monte Cassino.
**1100.1** Common root: *Winchcombe*[1] 1100.1. *Coventry*[1] abbreviates this item.
**1100.2** Common root: *Winchcombe*[1] 1100.2; *AC* (C) 1100. *Coventry*[1] abbreviates this item.
**1101.1** Common root: *Winchcombe*[1] 1101.1.
**1101.2** Common root: *Winchcombe*[1] 1101.2; *AC* (C) 1101.
**1102.1** Common root: *Winchcombe*[1] 1102.1.
**1102.2** Common root: *Winchcombe*[1] 1102.2.
**1102.3** Common root: *Winchcombe*[1] 1100.3. *Coventry*[1] abbreviates this item.
**1103** Common root: *Winchcombe*[1] 1103. *Coventry*[1] omits *de quodam fonte.*
**1104** Common root: *Winchcombe*[1] 1104; *APW* 1104; *AC* (C) 1104. *Coventry*[1] slightly abbreviates this item.
**1105** Common root: *Winchcombe*[1] 1105; *APW* 1105; *AC* (C) 1105.
**1106.1** Common root: *Winchcombe*[1] 1106.1; *APW* 1106.2; *AC* (C) 1106.3.
**1106.2** Common root: *Winchcombe*[1] 1106.2; *APW* 1106.1; *AC* (C) 1106.1.
**1106.3** Common root: *Winchcombe*[1] 1106.3.
**1108.1** Common root: *Winchcombe*[1] 1108.1; *APW* 1108.1; *AC* (C) 1108.1.
**1108.2** Common root: *Winchcombe*[1] 1108.2; *APW* 1108.2; *AC* (C) 1108.2.
**1109** Common root: *Winchcombe*[1] 1107.1.
**1110.1** Common root: *Winchcombe*[1] 1109.1; *APW* 1109.1; *AC* (C) 1109.1.
**1110.2** Common root: *Winchcombe*[1] 1109.2; *APW* 1109.2; *AC* (C) 1109.2.
**1111.1** Common root: *Winchcombe*[1] 1110.1; *AC* (C) 1110.1.

**1111.2** Common root: *Winchcombe*[1] 1110.2; *APW* 1110. *Coventry*[1] omits the comet.
**1112.1** Common root: *Winchcombe*[1] 1111.1; *APW* 1111; *AC* (C) 1111.
**1112.2** Common root: *Winchcombe*[1] 1111.3.
**1113.1** Common root: *Winchcombe*[1] 1112; *APW* 1112; *AC* (C) 1112.
**1113.2** Common root: *Winchcombe*[1] 1113; *APW* 1113; *AC* (C) 1113.
**1114** Common root: *Winchcombe*[1] 1114; *APW* 1114; *AC* (C) 1114.
**1115.1** Common root: *Winchcombe*[1] 1115.1; *APW* 1115.1; *AC* (C) 1115.1.
**1115.2** Common root: *Winchcombe*[1] 1115.2; *APW* 1115.2; *AC* (C) 1115.2.
**1116** Common root: *Winchcombe*[1] 1116; *APW* 1116; *AC* (C) 1116.
**1117.1** Common root: *Winchcombe*[1] 1117.1.
**1117.2** Common root: *Winchcombe*[1] 1117.3; *APW* 1117.
**1118** Common root: *Winchcombe*[1] 1118.1.
**1119.1** Common root: *Winchcombe*[1] 1119; *APW* 1119.1; *AC* (C) 1119.1.
**1119.2** Common root: *Winchcombe*[1] 1118.3.
**1120** Common root: *Winchcombe*[1] 1120; *APW* 1120; *AC* (C) 1120.
**1121** Common root: *Winchcombe*[1] 1121; *APW* 1121; *AC* (C) 1121.
**1122.1** Common root: *Winchcombe*[1] 1122.1.
**1122.2** JW*CC* 1122. The first continuation, which begins at this point, comprises material derived from the Dublin Manuscript of JW*CC* (D). See chap. 4 of the Introduction above.
**1123** JW*CC* 1123.
**1124** JW*CC* 1124.
**1125** JW*CC* 1125 (pp. 156, 160). H has *in episcopatum Couentrensem* for D's *ad presulatum Cestrensem*.
**1126** JW*CC* 1126 (pp. 166–68). The preservation of Robert Peche's obit may be significant. Cf. *EEA*, 14:xxxviii; *HBC*, 253.
**1127** JW*CC* 1127 (p. 174).
**1128** JW*CC* 1128 (pp. 174–76, 186).
**1129** JW*CC* 1129 (pp. 186–88). The preservation of the notice of Roger de Clinton's election as bishop of Coventry may be significant. Cf. *EEA*, 14:xl; *HBC*, 253.
**1130** JW*CC* 1130 (p. 192).
**1131** JW*CC* 1130 (p. 196).
**1132** JW*CC* 1132 (p. 208).
**1133** JW*CC* 1133, quoting from Walcher of Malvern's translation of Petrus Alfonsi's *Sententia de dracone*, ed. J.-M. Millás Vallicrosa, "La aportación astronómica de Pedro Alfonso," *Sefarad* 3 (1943): 65–105, at 87. See further P. McGurk's comments in JW*CC*, 3:210, nn. 2 and 3.
**1134** JW*CC* 1134.
**1135** JW*CC* 1135–6 (pp. 214–16). MS C divides this annal in two, putting one half under 1135, the other under 1136; but *Coventry* agrees with D[2] in placing all of this material under 1135. The words *Rex hic Henricus,*

*terrenis rebus optimus, / Ereptus penis, celi potiatur amenis* and *Potens inpotentem ui opprimit* are found only in the holograph and the Dublin manuscripts of JW*CC* (i.e. C and D), where they have been entered by the continuators $C^3$ and $D^2$ respectively.

**1136** JW*CC* 1136 (pp. 216–18). The long passage from *Questum super* to *uirtutum temperantia* is found only in the holograph and the Dublin manuscripts of JW*CC* (i.e. C and D), where they have been entered by the continuators $C^3$ and $D^2$ respectively. Like D, H omits the words *cum armis* in JW*CC* (C) 1136's "Vite necessariis castella et oppida muniunt, manu militari cum armis instruunt."

**1137** JW*CC* 1136 (p. 222).

**1138.1** JW*CC* 1137 (p. 228). H agrees with JWCC (D) in omitting *quod . . . Aprilis* from "Rex Anglorum Stephanus, mense Martio, ante pascha quod erat .iii. idus Aprilis mare transiens in transmarinis partibus moratur."

**1138.2** JW*CC* 1137 (p. 230). As with sections of 1135 and 1136, the words *miraculum Wintoniensis episcopus Henricus* and *multis aliis audientibus narrauit* in this item are echoes of the C and D manuscripts of JW*CC*. Note also the curious way in which the following sentence has been summarised in the present item: "Vt aure percepi, precedens miraculum Wintoniensis episcopus Heinricus, sequens uero narrauit Eboracensis archiepiscopis Turstinus, qui cum Særesbyriensi episcopo Rogero et quibusdam aliis episcopis et regni primoribus concilium tenuerunt apud Norðamtoniam, in plurimorum audientiam."

**1138.3** JW*CC* 1137 (p. 232). In JW*CC* (D) this material follows directly after the miracle-story which comprises **1138.2**, but in JW*CC* (C) it is separated from the former by a long passage on the papal schism and the politics of southern Italy.

**1139.1** JW*CC* 1137 (p. 234).

**1139.2** JW*CC* 1138 (p. 234). In JW*CC* (D) this material follows directly after the former item, but in JW*CC* (C) it is separated from the former by a long passage on the conquest of Thuringia by the Saxons.

**1141** Common knowledge, rightly dated.

**1143** The present continuator, evidently writing some time after the event, has confused the death of Miles, earl of Hereford, with that of Robert, earl of Gloucester. Miles was killed by an arrow in 1143 (see *Winchcombe*[2] 1143), whereas Robert died of natural causes in 1147 (see Gervase, 1:131).

**1148** Robert de Bethune, bishop of Hereford, died on 16 April 1148: see *Fasti*, 8:3; *EEA*, 7:xl; *HBC*, 250.

**1150** The settlement that ended the anarchy is rightly dated to 1153: see Gervase, 1:155–56; Diceto, *YH*, 1:296; Newburgh, 1.30.

**1154** Cf. *Winchcombe*[2] 1154.

**1156** A highly idiosyncratic entry.

**1157** Cf. *Winchcombe*[2] 1158; Newburgh, 2.5; Gervase, 1:165–66.

**1159.1** Cf. Gervase, 1:166–67; *Winchcombe*[2] 1160.1; Diceto, *YH*, 1:303.

**1159.2** Cf. Gervase, 1:167: "Hoc anno rex Henricus scotagium sive scuagium de Anglia accepit, cujus summa fuit centum milia et quater viginti milia librarum argenti."

**1160.1** Theobald died on 18 April 1161: see *Fasti*, 2:4; *HBC*, 232.

**1160.2** Some Continental chronicles report a lunar eclipse in August 1160 (e.g. the Beauvais *Continuatio ad chronicon Sigeberti Gemblacensis*, ed. Ludwig Bethmann, *MGH SS*, 6:461–63, at 463), but none is reported in any of the major English chronicles: see Newton, 655, 660, 662.

**1161** Richard Peche was consecrated as bishop of Coventry on 18 April, though there is some uncertainty as to the year since Gervase, 1:168, assigns it to 1160 and Diceto, *YH*, 1:305, to 1161. See also *EEA*, 14:xxiii, 109; *HBC*, 253.

**1162** Cf. Diceto, *YH*, 1:307: "Postquam autem induit vestes summis sacerdotibus Domino disponente collatas, habitum sic mutavit ut mutaret et animum." Gervase, 1:169.

**1164** Cf. Diceto, *YH*, 1:312–14. Gervase, 1:182–83. The decrees issued at Salisbury were the Constitutions of Clarendon (see *C&S I*, no. 159; Clarendon lies to the east of Salisbury), on 30 January 1164. For the complex series of events that led Becket to quit the kingdom in mid-October, see Frank Barlow, *Thomas Becket* (London: Weidenfeld and Nicolson, 1986), 94–116.

**1165** Henry led two Welsh expeditions in 1165, one in May and one in August: see *Winchcombe*[2] 1165.3, the commentary above, and Eyton, 79–82.

**1166** Not otherwise reported in any of the major chronicles.

**1167.1** Robert de Chesney, bishop of Lincoln, died on 27 December 1166: see *Fasti*, 3:2; *EEA*, 1:xxxvi; *HBC*, 255.

**1167.2** Robert de Melun, bishop of Hereford, died on 26 February 1167: see *Fasti*, 8:4; *EEA*, 7:xli; *HBC*, 250.

**1167.3** Cf. Diceto, *YH*, 1:330.

**1168.1** Robert II Bossu, earl of Leicester (d. 1168), was buried at St Mary of the Meadows, Leicester, which house of Augustinian canons he founded in 1143: see Dugdale, *Monasticon*, 6:463–64 (no. 1); Thomson, *St Mary of the Meadows*, 2.

**1168.2** Abbot Richard's obit is otherwise known from a list in MS. London, Lambeth Palace 585, fol. 215, a transcript of a list in a badly damaged MS. London, B.L., Cotton Vitellius F.XVII, fol. 46: *Heads I*, 170.

**1171.1** Prince Henry was crowned on 14 June 1170 (cf. RH*Chron.*, 2:4; Gervase, 1:219), which implies that the events of this year have been dislocated.

**1171.2** Cf. Gervase, 1:220–27; Diceto, *YH*, 1:342–44; RH*Chron.*, 2:14–16.

**1171.3** Cf. Gervase, 1:224; Diceto, *YH*, 1:343.

**1172.1** In emphasising the role of Strongbow the present account is not dissimilar to those in Newburgh, 2.26, and *Winchcombe*[2] 1170.3 and 1171.3. Cf. RH*Chron.*, 2:29–30; Diceto, *YH*, 1:348.

**1172.2** Cf. RH*Chron.*, 2:45–47; RH*GHS*, 1:41–44; Diceto, *YH*, 1:371–73.

**1173.1** Robert III ès Blanchemains, earl of Leicester (d. 1190), having joined the rebellion, Henry II's justiciar Richard de Luci besieged Leicester from 3 to 28 July, burning the town but without taking the castle: see Diceto, *YH*, 1:376; Newburgh, 2.30; RH*GHS*, 1:48.

**1173.2** Earl Robert III arrived in England on 29 September and was defeated at the Battle of Fornham on 17 October. Many chronicles of the period note the fate of his Flemish mercenaries. Cf. Gervase, 1:246; Diceto, *YH*, 1:377; Newburgh, 2.30; RH*Chron.*, 2:54–55; RH*GHS*, 1:61–62.

**1175.1** Richard of Dover was elected bishop of Canterbury on 3 June 1173 and consecrated on 7 April 1174: see Gervase, 1:244, 247; Diceto, *YH*, 1:369, 389; *Fasti*, 2:4; *HBC*, 232.

**1175.2** Compare Newburgh, 2.38; Gervase, 1:250–51; RH*Chron.*, 2:67–69.

**1176** Cf. Newburgh, 2.38: "Processu vero temporis cum eorum, quæ in se ab ingratis et infidis commissa fuerant, immemor videretur, muros Leicestrenses repente subrui, et munitiones omnium qui a se defecerant complanari præcepit: præcavens scilicet in futurum, confringendo cornua superborum, ne quid simile occasione aliqua in posterum attentarent." See also Diceto, *YH*, 1:404. These events took place after the release of Earl Robert III of Leicester from prison in January 1176: RH*Chron.*, 2:118.

**1177** See *Heads I*, 170, where Abbot William of Calwich's obit is dated to 1177/8.

**1179.1** This obit was also recorded in Dugdale, *Antiquities*, 1:111. Dugdale cited as his source the "Chronicle of Geoffrey," who was prior of Coventry from 1216 to 1235. See *Heads I*, 40–41, and the introduction, at pp. 164–66, above.

**1179.2** It is problematic for the placement of the present entry that Edmund's last datable attestation as archdeacon of Coventry belongs to early 1176 (see *EEA*, 16:113 and no. 45), whilst the first of his successor, Nicholas, as archdeacon of Coventry occurs *die sabbati proxima post oct' apostolorum Petri et Pauli anno regis Henrici secundi .xxij.*, that is, 10 July 1176 (see *EEA*, 16:114, citing *Final Concords of the County of Lincoln from the Feet of Fines Preserved in the Public Record Office*, vol. 2, *A.D. 1244–1272*, ed. Charles W. Foster [Lincoln: Lincoln Record Society, 1920], 312).

**1179.3** A reference to the renewal of the coinage in November 1180: Gervase, 1:294–95; Diceto, *YH*, 2:7.

**1181.1** Archbishop Roger de Pont l'Evêque died on 22 November 1181: RH*Chron.*, 2:264; *Fasti*, 6:4.

**1181.2** Alexander died on 30 August and Lucius was elected on 1 September 1180: Diceto, *YH*, 2:9.

**1181.3** Louis VII died on 18 September 1180, and Philip Augustus succeeded him, having been crowned in November 1179: Diceto, *YH*, 2:6–7.

**1182.1** Hugh II, earl of Chester (1153–1181), died at Leek on 3 June 1181: *ACestr.*, s.a. 1181 (pp. 28 and 125); RH*Chron.*, 2:265; RH*GHS*, 1:277. See also *Peerage*, 3:167; 14:170.

**1182.2** Bishop Richard Peche died on 6 or 7 October 1182: see *EEA*, 16:109; *HBC*, 253.

**1183.1** Cf. RH*GHS*, 1:292–95; RH*Chron.*, 2:273–80; Diceto, *YH*, 2:18–19. Henry the Young King died on 11 June. On the confrontation at the Citadel of St Martial at Limoges where Aimar, the rebel viscount of the Limousin, had been joined by Henry and his brother Geoffrey, see Gillingham, *Richard I*, 71–75.

**1183.2** Robert III, earl of Leicester, was arrested together with his brother-in-law, Earl William of Gloucester, and many other *potentes et ditiores regni* in 1183 (RH*GHS*, 1:294), but had evidently been released by the end of 1186, when he attended the Christmas court (RH*Chron.*, 3:3).

**1183.3** Walter of Coutances was consecrated on 8 July 1183: *Fasti*, 3:2; *EEA*, 1:xxxix; *HBC*, 255.

**1183.4** Master Gerard Pucelle was consecrated on 25 September 1183: see Gervase, 1:307; Diceto, *YH*, 2:21; *EEA*, 16:xxv, 110; *HBC*, 253.

**1184.1** Richard of Dover died on 16 February 1184: see Gervase, 1:308; *Fasti*, 2:5; *HBC*, 232.

**1184.2** Master Gerard Pucelle died on 12 or 13 January 1184: see *EEA*, 16:xxv, 110; *HBC*, 253. Cf. Gervase, 1:308: "Erat autem rumor in populo eum [Gerardum] interiisse veneno, quod et manifestis secundum physicos claruit indiciis."

**1185.1** Cf. Newburgh, 3.10; Diceto, *YH*, 2:32; *ACestr.*, s.a. 1185 (p. 33); Gervase, 1:325; Devizes, *AW*, s.a. 1185.

**1185.2** For the earthquake, see esp. RH*GHS*, 1:337, and RH*Chron.*, 1:303–4 (agrees as to date and notes the damage done to Lincoln Cathedral); Diceto, *YH*, 2:37 (no date).

**1186.1** An item seemingly unique to this source.

**1186.2** An item seemingly unique to this source.

**1186.3** Diceto, *YH*, 2:40, dates this eclipse of the moon to 16 April 1186, but agrees that the sun was eclipsed on 21 of the same month. Gervase, 1:334–35, dates the eclipse of the moon to 5 April, but places the eclipse of the sun on 1 May. See also Newton, 144–45, 655.

**1187.1** Cf. Diceto, *YH*, 2:49–50. Gervase, 1:373–75.

**1187.2** Philip Augustus invaded Berry in June 1187 in support of Prince Richard: cf. Diceto, *YH*, 2:49; Newburgh, 3.14; RH*GHS*, 2:6–7; RH*Chron*., 2:317–18.

**1187.3** A fuller version of this miracle story is to be found in Gervase, 1:369–70. There are some differences: Gervase does not connect the event with the loss of the relic of the true cross, he makes it a miracle of the Virgin Mary, and he uses it to explain why war was avoided. It seems certain that the two versions are independent of one another, but it is worth quoting Gervase's text in full because it helps to make sense of the terse account in the present chronicle:

> Est ibidem [i.e. juxta Castellum Radulfi] cœnobium monachorum habitus nigri, in honore Beatæ Virginis Mariæ dedicatum. Quo cum Braibanceni regis Angliæ stipendiarii festinarent, ut ea quæ in eadem ecclesia reposita erant absportarent, Lemovicensis vicecomes armatus accessit, eorumque ab ingressu ecclesiæ cohibuit furorem; fugatoque tandem latronum cuneo, remanserunt quidam ex ipsis in ipso atrio ecclesiæ ludentes. Cum ergo quidam ex ipsis, ut moris est, sorte perderent, alii vero lucro inhiantes eos qui perdebant probis irritarent, hi qui perdebant furore succensi in Deum et Beatam Ejus Genitricem nephandas blasphemias jactitabant, ac si eorum esset culpa quod hujusmodi infortunia eis accidebant; unus autem ex eis, insanior cæteris, arrepto lapide ad imaginem Sanctæ Virginis Mariæ in lapide sculptam projecit, quo infantem feriens, ejus manum dejecit in terram. Qua ruente, ipse quoque puer e gremio elapsus est inferiusque solito resedit. De brachio autem pueri, simul et manu, quæ jam in terram lapsa est, sanguis uberrime manavit, ac si viventis hominis vigor esset in lapide. Ipsa vero imago Mariæ, ac si suo compateretur filio, conjectis manibus ad humeros proprios vestimentum lapideum abrupit, et corpus proprium fere usque ad mamillas detexit. Hic vero, qui lapidem jecerat, absque mora corruit et expiravit; cæterique amentes affecti sunt. Vicecomes autem Lemovicensis accurrens, manum pueri sanguine madidam apprehendit, magnumque suæ defensionis præmium lætebundus absportavit. Interea exercitus utrimque in acies ordinatur, et hujus eventus miraculi circumquaque diffunditur. Terrentur hinc inde milites armati, et de belli eventu dubio plurimi suspicantur. . .
>
> There was there [next to Châteauroux] a monastery of black monks, dedicated in honour of the blessed Virgin Mary. When the Brabançon mercenaries of the English king made haste to it that they might carry off what had been placed in that church, the battle-ready viscount of Limoges drew near, and held back their ferocity from the entrance to the church; finally the formation of thieves withdrew, but some of them lingered playing dice

> in the forecourt of the church. When, therefore, these men were squandering their lot (as is their way), they angered others — those longing for lucre who lost in the toss of the dice. Those who were losing, enraged with anger, yelled out evil blasphemies against God and his blessed Mother, as if it were their fault that misfortune had fallen upon them in this way. And one of them, madder than the rest, grabbed a rock and threw it at an image of the holy Virgin Mary, sculptured in stone and in which she was carrying an infant, and its hand fell to the ground. Striking it, furthermore, the child fell out of her lap and came to rest below as normal, but from the child's arm and from the hand likewise, which had now fallen to the ground, blood was dripping copiously as if the spirit of a living human being was in the stone. Indeed, that same image of Mary, as if it were suffering with her son, broke off some stone clothing, her hands having been thrown to the ground before her, and exposed her own body almost as far as her breasts. Truly, he who had thrown the rock fell down and died without delay, and the rest were driven mad. But rushing up, the viscount of Limoges seized the hand which was wet with the child's blood, and, rejoicing, he carried off a great reward for his protection [of the church]. Meanwhile, each army was lined up in battle array, and the occurrence of this miracle was spread about, and thus the armed soldiers were then terrified, and many were suspicious about the dubious cause of the war . . .

For a more prosaic explanation as to why a full-scale battle was avoided in 1187, see Gillingham, *Richard I*, 83–85.

**1188.1** The date, 21 January, is the same as that in RH*GHS*, 2:29–30; RH*Chron.*, 3:334–35. Gervase, 1:406, dates the conference to around 22 January, and adds a similar miracle: "Cum autem de sumenda cruce hinc inde prodirent eloquia, signum eis apparuit in cælo, crux scilicet quinque stellarum, cum sereno cælo sol in sua luceret virtute." A similar miracle is said to have taken place at Dunstable on 9 August 1189: see RH*GHS*, 2:47; RH*Chron.*, 2:354; Newburgh, 4.6.

**1188.2** For comparable accounts of the tax raised in support of the Crusade, see Newburgh, 3.23; Gervase, 1:422; RH*Chron.*, 2:335–36; RH*GHS*, 2:30–31.

**1188.3** The present item is mistaken in its statements to the effect that Raymond V, count of Toulouse, died in 1188 and that Richard was asserting his power over his youthful successor, Raymond VI. Raymond V appears actually to have died in late 1194: see *Catalogue des actes des comtes de Toulouse*, vol. 3, *Raymond V (1149–94)*, ed. Emile G. Léonard (Paris: A. Picard, 1932–), xi; Roger Genty, *Les comtes de Toulouse* (Ferrières: Editions de Poliphile, 1987), 164. These are, however, notions that seem to have been current in England in the early 1190s, for they also figure in Gervase, 1:432–33, whose account seems, given that it offers no coverage of the confrontation at Gisors, to be independent of the present annal. Cf. also RH*Chron.*, 2:343–45; RH*GHS*, 2:40–46; Diceto, *YH*, 2:55. On Richard's quarrel with Raymond V of Toulouse and its development into a full-scale war with Philip Augustus, see Gillingham, *Richard I*, 90–95.

**1188.4** Apart from Gervase, the major English and French chroniclers of this period all have something to say about the meeting at Gisors and the cutting down of the great elm. Howden, for example, notes that the French king was so exasperated by Henry II's refusal to meet properly in order to make peace that he cut down a beautiful elm tree which was the customary meeting place of the kings of France and the dukes of Normandy, "giving orders that from now on no conferences will be held here" (RH*Chron.*, 2:345). Writing between 1214 and 1225 (see Delaborde, 1:lxvii–lxxx), William the Breton puts a different spin on this episode, investing it with prophetic significance. He describes the elm in great detail, emphasising its beauty and its immensity: it was a welcome sight, its branches reached back to the ground, its shady foliage was luxuriant, and its trunk was so massive that four men with their arms outstretched and fingers touching could only just encircle it (*Philippidos*, 3.102–10, ed. Delaborde, 2:69). The crucial point is made, moreover, by having Henry II boast that just as the trunk cannot be split or uprooted from the field, so the French will not be able to take any of it from him: "When I have lost it, then I will cast aside this land" (*Hunc cum perdidero, simul hanc volo perdere terram*) (*Philippidos*, 3.167–69). These words transform the felling and burning of the tree into a portent prophesying Henry's II's bitter end. For his part, Diceto, *YH*, 2:55, seems to confirm the claims which he makes for its size, stating that its branches reached out over the border into French territory (*intra fines Franciæ radicata*). The present chronicle's brief account of the episode is striking in as much as it attributes the felling of the tree to William III des Barres. The lord of la Ferté-Alais, Oissery, and a leading vassal of Philip Augustus, William III's chivalric exploits captured the imagination of chroniclers on both sides of the Channel (e.g. RH*GHS*, 2:46; RH*Chron.*, 2:88, 93–94), but no other chronicle attributes this act to him. A connection which might, however, explain why our chronicle was alert to William's exploits may have been his marriage to Amice, the daughter of Robert III, earl of Leicester, who would later, from 1204, style herself "countess of Leicester." For Amice and the marriage, which took place before 13 January 1188 when William took the cross, see *Peerage*, 7:537; Daniel Power, *The Norman Frontier in the Twelfth and Thirteenth Centuries*, Cambridge Studies in Medieval Life and Thought, 4th ser., 62 (Cambridge: Cambridge University Press,

2004), 239. On William, see also Jim Bradbury, *Philip Augustus, King of France, 1180–1223* (London: Longmans, 1998), 84–85. On the date of the conference at Gisors, see Diceto, *YH*, 2:55, who states that it began on 16 August and extended over three days; but compare RH*GHS*, 2:47, and RH*Chron.*, 2:345, where the conference is said to have begun on 1 September.

**1188.5** The conference took place at Bonsmoulins on 18 November 1188: cf. Diceto, *YH*, 2:57–58; Gervase, 1:435–36. On Richard I's act of homage to Philip, see also Gillingham, *Richard I*, 95–96.

**1189.1** This item is particularly striking for its emphases on (1) King Philip's role in reconciling Richard with his father before his death and (2) the actuality of that reconciliation. The usual sources imply that the settlement which was reached at Chinon on 4 July was entirely superficial. Thus Gerald of Wales, *De principis instructione*, 3.26 (ed. George F. Warner, *GCO*, 8:296), states that at this final meeting Henry II hissed in his son's ear as he gave him the kiss of peace, "God grant that I may not die until I have had my revenge upon you." Howden, furthermore, states that only the illegitimate Geoffrey Plantagenet had remained faithful to his father. When Richard came to view the body, blood spurted from Henry's nose "as though his spirit was angered by his approach," a sure sign that he was responsible for his father's death (RH*GHS*, 2:71; RH*Chron.*, 2:367). In short, the present item confirms this continuator's pronounced bias in favour of Richard's cause and the likelihood that he was writing before news of the events at Messina and Acre had reached England—that is, at a time when it was Richard's policy to present himself as Philip's man and ally. On the course of Henry II's war with Richard and Philip in the first six months of 1189, see in general RH*Chron.*, 2:362–67 (who also mentions the fall of Ballan); RH*GHS*, 2:60–71; and Diceto, *YH*, 2:62–64. Gervase, 1:448–49, is much less detailed on these events. See also Gillingham, *Richard I*, 98–100.

**1189.2** Richard was girded with the sword by the archbishop of Rouen on 20 July 1189: cf. RH*Chron.*, 3:3; RH*GHS*, 2:73. Diceto, *YH*, 2:67, 69. For the coronation in London on 3 September and the massacre of the Jews that followed, compare Devizes, *CTR*, 3–4; Newburgh, 4.1; RH*Chron.*, 3:8–12; RH*GHS*, 2:78–84.

**1189.3** Landon, 15: King Philip had sworn in a general council at Paris that he would be at Vezelay on 1 April prepared to start for Jerusalem. He then sent a letter dated October 1189 calling on Richard and the magnates of England to make the same oath. Richard on 12 November at London deputed William de Mandeville to swear before the French envoys that he would on no account fail to be present and ready to make his journey to Jerusalem on the specified day. See RH*Chron.*, 3:19–20; RH*GHS*, 2:92–93.

**1190.1** The date *post epiphaniam Domini* is somewhat problematic. Richard and Philip held a meeting at Nonancourt on 30 December 1189, some seven days before Epiphany (see Diceto, *YH*, 2:73; RH*GHS*, 2:104–5; RH*Chron.*, 3:30–31), but this annal evidently refers to the second meeting which took place two months after Epiphany on 16 March 1190, to which news was brought of the death of Isabel of Hainault, queen of France, the first wife of King Philip, and at which it was agreed that their departure for the Holy Land would be put off to the feast of St John the Baptist (see Diceto, *YH*, 2:77; Landon, 27; Gillingham, *Richard I*, 126). The most striking feature of this annal, however, is its neat balancing of the reasons for the delay in setting out on crusade. No other chronicle mentions in relation to the deferral that King William II, Richard's brother-in-law as the husband of his sister Joan, had also died at this moment—that Richard had as much reason for grief as Philip. The other chronicles mention only the death of Queen Isabel (e.g. RH*GHS*, 2:108; RH*Chron.*, 3:34). The accepted date for his obit in most modern accounts of William's reign falls some two months before Epiphany, under 18 November 1189 (e.g. Ferdinand Chalandon, *Histoire de la domination normande en Italie et en Sicilie*, 2 vols. [Paris: A. Picard, 1907], 2:417), and it was known to Diceto, among late twelfth-century English historians, that King William II had died in the middle of that month (see Diceto, *YH*, 2:73).

**1190.2** For the massacre of the Jews at Stamford on 7 March and for that at York on 16 March, see Newburgh, 4.8–10; Diceto, *YH*, 2:75–76. Newburgh, 4.9, also mentions a failed attempt to massacre the Jews of Lincoln. Howden describes the suicides of the Jews at York and Longchamp's punishment of the persecutors there (see RH*GHS*, 2:108; RH*Chron.*, 3:33–34). He states that he took a hundred hostages from among the citizens of the city. Newburgh, 4.11, likewise, goes on to describe Longchamp's expedition to York to punish those responsible for the massacre, but neither Howden nor Newburgh covers his actions in Stamford or Lincoln en route to York.

**1190.3** Cf. Devizes, *CTR*, 13–14: "Rex Ricardus sacramentum exegit a duobus fratribus suis, Iohanne uterino et Gaufrido non ex legitima, quod Angliam non intrarent imfra triennio peregrinationis sue, a die profectionis ab Turonis triennio computato." The oath appears to have been demanded in mid-March 1190. See also RH*GHS*, 2:106; RH*Chron.*, 3:32.

**1190.4** Robert III, earl of Leicester, is otherwise known to have been in England until at least 1 December 1189, when he witnessed a charter of Richard I for Canterbury Cathedral Priory (Gervase, 1:503). He is reported to have died on the journey to Jerusalem: Howden states that he died in *Romania*, that is, Greece (RH*Chron.*, 3:88; RH*GHS*, 2:148), while the

Melrose Chronicle has him die on the eve of the feast of St Giles (1 September 1190) while still at sea before being buried at the Byzantine town of Durazzo. His son Robert IV de Bréteuil was girded with the sword of his father's earldom at Messina on 1 February 1191. See Alan O. Anderson and Marjorie O. Anderson, eds., *The Chronicle of Melrose from the Cottonian Manuscript, Faustina B.IX in the British Museum* (London: Humphries, 1936), s.a. 1190 (47); RH*Chron.*, 3:94. See also Dugdale, *Monasticon*, 6:467; *Peerage*, 7:533–34, 14:429; Thomson, *St Mary of the Meadows*, 10.

**1190.5** Richard reached Marseilles at the end of July and departed for Messina on 9 August: see Diceto, *YH*, 2:84. On the arrangements for the armies' stay in southern Italy, cf. Devizes, *CTR*, 15–16; RH*Chron.*, 3:39, 55; RH*GHS*, 2:112, 126.

**1190.6** The present item clearly refers to the eclipse of the sun that took place on 23 June 1191. This eclipse is widely reported in English and French chronicles: e.g. RH*Chron.*, 3:115, and RH*GHS*, 2:172. See Newton, 143–49, 315–21.

**1194.1** RH*Chron.*, 3:253–4, reports that Robert IV, earl of Leicester (d. 1204), was captured by Philip on 15 June 1194. Rigord, *Gesta Philippi Augusti*, § 97 (ed. Delaborde, 1:1–167, at 127), adds that he was confined at Étampes. See also Paris, *CM*, 2:407.

**1194.2** The castle of Prince John at Nottingham was one of only two that were still holding out against Richard when he returned to England (13 March 1194). Richard went from Sandwich to join the siege, and he arrived at Nottingham on 25 March: RH*Chron.*, 3:239–40. The castle surrendered on 28 March. Richard held a council there on 30 March to 2 April, at which Hugh de Nonant was prosecuted for allying himself with Prince John and the king of France. RH*Chron.*, 3:240–42; Landon, 85–87. Cf. Diceto, *YH*, 2:114; Newburgh, 4.42; Gervase, 1:524. Given that Easter fell on 10 April in 1194 (*HDSBH*, 194), these events do indeed fall roughly within the compass of Passion Week (27 March–2 April).

**1195.1** Hugh du Puiset's obit is given as 3 March 1195 in RH*Chron.*, 2:284–85, and in local Durham obituaries: see *Fasti*, 2:30; *HBC*, 241.

**1195.2** This obit and appointment are otherwise unrecorded. Hamo makes his last appearance in other sources around March 1195: see RH*Chron.*, 3:285–86. The earliest datable reference to Master Roger of Rolleston as dean of Lincoln is in a source that has been dated to before the middle of June 1198: see "Prior Geoffrey's Memorandum" (below), and Frank M. Stenton, ed., *Documents Illustrative of the Social and Economic History of the Danelaw*, British Academy Records of Social and Economic History 5 (London: British Academy, 1920), no. 242, with *Fasti*, 3:9–10 and app. 42. See also *EEA*, 1: no. 97. Interestingly, both Hamo and especially Roger had connections with Leicester and Coventry. Hamo had been archdeacon of Leicester (*Fasti*, 3: app. 33, 35), as was Roger from before September 1193 (*EEA*, 4: nos. 11, 188A). Between July 1183 and March 1185, furthermore, Roger of Rollestion was given possession for his lifetime of the church of Checkendon in the diocese of Lincoln — a church that belonged to Coventry Cathedral priory (*EEA*, 1: no. 301). He resigned this post between c. 1187 and March 1190, at which point the priory granted it to Hugh of Rolleston (*EEA*, 4: no. 43). The cognomen suggests that Hugh was one of Roger's kinsmen. Moreover, according to the testimony of a monk of Coventry called John as reported in "Prior Geoffrey's Memorandum" (MS. London, B.L., Cotton Charters xiii.26, partly printed in Dugdale, *Monasticon*, 6:1244), Rolleston played a crucial role in the election of Bishop Geoffrey Muschamp which took place between March and June of 1198 (see **1198.3** below). In reality, of course, Muschamp owed his election to the say-so of the king, but the formal right to elect was contested, as on previous occasions, between the monks of Coventry and the canons of Lichfield. Asked to adjudicate, Archbishop Hubert Walter delegated "the power to the dean of Lincoln, Master Roger of Rolleston, because I am concerned that there should not be an argument between us over this office" (*Saluo iure utriusque ecclesie, do potestatem decano Lincolnie, Magistro Rogero de Rolueston, quia non curo quod hac uice sit inter nos contentio*). According to John, Roger went on to elect Bishop Geoffrey. However, in the testimony of the most vocal witness, Prior Geoffrey (Dugdale, *Monasticon*, 6:1242), the dean of Lincoln's role on this occasion was confined to that of first nominating Muschamp for the position of bishop on the occasion of his consecration in London. In any case, these fragments of information point to the existence of some kind of association between Roger of Rolleston and Coventry Cathedral priory, which may explain why his appointment as dean of Lincoln was considered a noteworthy event.

**1196.1** Robert IV, earl of Leicester, was set free in about 1196: see RH*Chron.*, 4:5; *Peerage*, 7:534.

**1196.2** An item seemingly unique to this source.

**1196.3** An item seemingly unique to this source.

**1197.1** For the full text of the Assize of Measures which was enacted on 20 November 1197, see RH*Chron.*, 4:33. Cf. *Annales monasterii de Waverleia*, s.a. 1196 (ed. Luard, *AM*, 2:129–411, at 250). A Henrican ell was 45 inches or 115 cm long. On the context of the Assize of Measures, see John Hudson, *The Formation of the English Common Law* (London: Longmans, 1996), esp. 135.

**1197.2** Bishop William Longchamp died on 31 January in Poitiers en route to Rome: see RH*Chron.*, 4:17; Diceto, *YH*, 2:150; *Fasti*, 2:45; *HBC*, 244.

**1198.1** The dissolution of the secular chapter created by Bishop Hugh de Nonant and the restoration of the monks to Coventry is covered in almost all of the major chronicles of the period, but most fully in RH*Chron.*, 4:35–37, who quotes Pope Celestine III's letter to Archbishop Hubert Walter ordering their return. Some confusion has been caused by disagreements in the sources as to the precise date of the monks' restoration (see Knowles, *MO*, 324; *EEA*, 17:xxxiv, n. 89), but this can now be resolved. Gervase, 1:550, states that the archbishop instituted the monks at Coventry in accordance with Celestine's mandate on 11 January, whereas Diceto, *YH*, 2:159, states that the monks were "reintroduced" on 18 January; the present chronicle agrees with Diceto, stating that the monks were "instituted" on the feast of St Prisca (i.e. 18 January). Jocelin of Brakelond, 94–95, provides the fullest treatment: he states that Abbot Samson, who was one of the prelates deputised by the pope with the task of restoring the monks, went with fourteen of them (whom he had received as the guests of his household) to Coventry as the feast of St Hilary (13 January) was approaching, but that he waited there for five days before the archbishop arrived, at which time the new prior (Joybert) was appointed and the monks were formally inducted. He also refers to a council at Oxford where the pope's mandate and the king's view of the matter were discussed before the judges, and this could conceivably have been the event of 11 January to which Gervase refers; but there can be little doubt that the monks were not, as Jocelin puts it, "instituted in person" until 18 January. The most striking feature of the present entry is the absence of any condemnation of Bishop Hugh de Nonant. This silence and the absence of any reference to his appointment (1186) or death (1197) seems to indicate an unwillingness to commemorate his acts: see introduction, pp. 159–62 above. See also Devizes, *AW*, s.a. 1198 (pp. 64–65).

**1198.2** Having been elected on 13 April 1189, Roger Beaumont was consecrated as bishop of St Andrews on 15 February 1198 (see *HBC*, 320), which was indeed the first day of Lent in 1198 (see *HDSBH*, 170). The presence in the chronicle of this obit and of **1202.2** below is explained by the fact that Roger was the third son of Earl Robert II and thus the brother of Earl Robert III of Leicester: see *Chronicle of Melrose*, s.a. 1198 (p. 50); Dugdale, *Monasticon*, 6:466.

**1198.3** Geoffrey Muschamp, sometime archdeacon of Cleveland, was elected bishop of Coventry after 27 March and consecrated on 21 June 1198: see Diceto, *YH*, 2:162–63; Gervase, 1:554; *EEA*, 16:110; *HBC*, 253.

**1198.4** Pope Innocent III was consecrated on 15 February 1198.

**1198.5** Having been elected on 10 August 1197, Eustace was consecrated on 8 March: see Diceto, *YH*, 2:159; *Fasti*, 2:45; *HBC*, 244.

**1198.6** John of Coutances, bishop of Worcester, died on 24 or 25 September: see *Fasti*, 2:100; *HBC*, 279.

**1199.1** The cardinal legate Peter de Capua arrived in France in December 1198, and peace negotiations between the two kings began at a place on the Seine between Les Andelys and Vernon on 13 January 1199: see RH*Chron.*, 4:79–80; Landon, 141–42.

**1199.2** The dates are mistaken and beyond repair in this annal: Richard was wounded on 26 March, and died on 6 April 1199 (see Landon, 144–45; *HBC*, 36), which was a Tuesday. Easter Sunday fell on 18 April in 1199 (see *HDSBH*, 210); Passion Week on 4–10 April. *Die vi° sequenti* ought, finally, to produce the Wednesday (14 April) rather than the Tuesday (13 April) in Holy Week. The entry is noteworthy, however, as a hitherto unreported instance of the legend that Richard besieged Châlus-Chabrol in order to force the viscount of Limoges to hand over some recently discovered treasure. It is clear that this dubious tale began to circulate widely in England as well as France within a couple of years of the king's death, for it was also recorded by Howden and Ralph of Coggeshall, both of whom were writing within two or three years of the event. Howden accepted its validity (see RH*Chron.*, 4:82–83), but Coggeshall (94) distanced himself from the story: "*Nonnulli vero referunt quod* quidam thesaurus inæstimabilis pretii in terra vicecomitis sit repertus, quem rex mandat et jubet sibi dari; quo a vicecomite negato, amplius regis animositatem erga eum exacuit" (emphasis added). On these and other accounts of how Richard died, see John Gillingham, "The Unromantic Death of Richard I," *Speculum* 54 (1979): 18–41, repr. in idem, *Richard Coeur de Lion: Kingship, Chivalry and War in the Twelfth Century* (London: Hambledon Press, 1994), 155–80; idem, *Richard I*, 321–34. On the dating of Coggeshall's annals for 1195–1200, see David A. Carpenter, "Abbot Ralph of Coggeshall's Account of the Last Years of King Richard and the First Years of King John," *EHR* 113 (1998): 1210–30 (esp. 1214–17).

**1199.3** John returned to England on 25 May and was crowned on 27 May 1199: see RH*Chron.*, 4:87, 90–91; Diceto, *YH*, 2:166; *HBC*, 37.

**1200.1** This is a striking entry because it exhibits aspects of the hagiographical pattern found in Adam of Eynsham's *Magna vita sancti Hugonis*, 5.18–19, ed. Decima L. Douie and Hugh Farmer, *The Life of St Hugh of Lincoln*, Nelson's Medieval Texts, 2 vols. (London: T. Nelson, 1961–1962), 2:208, 217–30, even though it was apparently written soon after the event. Book five of Eynsham's text was written, as its prologue indicates (see *Magna vita Hugonis*, 74), some thirteen years after Hugh died. Like the present entry, Adam also develops parallels with the life of St Martin of Tours. Among the many resemblances noted by Adam is the fact that Hugh died on the sixth day of the octave of St Martin, "bidding farewell to the light of this world" (*luci huius seculi valefaciens*) (*Magna vita Hugonis*, 208). This might suggest dependence on Adam, but it seems more likely that the Martinian theme was already being applied to Hugh in common discourse well before the writing of book five of the *Magna vita*. The present entry is much fuller, furthermore, in its coverage of the miracles at the funeral. Adam reports two posthumous miracles: the cure of a woman who receives her sight having been blind for many years, and the blinding of a thief who had stolen the purse of a woman in the crowd (*Magna vita Hugonis*, 230–31). See, likewise, RH*Chron.*, 4:142–44, who mentions the cure of a woman, "who had been blind in one eye for seven years." Coggeshall (110–12) is more cautious: "*Fama volitans perhibet* quod meritis ipsius sanitatem quibusdam ægrotis divine virtus contulit." But he goes on to say that it is not surprising that the Lord should work miracles in order to magnify his beloved. It is clear, then, that reports of posthumous cures began to circulate widely almost immediately after Hugh's funeral. On the precise date of Hugh's obit, see *Fasti*, 3:3.

**1200.2** Bishop John of Oxford died on 2 June and Bishop John de Gray was consecrated on 24 September: see Diceto, *YH*, 2:169; *Fasti*, 2:56; *EEA*, 6:xxxvi–xxxvii; *HBC*, 261.

**1200.3** This obit is not attested elsewhere: previously a subdean of Lincoln (*Liber benefactorum ecclesiæ Ramesiensis*, ed. William D. Macray, *Chronicon Abbatiæ Rameseiensis*, RS 83 [London: Longman, 1886], 310, 316), Winemer is otherwise attested as archdeacon of Northampton from 1192 × September 1193 until around 1198 (see RH*Chron.*, 3:278–81, 285; *EEA*, 4: no. 188A; *Fasti*, 3:31).

**1201** See, likewise, *Annales monasterii de Burton*, s.a. 1201 (ed. Luard, *AM*, 1:183–500, at 209): "Eodem anno sanctus Wlstanus Wigornensis et Sancta Modwenna Burthoniensis claruerunt multis et magnis miraculis." Cf. *Annales monasterii de Waverleia*, s.a. 1201 (ed. Luard, *AM*, 2:129–411, at 253). These annals all refer to a sudden outburst of miracles associated with the dedication of the church of St Andrew in the Isle (that is, on Andresey, an island in the River Trent) by the bishop of Coventry at some point between 1200 and 1208. This island was a subsidiary centre of the cult of St Modwenna, the patron saint of Burton-on-Trent who had once been buried there: see further Geoffrey of Burton, *Life and Miracles of St Modwenna*, ed. Robert Bartlett, OMT (Oxford: Clarendon Press, 2002), xxxii–xxxiii.

**1202.1** King John captured Arthur, duke of Brittany, the posthumous son of his brother, Geoffrey, at Mirabeau in Poitou in 1202: see Coggeshall (137–38), who preserves the letter John sent to all his barons in which he announced his victory and called upon them to give thanks to God. This letter was presumably the source of the item in the present chronicle, not least because it provided a date for the event: *die . . . Martis* (i.e. the Tuesday) *ante Ad Vincula Sancti Petri* (i.e. 1 August), namely, 30 July 1202. Cf. also Devizes, *AW*, s.a. 1202 (pp. 78–79). It may be significant for the dating of these entries that the continuator does not go on to mention that Arthur died in custody at Falaise in April 1203.

**1202.2** Roger Beaumont, bishop of St Andrews, died on 7 July: see *HBC*, 320. On his relationship to the earls of Leicester, see **1198.2** above.

**1202.3** Gilbert of Sempringham was canonised by Pope Innocent III on 11 January and his remains were translated to a new shrine on 13 October 1202: see *The Book of St Gilbert*, ed. Raymonde Foreville and Gillian Keir, OMT (Oxford: Clarendon Press, 1987), 186–91.

# Appendix A
# The Worcester Material in the *Annales prioratus de Wigornia*—Commentary

51 Common root: *Winchcombe* 13; *Coventry* 13.

52 Common root: *Winchcombe* 14.1; *Coventry* 14. The same item also appears in the calendar in T, fol. 35r (25 January): 'Conuersus Saulus uocitatur nomine Paulus'.

71 Possibly common root. The same item also appears in the calendar in T, fol. 37v (29 June): 'Cum Paulo Petrus passus petit æthera letus'.

220 Possibly common root. The same item also appears in the calendar in T, fol. 40r (22 November): 'Sponso cum Christo gaudes Cecilia uirgo'.

261 Possibly common root. The same item also appears in the calendar in T, fol. 38v (10 August): 'Astra petit iustus Laurentius igne perustus'.

654.1 Common root: *Winchcombe* 653.2.

654.2 Common root: *Winchcombe* 653.3; *Coventry* 653.2.

656 Common root: *Winchcombe* 653.3; *Coventry* 654.2.

678 Common root: *Winchcombe* 679; *Coventry* 679.

680 Common root (modified): *Winchcombe* 680.1; *Coventry* 680.

689 Common root: *Winchcombe* 689.2; *Coventry* 690.2.

692 Common root: *Winchcombe* 692; *Coventry* 692. But note that *APW* numbers Oftfor's reign.

693 Common root: *Winchcombe* 692; *Coventry* 692.

714 Common root: *Winchcombe* 715.1; *Coventry* 714.2.

717 Common root: *Winchcombe* 718.2; *Coventry* 718.2.

780 Source unknown.

742 Common root: *Winchcombe* 743; *Coventry* 743.

785 Common root: *Winchcombe* 784; *Coventry* 784.

787.1 Common root: *Winchcombe* 786.1; *Coventry* 786.

787.2 Common root: *Winchcombe* 787.1; *Coventry* 787.2.

832 Source unknown. Cf. *Winchcombe* 819; *Coventry* 819; JW*CC* (C), fol. 2r–p. 3 (ed. Dugdale, *Monasticon*, 1:607–9).

775 Common root: *Winchcombe* 774.4; *Coventry* 775.

778 Common root: *Winchcombe* 778.1; *Coventry* 778.1.

**781** Common root: *Winchcombe* 781.1; *Coventry* 781.
**850** Common root: *Winchcombe* 784; *Coventry* 784.
**855** Common root (modified): *Winchcombe* 955; *Coventry* 955.
**858** Common root: *Winchcombe* 956; *Coventry* 956.
**859** Common root: *Winchcombe* 957; *Coventry* 957.
**860** Common root: *Winchcombe* 957; *Coventry* 957.
**862** Common root: *Winchcombe* 958; *Coventry* 958.
**863** Common root: *Winchcombe* 959.1; *Coventry* 959.1.
**864** Common root: *Winchcombe* 960; *Coventry* 960.
**866** Common root: *Winchcombe* 963; *Coventry* 963.
**868** Common root: *Winchcombe* 967; *Coventry* 966.
**871** Common root: *Winchcombe* 969; *Coventry* 969.
**873** Perhaps distantly connected, to *Winchcombe* 969; *Coventry* 969.
**878** Common root: *Winchcombe* 972.1; *Coventry* 972.1.
**879** Common root: *Winchcombe* 972.2; *Coventry* 972.2.
**881** Common root: *Winchcombe* 973.2; *Coventry* 973.2.
**883** A candidate for inclusion among the material in the common root, but one which is unattested in the other witnesses.
**884** The same as 883.
**885** The same as 883.
**886** The same as 883.
**888** The same as 883.
**903** The same as 883.
**917** Common root: *Winchcombe* 915.2; *Coventry* 915.2.
**919** Common root: *Winchcombe* 916.1; *Coventry* 916.1.
**922** Common root: *Winchcombe* 922; *Coventry* 921.
**932** Common root: *Winchcombe* 923.1; *Coventry* 922.
**953** Possibly common root. The same item also appears in the calendar in T, fol. 37v (15 June): 'Celos Eadburga scandens nos crimine purga'.
**961** Common root: *Winchcombe* 951.
**992** Common root: *Winchcombe* 992.1; *Coventry* 992.1.
**993** Common root: *Winchcombe* 992.2; *Coventry* 992.2.
**1058** Common root: *Winchcombe* 1058; *Coventry* 1058; *AC* (C) 1058.
**1084** Common root: *AC* (C) 1083. A similar entry appears alongside the second Easter Table in J*WCC* (C), p. 56 (year 1 = 1083).
**1085** Not attested in the other texts, but a likely component of the common root.
**1104** Common root: *Winchcombe* 1104; *Coventry* 1104; *AC* (C) 1104.
**1105** Common root: *Winchcombe* 1105; *Coventry* 1105; *AC* (C) 1105.
**1106.1** Common root: *Winchcombe* 1106.2; *Coventry* 1106.2; *AC* (C) 1106.1.
**1106.2** Common root: *Winchcombe* 1106.1; *Coventry* 1106.1; *AC* (C) 1106.3.
**1107** Common root: *AC* (C) 1107. The source is probably J*WCC* 1106 and 1108.

**1108.1** Common root: *Winchcombe* 1108.1; *Coventry* 1108.1; *AC* (C) 1108.1.
**1108.2** Common root: *Winchcombe* 1108.2; *Coventry* 1108.2; *AC* (C) 1108.2.
**1109.1** Common root: *Winchcombe* 1109.1; *Coventry* 1110.1; *AC* (C) 1109.1.
**1109.2** Common root: *Winchcombe* 1109.2; *Coventry* 1110.2; *AC* (C) 1109.2.
**1110** Common root: *Winchcombe* 1110.2; *Coventry* 1111.2; *AC* (C) 1110.2.
**1111.1** Common root: *Winchcombe* 1111.1; *Coventry* 1112.1; *AC* (C) 1111.
**1111.2** Common root: *Winchcombe* 1111.2.
**1112** Common root: *Winchcombe* 1112.1; *Coventry* 1113.1; *AC* (C) 1112.
**1113** Common root: *Winchcombe* 1113; *Coventry* 1113.2; *AC* (C) 1113.
**1114** Common root: *Winchcombe* 1114; *Coventry* 1114; *AC* (C) 1114.
**1115.1** Common root: *Winchcombe* 1115.1; *Coventry* 1115.1; *AC* (C) 1115.1.
**1115.2** Common root: *Winchcombe* 1115.2; *Coventry* 1115.2; *AC* (C) 1115.2.
**1116** Common root: *Winchcombe* 1116; *Coventry* 1116; *AC* (C) 1116.
**1117.1** Common root: *Winchcombe* 1117.3; *Coventry* 1117.2.
**1117.2** Common root: *Winchcombe* 1118.1; *Coventry* 1118.
**1118** Common root: *Winchcombe* 1118.2.
**1119.1** Common root: *Winchcombe* 1119; *Coventry* 1119.1; *AC* (C) 1119
**1119.2** Common root: *AC* (C) 1119.2. The source is JW*CC* 1119: 'Post hec rex Henricus, consilio optimatum suorum, fecit pacem cum rege Francorum, in qua pace accepit Willelmus filius eius Normanniam, a predicto rege Francorum tenendam.'
**1120** Common root: *Winchcombe* 1120; *Coventry* 1120; *AC* (C) 1120.
**1121** Common root: *Winchcombe* 1121; *Coventry* 1121; *AC* (C) 1121.

# Appendix B
# The English Material in the C-Text of *Annales Cambriae* — Commentary

**1016** Common root: *Winchcombe* 1016; *Coventry* 1015.2.
**1017** Common root: *Winchcombe* 1017.1; *Coventry* 1016.
**1020** Common root: *Winchcombe* 1020; *Coventry* 1020.
**1022** There is nothing similar in either *Winchcombe* or *Coventry*, but compare the Norman Annals: *AC*, *AMSM*, *AU* 1031; *AG* 1035.
**1023** Common root: *Winchcombe* 1023; *Coventry* 1023.
**1024** Common root: *Winchcombe* 1024; *Coventry* 1024.
**1028** Common root: *Winchcombe* 1028.1; *Coventry* 1028.1.
**1029** Common root: *Winchcombe* 1029; *Coventry* 1029.
**1030** Common root: *Winchcombe* 1030; *Coventry* 1030.
**1031** Common root: *Winchcombe* 1031; *Coventry* 1031.
**1033** Common root: *Winchcombe* 1033; *Coventry* 1033.
**1035** Common root: *Winchcombe* 1035.1; *Coventry* 1035.
**1038** Common root: *Winchcombe* 1038; *Coventry* 1038.
**1039** Common root: *Winchcombe* 1039; *Coventry* 1039.
**1040** Common root: *Winchcombe* 1040; *Coventry* 1040.
**1042** Common root: *Winchcombe* 1042.1; *Coventry* 1042.
**1043** Common root: *Winchcombe* 1043.1; *Coventry* 1043.
**1044** Common root: *Winchcombe* 1044.1; *Coventry* 1044.
**1046** Common root: *Winchcombe* 1046; *Coventry* 1046.
**1050** Common root: *Winchcombe* 1050; *Coventry* 1050.
**1051** Common root: *Winchcombe* 1051; *Coventry* 1051.
**1053** Common root: *Winchcombe* 1053; *Coventry* 1053.
**1056** Common root: *Winchcombe* 1056; *Coventry* 1057.1.
**1058** Common root: *Winchcombe* 1058; *Coventry* 1058; *APW* 1058.
**1062** Common root: *Winchcombe* 1062; *Coventry* 1062.1.
**1066** Common root: *Winchcombe* 1066.1; *Coventry* 1066.
**1067** Common root: *Winchcombe* 1067; *Coventry* 1067.
**1068.1** Common root: *Winchcombe* 1068.1; *Coventry* 1068.1.
**1068.2** Common root: *Winchcombe* 1068.2; *Coventry* 1068.2.

**1069** Common root: *Winchcombe* 1069; *Coventry* 1069.
**1070** Common root: *Winchcombe* 1070; *Coventry* 1070.
**1071** Common root: *Winchcombe* 1071; *Coventry* 1071.
**1072** Common root: *Winchcombe* 1072; *Coventry* 1072.
**1073** Common root: *Winchcombe* 1073; *Coventry* 1073.
**1079** Common root: *Winchcombe* 1079; *Coventry* 1077.
**1080** Common root: *Winchcombe* 1080; *Coventry* 1078.
**1081** Common root: *Winchcombe* 1081; *Coventry* 1081.
**1083** Common root: *APW* 1084.
**1084** Not present in the other witnesses, but probably in the common root, since annals relating to Pope Gregory VII but naming him 'Hildebrand' occur in the first Easter Table in JW*CC* (C), p. 56 (year 11 = 1074).
**1085** Common root: *Winchcombe* 1085.1; *Coventry* 1085.1.
**1086** Common root: *Winchcombe* 1086.1; *Coventry* 1086.
**1087** Common root: *Winchcombe* 1087; *Coventry* 1087.
**1088** Common root: *Winchcombe* 1088; *Coventry* 1088.
**1089** Common root: *Winchcombe* 1089; *Coventry* 1089.
**1091** Common root: *Winchcombe* 1091; *Coventry* 1091.
**1092** Common root: *Winchcombe* 1092; *Coventry* 1092.
**1093.1** Common root: *Winchcombe* 1093.1; *Coventry* 1093.1
**1093.2** Common root: *Winchcombe* 1093.3; *Coventry* 1093.2.
**1095** Common root: *Winchcombe* 1095.1; *Coventry* 1095.
**1096** Common root: *Winchcombe* 1096; *Coventry* 1096.
**1097** Common root: *Winchcombe* 1097; *Coventry* 1097.
**1098** Common root: *Winchcombe* 1098.1; *Coventry* 1098.
**1099** Common root: *Winchcombe* 1099.1; *Coventry* 1099.
**1100** Common root: *Winchcombe* 1100.2; *Coventry* 1100.2.
**1101** Common root: *Winchcombe* 1101.2; *Coventry* 1101.2.
**1104** Common root: *Winchcombe* 1104; *Coventry* 1104; *APW* 1104.
**1105** Common root: *Winchcombe* 1105; *Coventry* 1105; *APW* 1105.
**1106.1** Common root: *Winchcombe* 1106.2; *Coventry* 1106.2; *APW* 1106.1.
**1106.2** This item must have been composed after Robert's death in 1134. Its source is unknown, but it can be seen as combining material from JW*CC* 1106 (p. 110) and 1134 (p. 212).
**1106.3** Common root: *Winchcombe* 1106.1; *Coventry* 1106.1; *APW* 1106.2.
**1107** Common root: *APW* 1107. The source is probably JW*CC* 1106 and 1108.
**1108.1** Common root: *Winchcombe* 1108.1; *Coventry* 1108.1; *APW* 1108.1.
**1108.2** Common root: *Winchcombe* 1108.2; *Coventry* 1108.2; *APW* 1108.2.
**1109.1** Common root: *Winchcombe* 1109.1; *Coventry* 1109.1; *APW* 1109.1.
**1109.2** Common root: *Winchcombe* 1109.2; *Coventry* 1109.2; *APW* 1109.2.
**1110.1** Common root: *Winchcombe* 1110.1; *Coventry* 1111.1.
**1110.2** Common root: *Winchcombe* 1110.2; *Coventry* 1111.2; *APW* 1110.

**1111** Common root: *Winchcombe* 1111.1; *Coventry* 1112.1; *APW* 1111.
**1112** Common root: *Winchcombe* 1112; *Coventry* 1113.1; *APW* 1112.
**1113** Common root: *Winchcombe* 1113; *Coventry* 1113.2; *APW* 1113.
**1114** Common root: *Winchcombe* 1114; *Coventry* 1114; *APW* 1114.
**1115.1** Common root: *Winchcombe* 1115.1; *Coventry* 1115.1; *APW* 1115.1
**1115.2** Common root: *Winchcombe* 1115.2; *Coventry* 1115.2; *APW* 1115.2.
**1116** Common root: *Winchcombe* 1116; *Coventry* 1116; *APW* 1116.
**1119.1** Common root: *Winchcombe* 1119; *Coventry* 1119.1; *APW* 1119.1.
**1119.2** Common root: *APW* 1119.2. The source is apparently JW*CC* 1119.
**1120** Common root: the second half of *Winchcombe* 1120, of *Coventry* 1120, and of *APW* 1120.
**1121** Common root: *Winchcombe* 1121; *Coventry* 1121; *APW* 1121.
**1122.1** Cf. *Winchcombe* 1122.3; *Coventry* 1122.3; *APW* 1122.
**1122.2** See *APW* 1122, which has the first half, but omits the obits.
**1124** See *APW* 1124, which has the first half, but lacks Ernulph's obit.
**1125** *Mutilatus* has apparently been transposed from the moneyers to Bishop Simon. See *AT* 1125; *APW* 1135 ('Monetarii totius Angliæ amerciati sunt').
**1128** See *AT* 1128—a possible source, but not in its existing form.
**1133** See JW*CC* 1133.
**1135** See *AT* 1135. *APW* 1135 has first half only.
**1136** See *AT* 1137; *APW* 1137, but in both Louis succeeds.
**1137** See *AT* 1137; *APW* 1137.
**1139** See *AT* 1139.
**1140** Source unknown.
**1141** See *APW* 1140 ('Facta est eclipsis solis die Sancti Cuthberti [20 March]').
**1142** See *AT* 1141; *APW* 1141.
**1143** See *AT* 1143.
**1145** See *AT* 1145.
**1147** See *AT* 1143.
**1148** See *AT* 1148. *APW* 1147 has Robert's obit, but not that of Roger of Chester.
**1150** See *AT* 1150.
**1151** See *AT* 1151.
**1152** See *AT* 1152.
**1153** See *AT* 1153.
**1154** See *AT* 1154.
**1155** See *AT* 1155.
**1156** See *AT* 1156.
**1157** See *AT* 1157.
**1158** See *AT* 1158.
**1159** See *AT* 1159.

**1160** See *AT* 1160.
**1161** See *AT* 1161.
**1162** See *AT* 1162; *APW* 1162.
**1163** See *AT* 1163; *APW* 1163.
**1164** See *AT* 1164.
**1165** See *AT* 1165; *APW* 1165.
**1166** See *AT* 1166; *APW* 1166.
**1167** See *AT* 1167; *APW* 1167 ('. . . Robertus episcopus Hereford' iv kal' Martii obiit, et G. archidiaconus Wyg'; successit S. Luvel').
**1168** See *AT* 1169.
**1169** See *AT* 1169; *APW* 1169.
**1170** See *AT* 1170.
**1171** See *AT* 1171.
**1172** See *AT* 1172.
**1173** See *AT* 1173.
**1174** See *AT* 1174.
**1175** See *AT* 1175.
**1176.1** See *AT* 1176; *APW* 1176.
**1176.2** See *AT* 1176.
**1177** See *AT* 1177; *APW* 1177.
**1178** See *AT* 1178; *APW* 1178.
**1179** See *AT* 1179; *APW* 1179.
**1180** See *AT* 1180; *APW* 1180 ('Baldewinus abbas de Forde consecratur in episcopum Wigornie die Sancti Laurentii').
**1181** See *AT* 1181; *APW* 1181.
**1182** See *AT* 1182; *APW* 1182.
**1183.1** See *AT* 1183.
**1183.2** *AT* 1183 has all of this material, except that Gerard is said to have been appointed to Chester rather than Lichfield. Cf. *APW* 1183.
**1185** See *AT* 1185.
**1187.1** Cf. *AT* 1187, 1188 covers all of these events except for the capture of the king of Jerusalem and the loss of the cross.
**1187.2** See *AT* 1187; *APW* 1187.
**1188** Simon Luvel, archdeacon of Worcester, was succeeded by Peter de Leche in 1188/9: see the *Later Winchcombe Annals* in F, fol. 21v; *Cart. Worcs.*, lxv; *Fasti*, 2:105.
**1189.1** *AT* 1189 and *APW* 1189 have the destruction of Worcester but not the date.
**1189.2** *Heads I*, 47. Neither *AT* 1189 nor *APW* 1189 have this obit.
**1189.3** *AT* 1189 and *APW* 1189 report all of these consecrations except for that of Richard of London.
**1190.1** *AT* 1190 and *APW* 1190 have William's obit, but date it to *v non. Maii*. For discussion, see *Fasti*, 2:100; *Cart. Worcs.*, liv, n. 2.

**1190.2** Cf. *AT* 1190.
**1191.1** *AT* 1190; *APW* 1191.
**1191.2** Cf. *AT* 1191.
**1191.3** Neither *AT* nor *APW* feature this item.
**1192.1** Cf. *AT* 1192.
**1192.2** Cf. *AT* 1192; *APW* 1192.
**1193** *AT* 1193 has all of these items except for the siege of Windsor. Robert's obit is also dated to *v. kal. Iulii*. Cf. *APW* 1193.
**1194.1** Cf. *AT* 1192, which is much briefer.
**1194.2** Neither *AT* nor *APW* feature these items.
**1195** See *AT* 1195.
**1196.1** *AT* 1196 records John's election, which it dates to *v. kal. Novembris*. *APW* 1197 notes both the election and the consecration, which it dates to *xiv. kal. Novembris*.
**1196.2** *AT* 1197.
**1197** *AT* 1197 and *APW* 1197 mention the earthquake, but not the time of the day.
**1198.1** *AT* 1198 also has these obits, but differs over their dates. Cf. also *APW* 1198.
**1198.2** *AT* 1198 dates this obit to *viii. kal. Octobris*. Cf. *APW* 1198.
**1199.1** Neither *AT* nor *APW* feature this item, but see Gervase, 1:573, who supplies the same date.
**1199.2** Cf. *Coventry* 1199.2 and the works cited there.
**1199.3** Cf. *APW* 1199, Coventry 1199.3 and the works cited there.